TUDOR CORNWALL

BOOKS BY A. L. ROWSE

History

THE COUSIN JACKS: THE CORNISH IN AMERICA

BOSWORTH FIELD AND THE WARS OF THE ROSES

TUDOR CORNWALL

THE ENGLAND OF ELIZABETH

THE EXPANSION OF ELIZABETHAN ENGLAND

THE ELIZABETHANS AND AMERICA

SIR RICHARD GRENVILLE OF THE *Revenge*

RALEGH AND THE THROCKMORTONS

THE EARLY CHURCHILLS

THE LATER CHURCHILLS

THE CHURCHILLS

THE SPIRIT OF ENGLISH HISTORY

THE USE OF HISTORY

ST. AUSTELL: CHURCH, TOWN, PARISH

Literature

WILLIAM SHAKESPEARE: A BIOGRAPHY

SHAKESPEARE'S SONNETS
Edited with an Introduction and Notes

CHRISTOPHER MARLOWE: A BIOGRAPHY

SHAKESPEARE'S SOUTHAMPTON: PATRON OF VIRGINIA

THE ENGLISH SPIRIT (*Revised Edition*)

TIMES, PERSONS, PLACES

A CORNISH CHILDHOOD

A CORNISHMAN AT OXFORD

CORNISH STORIES

A CORNISH ANTHOLOGY: *Selected*

POEMS OF A DECADE

POEMS CHIEFLY CORNISH

POEMS OF DELIVERANCE

POEMS PARTLY AMERICAN

POEMS OF CORNWALL AND AMERICA

SKETCH MAP OF SIXTEENTH-CENTURY CORNWALL

Towns : **PENZANCE**
Villages : Landulph
Houses : *Boconnoc*
Parliamentary Boroughs : <u>TRURO</u>. Grampound
Monasteries, Collegiate Churches : +
County Boundary : - - - - - - - - -

0 1 2 3 4 6 8 10 12
MILES

N

BIDEFORD

DEVON

+Hartland
Abbey

•Tonacombe
Kilkhampton
'Stowe

•Stratton
Launcells

Castle• Boscastle
•Bossiney
Tintagel

R. Tamar

Penheale
St. Clether +Newport
Lanwitton

LAUNCESTON

Roscarrock
Pentire
Point
•Padstow
St. Endellion
Port Isaac
Bokelly
Camelford
Altarnun

Trevose Head
•St. Merryn
St. Issey
Wadebridge
Egloshayle
St. Minver St. Kew
St. Breoke

R. Camel

BODMIN
MOOR

Tavistock•

Lanherne
St. Columb minor
Newquay
St. Crantock+
•Rialton
•Trerica

Withiel
St. Columb
major
•Lanhydrock
Restormel
Castle
•Roche

+BODMIN

•St. Neot
Liskeard
Menheniot
•Boconnoc

Cotehele
Halton
Quethiock
Landulph
Saltash

Buckland
+Abbey

Callington

St. Enoder
Luxulyan
Tywardreath
St. Austell

R. Fowey

LOSTWITHIEL
+St. Winnow
•St. Veep
Tregarrick
Trelawne

Plympton
+St. Germans

Tremeton
Castle
PLYMOUTH

Perranporth
Perranzabuloe
St. Agnes+

Mitchell
Probus

Grampound
St. Ewe
Golden•

FOWEY

W. Looe
E. Looe

Mt. Edgecumbe
Rame
Head

St. Nicholas
or Drakes Is.

CORNWALL

Helland

Tregony
Caerhays
Tregothnan
Talverne

Mevagissey

Dodman Point

TRURO
•Redruth
Camborne
Carclew•
Penryn
Glasney+
FALMOUTH
Tehidy

St. Ives
Lelant•
Clowance•
Marazion
Madron Godolphin
PENZANCE +St. Michael's
Newlyn Pengersick•
Paul•
•St. Buryan
Mousehole

Constantine
•Helston
Merthen+
Trelowarren

St. Mawes
St. Anthony
Pendennis

Hetford R.

•St. Keverne

•Erisey

Grade•

Lizard

Land's End

TUDOR CORNWALL

Portrait of a Society

by

A. L. ROWSE

Et dixit ad me: Fili hominis, putasne vivent ossa ista?
                                          PROPH. EZECH. XXXVII

CHARLES SCRIBNER'S SONS
NEW YORK

To the Memory of My Friend

CHARLES HENDERSON

First of Cornish Scholars

CONTENTS

ILLUSTRATIONS

MAP

The device on the binding is the arms of the Duchy of Cornwall

PREFACE TO THE NEW EDITION

THIS book was first published in 1941; since then it has had six reissues in Britain, with considerable intervals when it has been out of print. But it was never published in the United States – in the fateful year of Pearl Harbor Americans had other preoccupations. Now that it is necessary to reissue it again the opportunity has been taken to make it available in an American edition at the same time.

In my original Preface I stated that the book grew out of my intention, at first, to depict the process of the Reformation in microcosm, in the compact small area and society of my native Cornwall. My aim was to answer such questions as 'What *was* the Reformation when you come to study it under the microscope? What did it mean, and what did it do? How did it work out, and what were its effects upon the development of society?'

These questions led me far afield into the social history of that period in all its aspects, economic, political, military, religious, cultural. The attempt to give a complete picture, a rounded whole – to write what I came to think of as 'total history', cutting down through all the layers of the cake – took a good many years of research, more than a decade, mainly into primary sources, much of it in manuscript.

A study on such a scale – a one-inch ordnance map of this particular tract of history—can only be done for a small area. Fortunately that lay ready to hand in the little land of Cornwall, which, rated as an English county, actually has an independent life, a vital principle of its own, very evident in the sixteenth century and through the centuries since. It is obvious enough, for anybody with knowledge and imagination, even today; for the Cornish think of themselves as a distinctive people, even when they have emigrated overseas, where most of them are, the great bulk in America. So that I think of my later book, *The Cousin Jacks: The Cornish in America*, as in some sense an extension of this earlier book, *Tudor Cornwall*, overseas.

Up to the critical period of Renaissance and Reformation – the opening out of the modern world, the forging of the modern state – Cornwall was a remote Celtic province, like Wales or Brittany, speaking its own language, out of the mainstream of English life. Poor, except for its European tin-trade, and exploited by the English. It was forced into the mainstream in the course of the tensions of the sixteenth century. From being a far-away, insignificant corner of the land, sunk in its dream of the Celtic past, in its

9

own inner life of legends of Arthur and Mark, and Tristan, lapped in the faith and the cult of Celtic saints unknown to the Roman calendar, with its own miracle-plays (only just being studied and appreciated by American scholars), its own customs and superstitions and resistances, in the Elizabethan age it found itself in the front-line of the oceanic voyages and the long sea-struggle with Spain. The planter of the first American colonies in Virginia was a Cornishman, Sir Richard Grenville; the Gilberts and the Raleghs all had Cornish blood – Sir Walter Ralegh, swarthy and darkly glittering, was Lord Lieutenant of the county; Hawkins's right-hand man on the third fateful voyage to the Caribbean, Robert Barrett, was a Saltash sea-captain, burned at Seville.

Internally, the small backward-looking society at first struggled – so like the Celts – against the inevitable process. The Rebellions of 1497 and 1549 were to Cornwall what those of 1715 and 1745 were to the Highlands of Scotland – their leaders are even today remembered in Cornwall. But in the end the little province was drawn into the main stream, if not wholly absorbed, to make its distinctive contribution to the life of the nation and of the English-speaking peoples overseas.

That process of tension, struggle, adjustment is the story of this book, which developed from its original conception into something larger and more variegated. In the end it became a portrait of Tudor society in all its vivacious detail as reflected in the small but revealing mirror of Cornwall. In that a precursor of the larger work on the Elizabethan age upon which I have been engaged in later years.

The book had a reception quite beyond my expectations – when in my diffidence I was ready to offer the publisher a subsidy to publish it, it has often had to be reprinted! Even more rewarding has been the response in the minds of kindred spirits who have assured me that they were encouraged by it to go forward themselves in this field. The intervening years have seen a number of works following in the path opened up by this, with its aim to integrate local and national history, to cross-fertilise each other – particularly in the work of my friends, now leaders in this area, Professor A. G. Dickens and Dr. W. G. Hoskins.

This most fruitful of approaches to history is by no means fully explored, let alone over-exploited (as some are) – in fact I confess to some disappointment that it has not been more closely followed up: it offers richer rewards than most. I always hoped for a *Tudor Wales* – no subject more brilliantly lighted, with sharper colours or more vivacity. But, with all those Welsh historians working away at small facets, where is it? We can now look forward to a Norfolk in the Civil War, and an Essex in the early seventeenth century, but what about the North in the Wars of the Roses, the East Anglia of the Pastons, Georgian Kent or Victorian Lancashire; where is Stuart Hampshire?

When British historians fail to take their opportunities I am keen that young American scholars should come into these pastures – so much longer perspectives of time, such vastly richer sources and materials, such interesting subjects await them, more fun – if they have a sense of fun (it goes with imagination).

In my original Preface I specified the many obligations I incurred in the course of writing the book, to libraries, archives, other scholars, friends – particularly to All Souls College which enabled me to write it. Here I can only cite the encouragement I received from my long-dead friend, Charles Henderson, who accomplished so much himself and inspired so much Cornish scholarship in others in his brief life. The book is dedicated to his memory. I should now like to add two friends of a younger generation. T. M. Farmiloe of Macmillan in London and Thomas J. Davis of Scribner's in New York, who have been generously keen to renew the book in England and to give it its first appearance in America.

A. L. Rowse

All Souls College,
Oxford
2 *April* 1968

Note

For this new edition of a book that has had altogether seven impressions in Britain I have taken the opportunity to incorporate a number of corrections.

CHAPTER I

INTRODUCTION:
EVIDENCES AND SURVIVALS

THERE is no research more fascinating than to attempt to decipher an earlier, vanished age beneath the forms of the present and the successive layers that time has imposed. So it is that beneath the towns and villages, the roads and fields of to-day, we may construct under our very eyes, out of the evidences that remain, a picture of a former age. Nor is it at all difficult — in this case — to build up a picture of what Tudor Cornwall was like; for a good deal of evidence remains, under the skin of the later accretions of time. Only it demands the exercise of a rare faculty, to open our eyes to what is there for all to see — that of the historical imagination. That is to say, the imagination applied to the world as we see it, and limited in its working by the evidence we have; the acceptance of that limitation is what characterizes history as opposed to other forms of art. But it is rare for people to see what commonly lies around them and what they have taken for granted all their days.

In the case of Cornwall, as in that of any other English county, much survives. The land has not much changed. The area of cultivation has been extended; you can see how it has crept up the hill-sides, reclaiming downs and waste, constituting that homely, that intimate patch-work of small fields, brown and golden and green according to the seasons of the year, which you may observe from almost any point of vantage in the landscape. True, there are different methods at work now, and cultivation has been intensified. Population and stock were much more sparse; it was an emptier countryside; there was more room. It is one of the paradoxes of history that then, when the known world was in fact so much smaller, and so many fewer people inhabited it, it was in a sense larger; the spaces were greater and the time taken in going from one place to another so much longer. It was altogether easier for a man to be lost, in the sixteenth century. New roads have made their way across the face of the country; but in other cases widened and straightened highways follow the old routes. Many of the lesser roads, the lanes and footpaths are much the same; and in the villages, or even in the towns, the curves of the old oxen tracks determine still the line of the streets, forcing the traffic to conform to a distant past, a time out of mind.

Above all, the relation of the land to the sea is unchanged. The sense of the sea is over all, its scent and rumour everywhere. You are never far from the sea in Cornwall, though our dependence on it is less, perhaps, than it was. The conformation of the coast, the cliffs and estuaries, even the harbours and little ports — they call them creeks in the Tudor customs returns — are much what they were. For the rest, the changes of the seasons and their colours, the ardent blue of summer, the grey of winter, the purple and gold of the moors in autumn, the wind and the rain, are, we may suppose, what they have always been.

Of the works of man more has changed. Though even here, the most characteristic of all our buildings have not been much touched, at any rate in the exterior they present to the world: the Cornish churches are a legacy of the Middle Ages to a later age in which they are a curious, a revealing survival, evidence of what faith, what former hopes. Now, whatever tides have flown through and away from them, leaving them a little weathered and grey and empty, they have become part of, and give point to, the landscape.

The Cornish churches are to a large extent the work of the end of the Middle Ages. They were being rebuilt and refashioned on a larger scale throughout the fifteenth century and right up into our period, to the very eve of the Reformation, which put an immediate, a drastic, end to the work. Whatever the reasons for it may be — and one may suggest an increase in the community's disposable wealth, combined with a technical advance in building and tools as factors in it — the fifteenth century saw a great outburst in church-building all over the country. Cornwall participated in this, but it is notable how belatedly in this remote corner of the land. The finishing and decorating of our churches was still going on when the Reformation swooped down on them and put an end to it.

The rebuilding of Bodmin parish church, finest and largest of them all, was in full swing from 1469 to 1472; we are fortunate to be able to follow it in detail from the accounts that have survived.[1] The very ornately carved exterior of St. Mary Magdalen at Launceston dates from 1511 to 1524;[2] and the similar work on the south aisle of St. Mary's, Truro, belongs to the same date. The richly ornamented tower at St. Austell, of an exceptional design, dates to not much earlier — 1497 is the traditional date; while the finest of all Cornish church-towers, that of Probus, is also the latest. The tradition is that it was finished as late as the reign of Mary Tudor. Carew says that this 'high and fair church-tower, of hewed moor-stone, was builded within compass of our remembrance, by the well-disposed inhabitants';[3] and a Star Chamber

---

[1] *Camden Miscellany*, VII.   [2] Peter, *Histories of Launceston and Dunheved*, 305-11.
[3] Carew, *Survey of Cornwall* (ed. 1769), 140.

case of the reign of Henry VIII gives us new evidence of the lateness of its building – it was proceeding then and evidently not finished.[1] There is nothing impossible in the finishing touches being made as late as Mary's reign.

The last two towers are not, however, of the usual Cornish type, which is fat and rather squat, sitting squarely on its haunches, in keeping with the low-roofed churches of three equal aisles, without clerestories and with barrel or wagon roofs. Such is the characteristic Cornish church, and one sees its *raison d'être* when one knows those Atlantic gales in winter, especially if the church is in an exposed position, as many of them are, with the winds battering at the windows and blustering around the roofs.

The finishing of the interiors was even later. Characteristic of the Cornish churches was the seating throughout with substantial oak benches, with square-headed ends carved with vigour, if no great subtlety.[2] At Bodmin these were not begun till 1491 – the contract specified that they were to be like those of Plympton, or better – and were finished by 1495. The county was once extraordinarily rich in such woodwork. Even now a good deal is left: carvings of the arms of Arundells, Roscarrocks and so on, which point to the pre-Reformation appropriation of seats; the favourite symbols of the Passion, the Sacraments, evidence of their faith; occasionally a panel, such as that at St. Austell, of a fox in a surplice preaching from the pulpit to a credulous woman on her knees below, evidence of their humour. The rood-screens, more delicately carved, with their fan-vaulting and tracery, began to disappear much earlier. Yet the screens, from what remains of them, at Lanreath, St. Ewe and St. Winnow, show finer work; and painted as they were, added greatly to the general effect of richness and colour that these small churches must have given in their heyday.

To this the windows of stained glass contributed most; and what that effect was we can still see from the one church, St. Neot's, which has preserved its magnificent series of pre-Reformation windows almost intact. They were being put in at the end of the 1520s and into the 1530s, just when Henry VIII's first blows against the Church were being struck.[3] So also at Launceston, where the borough was contracting for the windows for St. Mary Magdalen in 1534; and as late as 1543-44 we find Sir John Arundell making a gift for glazing the altar window.[4] It looks as if the Cornish parishes had no sooner got their churches completed and well-furnished within, than the blows against the old faith and order began.

[1] Star Chamber Proceedings, Henry VIII, 17/209.   [2] Cox, *Bench-Ends in English Churches*, 62.
[3] cf. Rushforth, 'The Windows of St. Neot's Church', *Trans. Exeter Diocesan Architectural and Archaeological Society*, 1937.
[4] Peter, 312, 184.

But the very process of building those fabrics, which expressed and enclosed the storied world of myth in which their minds moved, is so much evidence of the character of their society at the end of the Middle Ages. For it was parish churches they built, not monastic; no additions were made to the latter, which were the work of the earlier centuries: monasticism was on the downgrade, losing real impulse and only holding on to what it had got. Whereas there was no doubt about the impulse in the parishes and towns; exuberant and vital as it displayed itself in church-building, this was in itself testimony to the increasingly secular character of society. For it was the whole society that ordered and did the work. There can be no doubt of the strongly local, and even competitive, interest behind it, nor even of a corporate compulsion to take part in it.[1] Yet the building was the outward and visible sign of the place of the Church in communal life: it was the real centre of life in the medieval parish; secular organizations even in the towns were far less important and only slowly developed an independent existence.

There are some houses, too, that remain from the times we are speaking of: a number of the larger ones date to just these years when Cornwall was waking from the long sleep of the Middle Ages, and a new stirring, new movement came over the land. Cotehele, most beautiful of Cornish houses, was built in the last years of the fifteenth century by the first Sir Richard Edgcumbe, the friend of Henry VII and founder of the family's fortunes. There it still is as he built it, in the groove of the hill above the gorge of the Tamar, looking out upon the woods where Sir Richard took refuge from pursuing Yorkists; he lived to see another day and his party's triumph.[2] Lanherne, the home of the Arundells, richest and best-beloved of Cornish families in our period, which saw their loyalty to the old faith cloud their fortunes, still stands by the parish church at St. Mawgan, though now there is a deep wall to divide them, the house itself become a convent. Other great houses were built as the century went on, and remain whole or in part: Trerice, a distinguished Elizabethan house with its great oriel window and fantastic gables, the home of another line of Arundells; Penheale, built by George Grenville in the 1570s, Sir Richard's favourite cousin; Arwennack, hard by the inner harbour at Falmouth, within the crook of Pendennis headland, where the Killigrews lived their exciting lives; Mount Edgcumbe, which, so the Cornish said, Medina Sidonia had chosen for his own before the sailing of the Armada.

[1] This comes out very clearly in the Bodmin Accounts; cf. Coulton, *Art and the Reformation*, 365-6.
[2] Carew, 114.

Then there are the remains of earlier castles and forts, Launceston, Restormel, Trematon, of which but the shells of their keeps and gate-houses survive.[1] Some of them were falling into ruin in the period of which we are writing. When Leland visited Cornwall in 1538, the castle of the Norman Earls at Liskeard was already fast disappearing: 'the site magnificent, and looketh over all the town: fragments and pieces of walls yet stand'. At Tintagel, *magni nominis umbra*, the ravages of time had even then gone a long way: 'the residue of the buildings of this castle be sore weather-beaten, but it hath been a large thing ... Belike it had three wards, but two be worn away by the gulphing in of the sea, insomuch that it has made almost an isle, and no way to enter into it but by long elm trees laid for a bridge'. The four centuries that have elapsed since then have completed the division of the main from that headland, full of so many memories of Mark and Tristan and Iseult, where

> all their past came wailing in the wind,
> And all their future thundered in the sea.

Yet two other castles, Pendennis and St. Mawes, were built in our period by Henry VIII, as part of his girdle of defences along the Channel coast and paid for out of the spoliation of the monasteries: a very precise example of the connection between the Reformation and the rise of modern nationalism. There they still stand, on either side of the entrance to the Fal estuary: Pendennis a little altered within, not much without; St. Mawes, most perfect and decorative of all Henrician castles, with the inscriptions that Leland wrote for John Treffry, its first governor, still decipherable upon the walls:

> *Henricus Octavus Rex Angl. Franc. et Hiberniae invictus*
> *Me posuit praesidium Reipublicae terrorem hostibus.*

It remains unchanged, the walls of its three-lobed batteries but weathered to a silver grey, the grass-slopes covered with mesembryanthemum and rock-plants down to the edge of the water.

Above all, St. Michael's Mount still presents the outline familiar to earlier ages: there it stands

> Where the great vision of the guarded Mount
> Looks toward Namancos and Bayona's hold.

A ghost from the Tudor age visiting his former places would not find the

[1] cf. Oman, *Castles*, 103-26.

17

Mount much altered from the shape it took at the hands of the priors in the fourteenth century.

Further back than all these in time are the fortresses, the earthworks, encampments of yet earlier, grimmer ages when life was indeed brutish and short, if it was not solitary, for men had to huddle together in order to survive at all. On innumerable hill-tops throughout the county, on headlands along the coast, are remains of such camps, with their vallums and ditches; of the type of Castle-an-Dinas, Tintagel, Castle-dore, around which the most persistent and enduring legends of the Celtic peoples lingered. These were a no less notable feature of the landscape in the sixteenth century than they are now; indeed more so, since as time went on men tended to plough in their sites, the weather eroded their ramparts and filled in their ditches.

There has been a considerable diminution too in the number of holy wells and crosses, most characteristic of Cornish monuments; though there is still a large number of crosses, both churchyard and wayside, strewn over the county. They are congregated most thickly in the westernmost hundred of Penwith, and taper away to hardly any at all in the north-eastern area, the borders of Devon.[1] For the most part they date to the early Middle Ages, from the eighth to the twelfth centuries; every church of Celtic foundation had its original churchyard cross, in many cases where it survives being centuries older than the church. Far the greater number of these monuments are wayside crosses, and that devout Cornishmen continued to erect them up to the threshold of our period is attested by the will of Doctor Reginald Mertherderwa, Rector of Creed and Principal of Bull Hall at Oxford, who in 1447 directed 'new stone crosses to be put up, of the usual kind, in those parts of Cornwall from Caer Beslasek to Camborne church where dead bodies are rested on their way to burial, that prayers may be made, and the bearers take some rest'.[2] But most of these crosses are to be found along the tracks upon the bleak uplands, where they served chiefly to guide the footsteps of our fathers across the moors.

Nor should one forget the little habitations that sheltered their families, the rude, hard life they lived. Hardly any of the simple dwellings of the cottagers of the time have survived, save here and there in remote places. But a few medieval and Tudor farm-houses are left; like the delightful Methrose in the parish of Luxulyan, with its diminutive enclosed courtyard and gateway, its one-storied hall going up to the roof of the house, its solar

[1] Langdon, *Old Cornish Crosses*, 1-9.
[2] ibid., 8.

18

and buttery. Among other things that remain are the few medieval bells in our church-towers which summoned the former inhabitants of those houses to church.[1] There are the brasses and monuments of stone which covered our forebears, the richer of them, when dead; and the sculptured and ornamented tombs, like that of Prior Vyvyan in Bodmin church, or of Lord Willoughby de Broke at Callington, which signalize to the world that here sleep the great.

So we may build up our picture of that earlier age, stone by stone, church by church, adding here a house, there a castle or a bridge, from beneath the debris of the centuries that have intervened since.

But there are other evidences that tell us something of what we would fain know, evidences more continuous, more loquacious, though no less incomplete and with tantalizing silences. These are of a literary character, documents: the letters that these dead men wrote to each other about their business affairs, or about their private sentiments, their feelings for their friends, their family affections, their griefs. Very rarely there is a diary; like that of William Carnsew, who was an old acquaintance of Sir Richard Grenville's.[2] From it we derive a picture of the daily routine of an Elizabethan gentleman; when he sowed his crops, sheared his sheep, planted trees, walked about his grounds or received his friends; how he idled and trifled the time away with his acquaintance playing at bowls or paying visits; what he read and thought about, the stirring and tragic events of contemporary Europe, like the 'Spanish Fury' at Antwerp in 1576 which so impressed itself upon his mind; the arrangements to be made for his two boys Matthew and Richard at Oxford, the payments he disbursed for their clothes, for books or to their tutor. But that is a very rare kind of document for the Tudor age; for Cornwall it is indeed unique.

Most important for our purposes is Richard Carew's *Survey of Cornwall*; and a very delightful book it is, perhaps the most attractive of Elizabethan topographical and historical descriptions of counties. It is a fascinating task to test the more formal documents, the official records that remain, by Carew's book, and his book by them, to note how well they corroborate each other. It gives one confidence in this strange business of reconstructing the past out of bits of paper and fragments and stones.

For the most part we are dependent for our continuous history upon official papers and records; the voluminous correspondence, constantly

---

[1] cf. Dunkin, *Church Bells of Cornwall*, and *Monumental Brasses of Cornwall*.
[2] State Papers Supplementary, vol. 16; cf. my *Sir Richard Grenville*, 126-9.

growing in bulk as the years go on, passing between the Council governing from Whitehall and their local representatives, the sheriffs, the justices of the peace, the Cornish gentry. There are the complaints that go up from all sorts and conditions of men to the high and mighty at Westminster — a prior is being oppressive to his townsmen, the townsmen are invading his liberties, a ship has been piratically spoiled by the men of Fowey or Looe or Falmouth, the Bretons or Flemings have taken retaliatory measures upon Cornish ships in their ports, there is an outcry against regrators putting up prices at a time of scarcity of corn, measures of defence have to be taken against the enemy upon the coasts, or obstinate Catholics fined for the luxury of non-attendance at church, dangerous quarrels leading to murder or bloodshed looked into, offenders punished. The Council sends down its instructions, writs, stays, warrants of arrest; there is all the interminable going to and fro in the 'endless adventure' of government. There are innumerable law-suits and cases before King's Bench, Star-Chamber and Chancery, the Courts of the Exchequer, of the Augmentations Office, the High Court of Admiralty, episcopal and diocesan courts, assizes and quarter sessions, records of manorial courts. Or occasionally there is a brief from King or Queen, those remote, semi-sacrosanct figures standing at the head of society, surrounded by their Court in distant Westminster, not one of whom in our period ever came into so remote a province under their dominion. Or there are such humbler documents as entries of births, marriages and burials written up by the parsons in their parish registers.

All this, and more, we have to go upon: the literary instruments by which a society is governed and held together; for the historian coming after, so much evidence.

Cornwall was then an integral part of the kingdom, like any other county; but it was also something more. It was a homogeneous society of its own, defined by language and having a common history underneath, like Brittany or Wales or Ireland, reaching back beyond Normans and Saxons, beyond even Rome in these islands, to an antiquity of which its people were still dimly conscious. Some memory of all this they carried in the legends of their race that haunted their minds. They remembered that they were a conquered people. Norden, writing in the reign of Elizabeth, says: 'So seem they yet to retain a kind of concealed envy against the English, whom they yet affect with a kind of desire for revenge for their fathers' sakes, by whom their fathers received the repulse.'[1]

We must allow too for the very remoteness of the county in accentuating

[1] Norden, *Description of Cornwall* (ed. 1728), 28.

ιts unity and homogeneity: a peninsula shut in on the east by the deep valley of the Tamar, with its ridge of hills and bleak moorlands on either side; on all the remaining sides, to north and south and west, the sea. This remoteness, this sense of separation, has been an abiding factor all through Cornish history. It has meant that the Cornish have kept rather to themselves, and up to comparatively recently have not mingled much in the general stream of English life. Whenever they have moved abroad in any number, it has usually been across the seas rather than 'up the country'. The innumerable ports and havens along the coast have been the most convenient point of departure, inviting to new lands across the oceans as they invited their forefathers in the fifth and sixth centuries, the colonizers of Brittany across the Channel. Up till this very century, Cornish life remained very much *enfoncé* in its old grooves: you can trace in the parish registers how long and how continuously a given family remains attached to its own village, its old places. All this had scarcely changed up to the last war. How much stronger then was that sense of separateness, a very real sense of isolation, when reinforced by difference of language and the geographical conditions of the Middle Ages, one may appreciate from the letters written by Grandisson, greatest of the medieval bishops of Exeter, to his friends the Pope and cardinals at the distant, gay court at Avignon, describing the state of his diocese: the western half of it, he writes, inhabited by a people speaking Breton, at the extreme westernmost tongue of land, and beyond St. Michael's Mount the immensity of the open sea extending without limit.[1] One has to remember that up to the sixteenth century, Cornwall was a last outpost of the known world.

Of the language that was spoken very largely in Cornwall up to the end of our period, various memorials remain, though little enough that can be regarded as an active and continuous survival from the past. Most notable in this latter category are the place-names, which are overwhelmingly Celtic and so mark off the county from English counties.[2] Indeed it is only along the banks of the Tamar and upon Bodmin moor that English names occur in any number. An active survival of the old language may be found in a number of dialect-words in English; and perhaps we may derive an idea of how it was spoken from the up-and-down, sing-song intonation with which English is spoken in such places as Mevagissey, Mousehole, Newlyn, around Falmouth, and in the far-western hundred of Penwith.

---

[1] 'At versus Occiduum Montis Beati Archangeli Michaelis pelagi inmensitas protenditur absque meta': *Register of John de Grandisson* (ed. Hingeston-Randolph), I, 95.
[2] Gover, Mawer and Stenton, *The Place-Names of Devon*, xxi.

Cornish was a Celtic dialect coming somewhere between Welsh and Breton, but inclining more to the latter in character.[1] Both Carew and Norden are agreed that it was a pleasant-sounding tongue. The latter says that whereas the north Welsh had difficulty in understanding the south, they could understand much of Cornish: 'The pronunciation of the tongue differs in all, but the Cornish tongue is far the easiest to be pronounced; for they strain not their words so tediously through the throat, and so harshly through and from the roof of the mouth; as in pronouncing Rhin, they fetch it with R[h] — Rhin, and LL with a kind of reflecting the tongue . . . But of late the Cornishmen have much conformed themselves to the use of the English tongue, and their English is equal to the best, especially in the eastern parts; even from Truro eastwards it is in manner wholly English. In the west part of the country, as in the hundreds of Penwith and Kerrier, the Cornish tongue is most in use among the inhabitants, and yet (which is to be marvelled) though the husband and wife, parents and children, master and servants do mutually communicate in their native language, yet there is none of them in manner but is able to converse with a stranger in the English tongue, unless it be some obscure people that seldom confer with the better sort. But it seemeth that in few years the Cornish language will be by little and little abandoned'.[2]

Carew's evidence is to much the same effect. By his time, he says, 'most of the inhabitants can no word of Cornish; but very few are ignorant of the English: and yet some so affect their own, as to a stranger they will not speak it: for if meeting them by chance, you inquire the way or any such matter, your answer shall be, "Meea navidna cowzasawzneck, I can speak no Saxonage" '.[3] Yet the Cornish retained a great devotion to their language, he says, 'for the Lord's Prayer, the Apostles' Creed, and the ten Commandments have been much used in Cornish beyond all remembrance'. Perhaps this may be taken as some evidence of the concessions the Catholic Church made to popular feeling, and may help to account for that devotion of the people to the old faith which led them to rise in rebellion against the Prayer Book in 1549. Carew adds that 'the principal love and knowledge of this language lived in Dr. Kenall the Civilian, and with him lieth buried; for the English speech doth still encroach upon it, and hath driven the same into the uttermost skirts of the shire'. Dr. Kenall was a much-beneficed ecclesiastic; he was Archdeacon of Oxford, Canon of Exeter, and among other things held the desirable rectories of Carhayes

---

[1] Jenner, *Handbook of the Cornish Language*, 7.
[2] Norden, 26–7.   [3] Carew, 56.

and St. Columb Major.[1] Carew speaks of the knowledge buried with him with a lingering regret. We also may regret that he did not commit to writing something of what he knew: was he too busy, or too devoted to his hounds?[2]

There are a few other evidences regarding the use of the language in our period. Sir William Godolphin writing in 1532 to Cromwell who had asked to have two Cornishmen sent up, 'proper fellows for the feat of wrestling', sends two of his household servants 'who are reckoned the best for that feat'; but 'their English is not perfect. The time is too short to make further search'.[3] Some few years later, in 1538, Godolphin sends up at Cromwell's request some Cornish tinners who are expert at blowing tin: 'for that work your servants Samson and John Herry have no fellows in Cornwall. You may call Herry to interpret these men's language, for their English is very bad'.[4] Even more interesting evidence as to the use of the language comes from the depositions of the Bishop's Consistory Court at Exeter. In a case of defamation in 1572, concerning words uttered before divine service in Lelant church, Wm. Hawysh deposed that upon 'dew whallan gwa metton in eglos de Lalant' (i.e. upon All Hallows day in Lelant church) the wife of Morrysh David 'called Agnes Davy "whore and whore bitch" in English and not in Cornowok'.[5] In a similar case at St. Ewe in 1595, a girl mentions that while weeding in a garden, two other women were 'talking together both in Cornish and English'.[6] The interest of this evidence of bilingualism is that it shows that Cornish still survived a long way east of Truro — for St. Ewe is near St. Austell — at the end of the century.

But in the next century the language was fast dying. The discontinuance of the miracle-plays in Cornish, the introduction of the English liturgy, the absence of any attempt to translate the scriptures were no doubt factors in its disappearance. But the increase of commerce, the rise in importance of the ports as opposed to the inland towns, consequent upon the naval developments of Elizabeth's reign and the war with Spain, by which Cornwall from being a remote, unimportant county was brought into the front line of the nation's offensive and defensive policy, were far more powerful factors. As that reign progressed, west-country harbours became the jumping-off point for innumerable sea-enterprises across the outer ocean; in the twenty years' naval warfare with which the epoch closed, Cornwall was in the most exposed position. Its isolation was ended; the

[1] Henderson, *St. Columb Major Church and Parish*, 12.
[2] cf. later, p. 340.
[3] *Letters and Papers of Henry VIII*, v, 1093.
[4] ibid., *Addenda*, i, 1342.
[5] Henderson MSS. (Truro Museum), vol. x, p. 124.
[6] ibid., p. 176.

process of absorption into the life of the English people was in motion. That process is the story of this book; the disappearance of the language was a natural, an inevitable consequence.

It left, however, literary remains on a more considerable scale than is usually realized. Most important of these are a number of miracle-plays, a trilogy known as the *Ordinalia*: the Creation of the World, the Passion of Christ, the Resurrection of Our Lord;[1] a later play, the *Gwyreans an Bys* (the Creation of the World), partly independent of, and partly based on, the *Ordinalia*;[2] and a long play dealing with the life and works of St. Meriasek, the *Beunans Meriasek*.[3] It is so much evidence that Cornwall played its full part in the 'vigorous and widespread dramatic activity throughout the length and breadth of the land' in the later Middle Ages.[4] Indeed there are indications that the devotion to the religious drama was deeper and more general, that it was more intimately bound up with the lives and minds of the people, in Cornwall than in most places.[5] The point, however, goes against the somewhat drastic opinion expressed by the editor of the *Ordinalia* that 'so far from these productions having any claim to be considered offshoots of the native genius or character, they are clearly exotics transplanted from English soil'. If indeed this opinion does not contradict what the same writer says of the language, 'that it was owing to their attachment to it, as the only surviving mark of their race, that the Cornish adhered to these plays with such remarkable pertinacity'. Sir E. K. Chambers refers to the 'great cycle' of the *Ordinalia*; and they are certainly worthy to be compared with the better known town-plays of Chester, Coventry and Beverley.

They are in many respects parallel to these, and yet have certain marked independent features of their own.[6] For one thing, the Cornish plays omit the whole of the Nativity from the subjects of which they treat; rather strangely, one cannot help thinking, for this part of the biblical narrative had an obvious popular appeal. But its place is taken by an elaborate treatment of the exquisite and moving legend of the Holy Rood: how Adam, weary of his life and sorrows, sends Seth to the gate of Paradise for the oil of mercy:

> ADAM   O dear God, I am weary,
> Gladly I would see now
> The time to depart.

[1] *The Ancient Cornish Drama*, trans. and ed. by E. Norris, 1859.
[2] ed. and trans. by Whitley Stokes, *Transactions of the Philological Society*, 1864.
[3] *Beunans Meriasek: the Life of St. Meriasek*, ed. and trans. by Whitley Stokes, 1872.
[4] Chambers, *The Medicval Stage*, II, 109.
[5] cf. Carew, 71b.   [6] Chambers, op. cit., II, 127.

> Strong are the roots of the briars
> That my arms are broken
> Tearing them up without number . . .
>
> *(to Seth)* Follow the prints of my feet, burnt;
> No grass or flower in the world grows
> In that same road where I went
> And we coming from that place . . .

Seth goes to the gate of Paradise and, looking within, sees the tree of knowledge all dry and made bare by his parents' sin. He is bidden by the angel to look again and sees the roots of the tree descending into hell. A third time he is bidden and sees a new-born child high up in the branches: He is the oil of mercy. Seth is given three seeds of an apple from the tree, which he is to place in Adam's nostrils and beneath his tongue when he dies and is buried. From these spring the three rods of Moses, the tree under which David repents of his sin with Bathsheba and commences the psalter (*Et tunc sub arborem sedens incipit psalterium: viz. Beatus Vir*, reads the stage-direction); and in the end, in the *Passio Christi*, it is from this tree that a portion is taken for the Cross.

The whole theme is very moving in its way; it is in its various developments and episodes interwoven throughout the plays, giving them a greater unity. Then too other legends are made use of: the miraculous release of Nicodemus and Joseph of Arimathea from prison, the death of Pilate, the episode of Maximilla in the Temple, the legends of Veronica and the bridge over Kidron. It would seem that a characteristic distinguishing the Cornish plays from the English is that they draw more upon legends for their material. And one sees with a certain historical satisfaction how well all this fits into its proper environment of the Cornish churches, how all of a piece it is with the painted rood-screens, carved bench-ends, the windows richly painted with biblical characters and the legends of the saints.

We know that the manuscript of the *Life of St. Meriasek* was finished by Dominus Hadton in 1504; and it is thought that he was a canon of Glasney College, near Penryn.[1] There is an even stronger case for the Glasney provenance of the *Ordinalia*, for they contain a large number of place-names mostly belonging to that locality. King David, preparing to build the Temple, rewards a messenger with 'Carnsew and Trehembys: make of them a charter for thyself'. Solomon, pleased with its progress, rewards his workers with 'the parish of Vuthek [i.e. Budock] and the

---

[1] Peter, *The Old Cornish Drama*, 34.

Carrak Ruan with its land'. On the completion of the Temple, they are given

> Together with all the field of Bohellan
> And the wood of Penryn wholly,
>   And all the water-courses;
> The island and Arwinnick,
> Tregenver and Kegellick. . . .

But it has not been hitherto noticed how large a part of the third play, the *Resurrectio Domini*, is taken up by the doubting of Thomas; and that the dedication of Glasney College was to Our Lady and St. Thomas.

There are, as one would expect, recognizable local touches everywhere in the plays. In the *Passio Christi*, one executioner claims that there is not a smith in all Cornwall who can blow the bellows better than he; another that there is not a fellow west of Hayle who can bore a hole better. One may imagine that such local claims as these were popular with the audience. The *Life of St. Meriasek* has a local *mise-en-scène*; for St. Meriasek was the patron saint of Camborne and the play has a number of references to places in the vicinity, mostly in Penwith and Kerrier. It seems very probable that the play was written for the feast-day of the Saint, who sometime in the early Middle Ages had lived as a hermit at Camborne, and given his name to a holy well there, before going back to Brittany where he died as Bishop of Vannes and has a number of dedications in his honour.

It is a very long and ill-constructed play, a mere string of episodes illustrating the life and miracles of the Saint; probably based upon the traditional Life which, as we gather from William of Worcester, it was the custom of the Cornish churches to keep — each perhaps its own saint. Interwoven with the Meriasek episodes, there is a good deal of extraneous material dealing with the legends of St. Silvester and the Emperor Constantine. No wonder the play took two days to perform. From the point of view of the dogmatic function of the Church, it is no less interesting than the *Ordinalia*. There is a long disputation between Meriasek and Teudar the pagan Cornish tyrant, on the respective merits of Christianity and Mohammedanism, in which the very sensible position of Moslems on the subject of the Virgin Birth is fairly put. Teudar puts the point that it is against reason 'that a child should ever be conceived without a man's seed in a woman's womb'. The Saint replies, 'As the sun goes through glass without breaking it, as thou seest, so Christ above went into Mary's womb without defiling any joint'. In that reply one seems to hear the voice of some long-dead priest expounding the central mystery of the Christian faith to his flock: a minute but direct shaft penetrating into the mind of the time.

These plays then give an extraordinary insight into the mental life of the people, moulded as it largely was by the Catholic faith. They enable one to form a coherent picture of the fabric of belief and teaching which held them up, the imagined world in which they lived and moved. It gave them standards, administered consolation in suffering, explained in terms of the universally accepted Faith how evil and good were rewarded, and so played an essential part in enabling society to discipline its members and hold itself together.

These remains of the ancient Cornish drama cover the century, and something more, with which this book deals. The *Ordinalia* cycle appears to date from the fifteenth century, and probably the second half of it. To the same period there dates a long narrative poem of 259 stanzas, on the Passion, the *Pascon agan Arluth*: a dull work which covers the same ground, though independently, as the second play in the trilogy. The *Life of St. Meriasek*, at the beginning of the sixteenth century, comes between the *Ordinalia* and the *Gwyreans an Bys*, the MS. of which is dated 1611 and is by William Jordan. The proportion of English words increases very much in the later plays: consistently reflecting the progress of the language in the county. Though even in the *Passio Christi* it is worth noting that when the women come to weep at the Tomb, it is an English hymn that they sing:

> Ellas mornyngh y singh mornyng y cal
> Our lord ys deyd that boughte ous al.

We need not concern ourselves with the remaining scraps of the language, the manumissions in the Bodmin Gospels, the Cottonian Vocabulary, the fragments of liturgy and scriptures that remain. A number of books, like Carew and Norden, record bits of talk, numerals and so on. And Andrew Borde's *First Book of the Introduction to Knowledge* includes a whole conversation for travellers going to Cornwall.[1] His book was published in 1547, and was perhaps the first of a type which has become universal since.

The concluding scene of *St. Meriasek*, in which the Saint takes leave of the faithful and promises absolution and healing to all who remember him, particularly those who come to pray at Camborne, points to a further field of evidence and survival from our period. The dedications of our churches are by common consent very distinctive of Cornwall. They are relics of the

[1] ed. Furnivall, Early English Text Society.

age of the Saints, that period which lies from the fifth to the ninth centuries. This is no place to go into its history; but we need not doubt the historicity of these missionaries who lived and worked in Cornwall, or passed through on their way from Wales or Ireland to Brittany, in that time of wandering; leaving behind them so many memories and legends enshrined in the popular memory, or in the dedications of churches and holy wells. Those memories remained very much alive throughout the Middle Ages, in spite of the efforts of the Church to bring about uniformity and the ministrations of the Bishops of Exeter in re-dedicating churches to received personages in the Roman calendar. One more testimony to the independence and vitality of Celtic tradition in Cornwall.

Devotions to the saints remained in full flood right up to the Reformation. When William of Worcester was in the county in 1478 he made notes of the feast days of many of these Cornish saints: St. Cadoc, St. Piran, St. Petroc, St. Germoe and a host of others.[1] At Bodmin priory and at St. Michael's Mount he took down lists of saints' days entered in their calendars and observed by the house. Leland, who visited us at the high tide of Henry VIII's religious changes, in 1538, and whose interests were distinctly more secular (he was a humanist), knew the story of St. Ia and had read her legend written and kept in the church of St. Ives.[2] Many other churches had similar written lives of their saints, as in Brittany. There too were their images in stone and painted upon the windows or upon the walls, some of which still remain; there were their name-days and rites, which do not. After the Reformation these things fell into disuse; the images were broken or whitewashed over, the devotions discontinued. Nicholas Roscarrock, himself a Catholic who suffered years of confinement for his recusancy in the reign of Elizabeth, set himself to compile a book of the saints, containing their legends, days and rites; and among them, in the years of exile from Cornwall, in prison in London or sheltering in Lord William Howard's house at Naworth in which he ended his days, he wrote down what he could remember from his youth in Cornwall of the observances kept there then.[3] *Super flumina Babylonis, illic sedimus et flevimus: cum recordaremur Sion.* Their names, if not their rites, have survived; and it is curious to reflect in how many Cornish parishes feasts and fair-days are still determined by the ancient commemoration of their saints.

But there are things more intangible still than these: the memories and

---

[1] cf. 'Itinerary' in *Parochial History of Cornwall*, IV; Supplement, 93-112.
[2] Leland's *Itinerary*, ed. Toulmin Smith, I, 192.
[3] Camb. Univ. Lib. Add. MS. 3041.

myths that haunt the mind of a people. No peoples are so haunted by memory as the Celts: therein lies their distinctiveness in Europe. Moreover so much of the folk-memory of the Celtic peoples, if we may use the phrase, seems to have attached itself to the Cornish scene. The Cornish have always been very tenacious of belief in Arthur: *quondam rexque futurus*. Nor is there much reason to doubt the historicity of such a person: the whole tendency of modern research goes to strengthen the tradition.[1] From the early Middle Ages at least the Cornish believed in him as alive still, and not dead. The story of the visit of the canons of Laon to the west country in 1113 is well known: how they passed through the *terra Arthuri* on their way from Exeter to Bodmin, and were shown Arthur's Chair and Oven on the moorland; and how, when they arrived at Bodmin, a tumult was raised in the priory church there by one of their servants disputing whether he were still alive.[2] Carew, who does not commit himself to much on this subject, yet appears to accept Arthur's existence without question and gives evidence of what people believed in Cornwall in his time: 'Upon the river of Camel, near to Camelford, was that last dismal battle strooken between the noble King Arthur and his treacherous nephew Mordred, wherein the one took his death and the other his death's wound. For testimony thereof the old folk thereabouts will show you a stone, bearing Arthur's name, though now depraved to Atry.'[3]

The Tristan story becomes more firmly attached to Cornwall as time goes on. Professor Loth argues for a Cornish provenance for the story told in the earliest French romances.[4] Carew is non-committal and half-sceptical: 'That Mark swayed the Cornish sceptre you cannot make question, unless you will, withal, shake the irrefragable authority of the Round Table's Romance'.[5] Loth investigated in detail the place-names of the romances, and shows how precisely they follow the geography of Cornwall. A curious concatenation of circumstances seems to connect Mark and Tristan with central Cornwall, the district between the Fowey and Camel estuaries. That Carew was well acquainted with the story may be gathered from his description of the son of John Winslade, one of the leaders of the 1549 Rebellion: who 'led a walking life with his harp to gentlemen's houses, where-through and by his other active qualities he was entitled Sir Tristram;

---

[1] cf. Collingwood and Myres, *Roman Britain and the English Settlements*, 321: 'the historicity of the man can hardly be called in question'.
[2] cf. Chambers, *Arthur of Britain*, 18, 184, from Migne's *Patrologia*.
[3] Carew, 122.
[4] 'Le Cornwall et le Roman de Tristan', in *Contributions à l'Etude des Romans de la Table Ronde*.
[5] op. cit., 77.

neither wanted he (as some say) a belle Iseult, the more aptly to resemble his pattern'.[1] For all that, we could have wished that Carew had told us more of what the people actually believed of the remote past in that land

> Where fragments of forgotten peoples dwelt,
> And the long mountains ended in a coast
> Of ever-shifting sand, and far away
> The phantom circle of a moaning sea.

For it is in such things, perhaps, rather than in institutions or their conscious history that the soul of a people lives. And though they are submerged now, it is in them that Cornwall has made its undying contribution to the mind and imagination of Europe.

[1] Carew, 131.

CHAPTER II

THE LAND

ANY sixteenth-century society lived more directly, more immediately off the land than we in the conditions of an industrial civilization are apt to realize. Yet our own dependence upon the land, if in the case of a large proportion of our people it is at a remove, is greater than we think. In the sixteenth century there could be no mistaking it, society was overwhelmingly agricultural in its basis; the dependence upon the land was so obvious as to be taken for granted, visible in all the institutions of society, a continually present influence in moulding its hierarchies, the social order, and reflected in its very prayers, in which a society looks inward upon itself. When the good people of the parish make their general confession in church, according to the Book of Common Prayer, they say: 'Almighty and most merciful Father, we have erred and strayed from thy ways like lost sheep.' When they pray for grace, they pray for 'the continual dew of thy blessing'; when they give thanks for God's mercies, they say: 'Be ye sure that the Lord he is God: it is he that hath made us and not we ourselves; we are his people and the sheep of his pasture.' We have become so accustomed to the liturgical droning of these words in our ears, that we forget how closely these phrases, and all the prayers for rain, or fair weather, or 'in the time of dearth and famine', re-echo the conditions of an agricultural and pastoral society.

Cornwall was in this fundamental respect like the rest of the country, but it has certain distinguishing characteristics of its own. There was, for one thing, the size and importance of the tin industry. Tin-streaming went on over a large area of the county, and mining for tin was just beginning in this age. That made a difference; it made Cornwall more of an industrial county than most. Then the proximity of the sea meant that fishing played a considerable part in its life, and the uses of sand and seaweed entered largely into its agriculture. A number of men, too, must have been employed, increasingly large as the century went on, in the shipping that went in and out of the Cornish ports. So that the Cornish population at this time must have been one mainly of peasants, tinners, fishermen and sea-going folk.

But there were differences within the land system itself which marked it off from other counties. It was a land of scattered hamlets as opposed to the centralized villages of the ordinary English countryside. In this it was, and is, like the other south-western counties, Wales and the 'Celtic fringe': a land of hamlets and scattered homesteads, where, Maitland tells us, 'old Celtic arrangements may never have been thoroughly effaced'.[1] It is evident that geographical determination was a yet more important factor: a country of hills and moors would obviously indicate scattered steadings, the way the ground was reclaimed from the waste, as against the 'nucleated' villages of the fat and comfortable plain.[2] It is only common sense to suppose too that geographical factors determined largely the amount and character of enclosure and commons respectively; the system of large open fields surrounding the centralized village was clearly inapposite to Cornish conditions, if not impossible over large tracts of the county. Carew says: 'The middle part of the shire (saving the enclosures about some few towns and villages) lieth waste and open, sheweth a blackish colour, beareth heath and spiry grass, and serveth in a manner only to summer cattle. That which bordereth upon either side of the sea, through the inhabitants' good husbandry of enclosing, sanding and other dressing, carrieth a better hue and more profitable quality. Meadow ground it affordeth little, pasture for cattle and sheep, store enough, corn ground plenty.'[3]

This already throws some light upon the question how far Cornwall was enclosed, how far it had an open field system of agriculture, with common fields and intermixed strips, like other counties at this time. The evidence on this subject has never yet been collected and very little has been known as to what prevailed.[4] Yet there is no doubt: it is clear from Carew that enclosure was going on in the sixteenth century, and of arable; so that there must have been the open field system in some places. Speaking of pasture and tillage, he says: 'What time the shire, through want of good manurance, lay waste and open, the sheep had generally little bodies and coarse fleeces, so as their wool bare no better name than of "Cornish hair". . . . But since the grounds began to receive enclosure and dressing for tillage, the nature of the soil hath altered to a better grain, and yieldeth nourishment in greater abundance and goodness to the beasts that pasture thereupon.'[5] More specifically, speaking of the divergence between Cornwall and other shires 'in husbandry matters', he says that the Cornish 'fall every where from commons to enclosure, and

[1] *Domesday Book and Beyond*, 15.
[2] cf. Gonner, *Common Land and Inclosure*, 125-31.   [3] pp. 5-6.
[4] cf. Tawney, *Agrarian Problem in the Sixteenth Century*, 262: 'It is a question how far there had ever been an open field system in some of these counties, e.g. Cornwall and Kent.'
[5] p. 23.

partake not of some eastern tenants' envious dispositions, who will sooner prejudice their own present thrift, by continuing this mingle-mangle, than advance the lord's expectant benefit after their term expired'.[1] And again as regards the husbandmen: 'These in times not past the remembrance of some yet living, rubbed forth their estate in the poorest plight, their grounds lay all in common, or only divided by stitch-meal', i.e. in separate strips.[2]

It is clear on which side Carew's opinion lay in this important agrarian issue of the sixteenth century; he was, like all expert opinion, in favour of enclosure; quite rightly, since that way lay economic progress. What is more, he indicates that the Cornish attitude to enclosure, by way of agreement with the lords and among themselves, was the right one, not the conservative resistance which lay behind so many of the agrarian disturbances elsewhere in this century. With this view recent authorities can agree; if only progress had taken this form in other areas, much distress would have been spared.[3] But here Cornwall had a great advantage; it had been following its own method of enclosure from early times. The large expanse of heaths and moors offered obvious opportunities for separate holdings and cultivation; the two went on concurrently; they were but two sides of one process. Such districts 'came into effective use late from a wild or nearly wild state, either by direct enclosure or under a system of cultivation free from the more complicating forms of common, and in particular from intercommoning over arable'.[4] The very nature and circumstances of the land encouraged enclosure in many parts, the steep hill-sides, the fertile but narrow valleys which are characteristic of Cornwall: obviously unsuitable for the open field system.

Yet there were other areas, level and fertile corn-growing lands, where common fields were not unsuitable; and there is considerably more evidence of their existence than has hitherto been realized. There is Carew for one, though he does not tell us the extent over which the open field system prevailed at the beginning of the century which saw its close; he speaks as if it were general, which is clearly going too far. It would seem that it obtained to some extent around the towns. Mr. Henderson writes of Helston that 'Gweal Hellis on the north side of the town was surrounded, after the Anglo-Saxon fashion, by great open common fields, in which each burgess had a number of strips, or "stitches". Nearly all the Cornish towns, notably in the Middle Ages, had such fields surrounding them . . . *Gweal* is the Cornish for an open field as opposed to *Park*, an enclosed field, and all the great fields round Helston (long since sub-divided by hedges) bore the name.'[5]

[1] p. 38.   [2] p. 66.   [3] cf. Tawney, 363.   [4] Gonner, 127.   [5] *Cornish Essays*, 67-8.

33

But we have direct evidence of the survival of common fields right up into our period. On the Cornish manors of the Earl of Devon, surveyed in the reign of Philip and Mary, none survived; but on one, the manor of Tinten in North Cornwall, not far from St. Tudy, they had but recently been enclosed. The surveyor, William Humberstone, writes: 'The lands of late in common fields, and now all enclosed and converted much into pasture, and employed to feeding and grassing of cattle.'[1] Humberstone, like all surveyors, was strongly in favour of enclosure; for he writes disapprovingly of the manor of Mudford and Hinton in Somerset which had three common fields.

A later survey of Courtenay manors in Cornwall, from the reign of Queen Elizabeth, yields some further examples.[2] From that of Treverbyn Courtenay may be drawn a precise picture of my native village of Tregonissey, an obscure hamlet in which the two chief tenants — they were copyholders — were then John Treleaven and Gregory Rowse. The former held one tenement with a close of land called Park en Gwene, 2 acres; a park called Higher Park alias Gwarre Park, of 2 acres; one close called Down Park, 2 acres, and one close called Park Carn of 3 roods; and the reversion to '8 les stitches containing 4 acres *divisim* lying in the common field called Westerfield'. The exciting thing to anyone who knows the village, now alas being swallowed up by the encroaching town, is how much of this is still recognizable. That holding has come down substantially unchanged and is now the Duchy farm; the name 'Down park' has survived; but what clinches the argument is that the 'Westerfield' — the name has not survived, but one recognizes in it the fields lying to the west of the village towards the town — is precisely the kind of land that might have been held and worked in common; for it is good rich soil, undulating in character, fairly broad and flat for Cornwall. There was no question of the upper parks — 'park Carn' means 'rocky park' — being anything but closes; they are far too hilly and heathy; it is quite evident that they were reclaimed waste, and as such, several and enclosed. ' All which substantiates the thesis of geographical determinism.

By the end of the century it would seem that the 'Westerfield' at Tregonissey had been enclosed. There is no mention of it in a later survey of John Treleaven's holding;[3] in its place we find the 'close next the churchtown' 5 acres, the undertown [i.e. the land lying below the farm] 2 acres, the further close 2½ acres, middle close 4 acres, the undertown close 6 acres, the further town close, 10 acres. The point is that these closes cover a great deal more ground than he had occupied in the first survey, and extend in the direction

[1] *Topographer and Genealogist*, I, 43 foll.   [2] E 315/414.   [3] E 315/414.

where the 'Westerfield' would have lain. One can test that because one knows where the undertown fields lie to-day: they still retain their name. Gregory Rowse also has large holdings and in such a position — for example, 'the close under the church way', 5 acres, Polkear 5½ acres, the great close 6¼ acres — that one cannot but think that they occupy some portions of the vanished 'Westerfield'.

Other examples occurring within this manor are at Rescorla, in the first survey, where Richard Rosevear holds 'six stitches lying in common field'; at Carveigh, in the later, where John Reynold holds a stitch of land called Polcatch, containing ¼ acre. Again at Rescorla, in the later survey, Thomas Rosevear has 'a little stitch above the house'. Has the Rosevear holding in the common field dwindled to this in the intervening years, one wonders? Similarly in a survey of the Earl of Oxford's manor of Roseworthy, in 1589,[1] we learn that at Coswinsawsen, Thomas Phillips holds a tenement 'the land whereof is holden in stitchmeal without division and contains to my Lord's part with 8 acres of moor enclosed, 25 acres'. At Porthveor, parcel of the Earl's manor of Bosowen, Henry James held a tenement to which belonged in stitchmeal 56 acres; and at Kestle, there is reference to the common field there, together with a moor, 80 acres, as being in the joint possession of the Earl and Sir John Arundell of Lanherne. Of the Earl's manor of Tresithney, there is at Tresausen a tenement of 30 acres 'holden in stitchmeal together with Nicholas Tredowden and one Isam whereof my Lord's part is the moiety'; and at Bosoghan-veor a tenement 'the ground whereof is in stitchmeal, viz the fourth part 12 acres'. At Trelast, belonging to the manor of Tregennoe, there is a tenement 'the land whereof lieth in stitchmeal with Piers Edgcumbe who hath one half, whereof my Lord's part is 60 acres'. As late as the reign of James I, about 1610, we learn from a survey of the manor of Leighdurrant, one of the Courtenay manors annexed to the Duchy of Cornwall, that 'some part of this manor lieth in common fields, which is hardly found in any manor of his Highness in Cornwall'.[2] From that we may deduce that the open field system was on its way to extinction by the early seventeenth century.

These examples suffice to show that the view that Cornwall had no open field cultivation, that all its arable land was from early times enclosed, is without foundation. How it was introduced we do not know; partly it may have been, in accordance with Mr. Henderson's view, radiated by the foreign influence of the towns in the earlier Middle Ages; partly it may have come into being, where appropriate, through the changes of the fourteenth century

[1] S.P. 12/31/30.   [2] L.R. 2/207.

consequent upon the Black Death, the break-down of serf-cultivation of the manor, the transition from villeinage to copyhold tenure. It is a mute process of which we have no evidence. The picture that we have of Cornwall in the sixteenth century is not that of static and complete enclosure of arable, but a process in being towards that end. In these few entries, taken from a handful of manors, we can still watch the shifts, the change-over from common field held in stitchmeal to enclosure taking place beneath our eyes. It may be that if we had more information from the far west of the county, we should find still more examples of open field cultivation. Moreover the process was an agreed and natural one, following in the wake of the enclosure of waste and moor going on all the time, and not enclosure forced upon recalcitrant tenants to rob them of their common rights. Hence it is that into the great Risings in our period, 1497 and 1549, very little of an agrarian element entered. Yet relics of open field cultivation were exceptional in the sixteenth century. Manor after manor of the Earl of Devon's estates is stated to have no common fields. The accepted view that Cornish land was mainly en-closed is substantially correct.

Far more important, and incomparably more extensive, were the commons in the usual sense, non-arable, pasture land, moor and heath and waste. Mr. Tawney says of the country in general: 'It must be remembered that the area under cultivation was everywhere an island in an ocean of unreclaimed bar-renness which cried out for colonists.'[1] If this seems a little excessive for the more fertile counties of the midlands, it at any rate conveys vividly the situation in the hilly north and west. We have already seen from Carew how much of Cornwall was, as it still is, barren heath fit only for summer pasture. In addition, there was in his day a large area which has been brought into cultivation in the centuries since. A process of nibbling away the waste has been going on all the time, testimony to the increasing efficiency of agriculture, the growth of population and man's necessity to wrest his living from the soil. *In sudore vultus tui vesceris pane tuo.*

The importance of the commons in the economy of almost every Cornish manor may be gathered from the surveys that survive. It is unnecessary to give examples: they are so general. Very few are the Cornish manors which have no due proportion of commons; nor are such manors of any size. The Courtenay manors of Landrene and Northill, for example, which had no commons, were extremely small; whereas the large manor of Treverbyn Courtenay in mid-Cornwall had an enormous area of commons of which the boundaries are given in great detail.[2] Typical of west Cornwall is the

[1] p. 88.   [2] E 315/414.

Earl of Oxford's moderate-sized manor of Roseworthy, which however
has attached to it the 'common called Roseworry down, wherein tenants
of the town of Roseworry claim common without stint, containing 80
acres of heath'; Penhale moor, where the tenants of Carnehell claim common
without stint, 40 acres of very good pasture; and Peanneaneth common of
16 acres in which the tenants of Tresausen claim common without stint.[1]
Here we see something of the economy of a Cornish manor: the hamlet of
Roseworthy with its common for pasture at its doors, the two smaller
downs shared by a couple of tenants each.

More interesting is to observe the process of enclosing the commons.
Of the manor of Tregennoe in St. Ewe we are told that 'there is no common
belonging to the manor other than the waste which hath been made several
by the said John Tregennoe alias Randall to the number of 200 acres belonging to the tenements of Tregennoe wartha and Tregennoe wallas'. In the
manor of Tregorrick in St. Austell, we learn that 'my lord hath the tenth
part of a wasterly moor not yet divided', i.e. 7½ acres. The implication is
that it will not be long before it is divided. It was easier to enclose waste,
since it was not divided into strips with various people's holdings scattered
about. How it was done we know from our present-day knowledge of
Cornwall, and the great hedges which people still raise around their holdings,
constructed with the stones cleaved from the surface of the moor. Such an
entry as this from a survey of Landrene is eloquent of the process: 'Noddon,
being a rocky piece of land enclosed, about 35 acres.'[2] Sometimes enclosure
was made with a quickset hedge, as we know from a case at Helston.[3] The
priory of St. John's Hospital there was seized of 40 acres of waste, which
used to be leased to the inhabitants of St. John's Street from year to year.
Then the Prior sold three acres of this land to Martin John Hycka, who
enclosed it with a quickset hedge. One of the inhabitants of St. John's Street
protested to the Prior, who told him 'to break down the hedge and promised
to defend him therein'.

Important as the commons were to the economy of the manor, they were
still more so to the towns. At Looe, Humberstone reports, there is a common
of 80 acres belonging to the borough, 'which is a great relief to the inhabitants, for all the summer the poor people keep there a cow or two as they
are of ability to buy them, and there is no rate or stint what every tenant
shall keep, for they do not much seek to overcharge the same, but apply their
study to the trade of living'.[4] Well-behaved inhabitants of Looe! It was not

---

[1] S.P. 12/31, 30.
[2] E 315/414.
[3] Early Chancery Proceedings, 1217, 25-6.
[4] Topographer and Genealogist, I, 345.

everywhere the same; for intercommon of pasture sometimes gave rise to quarrels and complaints; the well-do-do put more beasts to pasture than their quota, which ate up the share of the poorer people or those who had no cattle at all.

In the case of larger towns it was usually necessary to lay down with elaborate care the due proportion which different classes of inhabitants were to observe. The borough of Launceston possessed 'by time whereof no mind of man is to the contrary' certain town lands whereof some 'have been before this time enclosed and set to rent, to bear the yearly necessary charge of the town; and another parcel of these said possessions, called the open commons, lieth in quillets and furlongs, whereupon the inhabitants do maintain their tillage, and have hay for their cattle the winter time; and upon this commons every inhabitant doth freely pasture with his beasts, according to the customary stint of the town, after that the corn and hay is carried away'.[1] Then follows the customary stint: 'The Mayor for the time being to pasture with 12 beasts, every alderman with 10 beasts, every burgess that hath been common steward with 8 beasts, every burgess that hath been portreeve with 6 beasts, every other burgess with four beasts, and every inhabitant with two beasts.' One sees from this the inducements there were to hold office in the borough. 'Also there is another parcel of the said commons, of furze and heath, called Skardon, whereupon every inhabitant as well the rich as the poor may freely pasture only with two beasts during the time that the said quillets are in tillage, hayned and lopped. And upon this commons every inhabitant of the town may with hook and scythe cut and carry away upon his back as much furze brake and heath as his need shall require, without paying anything for it, so that he carry none with any cart or horse.' Launceston was fortunate in the extent of its town lands, though every borough and town had some common property. But there it was enough to bring in £50 a year, say £600 or more in modern currency, and this with the return from markets, courts and fairs seems to have been enough to meet all the expenses of the borough. This was surely a more important consideration than what Mr. Tawney calls, somewhat idealistically, 'the pride of common property'.

As some illustration of the difficulties that might arise when the town's claim to pasture upon commons was not clear, we may cite a case from Lostwithiel.[2] One Richard Curtis owned two moors there, Pylmore and

---

[1] Peter, *Histories of Launceston and Dunheved*, 158; it is clear that the date given, 1478, is incorrect, and from internal evidence that this document belongs to the reign of Edward VI.
[2] Star Chamber Proceedings, 2, bundle 24, 120.

Penkevelly; and of the first he had 'at great expense environed with hedges or inclosures' about four acres. The townsfolk of Lostwithiel proceeded to 'put their beasts into the said moors and to eat up and befoul his grass without any lawful authority'. Curtis thereupon impounded the cattle and 'immediately after in the parish church of Lostwithiel aforesaid . . . declared to the parishioners what he had done'. The townspeople promised, according to him, that if he gave up the animals, 'they would never after put in their beasts into the said moors and that they would never sue for common in the same'. However it would seem that they had some claims upon the moors, for the mayor of the town brought an action in Star Chamber on behalf of the burgesses and townsfolk.

It is evident from Carew's account that Cornish agriculture saw a great improvement in the sixteenth century, and that in a manner rather different from the trend in the country generally. For where the latter went in favour of pasture for sheep, to meet the demand of the growing woollen industry, in Cornwall it was in the direction of a greatly improved tillage. Here the county had much lee-way to make up. 'In times past', says Carew, 'the Cornish people gave themselves principally, and in a manner wholly, to the seeking of tin and neglected husbandry; so as the neighbours of Devon and Somerset shires hired their pasture at a rent and stored them with their own cattle. As for tillage it came far short of feeding the inhabitants' mouths, who were likewise supplied weekly at their markets from those places, with many hundred quarters of corn and houseloads of bread. But when the tinworks began to fail and the people to increase, this double necessity drave them to play the good husbands and to provide corn of their own.'[1] So much was this so that in the latter years of the century, in times of good harvest, Cornwall had a surplus of corn to export abroad or to other counties. Carew says that 'had not the imbargo with Spain, whither most was transported, foreclosed this trade, Cornwall was likely in few years to reap no little wealth by the same'. Here was an economic loss to the county on account of the long Spanish war; though some people attempted to counteract it by exporting surreptitiously to the enemy. On the other hand, there were years of dearth when not enough was produced to feed the people, and the Council had to take measures to meet the deficiency.

Carew describes the methods employed in Cornish husbandry as very laborious, 'the travail painful, the time tedious, and the expenses very chargeable'. He gives details of the method of breaking up the ground,

[1] op. cit., 19.

drying and burning the turf, and sanding the soil: charges which 'ordinarily amounteth to no less than twenty shillings for every acre: which done, the tiller can commonly take but two crops of wheat, and two of oats, and then is driven to give it at least seven or eight years leyre, and to make his breach elsewhere'. Cultivation was evidently not very intensive. Two sorts of wheat were grown, the bearded French wheat on the best soil, and notwheat (i.e. unbearded) on the less good. Rye was grown on the worst soil which would bear no wheat. 'Barley is grown into great use of late years, so as now they till a larger quantity in one hundred, than was in the whole shire before; and of this in the dear seasons past, the poor found happy benefit and the labourers also fed by the bread made thereof; whereas otherwise the scarcity of wheat fell out so great that these must have made many hungry meals, and those outright have starved. In the westernmost parts of Cornwall, they carry their barley to the mill, within eight or nine weeks from the time that they sowed it; such an hasty ripening do the bordering seas afford. This increase of barley tillage hath also amended the Cornish drink, by converting that grain into malt, which to the ill-relishing of strangers in former times they made only of oats.'[1]

These passages reflect back from the end of the century, when they were written, to the conditions that prevailed earlier, and yield information which is corroborated by official documents and surveys. Carew tells us that agriculture was more advanced in the east than in the west, and rents naturally higher around the towns than in the country. This is borne out by Humberstone who says roundly in his survey of Leighdurrant in S.E. Cornwall that 'the lands are very fineable, by reason there is such utterance and sale of all manner of victuals to the town of Plymouth, and the people more civil than in the west part of Cornwall, and better disposed to plant and set and furnish their habitations with orchards, and do use the making of cider as they do in Devonshire'.[2] Of the manor of Tinten in mid-Cornwall, he says that the soil is very good and fruitful, 'and the people more civil and wealthy than in the west part of Cornwall, but nothing given to plant or set, or to beautify their habitations with any commodity, but to apply themselves wholly to scrape and gather wealth'. It seems a characteristic of Celtic peoples not to have much instinct for beauty.

The improvement in tillage naturally meant a corresponding improvement in pasture and the size and quality of the animals: 'So as by this means (and let not the owners' commendable industry turn to their surcharging prejudice, lest too soon they grow weary of well-doing) Cornish sheep

[1] Carew, 20.   [2] *Topographer and Genealogist*, I.

come but little behind the eastern flocks, for bigness of mould, fineness of wool, often breeding, speedy fatting and price of sale . . . As for their number, while every dweller hath some, though none keep many, it may sum the total to a jolly rate. Most of the Cornish sheep have no horns, whose wool is finer in quality, as that of the horned more in quantity.'[1] Though Cornwall did not go in therefore for large-scale sheep-raising, like the Cotswolds or the downs of Berkshire and Hampshire, there had been a great improvement in quality and size since the beginning of the century. That the estates of the gentry were being made to bear a larger proportion of cattle may be gathered from the disparking of a large number of deer parks. The fashion in this respect was set by the Duchy of Cornwall, which, in the reign of Henry VIII, disparked its ancient deer-parks at Kerrybullock, Liskeard, Restormel and Lanteglos. Carew says that Henry was persuaded to this measure by Sir Richard Pollard; but since the results did not come up to expectation, 'the one was shent for the attempt, as the other discontented with the effect'. However, the site of the park at Kerrybullock became in time the Duchy's chief farm in the county, as it is to-day.[2] And we find the woods of these parks, when leased out, a profitable item in the economy of the Duchy.[3] The measure was not without its effect, for, Carew says: 'As Princes' examples are ever taken for warrantable precedents to the subject: so most of the Cornish gentlemen preferring game to delight, or making gain their delight, shortly after followed the like practice, and made their deer leap over the pale to give the bullocks place.'

Ploughing was everywhere done by oxen, as it continued to be upon the great farm of Bodrugan upon the coast near St. Austell until within living memory. 'Each ox', says Carew, 'hath his several name, upon which the drivers call aloud, both to direct and give them courage as they are at work.' This also remained right up to the last generation, as I remember hearing, upon the manor of Tregrehan near my home: one more illustration of the extraordinary continuity of the present with that distant past! Up to Carew's time and after, the Devon and Somersetshire graziers continued to 'feed yearly great droves of cattle in the north quarter of Cornwall and utter them at home, which notwithstanding, beef, whitsul, leather or tallow bear not any extraordinary price in this county, beyond the rate of other places. And yet the opportunity of so many havens tempteth the merchants (I doubt me beyond the power of their resistance) now and then to steal a transportation,

---

[1] Carew, 23.
[2] cf. Henderson, 'Cornish Deer Parks', in *Essays*.
[3] For Liskeard park, cf. S.C. 12/27, no. 10.

and besides, uttereth no small quantity for the revictualling of weather driven ships.'

There were very few horses of any quality in the county, as may be seen from the returns of horsemen made for defence purposes in the years before the Armada.[1] But Cornwall bred its own ponies, 'Cornish nags' they were called; we find a Cornish nag in an inventory of the Marquis of Exeter's horses in London: evidently from one of his manors.[2] 'The Cornish horses', says Carew, 'commonly are hardly bred, coarsely fed, low of stature, quick in travel and, after their growth and strength, able enough for continuance: which sort prove most serviceable for a rough and hilly country.'

In timber the county was naturally very poor, particularly as you went farther west (it still is) and the country became exposed to the full beat of the Atlantic gales, with few river-valleys for shelter. And in those days, with the innumerable uses of timber, and the much greater part wood played in all forms of construction, its dearth made a serious problem for the economy of many manors. All the manorial surveys and extents bear witness to the extraordinary care that was taken over the conservation of timber, and the elaborate arrangements made to regulate its use. It was usual to allow tenants enough loppings for hedgebote, firebote, and the repair of their houses; but to fell a tree it was necessary to have licence from the lord. And it is clear that in Cornwall many manors had not enough wood to be self-sufficing in this respect. In spite of all the elaborate precautions taken within the manor, the instructions laid down by royal commissioners in leasing church-lands, even Acts of Parliament, Carew says that the situation got worse: 'Timber hath in Cornwall, as in other places, taken an universal downfall, which the inhabitants begin now, and shall hereafter rue more at leisure. Shipping, housing and vessel have bred this consumption: neither doth any man (well near) seek to repair so apparent and important a decay.'

The improvement in agricultural conditions in the course of our period had the effect of very much increasing the competition for tenements, sending up rents and fines, the latter enormously, encouraging the tendency to consolidate holdings, and widening the disparity between classes on the land, the gentry, the larger farmers and small tenants. Other factors were at work, of which Carew was very intelligently aware. He was an enlightened economist, who for example did not share the prevailing opinion against the export of corn. His statement of the case, if brief, is worthy of modern marginal economics, none the worse for being founded on experience and observation.[3] And he thought that the increase of prices in his age was largely

---

[1] v. later, p. 388. [2] *L.P.* IV. 3759. [3] p. 23.

due to the influx of precious metals from America, a view with which modern opinion concurs. The other chief factor, in his view, was the growth of population, which he put down partly to 'the banishment of single-living votaries', i.e. the ending of monasticism and clerical celibacy — where again he is in sympathy with some modern schools of thought; partly also to 'younger marriages than of old, and our long freedom from any forewasting war, or plague, hath made our country very populous'.

Now for his evidence: 'In times past, and that not long ago', he says, 'holdings were so plentiful and holders so scarce, as well was the landlord who could get one to be his tenant, and they used to take assurance for the rent by two pledges of the same manor. But now the case is altered: for a farm, or as we call it, a bargain can no sooner fall in hand, than the survey court shall be waited on with many officers, vying and re-vying each on other; nay they are mostly taken at a ground-hop, for fear of coming too late. And over and above the old yearly rent, they will give a hundred or two hundred years purchase, and upward at that rate, for a fine, to have an estate of three lives: which sum commonly amounteth to ten or twelve years just value of the land. As for the old rent, it carrieth at the most the proportion but of a tenth part to that whereat the tenement may be presently improved, and somewhere much less: so as the parson of the parish can in most places dispend as much by his tithe, as the lord of the manor by his rent.'[1] This sounds rather over-optimistic, and Carew qualifies it by saying that it applies to East Cornwall, and to land about the towns above all. And he adds that Cornish people differ rather from other shires in preferring 'to take bargains at these excessive fines, than a tolerable improved rent, being in no sort willing to over a penny: for they reckon that but once smarting, and this a continual asking. Besides though the price seem very high, yet mostly, four years tillage with the husbandman's pain and charge, goeth near to defray it.'

The landlord's point of view is written all over this passage. But its substantial accuracy may be shown from the manorial surveys. In the survey of Roseworthy we read that David Angove occupies a tenement, late of John Rawe deceased, 39 acres at 26s. 10d. rent: 'the tenement is in the Lord's hands for the which David offereth fine £40'.[2] This may have been exceptional; but the following figures are hardly less eloquent of the trend:

[1] L.P. 37.   [2] S.P. 12/31, no. 30.

Holding	Tenant	Rent		Old Fine		New Fine		
		s.	d.	s.	d.	£	s.	d.
Roseworry	John Drewe	18	6	20	0	6	13	8
,,	Mr. Godolphin	46	8	20	0	30	0	0
Bosowen	John Rawlyns	22	2			30	0	0
,,	John Coswarth	13	6	13	4	} 33	6	8
,,	Margery Carthew	13	6	16	0			
Tresithney	John Coffer	53	4	40	0	50	0	0
Demyliock	—— Nancarrow	15	0			35	0	0

Some of the new fines are not after such an excessive rate; but the totals are revealing. The annual rents of the tenements then (1589) void within the manor are £18 14s. 1d.; the old fines upon these brought in £6 15s. 4d.; the new fines offered £267.

The disparity that had grown between the rents paid and the actual annual value of the land may be illustrated from the little manor of Austell prior, surveyed about 1610:[1]

Tenant	Holding			Term	Rent		Annual value	
	acres	roods	perches		s.	d.	s.	d.
Ric Kendall	3	2	10	2 lives	10	0	70	0
Joseph May	5	3	24	,,	7	0	40	0
,, ,,	0	0	5	,,	2	0	26	8
,, ,,	4	3	6	,,	1	2	40	0
Nich. Sawle (a mill)	1	0		3 ,,	46	8	70	0
,, ,,	1	1	0	10 years	9	0	22	8
John Stephens	3	2	19	12 ,,	5	0	70	0
J. Delamaine's tenement				34 ,,	2	0	3	4

Though the disparity varies, it is usually very large. Exactly the same holds good of the large manor of Carnanton, for which we are given the actual annual values of the holdings with which to compare the rents. The annual value is in many cases ten times the rent.[2]

All this is evidence of the truth of Mr. Tawney's thesis for the country in general. In the later fifteenth century and still more as the price-revolution got under way in the next, 'a manor on which there was a large number of customary tenants must have often seemed from the point of view of the owner a rather disappointing form of property, because the first fruits of

[1] L.R. 2/207.   [2] E 315/388.

44

economic progress tended to pass into the hands of the tenants. . . . The economic rent of unearned increment of their properties was intercepted by the copyholders, instead of being drained, as under leasehold, into the pocket of the lord.'[1] In the first stages of the depreciation of money and rising prices, the scales were tipped in favour of the tenants, against the landlords, with their fixed freehold and copyhold rents, and the wage-earning classes. The wage-earners tried to bring about a readjustment of wages to prices, but on the whole wages lagged behind and they lost ground. Landlords were in a better position; all over the country they faced their tenants with 'the alternative of surrendering their holdings or paying the full competitive price which could be got for them. And thus it caused an almost revolutionary deterioration in their position. . . . Now the unearned increment was transferred from tenant to landlord by the simple process of capitalizing it in the fine demanded on entry.' The tide of economic progress moved against the tenantry in the later sixteenth century, where it had been in their favour earlier.

It is this that underlies the new disposition of classes, the great strengthening of the position of the gentry, that is going on under the later Tudors — from the dissolution of the monasteries onwards, and with the dissolution itself as an important aid in the process. Cornwall is no exception in this fundamental development over the country in general. But it is interesting to watch the process in one county clearly, even microscopically, for evidences of its movement and for illustration of its effects. It was this rising tide of prosperity which enabled all the houses to be built by the Cornish gentry, and in so improved a style, when there were so few at the beginning of the century.[2] Then there were few, only Bodrugan, Lanherne, Cotehele, Stowe, Place at Fowey, of any consequence; by the end of the century there were Place at Padstow, Arwennack, Trerice, Morval, Mount Edgcumbe, Godolphin, Port Eliot, and soon after Penheale, Lanhydrock added to them. Where so many demesnes were leased out to farmers or customary tenants in the earlier period, or being possessions of the Church were run by bailiffs on behalf of the distant monks, by the end of the century they were coming to be occupied by a gentry on the spot, hard-working, avid of money and power, ambitious. Where the monks of St. Germans had prayed and (perhaps)

---

[1] op. cit., 304.
[2] cf. *Topographer and Genealogist*, I, 346. 'In those days men of worship sought no curious buildings, nor had any great regard to their estimation or calling and to seek to place themselves according to their estate, but to bear a low sail far under their degrees; but whether it were of policy or for need, or it were the fashion of the country, I know not. I see no great excess in the building of the country at this day, unless a few in number which swim in wealth; but I am sure the great number of gentlemen in the country be contented with their father's old house for want of a new.' This belongs to the reign of Mary.

ploughed, the Eliots came with their forward, rasping disposition; where the monks of Bodmin had their tithe-barn at Lanhydrock, the Robarteses settled and with the vast fortune they made out of tin-speculation and usury made a great estate. It was not long before these people, the new class they represented, were strong enough to challenge the King and the old social order.

Everywhere the gentry were on the upgrade and building up their estates around resumed demesnes, or vacated cells or lapsed holdings. The demesnes of the manor of Trelawne, which had belonged to Lord Bonville, were leased in 1504 to William Edwards, who was bailiff there.[1] A century later the place was bought by the Trelawnys, who until that time had resided at Poole, a smallish house in Menheniot. The cell of the Bodmin monks at Padstow, where they had their tithe-barn, became the fine house of Place, built by the Prideaux whose founder here was steward to the last priors; his family has been there ever since. Rialton, Prior Vyvyan's country manor near Newquay, was granted to the Mundys, relatives of the last Prior of Bodmin, who proceeded to raise up an interesting and varied stock there. The Chamonds got Launcells, the charming possession of the monks of Hartland; the cell of the monks at St. Anthony became Place near Falmouth. Nor was the process confined to lands late of the Church; all over the county, as all over the country, new men were stepping up into the larger farms, adding field to field and acre to acre, the younger sons of established families planting themselves out upon the soil; and once rooted, three centuries have not seen their hold essentially changed.

The manorial organization provided the basis of tenure and of services from the land all over the country. The manor was still, as it remained for long, the unit of juridical organization, and in many cases of economic organization. But the economic self-sufficiency of many manors was breaking up, owing to the growth of internal trade, the dividing up of manors by succession, their increasing variation in size, the lapse of ancient services. In fact time was disintegrating the economic organization of the manor, while preserving its utility as a legal and social unit. It is difficult therefore to draw an adequate picture of the manor and its working in the sixteenth century above all; for the preciseness and regularity of the earlier medieval system, with its boon days and work-silver, its all-embracing custom, was breaking down. The ancient services were ceasing to be rendered, the economic functions of the manor tending to be merged in something wider and losing their circumscribed and formal identity. But its system of courts, courts leet

[1] E 315/385.

BODMIN PARISH CHURCH

COTEHELE

and courts baron, remained, and in the eyes of the law the manor was what it always had been: the fundamental unit of land organization. We have to hold in mind therefore a somewhat imprecise picture of change going on beneath our eyes, in which certain functions of the manor gradually cease and are shredded away, while others remain.

'Every tenement', says Carew, 'is parcel of the demesnes or services of some manor. . . . That part of the demesnes which appertaineth to the lord's dwelling house, they call his barten or berton. The tenants to the rest hold the same either by sufferance, will or custom, or by convention. The customary tenant holdeth at will, either for years, or for lives, or to them or their heirs, in divers manors according to the custom of the manor. Customary tenants for life take one, two, three or more lives in possession or reversion, as their custom will bear.'[1]

What emerges from the study of manorial records is the overwhelming importance of the 'custom of the manor' in regulating its affairs. For the great mass of the peasantry, the customary tenants and what remained of the villeinage, the custom of the manor set the mental environment in which they worked. What had existed 'time out of mind', or was set down from time to time in the records of the courts as the custom of the manor, gave the peasantry what security they had, formed a barrier against change, and constituted an ultimate appeal which they relied on not in vain for the protection of their rights before the courts of the land. The appeal was always to that custom, and the King's courts made their decisions in the innumerable cases that came before them in accordance with it. Hence the extreme importance of knowing what it was, keeping it intact, writing it down. It was what governed the relations between the lord and the great bulk of his tenants. It was universal in character, and yet particular to its own manor. There were variations from manor to manor, yet these very variations were in accordance with a general pattern.

Humberstone wrote by way of preface to his survey: 'These customs are not so universal as if a man have experience of the customs and services of any one manor he shall thereby have perfect knowledge of all the rest. Or if he be expert of the customs of any manor in any one county that then he shall need no farther instructions for all the residue of the manors within that county.'[2] He then specifies customs which were universal throughout all the Earl's west-country manors: all customary tenants were bound to repair their houses and buildings at their own cost, but if there were timber growing within the manor the lord would find it; all tenants freehold and customary were bound

---

[1] p. 36.   [2] *Topographer and Genealogist*, I, 44.

to render suit at the lord's mills. He then promises to specify 'other customs ... which serve generally for the county of Cornwall', a promise which very significantly he does not fulfil. No doubt there were too many exceptions and variations.

Carew tells us that 'the ordinary covenants of most conventionary tenants are to pay due capons, do harvest journeys [i.e. days], grind at the mill, sue to the court, discharge the office of reeve and tithing-man, dwell upon the tenement and to set out no part thereof to tillage without the lord's licence first obtained'.[1] It was usual also upon Cornish manors to pay a heriot of the best beast upon the death of a tenant; and there was a custom that if a stranger passing through the county chanced to die, a heriot of his best beast was paid, or his best jewel, or failing that his best garment to the lord of the manor.[2] Such was the 'custom of Cornwall'; but Carew tells us it was dying out in his time.

Upon Cornish manors, as elsewhere, the demesnes were mostly granted out. That was naturally the case with all the Courtenay manors, for the Earls of Devon had never resided in Cornwall, though Sir Hugh Courtenay, son and heir of the Earl, lived at Boconnoc in the mid-fifteenth century. Let us take the manor of Tinten, for example; Humberstone says that 'one Sir John Taverney knight did inhabit within the said manor and kept great hospitality and occupied the demesnes in his own possession which are large and great, and now of late years granted out by copy for term of lives amongst the tenants, and the tenants at that time did custom services and works which are now converted into money'.[3] That may be taken as characteristic of most Cornish manors at this time. At Colquite, each of the first eight tenants held a portion of the demesne with his tenement: it had clearly been divided among them at some time.[4] At Portloe, in the reign of James I, the surveyor says: 'The demesne lands have been so long in grant by succeeding copies before the fee farm that they can hardly be distinguished from ancient customary lands.'[5] But there were certain lands allotted to three tenants that paid no work-money as the rest of the copyholders did, and therefore he supposed that these were demesne lands and 'henceforth most properly to be granted by lease'. This is interesting as showing how demesne became copyhold, and from copyhold came leasehold by the pressure of the lord's agents. At West Antony the demesnes were let by copy and divided among four tenants, and now reputed customary land.

[1] p. 38.
[2] cf. Survey of Leighdurrant (James I), L.R. 2/207.
[3] *Topographer and Genealogist*, I, 346.
[4] S.P. 12/109, 10.   [5] L.R. 2/207.

Almost everywhere the old boonworks, the labour services performed on the demesne at harvest time, had become disused; money payments had taken their place. At Leighdurrant, Humberstone reports, the tenants formerly did custom works, 'but it was many years past and clean without the remembrance of any man living'.[1] At Landulph, the lord had sometime inhabited there, but there was no remembrance among the tenants or in their copies; 'the custom works, if any were, are clearly drowned in their rents'. But these were manors in close proximity to the towns of Plymouth and Saltash, and much affected by that. Upon the remote Duchy manors of Boyton and Bradridge, formerly belonging to Launceston priory, relics of custom works survived into the reign of James I. The surveyor says that the tenants here were accustomed to work in the demesnes in time of harvest; now some of them, both free and conventionary, give money in lieu of services; but others continue to work.[2]

The most frequent term for which copyholds were granted was three lives in Cornwall, though terms for one or two lives were quite frequent and four not unknown. In one case a grant for five lives, upon the manor of Leighdurrant, is regarded by James I's surveyor as not good in the custom of the manor; but since the manor had been dismembered, it might have held good if it were not voidable on other grounds.[3] Upon the Earl of Oxford's Cornish manors the copy was for one life only; upon the Courtenay manors and those of the Duchy, the custom was three lives. This system of tenure continued to survive right up to our own time. Carew notes as a characteristic distinguishing Cornwall from other counties that the people 'always prefer lives before years, as both presuming upon the country's healthfulness, and also accounting their family best provided for, when the husband, wife and child are sure of living'.[4] He mentions also that upon some manors the widow had the right to hold her husband's tenement during her widowhood; this held good on practically all Courtenay and Duchy manors.

The fact is that the underlying bias of the custom of the manor was in favour of the tenants. It is extraordinary how conservative it was. Mr. Tawney says that it gave the dwellers on the land 'their social environment and their conception of social order', which if we do not grasp, 'we cannot understand their mental horizon'.[5] That conception of social order was, of course, a conservative one; all the agrarian risings of the sixteenth century were essentially conservative; it was the upper classes who were the innovators, the progressives. The custom of the manor impeded the free action

[1] loc. cit., 227. [2] L.R. 2/207. [3] ibid. [4] p. 38. [5] p. 124.

of the lords and their agents when they wanted to break through. By the end of our period a Duchy surveyor can write like this: 'Customs in this case [Landulph] are very nice, sometimes binding the lord, sometimes not; as it pleaseth the tenants to think most for their own behoof, that must be the custom. And the lord cannot dispose of his own, being in his hands, but according to the will of the tenants, whose will is the custom of most manors.'[1] This surveyor clearly has a mind of his own; but therein speaks the temper which made the lords press forward towards leasehold. No doubt the lesser gentry, being on the spot, were in a position to press more effectively than distant nobles who never saw their remote estates, still more than the Duchy which for long periods of time was swallowed up in the Crown and hardly maintained its administrative identity.

Mr. Tawney makes the point that Crown tenants got more favourable treatment than those of private lords; the Crown could afford not to be pressing, was in any case more conservative, and apt to be absent-minded. The long dormancy of the Duchy in the Crown from 1547 to 1603 meant much slackening in administrative efficiency; rents were lost or became submerged, encroachments were made upon its commons,[2] or private persons erected mills which diverted water from the Prince's. Here is the complaint of the surveyor at Boyton, when the Duchy administration was being tightened up under James I.[3] One Loveys had built a mill higher up the river, which took the water away, and the customary tenants no longer ground at the Prince's mill, which had been worth £10 a year, and now nothing: 'the principal reasons be for that any man may more freely abuse the King or the Prince (specially in former times) than any private person who will retain the customary or conventionary tenants to their suit or socorn, viz. to the custom mills. And will sustain no detriment by any, but will seek reformation. But his Majesty and his Highness have too many to have one to seek redress in things wherein they are in this nature abused.'

With the Duchy occupying so important a place in the land system of Cornwall, the conservative character of Cornish tenures must have been strengthened and a breakwater interposed which protected the tenantry against the too rapid changes which agitated other counties. The literature of the mid-sixteenth century is full of complaints of the depopulation of the

---

[1] L.R. 2/207.

[2] cf. Survey of the manor of Grediowe (L.R. 2/207): certain commons belong to the manor 'whereof is encroached and enclosed to the private use of certain freeholders as of customary or conventionary, who have thereby as I take it, forfeited the rest of the herbage. And what is encroached is *in primo jure* the Prince's and the rest of the common by his Highness to be improved ... How much there is encroached requireth a further inquiry to find'.

[3] ibid.

countryside to make sheep-walks. Nothing of that kind is true of Cornwall. A considerable improvement upon the poverty with which the period starts seems to be the story of the century. Only one instance of a depopulated manor appears, that of Bonealva in the parish of St. Germans. Here we learn that John James's tenement is 'now utterly ruined as are all the tenements that Mr. Kekewich holdeth, whereby the land is become surrounded, overgrown with bushes in many places, the fences decayed which much disableth and discrediteth the land. There is notorious waste to be observed in this manor punishable by statute, for it is a manifest depopulation converting the habitations to desolations, and the land from due maintenance for the common weal to far more unnecessary uses, though it may be conceived more convenient for Mr. Kekewich to dispose the tenements and to convert the same to his own use, whose mansion house and demesnes adjoin to this. And of four convenient farms there is but one left habitable, which is another man's possession.'[1] Mr. Kekewich had six of the seven tenements within the manor, and all the woods: perhaps he was engaged in making a park. We know that the town of St. Germans was impoverished by the loss of the monastery. But this case was altogether exceptional.

The bulk of the population on the land probably consisted of the customary tenants. The copyholders, says Harrison, are those 'by whom the greatest part of the realm doth stand and is maintained.'[2] And no doubt many would add: 'The whole wealth of the body of the realm cometh out of the labours and works of the common people.'[3] Mr. Tawney estimates that on a number of manors in the south-western counties, Wiltshire, Somerset and Devon, 77 per cent of all those holding land are customary tenants. The impression one derives is somewhat different for Cornwall; the proportion is not so high, even if they were a majority.

The daily routine going on within the manor, this life of physical necessity, so elemental and close to the soil, was much the same on the land in Cornwall as elsewhere in England, or for that matter in north-western Europe. Nor is it necessary to describe it in detail. Any series of court rolls, provided it extends over a sufficient length of time, will give you an idea of what it was: the slow process of change amounting almost to changelessness, the diuturnity of the routine, dated by the feasts and saints' days of the Church,

[1] cf. Survey of the manor of Grediowe (L.R. 2/207).
[2] Quoted in Tawney, 49.
[3] Quoted from Pauli, *Drei Volkswirtschaftliche Denkschriften*, in Tawney, 344.

the fabric of custom and customary morals within which simple men lived their lives. Mr. Tawney tells us, with a touch of imaginative sympathy for their human quality, that 'their silence was the taciturnity of men, not the speechlessness of dumb beasts'. Though that may a little be questioned, no doubt he is on the side of the angels. Yet it is probable that the information that speaks to us out of these records is that of the few intelligent men of the manor, spurred on by the active mind of the lord's steward.

For all that, each manor has something of a democratic unity – if that is not to misuse words, suggest later ideas. The men of the manor, the homage, have their responsibility: each of them is liable to be called on to be reeve. One knows so well what average human intelligence is like: the simplicity of mind, yet with it the capacity to carry burdens of responsibility, to render mutual help in the common labour of living. It is the give and take of primitive society, and social life at its simplest, at the base of the structure, has something of a self-governing, self-regulating character about it.

We may take, by way of illustration, among hundreds of such records, the series of court rolls for the little manor and borough of Michell, which extends with some gaps for a hundred years, from 1443 to 1546.[1] We have a complete record for the year 22-23 Henry VI, which enables us to see the full working of the manor, with its courts leet held twice, and its courts baron five times a year, by the steward of its lord, Sir John Arundell. The homage elect the reeve for the year and the two officers to taste the ale and weigh the bread. They then proceed to amerce all those who have brewed or baked without licence; it appears that the names of all brewers are regularly written down, as if all had been guilty as a matter of course, the innocent being afterwards acquitted with a *non brasiavit*. And so the common business of the manor was regulated: the homage presented the death of any free tenant and who the heir was; the reeve saw to it that he paid his relief and did fealty; stray cattle found within the manor were brought into the lord's pound; pleas of debt and trespass were heard, payments of fines and profits on the annual fair held on St. Francis's day collected. The manor made its contribution to the sustenance of the rich and gracious family living at Lanherne, building its fine house, bringing up its children, laying out its money upon rich stuffs, brocades, damasks, jewels, fine linen – all the things which appear in Arundell wills of the time – enabling it to play its part in Cornish affairs and farther afield. So these things are connected together, the small and the great, the produce of the soil transmuted into a higher way of life, of leisure and culture.

[1] Henderson, XIII, and *Essays in Cornish History*, 54-60.

Then comes a gap of forty years in the rolls, from 1450 to 1492, of civil war, of dynastic defeat, of a new royal house itself overthrown and displaced at length by an upstart Tudor — all the goings on of the great ones far away over their heads; and at the end of this time, the court rolls of Henry VII and Henry VIII's time take up exactly as they left off forty years before. There are much the same sums received as perquisites of courts; the parchment roll upon which the steward wrote his account costs 4d., as before; the same names appear, the same families go on for centuries in the country places, in that age-long routine of the manor which only came to an end in our own time.

CHAPTER III

INDUSTRY: TRADE: SHIPPING

TIN-MINING was the industry in which Cornwall was pre-eminent; it marked the county off from all other counties, except Devon, which shared in it to a decreasing extent; it gave Cornwall its distinctive place in the economy of Europe. From very early times right up to the modern age, Cornwall was the chief source of supply for the western world. With wool and lead, tin formed the bulk of England's exports, and as a commodity had 'an importance in international trade hardly less than most of the spices of the East'.[1] During the Middle Ages the centre of the industry had steadily shifted from east to west, from south-west Devon into east Cornwall, and later, in our period, within Cornwall from east to west.[2] It was this which raised to a position of pre-eminence in the industry, and of power and wealth in the county, the Godolphin family whose house on the slopes of Godolphin Hill in the far west lay very conveniently near rich alluvial tin-streams in the moor below and lodes leading into the hill above. It is a very nice, and a concrete example of economic determinism that that house and all its history, the greatness they afterwards achieved in national affairs, should have sprung from that hill and its lodes of tin.

Of course they were a family of ability to make use of their opportunity; hence their success, their rise to wealth and importance. The tradition is that the Godolphins took the lead in introducing new technical improvements which marked the sixteenth century in the industry, in importing German master-miners, or mining engineers as we should call them, to make improvements, and that they erected the first large stamps to be put up in the county.[3] It seems that this activity goes back to Sir William Godolphin, the head of the family in Henry VIII's time and a leading figure in Cornwall, for a period also Lord Deputy of Boulogne. But certainly these activities took a great extension in the next generation with Sir Francis Godolphin, who devoted all his ability to his mining affairs and public business within the county, and unlike the Grenvilles and Arundells took no part in affairs outside. So his concerns prospered; and when Carew at the end of the century came to write his account of the tin industry, he was much helped by

---

[1] Lewis, *The Stannaries*, xiii.   [2] ibid., 43.
[3] Hamilton Jenkin, *The Cornish Miner*, 53.

Sir Francis and his account is correspondingly the better for it. After paying tribute to him as a public servant, Carew says: 'By his labours and inventions in tin matters, not only the whole county hath felt a general benefit, so as the several owners have thereby gotten very great profit out of such refuse works as they before had given over for unprofitable, but her Majesty hath also received great increase of her customs by the same, at least to the value of £10,000. Moreover in those works which are of his own particular inheritance, he continually keepeth at work 300 persons or thereabouts, and the yearly benefit that out of those his works accrueth to her Majesty amounteth, *communibus annis*, to £1,000 at the least, and sometimes to much more. A matter very remorceable, and perchance not to be matched again by any of his sort and condition in the whole realm.'[1]

The sixteenth century saw an important turning-point in the industry, which was attended with considerable difficulties and towards the end a period of depression: this was the transition from tin-streaming to tin-mining. In the Middle Ages the industry was conducted almost wholly by tin-streaming operations; but with the gradual exhaustion of stream tin it became necessary to tap the lode itself and to mine for it. The process can never be said to be quite complete: you may still see tin-streaming going on here and there in remote places in Cornwall, little one-man shows like that at Perran Coombe, or at Polgooth, or along the desolate-looking 'bottoms' between Redruth and the coast. But mining in general developed with the sixteenth century: it is what is characteristic of the industry in our period.

This in turn necessitated all sorts of other developments; in the first place, technical advance in the art of mining. Germany at that time was the country of the most highly developed mining, and a number of German experts were brought in to survey for mines, supervise the sinking of shafts, introduce improved methods in smelting and so on. We hear of the elder Höchstetter and of a Hans Hering being employed in Cornwall: they were, of course, mining engineers. Sir Francis Godolphin employed a German to advise him as to improvements; Carew tells us that he 'took light from his experience, but built thereon far more profitable conclusions of his own invention'. Peter Edgcumbe was in touch with an odd German called Burchard or Burchard Cranach, who not only advised him as regards mineral matters but entertained medical notions too.[2] Of all these, little enough is known. But it so happens that among the State Papers we have a whole correspondence remaining between Ulrich Frose, another German master-miner, and his employer William Carnsew, which throws a flood of

[1] Carew, 153.   [2] Henderson, VII.

light not only upon the technical operations of mining in Cornwall in the 1580s, but upon its financial and social background.[1]

A further consequence of this development was that it necessitated larger financial backing. And we find a group of partners in the City — they are referred to as a company, with Mr. Customer Smyth at the centre and others such as Sir William Winter and Sir Lionel Ducket in association — interesting themselves in the possibilities of Cornish mines. It seems that their aim was to prospect for minerals of all kinds, especially for copper and lead, with a hope of finding silver and to reopen certain old abandoned workings and work them further. It was a time, the threshold of the war with Spain, when mineral enterprises were being set on foot in different parts of the country, with the active encouragement of the government, in order to make us independent of foreign supplies. The London company had also interests in South Wales and Cumberland; we hear of their smelting works at Keswick and at Neath, to the latter of which their Cornish ores were sent. At the Cornish end of the concern was a group of local gentry of whom William Carnsew of Bokelly was the most active, and through whom the correspondence passed.[2] A Mr. Weston seems to have been the financial agent employed and the overseer of the various enterprises on foot in Wales and Cornwall. Customer Smyth sent down Ulrich Frose, with a strong recommendation to Carnsew as to his honesty, skill and industry: he was to set the actual mining operations going, sink the shafts, overlook the workmen and so on.

Frose set himself to work upon Treworthy mine on the coast at Perran Sands, the modern Perranporth. There is a reference to this mine having been given over twenty-three years before by Carnsew who had worked it with the aid of the German Burchard: that would be about 1560. Frose sent his assistant Barnard, another German, prospecting for copper mines elsewhere in the county, and he returned with optimistic reports. Perhaps that is only characteristic of miners at all times and in all places, for their hopes certainly outran their finds. Later on we hear from Frose that Barnard had run away 'like a naughty deceitful *ungodly* [in the margin] man'. Barnard's reports of copper finds in the west had not come up to expectation. In addition there were German workmen employed, for Carnsew writes to Smyth protesting that they were more expensive than Cornish miners: 'Mr. Weston's prudence in bringing in the Dutch miners hither to [advance]

---

[1] The following account is based upon S.P. Dom. Eliz., vols. 163 to 199, *passim*.
[2] For Carnsew, see later, p. 426; and cf. Carew on him, p. 17: 'a gentleman of good quality, discretion and learning, and well-experienced in these mineral causes'.

such business in this country is more to be commended than his ignorance of our countrymen's [readiness] in such matters, who out of all peradventure be as skilful in mining, as hard and diligent labourers . . . in that kind of travail as are to be found in Europe.' Carnsew writes with conviction, and perhaps not without a certain Cornish patriotism. He makes the interesting suggestion that this might be brought to proof by allotting the German workmen a mine to work, while Ulrich set his Cornishmen on to similar work, and 'let it be considered which of them for one whole summer's day shall put you to most charges and gain you most'.[1]

Carnsew started with a good opinion of Frose, and asked him to stay at Bokelly over his first Christmas-tide in Cornwall. But the difficulties at Perran were too much for him and depressed his spirits. By employing Germans at the beginning the work had grown expensive; there was not enough capital to dig deep enough, according to German ideas (in Germany, he complained, they were willing to spend much more money in going deeper before expecting a profit). The mine was disappointing; when at last they got near a lode, the water burst in so that the men narrowly escaped with their lives. Frose became discouraged, despondent, lachrymose: it is odd to note how German his characteristics stand out after the lapse of so much time. He was fairly educated, wrote English well, though he was apt to spell it phonetically: he says 'bick-men' for 'pick-men', 'dender' for 'tender', and always 'hath' for 'have'. In these little peculiarities one can hear the accents of that far-away German in Elizabethan Cornwall. He mentions several times that his eyesight and head will not serve him to go down those dangerous cliffs where men were lowered on a rope. No wonder! It is curious to think of him, he leaves such a definite impression of personality, as one stands upon Droskyn Point and observes the workings, the adits and levels cut in the cliff, the heavy seas upon that coast rushing in and out of the channels made by those long-dead men.

Not only at Perran were they active, but also along the coast at St. Agnes, Illogan, and St. Just. At the last two there was a promising return of copper ore, but Perran and St. Agnes continued disappointing. Carnsew himself went down Treworthy with Frose and 'along the adit which is 50 fathom long under the old works'; but still they had not come to any ore, and they were at the expense of installing a pump. The fact was that the technical difficulties were outrunning their resources; in later centuries Frose's belief in the mine was justified by results. But as things were they had not capital enough to continue; the company in London doled out small sums of £50,

[1] S.P. 12/163, no. 74.

and then £20, and clamoured for results. These were not forthcoming and Carnsew, who had already had experience of losing money over mining ventures, became tired of Frose. Customer Smyth wrote to say that they proposed to move him to Wales to take charge of the smelting, 'being more a place for his quietness there than the following of the mines, as I conjecture by the imbecilities you write to be in him'. Hans Hering was to be brought back to Cornwall; but he too had his disadvantages: he was to 'use himself quietly and carefully in his office, better than (is reported) he did the last time of his being there, for his entertainment is like to be no longer among us, than that his behaviour and diligence shall be found good and honest'. There was no love lost between the two Germans: Frose wrote of Hering that 'when he was here before he said what he should do here, for here is no mines worth working; and that I had informed my master of good and rich mines, which is not so, and so he reported of me now being in the north country, which truly I do not mean to take at his hand . . . I do perceive Hans Hering is a great man with him [i.e. Mr. Weston]; the end will show all what he is.'[1] The usual quarrel of experts!

A year or two later, and we hear of Frose, after a sojourn in the North Country, evidently at Keswick, now in charge of the smelting at Neath. The copper mines at St. Just had turned out well: the man in charge there writes to Carnsew: 'I would to God we had a dozen such mines as St. Just's ore, for we have gotten of the said two mines from the 6 of July to the last day of October 50 ton and better.' Twenty men were employed at St. Just in addition to the captain. The ore was taken to St. Ives by boat, where it was freighted for South Wales and smelted under Frose's charge at Neath. The vessels brought back on their return timber for the mines, of which there was a scarcity in Cornwall. So that the collaboration between Cornish metal and South Wales smelting, which was such a notable feature of the Industrial Revolution of the eighteenth and nineteenth centuries, was anticipated in the Tudor age.

The correspondence comes to an end in the year 1587 with all that it has of the intimate and revealing of these undertakings to offer us: Frose's incessant complaints, Carnsew's efforts to keep things going, the men waiting for their pay, which is always in arrears. There is a charming touch of Carnsew preaching a sermon to his household: Otes concludes a letter to him, 'So with my humble duty remembered I commit your worship to the preservation of the Lord our God which art in heaven gives us this day our daily bread, as I shall remember the sermon which your worship did make upon

[1] S.P. 12/172, 32.

the same.'[1] Carnsew was a bit of a Puritan. It would be a little far-fetched to correlate this with nascent capitalism: is it not rather the natural and instinctive looking to providence to assure a man of his livelihood?[2] Besides, capitalism of a sort already existed in Cornish mining in the Middle Ages.[3] At Penrose the mine they had started was yielding very good lead, 'and there is also with the same lead other metal than lead, supposed to be tin by the judgment of most tinners of great knowledge'. But they could not pay the men, and the men would not work any longer without money; Otes was reduced to letting them work the mine at their own venture, himself providing them with the tools upon account. It was a method common enough in the tin-mines. Suddenly there came an arrest upon the mines at St. Just by Mr. Trevanion and his associates, no doubt due to financial difficulties: perhaps they were creditors, or possibly officials of the Duchy.[4] The correspondence ends with a characteristic lament of Frose's at the lack of ore for his furnaces at Neath. He had hoped to be in Cornwall again that summer, but had heard of Trevanion's stay of the mines and discharge of the men. Darkness descends upon them and upon their doings. It may be that the letters cease because Carnsew died; but there can be no doubt that an important impulse had been given to mining, for minerals other than tin, which continued from that time.

All the time the tin industry was of enormously greater importance. This is not the place to go into technical detail about its conduct — that may be gathered from a number of books and articles devoted to the subject. It is my purpose rather to sketch its general condition and its place in Cornish life at the time. Carew tells us that already in some cases men worked to a depth of forty and fifty fathom, and one can imagine, in spite of the rudimentary precautions of the time, under what conditions.[5] Notwithstanding ventilation-shafts 'their work is most by candle-light'. The toll of human life was beginning already: 'the loose earth is propped by frames of timber-work as they go, and yet now and then falling down, either presseth the poor workmen to death, or stoppeth them from returning . . . In most places, their toil is so extreme as they cannot endure it above four hours in a day, but are succeeded by spells: the residue of the time they wear out at quoits, kayles, or like idle exercises. Their calendar also alloweth them more holy-days than are warranted by the Church, our laws or their own profit.'

---

[1] S.P. 12/195, 50.
[2] I permit myself this reflection upon what has come to be known as the Tawney-Weber thesis.
[3] Lewis, op. cit., 189.
[4] S.P. 12/198, 68; 199, 5, 18.
[5] v. Carew 7-19 for his account of the industry.

Carew's was very much of an upper-class attitude: when you see the ingenuity of their workings, 'how aptly they cast the ground for conveying the water, by compassings and turnings, to shun such hills and valleys as let them . . . you would wonder how so great skill could couch in so base a cabin, as their (otherwise) thick-clouded brains'. He has a vivid passage, revealing very much the attitude of a cultivated country gentleman to the industry, wondering how it can be profitable when you consider all the charges of winning the tin before smelting it: 'whereto if you add his care and cost in buying the wood for his service, in felling, framing and piling it to be burned, in fetching the same when it is coaled through such far, foul and cumbersome ways to the blowing-house, together with the blowers' two or three months extreme and increasing labour, smelting heat, danger of scalding their bodies, burning the houses, casting away the work, and lastly their ugly countenances, tanned with smoke and besmeared with sweat: all these things (I say) being duly considered, I know not whether you would more marvel, either whence a sufficient gain should arise to countervail so manifold expenses, or that any gain could train men to undertake such pains and peril. But there let us leave them, since their own will doth bring them thither.'

But that is just the point: it was not their own will but natural necessity. The industry yielded its profits, at every stage, but not to them. The surplus-value skimmed off their labour produced large sums for the Duchy or the Crown — forty shillings upon each thousand-weight at coinage, in addition to customs at the ports. Coinage money was the largest item of revenue which the stannaries afforded: an average of £2400 a year in the first half of the century for Cornwall, compared with some £250 for Devonshire.[1] The highest sum reached was £2828 2s. 10d. for 1547, which drops markedly to £1976 19s. 11d. for 1549, the year of the Prayer Book Rising. In the latter half of the century the profits of the coinage fell to an average of under £2000 with the decline in tin production. But in addition the Crown derived a considerable revenue from the sale of licences to export, and from the toll tin raised on the numerous royal manors. Altogether Cornwall, through the dubious distinction of its liaison with the Duchy, was a fine milch-cow for the Crown and remained so for centuries: a long-continuing mark through the pages of history of its original condition as a conquered country.[2] No wonder Cornishmen as late as the sixteenth century remem-

---

[1] Lewis, op. cit., Appendix K.
[2] This was the view of Mr. Charles Henderson, in whose eyes it accounted for the comparative poverty of Cornwall in large houses and estates.

bered that they were a conquered people, and resented it.[1] They had cause to.

There were in addition other small taxes falling upon some of the stannaries, such as tribulage — a sort of poll-tax levied within the stannaries of Penwith and Kerrier.[2] There were too the profits of the stannary courts, the fines upon uncoined tin, occasional forfeitures. No doubt a good deal of tin was smuggled without paying duty: very understandable, particularly to a Cornishman.

Though enterprisers like Carnsew and Edgcumbe may have lost money by their ventures, there were families, besides the Godolphins, who made money out of tin. All landlords received a proportion, usually a fifteenth, called toll-tin, upon that raised within their manors. To a family like the Arundells of Lanherne, with their manors in the tin-bearing district of central Cornwall, their revenue from tin was not inconsiderable.[3] Carew tells us stories of two families, where a dream of one of their womenfolk led to a lode being discovered: in one case they found a work 'which in four years was worth well near so many thousand pounds'.

The great majority of the tinners were small producers, though there was a class, of whom the Godolphins were the outstanding example, of large producers. Various modes of employment were in use from the simple wage-labour to co-operative partnership and one-man shows on part-time, where a man alternated, as in Cornwall to-day, between work at a mine or tin-stream and looking after his small-holding.[4] Carew tells us that the wages were about 8d. a day, or 'for the year, between £4 and £6, as their deserving can drive the bargain: at both which rates they must find themselves'. One must remember that there would be many days in the year when, for one reason or another, work would be impossible and wages therefore not available. Mr. Lewis gives a number of instances from the early part of our period of miners receiving an average of 4d. a day, with more for washing ore.[5] But the Cornish, with their hankering after independence even at the cost of pecuniary loss, or perhaps owing to a curious speculative streak in their character which made them opt for the hope of a windfall rather than the certainty of a small return, made them prefer the tribute system. They have always been like that, and it really was not very intelligent of them.

---

[1] cf. before, p. 20.   [2] Lewis, 139-40.
[3] cf. also Henderson xxv, for account of Sir Piers Edgcumbe's toll-tin, aº 5 to aº 6 Henry VIII, by John Treveryan, his toller.
[4] Perhaps I may be allowed to cite, as examples, my friend Samuel Johns of Roche, and my grandfather, William Rowse of Tregonissey, who worked as a tin-miner, usually as a 'tributer', but also had a small-holding in the village.
[5] Lewis, 196-7.

Mr. Lewis says that 'the fact that Cornish miners as a rule preferred the illusory independence of the tribute system rather than the frank acceptance of the wage system tended to make them an easier prey for the dealer'.[1] We have already had an example of what the tribute-system was, at Mr. Penrose's mine, where the partners for a share of the profits allowed the tributers to work the mine for them and make what they could. Very often, and for long periods, they made nothing and their families went hungry.

There is no doubt that the general lot of the tinners was one of poverty and economic insecurity. Beare wrote in his survey of the stannary of Blackmore in 1586: 'The most part of the workers of the black tin and spaliers are very poor men — and no doubt that occupation can never make them rich — and chiefly such tin workers as have no bargains but only trust to their wages, although they have never so rich a tin-work; for they have no profit of their tin if they be hired men, saving only the wages, for their masters have the tin.'[2] Carew noted that 'the parishes where tin is wrought, rest in a meaner plight of wealth than those which want this damageable commodity; and that as by abandoning this trade they amend, so by reviving the same they decay again; whereas husbandry yieldeth that certain gain in a mediocrity, which tin-works rather promise than perform in a large measure'.[3] Thomas Cely writing to Burghley, stressing how important it was that someone holding position and rank in the west country should be made Lord Warden of the Stannaries, referred to the tinners as 'ten thousand or twelve thousand of the roughest and most mutinous men in England'.[4] It seems probable that of the Cornishmen who flocked into the risings of 1497 and of 1549, those despairing gestures of a people which mark our period, a great number were tinners.

One thinks of them in the end as the poor, pathetic human beings they were, at the mercy of wind and weather, of tin-dealers and merchants and usurers, with their gallant spirit, the affectionate, half-humorous names they gave their works, and the odd tinners' language that prevailed among them. Beare says: 'When occasion of talk is ministered of owls, foxes, hares, cats or rats, then it behoveth them to beware chiefly, for then must you speak in tinners' language and in no other language than tinners have decreed. The owl must be called 'a braced farcer', the fox 'a long tail', the hare 'a long ear', the cat 'a rooker', and the rat 'a pup'. The tinners often introduce these words of a set purpose that they may bring you to name some one of these.'[5]

[1] Lewis, 211.   [2] Quoted in Lewis, 198.   [3] Carew, 16b.
[4] v. Lewis, 217.
[5] Quoted in Hamilton Jenkin, 52.

INDUSTRY: TRADE: SHIPPING

Anyone who broke the rule, of course, paid a forfeit. It is a characteristic well-known in primitive societies, like the peculiar speech used among the boys at Winchester and other schools. Something of the same spirit survived up to the last generation among the miners and china-clay workers, in their almost universal habit of going by nicknames. Carew draws attention to the names they gave their works. One can see a little way into their minds from the Elizabethan survey of the great tin-bearing manor of Treverbyn Courtenay: the commons on the uplands above St. Austell, now pocked with china clay pits, were then full of little tin-works, half Cornish, half English by name: Great Beam, Gwethenbarra, Will Gummow's Work, Cricktoll and Good Fortune, Penweneff, Little Good Fortune, Little Space, Our Lady Beam and a score of others.[1] You may still see some of these workings out on the moor; some of the names remain the same: all that survives of these dead tinners, except their blood that runs in our veins.

The smallness of their operations, their defencelessness, made them the victims of blind economic forces and of all too sharp-sighted tin-merchants and dealers. The literature of the industry, reports and surveys, letters and state papers, Carew himself, all bear witness to the hardships they ran. The sixteenth century was a period of profound economic disturbance, of dislocation and new growth. Mr. Lewis says: 'The tinners' grievances were evidently smouldering through a long period, until under the Tudors matters reached an acute stage.' He regards the price-revolution as the underlying cause, throwing all costs out of gear. Food, clothing, and the necessities of their work, timber, rope, candles and other mining requisites, shot up in price out of all proportion to the increasing price fetched by tin. In addition there were the extra charges in working due to the deepening of the mines as time went on. The price of tin fluctuated wildly; and the century ended with a very severe depression throughout the stannaries. The annual output of tin declined to under 1000 thousand-weight; the coinage duty, a fair index, which averaged £2400 in the first half of the century, sank to under £2000 in the years 1597-1600.[2]

All this was, of course, the opportunity of the speculative dealer, the tin-merchant, the usurer. Carew gives a detailed account of the extortionate means employed, the surplus value of the tinners' labour squeezed out at every stage in the process.[3] They took advantage of his necessity to bind the labourer to deliver so much tin at the next coinage; but instead of handing over the money promised in return, they held out and then advanced him

[1] E 315/414. [2] Lewis, 212 foll.; and App. J and K.
[3] Carew, 14b foll.

63

wares instead, upon which to maintain a bare subsistence. In this way, supposedly independent tinners came completely under the bondage of the dealers. A species of usury ran throughout the industry, from the great merchant buyers at the top — chiefly the London pewterers — through the dealers and lesser merchants, to the small tinners at the bottom sustaining the burden. Mr. Lewis says that 'the ultimate profits of the tin dealers must have been large'; he instances cases where the 'poor tinners' sold to the dealers for £15 or £16 per thousand-weight, while the latter re-sold to the pewterers for £28 to £30. Fortunes were made by this apt combination of dealing and usury: there was Ezekiel Grose of Camborne, a nasty Elizabethan lawyer, who made a packet out of this and blossomed out upon the lands forfeited by the Tregians for religion.[1] The greatest example of all is that of the Robartes family, who having started as merchants at Truro, by tin-dealing and usury achieved an enormous fortune and bought a peerage from Buckingham.[2] They were, of course, on the Parliamentarian side in the Civil War.

There was a great deal of discussion of this state of affairs in the last years of the century and various remedies proposed, the most prominent of which was the revival of pre-emption, which had lapsed during the previous two centuries. The central idea of this was that the whole output should be bought by the Crown, at a fixed figure: this would give the tinners some stability of price; it would be necessary also to establish a loan-fund from which to advance them money between coinages, if the dealers were to be got rid of. They never were. Various offers were made by persons like Sir George Carey and Lord Buckhurst to take over the pre-emption. In the end it would seem that the Queen made an experiment in this direction, advancing the tinners some £8000 without interest. But the experiment, when it took place, did not last. The poor tinners clutched at the mooted pre-emption, like drowning men at a straw, but it was opposed by the rich tinners, 'since they make money out of the necessity of the poor men, who cannot wait for a better market, but are forced to borrow at twenty per cent and to sell their tin cheaply'.[3] Carew says that the rate was very often forty per cent.

There was a direct and fundamental cleavage of interest between the poor and the rich tinners, which one can see reflected in the institutions of the stannaries. For obvious fiscal reasons the Crown had throughout the Middle

[1] v. below, pp. 374-5.
[2] cf. Gardiner, *Constitutional Documents*, 17, 39; Coate, *Cornwall in the Civil War*, 5.
[3] Quoted Lewis, 220.

Ages a direct interest in their organization. The five stannary jurisdictions grew up around the chief areas of tin-streaming and mining operations: Foweymore, Blackmore, Tywarnhayle, Penwith and Kerrier.[1] These were organized under the direct control of the Duchy, to which all the Crown's mineral prerogatives had been handed over at its creation in 1337. For most of the Tudor period the Duchy lay dormant in the Crown, there being no Prince of Wales to bear rule as Duke; and the Crown's deputy was the Lord Warden of the Stannaries. There functioned under him a whole apparatus of courts with their final appeal to the Prince's Council. Henry VII, who had declared the stannary charters forfeit, to renew them on payment of a fine of £1000 in 1508, by this extended the privileges of the tinners to include owners, merchants, buyers, gentlemen bounders and others. The stannary parliament of 1588 divided all tinners into two classes: manual labourers, 'spaliers' and 'pioneers' as they were called, and gentlemen who shared in tin works or received toll tin as landlords, owners of bounds with all other workers required in the industry, smiths, blowers, smelters.[2]

But it does not seem that the Cornish tin convocations or parliaments, which were supposed to represent the whole industry, in fact represented any class but the large mine-owners and tin-dealers. At the tinners' parliament of 1588 they petitioned the Queen that the number of representatives from each stannary should be doubled, and the additional six be chosen, not by the mayors and councils, but by the stannary courts as in Devon, where the system worked more democratically.[3] But Mr. Lewis's analysis of the personnel attending the Cornish parliaments from 1588 onwards shows that they were recruited mainly from the leading county families.[4] The whole apparatus of the courts was in their hands and at their command; and how they were used by the county gentry, to serve their own purposes, whether the affairs were properly stannary affairs or not, may be seen from the example of Sir Richard Grenville — whom one would hardly have thought of as a tinner.[5]

The sixteenth century saw the jurisdiction of these courts encroaching until all kinds of cases, many of them remote enough from tin matters, came within their purview. For example, Sir Richard Grenville haled Thomas Hilling before the Stannary Court of Blackmore for slander of his father-in-law, Sir John St. Leger. At the same time there was a consolidation of the whole system of courts, a clarification of their position and a definite

---

[1] cf. for stannary of Blackmore, Henderson, *Essays*, 130-4.
[2] Lewis, 98-9.   [3] Add. MS. 6713.   [4] ibid., 129.
[5] cf. my *Sir Richard Grenville*, 150.

confirmation of their independence of the common law. By 1510 there was already a settled system of appeals from the steward's court in each stannary to that of the Vice-Warden, from him to the Lord Warden and ultimately to the Prince's Council.[1] This was confirmed by the leading case of Trewynnard, in the Court of Chancery in 1562 and in Star Chamber in 1564, which decided that a writ of error from a stannary court to the ordinary courts of law did not lie.[2]

In return for the special fiscal burden the industry bore, the stannaries were exempt from ordinary taxation; though they were charged with ship-money in the exceptional circumstances of 1588. They mustered their men separately from the forces of the county. This led to a good deal of friction in Devon in the crisis of 1588-89, where the Lord Lieutenant and Justices of the Peace complained that many men escaped their duty altogether on plea of belonging to the stannary.[3] It is worth while comparing in the two counties the proportions of the body of men to be raised by the stannary with that of the county. In Devon, the county was to furnish 1200 foot and 134 horse, of which the stannaries were to provide 200 foot. In Cornwall they were also to provide 200 foot out of a total of 600 foot and 66 horse: a much larger proportion.[4] In Cornwall too there were difficulties of adjustment, but these were got over by appointing Sir Walter Ralegh Lord Lieutenant of the county as well as Lord Warden; and after a certain tussle upon his first appointment, the steady support of the Crown enabled him to preserve the stannaries' independence in this as in other matters. In fact they constituted in all respects an *imperium in imperio*, whose great importance in the economy and social structure of Cornwall distinguished the county (and, to a lesser extent, Devon) from all others.

The county possessed, we are to suppose, the usual complement of domestic industries, though with some differences. For example, in the earlier part of our period, Cornwall produced not much good wool: the sheep were small, and of a coarse fleece. What they produced went under the name of 'Cornish hair', and as such had been exported from earlier times without paying custom.[5] But later, with the improvement of pasture and stock, Carew tells us, Cornish sheep grew to as good a size as those elsewhere and furnished good wool. So there would be spinning and weaving in Cornish homes as in other counties at the time. Perhaps rather more, for the west country was then the chief centre of the woollen industry, to which Wales

[1] Lewis, 112.
[2] cf. J. R. Tanner, *Tudor Constitutional Documents*, 355-6.
[3] cf. S.P. 12/209, 22; 216, 48.
[4] ibid., 206, 40.   [5] Carew, 23b.

and Ireland sent increasing supplies of wool for manufacture:[1] Exeter was the chief mart and place of export: the solid reality behind all those monuments to wool-merchants in the pleasant red-sandstone churches of the city. But though Devon and Somerset were more important in this respect, there was a certain export of cloth, known as 'Cornish straights', too.

Then there were the industries connected with building. The county has always had plentiful supplies of stone and slate of various sorts. Carew says: 'For windows, doors and chimneys, moor-stone carrieth chiefest reckoning. That name is bestowed on it, by the moors or waste ground, where the same is found in great quantity, either lying upon the ground, or very little under.'[2] It was in fact granite, in which the county is naturally rich. In the later Middle Ages the churches were built of moor-stone, where in the Norman period they appear to have used only the rarer 'cataclewse', from the cliffs near Padstow. Another famous quarry was on the coast near St. Austell and produced 'Pentewan stone', of which such fine churches as Bodmin and St. Austell were built. From the building accounts of Bodmin parish church we can trace payments for the carriage of this stone, by sea, from Pentewan to St. Blazey, and thence overland to Bodmin.[3] Along the coast, conveniently at the sea-ports, were the lime-kilns: the lime at Bodmin came from Padstow. Then there were masons, carpenters, plumbers, glaziers, who were all local men.

Carew notes the three different sorts of slate produced: the best, blue in colour, the second sage-leaf, 'the third and meanest grey'. He says that the first was held in good regard, 'as, besides the supply for home-provision, great store is yearly conveyed by shipping both to other parts of the realm, and also beyond the seas into Brittany and the Netherlands'. We remember the present that Sir Richard Grenville the Marshal made to Cromwell, of 18,000 slates from Cornwall for the roofing of his house, to advance his suit for the Marshalship of Calais.[4] And we find a Welsh boat, the *Speedwell* of Carmarthen, carrying a cargo of 10,000 slate stones back from Padstow in 1603.[5] There were various smaller local industries like the making of mats in the west of Cornwall 'of a small·and fine kind of bents there growing, which for their warm and well-wearing, are carried by sea to London and other parts of the realm, and serve to cover floors and walls. These bents grow in sandy fields, and are knit from over the head in narrow breadths after a strange fashion.'[6] Or there was the growing of garlic round Stratton,

---

[1] E. A. Lewis, *Welsh Port Books*, 1550-1603, p. xxviii; and A. K. Longfield, *Anglo-Irish Trade in the Sixteenth Century*, 86.
[2] p. 6.   [3] *Camden Miscellany*, VII.   [4] *L.P.* VII. 1475.   [5] Lewis, op. cit., 218.   [6] Carew, 18b.

'the countryman's treacle, which they vent not only into Cornwall, but many other shires besides'.[1] Tanning, to judge from the export of hides, must have had quite a place of its own among Cornish industries.

But, most important, after agriculture and mining, must have come fishing. Carew, who was an enthusiastic angler and wrote extraordinarily bad verses on the subject, has a long and boring account of fresh-water fish: altogether of less importance than the sea-fisheries, about which he does give some information, though unfortunately no figures.[2] It seems clear that our period was one of considerable development in the in-shore fisheries of Cornwall, as, farther afield across the Atlantic, there was the astonishing rise of the Newfoundland fishery to a dominant place in the western European markets. Upon the Cornish coast seine-fishing was introducing new conditions and displacing the older arrangements. It tended to cut out the smaller men; since the seine landed much larger catches, and the size of the net demanded the co-operation of three or four boats, each of them with six men or so apiece. This necessitated more capital and led in turn to the domination of the market by the merchants, dealing on a larger scale and chiefly for the export market. The needs of the export market brought about a change in the manner of curing the fish: instead of being smoked singly they were packed into hogsheads. Then they were pressed with great weights to squeeze the oil out of them. This 'train-oil' had a number of uses and was a commodity entering into export. In 1603, we find the *Nicholas* of Milbrook carrying 500 tuns of train-oil to Milford Haven.[3] The fish themselves, under the name of *fumadoes* (for they were formerly smoked), were exported in large quantities to Spain and Italy — as pilchards continued to be to Italy right up to our own time. Those intended for the French market were salted and packed in staunch hogsheads so as to keep them in pickle: the French, as always, had finer palates.

The consequence of the growing demand abroad and of the increasing hold of the merchants upon the supply was that the price of fish went up; complaints were made that there was a scarcity among the inhabitants while the merchants engrossed the profits. A further consequence was to enhance the price of cask, 'whereon all other sorts of wood were converted to that use': Cornwall already had a shortage of timber.[4] Towards the end of the century there was a prolonged and very interesting conflict between the fish-merchants of east Cornwall, who had engrossed the trade and built cellars at Cawsand to concentrate their catches for export, and the town of Plymouth to which the fish had formerly been brought for free sale in the

---

[1] Carew, 117.   [2] pp. 28-35.   [3] Lewis, 234.   [4] Carew, 33b.

market.[1] The struggle raged for a long time and gave a good deal of bother to the Privy Council, which made various orders in favour of the town and appointed Sir Francis Drake and others to see to their execution. In effect it affords a very precise example of the Tudor idea of controlling trade in conflict with new economic tendencies — in a word, progress.

Two surveys which were made in 1570 and 1582, at times when our relations with Spain were approaching a crisis, by way of knowing what the resources of the country were, give us a picture of the seafaring occupations of the west country, the number of ships, mariners and fishermen. The first of them is practically complete: it surveys the coasts parish by parish; only a few parishes like St. Blazey and Tywardreath and in the extreme north seem not to have sent in their returns; but we are given the shipping in harbour at the time.[2] What stands out in this respect is the extraordinary increase in the amount of foreign shipping at Falmouth: there were no less than four boats of Dieppe, two from Emden, two from Hamburg, and one each from Amsterdam, Bremen, Morbihan and Colchester in harbour at the time. This was a change from earlier in the century when Falmouth had very little importance, in fact hardly existed. Several factors combined to bring this about: Henry VIII's building of Pendennis and St. Mawes castles to defend the haven, the activities of the Killigrews who ruled there, the growth of western shipping with the new trade-routes, the war. Earlier in the century it was Fowey which was the most important of Cornish ports, as it had been throughout the Middle Ages. It still had more of the Irish and Welsh trade; Falmouth was rather a port of call for continental shipping.

This survey gives us a total of 40 masters, 1065 mariners, 72 seiners, 25 cargers for the whole county. The seiners are found, as we should expect, in the eastern parishes mainly: Rame, Looe, Talland, Fowey, and thereabouts, with a few in the far west at Lelant and St. Buryan. Very notable is the large number returned for St. Keverne, 4 masters and 104 mariners, more than for any other parish. True it was a large one, divided into four parts. But it may be that it was overpopulated, and this may throw some light on its restless record; St. Keverne men were very much to the fore in the risings of 1497, in the disturbances of 1538 and 1548, and again in the rebellion of 1549. For the rest, the parishes around Looe, Fowey, Padstow, St. Ives provided the largest totals, along with such big coastal parishes as St. Austell and St. Goran. Of the ships named, some were to win fame.

---

[1] cf. my 'Dispute concerning the Plymouth Pilchard Fishery, 1584-91', in the *Economic Journal* (*History Supplement*), Jan. 1932, from which I have taken some sentences.
[2] S.P. 12/73, 8.

There was the *Frances* of Fowey, owned by John Rashleigh, which a few years later sailed with Frobisher upon his third voyage to Meta Incognita;[1] it was probably a successor of hers of the same name which John Rashleigh set forth and sailed up-Channel to join the fleet against the Armada in 1588. At Plymouth there were, among the ships owned by William Hawkins, the *Judith*, in which the young Drake had returned from the disaster of San Juan de Ulloa the year before, and the *Pascoe* in which he was to sail in two years' time upon his resounding enterprise in the West Indies. There were at Fowey besides, the *Anne* belonging to Robert Rashleigh, and the *Violet*; these were of 40 tons. Practically all the Cornish boats were of small size, under 30 tons, and so not returned. But between 1571 and 1576 there were built the *Margaret* of Looe, of 160 tons, and the *Grace of God* of Fowey, 120 tons.[2]

The second survey, taken in 1582, is rather different in character.[3] It gives us 3 ships of 100 tons and upwards for Cornwall, all belonging to Fowey, compared with 7 for Devonshire and 62 for London; 2 ships of 80 tons, compared with 3 for Devon; and 65 ships, hoys, barks and so on of under 80 tons, compared with 109 for Devon and 44 for London. It is obvious that the bulk of west-country shipping was of small size, and that London possessed a smaller number, but of larger boats. The numbers of sea-faring men were calculated on a different basis: they were, for Cornwall, 108 masters, 626 mariners, 1184 seamen; for Devon, 150 masters, 1914 mariners, 101 fishermen. Evidently the Cornish fishermen are included along with the seamen.

Impossible to give a complete and detailed account of Cornish trade: it is a special subject of its own and would demand a book by itself. Nor would such an account be satisfactory; so many of the records are defective and wanting. But it is possible to give a sufficient idea of what the trade chiefly comprised in the early sixteenth century and to indicate certain trends.

First we may take the evidence of the customs returns: the Cornish trade came roughly under the heading of Plymouth and Fowey, most of the Devon trade being included under Exeter and Dartmouth.[4] It is to be noted that the receipt of customs at Plymouth and Fowey doubled between the first year of Henry VII's reign and the last: it went from £326 19s. 7½d. in 1485-86 to £646 14s. 8½d. in 1508-09. The last four years of the reign achieved a record; they returned three times the amount received in 1486-87. No doubt something of this was due to the increased efficiency of Henry VII's administration, and perhaps to the active pressure of his later years. The figures for

---

[1] Hakluyt, *Principal Navigations* (Maclehose ed.), VII, 236 foll.
[2] S.P. 12/107, 68. [3] ibid., 156, 45.
[4] In the following paragraphs I am summarizing the figures given by Schanz, *Englische Handelspolitik gegen Ende des Mittelalters*, II, 39 foll., 109 foll.

Exeter and Dartmouth were even more spectacular: they went from £515 4s. 7¾d. in 1485-86 to £1614 14s. 5¾d. in 1508-09. The increase at Bristol was nothing like so striking: from £887 6s. 1d. to £953 9s. 11¼d., though it had been a good deal more in the middle of the reign. One is impelled therefore to the view that there was a very real increase in west-country trade in the course of Henry VII's reign, no doubt in part due to his peace-policy, his effective keeping of the seas, and to his active encouragement.

The reign of Henry VIII affords something of a contrast. For the most part of the reign the figures maintained very nearly the level reached in Henry VII's time. But its closing years, 1542-47, witnessed an extraordinary decline, due evidently to the French War, and especially to the naval fighting in the Channel. For Bristol saw no such decline, except for the year 1543-44. Nor was the decline at Exeter and Dartmouth so marked, though it was considerable. Poole, however, was as adversely affected as Plymouth and Fowey. In these last the receipts went down from £778 18s. 7¼d. in 1541-42, the last year of peace, to £477 6s. 4½d. in 1542-43, reached bottom in 1544-45 with £133 12s. 1½d., and ended up in 1546-47 at £233 9s. 10d.

The same story is revealed by the figures of all the chief classes of exports and imports; and at the same time as the trade carried on by English subjects rapidly declines, that of foreigners to some extent increases. Take tin, the chief export. There is a considerable fall in the years of the French War: from 375,712½ pounds in 1509-10 to 81,525 pounds in 1543-44; by 1546-47 it had made up some leeway again and reached 293,600 pounds. At the same time the proportion exported by the foreigner increased somewhat. The trade from the Devon ports declined equally to one-third in the year 1543-44, but in general nothing like so much as in Cornwall. It may be that Cornish ships were more heavily engaged in privateering.

It would seem that this may be partly the explanation, to judge from the figures for the export of cloth. This was quite an important item in the Cornish export trade: rough, uncoloured woollens were made in the county, which on account of their narrow size were called 'Cornish straights'. These were exported in pieces; the figures speak for themselves:

| | Plymouth and Fowey | | Exeter and Dartmouth | |
Year	Inhabitants	Foreigners	Inhabitants	Foreigners
1509-10	439 pieces	58 pieces	4980 pieces	242½ pieces
1542-43	189 ,,	29 ,,	4417½ ,,	724¼ ,,
1543-44	62 ,,	91¾ ,,	3510½ ,,	682 ,,
1545-46	18 ,,	142½ ,,	1683½ ,,	2100 ,,

There is a very noticeable increase in the proportion of trade held by foreigners, which at once sinks with the end of the war. Hides were another item of Cornish export; the trade from Devonshire was inconsiderable. They were sent off in 'dickers' of ten hides each; the quantities varied very much from year to year, and there are many gaps in the figures. But the following will give some idea of the trade:

	Exported by		Value		
Year	Inhabitants	Foreigners	£	s.	d.
1509-10	11 dickers	——	11	0	0
1511-12	91½ ,,	64 dickers	180	0	0
1515-16	354½ ,,	37½ ,,	394	16	8
1534-35	208 ,,	32½ ,,	220	16	8

No doubt there was in addition a considerable quantity of all these goods which was smuggled, without paying customs or subsidy.

The chief import, at any rate in value, was wine; and here the import through Plymouth and Fowey came not far behind Exeter and Dartmouth. Both came a long way behind Bristol, which imported between two and three times their amount, or as much as Cornwall and Devon together. The import through all three was of unsweetened wine, upon which ordinary consumption depended. Sweet wines came in almost wholly through London and Southampton: the really rich families either bought their sweet wine there or imported their own direct. Here are some figures of wine imports, in tuns:

	Plymouth and Fowey		Exeter and Dartmouth	
Year	Inhabitants	Foreigners	Inhabitants	Foreigners
1509-10	214	—	182	147
1510-11	628	55	578	116
1540-41	865	98	739	361
1542-43	478·	8	687½	49
1543-44	104	—	258	4
1546-47	70	45	131	69

Here, too, one observes the same drastic falling-off during the war years. The foreigners played a larger part in the Devon trade, probably in return for woollens, than they did in the Cornish. At Bristol there was no such falling-off, doubtless because its wine-fleet was strong enough to defend itself, where the smaller west-country ports depended upon little ships not so capable of venturing out in war-time, unless perhaps they were engaged in privateering on their own.

From the Port-Books and Customs Accounts that survive we can trace in detail the little ships going in and out of the Cornish ports with their particular cargoes. Let us take an average year in the reign of Henry VII, 1498-99, the year after the risings in the west.[1] What stands out from the returns is that trade with Brittany is far and away more important than any other at all the Cornish ports. We find innumerable little boats of Ushant, Poldavy, Lantrégan, St. Brieuc, Concarneau, Blavet, Penmarc, Quimper, etc., arriving with their mixed cargoes of bay salt, linen, cloth and canvas of Breton manufacture, and taking away Cornish tin and hides, white and russet Cornish straights, fish — chiefly pilchards, herrings and congers.[2] In the early part of the century we have the impression that the trade is chiefly carried in Breton bottoms; the Cornish ships are fewer. But that tended to change as time went on, English sea-power grew and France suffered from the Wars of Religion — the last phase of which was fought out in Brittany, a complicated struggle in which Spaniards and English as well as French and Bretons took part. But trading relations between Brittany and Cornwall were so close, in addition to the link of a common speech, that it is not surprising to find a considerable Breton element in the Cornish population.[3]

In this particular year Fowey had much the largest trade of any Cornish port — and that remained on the whole true throughout the century, though Falmouth was catching up later on. Fowey was the chief port of export for tin, as to-day of china-clay. There were this year exported from Plymouth by inhabitants 21,250 lb., and by aliens 3350 lb.; while from Fowey the figures were 129,150 lb. and 14,250 lb. Thomas Eliot, who was himself one of the Customers of Plymouth and Fowey, had licence by letters patent this year to export a large quantity of tin. It is interesting to watch how he made up the amounts from small tinners all over the county, like Stephen Rowse who delivered five blocks of tin containing 1300 lb. which was taken on board the balinger *John* of Golant; John Rowse delivered 10 blocks containing 2500 lb. on board the *Magdalen* of Polruan. Various amounts too were laded for Eliot at Truro, Padstow and the Mount. He was a merchant on a large scale at Plymouth and Ashburton, the ancestor of the

[1] E 122/115/7.
[2] The word which frequently recurs in these accounts, *dentrices*, which would ordinarily mean pike, must I think be taken as meaning congers. We know that they were much eaten and appreciated in Tudor times; cf. John St. Aubyn's present of a barrel of congers to Lady Lisle, etc. *L.P.* VI. 589.
[3] v. below, pp. 95-6.

Earls at St. Germans. Almost everybody goes back to trade some time or other.[1]

Among the more unusual items entered, we find the balinger *Mary Clement* bringing in 27 portions of fruit, worth £54. Several Fowey boats, the *Julian*, the *Swan*, the *Grace Dieu*, bring in small quantities of wine. St. Ives is engaged chiefly in exporting fish, and imports salt, cresset cloth and some wine. Padstow has a more varied trade, still mainly with Brittany, but also with Ireland and elsewhere. The exports are mostly of fish, some tin and a little cloth. A typical return cargo from Brittany was that of the *Julian* of St. Brieuc, bringing 200 pieces of linen, 300 of canvas, 3 bolts of canvas, 3 pieces of checker ray and 1 quilt valued at 3s. 4d. A more southern cargo is that of the *Margaret* of Bilbao, which brought in 3 doles of fruit, 1 dole and 1 pipe of wine; some of her cargo she sold for victuals and repairs to the ship; a tale-telling entry: the voyage in those wintry waters (she entered harbour February 13th) had been too much for so little a craft. From Ireland there came the *Katherine* of Youghal with white fish and Irish mantles. These were staple Irish exports to Cornwall. There was a considerable export of Irish coarse cloth to the county — it was cheap — and also of mantles and rugs. In three months of the year 1505-06, 96 Irish mantles were exported to Fowey; in the first half of 1514-15, 213 to Plymouth.[2] In the latter half of the sixteenth century, with the ruin of Irish prosperity, these exports declined and raw materials were sent instead, wool, cowhides, fox and other skins. The same tendency is observable in the export of wood. There was a good market for wood, already prepared, in Cornwall: in 1505, 2633 boards were brought into the Cornish ports from Ireland. By the end of the century only unprepared timber, of less value, is entered. Then too the rise of the Newfoundland fishery adversely affected Irish exports: Cornwall, which had earlier taken fair supplies of Irish white fish, imported direct from Newfoundland. At Looe in this year 1498-99, a boat of Kinsale is entered with 150 boards and 12 mantles. The *Katherine* of Cork entered with a mixed cargo of 50 dozen cards, 800 pieces of canvas, 10 lb. of saffron, and departed with tin, lead, calf-skins, salt, hides.

Such was the character of the trade in these early years. When we look at the figures we find that at this time the trade of the Cornish ports coming under Fowey was as large as that coming under Plymouth. The development of Plymouth came later in the century; and at the same time there

---

[1] cf. Burghley, 'For gentility is nothing else but ancient riches'. (Precepts to his son, Robert Cecil: Peck, *Desiderata Curiosa*, 1, 48.)

[2] Longfield, op. cit., 84; and for the following sentences, 56, 66, 82-6, 119.

were new trends in Cornish trade. For example, there was a growth of the coal-trade from Cardiff, Neath and Swansea to Cornish ports, principally to Fowey, the chief centre of import.[1] An interesting cargo is that of the *Hart* of St. Ives which in July 1593 brought from Milford Haven for Sir Francis Godolphin, evidently for his mines, 100 packs of charcoal and 30 small oaks.[2] At the same time there was a notable growth in the Cornish shipping engaged in the carrying trade to South Wales: we find many cargoes of bay salt, wine, cheese and butter, Breton linen being brought in ships of Fowey, Looe, Falmouth, and Scilly.[3] Then too, with the great improvement in Cornish agriculture noted by Carew, Cornwall came frequently to have a surplus of corn for export. After the bumper harvest of 1582, for example, the Council gave licence for large quantities of wheat to be exported to Spain, and some also for Ireland.[4]

A multitude of cases, in the courts of Chancery and elsewhere, attest the life and concerns, the vitality, courage and quarrelsomeness of these merchants and seafaring men. Mr. Kingsford has studied the exploits of John Mixtow and his lads in the disordered reign of Henry VI: the Fowey gallants had a bad name on the other side of the Channel.[5] But these amenities were inseparable from trade; nor did they cease altogether when the orderly, watchful Henry VII came to the throne. A Breton ship had a safe-conduct from the King, but when she came in at Porth (possibly the modern Charlestown), on Lammas Day 1501, John Thompson the elder of St. Austell entered 'her with force and arms, and took away six pieces of crest cloth against the form and effect of the said safeconduct'.[6] Sir John Treffry and others took a ship of Croisic at Fowey, with a cargo of cloth, but that may have been under colour of arrest in time of war; anyhow there was trouble about the cloth which they took, for it belonged to Sir John Turberville and John Deboys.[7] We find a Fowey ship, the *Anne*, being made over to a son-in-law at less than her value, by way of dowry with the daughter: John Hartford, merchant, was to have her (the ship) for £120 by yearly instalments of £20, when her value was £200.[8] This must certainly be an early example of marrying on the instalment system. It did not work out well: the poor man got the wife, but not in the end the ship. Another case

---

[1] Lewis, op. cit., 2, 4, 9, 12, 15, 25, 27, etc.   [2] ibid., 159.
[3] ibid., 31, 42, 53, 60, 68, 72, 91, 97, 146, 206. In 1598, the *Hopewell* of Fowey carried a mixed cargo of salt, hops, canvas, pilchard train, prunes, etc., as far up coast as Beaumaris (ibid., 281).
[4] There is a schedule of these in S.P. Dom. Eliz. 161, 42.
[5] Kingsford, 'West-Country Piracy: the School of English Seamen', in *Prejudice and Promise in the Fifteenth Century.*
[6] Early Chancery Proceedings, 322/61.
[7] ibid., 228/68.   [8] ibid., 97/32.

reveals two merchants of Truro, Thomas Tregian and James Drew, breaking their contract with a London merchant: he had sold them a quantity of iron and some salt, and was to receive tin.[1] But since the contract was made, the price of salt had gone down in Cornwall, and they refused to receive it or to send the tin they had promised. No doubt this was the way the great Tregian fortune was made: by the 1530s the Tregian children were the best matches in Cornwall. Sir Richard Grenville the elder would have liked the son for his daughter; but he married an Arundell.[2]

So many of the Cornish families who later became prominent grew up in this way out of trade, and a number of them from the ports. The Treffrys of Fowey had already grown rich in the later Middle Ages and built themselves a castle overlooking the town, where they still are. The Rashleighs made a sixteenth-century fortune out of trade there: John lies sleeping grandly with his wife upon his Elizabethan tomb in Fowey church. But the family shortly moved out into the country, the delicious Gribbin peninsula which in time they came to own and where their house Menabilly is situated, still in sound and sight of the sea. They have been there ever since. So also with the Eliots of Ashburton and Plymouth, at the priory of St. Germans. The Killigrews profited from trade at Penryn, swam upwards (with some difficulties and setbacks) with the growth of Falmouth, until they came into haven – and a very merry time they made of it – at the court of Charles I and Charles II.

[1] Early Chancery Proceedings, 323/45.
[2] cf. my *Sir Richard Grenville*, 33-4.

CHAPTER IV

SOCIAL STRUCTURE AND GOVERNMENT

THE structure of Cornish society, by which I mean the classes, their character and relations to one another, was not essentially different from that of the rest of England. In Tudor England the dominant class was the country gentry, who formed the backbone of the ruling classes, shading off into the nobility on the one hand and into the town middle-class on the other; and there was much interchange between them: the younger sons of country families going into commerce, the heirs marrying sometimes into the ranks of the nobility. We find examples of this in Cornwall as elsewhere: a Trelawny going into trade at Plymouth, the Arundells marrying into the peerage. At the apex of all, and a cardinal influence in binding the society together, sat the sovereign, active, ruling, watchful, with the myth of sovereignty, in which everybody believed, powerfully aiding. Nobody could withstand it. Tudor history is full of instances — we shall find many in the course of this book — of persons, causes, armies being broken and shattered by it. It was not until the next century that the myth was questioned — by these same ruling classes.

Though Cornwall shared the common class-structure of English society, there were variations which gave it in this respect too a character of its own and made it more comparable to a palatine county like Chester or Durham, or like the principality of Wales, than any other southern, or western, or midland county. What made the difference was the importance of the royal connection, coming down from Conquest times, when William handed over the county, or a great part of it, to his half-brother Robert of Mortain — a connection which had been perpetuated through the Middle Ages by the Earldom and then by the Duchy.

It was the Duchy which was the 'peculiar institution', holding a strategical position in relation to Cornish life and responsible for more variation from the usual pattern than appears on the surface. For instance, Cornwall had no nobility. Carew notes this with the regretful, suggestive phrase that the 'king hath there no cousins'.[1] He proceeds to account for this through female heirs marrying out of Cornwall and carrying their 'inhabitance together with the inheritance, to gentlemen of the eastern parts'; and partly,

[1] Carew, 64.

77

too, to reluctance to live so remotely from the centre of affairs.[1] No doubt there was something in this last factor. Various noble families, the Bonvilles, the de Veres, the Warwicks and Spencers, and especially the Courtenays, held land in Cornwall, but the fact remains that they never lived there; they were foreigners. Another factor was the comparative poverty of the county, and its smallness. A contributing cause was the predominance of the Duchy, which made it unpromising for a local nobility to grow up under its shadow. On the other hand, what is less easy to observe but seems to emerge from a reading of Cornish history as a whole is that in consequence of this situation the smaller men had room to grow up, and this may in part account for the individualism and independence which have become a feature of Cornish life.[2]

The Duchy of Cornwall — it is important to distinguish it from the county and to use each term in its exact sense — has always had a peculiar character from the nature of its creation.[3] It was constituted by Edward III's charter of March 11th, 1337, to provide for the maintenance of the King's eldest son, the heir to the Crown. The charter itself differentiates the dukedom of Cornwall from the principality of Wales; for whereas the latter is conferred by special investiture of the King, his eldest son is born Duke of Cornwall.[4] The Duchy has always been a shifting possession from the Crown to the Duke and back to the Crown; for when the Duke dies or ascends the throne the Duchy reverts to the sovereign, unless and until he has a son. That is to say, the history of the Duchy has been one of long periods of 'dormancy' — as the legal phrase has it, when all 'those honours and revenues are drowned again in the Crown'. In our own period, owing to lack of male issue to the Tudors, the Crown was in possession of the Duchy most of the time: from Henry VII's accession to the birth of his son Arthur (1485-86), under Henry VIII from 1509 till 1537 when Edward was born, and throughout the reigns of Edward VI, Mary and Elizabeth, from 1547 to 1603. Nevertheless the Duchy organization persisted intact, with its own complement of officers administering it as a separate entity, though they were appointed by the Crown. There was no overlapping of the respective spheres, no confusion of

[1] Carew, 63.
[2] Small farmers and small-holdings are characteristic of Cornwall; and people on the land are, in general, less under the thumb of large landowners than in ordinary English counties. Nonconformity has also been a large factor. But for Duchy tenure, v. above pp. 49-50 and Coate, *Cornwall in the Civil War*, 12.
[3] cf. my 'The Duchy of Cornwall', *Nineteenth Century*, Jan. 1937.
[4] Sir John Doddridge, *The History of the Ancient and Modern Estate of the Principality of Wales, Duchy of Cornwall and Earldom of Chester* (1630), 79-80.

PORTRAIT OF A RESKYMER BY HOLBEIN

TOMB OF PRIOR VYVYAN, BODMIN CHURCH

substance even when the persons of the sovereign and the Duke were, as to-day, the same. In 1502, with the death of Prince Arthur, a difficulty arose: did the King's surviving son succeed to the Duchy under the Charter? The lawyers stretched a point to say that he did, and interpreted the phrase 'filius primogenitus' to mean 'filius primogenitus existens', and Henry succeeded his brother Arthur: a precedent which was followed in 1612, when Charles succeeded another Henry, James I's son.[1]

By the beginning of our period the Duchy had come to consist of a large body of estates, ranging as far afield as Knaresborough in Yorkshire, Wallingford in Berkshire, Kennington in Surrey, and a number of manors in Somerset, Dorset, Wilts and Devon, but with its nucleus in Cornwall. With the manors lying outside the county we are not concerned; but within, that nucleus was formed by the seventeen manors of the first creation, the 'antiqua maneria' which had originally been part of the earldom. With these manors went certain castles, parks and a few boroughs. There was Launceston Castle in its striking situation looking out over the valley of the upper Tamar and commanding the only passable road into the county. Here the assizes and quarter-sessions met, and within the castle was the county jail. The latter made such an impression upon the people, that though it has long disappeared it still lives on in a popular phrase. Launceston was an active Duchy centre, and in our period, the county town. But the real centre of Duchy administration was Lostwithiel; here the various offices, the shire hall where the county court met, the exchequer of the Duchy, the Coinage Hall for the stannaries and the stannary jail, were housed in the fine range of buildings built by Edmund, Earl of Cornwall, between the church and the river.[2] You may still see something of the hall, and remains of walls and archways built into adjacent houses there, the tidal waters of the Fowey moving by. Farther up the river, on an eminence overlooking the valley, was Restormel Castle with its park already by Carew's time beginning to go to ruin. There were three more castles that belonged to the Duchy: Tintagel upon its romantic headland and all that legendary past, Liskeard with its attendant park and borough, and Trematon with the borough of Saltash, guarding the lower passage into the county across the river Tamar. It is notable how these centres of the Duchy and most of its manors are concentrated in the eastern part of the county: going back to the Norman hold upon Cornwall, and before that to the conquests of the royal house of Wessex.

The drastic changes of the reign of Henry VIII, however, were not

[1] Coate, *Cornwall in the Civil War*, 10.   [2] Henderson, *Essays*, 47.

without their effect upon this. A vast amount of property coming into his hands with the Dissolution, and the attainder of the Marquis of Exeter, enabled Henry to effect a redistribution and an increased concentration of the Duchy estates. He severed from it the honour of Wallingford, annexing it to the Crown and linking it up for convenience of administration with that of Ewelme.[1] In return he annexed to the Duchy all the Cornish manors of the Marquis, the Courtenay inheritance, some fifteen in all, together with another fifteen manors belonging to the dissolved priories of Launceston and Tywardreath. This meant bringing the Duchy more powerfully into mid-Cornwall; and in the far west the Scilly Islands became Duchy property. The main concentration, however, still remained in the east, around the Duchy towns of Launceston, Liskeard and Lostwithiel where the annual audit was held. But the consequence must have been a considerable increase of the influence of the Duchy — that is, of the Crown in effect, in the county in general. It may be that the enormous extension of Parliamentary representation in Cornwall — to 44 members in all, which dates to the second half of this century when the Duchy was wholly in the hands of the Crown, has something to do with this.

Indeed, this peculiar association, the lapsing of the Duchy into the Crown, makes it not at all easy to disentangle respective spheres of jurisdiction, and led to difficulties later on. So long as the Duchy was attached to the Crown, things naturally worked smoothly, for appointments were in the same hands. Elizabeth treated the newly-annexed manors of Henry VIII as Crown property, like the rest of Church lands; and towards the end of her reign, owing to the financial pressure of the war with Spain, in the Netherlands, in France and Ireland, she was driven to sell eighteen of them. This was pronounced illegal upon the accession of James I, when the Duchy was put into order for Henry, Prince of Wales; the manors were held to come under the Charter of the Duchy, since they had been annexed by Act of Parliament, and were recovered. In Cornwall, so many rights which elsewhere belonged to the Crown belonged to the Duke by the Charter. There was the right of choosing the sheriff; of the escheators or feodaries, one each was nominated by the Crown and the Duchy. We have already seen that the stannaries came under the Duchy; they provided, in the coinage upon tin, the largest item of its revenue. But it had also the prises and customs upon wine, woollens and leather, the profits upon all the Cornish ports, such prerogatives as that of royal fish; together with the profits of the hundred and county courts, the goods of felons and fugitives, fines imposed and licences issued.

[1] Doddridge, 88-9.

SOCIAL STRUCTURE AND GOVERNMENT

We can get some indication of what these revenues amounted to from the figures given by Sir John Doddridge. Tudor arithmetic was apt to be unreliable; but separate items of revenue may usefully be compared. He tells us that the total revenue of the Duchy in 1377 was £3415 18s. 5¼d.; of which Cornwall provided '£2219 7s. 9½d., Devon £273 19s. 5¾d., and the other shires £922 11s. 2d.'[1] In 1524, before Henry VIII made his changes, the total revenue appears to have been £4769 13s. 4¼d.;[2] of which by far the largest single item was the profits upon the coinage of tin at £2771 3s. 9¼d. By that time the 'foreign' manors, outside Cornwall and Devon, brought in a larger revenue than those within: they produced £958, the Cornish manors £624 17s. 2¼d., Devon £170 14s. 3¾d. Lastly Doddridge gives us the figures for 1602, 'the last account extant'. What is notable, but does not surprise us, is the comparative stability of the regular revenue. For example, the total tin revenue in Devon and Cornwall, including that from the courts and various oddments, was in 1524, £2843 15s. 6¼d., and in 1602, £2726 7s. 8¾d. The yield from the ancient Cornish manors and boroughs had slightly increased to £686 2s. 9½d. The return from the annexed manors of Henry VIII was £254 8s. 3½d., of which the Courtenay manors provided £130 2s. 5¼d. To offset this gain, the revenue from the 'foreign' manors had fallen to £570 8s. 6¾d. From which we learn that the result of Henry VIII's changes was a net loss to the Duchy of £133 3s. 1¾d. per annum: typical of Henry VIII's financial transactions. However, what the Duchy lost, the Crown gained: also not uncharacteristic of Henry VIII. The sum-total of the regular Duchy revenues was in 1602 £4569 12s. 2¼d. compared with £4769 13s. 4¼d. in 1524, before he made his changes.

We have to take into account a consideration to which Doddridge draws our attention, and one which makes these figures of comparative rather than of absolute validity, namely that 'a certain yearly value, by reason it consisteth of casual profits, cannot well be drawn by consideration annual'. It seems that Duchy tenants were in an exceptionally favourable position, for neither rent nor fine could be increased; thus they were able to enjoy the whole of the increment due to the rise of prices, when fines upon the renewal of leases were in general increasing.[3] Meanwhile we have to allow for the fees and reprises which were paid out of the revenues: the salaries of the officials, which amounted to £138 3s. 4d. within Corn-

[1] Doddridge, 97.
[2] Doddridge gives the figure as £10,095 11s. 9½d., which is impossible: the separate items add up to no more than £4769 13s. 4¼d.
[3] Carew says (p. 64) as regards ordinary estates that 'their casualties of tin and fines … ordinarily treble the certain revenue of their rents'.

81

wall; while at the end of Elizabeth's reign, large sums for the maintenance of St. Mawes and Pendennis castles were charged upon the Duchy, which, as Doddridge notes, they had no right to be, for the castles belonged to the Crown.

Altogether the Duchy was a little government of its own, with a whole hierarchy of officials, from those in London attendant upon the King or the Duke down through the officials in Cornwall to the small men who had the deputy-keepership of the park at Kerrybullock or Liskeard, or the chaplain who said mass in the chapel of the Holy Trinity in the park at Restormel. Naturally the highest officials came and went with changes of government, since they occupied personal positions near the throne. Desirable posts in the Duchy administration were the rewards of personal service and reflected the sovereign's confidence in the fortunate recipient. Take the clearance effected, for example by Henry VII on coming to power, in the upper ranges of the administration. The leading Yorkist figures had been John, Lord Dynham, who held various offices of honour and profit, and John Sapcote, who was receiver-general of the Duchy, the active head of the administration in Cornwall.[1] These were replaced by the personal friends and supporters of Henry VII. Edward Courtenay, Earl of Devon, got the keepership of Restormel castle with the usual fees;[2] Sir Richard Edgcumbe that of Launceston, with the escheatorship of the Duchy, and later the keepership of Kerrybullock park and woods.[3] Sir John Halliwell became steward of the Duchy, Sir Robert Willoughby de Broke receiver and steward of the King's mines of gold and silver in Devon and Cornwall.[4] The latter became the leading figure later on in Duchy affairs,[5] and holding an estate within the county at Callington was buried in the church there, under that lovely alabaster tomb in the new Italian style that came with the first wind of the Renaissance into this country.

Or we may take the organization of the Duchy offices upon Henry VIII's accession which brought about a general post. Sir Henry Marney, friend of the King and Master of the Horse, succeeded to Lord Willoughby de Broke's position: he became steward of the Duchy, warden of the Stannaries, master forester of Dartmoor, etc.,[6] — offices to which Henry Courtenay, Earl of Devon, succeeded in 1523.[7] We now hear of 'the chamber at Westminster called the Prince's Council Chamber', and there is an usher

---

[1] *Cal. Pat. Rolls*, 1476-1485, 348, 386.   [2] ibid., 1485-1494, 81.
[3] ibid., 7, 93.   [4] ibid., 35; 13, 116.
[5] His son succeeded to his position, becoming steward of the Duchy, etc., in 1502 upon his father's death. *Cal. Pat. Rolls*, 1494-1509, 311.
[6] *L.P.* I. 54 (26).   [7] ibid., III. 3062 (26).

in attendance upon the 'Council of the said Chamber'.[1] It is evident that the organization is advancing to a fuller complement of officers. William Esyngton is appointed general attorney of the Principality of Wales and the Duchy of Cornwall; John Turner becomes auditor.[2] Within the county, Sir Piers Edgcumbe succeeds to his father's old position as constable of Launceston and keeper of Kerrybullock; Thomas Carmynow, one of the smaller Cornish contingent of personal attendants upon Henry — he was gentleman usher of the Chamber — succeeds the Earl of Devon as keeper of Restormel.[3] Sir John Arundell of Lanherne was appointed receiver-general of the Duchy for life, and so became the most important person in Cornwall in his time.[4] In 1516 we hear of a chancellor of the Principality and Duchy, Charles Booth, who had been appointed by the King when Prince, but to whom the auditors of the Duchy had refused to pay his fee, an expensive item of £60 p.a.[5] In 1518 there was a further step in organization: a body of commissioners and assessors for all the lands of the Duchy was appointed with the Bishop of Exeter, Sir Henry Marney and Sir John Arundell at its head.[6] This was renewed in 1521, and again in 1525 with the Marquis of Exeter presiding over it.[7] Evidently this is the Duchy Council in its early form.

Within the county the gentry ruled, as within every shire in England. They were the backbone of the government of the country: its effective political class. Locally they are seen in their public capacity as Justices of the Peace. The duties which fell to them as such were of every sort and kind: they were the natural leaders and rulers of the primitive society we are dealing with. Sir Thomas Smith says that they were 'those in whom at this time for the repressing of robbers, thieves and vagabonds, of privy complots and conspiracies, of riots and violences, and all other misdemeanours in the common wealth the Prince putteth his special trust . . .'[8] With the amplification of the scope of government and its increased efficiency, an underlying tendency of great importance throughout the sixteenth century — one of the ground-swells of our history which pass unnoticed when things of small importance bob up and down upon the surface — Smith notes the increase in the number of J.P.s: 'At first they were but four, after eight, now they come commonly to thirty or forty in every shire, either by increase of riches, learning, or activity in policy and government.'

[1] ibid., I. 1836 (2); 2861 (26).   [2] ibid., 709 (30); 2684 (72).
[3] ibid., 94 (85, 86); 190 (10).   [4] ibid., 54 (81).
[5] ibid., II. 1409.   [6] ibid., 4286.
[7] ibid., III. 1391; IV. 1533 (11).
[8] Smith, *De Republica Anglorum* (ed. Alston), 86, 88.

Cornwall shared in this general tendency. Where at the beginning of our period Henry VII's Commissions of the Peace contained perhaps a dozen names, by the end Elizabeth's contained some thirty, of whom about a half were of the Quorum. Their custom was in the earlier part of the century 'to begin the Quarter Sessions for the east half of the shire on the Tuesdays and Wednesdays at Bodmin, and to adjourn the same for the west half to be ended at Truro the Friday and Saturday following, leaving one day's space for riding between'.[1] This was later upset by the eastern J.P.s, who were in a majority, and fixed Sessions wholly at one place or the other: which led to considerable confusion. In the end a compromise was arrived at: they returned to the old arrangement, Sessions beginning alternately at Bodmin and at Truro, but with the safeguard that 'no recognisance should be discharged, or cause decided out of his own division'. This stopped what was done at one place being undone at the other — which had been liable to happen. It was a solution agreeable to all, and seems to have been suggested by Carew.

It goes without saying that it was the leading families that provided the bulk of the Justices. Sometimes a new recruit appears, a new name, which may mark the rise of a new family in the county, but which more often disappears and is submerged again after a while. There are the ups and downs of a society, the beginning and ending, the merging of families. But the constant burden, the bass to which other people sang treble, was borne by a core of long continuing families with larger possessions. In the Tudor period these were, as they had been for some time, Grenvilles and Arundells, Bassets, St. Aubyns, Carews, Treffrys, Trelawnys, Edgcumbes and Godolphins, Killigrews, Tremaynes. Others were less permanent; some few, like the Eliots, came in or arose, like the Robarteses, towards the end of the century. Others again were snuffed out, like the Reskymers, the Carmynows, the Carnsews; or came to a bad end like the Bodrugans, or a miserable end like the Tregians.

But we must confine ourselves to particularizing the character of the Cornish gentry. Carew, who wrote from the inside, said that they could 'better vaunt of their pedigree than their livelihood: for that, they derive from great antiquity (and I make question whether any shire in England of but equal quantity, can muster a like number of fair coat-armours) whereas this declineth to the mean'.[2] In other words, it was with us as with the Welsh, or Scots or Irish, rather than as the fat and prosperous midland or southern shires. It was the old story of the poverty of the county, the small area of

[1] Carew, 88.   [2] ibid., 63-4.

its cultivable land. Yet Carew admitted that there were exceptions, families with large patrimonies, which, when one considered the cheapness of living in Cornwall, enabled them to vie with eastern standards. He evidently had in mind such rich families as the Arundells, Grenvilles, Edgcumbes and Godolphins.

It was a consequence of the remoteness of the county, he adds — 'this angle which so shutteth them in' — that they were all inter-connected. 'All Cornish gentlemen are cousins.' They intermarried frequently with the gentry of Devon, but very much less so, one has the impression, farther afield. That came later. The consequence was a thickly coagulated west-country cousinage, which knit together the gentry of Devon and Cornwall and made them a factor of some importance in national politics. Ralegh's advancement of Grenville's interests is a case in point; Carew's dedication of his *Survey* to Ralegh witnesses to it. Carew proceeds to paint a rather idyllic picture of his own class, their keeping liberal houses, giving entertainment to strangers and living 'void of factions amongst themselves (at leastwise such as break out into any dangerous excess)'. The qualification is interesting; for in fact there were family feuds and jealousies which national issues sometimes fanned into flame.

Our period begins with the hostility that rankled between the Yorkist Bodrugan and Sir Richard Edgcumbe, who was a Lancastrian: when the former was defeated, the latter ate up most of his estates: hence the greatness of the Edgcumbes. A long rivalry divided the Grenvilles from the Arundells of Lanherne and was a factor in the attack upon the Tregians, connections of the latter. Every man's hand seems to have been against the Winslades. Sir John Killigrew and his son, Captains of Pendennis, terrorized the neighbourhood and made a host of enemies, most of them too unimportant to hit back; when they did try to get their own back, they found the Killigrews sheltered by their relatives at Court. Sir Richard Grenville was on bad terms with his neighbour Kempthorne at Tonacombe. The courts of law were pretty full with disputes concerning property, wills, forcible entry, mutual depredations, and not infrequently cases of loss of limb or life, coming up from Cornwall, perhaps more frequently than from elsewhere. In the end, there were two characteristics which distinguished the Cornish gentry above others: their litigiousness — Carew admits to that — and their clannishness.

A no less important rhythm to observe is that of the going up or down of families in accordance with the national movements they support. Yorkism brought Bodrugan and the Antron family down. The Prayer Book Rebellion ruined the Winslades and the Arundells of Helland. Devotion to Catholicism broke the Tregians and the Beckets of Cartuther; it adversely affected the fortunes of the Arundells, who were too rich however to be altogether extinguished and too loyal to be proscribed. On the other hand those families that swam with the tide, conforming to the changes of the Reformation, naturally went farther than those which tried to swim against it. A few who were forward Protestants, Tremaynes[1] and Killigrews, may be said to have jumped on the band-waggon.

One may distinguish two groups among the gentry of such a remote county: the home-keeping ones who looked after their affairs and those of the county on the spot, and those who went to advance their fortunes in London, at court, or who took some part in national affairs. Sir Richard Edgcumbe, an intimate friend of Henry VII, Comptroller of his household and sent on a number of weighty missions of state by the King, is a notable example of the latter type. Or there is a speaking contrast in the roles played by Sir John Arundell and his second son, Sir Thomas. The former remained in Cornwall all his life, with occasional incursions into grand affairs, such as attending the Field of the Cloth of Gold. Wolsey offered him a peerage, which he refused with the modest plea of inability to support the honour. He was content to remain at home, administering the affairs of the Duchy, taking his place at the head of the county for a great part of the reign of Henry VIII, providing well for the well-being of the Arundells. (Marriage had been their royal road to success: it might be said of them as of the House of Austria, *felix nube*.) His son Thomas, perhaps because he was a second son and able, went to London to make his fortune; and a conspicuous career he had. Starting in the households of Wolsey and Sir Thomas More, a young lawyer, he became Chancellor of the Court of Augmentations when the going was good for monastic lands. He married a sister of Queen Catherine Howard. But the times were dangerous. He attached himself too closely to the party of Somerset, and was executed as an accomplice of his. Nevertheless he had made enough to leave as a nucleus of his estates Wardour and its dependencies: the junior branch of the Arundells had outsoared the senior.

A similar contrast is provided in Elizabeth's reign by the careers of Grenville and Sir Francis Godolphin. The former spent his middle years, after a restless youth, mostly in the county performing his local and private duties; his last years he passed almost entirely away from home, attending Parliament, voyaging to Virginia, to Ireland, to the Azores. Godolphin succeeded to his position as first man of affairs in the county. But he went very little

---

[1] This refers to the Devonshire branch of the Tremaynes; the Cornish branch were recusants.

outside it; he remained at home supervising his mines and estates, his business as Receiver-general of the Duchy, the affairs of his station in the county, its defences, the fortifications of the Scilly Islands and so on. He was a man of culture and reading, all the same, and wrote a beautiful Italian hand. With the social life and culture of his class we are not here concerned; it will fall to be dealt with in its place.

But it is to be noted that all through the Tudor period there was a Cornish element at Court. After Sir Richard Edgcumbe, there was Catherine Edgcumbe as a lady in attendance. Thomas Carmynow was a gentleman usher at the funeral of Henry VII and at the coronation of Henry VIII; he was made keeper of the King's buckhounds by the latter and got various grants in Cornwall.[1] William Reskymer was gentleman of the Chamber to Henry VIII; it may be therefore that the lovely Holbein portrait of a Reskymer at Hampton Court, with the drawing for it at Windsor, is of him.[2] It is of a man with curiously shaped, round head, long thin beard, reddish hair and fine grey eyes: an expression of melancholy and refinement in the pose and appearance. Lady Lisle too was closely associated, through her great marriage, with the Court; her daughter, Anne Basset, a maid of honour to Jane Seymour, was rumoured as a likely candidate for the favour of the King just before, fortunately for Anne, he married Catherine Howard.[3] Under Elizabeth there were two notable royal servants of Cornish birth holding place near her. Edmund Tremayne was Clerk of the Privy Council, in a key position at Court, an able, reliable servant much used upon confidential business. William Killigrew was for many years Groom of the Chamber to Elizabeth and James I. He must have known them both as well as anyone; but he was discreet and kept his knowledge to himself. He did well enough out of his post to found a junior branch of the Killigrews at Hanworth in Middlesex.

In this rural world ruled by the gentry, the towns were to some extent an exception: they had a certain, and a growing, autonomy. (Carew's realization of this, and the natural dislike of a cultivated gentleman for the character and narrow outlook of small tradesmen, colours his account of the Cornish towns, which is, so he was himself aware, 'waspish', his pen 'somewhat deeply steeped in gall'.) During the sixteenth century English towns in general made great strides in self-government, consolidating their powers and freeing themselves from dependence upon local magnates. The Tudor

[1] *L.P.* I. 190, 10; 289, 50 etc.
[2] cf. Henderson, *History of the Parish of Constantine*, 103.
[3] cf. *Sir Richard Grenville*, 32.

monarchy was supported, it is true to say, more unitedly by the town middle classes than by any other class. This naturally led their government to be very sympathetic to appeals from the towns for increasing their rights. Narrow and confined as the outlook of the small townsmen was apt to be, we are observing in embryo the first stages in the growth of the great middle class that governs modern England.

This historical trend is not only observable, but indeed very marked, in Cornwall. For the Cornish towns it was the golden age of charters and grants of representation in Parliament. Not only had old boroughs like Launceston, Bodmin, Saltash, Lostwithiel, Liskeard, Truro, Helston, their charters renewed and greatly extended, but new boroughs were incorporated, such as East Looe, West Looe, Callington, and granted the right to return members to Parliament. The Reformation had some part in this process, for before it there were five boroughs which came under the wing of the Church: Bodmin belonged to the Priory there, Fowey to Tywardreath priory, Newport to Launceston, St. Germans to its priory, and Penryn to the Bishop of Exeter. At Bodmin and Fowey on the eve of the Reformation there was a good deal of ill-feeling between the town and the monastery: the townsmen, feeling their strength, were wanting to break through the antiquated bonds that bound them to the monks.

At Bodmin, which was the largest and busiest of Cornish towns with a population of 2000 — almost twice that of any other — the disputes were particularly bitter and prolonged.[1] They raged over the whole field of the Prior's rights in regard to the town, whether burgesses were liable to do suit of court at his courts, whether they had not right of common pasture in Dunmere Wood which he had enclosed and locked against them. They complained of his putting up a weir on Dunmere Water, and of causing them great annoyance by his mill-pool which flooded the ground about. They said that the Prior was a great farmer of benefices (which he was), and a great encloser; also that he was 'a great meddler with black tin and white tin, and that converteth into merchandise, and hath a blowing house of his own and bloweth tin'. The townsmen disputed the mortuaries and other charges which were exacted from them by the vicar, who was put in by the Prior (his brother). The vicar then got a dispensation from Wolsey not to reside, went to live in London and appointed a priest to serve his cure whom the parishioners disapproved of: they regarded their spiritual welfare as neglected. They petitioned the King that the mayor and burgesses were his

---

[1] v. *The Bodmin Register*, no. 17 (April 9th, 1836), containing a number of original documents then at Bodmin which have since disappeared.

and not the Prior's, who had service only of those who were his freeholders in the town. It may easily be imagined that these sentiments, which were of little avail so long as Wolsey ruled, were not unpleasing to Cromwell: in that difference lay a revolutionary change in English society.

Cromwell appointed a strong — and wholly secular — commission to go into these complaints of the town against the Priory; though right on the eve of its fall we find the mayor petitioning him that the town 'is greatly decayed and desolated by reason of certain trouble and certain vexations of the Prior, what in Edward III's days, Henry VI's days, and of late by Prior Vyvyan in the King's days that now is, and also by the Prior that now is'. That prior, Thomas Mundy, was the last of his line. One appreciated what a long stored up resentment in the towns Cromwell could rely upon in his attack on the monasteries.

Something of the same case obtained at Fowey, where the leading inhabitant, Thomas Treffry, was anxious to jockey the feeble monks of Tywardreath out of their ancient rights upon the town. Upon Treffry's complaints Cromwell administered a severe rebuke to the unfortunate Prior, a senile and lax old person who used to get overcome with drink in his study — no doubt he found the world depressing, the old order threatening to topple over round him.[1] The Lord Privy Seal wrote, by the hand of Treffry: 'Wherefore I require you to agree with the inhabitants of the town . . . that their liberties may be extended amongst them. And ye shall certify me in writing by Thomas Treffry the bearer hereof. For his Highness thinketh that the said port of Fowey ought to be his and to be held of him so that his Grace intendeth from henceforth to have it well provided for with good governance and for defence against the enemies of the realm. Wherefore his Highness thinketh that ye be very unworthy to have rule of any town that cannot well rule yourself. . . . And thus fare ye well.'[2]

It must have been very hard for the poor comatose and bibulous old Prior. But the Dissolution put an end to these difficulties; such towns were free to go forward on their way: it was the way of progress. And yet, on the other hand, it may be objected that a good many towns lost by the change, as Canterbury and Glastonbury so notably did. Bodmin must have lost too by the end of so popular a shrine as that of St. Petroc, all the moneys that ceased to flow in from the Priory estates, the great state that the Prior kept up with all his servants and dependants. It does not appear that Bodmin made any progress in wealth, or much in population, subsequently: it lost its lead

---

[1] cf. Baskerville, *The English Monks and the Suppression of the Monasteries*, 55, and below, pp. 166-8.
[2] *L.P.* VIII. 743.

over other Cornish towns: the rents of the monks were now drawn off to London, or went into the pockets of the fortunate purchasers of the priory lands. So too, in part, with Launceston;[1] though Bodmin, Launceston and Penryn, which lost the college of St. Thomas of Glasney, a less wealthy and important institution, still had their trade and their markets. St. Germans, however, which depended almost entirely upon the monastery, was very adversely affected by its coming to an end, and never much recovered.

But there was a general progress in independence, which is reflected in the flood of charters which Cornish towns procured for themselves at this time. The fact that they got them is so much evidence of their desire to extend their rights and liberties, have them defined and confirmed. One common characteristic that is worth noting is that in most cases these charters made a distinction between the chief or capital burgesses and the more numerous body of lesser townsmen. The Bodmin charter of 1563 appointed some twelve of 'the better and more honest burgesses' as capital burgesses and councillors; twenty-four of the 'more honest and discreet' were to complete the Common Council.[2] The Launceston Charter of 1555 appointed a mayor and eight aldermen, who were to admit as many burgesses and freemen as they thought convenient.[3] At Liskeard, under the charter of 1587 and the constitutions subsequently laid down, nine of the chief inhabitants were to be capital burgesses for life, and they chose for their assistance fifteen others 'of the most able and sufficient of the residue burgesses ... which shall henceforth be reputed inferior burgesses'.[4] At Helston, under the charter of 1585, the Common Council was to consist of a mayor and four aldermen, who were given the power to admit burgesses and freemen.[5] The Truro charter of 1588 set up a Common Council of a mayor and twenty-four burgesses, of whom four aldermen were to be elected each year.[6] These and similar charters for other towns at this period, mostly dating to the reign of Queen Elizabeth, are the beginning of the modern series. There is something definitive about them: they are sign-posts to show what the towns were achieving in ordering their own affairs. Some of the boroughs which received rights, including that to return two members each to Parliament, were no more than villages, like Mitchell, Grampound, St. Mawes, St. Germans; and naturally they and their rights were the property of the landowners who owned them. But the towns proper had gained the internal management of their own affairs. It was not without an element of patronage on the part of the greater

[1] Though cf. below.   [2] *The Bodmin Register*, no. 8 (Dec. 1833).
[3] Peter, *Histories of Launceston and Dunheved*, 196.
[4] Allen, *History of Liskeard*, 59.   [5] Toy, *History of Helston*, 168.
[6] Merewether and Stephens, *History of Boroughs*, II, 1326.

gentry outside and of propitiatory politeness on that of the burgesses. Hence the not infrequent offerings of sack and wine and sugar, which appear in the town accounts that survive and no doubt sweetened the visits of great persons and neighbouring gentlemen to the towns, and perhaps too their mutual relations. Sometimes we find the leading gentleman of the district named for office under the charter, as Jonathan Trelawny was named chief steward of Liskeard, or Richard Grenville first alderman of Bideford.

The fact was that these small communities were naturally oligarchies. They tended to be ruled by their men of substance, by those most competent and able to do it. It was in fact the survival of the fittest on the plane of municipal life.

This is the perspective in which to view the vexed question raised by the very large increase in the Parliamentary representation of Cornish boroughs in this period. The nineteenth century, which attached too much importance to Parliament in our constitutional history, gave a sinister interpretation to the fact. Reading back from the subsequent history of so many rotten boroughs, and with the seventeenth-century conflict of Crown and Parliament in their minds, it was natural for earlier writers to think that this remarkable increase in the number of boroughs sending members to Parliament — they were more than doubled in the latter half of the sixteenth century — was due to the desire of the Crown to pack Parliament with its nominees.[1] This interpretation, which is rather doubtful as it has been put, springs from an anachronistic view of the situation.

In the first place, there was no underlying conflict between Crown and Parliament in the sixteenth century. In the second, the new boroughs were represented by much the same people as the old, partly by members of local Cornish families, here and there a townsman among them, partly by persons from other counties or living in London. This state of affairs was continuous from the fifteenth century, when the six old boroughs which had representation throughout the later Middle Ages were represented half by local men, and half by outsiders.[2] The enfranchisement of so many new boroughs made no great difference in this respect. It is worth noting that two of the most obstreperous members of Elizabeth's Parliaments, Peter and Paul Wentworth, were members respectively for Tregony and Liskeard in 1572. Nor were members for Cornish seats behindhand in the opposition to Charles I. It is clear that the explanation has to be sought on other lines.

[1] cf. W. P. Courtney, *The Parliamentary Representation of Cornwall*, v-vii.
[2] M. McKisack, *The Parliamentary Representation of the English Boroughs during the Middle Ages*, 109.

The six towns which in the fourteenth and fifteenth centuries returned members fairly regularly to Parliament, in addition to the two knights for the shire, were Bodmin, Helston, Launceston, Liskeard, Lostwithiel, Truro.[1] One has the impression that in the earlier period the members were almost entirely local. Towards the end of the fifteenth century the outside element increased considerably; and this position did not change throughout our period. It does not seem to have been noticed hitherto, in spite of much writing on the subject, that the first increase in the Cornish representation comes, not in the reign of Edward VI, but with the Reformation Parliament of 1529, when the Launceston representation was doubled, and two members were returned for Launceston and two for Dunheved.[2] These boroughs are difficult to distinguish from one another; but Dunheved refers to the old borough of Launceston, while the newly enfranchised borough, around the ruins of the Priory at the foot of the hill, became more conveniently known later as Newport. The first members returned were Simon de Mountford and William Harris, the latter of whom was probably a local man. Neither of the members for Dunheved returned to this Parliament was Cornish. Sir Edward Ringley was Marshal of Calais; John Rastell was brother-in-law to Sir Thomas More, and a very active and interesting figure in the London of Henry VIII.

The Cornish returns for the Parliaments that sat between this and the last of Edward VI's reign are all missing. But with those for the Parliament of 1552-53 we find six new boroughs returning two members each: Bossiney, Camelford, Grampound, Mitchell, Looe, Saltash. It has been suggested that they were admitted in order to provide support for Northumberland's government.[3] This may well have been so, since we know that he was whipping up support elsewhere.[4] And further, it is to be noted that the new boroughs were mostly places which belonged to the Duchy, or were adjacent to Duchy lands. No doubt that was convenient. When we look, too, at the twelve new members returned, only two belong to recognizable Cornish families: Humphrey Cavell and George Kekewich.[5] Cavell may well have been a supporter of Northumberland, since he was on friendly terms with the Russells;[6] he was a lawyer living in London, of the Middle Temple, a partner in the famous literary enterprise *The Mirror for Magistrates*, to which

[1] In 1306, Tregony returned two members, instead of Lostwithiel: *Official Return of Members of Parliament*, Part I, 24.
[2] ibid., 308.
[3] *An Entire and Complete History . . . of the Boroughs of Great Britain* (1792), II, 81.
[4] cf. the letters printed in Merewether and Stephens, *History of Boroughs*, II, 1171-4.
[5] *Official Return*, 378. [6] cf. my letter, *Times Lit. Supp.*, April 15, 1939.

SOCIAL STRUCTURE AND GOVERNMENT

he contributed the poem on Michael Joseph, the blacksmith who led the rising of 1497.[1] Perhaps Saltash and Bossiney, in returning one local man each, may have been willing, like Grantham, to allow the government to nominate the other. It is possible that it nominated most of the twelve new members. The rest of the boroughs returned rather more local men than outsiders; though amongst the latter were Thomas Mildmay and Robert Ducket, both men of affairs in London, members for Helston. Launceston, Liskeard, Dunheved, on the other hand, like the county, all sent up local men. No doubt it was all satisfactorily arranged on both sides. The establishment of the right to return members was a convenience agreeable alike to the government and to those who wanted seats. These small places which qualified them to sit in Parliament were not likely to give trouble.

Through the reign of Mary the character of the representation does not change from what it was before. Outsiders like Sir Thomas Smith, Alexander Nowell, Christopher Dauncey, Sir Walter Hungerford, Thomas Mildmay, Thomas Roper, Francis Yaxley sit for Cornish seats along with Arundells, Roscarrocks, Cavells, St. Aubyns and the townsmen. One notes a number of Catholic sympathizers among these names. With the first Parliament of Mary (1553) the representation is increased by two members for Penryn: John Aylworth and Ralph Skinner, the first of whom was an official of the Duchy.[2] It was no doubt convenient that he should have a seat. In the last Parliament of her reign, two new members appear, for St. Ives: Thomas Randolph and William Chamber, neither of whom was Cornish.[3] Randolph was a Commissioner of the Exchequer, an official member. St. Ives continued to be represented by such members in all the Parliaments of Elizabeth up to 1601, when Thomas St. Aubyn and T. Breton, who were both local men, were returned. The borough came under the influence of the Paulet family; and in 1584 and 1588 the members are mentioned as expressly elected with the consent of the Marquess of Winchester and Lord Mountjoy, lords of the borough.[4]

The Cornish returns to the first Parliament of Elizabeth are lost; but with that of 1562-63 we find two more boroughs sending members, St. Germans and St. Mawes.[5] They each returned one Cornishman and one outsider. In the Parliament of 1572, three more boroughs are represented: Fowey, East Looe (in addition to West Looe), and Tregony.[6] These returned mainly non-Cornishmen: Tregony, for example, William Knollys and Peter Went-

[1] *The Mirror for Magistrates*, ed. L. B. Campbell, 46-7.
[2] *Official Return*, 381. [3] ibid., 396.
[4] J. H. Matthews, *History of St. Ives, Lelant, Towednack, and Zennor*, 497-8.
[5] *Official Return*, 403. [6] ibid., 408.

worth, the former an official at court and a cousin of Elizabeth; both forward-looking, aggressive Protestants. Fowey chose William Russell and Edward Harrington, who both had similar connections within the Protestant governing circle. To the Parliament of 1584 Callington returned members for the first time.[1]

With this last admission, the Cornish representation was complete, as it remained (except for the intermission of the Protectorate) up to the nineteenth century. There were now in all twenty-one boroughs, which meant that, with the two knights for the shire, forty-four members sat for Cornish seats. Later centuries which came to attach a more exact meaning to the idea of representation found this number astonishing. There is no evidence that the Elizabethans found anything remarkable in it. It was just that so many persons who took the trouble to qualify to attend Parliament sat for these seats. It was convenient for them, as also for the Crown. There was no conflict between the two. In 1584, Camelford and Newport failed to return members: the privilege cannot have meant so much to them. But with the increasing estimation of a seat in Parliament, the full complement of members was returned to later Parliaments of the reign. With so many seats available, too, it was natural that in these later Parliaments more persons who were not Cornish should find accommodation; even then, as was to be expected, there were among them members like Sir Henry Neville, Sir Walter Ralegh, Sir Francis Drake, who though not Cornish themselves had connections with the county. There is no evidence to show that the Cornish boroughs were specially selected for the favour of court representation. At this date, ministers of the Crown almost invariably, and officials more frequently, sat for seats with which either they had a family connection, or which were nearer at hand than the Cornish boroughs were. At the same time, a gentleman who had a seat in his keeping would not be averse to recommending himself to the powers that be by offering them the nomination. In 1601 John Trelawny wrote to Cecil: 'I am bold now again to present you with two burgess-ships for this Parliament.'[2] He had evidently done it before for the previous Parliament, and no doubt the seats in question were those of the neighbouring little borough of West Looe. It would seem then that the impulse for this remarkable increase in their parliamentary representation came not only from the Crown, but perhaps as much from the west-country gentry to whom it was convenient. In the next century, and later, it was something much more: it became a means to their hold upon power.

---

[1] *Official Return*, 413.   [2] *Salisbury MSS.*, XI, 40.

In the life of the Cornish towns at this time there was not much to mark them off from other west-country towns, except perhaps an even greater degree of narrowness, an extra dose of clannishness, in accordance with their remoteness from affairs. Within the towns there were the same class-divisions as elsewhere, and accepted as part of the permanent order of things. We have seen how the distinction between the well-to-do and the less well-to-do inhabitants was reflected in the constitutions of the boroughs, between the capital and the inferior burgesses. At Liskeard it was laid down, in the regulations adopted for the better government of the borough in 1588, that in washing at the town wells the poorer sort were 'to wash at the lower trough'.[1] At Bodmin the payments levied for contributions to the common purposes of the town in 1553-54 reveal the nice gradations of the social scale: 'after the rate of 2s. 8d. every of the twelve [i.e. aldermen]; 16d. every of the twenty-four [councillors]; 8d. 6d. 4d. or 2d. every other person of the said parish, according to their degree and ability'.[2] Some such rating was no doubt characteristic of other towns too. Nor do they the less exemplify the mutual help typical of such small societies. Society recognized its obligations; the poor were, within limits, succoured. At the same time they too were expected to render according to their ability — witness the gifts received for the rebuilding of Bodmin church in 1469-72.[3]

One respect in which the Cornish towns differed from most other towns, even in the west country, was the high proportion of foreigners they had resident in them. Mr. Henderson was of the opinion that our towns originally were plants of exotic growth, fostered and cherished by great landholders as profitable sources of revenue; that the Cornish, like other Celtic peoples, were essentially an agrarian people and not much given to urban living.[4] It is not until 1300, it seems, that Cornish names appear in the subsidy rolls for the towns; in 1327 Penryn was equally divided between natives and foreigners, while in Tregony and Grampound the foreign element still predominated. At Fowey as late as 1439 there were twenty-seven alien householders, Irish, French, Dutch, perhaps as much as a third of the town, or at least of the property-holders.[5] Bretons constituted much the largest foreign element — if indeed they are to be considered as foreigners at all in Cornwall, where they spoke the same language as the people. A Subsidy Roll of the reign of Henry VIII shows that at St. Ives there were twenty-three foreigners, all Bretons, of whom nine were fishermen, seven labourers,

---

[1] Allen, *History of the Borough of Liskeard*, 61. [2] Wallis, *The Bodmin Register*, 291-2.
[3] *Camden Miscellany*, VII. [4] Henderson, *Essays in Cornish History*, 19.
[5] ibid., 34-5.

four tailors, three smiths.[1] And there was a fair sprinkling of Bretons in the neighbouring parishes of Zennor, Towednack and Lelant. Again on the south coast we find them: in the parish of Constantine in 1544 there were fourteen Breton families resident; in 1558 there were still nine.[2] It is clear that in the early part of our period, up to the Reformation, they were still coming over in considerable numbers to serve for higher wages in subordinate capacities, as labourers, artisans, curates. But the Reformation, and the subsequent decline of the Cornish language, cut Cornwall apart from Brittany, and they ceased to come over. It may be that our population began to go up, and there was less room for them; certainly there were fewer openings. Our towns became inhabited mostly by Cornish people, at the same time as they were being assimilated to the English. They were ceasing to be so different.

Carew notes too that in his lifetime the sea-coast towns were prospering and becoming more populous as against those inland.[3] Tudor government recognized the decay of the latter as a problem to be dealt with, and produced an act of Parliament in 1540 'For the re-edification of towns westward', with a series of provisions for rebuilding fallen-down houses in the old Cornish boroughs.[4] It is hardly likely to have arrested a deep-rooted economic tendency, characteristic of the growing importance of the sea and the coastal towns throughout our period — one of the main rhythms in this history.

Carew has some speculations on the causes of these changes, and comments that anyhow what the inland towns lost the sea-coast gained. He does not state that the population of Cornwall was increasing, as it probably was, but he does confute the view that it was declining. He was of the opinion that the county was as well-inhabited as any other 'champaign shires'.[5] Of the western shires, it was usual in levying burdens upon the counties to rate Devon and Somerset together, as both larger and richer in resources than Dorset and Cornwall, which paired with each other. It is a pity that Carew does not give us his estimate of the total population of the county; but he suggests, since 'it cannot directly be summed' that it 'may yet proportionably be guessed at by the musters taken of the able men, which we will value at a third part of the whole, in ensuing Bodin's rate'. Now the total muster of able men for the county was at this time 6000; that would give, on this

---

[1] Matthews, *History of St. Ives*, 117-20.
[2] Henderson, *History of the Parish of Constantine*, 212-13.
[3] Carew, 57, 65-6.
[4] 32 Henry VIII, c. 19. *L.P. Addenda*, I. 769.
[5] Carew, 57.

computation, a population of perhaps 18,000 males. It seems that the Poll Tax Returns of 1377 indicate a population of 35-40,000;[1] while Mr. Henderson gives a figure of 105,800 for the year 1700.[2] There were some 160 parishes in the county.[3] If we allow them an average of 200-250 inhabitants, we arrive at an estimate of 32-40,000 persons. We have to allow for the old towns, the conventional figures for which at the time were Bodmin 2000, and the rest 1000. Altogether we may perhaps estimate the population in the sixteenth century at 40-50,000. That would not be incompatible with the slow growth of population in the Middle Ages, and at the same time allow for the figure attained at the end of the seventeenth century.

It is a commonplace to observe that the towns, though they had a growing autonomy in the governing of their own affairs from the fifteenth century, onwards, were closely knit into the fabric of this dominantly rural society. The fields came into the towns; most of them were no more than villages, and the administration of their affairs partook more of the nature of a manor than of a town — though as the critical surveyor of the Courtenay manors noted of one of the littlest of them, the fishing village of Crafthole, they held tenaciously to their rights and took what opportunity they could of expanding them.[4] The larger towns usually had some lands of their own, the town lands, with which they had been endowed to meet necessary expenses. Launceston was fortunate in this respect, in possessing both property within the borough and commons outside, with which to meet the town's charges — upkeep of bridges and highways, paving streets, repairing the church, maintaining the gildhall and officers' fees, paying tenths and fifteenths.[5] The towns, it may be supposed, from what fragmentary evidence remains, had the usual complement of gilds, which played such an important part in the social life of the time. At Bodmin there were over forty; almost the whole population seems to have been included in one or other of them, and it was through their organization that most of the money required for rebuilding the parish church was raised. Some five of them appear to have been craft gilds, and the remainder established for religious and social objects. The rules of the Cordwainers' Gild at Helston in 1517 survive; and from them we may gather the close connection between these two motives, so close as to become almost one, the keen sense of obligation to the craft and to society, the care for poor brethren, the provision for intercession at the gild's own altar in the church and for funeral ceremonies, the insistence upon the

---

[1] *Parochial History of Cornwall* (Truro, 1872), IV, App. 162.
[2] Henderson, XI.   [3] Carew, 57.
[4] *Topographer and Genealogist*, I. 344.   [5] Peter, op. cit., 158-9.

religious duty of doing good cobbling.[1] The whole life of society, as in primitive communities, was organized in one way or another.

Outside the bounds of the towns, there were the remaining classes of agrarian society. 'Touching the yeomanry', says Carew, 'I can say little worth the observing, for any difference from that of other shires.'[2] He might have added that, as elsewhere, they were a minority in Cornwall; and though one could cite a fair number of farmers who were prosperous, to judge from their wills, and others who shaded off into the gentry, the yeomen were possibly less particularised an element than in other counties. Of the peasantry the most numerous class, we have seen, were conventionary tenants, copyholders holding for term of three lives. Carew tell us what progress these had made in that century: how they had 'in times not past the remembrance of some yet living . . . little bread-corn, their drink water, or at best, but whey; for the richest farmer in a parish brewed not above twice a year, and then God wot what liquor! Their meat, whitsul as they call it, namely, milk, sour milk, cheese, curds, butter and such-like as come from the cow and ewe'. They went barefoot; their clothes and habitations were according, of the simplest, their lives of the hardiest. Yet he notes at the end of the century, 'now most of these fashions are universally banished and the Cornish husbandman conformeth himself with a better supplied civility to the eastern pattern, which hath directed him a more thriving form of husbandry'. As against this, he sets a large increase in the number of poor, with which he regards Cornwall as more pestered than most counties, though she did not produce them. They come in, he says, from Ireland, arriving daily in every ship; and he proceeds to a vehement diatribe which enables one to appreciate the temper of the country gentlemen who passed the Elizabethan statutes against vagabonds.[3]

For the rest, the county was organized and governed much as other counties. There were nine hundreds, East, West, Trigg, Lesnewth, Stratton, Powder, Pydar, Kerrier, Penwith, the origins of which, and the meaning of some of their names, are lost in antiquity. Carew tells us that there were no constables of the hundreds; their duties were performed by the deputy bailiffs.[4] This left the parish constables in a more independent position and gave them all the more influence; as was seen 'in the last Cornish rebellion [1549], how the constables' command and example drew many of the not worst meaning people into that extremest breach of duty'. It was a peculiarity of Cornwall that the sheriff, under the Duchy charter, was appointed

[1] Henderson, *Essays*, 75-9.   [2] Carew, 66.   [3] ibid., 67.   [4] ibid., 85-6.

by the Duke; but that in practice meant little, and the Duchy was in the hands of the Crown throughout most of our period.

The difficulties and discontent consequent upon the dissolution of the monasteries, the disturbed years from 1539 to 1549, account for the most interesting new constitutional development. The government thought conditions in the west sufficiently a problem to set up a special Council of the West, on the model of the Councils of the North and of Wales, to deal with it.[1] A large council of eighteen, headed by Lord Russell, with the Bishops of Exeter and Bath and the most important local figures serving on it, was constituted to deal with urgent questions of order, sedition, riots, disputes, and to enforce conformity with new Reformation legislation. Its jurisdiction covered the four western counties. The Cornish members of it were Sir Piers Edgcumbe, Sir John Arundell, Sir William Godolphin and Sir Thomas Arundell. The Council was set up in 1539, was active in settling disputes for the next year or two, and then lapsed. No doubt it had been useful in quieting the West and helping to bring it into line. In 1545 the war with France made its defence a more urgent matter, and Russell was made Lieutenant of these counties with the double object of maintaining internal order and providing for defence, raising levies, impressing seamen.[2] The rising of 1549 brought him again into the West as King's Lieutenant with a commission to repress the rebellion and establish order.[3]

From this time the possibilities of the office were grasped by the government; Parliament recognized the appointment of Lieutenants for any counties in time of emergency, and the system became general over the whole country. Francis, Earl of Bedford, Russell's son, succeeded to something of his father's position as Lieutenant of Devon and Cornwall in 1559 and so remained until his death in 1585. From their house at Tavistock, the priory which Henry granted Russell for his services, he and his son were in a favourable position near the Cornish border for overlooking what went on in the two counties. It was an important factor in keeping the Council in close touch with the situation there, one more means of binding the remote west to the central government. On Bedford's death, two Lieutenants were appointed, the Earl of Bath for Devon, and Sir Walter Ralegh for Cornwall.[4] It was a weakness in the latter's position that he was not resident in, though he had many family connections with, the county. In consequence, in the years of crisis and of the war with Spain, greater responsibility was thrown

---

[1] Skeel, 'The Council of the West', *Trans. Roy. Hist. Soc.*, 1921.
[2] Scott Thomson, *Lords Lieutenants in the Sixteenth Century*, 18-19.
[3] ibid., 26-9.   [4] ibid., 96.

upon those leading Cornish gentry who were made deputy-lieutenants; a whole martial organization, mustering all the able men of the county, drilling and exercising them with arms, grew up under them.

Of the spiritual organization of the county we shall speak later, for it is a whole subject of its own. Nor is this the place to describe in detail the social conditions of the people, the inner conduct of their lives. This whole book must be the revelation of the life of that society, as far as the evidences of it are recoverable, or it is nothing.

CHAPTER V

FEUDAL ANARCHY AND SOCIAL UNREST

CORNWALL lay, then, quiet, it might almost be said dormant, throughout most of the Middle Ages, a small conquered country on the remotest out-skirts of Europe, held in possession by its Anglo-Norman feudal class, its own inner life locked away in the secret of its now forgotten native language. The first stirrings of a new and altogether more active career in the history of the nation come about, significantly enough, at the full flood of the Renaissance period, with the break-up of the cohesion of the feudal nobility as a ruling class, their relapse into civil war and anarchy.

The county was not directly concerned in the Wars of the Roses, but all the same it was very far from being unaffected by them. Stubbs says: 'The south-western counties did not witness much of the military action of the time, and bore their share in the common burden quietly.'[1] In fact the Courtenays, most important of west-country families with large holdings in Cornwall, were leading participants in the struggle; they involved the county to some extent and brought in a number of west-country gentry in their wake. The head of the family, Thomas I, Earl of Devon, began by sympathizing with Richard of York's campaign for reform; but when he saw that York was aiming at the Crown, he drew back, swore fealty to Henry VI, and from that time the senior branch of the Courtenays were consistent Lancastrians and among the leaders of the party. The family made great sacrifices for the cause. Thomas II, Earl of Devon, was beheaded after the battle of Towton in 1461. Henry, his brother and heir, was executed at Salisbury in 1467; and his son John, titular Earl, was slain at Tewkesbury in 1471, while Sir Hugh Courtenay of Boconnoc, head of the Cornish branch, was beheaded after the battle. It was to the son of this last that the earldom descended; but the ill-fate dependent upon their dangerously exalted position continued to dog them, and the repercussions of the Wars of the Roses to pursue them, into our period, when ironically enough they were regarded with jealous distrust by the Tudors for having Yorkist royal blood in their veins, and the earldom came to an end with Edward Courtenay, candidate for the hands of Mary and Elizabeth, who died at Padua in 1556.

[1] Stubbs, *Const. Hist.*, III. 186.

The sympathies of Cornwall, like those of west and north in general, were with the Lancastrians. One Cornish family, the Trevelyans, owed their rise to the singular favour with which Henry VI regarded the young John Trevelyan, the founder of their prosperity. He was a prominent member of the Court-party, a follower of Suffolk's, an intimate of the King's; and Yorkist satires animadvert against his hold over Henry:

> The Cornish Chough oft with his train
> Hath made our Eagle blind.

And in the satire on Henry's favourites:

> *Libera me*, singeth Trevelyan, warre the rere,
> That they do no more so, *Requiescat in pace*.[1]

One has the impression of a very plausible and dexterous person; and he certainly did well for himself, getting all sorts of grants and offices at home in Cornwall, marrying a great heiress with estates in several western counties, managing to get a pardon from Edward IV and to survive Richard III, living on to the final triumph of his party with Henry VII.[2]

Other Cornish families besides, the Arundells, Treffrys, Edgcumbe, Nanfan, and certain of the Devonshire gentry with estates in Cornwall, Sir John Halliwell, Sir Robert Willoughby, were active Lancastrians. It is not surprising that when Queen Margaret returned to the country in 1471, she landed at Weymouth and was conducted by the Earl of Devon to Exeter, where she proceeded to raise an army, 'the whole might' of Devon and Cornwall, we are told, rallying to them.[3]

The career of the leading person in Cornwall during the Wars of the Roses was very characteristic of that disordered time. Sir Henry de Bodrugan was the last of a line which had occupied a prominent position in mid-Cornwall throughout the Middle Ages. Bodrugan, that great farm upon the cliffs between Mevagissey and the Dodman, was the centre of very considerable estates in the neighbourhood. Nevertheless, Sir Henry was in constant difficulties, due no doubt to over-spending himself, his ostentatious way of living, keeping a band of dependants and retainers, with which, to recoup himself, he committed constant depredations upon his neighbours. All very like what was going on with greater personages in other parts of the country.

Bodrugan had a root of instability and lawlessness in him; generous to his friends, extravagant, rash, hot-tempered, a familiar type of buccaneer, he

---

[1] *Trevelyan Papers*, I. 67, 70, 74.   [2] ibid., III. v-vii.
[3] cf. Scofield, *Life and Reign of Edward IV*, I. 583.

was popular with those whom he had not injured. He had enjoyed a long minority, with no father to restrain him.[1] He paid his addresses to someone else's wife; when the husband died, he seems to have married the lady; but her son, John Beaumont, was proved a bastard,[2] and everybody accepted the fact that he was Bodrugan's. The young Beaumont grew up at Bodrugan with his father and became a partner in all his regrettable, if enjoyable enterprises. On his wife's death, Sir Henry married the Viscountess Lisle;[3] but there were no children of the marriage. The prospect of his line coming to an end can hardly have been a settling influence.

At the time of the Earl of Oxford's descent upon the Mount in the autumn of 1473 — the last Lancastrian incursion against Edward IV — Bodrugan had played an odd, delaying, perhaps double, game.[4] After its surrender, we find him attacking Polwhele and threatening to burn the house down, in company with some of the Earl's freebooting followers.[5] In this unsettled time a series of charges mounted up against him: of forcibly entering James Trefusis's house and his ship, the *Bride* of Feock, and carrying away goods and chattels; of setting to sea two carvels, the *Mary Bodrugan* and the *Barbara* of Fowey, which chased a Breton ship into St. Ives and spoiled her of her cargo of wine and cloth.[6] He received his men and the goods at Bodrugan. These and other charges culminated in an act of attainder against him and his colleague in ill-doing, Richard Bonython; but they got it reversed. After that, a dependable Yorkist, a strong partisan, he had things very much his own way during the remainder of Edward IV's and Richard III's reigns. They knew that they could rely on him to defend their cause against the numerous west-country Lancastrians, and that explains why he was let off so lightly from the consequences of exploits and questionable doings too numerous to relate here.

Bodrugan's career comes to an end in a haze of picturesque stories as they have come down in Cornish tradition, from which it is now possible to disentangle the facts. There is usually something in tradition: in this case, in the part which Edgcumbe and Trevanion had in bringing him down. The older Cornish histories speak of Bodrugan fighting on the side of Richard III at Bosworth field, and of his escaping afterwards into Cornwall.[7] There is no evidence of this, nor is it probable — though there is no doubt on

---

[1] *Cal. Pat. Rolls*, 1446-1452, 126.   [2] ibid., 1461-1467, 539.
[3] *Rolls Parlt.*, VI. 133 foll.
[4] cf. Taylor, *St. Michael's Mount*, 121-32.
[5] *Rolls Parlt.*, loc. cit.   [6] ibid.
[7] cf. Davies Gilbert, founded on Hals and Tonkin MS. histories, *Parochial History of Cornwall*, II. 108.

which side his sympathies were. He is more likely to have lain low in Cornwall; for after Henry's accession, in February 1486, he was named along with the Earl of Devon, Sir Robert Willoughby, Sir John Halliwell, Sir John Treffry, and other triumphant Lancastrians to serve on yet another Fowey case of piracy.[1] But it was his last. Sir Henry had been too closely associated with Yorkist rule, and too well rewarded by it, to feel comfortable under that of Henry VII, with his former enemies now in the ascendant. The tradition is that at the time of Buckingham's conspiracy against Richard III, Bodrugan had taken the lead — it was to be expected that he should — in the pursuit of Richard Edgcumbe. Carew tells the story which had come down in the Edgcumbe family, how Edgcumbe was driven to hide in the thick woods at Cotehele overlooking the gorge of the Tamar; 'which extremity taught him a sudden policy, to put a stone in his cap and tumble the same into the water, while these rangers were fast at his heels, who looking down after the noise and seeing his cap swimming thereon, supposed that he had desperately drowned himself, gave over their further hunting, and left him liberty to shift away and ship over into Brittany';[2] from which he returned, of course, with Henry. Whatever Bodrugan's services to Richard III were, he was rewarded with the manors of Trelawne and Tywardreath.[3]

When Henry VII came to rule, it was then Edgcumbe's turn, and he was in a very powerful position, one of the chief agents in executing the King's policy. By 1487 Bodrugan's discontent with the new regime had betrayed itself. There is no evidence that he was with the Earl of Lincoln at the battle of Stoke, as has been said;[4] nor is he charged with having been there in his subsequent attainder. But on February 8th, 1487, a commission was granted to Sir Richard Edgcumbe to arrest Bodrugan and Beaumont and other rebels, 'who have withdrawn themselves into private places in the counties of Devon and Cornwall and stir up sedition'.[5] Edgcumbe must have leaped at the chance of getting his own back. The story is that Bodrugan slipped away out of his house to the cliffs nearby where there was a boat waiting for him: 'as soon therefore as he came to the cliff above an hundred feet high, he leaped down into the sea upon a little grassy island there without much hurt or damage, where instantly a boat which he had prepared in the cove attended him there, which transported him to a ship that carried him into France, which astonishing fact and place is to this day well known and

---

[1] *Cal. Pat. Rolls*, 1485–1494, 105.   [2] Carew, 114.
[3] Harleian MS. 433, 1616.   [4] cf. Blake in *J.R.I.C.* (1915), 64.
[5] *Cal. Pat. Rolls*, 1485–1494, 179.

remembered by the name of Henry Bodrugan's leap or jump'.[1] A later
story adds: 'into which boat they tell you when he got safe he turned about
and gave a curse upon Edgcumbe and Trevanion and all their posterity,
which the neighbourhood do not scruple to say hath in some part its effect
to this day. For so great was the love they bore this Sir Henry for his great
hospitality and generous way of living, that his memory is still held in
veneration, especially among the elder sort of people'.[2]

However that may be, Bodrugan and his son certainly left the country;
and that may well have been their manner of leaving. They went to
Ireland; on November 9th, 1487, an Act of attainder was passed against them
and their lands declared forfeit.[3] In the Act they were charged with
imagining and compassing the death of the King, in company with the
Earl of Lincoln there. But in a Star Chamber case of the next reign, John
Reskymer and Richard Antron, heirs to the Bodrugan inheritance, state
that Sir Henry 'departed into Ireland to a kinsman of his when he soon
afterwards there deceased'; but that he 'was never in company with the said
Earl, nor never spake with him, nor never sent him message by writing,
nor none otherwise, nor never committed treason'.[4]

It is a likely enough story. Perhaps the old man — he must have been over
sixty — had had enough. His wife, Viscountess Lisle, had died before him.
Early in 1486, he had tried to put himself right with Sir Robert Willoughby,
a leading supporter of Henry VII in the west, by granting him his manor
of Trethewe after his death.[5] Upon his attainder the Willoughbys took the
rents and profits of it anyhow, and afterwards bought it outright.[6] It was a
good time for those on the right side. Trevanion, for his part, got the
manors of Restronguet and Newham.[7] After various payments made to
Hugh Oldham, Walter Smert, citizen and skinner of London, and others to
whom Bodrugan was in debt,[8] the bulk of his manors, Bodrugan, Tregrehan, Tremodret, and many others, were granted on April 26th, 1488, to
Sir Richard Edgcumbe.[9] A junior branch of the Edgcumbes came to
inhabit Sir Henry's house out on the cliffs near Chapel Point, and were
buried in his parish church at St. Goran. It is through the inquisition taken
on the death of Sir Richard Edgcumbe that we learn the details of the

[1] Davies Gilbert, op. cit., 108.
[2] Polwhele, *History of Cornwall*, q. from Tonkin MSS.
[3] *Rolls Parlt.*, VI. 397; for Beaumont inheritance, v. Maclean, *Trigg Minor*, I. 552-3.
[4] Star Chamber Proc. Henry VIII 23/305.
[5] *Cal. Inq. post mortem*, Henry VII, I, 872.   [6] *Cal. Pat. Rolls*, 1494-1509, 503.
[7] ibid., 350.   [8] *Rolls Parlt.*, VI. 400.
[9] *Cal. Pat. Rolls*, 1485-1494, 224. There was an annuity charged upon them to Sir Thomas
Lovell; this was later extinguished and the Edgcumbes entered into entire possession.

economy of Bodrugan as it was in Sir Henry's time, his reeve's accounts: the forty-one kine, eighteen oxen (it was at Bodrugan that they ploughed with oxen latest of all in Cornwall, in the last century), the calves and heifers, the dutiful payments for blessed wax, to the brethren of St. John of Rhodes or St. John of Acre, which suggest those last, lingering days of the Middle Ages.[1]

Nor was Bodrugan the only offender among the Cornish gentry. Feuds, usually over property or office, were the order of the day, like the great Courtenay-Bonville dispute which, originating over the Stewardship of the Duchy, filled Devonshire with unquiet for years, culminated with an attack upon the cathedral at Exeter by the Earl and a private army of his adherents in 1455, and forced a petition from the Commons to Henry VI to imprison both Devonshire and Bonville and bring them to book for their offences.[2] The weak government of Henry VI was responsible for the deterioration of public order; but the civil war multiplied opportunities for private feuds, and not even Edward IV and Henry VII could at once catch up with disorder in the remoter parts of the country.

Twelve years after Edward's accession there was a feud going on in the Lizard peninsula, between the two chief landowners in that district, Thomas Trethewy of Reskymer and John Vyvyan of Trelowarren, evidently over the rights of the latter to his manor of Trelowarren.[3] On August 2nd, 1472, Vyvyan with his wife and children and servants was going on pilgrimage to offer in the chapel of St. James at Tregowris, when they were waylaid by a band of ten servants and followers of Trethewy's. An ambush had been set between the chapel and Treworgie; Vyvyan's party having heard of it, 'left and forsook the highway', but were pursued: several of them were wounded and John Merther, gentleman, nephew and servant of Vyvyan's, was killed. For a long time Trethewy with a band of forty kept watch day and night and 'made their espies throughout the country' to murder Vyvyan; they so menaced his tenants that they refused their tenures and the manor was left waste. On the Sunday after St. Bartholomew's Day Trethewy sent eighteen persons to Trelowarren, who took goods of the value of 40 marks. A nice Sunday occupation for the coroner of the county (which Trethewy was). Vyvyan declared himself so impoverished as not to be able to sue the process at common law, but petitioned Parliament. The offenders were attainted; but subsequently restored and the attainder revoked. No doubt there was fault on both sides.

A worse case was the long feud waged by Thomas Clemens against John

---

[1] Henderson, xxv.   [2] *Rolls Parlt.*, v. 285, 332.   [3] ibid., 52.

Glyn of Morval over the deputy-stewardship of the Duchy.[1] Clemens had held it, but for some reason Glyn had replaced him in the office. Accordingly on January 8th, 1469, when Glyn was holding the court of the manor within the castle at Liskeard, he was attacked by a band brought together by Clemens, his servants beaten, himself wounded in the face and imprisoned within the castle for five hours 'so that none of his friends might come where he was to relieve him with drink or staunch his blood, to the intent that he should have bled to death, except they suffered a priest to come to shrive and housel him'. Meanwhile they tore up the court rolls, cut off the purse hanging from Glyn's girdle containing money and bills; and in the end forced him to sign a bond in £200 not to take any action against them.

Next year in October, when the King was out of the realm — one can imagine the opportunity his withdrawal and the subsequent confusion gave to the disorderly — Clemens assembled a band and made a descent upon Morval. It seems to have been a regular raid, judging from the haul they made off with, £200 worth of goods, not only from Morval which they stripped of all its furnishings, goods, stocks, provisions, beasts, but also from the houses and farms dependent on it. Most of the goods were delivered to Clemens. Glyn issued a writ of appeal of robbery against him; for fear of which Clemens planned to murder him and many times lay in wait for him at Cargollen Bridge. Later Clemens learned 'by subtle and false espies' that Glyn would be at Tavistock Fair, and assembled a party of his men who 'on Saturday in the feast of the decollation of St. John the Baptist at Overwringworthy, lay in wait and at 4 o'clock in the morning horribly slew and murdered him, clove his head in four parts and gave him ten dead wounds in his body, and when he was dead cut off one of his legs, and one of his arms and his head from his body to make him sure'. They made away with his purse with £22 in it, his signets of gold and silver, his sword and dagger, his double cloak of 'mustardeviles'. Clemens received the men who had perpetrated this horrible murder and kept them in his house for a fortnight until it was known by whom the deed was done; then they all went into hiding. In this case too the offenders had so many connections 'by affinity' that neither the sheriff nor the coroner dared arrest the murderers nor serve a writ upon them. Glyn's widow was fain to petition Parliament for redress. This was in 1472-73. Yet three years later, on November 29th, 1475, we find a strong commission appointed, including Sir Robert Willoughby and Sir Henry Bodrugan, to arrest Thomas Clemens and two of his chief accomplices, Thomas Fleet and Thomas Knight, and bring them

[1] *Rolls Parlt.*, VI. 35.

before the King and Council.[1] They were to release Jane, Glyn's widow, who had been arrested by Clemens, and set her at liberty. In February 1476, another commission, this time omitting Bodrugan, was sent down to arrest and bring up Clemens and a good many more of his accomplices.[2] This is the last that we hear of him; it is to be hoped that he received his deserts at last. But if this was the kind of thing that a leading person in the county, whose name frequently appeared in commissions of the peace up to 1471,[3] was responsible for, it may be imagined what was the deterioration of order, the disturbed state of those times.

Along the sea-coast and in the Channel disorder was endemic. Spoliation, reprisals, privateering, piracy, were alike rife — so much so that it is difficult to distinguish one from another. They all are held to come under the generic term of 'piracy', though as Mr. Kingsford says, conditions might be described 'rather as a system of mutual reprisals than as piracy in the modern sense'.[4] In the absence of strong government with a royal fleet efficiently keeping the seas, with the chronic insecurity of our relations with France and Brittany varying with the changes of the civil war, it was a kind of mob-law which prevailed in the Channel punctuated by sporadic outbursts of private war between the west country and the Breton and Norman ports. Fowey was *longo intervallo* the leader in these exploits. This was the hey-day in the town's history — never was there such a time before or since: these were the days of the 'Fowey gallants' who filled the Channel with the rumours of their deeds and the fear of their name. The town seems to have prospered by them; for it was in these years that they were building the splendid tower of their church, erecting the blockhouses with a chain across to guard the entrance to the haven, while Thomas Treffry built his fair house of Place and embattled it, which is to this day 'the glory of the town building in Fowey', as it was in Leland's day when he stayed there with Thomas Treffry eighty years later.[5] The men of Fowey commended themselves, so Carew tells us, to the Earl of Warwick, 'whose ragged staff is yet to be seen, portrayed in many places of their church steeple and in divers private houses'.[6]

Their successes were innumerable. The Patent Rolls and Chancery proceedings of this time are filled with their depredations upon Breton ships, ships of St. Malo, of Normandy, of Bilbao, Biscayan barges, a ship of Plymouth trading to Fuentarrabia, spoiling them of their cargoes of wine,

---

[1] *Cal. Pat. Rolls, 1467-1477*, 552.   [2] ibid., 573.   [3] ibid., 610.
[4] Kingsford, *Prejudice and Promise in the Fifteenth Century*, 78.
[5] *Leland's Itinerary*, I. 204.   [6] Carew, 135.

oil, canvas, salt, bringing them back to Fowey to dispose of.[1] The town grew fat on the merchandise. In March 1455, eleven Fowey ships ordered for war captured and brought in half a dozen French ships, mainly of Norman ports.[2] It was open warfare, and reprisal was to be expected. In 1457 a Breton fleet sailed into the harbour by night, took the inhabitants by surprise who fled within the walls of Place, which was defended by the dauntless wife of Thomas Treffry in her husband's absence.[3] The invaders were driven off, but not until they had laid part of the town in ashes. It was after this that the blockhouses were erected, and Place embattled.[4] The town took no fall by this untoward event; such damage was easily repaired, and the gallants of Fowey went on in their courses much as before.

But Edward IV was determined to restore order in the Channel; as soon as he was firmly seated on the throne once more, and the threat of Oxford's hold upon the Mount removed, he took steps to bring the men of Fowey to book. He must have been tired of making restitution from the customs to Bretons and Spaniards upon whom losses had been inflicted by Fowey boats.[5] In November 1474 a commission was sent down to arrest all mariners, masters, pirates, victuallers of ships of Fowey, Bodinnick and Polruan for their depredations, and bring them before the King and Council, to seize their vessels, gear and goods, and place them in custody.[6] The captains were taken and sent to London, the Dartmouth men commanded to take their ships away — a great indignity, surely; they also took away the great chain that stretched across the harbour mouth.[7] Carew adds that the commissioners 'under pretence of using their service in sea affairs, trained thither [i.e. to Lostwithiel] the greatest number of the burgesses; and no sooner come than laid hold on, and in hold, their goods were confiscated, one Harrington executed, the chain of their haven removed to Dartmouth, and their wonted jollity transformed into a sudden misery: from which they strived a long time to relieve themselves: but now of late years do more and more aspire to a great amendment of their former defects, though not to an equal height of their first abundance'.[8] It was a notable fall, and Fowey was suitably chastened. Never quite the same high water mark was reached

---

[1] cf. *Cal. Pat. Rolls, 1452-1461*, 119, 168, 309, 441, 615, 650; *Cal. Pat. Rolls, 1461-1467*, 36, 233, 452; *Cal. Pat. Rolls, 1467-1477*, 249, 377; and cf. Kingsford, 'West Country Piracy', op. cit., 78-106.

[2] *Cal. Pat. Rolls, 1452-1461*, 302.

[3] *Leland's Itinerary*, loc. cit.; Pocquet du Haut Jussé, *François II et l'Angleterre* (1458-88), 37-8.

[4] So Leland states, and he had good reason to know, since he stayed with Thomas Treffry at Fowey when in Cornwall; as against the view of Oppenheim, 'Maritime History', in the *Vict. Cty. Hist. Cornwall*, I. 484.

[5] cf. *Cal. Pat. Rolls, 1467-1477*, 468, 474, 511, 602.

[6] ibid., 492.   [7] Leland, loc. cit.   [8] Carew, 135-6.

again; the glory and the old care-free jollity had departed. Carew states the position precisely: Fowey was to work its way back to a more respectable commercial prosperity under the guiding hand of the Rashleighs in the later years of Elizabeth, and to play an honourable part in the days of the Armada, but nothing like so conspicuous a role as in the later Middle Ages. It came to be overshadowed by Plymouth, and later, by Falmouth.

The advantage of Edward IV's closure of the Wars of the Roses and restoration of order was lost by the usurpation of Richard III and the murder of Edward's children. It reopened the whole question of the dynastic succession, produced a large exodus from the Yorkist party which linked up with the Lancastrian claimant, Henry Tudor, abroad in Brittany, and undermined public confidence at home. People could not be at ease with a crowned criminal on the throne. In the efforts which were made to overthrow Richard and make Henry king, the West, along with Wales, played an essential part; indeed, Henry VII's accession may be said to have had something of the character of a western victory.

The first concerted effort to overthrow Richard, Buckingham's conspiracy in 1483, had three elements: the Duke was to lead the rising in Wales, then march south to link up with the rising in the west country headed by the Courtenays, while Henry was to arrive upon the south coast from Brittany. The outbreak was fixed for St. Luke's Day, October 18th, but the plans were upset, and in the event ruined, by the great storm which swept the west of England a few days before. The country was deluged; rivers rose and broke their banks; two hundred people were said to have been drowned in and around Bristol. The Severn became impassable; Buckingham's army could not cross, the bridge-head being held against him; he himself became a fugitive and was betrayed and executed at Salisbury, where Richard halted on his rapid march west.[1]

Meanwhile Henry had been proclaimed at Exeter by the Courtenays — Peter, the ablest member of the family, who held the see, Sir Walter Courtenay of Powderham, the Bishop's brother, and their kinsman Edward Courtenay of Boconnoc, head of the family and later restored to the earldom by Henry VII. Associated with them were the Woodvilles, the Marquis of Dorset, the Bishop of Salisbury, and the leaders of the Lancastrian party in Devon and Cornwall, Sir Robert Willoughby, Sir Thomas Arundell, Richard Edgcumbe, John Halliwell, John and William Treffry, Richard Nanfan, John Trevelyan.[2] In Brittany, Henry was handsomely equipped

---

[1] Gairdner, *Richard III*, 138-9.   [2] *Rolls Parlt.*, VI. 273.

by the Duke with a squadron of five vessels and some three hundred men; but the same storm which had ruined Buckingham's rising scattered Henry's squadron and drove all his ships, save his own, back upon the Breton coast.[1] He arrived off the south coast by Poole to find the approaches well guarded; he then moved westward along the coast to Plymouth. Here too there were armed men waiting on shore. He was assured that they were Buckingham's men. The cautious Henry rightly placed no reliance on the information, and after hovering for a time off the cliffs of Cawsand slipped back to Brittany.[2]

It would appear that the Courtenays fell back on Cornwall; and on November 3rd, the Bishop and his kinsman of Boconnoc proclaimed Henry at Bodmin.[3] They were accompanied by Sir Thomas Arundell, Ralph Arundell of Penbugle, John Treffry, Geoffrey Beauchamp, Remfry Denzell, Thomas Borlase, John Rosogan and many others. But they were disconcerted by the rapid advance of the King to Exeter, where all opposition was stilled, and three prominent insurgents beheaded, of whom the most distinguished was Sir Thomas St. Leger, Richard's own brother-in-law.[4] There was no point in further resistance. The Courtenays fled abroad, accompanied by their chief adherents, Willoughby, Arundell, Edgcumbe, Treffry,[5] and a number of lesser men, such as Borlase, of whom a subsequent case informs us of his 'going beyond sea, by the commandment of the Earl of Devonshire'.[6] In Brittany the fugitives, of menacing number and importance, gathered; they kept Christmas Day at Rennes, where at high mass in the cathedral Henry solemnly swore to marry Elizabeth of York and received their homage as King of England.[7]

All this naturally did not improve relations between England and Brittany. They had been in a state of some insecurity with the complicated diplomatic game being played by England, France and the Empire over the Duchy's independence. Now relations degenerated into measures of active hostility. All Breton ships and goods in west-country ports were seized; the mayors of Dartmouth, Plymouth, Fowey and Penzance were ordered to hand them over for sale and to ransom.[8] Privateering became the order of the day once more. At the end of this year Charles Dynham sailing under the King's

---

[1] Pocquet du Haut Jussé, op. cit., 249-53.   [2] Gairdner, 142.

[3] There is no information in any of the histories of England as to this episode. It all rests upon a document mentioned by W. C. Borlase in his *Borlase of Borlase*, 29-30, as being then (1888) in the possession of Mr. C. D. Le Grice. But there seems to be no reason to question its authenticity, and it adds something to our information concerning the western end of the Buckingham conspiracy.

[4] Gairdner, 143.

[5] Polydore Vergil, *Angliae Hist.* (ed. 1546), 552; Hall's *Chronicle* (ed. 1548), King Richard III, fol. xxxix.

[6] Borlase, op. cit., 29.   [7] Pocquet du Haut Jussé, 252.   [8] Harleian MS. 433, 1627, 1639.

flag captured three Breton ships, the *Margaret* of Audierne, the *Katherine* of Nantes, the *Saint Gremon* of Penmarch.[1] Their cargoes, however, 990 bales of woad being transported from Guyenne to Flanders, were ordered to be restored, since they belonged to Spanish subjects. This condition of affairs lasted all the winter. The Duke of Brittany armed his subjects and ordered them to keep watch on the coasts.[2] Even after a truce had been arrived at, in the spring of 1485 we find the *Little Anne* of Fowey entering harbour at Southampton, seizing the *Sainte Marie* of Portaly lying at anchor there, and carrying off her cargo of wine, salt, linen, all her gear, sails and anchors, with 200 crowns of gold 'to the parts of Cornwall'.[3] The King ordered restitution of the goods and the arrest of the offenders.

While Henry Tudor and his supporters went on with their preparations in Brittany and later in France for a second expedition, Richard III and his adherents made hay with their enemies' properties while the sun shone. From a docket-book of Richard's grants, we learn the names of others who had taken up arms against him: a balinger which had belonged to Stephen Calmady, 'our rebel', was granted to Thomas Young;[4] the goods and chattels of Thomas Bonython, 'gentleman, late of Penryn, our traitor', were confiscated.[5] A shower of grants of land and offices descended upon Richard's chief supporters and instruments in the west, Halnath Malyverer, Avery Cornburgh, Sir James Tyrrell, Lord Dynham. The King had all the lands of his opponents in his hands, and he was by nature a spendthrift. Sir James Tyrrell, most odious of his instruments, for it was he who took the fatal message to the Tower by which Edward IV's children were put to death, got the lands of the Arundells, his relations by marriage, with whom he was in dispute at law.[6] John, Lord Dynham, was given many of the Courtenay lands and offices;[7] Malyverer got Boconnoc, home of Edward, later Earl of Devon.[8] Bodrugan was granted the manors of Trelawne and Tywardreath.[9] The fact was that the King, whose star was in decline, was having to purchase support by his largesse: so many grants were so many indications of the weakness of his position: so much transference of land and changes of ownership cannot but have increased the disquiet, the restlessness and general lack of confidence.

Meanwhile Henry Tudor was completing his preparations in France and in correspondence with his friends in this country. On August 1st,

[1] *Cal. Pat. Rolls*, 1476–1485, 426.
[2] Pocquet du Haut Jussé, 254.
[3] *Cal. Pat. Rolls*, 1476–1485, 545.
[4] Harleian MS. 433, 1565.
[5] ibid., 1704.
[6] ibid., 1557.
[7] ibid., 601, 602, 699, 700.
[8] ibid., 1068.
[9] ibid., 1616.

1485, he embarked at Harfleur for Milford Haven and the campaign which ended so triumphantly at Bosworth. He had a body of French troops on board, and a number of his leading west-country adherents; for John Halliwell and John Treffry were among those knighted at his landing, and Richard Edgcumbe after the battle at Bosworth.[1] The Lancastrians of the west had come into their own.

[1] Shaw, *Knights of England*, II. 22-3; *Dict. Nat. Biog.*, sub Edgcumbe.

CHAPTER VI

THE REBELLIONS OF 1497:
HENRY VII AND PERKIN WARBECK

ON gaining control of the kingdom, Henry handsomely rewarded his western supporters; they now came into their own, and rather more than their own. They were not only restored to their possessions in the west country, granted new offices and perquisites there, but they formed an important section of the inner circle that held power about the King. The Courtenays got their reward. The earldom of Devonshire was restored in the person of Edward Courtenay of Boconnoc, the heir male of the last Earl, though it was shorn of a few manors which went to that Earl's sisters.[1] Sir Walter Courtenay was granted the Duchy offices which had become almost hereditary in their family; forester of the chase of Dartmoor, steward of the manor and borough of Bradninch and of all the Duchy lands in Devon, warden of the stannaries there.[2] His politic brother, the Bishop of Exeter, became keeper of the privy seal and, the ablest member of the family, an important member of the government. He was seneschal at Henry's coronation, active in the Parliament which reversed Richard's attainders, and served on all the important commissions in the west country.[3] At Exeter he continued his building activities, broken into by his enforced absence abroad; he is said to have already completed the north tower of the cathedral with its pinnacles, installed Great Peter, the largest bell in it, and had the curious great clock made which is still the glory of the north transept. He now set to work altering the palace, which Richard III had found so well stocked on his arrival at Exeter; the bishop celebrated the union of the houses of Lancaster and York with the magnificent mantelpiece which still remains there.[4] In 1487 he was translated to Winchester where he died five years later. One of the first English students at Padua, this cadet of a noble house was, in his tastes and in his career, a typical prelate of the early Renaissance.[5]

Still closer to the King stood Sir Richard Edgcumbe whom Henry made comptroller of his household, a chamberlain of the exchequer and

---

[1] *Cal. Pat. Rolls*, 1485-1494, 28.   [2] ibid., 21.   [3] ibid., 44, 49, 69, etc.
[4] J. F. Chanter, *The Bishop's Palace, Exeter*, 31-3.
[5] cf. art. in *Dict. Nat. Biog.*; Oliver, *Lives of the Bishops of Exeter*, 109-12.

member of the Privy Council. We have seen the various grants he was made within the Duchy,[1] and there were many others he received in the west country and elsewhere. In 1487 he was sheriff of Devon; he received many rewards and douceurs, the stewardship of various lands and estates, the custody and wardship of a number of west-country heirs (a profitable office), a grant of 100 marks during his shrievalty, better still a licence to beard, clack and cleanse 100 sacks of Cornish wool and export them through the straits of Morocco; and much else.[2] But Henry used him for more important diplomatic services outside the country. After the battle of Stoke in 1487, to which field Edgcumbe brought the King reinforcements, he was sent on to Scotland with Fox, afterwards Bishop of Exeter, to treat with the Scots for peace. They arranged a truce for seven years; and in the same year Edgcumbe was sent again as ambassador to arrange a marriage treaty.[3]

Next year a still more difficult and ticklish mission was confided to him, to negotiate and receive the submission of Ireland, taking the oaths of allegiance of the chief nobles, the gentry and the towns.[4] A detailed account of his voyage and transactions there, which may come from his hand, survives.[5] From this we learn that he took shipping from Mountsbay, June 23rd, 1488, in the *Anne* of Fowey — we have heard of her upon other, less lawful occasions — attended by four other Fowey ships, one a barque of Sir John Treffry's, and five hundred men in them. They made for Scilly that day and night against the wind, arriving there to hear that certain sea-rovers had made off on rumour of their expedition. But Edgcumbe made a diversion up the Bristol Channel to look for a 'great Fleming ship of war' which was preying on the King's subjects there along with other rovers; they too were warned however of the expedition and got away. It seems that clearing the seas of pirates was almost a subsidiary purpose of the voyage; for, arrived upon the Irish coast, Edgcumbe made search for others. He landed at Kinsale, where he received the oaths of allegiance of Lord Courcy and the townspeople, and thence went on by sea to Waterford and Dublin. At Dublin the negotiations with the Earl of Kildare and the Irish lords were long and difficult. In the end after a good deal of hard bargaining, much good cheer and plain speaking, Edgcumbe prevailed with them to swear allegiance

---

[1] v. before, p. 82.
[2] cf. *Cal. Pat. Rolls*, 1485-1494, 7, 17, 27, 93, etc.; Campbell, *Letters and Memorials of the Reign of Henry VII*, I. 18, 19, 195, 290, 448, 451, 577; II. 78, 85.
[3] Rymer's *Foedera* (3rd edition), v, pt. III, 193.
[4] Campbell, *Memorials*, II. 315.
[5] Brit. Museum: Titus XI, 282-6; cf. *Dict. Nat. Biog.*, sub Edgcumbe; but more probably it is from the hand of Robert Bolman, one of the clerks of the privy seal, who was appointed to accompany Edgcumbe, v. Campbell, II. 318.

to Henry VII. It was a tricky mission most successfully accomplished. Edgcumbe laboured home slowly through the stormy seas of that year, arriving at St. Ives upon August 7th and at Fowey next day where he landed and went on pilgrimage to St. Saviour's chapel.

At the end of the year Edgcumbe was entrusted with another highly responsible mission. He was sent as ambassador along with Dr. Aynsworth to the young Duchess of Brittany with an offer of English help in her forlorn attempt to defend the independence of the Duchy against the advance of the French.[1] On his landing at Morlaix, he narrowly escaped being captured by the French, who besieged and took the town.[2] However he got away, and by February 10th, 1489, he had concluded a treaty completely in accordance with Henry's wishes: the Bretons were forced, in return for the promise of help, to subject the Duchess's marriage and her foreign policy to Henry's approval, and to give pledges of land as security.[3] In April, Henry was writing to the Earl of Oxford that the duchess was in her city of Rennes and 'our right trusty knight and councillor Sir Richard Edgcumbe there also, having chief rule about her'.[4] Actually Edgcumbe's position was a very awkward one, with the Breton government divided against itself and the French constantly advancing; while Henry was anxious to limit his liabilities in the war in which he was involved with Spain and the Netherlands against France. Edgcumbe was apparently sent once again on a mission to offer mediation between France and Britain; but on September 8th he died at Morlaix where he lies buried in the church of the Dominicans.

In the wider field of diplomacy into which Henry's policy was leading, he employed yet another of his Cornish supporters, Sir Richard Nanfan. Henry's objective was to strengthen his dynasty by a treaty of alliance with the Spanish royal house, cemented by a marriage of his son Arthur with the little Katherine of Aragon — a marriage from which there sprang so much later trouble. Nanfan was appointed ambassador, along with Dr. Savage, at the end of 1488 to proceed to Spain to treat with Ferdinand, and to go on to Portugal to confer the Order of the Garter upon its King.[5] Nanfan was created a knight at the King's hands between Westminster and Sion the same day that he set out. The party set sail from Southampton on January 19th, but next day, we learn from the Journal of the voyage which remains,[6]

[1] Campbell, II, 378; cf. Busch, England under the Tudors, 45.
[2] Paston Letters (ed. Gairdner), III. 907.   [3] Busch, 46.
[4] Paston Letters, III. 358.
[5] Pollard, The Reign of Henry VII, III. 2.
[6] Gairdner, Memorials of the Reign of Henry VII, 328 foll.

they were forced by the wind into Plymouth, where Nanfan stayed with
Alderman Thomas Tresawell, the chaplain of the Ambassador of Castile
and the Herald of Scotland with John Treville, and Richmond King-at-
Arms with the mayor. They did not set sail again until February 1st.
They had the wind against them that eve and all next day, which was Lady-
day, and on February 3rd they landed at Falmouth in 'a great tempest of
wind, rain and bad weather'. Here — it must have been at Penryn that they
stayed, for there were hardly any houses at Falmouth then — they remained
for ten days. The returning ambassadors of Castile, who were among the
party, lodged with a merchant, John Luck; the Knight, Chaplain and Herald
of Scotland with Thomas Killigrew; Dr. Savage with Piers Luck, Nanfan
with the provost of Penryn, Sir John Oby. It must have been a great excitement for so small and so poor a community, and put a considerable strain
upon their resources to entertain them suitably; though it must have been
even more so in the early months of 1506, when the Venetian ambassador
to Castile, and King Philip with his Queen Juana themselves, were detained
for some weeks by bad weather at Falmouth on their way to Spain. 'We are
in a very wild place', wrote the cultivated Italian somewhat ungratefully
to the Signory of Venice, 'which no human being ever visits, in the midst
of a most barbarous race, so different in language and custom from the
Londoners and the rest of England that they are as unintelligible to these last
as to the Venetians.'[1]

Nanfan and his party, more fortunate, took to the ship on the tenth day
after dinner; coming into the Road they found the wind contrary, and that
night they lodged on shore again near the Road, probably at St. Mawes, off
which the ships were lying. At midnight, the wind having abated, the
sailors came to fetch them by boat and they set sail for Spain. They made a
quick crossing in two or three days, arriving in Biscay on February 16th,
whence they went on to Burgos, Valladolid and Medina del Campo, where
the court was. We have a record of their audiences with Ferdinand and
Isabella, of the jousts and lists, dances and a bull fight given in their honour,
their sight of the little Princess of Wales, the presents given on their departure, including twenty-five yards of silk stuff and a mule to John Nanfan,
Sir Richard's bastard son. The mission was a great success; the ambassadors
had concluded on Henry's behalf the treaty of Medina del Campo, the first
alliance of a great power with the Tudor dynasty. From thence they went
on to the pleasant amenities of Portugal, where Nanfan put the Order of the
Garter upon the King. At Lisbon, where they were entertained by the

[1] Pollard, op. cit., I. 277.

English merchants, Nanfan freighted a Bristol ship with salt to return home. Arriving on the Cornish coast, they had great trouble in doubling Cape Cornwall, and when they succeeded, there was a wind offshore so they could not recover the land. Early in the morning of St. Mary Magdalen's day Nanfan and his company landed at Padstow, Savage going on to Bristol. That night Sir Richard slept at Launceston, and thence made his way to the court at Windsor.

Nanfan, like Edgcumbe, as a trusted servant of the King, received a number of grants and stewardships of land.[1] Nanfan's were mostly away from Cornwall — he had larger interests elsewhere; but in May 1488, he was granted the manors of Blisland, Carnanton and Helstonbury, which had belonged to the Countess of Warwick.[2] In 1489 he was sheriff of Cornwall. After this his interests moved away from the county, for he was appointed to the important post of Lord Deputy of Calais; he took some of his Cornish clientèle with him, for we hear of his brother William Nanfan and John Flamank being there.[3] He continued to be used by the King in important negotiations: he concluded a trade-treaty with Riga in 1499, the object of which was to break the Hansa monopoly, and in 1505 he was empowered to negotiate an alliance and commercial treaty with the Duke of Saxony.[4] He died in 1507, leaving the young Wolsey, whom he had befriended and made his chaplain, as his executor, along with James Erisey to whom he left his Cornish estates and in whose family they descended.[5]

Of the rest of Henry VII's Cornish clientèle the Treffrys of Fowey did perhaps best; it was in this early Tudor time that that family spread its wings, and the brothers Sir John and William must have been men of ability who knew how to take their opportunities. Sir John had been knighted at Milford Haven on Henry's landing, and he probably brought aid to the King at the time of Simnel's Rebellion before the battle of Stoke, for next year (1488) he was granted the manors of Langham and Launden, 'forfeit by Lord Zouche, the traitor'.[6] William Treffry became an usher of the King's Chamber, and on October 16th, 1485, was made surveyor of customs within the city of London, a lucrative appointment; next day he got that of controller of the coinage of tin in Devon and Cornwall, and keeper of the stannary jail at Lostwithiel, 'for service done at his great cost and expenses'.[7] Later he was granted the manors of Pedington, Avenescourt, Wike in Gloucestershire, forfeited by 'John Kendall the traitor'.[8] This younger brother of a not as yet

[1] Campbell, op. cit., II. 11, 25, 38, 313.   [2] ibid., 315.
[3] Pollard, op. cit., 240 foll.   [4] ibid., 311, 315.
[5] Cal. Pat. Rolls, 1494-1509, 594; Maclean, Trigg Minor, III. 308-9.   [6] Campbell, II, 232.
[7] Pollard, op. cit., I, 88, 90.   [8] ibid., II. 397.

very well to do Cornish family died a rich man; we have his will, one of great elaboration and care, making all the arrangements for his nephews to succeed to his estate, for he had no children of his own.[1] From it he appears a kindly, generous, conscientious sort of man. He asks his fellow Hugh Denis and Mr. Weston of the King's Chamber: 'I beseech you commend me unto my sovereign lord the King, he to be good and gracious lord unto my nephews, and show his grace that I never had none of his money untruly in all my life, and thus I beseech you in the way of charity to pray for me.' He leaves tokens of remembrance to his friends Lord Willoughby de Broke, 'an uche [brooch] for his pleasure a heart enamelled, wrapt in a towel wherein is couched a fair diamond, a ruby and a pearl', and to Sir John and Lady Arundell, cloth of diaper of damask, and 'a pawnce with diamonds with a great pearl hanging under'. He leaves money to the poor of the parishes round Fowey, horses to his menservants, dowers for his maidservants. His chief concern was to provide for the succession to his nephews, to whom he bequeaths a mass of plate which was to remain in the grocery at London till they came of age: the prongs for green ginger, the apostle spoons, the Spanish dish of silver all gilt on the inside, the silver ewers and candlesticks and Paris bowls. For himself he wished his body 'to be buried at the ambulatory on the south side of our Lady chapel in the church of St. Barry at Fowey . . . And as soon as the ambulatory is made I will mine executors cause to make a tomb with three images, one of my brother, another for me and another for my wife after their discretions and like unto a tomb which lieth on Mr. Browne in the Crutched Friars of London with the pity of St. Gregory'. He had his will; his tombstone remains, in the chapel at Fowey, which was being built at that time in the spring of their family's fortunes.

We have already seen how Henry having the Duchy in his hands was able to reward his supporters with its offices, Sir Robert Willoughby becoming Receiver, Sir John Halliwell Steward, and so down to the small men like John Upcote, who 'in consideration of the true and faithful heart which our humble subject hath borne and done unto us, as well beyond the sea as at our late field and journey' was rewarded with the offices of captain of Tintagel castle and bailiff of the manor of Helston.[2] James Bonython for his services overseas as well as on the happy return to this country was made surveyor of customs in Devon and Cornwall.[3] Sir Thomas Arundell got back the lands which had been annexed by his too clamant relative, Sir James Tyrrell.[4]

[1] *J.R.I.C.*, Sept. 1875.
[2] Campbell, I. 44; and cf. other such grants, ibid., 19, 27, 28, 42, 43, 76, 341, etc.
[3] ibid., 200, 201.   [4] *Rolls Parlt.*, VI. 273.

It was not to be expected however that after so much disquiet, and so many disturbances of the peace, entire order should reign in so remote a part of the realm, in spite of Henry's firm and able rule. A sputter of piracy still went on upon the coasts, mostly from the hardened sinners of Fowey as before. In 1486 certain merchants of the Hanse had to complain that two ships, the *Grasinius* amd the *Marie* of Hamburg, when sailing by the coast near by Fowey were seized, carried into harbour, and plundered.[1] About the same time the *Anne* of Fowey captured a Breton ship, of Bréhat, laden with wheat, wine, salt, mercury to the value of 2500 crowns, on her way towards Ireland; she was brought into Fowey and plundered, and the offenders disobeyed the King's signet letters to make restitution.[2] It was not to be wondered at that foreigners tried to get their own back. In 1496 four French ships came into harbour at Falmouth and carried off the *St. John* of Fuentarrabia into which two London merchants had loaded their goods for Spain, wheat, cloth, tin, skins.[3] The King granted them letters of marque to recover their losses, allowing a goodly margin for interest. It was an elaborate game of tit-for-tat which was played across the Channel.

Inland, some evidences remain of the disturbed state of affairs, the constant breaches of the peace.[4] Many of them were usual enough, house-breaking, horse-stealing, carrying off cattle, assault — the small change of medieval social life. But some offences are rather more particularized, others on a larger scale. In 1493, Stephen Tregasow, gentleman, with two yeomen and a holy-water clerk, was charged with carrying off six silver chalices, worth £40, belonging to the parishioners of Lanreath. On July 10th, 1492, a large body of tinners attacked the Franciscan friary at Bodmin and 'put Simon their servant and messenger in despair of his life with threats'; no doubt some dispute over tin-rights. There are several cases of tin being carried away from the works; for example, in 1490 a band of some forty men entered the tin-works of Peter Edgcumbe at Tremodret and took 28 feet of black tin, worth 14 marks. Two Calwodeleys, of an old North Cornwall family, attended by a band of their followers, attacked John Tresithney and John Butler at Padstow on Thursday after Michaelmas 1495, and carried them off to Blisland upon Bodmin Moor and kept them there for four days. There is a whole series of complaints, twenty-six in all, laid against Roger Whalley of Park, near Egloshayle, depredations upon his neighbours, driving off their cattle, killing their sheep with his dogs, refusing to pay his tithes, assaulting John Trenowth, beating his wife and shooting in at his windows. He must

[1] *Cal. Pat. Rolls*, 1485-1494, 105.   [2] Campbell, I. 328.
[3] *Cal. Pat. Rolls*, 1485-1494, 61.   [4] cf. *J.R.I.C.* 1915, 80-6.

have been a holy terror to the neighbourhood. In fact, he was the servant of Sir Richard Nanfan; perhaps this was how he looked after his master's interests. But the interesting point is that a number of these names, the Calwodeleys, Tresythney, Roger Whalley, we come across again in the risings of 1497: they were evidently restless men, and there was a spirit of unrest abroad. The inarticulate people of Cornwall were stirring and waking to life.

What brought all this to a head was the heavy taxation voted by Parliament in January 1497 for Henry's Scottish war.[1] Henry had received great provocation from the Scots, who were supporting Perkin Warbeck as a pretender to the English throne and raiding along the borders. This interested the Cornish very little; they regarded the Scottish borders as no concern of theirs; what did concern them, and that very seriously, was the weight of taxation imposed. Parliament voted two whole fifteenths and tenths payable in May and November, and a further subsidy of £120,000 without the usual abatements. Bacon comments on this measure that Henry's wars 'were always to him as a mine of treasure, of a strange kind of ore; iron at the top, and gold and silver at the bottom'.[2] Some attempt was made to exclude the poorer folk from its operation, but that was likely to fail where the collectors of the tax were exacting; and we know that the Cornish of the western district particularly resented the exactions of Sir John Oby, provost of Glasney College by Penryn. Subsidies, according to Sir Walter Ralegh later, were imposed 'for the most part upon the meaner part of her Majesty's subjects'; while Paget under Henry VIII expressed his preference for benevolences over parliamentary taxation, since they 'did not grieve the common people', but were paid by those who could best afford to pay.[3]

Four commissioners for assessing the subsidy in Cornwall were appointed, to be associated with the justices of the peace: John Arundell, Richard Flamank, John Trevenor and Thomas Erisey.[4] A letter of Sir William Godolphin's a generation later informs us that the people began to stir first in the parish of St. Keverne in the Lizard area, where dwelt Michael Joseph, the blacksmith, a man of great force and stout courage who became their

---

[1] The basic authorities for the Risings of 1497 are Polydore Vergil, *Angl. Hist.* (ed. 1546), 599-602, 604-6; Hall's *Chronicle* (ed. 1548), sub aº 12 Henry VII; Kingsford, *Chronicles of London*, 213-23; *The Great Chronicle of London*, ed. Thomas and Thornley, 175 foll. cf. also Bacon, *Henry VII* (Cambridge 1881), 148 foll.; Busch, op. cit., 110 foll.

[2] Bacon, 147.

[3] Pollard, I. xliii. 'Those who paid benevolences were the chief beneficiaries of Tudor government, and they contributed least to the regular forms of taxation. Tudor autocracy, in this as in other respects, attempted by extra-legal means to redress a balance unfairly tilted by middle-class predominance in the House of Commons.'

[4] *Rolls Parlt.*, VI. 518.

leader.[1] It is worth noting that St. Keverne would fall within the sphere of the provost of Glasney as collector; it was a large populous parish which now started a tradition of unquietness. But resentment rapidly spread throughout the county and found itself leaders from all parts. From the far west there came John Trevysall of St. Madron and William Antron, both of the lesser gentry, John Rosewarne of Rosewarne; from mid-Cornwall, Ralph Retallack of St. Columb, Richard Borlase of St. Wenn, Thomas Polgrene of Polgrene; from the north of the county, John Allen and William Ham of Stokeclimsland.[2] But it was at Bodmin that they found their intellectual leadership in Thomas Flamank, an able, persuasive lawyer, a member of an old family, son and heir of Richard Flamank, one of the commissioners for the collection of the subsidy.

All the evidence goes to show that this combination of the powerful blacksmith, a natural leader of men, and the plausible lawyer made a very effective leadership. And they had much to go upon. If we can judge from the King's historian, Polydore Vergil, the government was not without sympathy for the lot of the Cornishmen, poor in the extreme, wretched, many of them tinners whose work lay underground. Flamank's eloquence persuaded them that the law was on their side; that, as Bacon says, 'subsidies were not to be granted, nor levied in this case, that is, for wars of Scotland; for that the law had provided another course, by service of escuage for those journeys; much less when all was quiet, and war was made but a pretence to poll and pill the people'.[3] The last fell with all the more conviction upon the ears of the people because there was so much in it. Flamank was able to persuade them that they meant no damage to any creature, still less against the King's person; all their resentment was directed against Cardinal Morton and Sir Reginald Bray, who were the most intimate of the King's councillors and were held responsible for this measure. In fine, Bacon says, this man talked 'as if he could tell how to make a rebellion, and never break the peace'. One recognizes the type across the centuries.

Armed with these persuasions, and for the rest 'with bows and arrows and bills, and such other weapons of rude and country people',[4] they marched out of Cornwall and into Devonshire gathering support from the people as they went. There can be no doubt that there was a great deal of popular sympathy with them; the parishes on their route nourished them, and the motley army conducted themselves well in the counties through which they passed. A few more recruits of the yeoman class joined them on their way through Devon and into Somerset: John Tolle of Lamerton, John Broke of

[1] *L.P.* XII. I, 1001.   [2] *Rolls Parlt.*, VI. 544.   [3] Bacon, 148-9.   [4] ibid.

Doddebroke, Robert Warwick of Plymouth, Richard Fader of Suttecombe.[1] They made their way, 'without any slaughter, violence or spoil of the country' towards Taunton. Thence they marched to Wells, where they got their most notable recruit, James, Lord Audley. The Cornish leaders had apparently had some secret intelligence with him before: an unquiet spirit among the old nobility, entertaining popular aspirations and cherishing some disappointment that his services had not been better rewarded by the King.

He now became the leader of the rebels, who were much encouraged by the accession of one of the nobility. It is plain that Somerset gave them a good deal of support. In a complaint next year that one William Rawlyns of Wareham had evaded paying his fines, it states 'except it were that he paid his mother's fine dwelling at Castle Cary in Somerset which aided, supported and comforted the Cornishmen indeed'.[2] Thomas Trowe of Playnesfield joined them here — perhaps also John Audley, gentleman, of London, either here or later. It would appear that the rebels had sympathizers among the cathedral chapter, for fines were subsequently laid upon Master John Stephens, Dr. Bokett, and Master John Austell — evidently a Cornishman.[3] At the time when the rebels were thronging the narrow streets of the little town, crowding within the walls of that now quiet close, there was another Cornishman who ruled there as suffragan of the see. One wonders what Bishop Thomas Cornish thought of it all — one can still see the recognizable outline of his figure, in vestments and mitre praying before an altar to the Virgin and Child, in the matrix upon his tomb, with the Cornish choughs and the sheaves of corn upon it, in the north transept of the cathedral.

Leaving Wells, the rebels marched first to Salisbury, thence to Winchester and across Surrey to the very borders of Kent. They were encouraged by Flamank to expect that the Kentishmen would join with them, for Kent had a strong tradition in popular risings, with Wat Tyler and Jack Cade. But they were disappointed of their hopes. The Kentishmen not only refused to join with them, but lined up behind their leaders, the Earl of Kent, Lord Abergavenny, and Lord Cobham, to resist. Bacon says that at this discouragement, some of the simpler sort among the rebels stole away; 'but the sturdier sort, and those that were most engaged, stood by it, and rather waxed proud than failed in hopes and courage'.[4] It was a sufficiently astonishing achievement in itself to have marched the whole length of southern England

---

[1] *Rolls Parlt.*, VI. 544.   [2] Gairdner, *Letters and Papers*, II. 75.
[3] E 101/516: 24.   [4] Bacon, 150.

from Cornwall to Kent without let or hindrance. Bacon tells us that they began to aim higher now than Morton and Bray, and were not afraid to give battle to the King.

Henry seems really to have been caught by surprise, certainly at the dimensions the rebellion had reached and the rapidity of its onset. He was immersed in the preparations for the war with Scotland; it was only when he heard of the accession of Audley to the rebels that he realized how dangerous the situation was. Bacon tells us that he was 'much troubled therewith', for what could be worse than the concurrence of three dangers, 'knowing well that it was a dangerous triplicity to a monarchy to have the arms of a foreigner, the discontents of subjects, and the title of a pretender to meet'? It was the crisis of Henry's reign; but now that it had come he was well prepared for it. He had the moneys recently voted by Parliament in hand, and the army of some 8000 men being prepared for Scotland under the able command of Lord Daubeney, the Chamberlain. The latter was at once countermanded and ordered to hold his army in readiness to meet the Cornishmen; the Earl of Surrey was dispatched to the Scottish border with orders to act on the defensive until the crisis in the south was overpast. Henry determined to await the rebels outside London, even at the cost of some panic to the city. It was contrary to his earlier practice, which had always been to meet dangers at once. 'But now', Bacon says, 'besides that he was attempered by years, and less in love with dangers by the continued fruition of a crown; it was a time when the various appearance to his thought of perils of several natures and from divers parts, did make him judge it his best and surest way to keep his strength together in the seat and centre of his Kingdom.' There was further the consideration that he would have the rebels at a vantage, harassed and weary with their long march, cut off from their own country and unable to retreat, while allowing time for those dissensions to develop which always afflict popular movements.

Lord Daubeney left Richmond, where the Court was, on the Sunday before St. Barnabas; the King left the Monday after, and next day the Queen with the little Henry Duke of York moved to Coldharbour, whence the Monday following they went for safety to the Tower of London.[1] That same day tidings came to the Mayor that the Cornishmen were at Farnham; they were accounted to be some 15,000 strong, almost certainly an exaggeration. As they drew nearer to London, panic grew in the city. Hall tells us, 'In the mean season there was great fear through the city and cries were made, "Every man to harness! To harness!" Some ran to the

---

[1] Kingsford, op. cit., 213.

gates, others mounted on the walls, so that no part was undefended, and continual watch was kept by the magistrates of the city lest the rebels being poor and needy would descend from their camp and invade the city and spoil, and rob the riches and substance of the merchants.'[1] On June 13th general watch was kept in the city; and that day Lord Daubeney arrived upon Hounslow Heath with his army of eight or ten thousand men, to whom the Mayor sent provisions of wine and victuals.[2]

Next day the news was that the Cornishmen were at Guildford; and upon Gill Down there was an encounter between some of Daubeney's spearmen and the rebels, two of whose spearmen were taken and brought to the Lord Chamberlain. On Thursday, late at night, Daubeney brought his army into St. George's Field for the protection of the city. The rebels moved to Banstead Down, and the next night to Chussex plain. The King lay with his army about Henley on Thames; a great many of the nobility and gentry, with their followers, from the nearer counties had flocked to his standard. That night a message was sent from some among the rebels to Daubeney, suing for a general pardon and offering to surrender the leaders, Audley and the Smith. Early next morning, Friday, June 16th, Daubeney moved from St. George's Field towards Croydon to reconnoitre in the direction of the rebels, but came back in the afternoon to be joined there by the King with his forces. The Mayor and aldermen with all the chief crafts of the city, their courage somewhat restored, understanding that the King would lie that night at the Tower, stood in their harness all along the streets from London Bridge to Gracechurch Street to receive him. But tidings came that he would pass the night on the south bank of the river, at Lambeth, so that the people went home; that evening Henry was among his army in St. George's Field, 'abrewing and comforting of his people'. They were in all some 25,000 men against the rebels' estimated 15,000: a comfortable, a safe, superiority.

The same afternoon the Cornishmen reached Blackheath and there pitched their field; they made their camp upon the hill far into the heath, whence they could look down upon London and the Thames in the evening light. It was high summer — June 16th — and they had come a long way. The city chronicler tells us that they lay there 'all that night in great agony and variance; for some of them were minded to have come to the King and to have yielded them and put them fully in his mercy and grace; but the Smith was of the contrary mind'.[3] In the night many of them stole away secretly

---

[1] Hall, *Chronicle*, The Reign of Henry VII, fol. xlii.
[2] Kingsford, loc. cit.　　[3] ibid., 214.

from the field, so that in the morning there were not left above nine or ten thousand. The rebel captains gave orders that night to their remaining followers how they were to fight. At Deptford Strand they placed a number of guns supported by archers to impede the passage of the river: a measure which 'wrought wonders' on the morrow, for there several of the King's spears were slain before the passage was taken.[1] Henry had his plans well laid; he had even given out that he proposed to give battle on Monday, so as to catch the poor fools of the rebels unprepared and in disarray. He had divided his forces into three 'battles', one to attack the hill on either side, that towards London and in the rear, so as to surround the Cornishmen and prevent their retreat, while he held himself in reserve. Everything worked according to plan. Early next morning he sent the Earls of Oxford, Essex and Suffolk, to surround the hill and stop all the ways leading from it, while Daubeney was sent with the main battle to attack the position in front. The bridge at Deptford Strand was attacked by a company of spears under Sir Humphrey Stanley, who won it after a sharp tussle, in which a number of the Cornish archers were killed. The leaders had neglected to place any men upon the high ground above the bridge to second the archers below, nor had they brought forward their main battle, 'which stood in array far into the heath, near to the ascent of the hill'.[2]

The bridge was won, and Daubeney gained the heath, where he charged forward at the head of his troops with such force that he was surrounded and taken by the rebels, who could have killed him, but omitted to do so: 'whether it were for fear or for hope of favour, they let him go at liberty without any hurt or detriment'.[3] He regained his men, the Cornishmen bravely enough maintaining their fight for a time, though the battle was already lost and they were surrounded on all sides; 'being ill-armed, and ill-led', says Bacon, 'and without horse or artillery, they were with no great difficulty cut in pieces and put to flight'. Michael Joseph fled from the heath to the Friars' Church at Greenwich, but he was so hastily pursued that he was taken 'or he came within the church'. Audley and Flamank were captured on the field.[4] Of the rebels some 200 were slain, but of the King's people few or none except those eight killed at Deptford Strand.[5] It was noted that the arrows gathered afterwards were a full yard in length: 'so strong and mighty a bow the Cornishmen were said to draw'.[6]

After the battle the King rode to Blackheath where he dubbed a score of

[1] *Great Chronicle*, 277.   [2] Bacon, 154.   [3] Hall, loc. cit., xliii.
[4] Audley seems to have been taken by a servant of Lord Dacres; there are several rewards for him noted in *Excerpta Historica* (pub. Bentley), 112.
[5] *Great Chronicle*, 277.   [6] Bacon, 155.

knights for their services, and at the bridge foot upon his return a further batch — it was a cheap way of reward. At two in the afternoon he came over London Bridge, where the mayor and his brethren in scarlet were waiting at St. Magnus Church to receive him; he gave them thanks for their good keeping of the city and for so plentifully victualling his army, and 'with his own sword which was girt about him', he dubbed the mayor, one of the sheriffs and the recorder knights.[1] Then he went on to St. Paul's where he offered. Shortly after he passed there came 'riding behind a yeoman of the guard, the Smith, being clad in a jacket of white and green of the King's colours and held as good countenance and spake as boldly to the people as he had been at his liberty'.[2] After the service at St. Paul's the King returned to the Tower, where he found the Archbishop of Canterbury who had taken refuge there the Thursday before. Proclamation was made that afternoon giving the goods of all the prisoners to those that had taken them, either to take them in hand or to compound for them, as they could. We learn that some of the prisoners were sold for 12d., some for more. On the Monday following, the three rebel leaders were brought before the King and Council in the Tower and there examined. On Midsummer's Day there was a further creation of knights within the Tower, including the other sheriff. Sir John Arundell was granted Audley's manor of Honybere for life, for his services against the rebels.[3]

Then as Bacon says, 'after matter of honour and liberality followed matter of severity and execution'. On Monday, June 26th, the Smith and Flamank were arraigned in the White Hall at Westminster and sentence passed upon them; next day they were drawn from the Tower through the streets of the city to Tyburn where they were hanged, drawn and quartered. The same day Lord Audley was brought to Westminster, the sinister axe of the Tower borne before him;[4] after being sentenced he was taken to Newgate, where he remained all night. Next day, about nine o'clock, says the chronicler, he was 'drawn from the said gaol of Newgate unto the Tower Hill with a coat-armour upon him of paper all to torn, and there his head stricken off: upon whose soul and all christen God have mercy! Amen!'[5] The proprieties were observed, society satisfied. But not so with the brave blacksmith: it is said that as he was being drawn on a hurdle to Tyburn, he gloried in what he had done and boasted that 'he should have a name

---

[1] Kingsford, 215.   [2] Great Chronicle, 277.   [3] Cal. Pat. Rolls, 1494-1509, 107.
[4] cf. Cal. Pat. Rolls, 1494-1509, 115. Commission to Sir John Dynham, Lord Treasurer, Sir John Digby, King's Marshal, Sir William Vampage and Robert Rydon, clerk of the Council, to execute the office of marshal upon Audley and pass sentence upon him.
[5] ibid., 216; the payments for two coat-armours for him are given in Excerpta Historica, 114.

perpetual, and a fame permanent and immortal'.[1] And so he has, after a sort: though the Cornish have forgotten him, he has his place in history. When the *Mirror for Magistrates* came to be planned and written, one of the most popular of Tudor works of literature with its tragic tales of the fall of princes and great men — themes which were to be taken up later by the greatest of poets in his historical plays, it was a fellow Cornishman, Humphrey Cavell, who wrote the poem on Michael Joseph and the Rebellion of 1497.[2]

Henry at first intended to send down the bodies of the Smith and Flamank to be set up in different places in Cornwall as a warning to the people. But hearing that the Cornish 'were by this scourge little mollified or quieted, and were ready to move again and begin new commotions and conspiracies, if any ungracious or evil minded person would either move or prick them forward, he turned his purpose and caused them to be set up in London and other places'.[3] Audley's body was buried in the Blackfriars church within Ludgate.[4]

Actually Henry was content with very little bloodshed; in the hour of victory he showed himself extraordinarily clement. Bacon suggests various reasons why 'the King did satisfy himself with the lives of only three offenders for the expiation of this great rebellion . . . Whether it were that the King put to account the men that were slain in the field, or that he was not willing to be severe in a popular cause, or that the harmless behaviour of this people that came from the west of England to the east without mischief almost, or spoil of the country, did somewhat mollify and move him to compassion; or lastly that he made a great difference between people that did rebel upon wantonness and them that did rebel upon want'.[5] The end of the month saw a spate of commissions issued, too numerous to detail, with the purpose of ordering and clearing up the situation: mandates to the sheriff of Cornwall and all the western counties to pardon all offenders who submitted to the King's mercy, strong commissions appointed to inquire in all the southern and western counties affected by the rebellion with power to punish or pardon the delinquents.[6] Whether it was wiser to let the rebellion go unpunished, since Cornwall was still seething, or whether it would have been more salutary to have exacted retribution, we cannot say; but in the event the county was undismayed by the disaster of Black-heath and ready for a new outbreak.

The Cornish Rising was Perkin Warbeck's opportunity. This is not the

[1] Hall, loc. cit.
[2] cf. *The Mirror for Magistrates* (ed. L. B. Campbell), 46-7, 402-18.
[3] Hall, loc. cit.   [4] Kingsford, 216.   [5] Bacon, 156.
[6] cf. *Cal. Pat. Rolls*, 1494-1509, 115, 117-19.

place to go into the astonishing career of that romantic adventurer, the son of a burgess of Tournai, whose personal charm was his greatest asset, and who posed before the courts of Europe as Richard, Duke of York, the second son of Edward IV.[1] He was backed by Yorkist adherents and malcontents with Henry's regime in various places; his pretensions suited the interests of a number of powers: he was a pawn in the diplomatic game. Good-looking and gifted with address and social grace, he not only played his exalted part with skill, but won peoples' hearts and affections in the process. Having made his first appearance at Cork in 1491, he was received in France, in the Low Countries and at Vienna with the honours accorded to a royal person, and he developed the manners, handsome and gracious, which went with his supposed station. In 1495 he was in Scotland where he won the heart of the young James IV, who not only supported him politically but gave him the beautiful Lady Katherine Gordon, daughter of the Earl of Huntly, and a cousin of his own, to wed.

On the news of the Cornish Rising, early in June Warbeck left Scotland, with his wife and a few followers in three small vessels from the Firth of Clyde. He arrived at Cork on July 25th, where he was received by his old friends, and remained in Ireland for more than a month. During this time he had some communication with Cornwall; he certainly judged the situation there encouraging, while in Ireland it was not. Loyal Waterford sent the King news of his presence and of his intentions. They set out ships to catch him; Kildare and Desmond were on the look out for him. Perkin's friend John Walter conveyed him secretly in a boat to Kinsale, where three Spanish ships were awaiting him — it seems that Ferdinand wanted to get hold of him too. But by some means he persuaded the captain to take him over to Cornwall, with his wife and followers; and to such good effect that when the very ship he was in was stopped by a King's vessel, the sailors hid Perkin in a cask in the hold and denied his presence, resisting the high reward that was offered for him. On September 7th, he landed, according to Henry's information, with two small ships and a Breton pinnace and some 100 or 200 men, at Whitsand Bay near Land's End.[2]

Leaving his wife in the safe custody of the priests at St. Michael's Mount, Perkin marched rapidly to Bodmin, the restive county town by no means yet appeased of the late discontents. Here he proclaimed himself Richard IV, and within a few days some 3000 men flocked to him. He was advised by a council of three: John Herne, a mercer of London who had fled for debt,

---

[1] For his career in full, v. Gairdner, 'The Story of Perkin Warbeck' in his *Richard III*.
[2] Ellis, *Original Letters* (Series I), I. 32; Kingsford, *Chronicles of London*, 217.

Richard Skelton, a tailor, and John Asteley, a scrivener. They determined upon an immediate attack on Exeter, a course which had obvious advantages, as Bacon says, 'as well to make his men find the sweetness of rich spoils, and to allure to him all loose and lost people by like hopes of booty, as to be a sure retreat to his forces in case they should have any ill day or unlucky chance in the field'.[1] Henry heard the news at Woodstock, where he was, within the same week and at once commanded Lord Daubeney to go west gathering forces as he went, and Lord Willoughby de Broke to go by sea keeping a look out in case Perkin took to sea again.[2] At the same time summons was sent in every direction to nobles and gentry to gather their men and join the King. In one of these letters written a week later to the Bishop of Bath and Wells, Henry said that though the commons of Cornwall took Perkin's part, amongst them 'on Monday last, 18 September, there was not one gentleman'.[3]

But this does not wholly represent the situation. Though Henry was right in that none of the greater gentry of Cornwall, the Anglo-Norman families which ruled there, joined the rising, it is evident that many of the lesser gentry, the smaller landed families which stood on the border between gentry and yeomanry, did join. These sprang from the Cornish people themselves, and had Cornish names; they would naturally have more sympathy with the common folk to whom they were allied, and it may not be fanciful to suggest a common element of Cornishry, of that resentment of a conquered people against the English which Carew noted as surviving long after. When the Act of Attainder was passed against the leaders of the western risings, we find among those who supported Perkin John Nankivell of St. Mawgan, Walter Tripcony of St. Columb, Humphry Calwodeley of Helland, Otis Philip of Polwhele, among the lesser gentry; Walter Grigg, Nicholas Polkinghorne of St. Gwinnear, Thomas Gosworthdogga of St. Crowan, John Trehanneck of St. Teath, John Tregennow of St. Columb, among the yeomanry.[4] It is worth noting that they come mainly from mid-Cornwall. To these there were added from Devon John Giles of Samford Spiney, Robert Sturridge of Ashburton, Thomas Hart of Barnstaple. The leading gentry were unable to make head against the commons now any more than earlier in the year; it is said that Sir Piers Edgcumbe opposed them at the head of the posse comitatus at Castle Kinnick on the downs east of Bodmin, but that his men deserted to the rebels — one more indication, if so, of the strength of the popular feeling.[5] There can be no

---

[1] Bacon, 164. [2] Ellis, 33. [3] ibid., 34. [4] *Rolls Parlt.*, VI. 544.
[5] Gilbert, *Parochial History of Cornwall*, II. 187-8.

doubt of Perkin's popularity with the Cornish, and he on his part 'assumed majesty with such a born grace and affable deportment that immediately he won the affection and admiration of all that made addresses unto him'.[1]

By Sunday, September 17th, at one o'clock in the afternoon, Perkin was before the gates of Exeter, his forces now swollen to about 6000.[2] He drew up his ranks in order of battle for some two hours before the city, summoning it to surrender. The citizens closed the gates and sent messengers for help, letting them down by cord over the walls. They made what preparations they could against an attack, piling faggots ready to fire against the gates and posterns, digging trenches and making ramparts behind them. Meanwhile some of the greater gentry had come to the aid of the city under the leadership of the Earl of Devon and his son Lord William Courtenay, 'a man of great force and valiantness'; there also came, or were already within the city, Sir William Courtenay, Sir Edmund Carew, Sir Thomas Trenchard, Sir Humphry Fulford, Sir John Halliwell, Sir John Croker, Sir John Sapcotes, Walter Courtenay, Sir Piers Edgcumbe.[3] The anxiety aroused in Plymouth may be illustrated by two small straws of evidence from the Town Accounts: 'Paid unto a man that was sent unto Exeter when the Captain was at Exeter to spy tidings, 2s. 6d. Item paid to Thomas Martyn and his company to sail to Penlee to speak with Mr. Treffry: 16d.'[4]

Outside Exeter Perkin determined upon an immediate assault, and that same Sunday attacked both the north gate and the east gate. There was no point in attacking the west gate, it was much too strong a position naturally, as those who know Exeter will realize; there was first the flat, low-lying Exe Island to cross, then the bridge over the river immediately under the ramparts and their defenders, and within, the steep declivity of the High Street. Perkin wasted no time here, but attacked the north gate. Driven back, the Cornish made their main attack on the east gate, where conditions were less unfavourable — though they had no guns, nor any of the proper engines for a siege. They broke down the gate, however, and in the hand to hand fighting which ensued, they penetrated into the city as far as Castle Street, when the Earl and his son rushed up from Blackfriars with reinforcements and caught the rebels on the left flank. The fighting grew 'very hot and fiery', but bit by bit the Cornish were pressed back out of the city. No attempt was made to restore the gate; huge bonfires were kept going

---

[1] The fullest account of the events at Exeter is to be found in Cotton and Woolcombe, *Gleanings from the Municipal and Cathedral Records of Exeter*, 19–47.
[2] Hall, loc. cit., fol. xlvi; Ellis, 34.   [3] ibid.
[4] Worth, *Plymouth Municipal Records*, 94.

within all that night to defend the entrance and observe the movements of the enemy.

Next day the attack was renewed, especially upon the north gate; but by this time guns had been brought to bear upon the untrained, undisciplined Cornish, and Perkin was very glad to leave the city without further molestation. His request was granted by the Earl, who explained in his letter to Henry that the citizens were not able to encounter the rebels, and that his company were weary and some hurt.[1] He himself had been wounded in the arm by an arrow that morning — evidently the bow was the Cornishman's chief speciality and reliance in warfare. By eleven they had left the city, and by twelve were all out of sight. They made their way towards Cullompton; discouraged by their defeat, some of the men deserted. The London chronicler says that 200 of them had been slain;[2] this was surely an exaggeration; the Earl merely reports 'twenty of theirs hurt and many slain'.[3] The affair does not appear to have been on a very large scale — nothing like the disaster of Blackheath field.

Meanwhile Henry had despatched what aid he could westwards, while he gathered his forces at Woodstock. Empson was sent at once to Exeter, with 1000 marks; on September 20th Sir John Cheyney was allowed £500 for his retinue; another 1000 marks were forwarded to Daubeney. Perkin marched northwards to Taunton, his courage foundering within him; he could put 'small trust and less confidence in the remnant of his army . . . because the most part of his soldiers were harnessed on the right arm and naked all the body, and never exercised in war nor martial feats, but only with the spade and shovel'.[4] In this condition they reached Taunton on September 20th. The royal forces under Daubeney, Willoughby de Broke and Sir Rhys ap Thomas were approaching; the young Duke of Buckingham with a great concourse of west-country gentry, Berkeleys, Paulets, Luttrells, Cheyneys, and so on, joined them on the way. Henry pursued the same cautious tactics as before Blackheath; holding himself in reserve, he sent Daubeney ahead to engage the rebels.[5]

But his careful plans were rendered unnecessary by Perkin's flight. When Perkin heard that Daubeney's vanguard was at Glastonbury, not twenty miles away, his courage failed him. Their respective forces were too unequal. That day, probably Thursday, September 21st, he 'dissimuled all

---

[1] Ellis, 36-7.   [2] Kingsford, 217.

[3] We read in the Receiver's Accounts of the city for that year of the sums expended for renewing the destroyed east gate, and various other repairs about the walls, streets and gates. Cotton and Woolcombe, 31-3.

[4] Hall, loc. cit.   [5] Polydore Vergil, 605.

the day time with his company as though nothing could make him afeared';[1] then at midnight he stole away with some sixty horsemen and made for the south coast. On hearing the news Daubeney at once sent 200 spearmen to head him off from the sea-coast and if possible bring him back.[2] But Perkin and his three followers had outsped their company and arrived in safety at Beaulieu Abbey near Southampton where they took sanctuary. The poor Cornishmen were 'amazed and disconsolate' at the news of their desertion; Hall tells us that Henry heard it with 'great commodity and quietness, by reason he was not forced to fight with the Cornishmen, whose hearts and courages were so increased and inflamed by deadly desperation that they earnestly determined and were steadfastly bent either to win victory and overcome their enemies or else not one of them all to live any day or hour longer'.[3] In this mood, and at this time, a band of several hundred sea-rovers, who had come to aid Perkin under the lead of one James, met with the unfortunate Provost of Glasney, whose exactions had been remembered against him. It was said that he had 'gathered more money than came unto the King's use'. They brought him to Taunton, and 'there in the market-place slew him piteously, in such wise that he was dismembered and cut in many and sundry pieces'.[4] So he perished, an example to too officious and eager tax-collectors.

News of Perkin's flight was brought to Henry at Woodstock on the 25th, and at once the King set out westward. We may trace his progress in the record of his privy purse expenses: he was at Cirencester on 27th, Malmesbury on 28th, Bath on 29th, Wells on 30th. Thence he came on via Glastonbury and Bridgwater to Taunton which he reached on October 4th.[5] No doubt many of the Cornish had fled by this time, humiliated and broken by the desertion of their leader; those who remained readily submitted to the King, 'holding up their hands in asking mercy, offering and promising him faith, loyalty and obeisance'.[6] Henry, glad at the turn of events and the avoidance of bloodshed, readily pardoned the offenders, all except their leaders who were attached or gradually gathered in. That night the King played at cards and lost £9, some tribute to his high good humour in one so careful of his money.[7] Next day Perkin was brought into his presence: the sanctuary at Beaulieu had been surrounded with troops while Henry was moving west, and Perkin had chosen to throw himself on the King's

---

[1] Hall, fol. xlvii.
[2] The London Chronicle gives this figure; I prefer it to the 500 of Hall.
[3] Hall, loc. cit.   [4] Kingsford, 218.   [5] *Excerpta Historica*, 113-14.
[6] Hall, loc. cit.   [7] *Excerpta Historica*, 114.

mercy, which was readily granted on his surrendering himself.[1] He was carried along with the King, a prisoner to grace Henry's triumphal entry into Exeter two days later, October 7th.

The King remained at Exeter for nearly a month; it was his intention, he wrote to the mayor of Waterford ten days later, not only to clear up the remains of the rebellion, but 'so to order the parts of Cornwall as the people may live in their due obeisance unto us, and in good restfulness for themselves in time to come'.[2] It was the first and last time that a Tudor sovereign came into the far west, to this city which had been and was to remain so faithful to their cause; and after so recent a trial its reception of the King was all the more jubilant. The Receiver's Accounts bear witness to the charges the city was at for his entertainment: a cask of wine presented to him, four oxen and forty sheep, a douceur to the official in charge of the King's footmen and henchmen, wine for Lord Broke, payments to the Earl of Devon, charges for the horsemen employed on Henry's personal service during his stay.[3] The Treasurer's house in the cathedral close — it stood at right angles to the north tower, and was pulled down, alas, a century ago: the line of its gable still remains against the tower — was prepared for the King's reception. Half a century later, in the reign of his granddaughter Mary, an old man of eighty remembered the King's stay here and how eight of the sixteen trees that stood before the house were felled so that Henry might look down from the new window made and see the rebels that thronged the close with halters round their necks crying for mercy and pardon.[4] As usual he was merciful; a few of the ringleaders among the Cornishmen were executed, all the rest were pardoned. The King spoke once and again from his window to the crowds in the close below; upon his clemency 'they made a great shout, hurled away their halters and cried "God save the King"'. These were memorable days for Exeter: some small speaking evidence remains in the entry upon the margin of a thirteenth-century psalter in the Cathedral, 'M. qd proximo Ste Fidei Ao. dm 1497 intravit in Exon H. septimus'.[5] We find too from the records of Plymouth that their mayor went up at some cost to Exeter while the King was there: no doubt to swear fidelity and receive instructions.[6]

---

[1] There is a direct contradiction in our authorities as to where Perkin was brought to Henry. Polydore Vergil definitely implies Exeter, and is followed by Hall and Bacon who embroider on the negotiations between Henry and Perkin in sanctuary, as if conducted by the King during his stay at Exeter. But there is no doubt that Perkin was brought to the King at Taunton. This is clear from the *Excerpta Historica*; it is corroborated by the London Chronicle (218), and made certain by Henry's letter to the mayor of Waterford (quoted in Cotton and Woolcombe, 36). After all, Henry should know best where he met Perkin. Gairdner accepts this course of events (*Richard III*, 328); so also Busch, 117.

[2] q. in Cotton and Woolcombe, 37.　　　[3] ibid., 34.　　[4] Oliver, *History of Exeter* (ed. 1861), 87.
[5] Cotton and Woolcombe, 34.　　　　　　[6] Worth, *Plymouth Municipal Records*, 95.

The Earl of Devon, Lord Willoughby de Broke and Lord Daubeney were sent as commissioners into Cornwall to receive the submission of the county. It was probably at this time, though it may have been earlier, that the town of Plymouth despatched their little contingent of eight men in green and white jackets to aid the Earl in Cornwall.[1] Horsemen were sent to St. Michael's Mount to escort Perkin's wife, Lady Katherine, to the presence of the King: we have payments noted for horses and saddles for her conveyance, and £20 for her diet from Bodmin to the Queen 'wherever she be'.[2] But first she was brought to Henry's presence at Exeter; he seems to have confronted Perkin with his wife and made him confess to her the whole veracious story of his imposture. Henry appears to have been not a little struck by her beauty and to have declared her a lady fit, not for a captain, but for a commander in chief;[3] he treated her with great courtesy, and providing her with a suitable escort of matrons and gentlewomen ('because she was but a young woman') sent her on to the Queen. She was honourably entertained at court, and subsequently married Sir Matthew Cradock; she lies buried beside him in Swansea church.

It is not our business to trace the brief remainder of Perkin's pathetic career. Henry treated him well enough for a time. The Milanese envoy wrote that 'it was necessary to guard him well, in order that the men of Cornwall may not murder him, as they are incensed since they have learned from the King that they have been worshipping a low born foreigner as their sovereign'.[4] He was taken back by Henry and paraded through the streets of London, 'upon whom the same season and other days following was much wondering and many a curse thrown at his head'.[5] He was not imprisoned, but kept about the court — a restraint which after so many years of strange adventure he could not endure. He got away once, but no farther than to Richmond; he was brought back, set to stand in the pillory at Westminster, where he 'was wondered again upon, as he had been oft time before'.[6] Sent to the Tower, he was given just enough latitude to involve his fellow-prisoner, the young Earl of Warwick, last of the Plantagenets, in a forlorn attempt to escape, and both were sentenced to death. So 'it was ordained that this winding-ivy of a Plantagenet should kill the true tree itself'.[7] The oddity of this phantom's crossing the page of Cornish history for ever remains.

[1] Worth, *Plymouth Municipal Records*, 94.
[2] *Excerpta Historica*, 115; Gairdner, *Letters and Papers*, II. 73.
[3] Polydore Vergil, 606.   [4] q. in Pollard, I. 177.
[5] Kingsford, 219.   [6] ibid., 223.
[7] Bacon, 176.

Henry had good reason to be satisfied with his stay in the west. He had surmounted in this year 1497 the very crisis of his reign: henceforth he was secure to rule as he willed. In recognition of the fidelity of the citizens of Exeter, he presented to them his sword and his cap of maintenance, ordering them to be carried in state before the mayor — as they still are. On returning to London he granted the city a new and more generous charter. He left Exeter on November 3rd, and travelling by Dorchester, Salisbury and Andover, reached Richmond on November 18th, and made his entry into Westminster the following week.[1]

It was characteristic of Henry that while sparing of bloodshed, he should have determined to make his western subjects pay for their pleasures in rebelling, and turn their disobedience to his own financial profit. At Exeter he had issued a commission to Sir Piers Edgcumbe, sheriff of Devon, Roger Holand and others to seize all the lands, goods and chattels of those who had been killed in the risings, or had been executed afterwards, or had refused to submit after his proclamation.[2] Now he determined to levy fines throughout the western counties not only upon those who had taken part, but upon all who had in any way aided or abetted the rebels, or who had helped or supported them on their way to Blackheath, or on their flight back into Cornwall on both occasions. Commissioners were appointed to go through the western counties, comb them for offenders and rake as much as they could out of them by way of fines. Sir Thomas Darcy, Sir Amyas Paulet and Robert Sherborne, Dean of St. Paul's, were first appointed as commissioners for Devon and Somerset;[3] later William Hatcliff, clerk of accounts of the Household, Thomas Harris, chaplain, and Roger Holand were added, and the activities of the commissioners were extended into Dorset, Wiltshire, Hampshire, and into Cornwall.[4] It seems to be agreed that they did their work thoroughly; though the rebellion had broken out in the first instance because of the financial exactions of the government, there could be now no resistance: the Cornish were not only defeated but humiliated. Bacon comments that the 'commissioners proceeded with such strictness and severity as did much obscure the King's mercy in sparing of blood with the bleeding of so much treasure'.[5]

Various papers attest their nefarious activities in the west country.[6]

---

[1] *Excerpta Historica*, 115; Kingsford, 219.
[2] *Hist. MSS. Comm., Second Report*, 20.   [3] Hall, loc. cit., fol. xlviii.
[4] cf. their commissions, September 13th, 1498, given in full by Pollard, II. 111-16; and for their warrants to grants receipts later, March 11th and August 6th, 1500, Bain, *Cal. Docts. relat. to Scotland*, IV. 334.   [5] Bacon, 169.
[6] The roll of fines for Som., Dor., Wilts and Hants in Royal MS. 14 B. vii is summarized in Gairdner, *Letters and Papers*, II. 335-7.

Somerset was made to pay particularly heavily for the support it had given the Cornishmen; and it is interesting to notice that a number of heads of monastic houses appear in the list of fines: they must have entertained the rebels hospitably. They were the abbots of Athelney (100 marks), Cleeve (£40), Ford (£60), Muchelney (£60); while Sir John Speke of White-lackington paid as much as £200. The borough of Taunton paid £441 6s. 8d., Bridgwater £166, Wells £313 13s. 4d., Dorchester and Bridport £226 13s. 4d. Then the hundreds are fined separately; there follow a few individual fines taken at Greenwich, while the sum raised from the goods of those dead is in this list £123 13s. 4d. The number of names on this roll is some 3400, and the total amount of fines raised is £8810 16s. 8d. The King, deeply interested in all financial matters, endorsed it himself.

But this was by no means all. The process of raking in fines went on for several years in the west country, though naturally the amounts got smaller as the comb got finer and the country more impoverished. A roll of the year 1500, covering the same counties as before, enables us to see the process at work, the fines collected deanery by deanery, usually in three lots to make payment easier.[1] The county of Dorset, for example, paid on this roll three instalments, £320 10s. 0d., £333 6s. 8d. and £405 3s. 4d. — in all a sum of £1059. The total sum raised from these counties on this roll amounted to £4629 8s. 8d.

Two further rolls show us what happened in Cornwall and Devon.[2] The returns were made by Thomas Harris, chaplain to the King, and Roger Holand. They were made parish by parish, in each a leading inhabitant, or someone from outside, making himself responsible as mainpernor for the rest, raising the fines and paying over to the royal officials.[3] Sometimes the parson was the mainpernor of the parish: Master William Piers, vicar of Breage, and John Godolphin junior were mainpernors for that parish, which paid 4 marks. Master Alexander Penhill, rector of Illogan, was responsible for several parishes: Illogan 5 marks, Redruth £4, Camborne £4, Grade 40s., St. Stephen-in-Brannel 4 marks, Wendron 40s., St. Agnes 5 marks, Lawhitton 4 marks. No doubt he made something out of it. Several persons were very much to the fore in the matter, taking several parishes under their charge, Piers St. Aubyn of Helston and St. Michael's Mount, Thomas Tregos, William Trewynnard, Stephen Calmady, Richard Coode

---

[1] E 101/516. 24.
[2] E 101/516. 27 and 28. When Mr. W. J. Blake wrote his account of the Rebellions in *J.R.I.C.* in 1915, he came to the conclusion that these returns were no longer extant. I am indebted to the late Mr. J. R. Crompton for tracing them.
[3] Mainprise is legally a form of bail.

of Morval. A few persons are fined individually: Master Thomas Allen, vicar of Newlyn, paid £20; Thomas Tregos of St. Anthony and Thomas Budockside of Budock paid 10 marks for Master Nicholas Wyse, vicar of Constantine; Nicholas Enys of Luxulyan paid 8 marks for Remfry Enys and William Penrose; while William Trewynnard and Nicholas Enys paid as much as £30 as mainpernors for John Tresynny of Penryn — an important offender. The sums for which the parishes were assessed varied a great deal, the most frequent being 40s. The total raised from Cornwall on this roll — and it seems fairly complete — was £623; from Devon £527.

There can be no manner of doubt as to the loss inflicted upon the west country by the King's financial rearguard action. And some few evidences remain of the disturbance that the year 1497 brought about in Cornish life. There were the attainders and the property changes consequent upon them. In 1506 Roger Holand, who was in a good position for picking up such trifles, was granted the manors of Cadbury and Calwodeley which had belonged to Humphrey Calwodeley, who had taken part with Perkin and been attainted; Holand was also given the lands of Oliver Calwodeley of Padstow, within the city of Exeter, forfeited for a murder committed at Padstow by the latter, who had then fled the realm.[1] It seems that the Calwodeleys were a restive lot. Humphrey's attainder was reversed in 1507, and his lands restored to his eldest surviving daughter[2] — so that it is probable that the father had been one of the ringleaders executed by Henry at Exeter. In 1500, William Barrett of Tregarne, Flamank's brother-in-law, was pardoned.[3] The year 1506 saw a whole crop of reversals of attainder: in favour of James Tripcony, son and heir of Walter Tripcony, who must have been among those executed: of William Brabyn, son and heir of John Brabyn, deceased, of St. Mabyn, of all matters relating to his father; Thomas Polgrene of Polgrene, Thomas Gosworthdogga of St. Crowan, Nicholas Polkinghorne, John Trehannek, and John Tregennow, all of whom had been attainted in the Parliament of 1504.[4] William Antron of Antron, who had been a member of Parliament for Helston in 1491-92,[5] was among those executed after Blackheath and attainted in 1504. In 1512 a commission was appointed to inquire concerning his lands; they were restored to his son and heir, Richard.[6]

A few scraps of evidence remain of all that disturbance. John Pendyne was fined £40 for 'the unnatural rebellion by him and others committed and

[1] *Cal. Pat. Rolls*, 1494-1509, 443.   [2] ibid., 527, 622.   [3] ibid., 217.
[4] ibid., 509, 514; and cf. James Tripcony's petition for his father's lands, C/1229. 25.
[5] Wedgwood, *History of Parliament*: Biographies, 14.
[6] *L.P.*, I. 1123 (6); 1415 (26).

done against our sovereign lord the King as well with the smith who named himself the Captain of Cornwall as with Perkin Warbeck'[1]: this man, who owned the estate of Pendeen near St. Just, belonged to the class of small Cornish gentry. Mr. Borlase says that his daughter Jane conveyed her lands to her father's captor, John Thomas, serjeant-at-arms.[2] Sir Richard Nanfan's irrepressible servant, Roger Whalley, appears again in a petition to the King.[3] It seems that he was present at Blackheath against the rebels, and that afterwards at Padstow he was beaten up by John Tresynny, who had been a captain with the Smith, who 'upon trust of the landing of Perkin Warbeck, with certain of the late Lord Audley's servants your rebels . . . assaulted your said suppliant as he was coming from his church, and there sore beat and wounded him, and that done went into the house of your said subject where he took robbed . . . all his money and stuff of household [goods?] in value of £50 and better'; then they went off to be present at Perkin's landing in the west near St. Buryan. The importance of this is that it is so much evidence that Perkin was expected in Cornwall — the only scrap of evidence that remains; it is all the more likely that the contact would be made through the port of Padstow which traded regularly with Cork. Whalley ends by asking for some of John Tresynny's forfeited land, not exceeding 6 marks value per annum, for life.

The rebellions of 1497 left their mark upon the history of England: they were the first notice served upon the country of the existence of an obscure, hardy people in the west not yet wholly absorbed into the nation. These events made that year memorable. When in his *Utopia* Thomas More asks Raphael Hythloday: 'I pray you, sir, have you been in our country?' the latter replies: 'Yes, forsooth . . . not long after the insurrection that the western Englishmen made against their King, which by their own miserable and pitiful slaughter was suppressed and ended.' And when they speak of vagabonds and idlers, Raphael says, 'I will speak nothing of them that come home out of the wars, maimed and lame, as not long ago out of Blackheath field . . .'[4] We know from a sermon of Latimer's that as a lad he buckled on his father's armour when he went to fight for the King at Blackheath field. When, fifty years afterwards, the Cornishman, Humphry Cavell, contributes his poem on the Blacksmith to the *Mirror for Magistrates*, he enforces the moral of it all:

[1] C 1/209. 1.   [2] *Borlase of Borlase*, 31.
[3] Spec. Coll. 8/345, no. E 1335.
[4] cf. *L.P.*, I. 519, 43. 'William Morgan of Carmarthenshire, for good service done to the late King against the rebels of Cornwall upon Blackheath, where he was sore hurt and maimed, to be constable of Tenby.'

How can he rule well in a commonwealth,
Which knoweth not himself in rule to frame?
How should he rule himself in ghostly health,
Which never learned one lesson for the same?
If such catch harm their parents are to blame:
For needs must they be blind and blindly led,
Where no good lesson can be taught or read.[1]

The effect of the Risings, and perhaps even more of their punishment with such economic severity at a time when currency was scarce, must have been very heavy upon Cornish society. There is evidence that the county was much impoverished and wasted by it all. Cornwall's first irruption into English society was singularly unfortunate for itself; its exhaustion kept the county quiet for half a century until the Reformation brought renewed disturbances.

---

[1] *The Mirror for Magistrates*, ed. L. B. Campbell, 407.

CHAPTER VII

THE CONDITION OF THE CHURCH BEFORE THE REFORMATION

THROUGHOUT our period, as indeed from the early Middle Ages right up to 1876, Cornwall formed part, a separate archdeaconry, of the diocese of Exeter. It looked to the cathedral of St. Peter there upon its hill over-looking the city, still more to the hierarchy with the bishop at its head, for the impulse which kept the system of the Church regulated and in working order. That system, even in the days of its decadence when things were moving towards a decided change, was infinitely more important than we realize to-day. The Church was coterminous with the whole of society; it met and ordered social life at a hundred points; its claims were universal, and covered the whole life of man. Indeed it was inseparable from medieval society; it may be said to have been society itself regarded in a certain light, *sub specie aeternitatis*, a reflex of men's ordering of their affairs in this world.

That makes it a difficult, if not from the beginning a hopeless, task to dis-entangle one from the other — but at the same time one that is necessary in the writing of books. In addition to its spiritual and pastoral function, the essential part which it played in social organization, the Church had its own organization, with roots and tentacles extending widely into property of every kind, to provide for it. There fell to its officers, the clergy and their courts, not only the general function of watching over the moral life of the people, but much business of a miscellaneous character. The Bishop's Registers and his consistory court bear witness to its extent: the proving of wills and cases concerning them, cases of defamation and slander, all matri-monial causes, of custom of tithe, in addition to the episcopal routine in running the diocese. Lastly there were the monasteries and colleges, the regular clergy, to whom the bishop stood in a special relation.

The medieval bishop needed to be an able man. And, indeed, they usually were, marked men, men of learning and character in a society all too rude and primitive. The medieval bishops of Exeter were a distinguished lot, from the great canonist Bartholomew and the builders and founders, William Warelwast, Walter Bronescombe, Stapledon and Grandisson right up to the Reformation. Some of them were great men. Nor were the immediate pre-Reformation bishops exceptions to this. They fell rather into two classes, sons of noble families and distinguished court officials; in both respects contrasting with the post-Reformation bishops. Peter Courtenay, who held the see from 1478 to 1487, belonged to both classes, as a Courtenay and keeper of the Privy Seal. Richard Fox, who succeeded him (1487-92), was of the official class; he too became Lord Privy Seal and was one of Henry VII's most trusted ministers. So also was Oliver King (1492-95), principal secretary to Edward IV and Henry VII. Richard Redmayne (1495-1501) followed, then John Arundell (1502-04), third son of Sir Remfry Arundell of Lanherne. As a member of one of the foremost west-country families he had received a good deal of royal patronage before becoming Dean of Exeter, Bishop of Lichfield and Coventry, and ultimately of Exeter. During his brief episcopate he lived in state, maintaining his family's tradition of generous hospitality; he had a daily distribution of alms made at the palace-gate.[1] He was followed by Hugh Oldham (1504-19), who was advanced by the favour of Henry VII's mother, the Lady Margaret, and proved a most exemplary bishop. Fox and King were unable to reside owing to their duties at court; Oldham devoted himself to the duties of his diocese. He had things in good order, and was moreover able to direct the surplus arising from his revenues to his two foundations, Corpus Christi at Oxford of which he was co-Founder with Fox, and Manchester Grammar School.[2]

Last of these bishops was John Veysey who held the see for more than thirty years, from 1519 to 1554, with the intermission of two years 1551 to 1553, when he had to make way for the Reformer, Miles Coverdale, after which he was restored in his extreme old age by Mary. Veysey belonged to the official class; a good clerical courtier, a man of 'accomplished manners and business talents', he accumulated a mass of preferments by the favour of Bishop Arundell, Wolsey and the King. Already connected with Exeter from 1503 as Canon, and Dean from 1509, he became also Dean of the Chapel Royal and of Windsor. He was necessarily much about the Court. We have a pleasant pen-portrait of him in one of More's letters to his daughter Margaret, describing how he had read one of her Latin letters and some verses to him, and how he had expressed himself charmed with them, so that 'his words were all too poor to express what he felt'. 'He took out at once from his pocket a portague which you will find enclosed . . . I tried in every possible way to decline it, but was unable to refuse to take it, to send you as

---

[1] Oliver, *Lives of the Bishops of Exeter*, 117.
[2] v. Mumford, *Hugh Oldham*.

a pledge and token of his good will. This hindered me from showing him the letters of your sisters, lest it should seem that I showed them to obtain for the others too a gift which it annoyed me to have to accept for you. But, as I have said, he is so good that it is a happiness to be able to please him. Write to thank him with the greatest care and delicacy. You will one day be glad to have given pleasure to such a man.'[1]

That was very characteristic of Veysey: generous to a fault, cultured, affable, easy-going, in fact a spendthrift: a regular Renaissance prelate; one thinks — it is not a far cry from Exeter to Rome — of Leo X. But Veysey was a good man of affairs. On being appointed to the see, he made his visitation of the diocese; he reduced to order the statutes of the cathedral,[2] and at first, in spite of the calls of the Court, attending the King to the Field of the Cloth of Gold, meeting the Emperor at Dover, he spent some part of every year in his diocese. Then, in 1526, he was made Lord President of the Council of Wales, given charge of the Princess Mary and took up residence at Ludlow. He was already an oldish man, and this effectually uprooted him from Exeter. Later he lived in retirement at his native Sutton Coldfield, in great profusion and hospitality, where he lavished the revenues of the see upon the little town, paving it, building houses and bridges, founding a grammar school, introducing the manufacture of Devonshire kersies, constructing market-place and moot-hall, procuring a charter, granting it his manor, park and chase, rebuilding the aisles of the church and making himself a magnificent tomb in which he now lies.

Partly in consequence of all this, but still more of the pressure put upon him to grant away the possessions of his see, Exeter from being one of the wealthiest became one of the poorest of English sees. With its numerous, delectable estates in Devon and Cornwall, its conveniently spaced manors in Hampshire, Surrey, Middlesex on the way up to the Bishop's town-house in London, its revenues amounted to £1566 14s. 6½d. in 1535: a sum which one must multiply by twenty for a contemporary valuation.[3] That gives you the scale on which the pre-Reformation bishops lived. It was the deliberate intention of Reformation government, of Henry, Edward and Elizabeth, to reduce this, and very rightly. It exactly reflected the changed status of the Church in society consequent upon the Reformation. Where the pre-Reformation bishops, with their great possessions, took their place along with the nobility, the post-Reformation bishops took theirs alongside

---

[1] q. in Routh, *Sir Thomas More and his Friends*, 133-4.
[2] They are given in Oliver, op. cit., 471-6.
[3] *Valor Ecclesiasticus*, II. 289-91.

the gentry. There were no churchmen in Elizabeth's Council, save the Archbishop. Where the Church had been co-equal, it was now subordinate. The revenues of Exeter under Elizabeth amounted to the more appropriate figure of £500 per annum. Bishop Bradbridge found this insufficient and was given licence to hold two benefices in commendam, Newton Ferrers in Devon, and Lezant in Cornwall.[1]

But to return to things as they were at Exeter and in the diocese while the old order still prevailed, and the Bishop bore rule in person, as in Arundell's day and Oldham's and in the first years of Veysey — some idea of their multifarious activities may be gained from their registers: more rarely, if we listen to the still accents in which they speak to us, some feeling of the atmosphere in which these men lived their dedicated, formal lives: the ordered household, the chaplains and prayers and devotions, the episcopal routine punctuated by the sacraments, the procession of the seasons, autumn falling upon the oaks in the park at Bishop's Clyst, the first spring flowers in the hedges at Chudleigh, high summer upon visitation in Cornwall, the feast of the Nativity spent in the palace beneath the shadow of the Cathedral, the great fires burning in the hall to keep out the cold, the winds that whip round the corners in the city outside. Some inner sense of the life lived in that household breathes in the phrase with which the registrar breaks the formal record to note his lord's death: 'ipsoque eodem die . . . in palatio suo Exon., Dominus ab hac luce migravit. Cujus animae propitietur Deus. Amen.'[2] Or perhaps one penetrates even more intimately, if less literally, the stillness of these men's minds as one watches by their tombs, their painted effigies in their glory, jewelled mitres and vestments, the croziers in their hands, princes of the Church vested for mass — and underneath the lean skeleton of the dead man: sic transit gloria mundi. Perhaps one is not far from them as they lie through sleepless nights and days upon their tombs, the shifting lights of morning and evening, the half-lights of the night, lending them life in the silence round the choir where they once ruled. Or perhaps, again, one is at all times equally remote from them, and the historian's task ultimately impossible, a fugitive chasing of shadows that for ever elude him, an attempt to make dry bones live.

The episcopal routine as it moved slowly on its immemorial way, setting in motion innumerable small processes, responding in the accustomed ways to the secular needs of that society, the whole fabric so familiar, so sure that men were content to assume it like the seasons and live their lives within it,

[1] Oliver, op. cit., 140.
[2] q. ibid., 120.

cradled, fortified and consoled by its rites, nor ever think of the change that was going on within — that routine as it affected Cornwall was in no way dissimilar from what went on in other dioceses. It was what bound that westernmost outpost to the Catholic Europe of which it was part. In addition to the usual routine of ordinations, confirmations, presentations to livings, consecration of buildings, visitations — a life of ordered ceremonial, in which we can hear the bells ringing in the city, in the country churches, can smell the incense and mark the accustomed gestures — in addition there was the more specialized work of the bishop as mediator and judge.

There were disputes and agreements as to the rights of parishes and their dependent chapelries. There is a long document of Bishop Courtenay's of 1482 concerning the chapel of St. Agnes dependent on the parish church of St. Perranzabuloe, which may serve as model for the rest.[1] It starts with the petition of the people of St. Agnes to the Bishop while on visitation, reciting their difficulties in attending the mother church on account of distance, bad weather in winter, and praying for the consecration of a cemetery at St. Agnes. The Bishop summons the parties by proxy to Exeter Cathedral, where they swear to abide by his decision. He concedes to them the right of burial at St. Agnes, a chaplain to be maintained there at the cost of the vicar, a house and stable to be found for him by the inhabitants, who are to maintain the fabric of the chapel, its books and ornaments, seats and vestments and windows; the vicar is to maintain the chaplain's house, but to receive all mortuaries as usual. On St. Piran's feast the inhabitants were to offer ½ lb. of wax at his image in the parish church in sign of subjection and filial obedience. The relics of St. Piran were to be lodged in the chapel at St. Agnes if required. The deed concludes by reciting the penalties of interdiction if the composition is broken.

The appropriations of churches to monastic houses necessitated a number of such compositions, particularly in the Launceston district where so many of the churches belonged to the priory. Bishop Redmayne sent as deputy John Nans, canon of Exeter, to settle the dispute concerning the chapels of St. Giles and Werrington, dependent upon St. Stephen-by-Launceston, which in turn belonged to the priory.[2] The prior and convent were to maintain a chaplain there to serve each chapel on alternate Sundays, alternating with a canon of Launceston. A similar composition was made by Bishop Oldham in 1506 touching the chapels of Tremaine and Egloskerry: a chaplain was to be maintained by the prior to serve both on alternate

---

[1] Henderson, x. 347-53 (from the Bishop's Registry, Exeter, no. 1064).
[2] ibid., 292.

Sundays as of old custom; the bishop agreed to consecrate the chapel and cemetery at Tremaine, the tithes belonging to the altilage to be offered before the image of St. Winwalo there, and 12d. with a candle of 1 lb. of wax to burn before the image of St. Stephen in the priory church before high mass on the morrow of Christmas.[1] In 1509 Oldham made a similar composition between the inhabitants of Golant and Tywardreath priory.[2] The Golant people 'being merchants and artificers' cannot leave their craft, boats and nets — the village lies on the bank of the Fowey river — to go all the way to Tywardreath. The bishop consents to consecrate their chapel and cemetery; the inhabitants to pay as fish tithe to the priory, the eighteenth fish 'salsum de clavo absque onere aliquali', the eighteenth bushel of all grain brought in ships to the shore, and the eighteenth barrel of all herrings landed. One sees what a fertile ground of dispute tithes provided. But the parishioners needed the intervention of the bishop in their dealings with the monasteries. In 1524 there were complaints that the abbeys of Hayles, Beaulieu and Rewley, owners respectively of the sheaf tithe[3] of Paul and Breage, of Wendron and Stithians, of Crowan and St. Wenn, had not made certain distributions of alms to the poor. In consequence Veysey sequestrated Breage with its three chapels and distributed £6, a fair sum, to the poor.[4]

Of the multifarious activities of the bishop's routine his register provides full evidence. There are the licences to clergy to preach — these are few in number and increase after the Reformation — sequestrations of benefices for good cause, licences for non-residence for sufficient reason, such as study at Oxford; Papal bulls giving permission to hold benefices in plurality are enregistered; commissions are granted for such purposes as reconsecrating a polluted church or churchyard, to suffragans to perform various episcopal acts. Indulgences are granted to those who contribute to making or repairing certain bridges — in 1504 those at Launceston and Bodmin, in 1521 at Looe and Camelford.[5] In 1535 Veysey while at St. Germans granted an indulgence to all penitents visiting the chapel of St. Benet's in Lanivet and contributing to the repair of the road there, which was not usable in bad weather.[6] It was, and still is, a damp spot.

The register of the consistory court gives us evidence of the judicial business of the diocese. This includes all matrimonial causes, breach of contract, tithe cases, cases concerning parish custom, the rights of parishioners, slander. The people of Golant were still in trouble about their parish church at Tywardreath.[7] They had contributed £4 towards the building

<hr>

[1] Henderson, x. 299.   [2] ibid., 300a.   [3] i.e. the rectorial tithes.
[4] ibid., 104.   [5] ibid., 298, 301.   [6] ibid., 302a.   [7] ibid., 123a.

of the new aisle, £10 to buying the bells, and had made at their own charges a window painted with the figure of their patron saint, St. Sampson; when the wardens of Tywardreath demanded that they should contribute to the new rood-loft, they refused; they had given enough. At Stratton, we learn the custom was for the vicar to have a flagon out of every bridgin of ale sold, and of every half-bridgin one pottel. From another case we learn that during the archdeacon's chapter in Michaelstow church, Richard Broad of Minster used many opprobrious words against Sir John Trelawny imputing to him the sin of incontinence, saying that one John Cole 'diversis noctibus adduxit ad eum quandam mulierem indutam vestibus virilibus'. If so, Sir John had at least the merit of being somewhat original.

No doubt so long-established, so well-worn a routine worked largely by its own momentum, with its complement of officials and commissaries, even during the episcopate of absentee bishops. There is no evidence that the diocese of Exeter was not well governed in these years before the Reformation. In any case it was so large that the bishops needed suffragans to help them. We find mention of three or four in Cornwall. The chapelry of Tremaine was dedicated by the Bishop of Sebaste in 1504.[1] The titular Bishop of Solubria was provided for by the livings of St. Goran and St. Gluvias between 1511 and 1514; it was he who consecrated the chapel and cemetery at Golant after Oldham's composition in 1519.[2] Much of Veysey's functions were in Devonshire performed by William, Bishop of Hippo;[3] in Cornwall, from 1519 to 1533 by Thomas Vyvyan, Prior of Bodmin and titular Bishop of Megara.

This ecclesiastic was much the most important churchman in Cornwall right up to the threshold of the Reformation. A Cornishman himself, and the holder of much preferment within the county, he was the last figure, on the grand scale, of the old order. With him bearing rule at Bodmin, it was as if Cornwall had its own bishop, as in the days before Exeter was a see at all. When Prior Vyvyan died, and was buried in state in the tomb which Leland describes,[4] and which still survives, though then it stood before the high altar of the priory church, men must have felt that the old order was changing. Not that he was popular: he was too high-handed and acquisitive for that: a sort of local Wolsey with whom his career was closely contemporary. He was ordained to the first tonsure and acolyte, as canon of Bodmin

[1] Henderson, x. 298.
[2] ibid., 61, 300.
[3] He is said to have held the last ordinations in Bodmin Priory in March 1539. Oliver, *Monasticon Dioc. Exon.*, 17.
[4] Leland's *Itinerary*, I. 180.

Priory, by Bishop King's suffragan on September 15th, 1493.[1] In 1508 he was elected prior and confirmed by Bishop Oldham.[2] Next year he was collated to the vicarage of Egloshayle. In 1516 he presented his brother to the vicarage of Bodmin. On May 4th, 1517, he was consecrated Bishop of Megara, in order to act as suffragan to Oldham to whom his abilities had evidently recommended him. Next year we find him holding an ordination in Exeter cathedral, and thereafter a number of ordinations at Bodmin.[3] On June 16th, 1519, he consecrated the chapel of St. Christina at Stowe in Kilkhampton; and in 1522 received Veysey's commission to confirm, bless chalices, bells and vestments, and dedicate portable altars, during the bishop's pleasure. In 1523 he was instituted to the rectory of Withiel, and in 1524 to the Bodmin prebend in St. Endellion church, both in the patronage of the priory. In the same year he received the commission from Veysey to consecrate the chapel of St. Mary Magdalen at Launceston. He died on Pentecost Sunday, June 1st, 1533.

With these various preferments, which he held till his death, the prior was well able to support his position with some state. He is said to have rebuilt Withiel church and rectory, and the delightful country house at Rialton, of which a fragment remains, where he much resided.[4] And no wonder; for it is a pleasant place, situated a little way in from the mouth of the valley upon the sea, sheltered from the winds, the house turning its back upon the coast and looking south up the valley. From the large oriel window in his study, which he built for himself — the arms of the priory, the three fishes, with his initials, are still to be seen in the glass panes — he looked out upon the little courtyard with its holy well and into the orchards, fringed by the wind-blown elms. It was a very Cornish scene, and a very suitable retreat for an ecclesiastic burdened with so much business, the sound of the sea upon the shore somewhat subdued in that quiet valley, the pleasant noise of the stream running by the house to accompany his thoughts and meditations.

The Archdeacon of Cornwall was not such an important personage; though he had his stall in the cathedral — the second on the left as you passed through the screen into the choir, next to the Precentor — a prebend in Glasney college at Penryn, and the advowson of the little priory of St. John

---

[1] Henderson, XXXI: Materials for a History of Bodmin Priory; cf. also Maclean, *Trigg Minor*, I. 133-5.
[2] Bro. John Symon and Robert Hooker, notary public, brought the decree of election to Bishop Oldham at Clyst, April 13th, 1508.
[3] Oliver, op. cit., 17.
[4] v. Henderson, 'Rialton', in *Old Cornwall*, Winter, 1936.

at Helston, with rights in relation to probate of wills, inductions, visitations, and so on. The archdeacon as such was on the downgrade compared with what he had been in the earlier Middle Ages; but he still had an important part to play, in a position rather independent of the bishop, on the more secular side of diocesan administration, dealing direct with the clergy, holding courts of his own and, of course, receiving the fees. Archdeacons were somewhat secular persons; they were usually non-resident, performed their office by deputy, and were sometimes arrant scoundrels. The job was regarded as a step to preferment for the sons of important persons, and not unnaturally looked at mainly from the point of view of its financial profits. The archdeaconry of Cornwall provided a case in point during these years, a long dispute as revealing as anything could be of the underside of clerical life, much litigation, which vexed the bishop and tormented his respectable chancellor (a Fellow of All Souls, moreover) to death in prison: in short, altogether a pretty story.

On October 8th, 1537, Wolsey's illegitimate son, Thomas Winter, was collated to the archdeaconry of Cornwall and two days later was installed by proxy.[1] In his lifetime the great Cardinal had been fond of this child of love, and the lad had been coddled with much ecclesiastical preferment and brought up in the lap of luxury.[2] He lived a good deal abroad, studying at foreign universities, Louvain, Padua, Ferrara, Paris, everywhere treated with the deference due to his high connection; a good Latinist, he liked a life of cultured ease: he was of a gentle, easy disposition, with all the extravagant tastes of his father, and none of his energy or business sense; the young man was always overspent and in debt, in spite of his numerous preferments. On his father's fall he had to resign most of these and lived in penury for a time at Padua. In 1534 he returned to England and three years later obtained the archdeaconry of Cornwall, no doubt through Cromwell's influence. He then — and this was clearly part of the bargain — on November 9th, 1537, leased the archdeaconry, with all its offices, properties and rights, for a term of 35 years to a layman, one William Body.[3]

Body was one of the underworld of Cromwell's agents, a bold, unscrupulous man used on the shady side of the great man's multifarious business. He played a by no means clear part in bringing Lord Leonard Grey, Lord Deputy of Ireland, to the block. Winter must have known him in Cromwell's entourage: he became one of the gentlemen ushers of the King's

[1] Henderson, x. 265.
[2] The kindly Oliver calls him Wolsey's nephew (*Lives of Bishops of Exeter*, 289); but v. Pollard, *Wolsey*, 306-12, for his career, and Rose-Troup, *The Western Rebellion of* 1549, cc. iii-iv.
[3] Early Chanc. Proc., v. 60, and file 950/37.

Chamber. It seemed that Winter had made a profitable bargain; for Body agreed to pay him £30 yearly out of the revenues of the archdeaconry, and paid him £150 down — £100 in ready money and £50 in discharging a bond of Winter's against one Giggs, mercer of London. Body also lent Winter £32 12s. 2d., some of which he paid to various merchants in the city, and gave him 'by the way of love . . . 5½ yards of fine woollen cloth of the colour of French black, price £6; a nightgown furred with old marten and new faced with foynes, price £6; and a bible in Latin, price 15s.'. The proceedings sound very questionable, but it is possible that the arrangement was the less noticed at first because the duties of the archdeacon continued to be carried out by Winter's deputy as before.

But a storm blew up at the end of the first term of three years. The bishop took notice of Winter and had him cited before his chancellor, Dr. Brerewood, for using 'unlawful games' and other offences such as felling timber on his glebe. This may have been purely *pro forma* in order to end Winter's lease of the archdeaconry to Body. For Winter was no less anxious to end it: he claimed that Body had added in his own hand certain fraudulent articles to the original indenture between them. Now, probably with the advice of the bishop, he appointed the bishop's commissary, John Harris, prebendary of Glasney, to exercise his rights as archdeacon. Body determined to put them to the test by exercising them himself in person. He procured a letter from the King to the bishop and dean and chapter, confirming his grant and asking them to confirm it with their seals.[1] He then went down to Cornwall where the archdeacon's visitation was being held in the church of St. Stephen's by Launceston. Here there was a regular scene. Harris, with Winter's authority and the bishop's, forbade Body to exercise the office of archdeacon and exhorted the clergy not to pay him their procurations. When Body took the book and proceeded to call their names in order, Harris 'raught' it out of his hand. Body half-drew his dagger, but was overpowered, carried out of the church and the doors locked against him. It certainly seems that he was hardly treated after all the money he had spent on Winter.

There followed a good deal of litigation; and Body brought an action against the bishop and his deputies, threatening them with the penalties of praemunire. In the House of Lords Gardiner defended his brother of Exeter, contending that as the bishops were no longer subject to Rome but to royal authority, they could not fall under praemunire; until the Lord Chancellor, Cromwell's associate Audley, 'bade him hold his peace for fear of

[1] *L.P.*, XVI. I, 522.

entering a praemunire himself'.[1] The world was not what it had been for bishops: no wonder Veysey became a defeated and disillusioned old man. Both his chancellor and registrar were arrested and committed to prison; early in 1544 they were charged with a breach of praemunire before the King's Bench, and sentenced to imprisonment.[2] The registrar paid a large fine; Body agreed to release him from any further actions and he was freed; Brerewood, the chancellor, died in the midst of his troubles. Body had won.

The year before, 1543, Winter had resigned the archdeaconry; and a new lease of it to Body was made by the Bishop, John Pollard, Winter's successor, and the dean and chapter.[3] Body was to pay the archdeacon £10 yearly: it represented a handsome compensation for his losses through Winter; it was the new archdeacon who was the loser. The latter, on succeeding, seems to have agreed to pay Winter an annuity of £16 for life out of the archdeaconry, and to have paid a sum of £50 down to meet some of Winter's debts — one of £49 to a London tailor is a further indication of the extravagant tastes which Winter inherited from his great father, the Cardinal.[4] We learn that for non-payment of these debts Winter had been attached; and nothing more is ever heard of him. Can it be that he died in prison — that prison was too much for him; or that he was carried off by the sweating sickness which ravaged London in that year and carried off Holbein? As for Body, a worse fate was in store for him: within a very few years he was murdered by a mob at Helston, in the archdeaconry which he was so determined to hold in his grip.

Of the state of the clergy there is no reason to suppose that it was very different in Cornwall from elsewhere. Conditions differed a little in that the people spoke Cornish; but that mattered the less when the language of the Church was Latin: hence the attachment of the Cornish to it. Dr. Moreman, the learned vicar of Menheniot (1529-54), we learn from Hooker of Exeter, was 'the first in those days that taught his parishioners and people to say the Lord's prayer, their Belief and the Commandments in the English tongue, and did teach and catechise them therein'.[5] But Moreman was an exceptional man: a former Fellow of Exeter College, he was a scholar and at Menheniot kept a school, at which Hooker was a pupil. 'He wrote upon St. Paul's Epistle to the Romans by the hand of Lawrence Travers, vicar of Quethiock, for his own hand was very bad and scarce legible': in that like other scholars. Moreman was a convinced and prominent

[1] Muller, *Letters of Stephen Gardiner*, 391.   [2] Rose-Troup, op. cit., 67-8.
[3] Henderson, x. 106.   [4] Early Chanc. Proc. 1124/27-29.   [5] Harleian MS. 5827.

Catholic: at Oxford he had been opposed to Henry's divorce — which did not prevent him being made canon of Exeter in 1544. But in Edward VI's reign he was imprisoned. One of the Articles of the rebels in 1549 demands his and Dr. Crispin's release, 'which hold our opinions . . . and to them we require the King's majesty to give some certain livings, to preach among us our Catholic faith'.[1] On Mary's accession he was released and greatly in favour: he was appointed one of the divines to dispute with the Protestants in convocation and returned to Exeter, where it seems that he was destined to succeed Veysey as bishop. But by this time he suffered from that fatal disease which afflicted the supporters of Mary — old age — and died about the same time as Veysey who was then over ninety. His name has, however, come down as that of the most distinguished parish priest of his time in Cornwall.

There were few others. Some of the cathedral dignitaries held Cornish livings, like Brerewood, the chancellor, who held the good rectory of St. Ewe from 1524 and a prebend at St. Endellion from 1533 to his death;[2] but it is unlikely that he, or such persons in general, resided. The most exciting holder of a Cornish benefice at this time was the famous poet Alexander Barclay, who was collated to the living of St. Allen in 1530 and resigned it next year.[3] Barclay had been a chaplain at the college of Ottery St. Mary and while there wrote his best-known work, his version of Brandt's *Ship of Fools*. The work was dedicated to Thomas Cornish, suffragan bishop of Bath and Wells, warden of the college: he had, according to the dedication, ordained Barclay and conferred many benefits upon him.[4] A later work, a translation of Sallust's *Jugurthine War*, was dedicated to Veysey.[5] Most of the details of Barclay's life are lost; but he seems to have left the Benedictine order to become a Franciscan friar, and when the dissolution came to have gone about the country preaching. His sympathies, like those of his fellow-poet Skelton — whom for the rest he disapproved of — were conservative and catholic. In 1538 he was in the west country once more, for Latimer wrote to Cromwell that 'Friar Bartlow does much hurt in Cornwall and in Devonshire both with open preaching and private communication'.[6] We find him stopping at St. Germans at this time just before the end: the conversation which took place at supper with the prior, between Barclay and a westcountryman sympathetic to the religious changes, is very revealing of the temper of the time.[7]

[1] q. Rose-Troup, 221.   [2] Henderson, X. 26, 66; this corrects Rose-Troup, 68.
[3] ibid., 68.   [4] *Barclay's Eclogues*, ed. White (E.E.T.S.), xi.
[5] ibid., xxxviii.   [6] L.P., XIII. 709.   [7] See below, pp. 182-3.

In addition to the numerous benefices appropriated to monasteries, their priors were not averse to nominating themselves, or their relatives, to livings in their patronage. We have seen the preferments enjoyed by Prior Vyvyan. In 1516 the prior of Taunton was, for some reason, presented to the living of Lanlivery; the prior and convent of Tywardreath were patrons, so there must have been some arrangement.[1] Let us look at this prior of Tywardreath, Collins by name. He was elected prior in 1507, but at the same time continued to hold the priory living of St. Anthony-in-Meneage till 1514. Meanwhile in 1513 he was presented to St. Clether by the chaplain of St. Michael's chantry at St. Austell, himself an appointee of the priory. The prior held this little benefice — small indeed, but all was grist that came to the mill — till 1518 when he resigned it to succeed to the priory living of Fowey. This he held until 1528, when, frightened by the unfriendly letters he received from Wolsey and the Marquis of Exeter urging his retirement from being prior, he did at last vacate his vicarage, to nominate a relative, Henry Collins, in his place; but he was careful to reserve himself a pension of £8 a year upon it: its value was only £10. When his nominee died next year, the prior presented yet another member of his family, if on the wrong side of the bed, Edward Collins alias Harris.[2]

Similarly Robert Swymmer, the last prior of St. Germans, enjoyed the vicarage of Talland (1520-38), to which Launceston Priory appointed him.[3] In 1537 he was presented to the more remunerative rectory of Minster, and next year resigned Talland. The last prior of Tywardreath, Nicholas Guest, held the vicarage of St. Winnow from 1538 to 1545.[4] But with this we are over the threshold of the Dissolution, when it was natural and fairly frequent for uprooted monks to take livings.

The relations of the heads of religious houses did well for themselves in this as in other ways. We find Richard Carlyan, a relative of the prior of Launceston, chopping and changing preferment in this area a good deal, and reserving for himself a pension on the vacated living.[5] That was one way of doing it. Prior Vyvyan presented his brother, another Thomas, to the vicarage of Bodmin, between whom and the townsmen there was a great quarrel, which lights up something of the background of parish life. It formed another article in their indictment of the prior. They complained that the prior's brother had 'departed from his vicarage by the labour of the said prior and lieth in London, where he by citation otherwise procureth un-

---

[1] Henderson, x. 63.   [2] ibid., 59, 62, 64, 67, 68, 295; Oliver, *Monasticon*, 35-6, 45-6.
[3] Henderson, x. 27, 33; Oliver, 3.   [4] Henderson, 27.
[5] He reserved a pension of 20 marks on resigning Liskeard in 1529 (Henderson, 25).

just vexation against the inhabitants of the town'. In his absence, they said, the prior had appointed a priest of ill-living and disposition, who had been put out of three or four other parishes before, to serve the cure; and he had done this to provoke them 'to do something against your Highness' laws', while his servants told them that the prior would cause them to be hanged, saying that 'they should wear halters as their predecessors did at Blackheath field': that memory had evidently not been forgotten in the town of Bodmin.[1]

The dispute between the vicar and his parishioners was over the custom of tithe and mortuaries — a fertile source of trouble.[2] Their counsel in London went to meet the vicar in St. Paul's, where a lot of such business was done.[3] The latter stated that he claimed 'nothing of your town and parish for the right of his church but such duties as he can well prove by old precedents had been paid and received by his predecessors in times past'. He complained bitterly of his parishioners, said that they had caused him to depart out of that town by force, 'for he could not tarry among you'; that 'ye be so unreasonable and so full of malice and dissimulation that no man can trust you, for ye speak fair words and think otherwise in your hearts, and he hath proved you many days'. He went so far as to say that 'ye be so full of craft and so full of malice that if Christ were here again and dwelling with you, ye would hang him on the cross and crucify him again'. The vicar was evidently moved and ended with defiance: 'and whereas ye do malign and grudge against his priest that serveth his church, he purposeth not to change him for your pleasures, for he payeth him his wages, and also he is admitted by the ordinary to serve there; and if ye can find any fault or cause reasonable against him, ye may complain to the ordinary if ye will'. Their solicitor learned that the vicar had sued out of the Cardinal's court a licence of non-residence for two years, 'whereby ye may perceive that he intendeth to tarry here for two years, and all is to put the town and parish to vexation and trouble'. The lawyer warned him that if he went to the law, 'he should be answered and have trouble enough, his handful'. We know no more of this business. In 1534 a commission was issued by Veysey to the prior and the vicar touching the pollution of the cemetery; so there must have been trouble and bloodshed.[4] But the vicar continued, though by this time his powerful brother was dead.

A survey of the institutions shows that the great majority of those holding livings were not recognizably Cornish. Indeed, a considerable number

---

[1] *The Bodmin Register*, 304-6.   [2] ibid., 36-8.
[3] ibid., 309-12.   [4] Henderson, x. 302.

were, for various reasons, non-residents. Veysey stated in making his return to Wolsey of the payments made by the clergy to the loan of 1522, that the holders of about 100 benefices were residing outside the diocese:[1] that figure must apply to both Devon and Cornwall; perhaps we should not be far wrong in allowing 25 of these to the latter. A few of the clergy were younger sons of important families: they got the local family living, and sometimes others too; though this feature of social life was by no means so marked in the sixteenth, as it became in the eighteenth, century. William Reskymer became rector of Ladock, in which parish the family had property, in 1520; in 1536 he also became vicar of Constantine, where the Reskymers dwelt at Merthen, that delightful Tudor house above the Helford River which still remains.[2] Thomas Godolphin was vicar of Breage, the parish church of Godolphin, from 1504 to 1510.[3] The best example of all is perhaps John Grenville. A younger son of Sir Thomas Grenville of Stowe, his father willed that he was 'if he be disposed to be a priest, to have the next avoidance of one of the benefices of Bideford or of Kilkhampton'. The latter fell vacant in 1524; he was presented and retained it, with Launcells from 1533 to 1545 and Week St. Mary from 1558, through all the changes of Henry, Edward, Mary and Elizabeth, till his death at a patriarchal age in 1580.[4] His comfortable, conforming career was an epitome of the attitude of the average clergyman through all that time of change.

There was, of course, a fairly clear class-division between the richer and the poorer clergy, between the well-beneficed, the pluralists, and those who had small benefices or none. Where the former in life lived in their comfortably-stocked rectories off the fat of the land, and in death sleep beneath their admirable, expensive brasses, leaving their wills behind them, the latter lived poorly beside the peasant, sharing his life and in death mingling their dust with his, leaving nothing by which we may remember them. There is Master Warren Penhalurick, who among Cornishmen of no particular family, attained to good things through the church. Vicar of Wendron in 1503, he was presented to Stithians in 1513 and St. Just-in-Roseland in 1529.[5] In addition he was a prebendary of Glasney. In the Return of 1522 he is rated as one of the most well-to-do of the Cornish clergy, with goods valued at £120 and taxed at £14 13s. 4d.[6] No wonder he could afford, when he died in 1535, a fine brass in the church of Wendron upon

---

[1] Henderson, x. 366 (11).   [2] ibid., 65, 68.
[3] ibid., 57, 61.
[4] ibid., 25, 26, 28, 33. This corrects my account in *Sir Richard Grenville*, 28.
[5] ibid., 57, 62, 66, 69.
[6] ibid., 366 (6).

which he is depicted in processional vestments, cope and alb and stole, with an inscription reciting his benefices.[1]

On the other side we have the clerical proletariat: those whose livings were worth little — there were some in Cornwall worth only £5 or £6 a year compared with the £53 6s. 8d. of St. Columb Major, which was (and is) the fattest;[2] the simple massing-priests, chaplains, curates. The pluralist parson of Marhamchurch, Richard Carlyan, engaged a curate 'to say and celebrate all divine service in the church there and also to administer all sacraments and sacramentals there' for four years at £6 a year. The curate averred that he was to receive a quarter's warning before being put out; nevertheless the parson put him out without warning, so that he lost 30s. thereby, besides 33s. owing to him. Carlyan farmed his benefice to him for a year, promising that he should not be the loser if the profits decayed in that time; as it happened that year many sheep died in that parish, and the curate lost 46s. 8d. for altilage money. When Carlyan died, he was worth £100, but his executors refused to compensate the curate for his losses.[3]

Matters of this sort provided frequent cases in the courts. From one such we learn of the foreign incumbent of Calstock, Sir John Baptist de Bazadonis, who leased his parsonage for 7 years at £20 a year, to someone who sub-let it for £24 and cut down 'the great old oaks' and ash trees growing in the glebe.[4] From another we learn of the parson of Grade, who had quarrelled with his chief parishioner James Erisey, and setting his benefice to a Breton priest to serve, went off to take shelter at St. Keverne, which was a sanctuary, like Beaulieu to which it belonged.[5]

Yet other cases throw light into still darker places — the morals of the clergy. There is the vicar of St. Veep, early in the reign of Edward VI: John Winslade charged him with keeping one Jane Erle 'as his concubine in his house at St. Veep by the space of ten years or more and by her had divers children', which he did 'openly confess at a general sessions holden at Bodmin' at Midsummer 1547; 'which said Jane Erle came to death in the house of the same complainant at St. Veep . . . and was secretly buried in the night time within the parish church . . . under the sieges or seats, whose death was not known unto the parishioners by the space of three years.'[6] There was a long record of ill-feeling between the parson and Winslade. The former stated that he had offended Winslade by giving evidence in a case of forcible entry against a friend of his, and that Winslade swore he

---

[1] Dunkin, *Monumental Brasses of Cornwall*, p. 11, pl. vi.
[2] *Valor Ecclesiasticus*, II. 400.   [3] Early Chanc. Proc. 1055, 34-5.
[4] Court of Requests, Bdle. 3, 37.   [5] Star Chamber Proc., Bdle. 20, 130.
[6] Early Chanc. Proc. file 1201, 15-16.

would displease him for it. The latter brought a charge of murder against him at the inquest on Jane Erle, but there was insufficient evidence. They then caused him to be indicted 'on the statute of incontinency of priests' at quarter-sessions at Bodmin, charging him with frequenting 'the company of one Alice Hogges, wife unto one Richard Hogges': which he traversed. He was then charged with murder at Launceston Assizes, but it could not be proved. Next they caused the coroners to hold another inquest and 'found him guilty of murdering the said woman whereas of truth the said woman . . . died of God's visitation'. Afterwards the verdict was made void for insufficiency. Again they caused him to be indicted at Bodmin for a breach of the Six Articles, but though John Winslade was foreman of the jury and John Birt, his kinsman, constable of St. Veep, there was no proof. Whether the priest was guilty or no, it was an unpleasant case. It is curious that he should have been able to keep his woman so quiet in the house all that time, away from the inquiring nose of archdeacon or bishop's commissary. But St. Veep was a remote place, and so close had he kept her that in 1544 he was able to get the additional living of St. Neot.[1] It is no less interesting that the Prayer Book Rebellion should bring these two enemies together, the priest and Winslade, who seems to have been a bit of a moralist. For they both were hanged for their part in the Rising.[2]

It strikes a pleasanter note, so much light relief, to come upon the evidence against the vicar of St. Austell in a case in the Bishop's consistory court in 1557:[3] 'On Shrove Tuesday last', the deponent 'came through St. Austell churchyard and saw Joan Suer sitting in the church porch and said the vicar would not hear her confession, and had taken her sister into the church and locked the door. Therefore he smote the church door and asked the vicar whether he used to shrive women and the church door locked upon them.'

Such were the difficulties, if that is the right word, that attended upon an unmarried clergy. The graver difficulties that marriage incurred under Mary, namely deprivation or putting the lady away, will be dealt with later.

Though Exeter was one of the larger dioceses — was in fact geographically the largest of the southern sees, it was not one of the richer: so much of Devon and Cornwall was infertile moorland. Of the tax upon the clergy, upon the excuse of a papal crusade against the Turks in 1502, Exeter paid £464 13s. 4d., Bath and Wells £617 16s. 8d., Winchester £973 6s. 8d., Salisbury £1228.[4] Not that these figures are necessarily conclusive; they are only a comparative indication. But with the *Valor Ecclesiasticus* of 1535 we

---

[1] Henderson, x. 28.   [2] See below, p. 284.
[3] Henderson, x. 118b.   [4] Wilkins, *Concilia*, III. 646.

are enabled to gain a full view of the revenues, the property, the economic condition of the Church. This famous survey was compiled in pursuance of the Act of First Fruits and Tenths, which had been annexed to the Crown, and it provided the government with the material upon which to base its taxation of the Church throughout the country.[1] Commissions were appointed in every shire, who were to return the revenues of all benefices and ecclesiastical bodies, deanery by deanery; the Bishop was made responsible for the return from the whole diocese, and for its quota of taxation.[2] This meant that Veysey, who was already very old, was back at work in the diocese for most of this year. He was in Cornwall in March, for on the seventh he subscribed to the Act of Supremacy and renounced papal jurisdiction in the chapel of St. Mary in the priory church of St. Germans, before the prior, Dr. Brerewood, Dr. Moreman and a gentleman usher of the King's household who had doubtless brought the instrument from court, as witnesses.[3] He was at Shaftesbury in October, for he wrote from there to Sir Thomas Arundell complaining that his revenue of tithe-tin from Devon and Cornwall had remained unpaid by the latter's deputy now for three years, though he had records to show that it had been paid to the see of Exeter since before King John's days: perhaps a reminder due to the work he had put in on his revenues that summer.[4] He thanked Sir Thomas for his venison, wine and other gifts, and said that he had been with the King on the Friday before — Henry and Anne were on a tour of Wiltshire and Gloucestershire that summer and autumn: he had found them in good health and merry.

The total revenues from the benefices and monastic houses in Devon were £17,316 13s. 10½d.; those from Cornwall, £4082 14s. 8¾d.[5] The revenues from the latter were less than half those of the archdeaconry of Exeter, which were £8799 15s. 3¼d.; though the Devonshire archdeaconries were much smaller. Everything goes to show the comparative poverty of Cornwall. Yet there was in addition a substantial drain upon the resources of the county, large sums going out of it every year to the bishop (who spent it upon Sutton Coldfield), to the dean and chapter of Exeter (the dean, who was Reginald Pole, spending his in Italy), to religious houses in Devon and other counties, who consumed theirs in the good things of this world, and the contemplation of the next — but not in Cornwall.

Let us look at the figures more closely. Of the bishop's princely revenues

---

[1] cf. Sabine, *English Monasteries on the Eve of the Dissolution*, which studies the *Valor* on its monastic side. The secular side still awaits its student. I make my contribution, so far as Cornwall is concerned, below.

[2] Veysey's commission is given in *Valor Ecclesiasticus*, II. 289.

[3] *L.P.*, VIII. 311.   [4] *L.P.*, IX. 555.   [5] *Valor*, II. 391, 408.

of £1566 14s. 6½d., rather more than a quarter (£435 17s. 6⅛d.) came from his fat Cornish manors: that is to say a sum almost equal to the revenues of the Earl of Devonshire from all his lands, over several counties. The bishop's income arose almost entirely from temporalties, not spiritualties (i.e. from lands, not tithes), and his manors were good ones: his manor of Pawton, which included the whole country west of Wadebridge between St. Breoke Downs and the River Camel, was the richest in the county (it was worth £105 15s. 6¾d.) and several of the others were not far behind.[1]

The cathedral establishment at Exeter, the dean and chapter, the various officers like the chancellor, treasurer, archdeacon of Cornwall, and the vicars choral, derived a total revenue of £323 17s. 2½d. out of Cornwall.[2] It was mostly in spiritualties, from appropriated benefices. The dean and chapter had no less than a dozen livings,[3] while Newlyn East and Probus were appropriated to the chancellor and treasurer respectively. That is to say, they took the rectorial tithes, while the lesser went to the vicar for his stipend. This meant draining away money, the profits of the harvests, the fruits of the soil, from the parishes. It is rather wonderful to reflect how all through history the labourers on the soil, willing beasts of burden — with some few revolts now and then, have carried all this superstructure, bishops and deans and clergy, kings and lords and squires, upon their broad uncomplaining backs.

Still more is this the case with the moneys which trickled, and in some parts flowed, from the parishes into the monastic houses. The monasteries of the neighbouring county took a total sum of £246 11s. 6d. out of Cornwall yearly; no less than £76 went from the parish of Lelant (with St. Ives) to the college of the Holy Cross, Crediton. Monasteries and colleges in other counties, like Hayles Abbey, Rewley, Beaulieu, Bridgwater Priory, Sion Abbey, Windsor, took a further sum of over £400 out of the county. In all some £1500 — and this is a minimum figure — went out of Cornwall: about a third of the total Church revenues of the county.[4]

A clear analysis of the *Valor* reveals a further point of some importance:

---

[1] *Valor*, II. 289-91.　　[2] ibid., 292-9.

[3] They were: St. Perran, St. Erth, Gwennap, Veryan, St. Issey, St. Merryn, St. Eval, Constantine, Sancreed, Gwinnear, Mullion; they held the advowsons of St. Erth, Gwennap, Sancreed, Altarnun, St. Perran, St. Issey, St. Eval, Elerky, St. Winnow, Constantine, St. Breward, St. Merryn, Trevalga, and the manors of Methleigh in Breage, Lamberran in Perranzabuloe, with lands at Treworthen: a goodly heritage.

[4] These latter are approximate figures, for there are a few gaps in the returns in the *Valor*. Nearly all of these I have been able to fill from the Ministers' Accounts given in Dugdale, *Monasticon*; but one or two still remain, for which I have allowed an average on the low side. It must be insisted that these are minimum figures; the conclusion in the text therefore not only holds good but is a rather moderate statement of the position.

namely that Cornwall enjoyed, if that is the word, a much higher proportion of its Church revenues being devoted to the upkeep of the monasteries, than Devon or most other counties. The total income of the religious houses and collegiate churches in Cornwall was £1454 2s. 8¾d.: yet another third of the county's total church revenues. That is to say that only a sum of £1248 11s. 5⅞d., or rather less than a third, remained to sustain the parish clergy.

The situation can be best illustrated deanery by deanery:

Deanery	Benefices	Approp.	Value £	s.	d.	Unapp.+ vicarages: value £	s.	d.
Kerrier	17	11	245	3	8	268	7	9
Penwith	17	11	296	12	4	341	14	4
Powder	29	13	214	6	9	438	8	6½
Pydar	17	10	185	9	6	323	0	8
Trigg minor	19	7	124	3	8	247	11	5
Trigg major	17	12	127	13	7½	238	8	3
East	23	8	120	6	8	486	16	6
West	18	8	115	7	8	305	7	8

Comparing these figures with those for other counties, one is enabled to draw the conclusion that the proportion of benefices appropriated to monastic houses was in Cornwall above the average, and notably above that in Devon. The figures reveal the further point that it was in the western part of the county, Penwith and Kerrier, that the proportion was at its highest and most money left the parishes to flow into the coffers of monks or canons. It was these parts which were already the poorest and most restive. As you went towards the eastern boundary of the county, fewer livings were held away from the parishes. Perhaps that was something as against the fact that the Duchy estates were mostly in the east and took a good deal of money away from those parts.

There is no need to go into detail as to the values of Cornish livings. They were very much what they were in Devon, with a large number averaging round about £15. There were not many rich ones: the best were St. Columb major, worth £53 6s. 8d., St. Breoke £41 10s. 8d., Stokeclimsland £40. There were several worth over £30. On the other hand there were some very small ones, worth only £5 — moorland parishes in the Lizard or Bodmin moor districts, where one can imagine the lives of the poor priests alongside their peasants.

As for a picture of the economic hold of the Church in Cornwall, a map would show that certain whole districts were predominantly in the hands of the Church, as others of the Duchy. There were certain well-defined ecclesiastical districts. The country round Launceston and the pleasant streams running down to the Tamar there, was one, where the priory and the bishop together owned a good deal of land. So also round about St. Germans, where the bishop and the priory almost divided the country between them. Around Bodmin and from there to Padstow, in fact most of the land on both sides of the lower course of the Camel, belonged to the Church: which was not surprising since it was St. Petroc's own country; on one side it belonged mainly to the priory, on the other to the bishop, with the livings in the hands of the dean and chapter. Farther down the coast near Newquay, the college of St. Crantock owned the land round the Gannel estuary. On the south coast, Tywardreath possessed a number of small manors, besides the livings, round St. Austell and Fowey. Farther down, the bishop had large possessions on both sides of the estuary of the Fal; he owned Penryn and the land where Falmouth stands; here and in the Lizard district Glasney college possessed many of the livings. In the far west, the Land's End area was dominated by the royal foundation of St. Buryan, with its dean and prebendaries. Many of these lands went back in the hands of the Church to time immemorial, before the Norman Conquest, before the time even of the Saxons, to the dim dark ages of Celtic Christianity. Perhaps it is not surprising therefore if simple people did not welcome the Reformation, it meant such a breach with so long a past. If they consulted their interest, it should have been popular; for Cornwall had little reason to regret the Reformation. Yet, such is the irrationality, the conservatism of human beings, that some did.

CHAPTER VIII

THE DISSOLUTION OF THE MONASTERIES

THE Cornish religious houses were not large as monasteries went, notably in Somerset and Gloucestershire, to take only the west. There was nothing even to equal the rich abbey of Tavistock and Plympton Priory, each of which had an income of over £900. Yet the Cornish houses were not inconsiderable, seen in relation to the county, where everything was on a smaller scale, estates, gentry, farms, churches, landscape. Their properties were a factor of some importance in the total economy of the county, even if they did not occupy as large an area relatively as in some others. There were three houses with an income of over £200, which thus escaped the Act suppressing the smaller monasteries in 1536: Launceston Priory with a net revenue of £354 0s. 11¼d., Bodmin with £270 0s. 11d., and St. Germans with £227 4s. 8d.[1] Then there was the little Benedictine priory of Tywardreath with £123 9s. 3d. Glasney college at Penryn, a college of secular canons and vicars choral, enjoyed a gross income of £210 13s. 2d.; the college of Crantock with its dean and prebendaries, £89 15s. 8d.; the deanery of St. Buryan, £58 7s. 11d. In addition there was St. Michael's Mount, served by an archpriest and two chaplains, which was a cell of Sion Abbey and worth £33 6s. 8d. Upon Tresco in the Scilly Islands was the cell of St. Nicholas which belonged to Tavistock and was served by one or two monks; similarly Plympton had a cell at St. Anthony-in-Roseland. Probus church had a vicar and five prebends, with an income of £32 6s. 4d.; St. Endellion a rector with three prebends, worth £25; St. Teath with three or four, worth £26 3s. 0d.[2] But these last were only parish churches with a peculiarity. There were, besides, a Franciscan church at Bodmin and a Dominican at Truro. Such were the religious establishments of Cornwall, monastic and collegiate; the chantry foundations in the parish churches will be dealt with later.

The three larger houses were Augustinian; their inmates were not in the strict sense monks, but canons wearing black habits like the Benedictines, living under a regular rule. In practice it was as near as made no difference. Perhaps there was a certain distinction of class: Augustinians were apt as a

[1] These figures are those of the *Valor Ecclesiasticus* (II. 392 foll.). The later surveys of the Crown officials increased these figures by some 25 per cent.
[2] Oliver, *Ecclesiastical Antiquities*, II. 187-92.

whole to be of rather a lower social level; it is noteworthy how few people there were of any distinction in the Cornish houses — in fact, apart from one or two priors, none at all. Beginning as these orders did as a reform and a return to stricter rule, by the time of the Reformation the Augustinians were the most indifferent, where the Carthusians and Cistercians were the most devoted.[1] There were none of the latter in Cornwall.

The Augustinian houses had been refounded in the great religious age of the twelfth century when the early Bishops of Exeter were getting their diocese in order. But they all went back to a remoter past. St. Germans had been the seat of the Cornish see from 926, when it had been founded by Athelstan, to 1043 when it was united to Crediton, to be removed later to Exeter.[2] It had probably been a Celtic monastery before this. Certainly Bodmin had been. When Leland was there about 1540, he wrote: 'There hath been monks, then nuns, then secular priests, then monks again and last canons regular in St. Petroc's church'; and that about describes its history.[3] It had begun at Padstow (Petrocstow) with St. Petroc himself, but was moved inland because of the Danes ravaging the coast.[4] Athelstan refounded it with secular priests, instead of the Celtic monks and nuns side by side, as he did elsewhere, at Launceston, St. Germans, St. Buryan, Crantock, after his conquest of Cornwall. Then Bishop Warelwast (1107-38) reconstituted Bodmin with canons regular. A new priory church was built some 100 yards to the east of the parish church, across the road, and the shrine of St. Petroc shifted to it. At Launceston the same thing happened. Warelwast reconstituted the priory away from the parish church of St. Stephen on its hill, on a fertile agreeable spot in the meadows by the little river Kensey.[5] St. Germans was converted to the Augustinian rule by Bishop Bartholomew at the end of the twelfth century. Sometime in the same century the smaller priory of Tywardreath was founded by one of the Cardinhams as a dependent cell of the abbey of Angers.[6] Hence as an alien priory it was taken into the hands of the Crown by Henry V, restored as a Benedictine house and counted henceforth as a royal foundation. St. Michael's Mount, which had been a dependency of Mont St. Michel, was handed over to Sion Abbey.[7] St. Buryan and St. Crantock were royal foundations dating from the time of Athelstan's reconstitution of them.[8] Glasney, the latest in time, was founded

[1] cf. Baskerville, *The English Monks and the Suppression of the Monasteries*, 148.
[2] Henderson, *Records of the Church and Priory of St. Germans*, 2-5.
[3] *Leland's Itinerary* (ed. Toulmin-Smith), I. 180.
[4] Henderson, *Concerning Bodmin Priory*, 2-5; and *Essays*, 219-28.
[5] Peter, *Histories of Launceston and Dunheved*, 3-5.
[6] Oliver, *Monasticon*, 33.   [7] Taylor, *St. Michael's Mount*, 35.
[8] Henderson, *Essays*, 96-7.

as a college of secular canons, under the same statutes as Exeter cathedral, by Bishop Bronescombe in 1264.[1]

The medieval history of these houses was an undistinguished one — appropriately enough for institutions whose main function was the life of prayer. Their quiet routine proceeded through the ages punctuated with occasional excitements, quarrels over relics or over the election of a prior, disputes with the townsmen over their rights; they never produced anybody of importance. We are fortunate in possessing a survey of them on the threshold of our period, while they still were flourishing and all was going on as it had been for centuries — no question of dissolution: a starting-point for the investigation of their last years. In the interval after Fox's translation to Bath and Wells, in 1492, Archbishop Morton held a visitation of the Exeter diocese by his commissary Robert Sherborne, Treasurer of Hereford Cathedral.[2] He was at Launceston on the vigil of St. Peter and St. Paul, where the prior and sub-prior reported that all was well, but that they were ten in number where they should be thirteen. A monk who had been professed two years ago had left the house without the prior's leave; the latter was to make strict inquiry for him. Dan William Symon said that the sub-prior lately sold a silver chalice worth £4 at Exeter, had given a law-book worth 10 marks to Master Thomyow, and had wasted a great many other goods and valuables of the house, putting divers ornaments in pledge, in particular a furnished bed to a man of Tavistock. This monk must have had some dislike of the sub-prior; it is all the small change of monastic life. The commissary ordered these matters to be reformed.

The Sunday after he was at Bodmin. Here there were similar small complaints. The sub-prior deposed that they were not in full number, which by old custom was ten; one monk refused to bear the lantern as he was obliged to do, or to obey the usages and commands of the Order. Another canon said that certain alms were wont of old to be distributed in the cloister and now are in the porch of the hall; there used to be an almoner appointed for the purpose. Dan David Brooke said that there used to be a priest to serve perpetually in the chapel of the Blessed Virgin and now there is not. Another said that there used to be a candle burning before her image. It is all, what we should expect, very small beer. There were seven monks in all, including the prior.

At Crantock the following Wednesday, the dean was sworn to continual residence according to the statutes; the eight prebendaries were supposed to

[1] Peter, *Glasney Collegiate Church*, 3-6.
[2] There is a photostat of the original from Morton's Register at Lambeth in Henderson, XI. There is a study of this visitation by Canon Claude Jenkins in 'Morton's Register', *Tudor Studies presented to A. F. Pollard*, 60-2.

THE DISSOLUTION OF THE MONASTERIES

be in deacon's orders at the time of their collation. They had their proper complement of four vicars, but were supposed to have two or three boys and one clerk for the sustentation of the prebendaries; at present they had not one, but were to remedy this by Michaelmas. No doubt the fewer they were, the more there was to go round; this consideration must have been an inducement to keep numbers low in all such institutions. At Glasney the provost, Master John Oby, said that they did not say matins at midnight according to the statutes. He was ordered to bring up the vicars to the statutory thirteen; they were at present only seven. Among the non-residents, who have a whole section to themselves, several did not appear; the houses of three of them were not in good repair, in fact almost destroyed, and the fruits of their prebends were accordingly sequestrated. One prebendary said that they were bound to distribute 40s. a year among the poor, and now they do not give a penny. They one and all agreed that the faculties now coming from the church were not sufficient to provide this alms. One of the vicars said that the statutes were not publicly read and that their steward did not pay them what he received. They were given till Michaelmas to provide themselves with new copies of the statutes. Master William Breberveth, who was also vicar of Gwinnear, was told to reside in his own vicarage.

At Tywardreath there were seven monks, including the prior, who said that all was well except that Richard Haringdon of Lampetho detained a tenement worth 20s. a year from them and had done so for four years. The prior of St. Germans deposed that a recently professed monk had left the priory and gone they knew not whither. They were seven in number there and all was well.

So far things were going on much as they had done for so many years before. But the mechanism was running down, the vital impulse of monasticism flagging. Within a few years the biting wit of Erasmus, himself a confrère of the Cornish Augustinians and the most distinguished figure the Order ever produced, would undermine the respect of European opinion for the institution; while the German princes, aided by the resounding voice of Luther, made a revolutionary onslaught upon the system. In England Wolsey himself set the precedent of expropriation with the suppression of a number of small houses to found his colleges. Economically they were rentiers living on their revenues,[1] and thus especially open to the hostility of the townsmen with their active commercial spirit, who found their maintenance of their passive property rights galling and cramping to enterprise. We find this clearly the case in Cornwall as elsewhere.

[1] Savine, *English Monasteries on the Eve of the Dissolution*, 125.

The picture of their condition that arises in our minds from the evidence is not that of the old popular view that they were dens of vice — whatever that may mean; but rather that they were antiquated, wellnigh useless corporations faltering to decay, such as society has to reform out of existence from time to time. Let us take the last years of Tywardreath for a case of gradual deliquescence. Prior Collins succeeded in 1506, having arranged for a good pension to his predecessor charged upon the tithes of St. Austell.[1] He proceeded to petition the Pope and Wolsey for licence to hold benefices to the value of £100 for the benefit of the convent on the plea of poverty and depredations from pirates in time of war owing to their proximity to the sea. He must have in part succeeded, for we knew that he held certain benefices.[2] But the convent can hardly have been in good condition, to judge from Oldham's injunctions upon his visitation in 1513: the prior was to exhibit a faithful statement of income and expenditure to the community once a year in the chapter-house; novices and others were to be instructed in grammar; no lay servant was to be employed who was not of approved character; none was to go out of the enclosure without leave of the prior, and then two by two; they were never to frequent taverns or converse with women, at least with those of suspect character, and on no account to admit them within the enclosure. These admonitions were to be read four times every year in the chapter-house. It was evidently necessary.

Some years later, in 1521, Bishop Veysey on visitation heard a very unfavourable account of them from almost every mouth.[3] He wrote that hardly a shadow of the rule of St. Benet appeared to be observed by them, of divine service, obedience or of the silence of the cloister; that it was more healthy not to enter into religion than daily break the rules they had professed. He enjoined upon them that they were to say matins a little after midnight as in other religious houses, that no brother was to leave the precincts without leave and then only with a companion; that all windows and places by which women might enter or brothers go out were to be closed. The vow of purity was to be strictly enforced. It is not difficult to see what the trouble was at Tywardreath. They were given till the last day of April to correct and reform the brothers notorious for incontinency.

Not unnaturally the authorities — Veysey, Cardinal Wolsey, the Earl of Devon to whom the King had resigned his rights of patronage — were anxious to get rid of the prior. The Cardinal wrote him, politely mentioning his good administration in times past, but suggesting that he should now resign of his own good will, thereby making sure of a pension such as he should

---

[1] Oliver, *Monasticon*, 35. [2] cf. above, p. 153 [3] Henderson, x. 302.

'have good cause to be contented with'.[1] The Earl of Devon wrote in no such polite tone, but desiring him 'the rather at this mine instance, and at this my request' to resign his place unto a protégé of the Earl's, who had been granted the next advowson by the King. This fortunate person, it was intended, was Dan Robert Hamlyn, monk of Tavistock who wrote the prior a couple of disingenuous letters which portray an unattractive side of the monastic character. The Cardinal and the Earl, who were his good friends, he wrote, did not intend to force the prior to resign; they were only considering his welfare, his great age, etc. But the prior was alarmed and not to be lulled into a sense of false security. Dan Robert wrote to say that he had never intended to depose him, but that if he were minded to resign, 'I would be content, ye to execute the active voice and I the passive, and so should ye and I pass our time merrily to the pleasure of God and to the wealth of the house. Sir, ye nor I have nor may have but the living of one man, nor no man has more in this world. Commonly they that have a competent living live more merrier than they that have much more. St. Ambrose saith . . .' and so on.

The prior, however, was not to be persuaded; nor did a visit from two gentlemen who were the Marquis's servants, with 'my friend William Kendall', move him, in spite of their threat 'if I would not so do, that there should such things be laid to me that I should leave it whether I would or no'. He answered them that he trusted 'my lord would continue my good lord, as he hath been in times past, as I have been and shall be his continual poor beadsman. But as to resign or put away from me that poor living that it hath pleased Almighty God to call me to, I intended not during my life nor never was minded to do'. Nor did he. Instead, he stirred up his friends at Exeter, the subdean and chancellor, and Sir Thomas Denys, his patron. At any rate the authorities got no further for the present, such was the *vis inertiae* of an obstinate old prior. Dan Robert had to content himself with something much better: the rich abbey of Athelney.[2]

Prior Collins held on for another nine years or so, getting more and more lax. How he attempted to avoid deposition even to the last may be seen from a case in the Court of Augmentations: he apparently borrowed £40 from William Kendall, who was bailiff of Fowey for the house, 'or else', said John Arundell of Trerice, 'the said prior had been like to be deposed of his room'.[3]

---

[1] This amusing correspondence is printed, but not dated, in Oliver, 45-6. But it must date to 1524-25, for in the course of it the Earl of Devon becomes Marquis of Exeter. He was created Marquis in 1525.

[2] Baskerville, 56.

[3] Augmentations: Misc. Books, 133.

Another witness followed this up by saying that he had delivered the money 'being all gold saving one groat' from Kendall to the prior, who told him to give it to two gentlemen of the King's household. But not even this saved him: he had to resign. It was not only old age that enfeebled him, but drink. Many years later, well on in the reign of Elizabeth, in a case concerning some of the priory lands, an ancient gardener aged about 90 gave evidence that 'he did well know Prior Collins and saith that he would be overcome with drink, and that after the said prior was deprived of the house of Tywardreath, one Sir Nicholas Guest sub-prior of St. Germans, was made prior of Tywardreath'.[1] Another old boy aged 80, who had been a wine-merchant's apprentice at Lostwithiel, remembered the prior's butler coming several times to his master's house 'to fetch divers bottles of wine . . . and then it was reported by divers credible persons that did well know the said prior that the said prior would be oftentimes overcome with drink'. There can be no doubt, from other evidences, that Collins was prevailed on to resign some two years before the suppression, i.e. about 1534; he was succeeded by the sub-prior of St. Germans, who upon the suppression was awarded a pension of £16, and afterwards took a benefice.[2] The old prior lived on till 1539, a visible embodiment of the decay of the old order. His tomb, with the pastoral cross carved upon it signifying the duties of the office which he so negligently performed, may be seen up-ended in the parish church of Tywardreath.

His senility did not prevent him from providing for his relations. We have seen with what tenacity of purpose he presented Collinses to the priory living of Fowey. Before the end of his rule he made out a beneficial lease for 90 years, which was doubtful in law, of some priory land to his cousin Nicholas Collins of Fowey.[3] It was dated 1530; but John Rashleigh said that the lease was 'in truth but a blank given by the said prior to his cousin Nicholas Collins and afterwards written in form of a lease, and then hanged in the smoke to the end the same should seem old'. It is not surprising that the Collinses have cut a fair figure in these parts ever since.

A few fragments from another case add some touches to our picture of the last years of this house. There was, as so frequently, a dispute over tithes, in this case the tithe-fish of Fowey.[4] It seems that the vicar enjoyed tithe-wool, tithe-lamb and smaller tithes, while those on corn and fish went to the priory. A barber at Lostwithiel gave evidence that when he was a scholar in the priory with one Thomas Reyne, chancel clerk, as his schoolmaster, and the fish used to be brought home by servants, 'at dinner times he

---

[1] Excheq. Depos. 31 Eliz. Hilary 24.   [2] L.P., XIII (2), 1520 (iii).
[3] Excheq. Depos. 31 Eliz. Hilary 24.   [4] ibid., 26 Eliz. Easter 14.

was appointed by his schoolmaster to keep the tithe fish brought home when it was laid forth in the sun to be dried for the provision of the said house'. A pleasant picture it is of the life of that house, of which hardly a scrap remains, standing as it did in the valley below the church, looking down the creek to the sea, the coast along the Gribbin covered in early summer with drifts of blue-bells and red campion, the bay itself, according to the story, sometimes echoing with the sound of bells which were never hung in the priory tower, for the ship which was bringing them from abroad went down in sight of it.

The evidence of the gradual running down of the monastic life is no less clear in the case of Launceston, the largest of the Cornish houses. The last years of this house were filled with a furious faction-fight between their newly-elected prior and a party among the canons, each side with its supporters in the town and among the west-country gentry, and clamouring for aid from the higher powers at Court.[1] It began with the election of John Shere, a comparatively young man of twenty-seven, as prior in 1534;[2] though it appears that his predecessor, Prior Baker, had resigned because he could not reduce the unruly brethren to obedience. The defeated party among the canons, who had hoped to elect William Gennys and were supported by William Kendall, the Marquis of Exeter's chief agent in Cornwall, at once petitioned the King.[3] They complained that Prior Baker, who during his rule (1521-34) had brought the monastery out of £1000 debt, had new roofed the church throughout and garnished it with copes, vestments, altar-cloths and organs to the value of £400, had been deposed by the instant labour of Sir William Courtenay of Powderham and the chancellor of Exeter. That these had promised them a free election and then compromitted it so that Shere was advanced, 'which not three years before was chamber lad to the same Baker before prior'. They charged him with bringing the house in debt for 1000 marks within six months, selling woods and pledging jewels to meet the same, and taking 'other men's money which was laid in pawn in the common coffer of the said house for the indemnity of certain pensions'. The bill of complaint, asking for Shere's deposition, was presented by Kendall to the King, who ordered Bishop Veysey to examine into the matter in January 1535.[4]

The latter deputed Sir John Chamond, who was chief steward of the house, to take evidence at Launceston in February.[5] It is clear that the chief

[1] For the full story of this v. Robbins, 'The Closing Days of Launceston Priory' in *Devon and Cornwall Notes and Gleanings*, IV.
[2] Henderson, X. 27.   [3] *L.P.*, VIII. 224 (2).   [4] ibid., 92.   [5] ibid., 224 (1).

charge against Shere was that his election was simoniacal and procured by a compact with Sir William Courtenay. John Pearce, a townsman who was examined, said that he knew of no money that had passed nor was it spoken of in the town, nor did he know of the election until he heard the bells of the priory ring at the time; but afterwards when Sir William departed out of the town, the rumour ran that the prior had given money 'to have the room'. Men said too that he did not fulfil his covenants with the old prior but dealt unkindly with him, and that he 'occupied' some £60 that was left in gage for the pension of one Mr. John Cork, against which he had pledged a gold chalice.[1]

Meanwhile Kendall was at work at Launceston trying to get evidence against the prior. In February Veysey himself examined a number of witnesses upon questions put to them by Kendall.[2] The mayor, Thomas Hicks, denied that he had been 'laboured' by any one in favour of the prior, but admitted that he had been 'specially laboured and desired by his own natural brother, John Hicks, canon of Launceston, to the intent the same Sir William Courtenay should cause his brother, Sir John Hicks, to be prior there'. That was all very natural, but it did not come off. On the other hand he did stand bound to Sir William for a certain sum on behalf of the prior — he took it that it was in return for Sir William's charges in coming to Launceston for the election. The prior had also borrowed 150 marks after his election from John Wise; while Richard Carlyan, the pluralist vicar of Stratton, raised £20 from a friend to lend the prior 'as then destitute of money'. That too was a natural enough condition for a newly elected prior. But it looks as if some money had passed. Sir William Courtenay, writing to Cromwell in March about the similar conflict at Hartland where he was engaged on the side of the new abbot against Sir Thomas Arundell and the old one, took the opportunity of adding: 'Kendall makes many cracks in your name at Launceston.'[3]

In April the bishop came down and examined the prior and others in person; the results of the examination exonerated the prior but revealed the sad state of affairs in the convent.[4] The prior made it clear that Kendall's motive in all this was revenge for refusing to let him have the farm of the rectory of St. Thomas's, Launceston, at a rent far under its value. With

[1] These transactions are of interest in showing how to some extent monasteries performed the function of banks in those days. It was also customary to leave title-deeds and bonds in their care; cf. Baskerville, 33-5.
[2] *L.P.*, v. 837, where it is wrongly dated to 1531-2; the document obviously belongs here. cf. Robbins, loc. cit., 21.
[3] *L.P.*, VIII. 359.   [4] ibid., v, 837.

regard to his recalcitrant canons, he said that some of them 'living insolently' had fallen in debt in the town; on the advice of the archbishop's commissary he had posted a schedule on the church door asking the townsmen to let him know the debts of the brethren. Whereupon Sir William Gennys and others had pulled it down and would have slain him, for they had weapons in their chambers for the purpose; and for this he had committed them to prison according to the rules of the Order. The bishop himself stated that Gennys was noted to be of vicious living and little learning, and to have made simoniacal compacts and promises; the complainants confessed that they intended to have chosen him prior. Instead, the election had been compromitted to one John Stubbs, a priest, who had named Shere and he had been installed with accustomed order; whether it was due to the inspiration of the Holy Ghost or the procurement of Sir William Courtenay, it was evidently better than by vote. Shere had occupied the office of steward within the priory and was commended by Sir Piers Edgcumbe, Sir John Chamond and other gentlemen. He was easily able to explain the pledging of the chalice and the sale of Bradbridge wood to meet the debts of the convent. These depositions Veysey forwarded to the Council.[1]

A week later, Sir William Courtenay, writing to Cromwell about the far worse state of affairs at Hartland owing to the negligence and feebleness of the late abbot, desired him to 'be good to my prior of Launceston which is troubled with that wretch Kendall and four or five of his unthrifty monks, which be as unthrifty as any be in England'.[2] Next month he wrote somewhat nervously defending himself and the prior: 'As touching any simony I promise you upon mine honesty he is guiltless; howbeit since the time that I made him I have had 200 marks of him, and as God shall help me without any promise of him or any man for him . . . And by my faith and troth I refused of other naughty persons of the said house £600, and £40 fee of one of the said canons to have made him, which is the greatest procurer of this business against the said prior: which is a naughty priest and of very ill conversation, which caused me to refuse it'.[3] Sir William's candour is very revealing: it leaves no doubt that it was he who made the election. He proceeded to attack the character of the prior's enemies, 'some of them burned in the hand': Sir Lamprey, for instance, had been turned out of the cure of Launceston by the prior because he was 'a common lecher and a maintainer of thieves'. Sir William said he had a near kinsman who had long been a thief: when the latter had stolen in Devon or Somerset he always repaired to this priest; when on two or three occasions he had been indicted at

---

[1] *L.P.*, VIII. 533.   [2] ibid., 569.   [3] ibid., 690.

Launceston, the priest bribed the parties to give no evidence; by this means he was said to be worth 100 marks.

Sir William Courtenay died at the end of that year, but his protégé triumphed; Gennys had to leave the monastery. The prior began a correspondence with Cromwell which was to stand him in good stead later. He wrote him a letter in January 1536, under the superscription 'Jesus' usual with such religious persons, asking for power to deal with the case of the vicar of Stratton.[1] This acquisitive priest, who was a brother of Prior Carlyan (1507-21) enjoyed in addition to his livings, one of them in the gift of the priory, a large pension of £13 6s. 8d. out of the priory manor of Launcestonland. The prior, who was getting things in order, wanted to put this right. He had certainly entered upon the right terms with Cromwell, for in October he wrote sending him his fee, 'for all my hope and trust consisteth in the continuance of your leanful favour and supportation'.[2] This was well, for in the very next year he had need of all his credit with the great man. In January 1537 his old enemies Kendall, Gennys and Lamprey, the appropriately named chaplain, got together and brought a renewed charge against him of dangerous political character.[3] This winter of 1536-37 was the interval between the two waves of the Pilgrimage of Grace, the very crisis of the Reformation in England. Gennys deposed before the aforesaid witnesses that on January 19th, when riding with his late prior between Okehampton and Launceston the latter had said 'that if the Northern men should continue rebellious against the King's grace, that a scholar of Oxford should show him that his grace should be in danger of his life, or else avoid his realm before the end of March next coming'. The prior was informed of the charge in the chamber chapel of the priory before witnesses on February 1st.

The prior recognized his danger and at once wrote to Cromwell protesting his innocence and that 'mine old mortal enemy never ceaseth to imagine my destruction, and hath now of late most devilishly invented and surmised a lie against me'.[4] Not content with writing he placed his case in the hands of Sir John Chamond and Richard Pollard, both of them men whose word Cromwell could rely on. And so Shere surmounted this new danger. For his help Chamond was granted an annuity of 26s. 8d. for life, in addition to the same amount which he received as steward of the priory lands.[5] In November 1538, the prior made out a patent for an annuity of £5 to Cromwell and his son Gregory for the term of their lives; but this was no doubt even more in anticipation of future reward than of past services.[6] It was

[1] *L.P.*, XII. (ii) App. 3.   [2] Robbins, 72.   [3] *L.P.*, XII. i, 298.
[4] ibid., XII. (ii) App. 3.   [5] Robbins, 74-5.   [6] ibid., 85.

almost *de rigueur* for the monasteries to make these gifts to the minister, in addition to all the gifts in kind, the fish, the congers, the hake, the delicacies, the jewels, for by now the monasteries were on their last legs, every day expecting the *coup de grâce*, and their heads were anxious for their future. 'I see this world is but every man to serve his turn,' said John Hussey wisely about this time: a characteristic Tudor sentiment; he was the confidential agent of Lord and Lady Lisle, and had good reason to know.[1] The prior of Bodmin was up to the same game, and had sent Cromwell a patent for £6 a year for life, the year before.[2] Neither the prior of Launceston nor his brother of Bodmin need have feared for their livings; it was the policy of the government to pay them generously, far too generously, for their compliance. On their surrender next year, Shere was awarded a pension of £100, and the prior of Bodmin £66 13s. 4d. a year, a good £1500 − £2000 a year in our currency.[3] Their acquiescence could have been purchased at less than half the price; and in view of the state of affairs in these houses, who can doubt that it was just as well that they should cease to exist?

Their heads had realized for some time now that their end was inevitable; it was a question of making good terms. Already at Launceston, Shere was making out nice little patents for his friends and relations, pensions upon lands, or profitable long-dated leases. Everybody was doing it everywhere. Richard Shere, the prior's brother, was steward within the priory for three years before the dissolution;[4] Henry Shere was bailiff of the priory borough of Newport Pound.[5] The prior made a lease of property at Overtrelabe to William and John Shere, and Lawrence their son.[6] His election had been very well worth while to his family. John Amadas, who was a King's serjeant and servant of Cromwell's, and therefore a useful person, received an annuity of £2 for himself and his son for their lives; just before the end, in January 1539, Richard Pollard received his reward from the prior in an annuity of 4 marks.[7] All these grants totalled up and made a drain upon the monastic resources before they were finally taken over. But there are other evidences of the slowing down of the machine. In a case of the year 1564, concerning the water-mills along the little river Kensey that stood two outside the priory gate and one within, one of the former monks turns up to give evidence, now an old man of 70.[8] The witnesses agreed that during Prior Shere's time, all the last five years of the priory, the mill within had decayed out of use, where before Prior Baker had ground his corn for the

---

[1] *L.P.*, XI. 47.   [2] ibid., XII. i, 194.   [3] ibid., XIV. 361, 384.
[4] Excheq. Depos. 6 Eliz. Easter 2.   [5] *Valor Eccles.*, II. 403.
[6] Excheq. Special Com. 527.   [7] Robbins, 85.
[8] Excheq. Depos. 6 Eliz. Easter 2.

provision of the house; and in Prior Carlyan's time, before that, the water went from there to a tucking-mill which was also the prior's then and leased out. But latterly all corn for the house had been ground outside the gate and 'was borne in and out in a great willow basket between two men upon a staff'. With that image of the convent life slowing down, if that is the word where there was so much quarrelling, with the picture of the brethren in the almuces of grey fur which they were so anxious to obtain permission from Bishop Oldham to wear in choir,[1] like the canons of Exeter Cathedral, they disappear from our view.

Conditions at Bodmin were not essentially dissimilar, though there the disputes were more varied, and with the outer world. At the same time there is some evidence of faction within in the last years, though it was prevented from coming to a head. We have already seen what conflict raged between the townsmen and the prior, over the vicar and their respective rights, during the rule of Prior Vyvyan.[2] When that memorable man lay on his deathbed, so it was said in evidence many years later, he declared to his servant Nicholas Prideaux that 'none of his brethren, being canons of the said priory, was meet and able to be prior there and to succeed him'.[3] According to Prideaux, the dying prior desired him to do all he could to get Thomas Mundy (alias Wandsworth), then a canon of Merton Abbey in Surrey, elected as his successor. Which Prideaux proceeded to do. But meanwhile by the 'great labour' of Sir John Arundell of Lanherne and others, John Symons was elected, according to custom in the chapel of the Virgin, and on July 6th his election was confirmed by Veysey.[4] He did not last for more than nine months; in the following spring he had to make way for Mundy, who had Cromwell's support, and resigned on a good pension of £40.[5] But he had just time to assert the rights of his house in regard to the tithe upon fish landed at Padstow, and this led to a series of informative cases.

It appears that the fish tithes of Padstow had been leased by the convent to Christopher Tredennick for forty years at £4 per annum.[6] Some time before his death, he made over his lease to his young children. On November 4th, 1533, the prior had caused Thomas Coles, one of his monks, Nicholas Prideaux, William Vyvyan, Richard Sawle and a body of yeomen and labourers, some sixteen in all, to pounce upon the young Tredennicks, seize

---

[1] Oliver, *Lives*, 23.   [2] v. above, pp. 153-4.
[3] Excheq. Depos. 18 Eliz. Trin. I. Cornwall.
[4] Henderson, x. 25.   [5] Oliver, op. cit., 17.
[6] Star Chamber Proc. Henry VIII, II. 18/25.

their father's lease of the tithes and a quantity of fish, 6 barrels of white herring worth £4, and 20 couples of hake, mullet, etc., worth £4. On November 24th the prior in person with the same following of servants, made a more interesting catch.[1] It had been the custom at Padstow 'time out of mind' for some of the inhabitants to make joint-stock voyages to Ireland for fish, dividing the proceeds among those who had set out the ships on their return. In September 1533 John Carmynow set forth the tenth part of three ships, the *Joan*, the *Anthony*, the *Nicholas*, with 28 bushels Cornish of salt, 7 bushels of flour, 3 hogsheads and 3 barrels of beer, and 33s. sterling in ready money. On their return, the prior's band entered the ships and took 6 barrels of white herring, 400 hake, etc., to the value of £7. John Carmynow was determined to get something of his own back; and on December 3rd he took his opportunity, attacking Richard Sawle, the prior's servant, with a band of seven, and wresting from him £2 worth of fish.[2] Sawle claimed that Carmynow was 'a man of great possessions and kindred' within the county and that he himself was but a poor man unable to sue him at common law. The case came before Star Chamber. The prior was determined to assert his rights; it meant that there was no love lost between the priory and people like Carmynow, who belonged to the class which was to prove most dangerous and most hostile to the monasteries.

In the spring of 1534 Prideaux's efforts with Cromwell and others to procure Mundy's election were successful. It may be that the impulse came from Cromwell himself, spurred on by Prideaux, rather than from the dead Prior Vyvyan who can have been very little out of Cornwall; for Mundy was a member, if perhaps an illegitimate one,[3] of a well-known family in the city of London which had provided a Lord Mayor and must have been known to Cromwell with his contacts in the city, while Prideaux was an able and aspiring lawyer of an old Devonshire family. In February Cromwell wrote to Veysey insisting upon Mundy's preferment, and the bishop wrote from Ludlow, where he kept his state as Lord President of the Council of Wales, to the prior of Bodmin to make way for Mundy.[4] The latter was evidently an able man of business. He was faced with a demand from Cromwell to reward his servant with a grant of the fish-tithes of Padstow. Mundy replied that he had moved his brethren, in the presence of Sir William Godolphin, in the matter, but that they were unable to comply, for

---

[1] Star Chamber Proc. Henry VIII, vol. IX, no. 44.
[2] ibid., Henry VIII, II; bundle 29, no. 55.
[3] I think this is the most probable explanation of the fact that he is usually referred to as Wandsworth, his brother as Mundy.
[4] *L.P.*, VI. 169.

the larger part of them was already granted and the rest reserved for the maintenance of the house.[1] Instead, however, they had given Cromwell's servant an annuity of 5 marks, and they sent his master eight congers, 'and if anything in Cornwall can do your pleasure you may command me'. The prior takes advantage of this approach to complain of the state of the house, 'oppressed with debts and daily resort'. We need not take very seriously his plea that 'it lies common trade of the shire near the coast whereby ambassadors and strangers pass': that merely leads to a request for the appropriation of more benefices to maintain hospitality, since 'in the days of my predecessors worshipful men of the shire and others at sessions and on commissions were entertained here'. Certain suffrages and masses are celebrated in their church, he says, for Henry VII who promised to appropriate Lanteglos to them; he asks Cromwell now to use his endeavours with the King to carry out his father's intentions. It is rather surprising to see the monasteries stretching out their dead hand at this late date for yet more benefices. It does not appear that Mundy was successful.

The prior's troubles were but beginning. He wrote next year to Cromwell that 'through your wisdom I am in quietness with my brethren and trust they will be conformable'.[2] This happy state of affairs was not lasting. No wonder Cromwell, who knew more than anyone alive what was going on in the monasteries, was making up his mind to bring them to an end. There was also trouble with Roger Arundell of Helland, son of Sir John, who naturally resented their defeat at Cromwell's hands and Mundy's intrusion. He maintained a faction among the canons against the prior and supported the townsfolk in their depredations upon the priory weir. 'He hath of late fetched one of my canons out of my house with violence, and is yet out in apostasy' — the prior wrote, his indignation getting the better of his grammar. 'He has issued a commission to pluck down a weir belonging to this house, and will do so unless we obtain a supersedeas from you. He maintains a number of disorderly persons, who boast in taverns "that it is not Cromwell that shall rule their master".' The prior sent on an opinion of Dr. John Tregonwell, the eminent Cornish civil lawyer who was much employed later in the business of the suppression — an opinion which was entirely favourable to the priory's rights in the matter: an episode which shows that Tregonwell was not biased against the monasteries.[3]

But they were on their last legs now and difficulties naturally increased for them. The suppression of the smaller monasteries in the spring of 1536, with the provision which the Act made for 'capacities' to those monks

[1] L.P., VII. 222.   [2] ibid., IX. 908.   [3] cf. Baskerville, 129.

who wished to leave religion and go out into the world in some more useful occupation, added to the restiveness of those who remained in the larger houses. The evidence shows conclusively that the large majority of monks wished to leave the monasteries. Of the forty-two monks and canons in seven small Sussex houses, of which we have a report, 'no fewer than thirty-eight wished to have "capacities", and only four to remain in religion'. Mr. Baskerville concludes, 'it can hardly be pretended that zeal for religious life was rife in the county'.[1] Nor was it any more in Cornwall; though, we must remember, Augustinians were the most indifferent of all. Of the five or six monks of Tywardreath at the time of its suppression, not one chose to continue in religion and be drafted to some larger house still remaining; nor, to do them justice, should we expect them to, from what we have learned of their conduct.

On May 28th, 1536, the prior wrote to Mr. Lokes, a mercer in Cheapside and a confidant of Cromwell, a letter which depicts very clearly the state of affairs in the convent.[2] His canons lived very unthriftily, and were very discontented with the injunctions the bishop had laid upon them at his visitation — though these were no harder to keep than their own rule. Most of them intended to depart with capacities without his consent; one of them had purchased a capacity without his licence, and he had stopped him from going: 'if he allowed him to go, he would never have a canon to abide with him' — a most illuminating sentence. Roger Arundell maintained their cause and threatened to bring him before the Council for not allowing the monk to go. He asks Mr. Lokes to place this before Cromwell and to refer any complaints to the gentlemen of the county, for he is too much in debt to be able to come to London. Lastly, Arundell had procured a commission to pull down a weir which had belonged to the house this 400 years.

The trouble with the town was coming to a head: no doubt the townspeople were quick to take advantage of the weakened position of the lord prior. In July he had to write to Cromwell to favour his house, 'for his neighbours of Bodmin would undo it without his help'.[3] They make common the woods and waters which have been several to his house since King John's time. They forbid his fishing in his water, have cut his net twice this summer, and last night, nine or ten persons well appointed with weapons, took the fish from his servants by force and put them in jeopardy of their lives saying that 'I bear me bold on the Secretary, willing him to mend it if he could'. They have fetched stray cattle out of his pound, burnt his weir and so on; nor can he get any remedy at sessions, unless Cromwell writes

[1] cf. Baskerville, 145.   [2] L.P., x. 981.   [3] ibid., XI. 133.

to the rulers of the country to see these misdoers punished: otherwise he will not be able to remain in the country. He mentions that he has helped Cromwell's servant, the bearer, in conveying his hawks and hounds, two falcons, three merlins, a brace of greyhounds, 'a fair dog and a mean bitch'.

The all-receiving Secretary was also being lobbied by the townsmen, who petitioned that all liberties and franchises in the borough, with rights over rivers and streams belonged to the King, and desiring 'some remedy against the cruel vexation and trouble that of long time we have had and sustained, and now have by the priors of Bodmin who have been there as lords of the leet, and so take unlawfully much profit by the same'.[1] Cromwell sent down a commission, very lovingly worded, to the leading gentlemen of the county to examine into the matter in February 1537; and as the result of their labours, an agreement was concluded.[2] The prior granted the mayor and burgesses, a court leet and view of frank pledge at a rent of £4, licence to build a market-house and to hold a fair at Berry Tower; in return they renounced their claim to fetch wood from the prior's wood at Dunmere. It cannot escape notice that the town had largely won.

The suppression of the larger monasteries was now well on the way. The defeat of the Pilgrimage of Grace in 1536-37 made it only a matter of time and convenience. After the crisis the air was full of rumours; it was for the prior to look to the future. In January he wrote to Cromwell sending him a patent of £6 for life, 'trusting you will continue my good lord, as ye have ever done, and remember me and my poor brethren to the King's commissioners at their coming into Cornwall for our poor living'.[3] He was already, like the Wise Steward in the Gospel, making his own dispositions, turning his business capacity to good account on behalf of his family and friends, disposing of convent leases in their favour to such an extent as to leave a permanent mark in the rooting of the Prideaux family in Cornwall. The evidence of his activities in this direction, which is fuller than in most cases, makes significant study for the history of the English Reformation.

It seems that Nicholas Prideaux was his chief agent, and perhaps inspirer, here as in his election: that gentleman certainly did well for himself the day he rode to London to bring it about. He received his reward with a lease of the great tithes of the four parishes, Bodmin, St. Minver, Cubert and Padstow, for thirty years at a rent of £73 per annum.[4] Three years later, in August 1538, the prior granted him a further 78 years from the expiry of the first lease, at a rent of £56 12s. 10d. This was so much less than on the first

[1] Wallis, *Bodmin Register*, 293-4.   [2] ibid., 294-7.
[3] *L.P.*, XII. i, 194.   [4] Excheq. Depos. 18 Eliz. Trin. 1.

lease, for Prideaux had claimed the tithe-fish of Padstow and the oblations at St. Cadoc's as coming within it; on dropping the claim, he got the second lease at so much less rent. Prideaux's former servant gave evidence of all this in 1576, since he had carried 'the same lease to the vicars of the four parishes aforesaid, which was read to the parishioners', and he had been present in the parlour of the priory in 1538 when the prior before his dinner delivered the second lease to his master, and after dinner granted the manor of Bodiniel to Sir John Chamond. The prior must have had a good digestion that day.

Prideaux was getting the second lease at below its value; while the fact that it was to run for so many years meant that the usual fines on renewal would not be paid. This was equivalent to making him a present of several hundreds of pounds in all. These long leases granted by the monasteries towards the end, by way of endowing friends and relations, meant a great loss to the Crown on taking them over; and an act was passed invalidating grants made within a year of the surrender. But grantees clung tenaciously to their property: there was no separating them from what they clasped so fast: they proved as slippery as eels in evading detection: they covered up their tracks to admiration — after all they were not lawyers for nothing — and when hard put to it they could always ante-date the leases and smoke them so that they looked old, as at Tywardreath. Besides the government was not over-anxious to run them down: it needed their support. In the event they mostly got away with their loot. Upon them rests the greatness of modern England.

This was by no means the end of the gains of the Prideaux family: Nicholas and the prior together constructed a whole dynastic structure, knit by various marriages between their families and solidly founded upon the acres and in the tithes of the priory. When the prior came to write his will in his later troubles in 1548, he wrote that Nicholas Prideaux 'oweth me a great sum of money as he knoweth in conscience and was the setter forth of all these foresaid bargains', and added a little sadly that if he would testify the truth and help carry out his will, paying his true servant, Richard Vele, mason, a small annuity, 'as he is in conscience bound to do . . . I clearly forgive him and discharge him and his conscience of all his debts and other matters betwixt him and me'.[1] What passages between them this laconic reference must cover up, from the time of his election forward! For Humphrey Prideaux, Nicholas's brother, the prior had disbursed and laid out £145 at divers times, which he agreed to remit to him upon condition that his

[1] P.C.C. 19 More.

179

nephew William Mundy should marry Humphrey's daughter, Elizabeth, as soon as she came to lawful age. Then too, Humphrey's son William Prideaux, married the prior's niece, Joan Mundy, daughter of his elder brother John, whom he brought into Cornwall and to whom he made a long lease for ninety-nine years of the manor of Rialton.[1] That henceforward for a century or so, became the family seat of the Mundys. To the happy couple, William and Joan, the prior granted the manor of Padstow, with all its appurtenances and rights, including wreck of the sea and Gulland Rock and Garth Wood, and the advowson, for ninety years, at the low rent of £10 7s. 8d. This grant was allowed later by the Court of Augmentations, though it was made but a few months before the surrender. Nicholas Prideaux was already in possession of the fish-tithe of Padstow, in addition to everything else: he does not seem to have paid any fine upon receiving it, as was usual. By a later transaction, in 1545, along with John Pope, a rich speculator in monastic lands, Nicholas Prideaux purchased the fee-simple of Padstow outright and made it their property.[2] And so their patrimony was built up. Nicholas's motives were purely dynastic; he was a bachelor himself, and his nephew was to carry on the family there. In the next generation they built their Elizabethan house upon the hill looking down over the little town and across the lovely expanse of water of that harbour. They have been there ever since.

Another niece of the prior's, Katherine Mundy, was to marry Lawrence Kendall, and upon that condition they were granted the manor of Withiel with the advowson of the church, for ninety-nine years. In addition the prior made them some small bequests in his will. Truly the priory was a marvellous milch-cow for them.

But other people had to be squared, too, or rendered complacent. It was said that the under-steward of the priory would not be a party to these dubious leases; he was therefore displaced by John Tubbe, who received a grant of the manor of Fosnewth for his compliance, though to the day of his death he never paid a sum of £40 which he owed to the prior, probably for this grant.[3] Sir John Chamond had only paid £10 out of £40 which he owed the prior, almost certainly for the grant of the manor of Bodiniel. After the Dissolution Chamond advanced a claim to the woods on the west side of Dunmere as belonging to the manor, as well as those on the east. In fact they belonged to the manor of Pendewey. But he forced Roger Tollet 'to swear against his conscience touching the manor of Bodiniel and the fishing in Dunmere and Allen waters, threatening him that if he

[1] Maclean, *Trigg Minor*, I. 136-7.   [2] *L.P.*, xx. 282; 19, 52.   [3] P.C.C. 19 More.

had not sworn so he should have lost his living and not have remained in the country. Whereof he often repented continually to his dying day'.[1]

There were other grants, too, like the annuity of £4 to Dr. John de Coloribus for his good and faithful service to the prior and convent.[2] But not all these transactions passed without difficulty or comment. To get Withiel Lawrence Kendall had been reduced to promising the brethren a large sum, which needless to say they did not receive.[3] The prior had some difficulty in getting the convent's assent to his transactions. Years after, the scene was described by one of the surviving canons: how the prior had 'called his brethren together in the dortor-house where the coffer that the convent seal was in lay'; taking it out of the chest, the prior desired his brethren to seal 'certain writings which he set forth out of his bosom'.[4] The sub-prior, Richard Oliver, was unwilling and was reviled by the prior. The latter reasoned with the brethren that if 'the convent stand, these writings shall stand for none effect', and that it was better 'that the gentlemen of the country should be the better for the same rather than any stranger'. (No doubt, where Prideaux and Kendalls were concerned.) But the prior evinced a better reason still when he paid £5 to each of the brethren for sealing the writings, which were never read to them. Upon that they went further and sealed various blanks to please the prior. Opposition was stilled by this, and the promise of £20 each if the deeds held good, moreover the advowsons of the priory were shared out among them, the sub-prior receiving that of Padstow for his compliance. And sure enough we find him in time enjoying the vicarage of Padstow after the Dissolution, upon the kind, but surely not unrewarded, presentation of Dr. Tregonwell.[5] So all was arranged.

The feeling about these leases may be glimpsed from a scrap of reported conversation between Nicholas Glyn, who wanted to buy Margaret Wood of the prior, and Nicholas Prideaux who got it. After the surrender, Prideaux who wanted to propitiate Glyn offered him a part of the wood; the latter replied: 'I am afraid to bargain, for fear of the statute, for you know, Mr. Prideaux, that I do know how the case standeth.' Prideaux, annoyed by this, replied: 'Sir, if ye be at that point, do what ye can.'[6]

After this tale, complete as it is in its revelation of the methods of disposing of monastic property, it may come as something of a surprise to learn that Prior Mundy was a convinced and even a devoted Catholic, who later ran

[1] Excheq. Com. & Depos. 20 Eliz. 525.
[2] Early Chanc. Proc. File 1207, no. 33.
[3] Maclean, I. 136.   [4] Excheq. Com. & Depos. 20 Eliz. 525.
[5] v. below, p. 209.   [6] Maclean, I. 138.

the risk of his life for the sake of his convictions.[1] Whether it were repen-
tance or no — his will shows how anxious he was that his soul should be
prayed for — this fact should upset some preconceived notions about the
nature of the Reformation in England.

Of St. Germans there is little evidence, and we may presume therefore
that all was well. It seems to have been well-conducted under the rule of its
last prior, Robert Swymmer, who bore rule there from 1509 right up to the
surrender thirty years later.[2] Nicholas Guest, the cellarer and sub-prior,
was an inmate of the house for twenty-eight years before he was drafted to
Tywardreath to replace the bibulous Collins two years before its dissolution: he must have been a respectable person.[3] In consequence there
seem to have been no faction-fights within the house — at least, none that
left any evidence. They had their little troubles occasionally, like everybody
else, over letting their lands. In 1519, John Seymour of Launceston complained that the prior and Guest and others had assaulted him at St. Germans,
imprisoned him in the prior's house for twenty-four hours and taken his purse
and money from him; and that they had entered his tenement at Landulph,
which had been leased him by the previous prior.[4] Swymmer denied that
it had been; the convent was evidently capable of standing up for itself.

In 1534 there were seven all told who acknowledged the Royal
Supremacy here; in 1539 at the surrender they were eight; the only Cornish
house to show an improved position in the interval.[5]

It was here at St. Germans that there took place in the autumn of 1538,
when the monasteries were going down all over the country, a conversation
at the prior's board which gives us as revealing a glimpse as any anywhere,
of the state of mind and feeling with which the religious changes were
regarded: the suspension of judgment, the mixture of apprehension and
part-approval, the enthusiastic agreement of some, the opposition of others.[6]
The famous friar and poet, Alexander Barclay, had been preaching in honour
of the Blessed Virgin, though not so much — so William Dynham, another
visitor, thought — 'to the edifying of his audience as his demeanour was
next day, I heard, to their destruction'. So the latter put certain questions
to him at supper for the benefit of the audience. 'After a sudden dump he
brake silence as a man that had spoken too well (and yet a friar in a somewhat

---

[1] v. below, p. 207.   [2] Oliver, *Monasticon*, 3.
[3] Augmentations: Misc. Books 118, 231-3.
[4] Star Chamber Proc. Henry VIII, bundle 22, 353.
[5] Deputy Keeper's Report, VII. App. 2. 9; VIII. App. 2.
[6] *L.P.*, XIII. ii. 596.

honester weed), and glorified himself.' He protested that he would not preach any new things not set out by the King and his Council. Dynham led him on, wondering what he meant when all men of literature and judgment knew that 'our so Christian a Prince and his Council set forth no new thing but the gospel of Christ and the sincere verity thereof'. Barclay replied: 'I would to God that at least the laws of God might have as much authority as the laws of the realm.' Dynham asked him what he meant. Barclay said: 'Nothing'; but he added that men were too busy pulling down images without special commandment of the Prince. Dynham replied that he knew of none except such as idolatry was committed unto and reminded him of St. Margaret Pattens' Rood. (Which had been exposed to the people as a manifest fraud, and so was of propaganda-value to the government.) The company did not much like this, but they tolerated it 'for the intent and good fact thereof'. Barclay asked, What followed? And when Dynham put the question to him, he said they knew how many tenements and some people were burnt in consequence. Dynham took advantage of this to push his attack home: 'What, Barclay? Here is somewhat moved; ye have a versatile ingeyne, that were ye so slipper as an eel, here will I hold you. Would you infect this audience with that opinion, that God for such cause plagued them? Your cankered heart is disclosed. My true little stomach, with reverence of the prior and his board, must be opened lest it break. You are, Barclay, a false knave and a dissembling friar. You get no pence might I rule here. You seek your own profit vocal to hinder the truth more than unity to set forth the true and princely endeavour of our most Christian King and of his Church Supremest Head's most laudable enterprises; whereof I trust thou shalt hear.'

Dynham, of course, wrote off to Cromwell. Nothing seems to have happened to Barclay, though Latimer heard of his preaching in Cornwall and Devon and reported it to the Secretary; in the end Barclay conformed, like most other people. But the scene is very suggestive: the attitude and provenance of the two disputants, the credulity on one part, the sycophancy on the other, the fear: it is not unlike the atmosphere of contemporary Germany.

There were two houses of friars in Cornwall: the Franciscans at Bodmin and the Dominicans at Truro. Little enough is known of their history, though rather more of the former than of the latter. They were chiefly engaged in preaching to the poor, ministering to the sick, hearing people's confessions: theirs was missionary work among poor people, rather like the Salvation Army to-day. They were essentially popular in character; many were the bequests, usually small amounts, made to them, and greater people liked to be buried in their churches. In the Grey Friars at Bodmin there were several tombs of the Peverell family.[1] When William of Worcester was here in 1478, they regarded Edmund Earl of Cornwall as their founder, and they kept the obits of several Carmynows, Peverells and Sergeaux, who were benefactors, and of Walter Stapledon, Bishop of Exeter, as a principal benefactor.[2] At Truro the Black Friars kept the obits of a Reskymer — who seems to have been held to be a founder — a Blanchminster, a Beauchamp and a Bodrugan.[3]

By the sixteenth century they were much less popular; perhaps parish work needed less to be supplemented by them and their numbers dropped off. Since they stood outside parish life — many of them were not resident in their houses but up and down the country preaching, or assisting the clergy elsewhere, and since they were not rooted in landed property, they were exposed first to the reforming energy of Henry's government. In themselves they were very much divided over the new measures, though in the end the great majority of them went over to the new order and provided some among the leading reformers: Miles Coverdale, for example, the Edwardian Bishop of Exeter (1551-53) was an Austin friar.[4]

At the beginning of the religious changes, in 1533, the obstinate devotion of many of them to the cause of Katherine of Aragon and the Papacy, and their preaching, invited the attention of the government. In April, James Horswell wrote up from Plymouth to Richard Cromwell: 'There be knave friars here that play their parts', and recommending him to summon Prideaux, servant to the prior of Bodmin, and friar Arthur 'who move sedition in all their communication'.[5] It is interesting to see that Prideaux, who ultimately did so well out of the religious changes, was not in favour of them at the beginning. There was also murmuring among the Grey Friars at Plymouth: Sir Piers Edgcumbe had to examine the warden and two of the brothers and send up their examinations. He committed Friar Gawen, the warden, to Launceston Castle; and punished all persons who spoke opprobrious words of Anne Boleyn, now Queen, by pillory and the stocks.[6]

In 1534, the Observant Friars, who were entirely devoted to Katherine and the old order, were suppressed: it was a very signal pointer to the future. Two of them, who were attempting to fly overseas, were pursued into the west country by John Hilsey, Provincial of the Dominicans. He and George

---

[1] Maclean, *Trigg Minor*, I. 188.
[2] *Parochial History of Cornwall*, IV. Supplt., 101-2.
[3] ibid., 107.   [4] cf. Baskerville, 234-6.
[5] *L.P.*, VI. 394.   [6] ibid., 1503.

Browne, Provincial of the Austin Friars, had been given the job of conducting a general visitation of the friars throughout the country. Hilsey wrote to Cromwell that he had pursued these recalcitrants through Somerset, Devon and Cornwall so closely 'that they cast off their clothes for secular raiment, as they are now brought to you'.[1] They were taken in Cardiff: they probably got across by sea from Cornwall.

The suppression of the friars, like that of the monasteries in general, even some of the smaller houses which the Act of 1536 dissolved, was held up by the critical events of 1536-37, the Pilgrimage of Grace and its consequences. But in the course of 1538 the friaries were all suppressed. The pleasant task, which he evidently much enjoyed, was given to the Bishop of Dover, himself a Dominican. In August he wrote from Haverfordwest to Cromwell to say that he had suppressed twenty-eight since departing from him, and asking for warrants for the friars to serve as secular priests and take livings.[2] In many places, he said, men were clamouring for the debts of the convents, and without some consideration from Cromwell, poor men would lose money by the friars and would murmur. He had collected various relics, including 'Malchus' ear that Peter struck off'.

In September Hilsey came down through the west from Bristol to Exeter and Plymouth, and on the 20th received the surrender of the Grey Friars at Bodmin.[3] There were a warden, Walter Rodd, two brothers and six lay-brothers. The house was some £16 in debt, against which the warden had a suit of white vestments, not yet all paid for, a pair of organs, a little mazer and two spoons. The kitchen and brewhouse furniture was mostly sold to pay costs for 23s. 1d.; two old feather beds fetched 10s. The furniture of the chambers, frater and buttery, the various vestments, an alabaster relief above the high altar were handed over to the mayor for the King. The Visitor took over 286 oz. of plate — mostly poor stuff, one imagines. 'A chest of evidences belonging to three divers gentlemen' was sealed and left with the prior of Bodmin: which shows that the friaries like the monasteries were used as repositories to hold title-deeds in safe keeping.

Two days later the Visitor was at Truro, where friars John Reskarnan, John de Coloribus and nine other brothers resigned the house to the King.[4] Here too there were title deeds in safe keeping, which were handed over to the mayor; so also was all the stuff, the furnishings of the house, the table over the high altar new painted at the prior's charges, altars, books, sacring bells, stalls 'poor and old'. In the steeple were three bells. The stuff in the

[1] *L.P.*, VII. 939.   [2] ibid., XIII (2), 200.
[3] ibid., 396.   [4] ibid., 405.

vestry was very poor: it was valued by the mayor and sold to meet the debts of £16 13s. 4d. The Visitor took 360 oz. of plate. Friar John de Coloribus was one to whom the prior of Bodmin granted an annuity for his services to the priory: he must have been a popular preacher. That he had the ear of the Arundells may be gathered from a letter of his to the influential Sir Thomas, saying that 'my master, your father, had written desiring you to speak in my favour now that I am called to the house of the Bishop of Lincoln, that I may obtain some good provision to return to Cornwall. The King remembers my name'.[1] (Who wouldn't? one may ask.) He goes on to say that he would rather have £20 near Sir Thomas's father, than £40 elsewhere. He seems to have obtained his desire and not left Cornwall.

We do not know when or how or by whom St. Michael's Mount was suppressed; presumably along with Sion Abbey to which it belonged. In 1537, John Arscott, archpriest of the Mount, was granted a dispensation by Cranmer to hold another benefice provided it did not involve the cure of souls; and the abbess of Sion presented him to the living of St. Clement near Truro.[2] Only an inventory remains, of about this time, from which we learn how richly furnished the church was. The cult of St. Michael, which brought so many pilgrims, was a profitable one; and this is reflected in the furniture of the church, which must have received many presents, though the offerings to the saint, over and above the stipends of the chaplains, went to Sion. His image was of silver gilt and weighed ten ounces; there were two bonnets for him, one of tinsel satin embroidered with gold, the other of blue velvet fringed with gold; he had two coats, one of cloth of gold, the other of purple velvet embroidered with IHS. He wore a chain of gold, a baldric of silver and gilt, a flower like a rose, of gold of Venice set with pearl and stone, and a little silver bell. He must have cut a pretty figure before the devout eyes of the faithful.

It was evidently stimulating to their piety, for there were 'two cloths hanging beside St. Michael and 43s. 6d. in money upon it and five ships of silver, 43 rings of silver, a plate of silver with a woman's image upon it and an image of silver kneeling, and divers other small images and tokens of silver upon it. Upon the same a royal, 4 nobles and 2 ducats of gold, a ring of gold valued at 10s., a little image of St. Michael of gold valued at 51s. 8d.'. St. Michael shared the devotions of the people with other saints and relics; there was a cloth with an image of St. Bridget which attracted

---

[1] L.P., v. 214.
[2] Taylor, *St. Michael's Mount*, 78-90, to which I am indebted for the following paragraphs.

offerings, a sword and a pair of spurs of copper and gilt that had belonged to the sainted Henry VI, and, not least interesting, the jaw-bone of St. Apollyen enshrined in silver and gilt. The church was very rich in vestments and plate: there were pyxes and chalices and monstrances, wrought cloths and silver rings and beads; there were copes and albs, books and frontals, two pairs of organs — all the equipment for the constant services which were appropriate to so popular a resort of pilgrims. In addition there were certain habiliments of war: bows, sheaves of arrows, breast-plates, handguns, and a firkin of gunpowder. These accoutrements give the impression of being somewhat out of date. It was one of the consequences of the Dissolution that they were brought up to date and the Mount from being primarily an outpost of faith became an outpost of power: in that an apt epitome of the Reformation. Now that with the passage of centuries it has ceased to be either, but is just a private possession of an old, long-rooted Cornish family, it remains not so very much changed, where the greater religious houses of Cornwall have hardly a vestige left of them, the place of the pilgrims up that steep rocky path taken by the hardly less constant succession of tourists, the west wind blowing strong across the bay, besieging that ancient fortress in vain.

The government's chief agent in carrying out the surrenders in the west was a Cornishman, Dr. Tregonwell,[1] whose career is well worth studying as that of a person whose fortune was largely made by the opportunities afforded by the Dissolution. At the same time it is worthy of note that he was no forward-looking Protestant with radical inclinations; he was essentially a civil-servant whose religious tendencies were conservative and grew more so with time and prosperity.

He was of no family of consequence, perhaps of yeoman stock; we do not know where he was born, probably at Tregonnell in the parish of Manaccan near the Lizard. It was his education which made him, and his ability to profit by it. At Oxford he studied civil law, which proved to be the high road to promotion in the world, though for some time he hesitated between that and the Church. For in 1519 he was presented by the dean and chapter to the living of St. Issey, which he resigned three years later to Robert Tregonwell, Vicar of St. Austell, perhaps a brother.[2] He was probably in deacon's orders; and before leaving Oxford became Principal of Peckwater Inn and Doctor of Civil Law. Removing to London he became a judge in the Court of Admiralty, and began to be employed by the King upon confidential missions and in diplomatic and commercial

---

[1] The name was pronounced Tregúnnell.   [2] Henderson, x. 65-6.

negotiations. In all these he seems to have displayed an equal tact and skill. He was made proctor for the King in the divorce-case, and sent to the Continent on that business in 1530. By 1531 he was one of the King's learned counsel and was sent next year to the Netherlands to settle commercial disputes. For his services in the long business of the divorce he was, upon its conclusion, awarded a pension of £40 a year.[1] In 1534 he signed the treaties of peace with Scotland and later was employed as a lawyer in the proceedings against the Carthusians, Sir Thomas More, and against Anne Boleyn. He was a reliable servant of the Crown: a man of the centre. Cromwell talked of him for the office of Master of the Rolls; but though Tregonwell asked for it, for his 'credit's sake', he did not get it.[2]

As early as 1533 Cromwell had employed him in monastic business, over the election of the abbot of Tewkesbury.[3] Two years later, when Cromwell was made Vicar-General and ordered a general visitation of all monasteries and churches throughout the realm, Tregonwell became one of the Royal Visitors. In September he visited the University of Oxford and thence turned his steps south-west. In November he was riding into Devonshire, and that he visited Bodmin we know from the prior's letter forwarding his judgment in the dispute over the priory weir to Cromwell.[4] In the west country he was able to do Cromwell various little services, as at Exeter where he obtained the stewardship of the lands of the dean and chapter in Devon, with an annuity of £5 for him — which they granted, they wrote submissively, 'on being reminded by Mr. Tregonwell that such small office would be a treasure to you'.[5] The dean and chapter of Salisbury were similarly moved, to the same amount.[6] Tregonwell in turn asked Cromwell for the farm of one of the smaller houses there.[7]

In the summer of 1536 he was in the west country; no doubt — though little of his correspondence survives — engaged in suppressing the smaller monasteries and setting forth Cromwell's reforming Injunctions. The clergy were ordered to preach the new dispensation; the people were not to observe the old superstitious holy days now abrogated from above, nor to extol images and relics, nor to gad about on pilgrimages. Parents were to teach their children the Paternoster, the articles of the faith and the Ten Commandments in English. The rumour preceded Dr. Tregonwell that he 'was coming to take away crosses, chalices and other idols of the churches'.[8] He thought it had been set on foot by a sumner about Bridgwater, whom he hoped to catch on his return. Arrived in Cornwall he

[1] L.P., VI. 578 (10).   [2] L.P., VII. 743.   [3] L.P., VI. 328.   [4] See above, p. 176.
[5] L.P., X. 4.   [6] ibid., 153.   [7] ibid., 388.   [8] L.P., XI. 405.

admonished the leading justices to seek out spreaders of the report, notwith-standing which he found 'everyone ready to obey the King's Injunctions and orders. The country is as quiet and true to the King as any shire in the realm'. It would appear that some concession had been made with regard to the observance of feasts of the dedication of their churches, to which Cornish-men were very much attached; Tregonwell wrote that 'the people are marvellously pleased that the King has allowed the *festum loci* of every church to be kept holy, at Cromwell's intercession'.[1] It is curious to reflect that to that we owe the retention of the local feasts which for centuries have been such a feature of our parish life, and up to our own time have remained a survival from the world of medieval catholicism. Tregonwell trusted that Cromwell would not hear henceforth that the sacrament of the altar had been irreverently handled in Cornwall. The pestilence was reigning very sore there, he wrote; hardly any place was clear; if it had not been for fear of Cromwell's displeasure he would have turned back at his first entry into Somersetshire.

On his way back, he received a letter from Cromwell on the highway between Blandford and Salisbury asking for his lanner to present to the King. 'She is at the mew at Langley'[2]; he would send her with all diligence. On his return he offered Cromwell £100 to move the King for a pleasant morsel, the nunnery of St. Giles in the Wood in Hertfordshire.[3] Two years ago Cromwell had moved the King for an annuity of 50 marks; the bill had not been signed nor the money paid, he said. He wrote also to Wriothesley asking him to remind Cromwell of his suit; he had long been a suitor for some recompense for the service he had done the King for eight or nine years and he hoped now for some provision for his old age.[4]

A great part of the next year Tregonwell was taken up with examining the numerous prisoners implicated in the Pilgrimage of Grace; and the rebellion itself held up the government's course, the further progress of the Reformation. With the rebellion out of the way and opposition suppressed, the government could go forward with its plans. In January a new royal visitation was begun. At Exeter the Bishop commanded every canon to preach the King's title as Supreme Head; and Tregonwell enjoined them not to execute any statutes of the chapter contrary to the King's laws.[5] In May Veysey issued his Injunctions, and ordered the clergy to procure copies of the Royal Injunctions given them by Tregonwell.[6] In September a new set were issued by Cromwell going a great deal further in reform: images were

---

[1] For more fully about this see below, pp. 436-7.   [2] L.P., XI. 524.
[3] ibid., 1390.   [4] ibid., 1391.   [5] L.P., XIII. i, 175.   [6] ibid., 1106.

to be taken down, lights put away, the Bible set up in the churches, the clergy to preach against idolatry; registers were to be kept of births, marriages, deaths.

Meanwhile the greater monasteries were beginning to go down all over the country; Tregonwell took the surrenders of houses as far apart as Llanthony and Robertsbridge in Sussex. In January 1539, he came west again, with Petre, into Wiltshire, receiving surrenders as they came. At Hinton there was one monk who expressly denied the King's Supremacy, affirming the Pope to be Vicar of Christ and Supreme Head of the Church; but 'the prior says he is a lunatic'.[1] How had times changed: one sees the picture of the poor old *fainéant* who could not get used to the new ideas. From Exeter Tregonwell wrote that in Somerset and Devon they 'had found as much conformity as might be desired, except that in many they found great waste, and many leases lately passed, which they have stayed and called in again'.[2] Then the commission divided into two parts to get through their work by Lady Day, so that the Crown might get the half-year's rents.

Tregonwell and Smith came on into Cornwall where they received the surrender of Launceston on February 24th.[3] They found 'the prior and convent very conformable, and all things in good order'. The house was out of debt; the plate, bells and buildings in good condition. Tregonwell handed over to the prior certain plate and stuff as Cromwell had commanded him; he referred the assignment of their pensions to the latter's decision. In the event the prior, like all such persons who were ready to accept the inevitable, was very handsomely treated: he received a pension of £100 a year, equivalent to some £2000 in our money. It was not only generous, it was even extravagant. There were eight brethren remaining in the house, the factious Gennys having been removed, and the old Prior Baker having died since the convent acknowledged the Royal Supremacy in 1534: they had then been twelve in number including the prior. One of the canons was awarded a pension of £10, three others £6 13s. 4d. each, the four remaining £5 6s. 8d. The priory seal, affixed for the last time after so many centuries, shows the tower with its cupola and the conventual church with its steep roof which Prior Baker had been at such pains so recently to repair.[4]

Tregonwell was at Bodmin three days later, where the prior and convent sealed their surrender in the chapter-house according to the formula 'sponte ac voluntarie' on February 27th. Part of the convent seal remains upon the document: the Virgin and Child, and St. Petroc in chasuble and holding his crozier, in their decorated niches of gothic design. Prior Mundy, who

[1] *L.P.*, XIV. i, 145.   [2] ibid., 324.   [3] ibid., 361, 367.
[4] Deputy Keeper's Report, VIII. App. 2.

signed as Wandsworth, was given a pension of £66 13s. 4d., the sub-prior, Richard Oliver, £8; Richard Lewis, 'blind and of the age of 100 years', £10 and six dozen woods yearly; two more £6 each; three others £5 6s. 8d.; two lay-brothers £2, and Thomas Rawlyns, 'blind and aged, for his corrody', £2.[1] Somehow they give the impression of being rather an infirm lot. There had been ten canons, with the prior, who acknowledged the royal supremacy,[2] now there were seven who subscribed to the surrender (omitting the blind centenarian).

On March 2nd Tregonwell received the surrender of St. Germans.[3] There they were eight in all, including the prior and a novice. Prior Swymmer got a pension of £66 13s. 4d., four of his canons £5 6s. 8d., another £6 13s. 4d., and the novice £2. The worn seal displays the Virgin seated with the Child raising his right hand in blessing. Provision was made in the surrenders for the first quarter of the pensions to be paid at Lady-day; and these continued to be a first charge upon the revenues from the monasteries, and to be paid regularly, as we shall see, until their recipients died off. There is not the slightest doubt that the monastic heads were extremely well-treated by the government; as for the monks, it was open to many of them to take livings and serve the Church more usefully than they had done. Upon a few who were feeble and incapable, the smallness of their pensions may have weighed a little hardly; where there was actual infirmity allowance was made, as we have seen. But when one considers the state of affairs in the houses, the laxness of discipline, the factiousness, the futility, still more the rapid making over of monastic property when the Dissolution became inevitable, it did not come a moment too soon. In fact by its slowness, taking from 1535 to 1539, the Crown lost a good deal of what might have accrued to it. This could not have been prevented entirely, and it would not have been good politics to do so. Perhaps the best summing-up is in Cromwell's own words: 'I perceive', wrote Sir Thomas Arundell to him, 'as you have often said, you are slow but sure.'[4]

Thus was what has been called 'the first and greatest example of nationalization' accomplished.

We do not need to follow in detail the remainder of the career of him who was the chief agent of the Dissolution in the west country. Before Tregonwell came west on his final campaign, in 1538 he seems to have achieved something of his aim and got a lease of St. Giles in the Wood.[5] But shortly

---

[1] *L.P.*, XIV. i, 384.   [2] Deputy Keeper's Report VII, App. 2, 9.
[3] *L.P.*, XIV. i, 420.   [4] *L.P.*, VI. 629.   [5] *L.P.*, XIII. i, 585.

afterwards the King ordered him to leave it for someone else. He had 140 acres of corn on the ground, and hay and wood already housed; he did not know where to go, he complained.[1] But it took more than this to uproot someone so tough. In August 1539 he was still at St. Giles's, for he wrote from there reminding Cromwell how he had 'often said that he would make him spend £100 a year'.[2] The King when he called him from the Arches said he would provide for him and his posterity; he hopes the King has not suspected his fidelity and diligence — he has been a long suitor, yet nothing had fallen to his lot.

It is probable that Henry, who had few illusions, except in regard to himself, considered that he was sufficiently well-rewarded; and Cromwell must have known that he would make good use of his opportunities. We now know that he did. Upon his visits to the western houses he was in the enviable position of being able to accept here a patent for £2, there another for £5 and so on. From the late monasteries of the five western counties he received annuities amounting to £41 13s. 4d. — which the government continued to pay out of their revenues after their suppression.[3] And that is excluding what he must have received from other houses elsewhere. In addition a certain amount of patronage was made over to him by priors anxious to stand well in his eyes and gain the favourable consideration of the great minister when their day came. In the next decade we find Tregonwell presenting to a number of livings in Cornwall alone: in 1543 to the vicarage of Maker by grant of Plympton Priory when he was there in October 1537; in 1544 to St. Neot, by grant of the late priory of Montacute; in 1549 to Gulval, by grant to him and Robert Tregonwell from St. Germans; in 1551 to St. Minver by grant of Bodmin Priory.[4] If this was true of Cornwall alone, he must have had grants of a great many more presentations in other counties, many of them bringing something in: a pretty penny all told. The fact was that he was now a rich man, and well able to afford the £1000 which he gave for the fee-simple of Milton Abbey in Dorset in 1540, whose surrender he had taken not two years before.[5] Like others too, he had a number of further transactions in monastic lands; particularly in 1544, when, with John Southcote of Bodmin, who seems to have been his brother-in-law, he bought several more manors and properties in Dorset, which had belonged to Abbotsbury and Shaftesbury.[6] Few men were in a better position to know their value. He was engaged in rounding off his estates, founding a family.

[1] *L.P.*, XIII. ii. 74.   [2] *L.P.*, XIV. ii. App. 35.
[3] E 164/31 (Cardinal Pole's Pension Book).
[4] Henderson x, 28, 72, 30.
[5] *L.P.*, XIV. 282, 90.   [6] *L.P.*, XIX. 527 (36).

His legal abilities continued to be employed by Henry's government. He was appointed to draft a bill to punish offenders against the Six Articles; he was in the Anne of Cleves divorce proceedings; his commission as principal judge of the Admiralty was renewed. [1] In 1550 he was made one of the commissioners of the great seal during the sickness of Lord Chancellor Rich; but otherwise he was not much in evidence in the reign of Edward VI. [2] It is likely that, a conservative in religious matters, he did not approve of the new trends. There is no doubt that he was in favour under Mary. He was one of those to be knighted after her coronation, and he was a member of her first Parliament. When Gardiner died, he was one of three appointed to perform the duties of the Lord Chancellor in Chancery. [3] In June 1558 he was given licence to retain thirty gentlemen over and above those daily attendant upon him in his household. [4] So that, rich and esteemed, he lived in some style. He took not much further part in public affairs, but concentrated his attention upon the patrimony he was building up in that delicious Dorsetshire valley with the fine church looking away to the hills. Here he died, January 13th, 1565, and was buried under an altar-tomb with the old formula inscribed upon it: 'On whose soul God have mercy'. Out of his mouth there issues the sentiment: *Nos autem gloriari oportet in cruce Domini nostri Jesu Christi*, with who can say now what backward glance at the monks whose place he had taken? It will not be denied that his cross was a considerably more profitable one.

---

[1] *L.P.*, XIV. 860-1, 979.
[3] Pat. Rolls. Mary, Nov. 29, 1555.
[2] Hutchins, *History of Dorset*, I. 431.
[4] ibid., June 20, 1558.

CHAPTER IX

CONSEQUENCES OF THE DISSOLUTION: ECONOMIC, POLITICAL, RELIGIOUS

THE learned Dr. Savine, whose study of the economic basis of the monasteries at the moment of the Dissolution is the best guide to that difficult and labyrinthine subject, pays a remarkable tribute to English administration.[1] Where the history of English political liberty is well-known abroad, he says, that of English administration is not, though it has a not less claim to public attention. He regards the long record of administrative success as being due to a powerful government having been developed early upon the island. It demanded habits of business routine which became firmly rooted both with the official class at the centre, and, even more important because so much of their work was voluntary, with local officials and the J.P.s in the country. From time to time, for some specific purpose of government, a great official survey was demanded which required, and received, the full attention of both; nor did it tax their joint resources. If there was anything which might have been expected to do so, it was the whole business of the Dissolution, the surveys, the surrenders, the dispersal of lands on a scale amounting almost to a land-revolution. It was a stupendous undertaking. Yet it was carried through successfully. It is probable that Tudor administration, less spectacular as it now seems, was one of the greatest of their achievements, and the clue to much of their success.

The *Valor Ecclesiasticus*, taken on the eve of the Dissolution, gives us a conservative estimate of the value of church-properties. It is on the whole reliable enough. But in the case of the monasteries there were certain sources of income which were not taken fully into consideration; the most important of these was the income arising from the demesne land around the monastery, which, because it was originally cultivated by the monks themselves, was not counted as producing revenue. Sales of woods and profits of courts, though less important, had also tended to be omitted. There was also a certain increase in the income from land in the interval. When, with the Dissolution, the Crown's officials took over the lands, they naturally made a closer scrutiny of their revenues, attaching the proper value to the monastic demesnes, ferreting out small rents and profits which had been for-

[1] Savine, op. cit., 17.

gotten. In consequence it was found that the revenues were larger than the *Valor* had estimated; Savine puts it at something under a fourth.[1] The disparity in Cornwall may be seen from the following table:

	Valor Ecc.			Ministers' Accounts, 1540[2]		
	£	s.	d.	£	s.	d.
Launceston	392	12	11½	440	7	0¾
Bodmin	289	11	11	340	6	8½
St. Germans	243	8	0	283	9	0¼
Tywardreath	123	9	3	201	10	8½

That is to say that in the case of the three larger houses the disparity was only some 12 or 13 per cent. In that of Tywardreath it was no less than 66 per cent: a further and eloquent indication of the lax state of affairs which prevailed there under the long regime of Prior Collins.

Let us go into the figures for Tywardreath. The *Valor* returns Tywardreath manor as worth £8 7s. 11d. The Ministers' Accounts for 1540 go into detail; they give the site of the manor and its lands as worth £9 9s. 4d., rents of assize £12 11s. 4d., of free tenants £1 11s. 0d., and profits of courts 8s. 2d.: a total value of £23 19s. 10d. It is reckoning in the value of the demesne which accounts for most of the difference; but there are smaller differences between the earlier and the later valuations in the case of all the manors, and even as regards some of the rectories. That of St. Austell, for example, is given as £23 7s. 6d. by the *Valor*, and £27 according to the Ministers' Accounts. The latter always goes into greater detail: at St. Germans, where the *Valor* returns the manor at £13 12s. 10d., in 1540 we have the farm of the site and the demesne lands returned at £6 15s. 11d., the rents of customary tenants in the parish at £28 17s. 7d.; within the borough, customary tenants at £11 6s. 2½d., free tenants at 7s. 1½d., and profits of court at 14s. 4d.: £48 1s. 1½d. in all. It is not possible always to compare the figures exactly; but there is no doubt about the totals, or about the value of the demesnes. At Launceston in 1540 the site of the monastery with its demesne was valued at £15 19s. 6d. p.a.; at Bodmin at £8 17s. 10d., while the farm of the demesne was returned at £13 3s. 5d.

The place of the demesne in the economy of a monastery, with some light on how the monks managed their property, may be gathered from an interesting series of cases relating to St. Germans. There was a dispute over certain lands and tenements called Tolvans, Torton down and Lancolyn.

[1] ibid., 74.

[2] These figures are from Dugdale, *Monasticon*, VI. 212; II. 463, 468; IV. 658.

Thomas Godwyn claimed that he had a lease of these lands from the King at a rent of £12 6s. 8d.; they had formerly been in the tenure of William Swymmer, the prior's brother, to whom they had been leased on November 21st, 1538, for 60 years at a rent of £3.[1] Such a lease would have been invalid; but the defendants claimed that Lancolyn was parcel of the monastic demesne and was 'always occupied and manured for hospitality by the prior and convent'. In July 1544 Nicholas Guest, who had been cellarer of the house, deposed that he had known these lands for twenty-eight years — he was now sixty-seven, 'for he was a brother and professed in the said house and continued thereby all that time'.[2] He said that during that time these lands had not been leased under the convent seal, but kept for the maintenance of hospitality, 'except part of it set at will of the prior'. For nine years during which he was cellarer he 'had the governance of the premises and had certain sheep and other beasts and cattle depasturing on part thereof and the other part tilled'.

William Lawry, who was now twenty-eight and had been in the priory since he was twelve, let the cat, or some part of it, out of the bag. He gave evidence that six weeks before the Dissolution Torton down was let under the convent seal to Thomas Spry and Walter Trelawny, and Tolvans and Lancolyn to Peter Coryton and William Swymmer respectively. He said that John Champernowne, who had got a grant of the priory, showed him 'that William Swymmer gave him money that he might enjoy the said close called Lancolyn'. Some months later further evidence was taken.[3] The late prior (now a man of 60) was called, and said that Tolvans was divided into two by a hedge, and that he had let one half with Torton down for £14 13s. 4d. yearly 'in victual for the provision of the said house'. Three months before the Dissolution he had let these two closes to Peter Coryton for three lives at £6 rent. One part of Tolvans was 'by lease of word letten to divers persons to plough and sow, yielding and paying therefor yearly the third sheaf thereupon growing' — which third sheaf was to go to Mrs. Buller by a previous grant of the prior. Roger Davyn deposed that immediately after the Dissolution, John Champernowne and Peter Carew claimed the demesne and these closes with it at a court at Landrake; but that John Benny aged 90 had witnessed that Tolvans and Torton down were 'parcel of the barton of Landrake and no part of the demesne of St. Germans, and so it was presented by the homage, and Champernowne's and Carew's claim voided'.

What a confusion of evidence there is! We do not know what happened

[1] E 321/18/94.   [2] Augmentations, Misc. Books 231-3 (245-7).   [3] E 321/28/39.

in the end;[1] nor does it matter. Certain points of interest emerge: the un-certainty of status of some lands, the reliance upon the memory of old men to know the custom, the homage following, the method of provisioning the house, the prior's very natural anxiety, like other priors, to do his brother a good turn.

We do not need to repeat here the detailed analysis of Dr. Savine on the administration of monastic property, especially since a minute study of the figures for the Cornish houses bears out his conclusions, and reinforces them. It will be enough to bring out certain salient points. The monastic income came from two sources: tithes, mainly from churches whose rectories were appropriated to them, and revenues from their manors and other lands. These two sources are denoted as 'spirituals' and 'temporals' respectively. Dr. Savine tells us that monastic tithe was a considerable portion of the monastic budget and of total tithe-income. A very small portion of tithes appropriated to monasteries came back into the hands of the Church upon the Dissolution; the vast bulk was thrown on to the market and into the hands of the laity. The consequences of this were enormously important. It provided a large and varied field for investment for county families, in addition to the monastic lands themselves. The purchase of tithe greatly strengthened the economic hold of the gentry all over the country; it was a new field of expansion for their interests. There are hundreds of transactions of this character which take place from now on in any given county like Cornwall: we shall only have space to follow the general movement, though our conclusions rest upon innumerable cases and documents. The social consequences are of great importance and fascinating to study; for it was this which gave the laity, or rather the country gentry, its hold over the Church of England. It is probable that this underlying fact, which does not attract much attention on the surface of history, has had as much influence in determining the subsequent character of that Church as the more spectacular legislation of the Tudors in regard to it.

The transition was made easier by the fact that for years the collection of monastic tithe was in the hands of the secular bailiffs of the monasteries. Hence there was a natural tendency for tithe to be regarded in the same light as temporal rents, especially when they were both collected by the same person. People became accustomed to the lay control of spiritual revenue. The leasing of benefices to lay persons to farm carried the tendency to secular-

---

[1] Except that in June 1545 Richard Buller sent a band of his servants to eject Coryton from Tolvans and Torton down; he claimed that the latter had no lease either from the prior or the King. E 321/11/39.

ization still further. The monks became only receivers of rent; it was the farmer of the tithes, as in the case of Nicholas Prideaux and the four parishes of Padstow, St. Minver, Cubert and Egloshayle, who entered into direct relations with the parish. Of course, in time he became the squire of it: in that lies the kernel of much of English social history. And so, as Savine concludes, 'the clerical property dropped by the monks could never return to the parochial clergy, but passed for ever into the hands of the laity'.[1]

In the Cornish houses, except for Bodmin, the proportion of their income which came from tithe was very large, as the following table shows:[2]

	(1) Spiritual Income			(2) Temporal Income			Proportion of 1 to whole per cent
	£	s.	d.	£	s.	d.	
Tywardreath	99	17	10	51	18	3	66
St. Germans	123	16	8	119	11	4	51
Launceston	159	8	8	229	2	6¼	40
Bodmin	72	2	0	217	9	11	25

In addition there was the large part already played by laymen, before the Dissolution, in managing the monastic estates. Some part of this is reflected in the *Valor*, in the tax-free allowances which were made for the fees paid to stewards, receivers, bailiffs. No allowance was made for inferior officials, or for expenses. So that we do not get a complete picture of the expenses of monastic administration, or of the good pickings it afforded to lesser laymen. But of what the privileged and the great got out of it we have some idea. We know that the nobles at court were not averse to accepting the chief stewardships of houses, the duties of which were negligible: the Earl of Shrewsbury had eleven, the Earl of Derby seven, Cromwell six, up to 1535.[3] The Marquis of Exeter, among several such offices, was chief steward of St. Germans, with a fee of £2.[4] Stephen Gayer was auditor and Walter Trelawny general receiver with the same fees. Sir John Chamond was the chief layman connected with the Cornish houses: he was chief steward of Tywardreath (66s. 8d.), of Launceston (53s. 4d.), and of Bodmin (£5).[5] The office was largely a sinecure; but it put Sir John in the way of picking up desirable bits of monastic property when the Dissolution came, like the manor of Bodiniel which he purchased: he was in a position to know its value.[6]

Among Bodmin Priory's complement of officials we find Sir Richard

---

[1] op. cit., 113.   [2] These figures are from the *Valor Ecclesiasticus*.
[3] Savine, 255.   [4] *Valor*, II. 405.   [5] ibid., 396, 400, 403.   [6] v. above, p. 179-81.

Grenville as steward, and Nicholas Prideaux as bailiff, of its very exiguous lands in Devon. John Kempthorne was under-steward of Launceston, and bailiff of Treworgy and Trewosell; at Tywardreath he was steward of the manor-courts and bailiff of Porthea. Walter Kendall was water-bailiff of Fowey. John Tregian, a rich merchant of Truro and Probus, was auditor of both Bodmin and Tywardreath. Among relatives of various priors we find Henry Shere as bailiff of Newport borough at Launceston, John Vyvyan as receiver of the manor of Bodmin, William Vyvyan, bailiff of Pendewey manor. 'Even before the Dissolution', Dr. Savine concludes, 'economic initiative had, on monastic territory, passed from the monks to the gentry.'[1]

We have already seen to what an extent the greater gentry could intervene in the affairs of a monastery, in the case of Sir William Courtenay at Launceston. It was conceded that the families of founders and benefactors were in a special position, and this we find Edgcumbe pleading in relation to Totnes Priory.[2] They often had the right to appoint to a corrody, by which some deserving (or undeserving) person was maintained as a kind of pensioner in the house. At Tywardreath the King as founder had granted a corrody to William Huchyn, valued at £3 6s. 8d. That was all that this house was allowed tax-free by way of alms — they are not likely to have distributed much. We know that the chancel-clerk there had a scholar under him — but his instruction is likely to have been of an informal character. At Launceston allowance was made for those alms which were distributed in accordance with the will of the founder: *in cena Domini* and on Wednesday in Quadragesima for the founder's soul, £4 2s. 2d.; to paupers in the hospital of St. Leonard similarly 6s. 8d.; to prisoners in the Castle by will of the founder 20s.; to paupers on the day of his obit 20s. and annually for his soul 20s. Then there was a chaplain to celebrate in the chapel of Launceston Castle, and a foundation to say mass twice a year at Penheale for the soul of the founder. The alms distributed by the founder's will at Bodmin were calculated at 52s. At St. Germans *in cena Domini* they were £4; to paupers in Lent three loaves and nine herrings for the founder's soul, 10s.; an obit for souls of John and Roger Cole in Callington church 6s. 8d., with a foundation to keep a light burning there, 26s. 8d. The Bishop had granted a corrody here to Robert Goldson, valued at 53s. 4d. It will be seen that the amount allowed for alms, in relation to the total income of the monasteries, was very small; though no doubt other alms and much hospitality were given for which no allowance was made. But the real purpose of the monasteries was prayer, especially for the souls of the departed. It was a very

---

[1] op. cit., 261. [2] *L.P.*, x. 551.

penetrating remark of Bishop Latimer, which went to the very root of the matter, a very just judgment too of human affairs and human methods, when he said 'As the founding of monasteries argueth purgatory to be, so the putting down of them argueth it not to be'. [1]

At first the monastic lands were slow in being sold. [2] It may be that it was not the government's policy to sell them; certainly Henry and Cromwell can hardly have wished to do so, and the latter had promised to make his master the richest prince in Christendom. If only the lands of the Church could have been retained, he would have been; and not only that, it would have formed the economic foundation for an absolute monarchy in this country. It does not seem that Henry VIII would have parted with them, at any rate permanently, if it had not been for the enormous expense of the French War of 1543-46. So also with the government of Edward VI; so also with Mary at the end of her reign, when Philip involved her in another war with France; so also with Elizabeth. By the end of her reign, most of the Church lands had gone from the Crown irrevocably. The country was the wealthier for it.

If we are to trace the process in the concrete, let us take the case of St. Germans. Carew tells us the delightful story which had come down to the next generation, how 'John Champernowne, son and heir apparent to Sir Philip of Devon, in Henry VIII's time followed the Court, and through his pleasant conceits, of which much might be spoken, won some good grace with the King. Now when the golden shower of the dissolved abbey lands rained well-near into every gaper's mouth, some two or three gentlemen, the King's servants, and Master Champernowne's acquaintance, waited at a door where the King was to pass forth with purpose to beg such a matter at his hands. Our gentleman became inquisitive to know their suit; they made strange to impart it. This while out comes the King. They kneel down; so doth Master Champernowne. They prefer their petition; the King grants it. They render humble thanks, and so doth Master Champernowne. Afterwards he requireth his share. They deny it; he appeals to the King. The King avoweth his equal meaning in the largesse; whereon the overtaken companions were fain to allot him this priory for his partage'. [3]

The story has achieved such form, such balance and antithesis, that one may well imagine how often it was told over the dinner-table, when the meats had been removed to make way for a dish of raisins and the wine, at

[1] q. Baskerville, 22.
[2] cf. Liljegren, *The Fall of the Monasteries and the Social Changes in England*.
[3] Carew, 109.

Antony looking out over the St. Germans river. One does not need to take it *au pied de la lettre*; and yet it certainly incorporates something, as traditions do, of the manner of the grant. For the interesting thing is that among the first grants of monasteries in the west, no less than three are to gentlemen of the King's household. This is the first; then Bodmin was granted to Thomas Sternhold, groom of the robes and metrical versifier of the Psalms; while Hartland went to William Abbot, serjeant of the King's cellar. All that was natural enough, since they were in a position to press their suits. But it is a mistake to imagine that they got these grants for nothing; only very exceptional persons were given anything by Henry VIII; the utmost they got, if they won the King's favour or performed him some service, was to get a grant cheap.

On June 19th, 1540, Henry leased to John Champernowne, esquire, of the King's household, the site, house and demesnes of St. Germans for 21 years at £6 15s. 11d. rent; and Totnes Priory for £17 6s. 4d.[1] In the Particulars for Grants we find a survey of these properties, giving details of the closes, pastures and meadows, and rating the two properties at 20 years purchase, less the tenth upon them, at £434. It does not seem that John Champernowne lived to complete the transaction; it was his widow who paid the money to the Crown.[2] After her death, Henry Champernowne succeeded. He was a young fighting man, bent upon the wars abroad.[3] Before he left the country with a band of his west-country cousins, young Richard Grenville among them, he made over St. Germans to John Eliot, who had recently come there as lessee of the Bishop's manor of Cuddenbeak.[4] John Eliot was a merchant engaged in trade at Ashburton and Plymouth. In 1565 there were several transactions between him and young Champernowne. In March Eliot paid him £50, and on Ash Wednesday took formal possession of the priory, as the custom was, in the presence of witnesses. There was a deed of bargain and sale, now illegible; it says, 'the consideration five h . . .', probably £500. There were further payments made later; but when Henry Champernowne made his will in October 1568, before going abroad to the French wars, from which he did not return, there was still £200 due to him from John Eliot. By July 16th, 1574, this was paid off, and John Eliot was released of all claims upon him. And so the Eliots came into full possession of St. Germans; they have been there ever since.

By 1576, when Eliot made his will, it was already called Port Eliot. He

[1] Particulars for Grants, Supp. Henry VIII, 1307.
[2] These two paragraphs are based upon the Port Eliot MSS. transcribed in Henderson, **xxiv**.
[3] cf. my *Sir Richard Grenville*, 62-3.
[4] Henderson, *Records of St. Germans Church and Priory*, 30.

seems to have been proud of the ceilings of the house, probably decorated plaster ceilings like those which Richard Grenville was putting up at the very same time at Buckland Abbey; for Eliot writes, 'my will and mind is that my executors nor any of them shall at any time remove or take away any of the ceilings of the house called Port Eliot, but leave them as implements appertaining to the house'. John Eliot was not rich; his only property outside St. Germans was, as befitted a man of the middle-class, house-property mainly in Ashburton and Plymouth. The total value of his estate was £34 5s. per annum. He was succeeded by his nephew, Richard Eliot, who on his death-bed married his young son, then aged seventeen, to the daughter and heiress of a wealthy local yeoman, also going up in the world. This move was very successful and established the fortunes of the family. Their son was the great Sir John Eliot, who was knighted by James and led Parliament in opposition to Charles I. He was an able man of business and much increased the value of his accumulating properties. In 1624 he bought the borough of St. Germans with its liberties, which had formerly belonged to the priory. This brought with it the patronage of two seats in Parliament, the source of the family's political influence in the eighteenth century. How it all points to the future, the peerage at the hand of the younger Pitt in 1784 in return for political support, the rule of the oligarchy. Sir John Eliot was the spokesman of his class. Able, eloquent, uncompromising, doctrinaire—an inspiring leader, his voice was the voice of a new class demanding power. When he died in the Tower, he became its martyr — an even more important role. The priory church of St. Germans, shorn of its choir and north aisle, is now a mausoleum of the virtues, the family piety of the Eliots, the memory of the monks quite overlaid. In that again, lies much of the history of modern England.

If we would visualize what the priory buildings looked like at the time of the Dissolution, we have to think away the eighteenth-century landscape, the great rolling park with its deliberate trees, designed by Repton. In Tudor days, as we can judge from the Particulars for Grants, all was on a smaller, more domestic scale; there were the priory buildings in the middle of orchards and gardens, with fields and closes and open down around. A creek of the river came right up in front of the buildings, so that they looked out upon the water at high tide, the mud at low tide; the monks' fishing was at their door. In the eighteenth century the creek was dammed and turned into park-land; the house itself was a good deal rebuilt and given a Georgian form. Its lines, however, would still be recognizable to Prior Swymmer. In 1550 he bought a tenement in Bakewell Street, to which his brother afterwards succeeded: this street ran on the west side of the priory almost on the lines of the present drive. As time went on the Eliots managed to move back the frontiers of the village, incorporating the old closes and lanes that came up to the priory, so as to get privacy and a park. At Tregonwell's Milton Abbas, the eighteenth-century owner boldly transplanted the whole village a mile away.

What happened to the monks? The prior was well provided for: he had the large pension of £66 13s. 4d., and there was a more useful career in the church open to the former religious. Swymmer held the vicarage of Talland, by grant of his brother-monks of Launceston, along with his priory from 1520 to 1538. The year before he resigned Talland he was presented to the rectory of Minster. When in 1554 William Todd was deprived under Mary of the rectory of Northill, probably for the sin of clerical marriage, Swymmer was presented. He held both livings very comfortably till his death in 1558.[1] Nicholas Guest, late sub-prior of St. Germans and prior of Tywardreath, was provided for with his pension and the living of St. Winnow, which he held from 1538 to 1545, when he died. Two more canons got livings in Cornwall later: Robert Vyan was vicar of Altarnun 1564-71, John Rich died in 1547 as vicar of St. Martin-by-Looe: we do not know when he was presented.[2] The rest had their pensions to live upon. In 1555, four of the canons were still receiving them: the prior, Stephen Sedge-moor and Robert Vyan (£5 6s. 8d. each), and Robert Capell (40s.).[3] They had not done so badly out of the Dissolution.

Bodmin Priory, with its buildings and demesnes, was sold to Thomas Sternhold in 1544.[4] Mr. Henderson tells us that it had been already leased to him since 1540.[5] A scrap of evidence remains of the early dismantling of the church, for in July 1538 John Tregons, the King's agent, sold four of the largest bells of the priory, the heaviest excepted, to the parishioners of Lanivet for their church for £36 13s. 4d.[6] The fact was that Bodmin did not need a second large church, and so the priory church must have been stripped of its lead and early allowed to decay. But the domestic buildings, which in this case were on the south side, on a gentle slope down to the stream, remained.

Sternhold was a groom of the robes to Henry and undoubtedly in his favour; for he was not only allowed to purchase the priory for less than its value — Henry sold it to him for £100 when its market-value was £153,[7] but the King left him 100 marks in his will. It was his literary and musical

---

[1] Henderson, x. 27, 31, 33; and xxi. 'Notes on St. Germans'.
[2] ibid., 28, 29, 34, 37.   [3] E 164/31.   [4] L.P., xix. i, 1035 (21).
[5] Henderson, *Cornish Essays*, 226.   [6] Dunkin, *Church Bells of Cornwall*, 50.
[7] Particulars for Grants, E 318/1056.

talents which recommended him. Sternhold has his place in the history of the
nation and its literature as the first to versify the Psalms in common metre.
It was an undertaking much in request at that time when the English
liturgy was coming into being and the English Bible being set up in the
churches. At the French court the distinguished poet Marot was engaged on
the same task; and like him Sternhold got into passing trouble for his
sympathy with the new learning. He was no poet like Marot, but his work
had none the less influence for that. He was the first in this field; and before
his early death he had set nineteen of the Psalms into verse, dedicating his
work to the young Edward VI in gratitude for a King 'that forbiddeth not
laymen to gather and lease in the Lord's harvest', and trusting that as his
'grace taketh pleasure to hear them sung sometimes, so he will also delight to
see and read them and command them to be sung by others'.[1]

There was something simple and affecting in Sternhold's verses, something
appealing about his personality. His work attracted a host of followers, all
of them less good than himself, of whom the chief was John Hopkins, who
added his work to Sternhold's in a joint version, but deprecating any intention of fathering his work upon the dead man, since it was 'not in any part
to be compared with his most exquisite doings'. And so Sternhold and Hopkins came into being, that version of the Psalms which has had a greater
circulation and more general usage among Protestants than any other work,
outside the Bible and Prayer-Book, those Psalms to which Cromwell's
russet-coated troopers went into action, to which upholders of the Parliament turned for consolation in defeat and joy in victory, and whose strains
were heard for some three centuries in our country churches.

Such was the man who came into possession of Bodmin Priory. He was
not there long. We find him bringing a case against some Bodmin men who
had trespassed upon his fishing at Dunmere, which he held had been granted
him with the priory.[2] He tried also to challenge the Chamonds' right to the
manor of Bodiniel.[3] Richard Chamond answered that it had been granted
to his father by Prior Wandsworth for a rent of £5. Sternhold replied that
it was void by the statute which made grants made within one year of the
Dissolution illegal. Then, in 1549, he was dead. We have his will, which by
its terms shows that he was a Protestant, commending his soul 'into the hands
of Almighty God my Creator and only Saviour'.[4] He appointed his wife as
his executrix on behalf of his little daughters, who were three years and one
year old respectively, between whom his property was to be divided. They

[1] *D.N.B.* art. Sternhold.   [2] E 321/21/95.
[3] E 321/14/89.   [4] P.C.C. 37 Popplewell.

204

came of age in 1564 and 1565, married up-country, and in 1567 the priory was sold to John Rashleigh of Fowey, for £360.[1]

The Rashleighs, as befitted a prospering merchant-family, like the Eliots, were already in the field for monastic property; it was the obvious road from trade to becoming country gentry. John's father, Philip, the first of the family to come down into Cornwall from Devon and engage in trade at Fowey, had in 1545 bought the manor of Trenant, parcel of the possessions of Tywardreath, and paid £209 6s. 8d. cash for it.[2] It was this which was the beginning of their hold upon the lovely Gribbin peninsula between Tywardreath and Fowey, of which they came in time to have a monopoly. John Rashleigh was the second son, though he inherited the ability and carried on the business in Fowey. His town-house may still be seen there, now the Ship Inn, with the richly-panelled chamber which he furnished for his wife Alice in 1570: their names are upon the carved mantelpiece with its caryatids and Renaissance motifs. Now they lie across the churchyard in that church musty with so many memories, of the Hundred Years' War and the burning of Fowey, of the Spanish Armada and John's son, another John, sailing his ship the *Francis* up to Plymouth to serve under Drake.

Rashleigh decided not to live at Bodmin, but to remain on the south coast convenient to Fowey.[3] And so the priory was divided and let off in separate tenements: we hear of one consisting of the kitchen, garner-house and 'the whole foundation whereon the great brewing-house hath stood'; another consisted of 'the great hall house and buttery in the end of the same, the gate-house with the chamber over it, the garden behind the brew-house, the prior's pool, the corn-mill etc.' Someone later held the cloister, the dorter closes and St. Guron's well. As late as 1636 there was reserved to Mr. Rashleigh 'a chamber called the great chamber with bedding and furniture to be provided for him whenever he shall have occasion to visit the same'. This was probably part of the prior's lodging. But by this time the Rashleighs had built their house at Menabilly, in the most exquisite situation by the Gribbin looking out to sea; and the priory was still further sub-divided and parts of it left to become ruinous. It was all a pity; for if they had chosen to live there, like the Eliots at St. Germans or the Bassets and St. Aubyns at the Mount, it would have saved something of the buildings, if not of the church, where now nothing remains.

We have seen in what manner Prior Mundy had granted away the bulk of the priory lands before the Dissolution: he was not the son of a London

---

[1] Maclean, I. 140-1. [2] E 318/923.
[3] For this paragraph I am indebted to Mr. Henderson's *Cornish Essays*, 226-8.

business man for nothing.[1] Not unnaturally his proceedings gave rise to much talk and several law-suits. Benet Killigrew, who was a page of the Chamber and later havenor of the county, claimed that the King had leased him the barton of Rialton for 21 years from Michaelmas 1539; but that John Mundy by virtue of a grant from his brother the prior had entered the premises, while the prior 'had not only declared with the justifying by open perjury of the feigned and void estate aforesaid, but also by like fraud and deceit intendeth to avow and maintain divers such like estates made unto sundry persons of other the possessions of the said late priory to the yearly decay of the King's revenues of 100 marks'.[2] Nor were the tenants of the manor any more satisfied. For when Sir Thomas Arundell and other commissioners were appointed to go into the question of the King's rights against the Mundys, the latter had such reason to be displeased with the tenants' evidence that they had 'ever sithence conceived and borne such malice and inward grudge towards your said orators' that they had set on their bailiff to 'imagine and invent by all means and ways they can to break and subvert the said ancient and reasonable customs'.[3]

The grants at Padstow to the Prideaux had their questioners. Thomas Strowde brought a case against the ex-prior and Humphrey Prideaux, stating that the King had leased him the tithes of Padstow from Michaelmas 1539; but that Humphrey Prideaux was taking the fish-tithes 'by colour of a certain feigned and void estate' made him by the prior, and that the rents charged for it were much less than in the royal grant.[4] He too stated that the prior intended to maintain this grant along with the others he had made. And the prior, or his relations, had so covered up his tracks that he succeeded. Most of the leases had been made presumably, with commendable foresight, more than a year before the Dissolution, and so held good. Once these people had got their teeth into land they did not let go. The Mundys' lease of Rialton was renewed at an increased rent by Queen Elizabeth in 1599, and they held it until the Civil War when it was seized by the Commonwealth.[5] At the Restoration, the lease was granted to the Godolphins, and to-day it remains Duchy property.

But the ex-prior seems to have had a bad conscience about these doings. We have noted the uneasy tone of his will — though that may be due to the much more serious trouble he got into in 1547, which brought him very near to losing his life. It is an interesting story, which shows how careful one has to be of too hard and fast generalization about any movement so

[1] See above, p. 175.   [2] E 321/17/89.   [3] E 321/16/70.
[4] Augmentations Proc. 3/96.   [5] Henderson, 'Rialton', in *Old Cornwall*, 1936.

complex as the Reformation; for it turns out that this *bourgeois* prior, with his strongly developed acquisitive instinct for his family, was not, as one might have expected a Protestant, but a devout Catholic.

At the Dissolution he was very well provided for. He had his pension of £66 13s. 4d.; and already in January of that year, he had taken steps to safeguard the future by getting himself presented to the living of Lanlivery by Nicholas Kendall, a member of that family into which the prior proposed to marry his niece.[1] This little group certainly knew how to look after themselves. After the Dissolution he returned to London, where he was instituted to the rectory of St. Leonard's, Foster Lane, on July 12th, 1542.[2] The next we hear of him is his arraignment for high treason on July 1st, 1547.[3] It appears that Mundy, with his friend Thurston Hickman, a former Carthusian, had helped John Foxe, parson of St. Mary Magdalen, Queen-hithe, to escape overseas to Louvain. Foxe had been a monk of the London Charterhouse, a colleague of those Carthusians who had been executed for denying the King's supremacy in 1535. Though he had himself conformed, he kept the left arm of the martyred prior Houghton secretly as a relic upon his altar. Upon its discovery he fled abroad, to renew his profession at Louvain. Mundy and Hickman aided him, and had planned to convey 'the said arm with other baggage that they called relics over sea to the said Foxe as they had promised'. They were indicted at the Guildhall, condemned of high treason and sentenced to be hanged, drawn and quartered like the Carthusians before them. If Henry had been alive the sentence would undoubtedly have been carried into effect; but the government of Protector Somerset was a merciful one and the sentence was not carried out. We know from his will that Mundy was imprisoned in the Tower, and that Hickman, whom he made his executor, 'hath been my keeper all the times of my sickness'.[4]

An echo of the case is to be found in the pages of Bishop Hooper, who wrote: 'In a certain church in England was an inquisition made for the Bible for the King's majesty's officers, that instead of the Bible found the left arm of one of those Charterhouse monks that died in the defence of the Bishop of Rome, reverently hid in the high altar of the church, with a writing containing the day and cause of his death: doubtless a very sacrament and open sign that they be hypocrites and dissemblers, and not persuaded of the truth in their hearts. And I trust to hear that the King's majesty never put his officers to great pain to bring them to Tyburn, but put them to death in the

[1] Henderson, x. 70.
[2] I am indebted for this fact to Mr. G. Baskerville, v. Newcourt's *Repertorium*, I. 394.
[3] *Wriothesley's Chronicle* (Camden Soc.), I. 184-5.
[4] P.C.C. 19 More.

church, upon the same altar wherein this relic was hid, and burnt there the
bones of these traitorous idolaters, with the relic, as Jehoiada did all the false
priests, 4 Reg. xxiii. And the doing thereof should not have suspended the
church at all, but have been a better blessing thereof than all the blessings of
the bishops of the world: for God loveth those that be zealous for his glory.'[1]
What a horrible temper this Old Testament spirit reveals; how these religious
persons loved one another. The Catholics were no better; it was Bishop
Hooper who was burned, under Mary. It would be anachronistic perhaps
even to disapprove; but one can hardly help noticing the idiot identification
on both sides of 'the Truth' and 'God' with themselves.

This awkward passage leaves its mark in the will which Mundy made
February 17th, 1549; and his benefices became vacant upon his condemnation. On October 29th, 1547, a new parson was instituted to Lanlivery, 'per
attincturam ultimi incumbentis'.[2] His will mentions a deed of gift for £4 to
William Gainsford, gaoler of the Tower. The ex-prior was a creditor on a
large scale in Cornwall: several people in his immediate entourage at Bodmin had screwed money out of him. The Chamonds owed him £30,
evidently for Bodiniel; John Tubbe's executors owed £40; Humphrey
Loves £9; Humphrey Prideaux £145 — this large sum the prior had agreed
to remit 'at my last being with him at his place of Thuborough ... as I
certified King's counsel by my writing what time I was judged to die'.
Thomas Opy, tanner, of Bodmin, owed £9 odd; the prior willed him to
pay Elizabeth Rosemund, widow, a small annuity 'for the rent of a chamber
which I promised her during my life': she was evidently the mother of
Thomas Rosemund, one of his former monks. Robert Sturgyn of Bodmin
owed him some money out of which he desired him to pay John Blight,
draper, '6s. 8d. the which I owe him for a coat cloth for Peter my man.
And also I desire him to be good to poor Hugh Deakin my old servant and
Roger Turrell'. He left a number of small loans due to him by 'Master
Trevelyan, his son and heir Humphry Trevelyan' and others, to Lawrence
Kendall his nephew and Katherine his wife. Other small sums were to be
devoted to prayers and masses for him; he willed the fellows and company of
Holmes college to pray for him, so also the vicar of Greenwich, Sir William
Bray, priest, Lawrence Kendall; Sir Walter Preston, priest, was 'to say for my
soul ten masses and ten dirges and commendations'. The prayers of
Nicholas Prideaux were not desired. It would seem that the prior no less than
the priory had been a veritable milch-cow for this family, by the schemes of
this man. The prior had so much money out on loan and owing to him, that

[1] *Early Writings of Bishop Hooper* (Parker Society), 202.   [2] Henderson, x. 71.

one cannot but wonder whether he had not been something of a money-lender to the neighbourhood. His will expresses a contrite heart, very understandable in the circumstances; he can never have expected such a fall. Perhaps his troubles were due to a too easy good-nature, a spirit of complaisance and a readiness to fall in with the plans of others, rather than any ill-nature in himself. He died in the winter of 1553-54.

The story of the remainder of the Bodmin monks is not long to tell. Richard Oliver, the sub-prior, who got a pension of £8, became vicar of Padstow, 1547-63, on the presentation of Dr. Tregonwell, who had it by grant from the priory.[1] John Dagle, who had a pension of £5 6s. 8d., had a successful career in benefices. In 1549 he was instituted to Morval, being presented by Walter Trelawny who had the grant from St. Germans; next year he became vicar of Bodmin, to which he was presented by the Chamonds by grant from the priory. In 1551 he resigned Morval; but in 1557 got the good rectory of St. Breoke. This he held with Bodmin until his death in 1564.[2] The changes and chances of Henry, Edward, Mary and Elizabeth do not seem to have made much difference with him, as with most sensible people. He seems to have resided, unmarried, at St. Breoke, and was buried at Bodmin.[3] Benet Carter, who received a pension of £6, was vicar of Grade 1540-50, when he died.[4] John Wilcock, pensioned at £5 6s. 8d., was rector of Jacobstow, 1545-57.[5] Thomas Rosemund and Thomas Marshall received pensions of £6 and £5 6s. 8d.: we do not know that they afterwards took livings. Michael Plemyn and John Best, who were lay-brothers, had pensions of 40s. They were still on the list of pensioners, along with four of the canons, in 1555.[6] The others had disappeared by then.

Tywardreath, as the one Cornish house to go by the Act of 1536, was the first in the market. In October its site and demesnes, with the grange of Trenant, were leased to John Grenville, an active, pushing younger son of the house of Stowe, who had his way to make in the world.[7] His lease was for 21 years at a rent of £9 9s. 4d. But there were two others after Tywardreath, Sir William Godolphin and Sir John Arundell. In August 1537 Godolphin wrote pressing his suit upon Cromwell, no doubt for the sale of the priory. He added: 'John Arundell, son and heir to Sir John, boasts that I shall never have it, and that my lady of Sussex has sent him word to come to court and

---

[1] Henderson, x. 71, 76.   [2] ibid., 29, 30, 74, 77.
[3] ibid., XXXI. 'Notes on Bodmin Priory'.   [4] ibid., and x, 70, 72.
[5] ibid., 29, 32.   [6] E 164/31.
[7] E 318/573. In 1543 he got the office of surveyor of all copyhold lands of the suppressed houses in Devon and Cornwall belonging to the King. L.P., XVIII. i, 546.

make sure of it, for John Grenville's lease of the mansion is the only grant of it.'[1] The latter found it less profitable than he had hoped, for he complained to Lord Chancellor Audley, to whom he was serjeant-at-arms, that he was so molested by Mr. Arundell that he got little profit out of it.[2] There was a good deal of ill-feeling between the Grenvilles and Arundells at this time; it lasted for many years. Neither of them got possession of Tywardreath, however, but some altogether more exalted, or at any rate more fortunate person, the Earl of Hertford, brother to Jane Seymour, afterwards Protector Somerset. He received a grant of the priory demesnes, the manor (valued at £14 5s. per annum) and advowson, in exchange for a number of Somersetshire rectories which had belonged to Muchelney and now went back to the Crown.[3] It does not appear that he paid anything: that was one of the advantages in being the King's brother-in-law.

At some time Hertford alienated Tywardreath to the Duke of Suffolk: there was a great deal of chopping and changing of Church lands among the greater nobles at Court. In 1564 the manor, and a sixth part of the demesnes (the latter had been previously leased to Nicholas Kendall) were sold outright to John Young, who sold them soon after to Christopher Copleston.[4] The value of these properties had gone up a good deal in the interval, and they fetched a good price: £1466 10s. The Coplestons, who were seated in Devonshire, had no need of another house in Cornwall. In 1570 we find a moiety of the house and site of the priory, and of the manor and advowson in the hands of the St. Aubyns;[5] and in 1573 Copleston alienated more of the demesnes to one of the Rashleighs.[6] In these sales we trace the break-up of the monastic estate. Nor was there any purpose for a second church immediately adjoining the parish church on the south side. It was still standing when Leland was here a few years after the Dissolution, and he noticed a tomb to Robert FitzWilliam at the west end.[7] But in time both church and priory buildings mouldered and were quarried away so completely, that hardly any fragments remain to show where it stood.

Apart from the prior, Nicholas Guest, it does not seem that any of the monks received preferment: from their previous record it would hardly appear that they were up to it. They received very small pensions. In 1555 William Huchyn was still alive and receiving his corrody of 66s. 8d.; John Fountain got 26s. 8d., John Nowell 20s., and David Harry two portions of 20s. each.[8] Lawrence Kendall, the husband of Prior Mundy's

[1] *L.P.*, XII. ii, 595.   [2] ibid., 738.   [3] E 318/573.
[4] Pat. Rolls 6 Eliz. 23 April, 1 May.   [5] ibid., 1069.
[6] ibid., 1109.   [7] *Leland's Itinerary*, I. 202.   [8] E 164/31.

niece, was the largest beneficiary of the convent still alive: he was being paid £6 a year, a grant from before the Dissolution. After all, he was the nephew of Prior Collins's old friend William Kendall.[1] The Kendalls of Pelyn nearby have been a family of consequence in that neighbourhood ever since those distant, fortunate days.

In 1546 the tithes in and around Tywardreath were valued for Robert Curzon by the Court of Augmentations.[2] We may take this transaction as typical of the hundreds that took place after the Dissolution. The tithes in question were: those on corn within the demesne lands of the priory, upon wool, lambs, offerings and other small tithes within the parish, and upon fish there; upon corn and other tithes on the demesne lands of the monastic grange of Trenant; and the tithe upon tin coming from all lands in the tenure of Nicholas Kendall. These were valued by Matthew Colthurst, the Court's surveyor, at 24s. 7d. a year over and above the £5 6s. 8d. allowed for the curate's wages to serve the parish church of Golant. An official of the Court has written upon the document: 'Mem. to certify whether you mean the tenth of the toll of lead within the parish or in all the lands belonging to the abbey, and whether the chaplain be serving in the parish or in another parish, for as it is written it cannot pass.' The reply is appended: 'The toll tin ... groweth of all the lands and tenements pertaining to the said late priory being in the King's Majesty's possession, which be of the clear yearly value of £33 2s. 10d. Also the chaplain serveth not the cure of the parish church of Tywardreath above said, but at the parish of St. Sampson, where always a monk of the said house did serve the cure, and of necessity must have a priest continually to serve the same.' One might say like someone else on a celebrated occasion 'On ne voit pas la nécessité'. But the sixteenth century thought otherwise, and the government did its best to provide for chaplains to say the services which the monks had provided. There were some difficulties over the matter; here and there lessees refused to fulfil their obligation to provide a curate, or more frequently there was some doubt as to where the obligation lay. However, these tithes, which had been leased to Nicholas Kendall, were granted to Robert Curzon in 1548, along with some other property: it was in part a gift, a small exemplar of the enormous grants which the governing oligarchy around Somerset handed out to themselves at the death of Henry VIII 'in fulfilment of his will'.[3] Later on, these tithes, like much else in this vicinity, came into the hands of the Rashleighs; in the nineteenth century they were worth £400 a year.[4]

[1] Vivian, *Visitations of Cornwall*, 258-9.   [2] E 318/340.
[3] *Cal. Pat. Rolls. Edward VI*, 1. 383.   [4] Grove, *Alienated Tithes*, 104.

It does not seem that the Crown was anxious to sell Launceston Priory, with its chief possession the manor there, outright. Doubtless the reason was its proximity to the Castle and the fact that the manor lay very conveniently to the Duchy estates in the neighbourhood. That it was not sold was not for want of a prospective purchaser, or at least of someone to ask for it. Sir Richard Grenville, High Marshal of Calais, was early in the field. That same summer of the Dissolution he had come over from his post of duty and paid a visit at Court.[1] Riding down to the west he had much to think about: what passed in his mind we may guess from the fact that as soon as he arrived at Stowe, he sat down to pen a long letter to Cromwell.[2] It was what was passing in the minds of a great many gentlemen at that historic moment, though no one expressed it more fully, more perfectly, than Sir Richard. His letter is a document of the first importance: in it is portrayed the mind of his class as in a mirror. When last he was with Cromwell, he wrote, he said that he had no suit to the King for land or fee. Since then he has bethought him that if he has not some piece of the suppressed land, by purchase or gift, 'I should stand out of the case of few men of worship of this realm'. He is as glad as any man of the realm at the suppression of 'these orgulous persons and devourers of God's word and takers away of the glory of Christ', who, he reckons, were also 'takers away of the wealth of the realm and sprys to the devilish Bishop of Rome'. Then follows the most revealing passage, which might have been taken as their text by the government, so well does it describe the motives to which they appealed, and on which they relied, in carrying out their revolutionary policy. *That his heirs may be of the same mind for their own profit*, he would gladly buy some of the suppressed lands in these parts and would find the King sureties for payment of his money and would sell part of his inheritance to pay the rest: a not over-delicate way of putting that he wanted them as a gift. But could the fundamental appeal of the Dissolution to cupidity and class-interest have been more expressively put? The Reformation could not possibly fail resting as it did upon this sure foundation.

The lands he wanted were the priory of Launceston, with a parcel of the demesnes called Newhouse, valued at £14 per annum; and the manor of Norton at £19. He probably had had a look at them on his way home to Stowe. If the King would give him the purchase of £8 p.a., he coolly suggested, he would give twenty years' purchase for the rest. If the lands were now worth more, he would give it, and if the woods were worth more than £40, he would answer the overplus. He did not obtain his request. Only those who had the intimate favour of the King, a personal servant like

[1] cf. my account in *Sir Richard Grenville*, 34-5.   [2] *L.P.*, XIV. i, 1338.

212

Sternhold, Cromwell himself, above all in the west, Lord Russell, got gifts of land. Others had to buy in the market.

In 1540 the site of the priory was leased to Gawen Carew for 21 years, with various dependencies, the rectory and chapel of St. Giles, Werrington, certain of the tithes of St. Thomas by Launceston, the rectory and chapel of Tresmere.[1] Carew, who was connected with the Court, made no attempt to live at Launceston, or apparently to buy it. He paid £15 19s. 6d. rent for the priory, £16 9s. 8d. for the tithes of Werrington, £2 for the lesser tithes of Tresmere.[2] Later, after the changes and chances of the intervening years, in which he took a prominent part in suppressing the Rebellion of 1549, and in the western conspiracy against Mary, he took on a much larger proposition, the manor of Launceston with its borough of Newport: this he leased in 1568 for a rent of £128 6s. In 1575 he took out a new lease of the priory and the above dependencies for sixty years at £34 19s. 2d. per annum.[3]

It seems that Carew's purpose was purely to make a profit out of his leases and not to build up any patrimony here. He showed himself unwilling to fulfil the obligation of maintaining curates to serve the churches whose tithes he had leased. This caused a good deal of trouble to the parishioners. Upon taking up his lease of the priory, he refused to pay the stipend of £5 allowed by the King's commissioners to the curate of Tresmere.[4] The parishioners sent a deputation to see him in London; he again refused to pay the chaplain, but offered them the tithes if they would support the chaplain, and pay himself 20s. a year in addition. At this they went to Sir Thomas Arundell, 'who then was in some trouble and could not help them, but willed them to retain some lawyer and go to the officers of the Augmentation Court'. Carew leased again the small tithes of St. Stephen's to William Heddon, for a fine of £22, and for a discharge from paying the curate for a number of years. Later on, he assigned the lease of the manor which he obtained from Queen Elizabeth to Thomas Hicks, a leading merchant and sometime mayor of the town.[5] In 1585, the woods of the manor which were for Cornwall very extensive, some 178 acres in all, were leased out in five parcels.[6] In 1600 the rectory of St. Stephen's, with its tithes, was sold for a large sum to Best and Holland, who were big London speculators in church property.[7]

The priory site itself was sold by the Crown at last in 1614, to Richard Connock, whose father, a Liskeard man, had made money in Elizabeth's reign, as an attorney, in commerce, and by various dubious means, and so

[1] ibid., xv. 1032. [2] Excheq. Spec. Com. 12 Feb., 21 April 1575.
[3] Pat. Roll. Eliz. 1126. [4] E 134/30 Eliz./Easter 7.
[5] Robbins, *Launceston*, 86. [6] E 311/27 Eliz. 244, 247, 248, 252, 253.
[7] Peter, *Launceston and Dunheved*, 33-4.

was enabled to go out of the town and settle at Treworgy as a country gentleman. Connock sold it to the Drakes of Buckland Abbey during the Commonwealth; thence it passed to Sir William Morice of Werrington, and so to the Duke of Northumberland. Werrington itself passed from the Duke to the great, but modern, clan of Williams, who made their fortunes out of the Industrial Revolution. One observes the process of breaking up the priory possessions in Launceston. The buildings themselves were quarried away early, as the castle walls were to be later, by the acquisitive inhabitants of the town. There was indeed no use for the fine Norman church, with its new roofing throughout carried out by Prior Hopkyn: there was the parish church of St. Thomas immediately outside the precinct, a bow-shot up the hill was the mother-church of St. Stephen's, while in the town itself was the newly-built church of St. Mary Magdalen. So Launceston Priory joined the other Cornish houses of which hardly anything remains.

Of the canons of Launceston after the Dissolution there is little record. That unsatisfactory person William Gennys, who gave Prior Shere so much trouble, had already left the house to become vicar of Poughill in 1538, to which he was nominated by one to whom the convent had granted this turn.[1] It was a way of getting rid of him. He received no pension. He died as vicar of Poughill in 1547.[2] Prior Shere took no living in Cornwall. His large pension of £100 — at least £2000 a year in our money — was enough to keep him in affluence. He was still in receipt of it in 1555.[3] There is an interesting, but tantalizing reference to a John Shere in a list of prisoners still in west-country gaols in September 1551, two years after the Prayer Book Rebellion: they were being held over to the next assizes.[4] Among them was a Peryn, a Donne, a Hayman, two Hores: names connected either with west-country monastic houses or subsequently recusant families. It would not be surprising if the ex-prior's Catholic sympathies got him into trouble at the time of the Rebellion. In Mary's reign we find the little priory manor of Tottisdon in Devon rated for him at £4 4s. 1d. per annum; i.e. at 30 years' purchase £126 2s. 6d.[5] With his large pension he could well afford it. John Ham, John Hicks, John Morley got pensions of £6 13s. 4d., Stephen George of £10, Thomas Webb, Richard Tredennick, John Lawrence and John Fick of £5 6s. 8d.[6] Of these, only the last got a benefice in Cornwall: he was vicar of St. Eval, 1563-79.[7] In 1555 five canons were still alive receiving their pensions, besides the prior.

[1] Henderson, X. 27.   [2] ibid., 29.   [3] E 164/31.
[4] A.P.C. 1550-52, 368.   [5] Harleian MS. 607/239.
[6] L.P., XIV. 361.   [7] Henderson, X. 76, 81.

The Crown kept the ownership of St. Michael's Mount in its hands until the end of the century; when, hard pressed for money to sustain the wars on so many fronts, Elizabeth's government sold it, like most of what remained of the church lands in the county, including even the manors annexed to the Duchy. The Mount and its manors of Lambesso and Traboe were sold for a very large sum — the value of land had greatly increased — to Bellot and Budden, two dealers in church lands, and from them passed to Sir Robert Cecil.[1] Hence it is that the cartulary of the priory is preserved to this day at Hatfield. From the Cecils it passed to the Bassets, and from them to the St. Aubyns with whom it has remained.

In the days of the abbess of Sion, the most important secular person connected with the Mount was the Receiver of its revenues. In the last days of the priory, this office was combined with that of the captaincy of the Mount — perhaps a consequence of the French raid upon Mount's bay during Henry VIII's first French War. From 1521 these offices were held by the Millitons of Pengersick, a castle of which the keep remains in a delightful situation a little way inland from the bay. In 1560 their lease was renewed for 40 years at a rent of £26 13s. 4d.[2] They were to maintain a priest there and five soldiers to defend the Mount; one notices the diminution of the religious element and the increase of the militant. This lease was granted without fine in consideration of the £44 16s. 11d. spent by them upon the repair of the pier, church, chapel and hall, where a commission had estimated that it would cost at least £200.

So the Mount, like other monastic edifices, was decaying; this step saved it, and in fact it is the only one in Cornwall which remains substantially unchanged, though it has been much added to. When Leland was there, he wrote: 'Within the said ward (i.e. the outer ward) is a court strongly walled, wherein on the south side is the chapel of St. Michael, and in the east side the chapel of our Lady. The captain and priest's lodgings be in the south side and west of St. Michael's chapel.'[3] Those buildings have vanished; the later house lies mainly upon the north side. In 1565 the advowson of St. Hilary also was granted to William Milliton. He died before his lease was up and was succeeded as captain of the Mount by Arthur Harris, who in 1596 received a grant of the office for life. This held good when the Mount went out of the possession of the Crown, and became, like almost everything else which had belonged to the monasteries' private property. To-day it is the noble residence of a peer.

---

[1] Taylor, *St. Michael's Mount*, 89.　　　[2] Pat. Rolls. Eliz. 8 April 1560.
[3] *Leland's Itinerary*, I. 320.

In 1546 William Abbot, of the King's household, bought Hartland Abbey just over the border in Devon, in its beautiful situation in the neck of the lovely valley, which, with its water-meadows and gardens, breaks the rigour of that iron coast: a little paradise. From the survey one derives the same impression as at St. Germans: a monastic landscape with its small closes and orchards and downs with little patches of wood: all transformed by the disciplinary hand of the eighteenth century into a gentleman's seat in its regular park. William Abbot, like the Eliots, made the place his home, established his family there, and it has come down in succession through heiresses to the Luttrells, Orchards, Bucks, Stucleys. But this is, properly, outside our province. What is not, is that Abbot's purchase included the site and house of the Greyfriars at Bodmin, with its gate-house and gardens.[1] This he sold next year to William Vyvyan and others, who evidently bought it as a speculation; for in 1566 they sold it to the mayor and burgesses of Bodmin.[2] In their hands the property remained. The church was a fine one, some 150 feet in length, and right up to the last century was used as an assize-hall, when it was destroyed to make way for new assize-courts: destroyed like other monuments of the past in Bodmin, leaving what should be one of the most interesting of Cornish towns, one of the least. Similarly at Truro, the site of the Blackfriars which was valued at £2 per annum, was sold in 1553 at 16 years' purchase to two Warwickshire speculators.[3] A few months previously it had been rated for Henry Killigrew, servant to the Duke of Northumberland. No doubt very soon it passed into local hands, and the church there disappeared much earlier and even more completely than the Greyfriars at Bodmin: some few fragments of the latter remained until lately: at Truro only a line of wall and a name, St. Dominick Street.

So much for the dispersal and devolution of the Cornish houses themselves, their churches and sites, buildings and demesnes. It is not possible here to trace in detail the location and descent of all their lands, precisely who got them and what they paid for them, the subsequent transactions in them: that would demand a whole book to itself. This study rests upon such a survey. Here it will be enough to notice various transactions, typical or interesting in themselves, which will enable us to build up a picture of Cornish society at this time. Here, for example, is what happened to two cells of larger houses. In the parish of St. Veep, in the delectable country on the east bank of the River Fowey, hilly but fertile, was the cell of St. Caroc belonging to Montacute, with the manor of Gonan and lands in several parishes hereabouts.

[1] *L.P.*, XXI. i, 149 (37).   [2] Maclean, I. 191.   [3] Particulars for Grants, Edward VI, No. 1595.

This nice little property had been leased in 1537; in 1546 it was purchased by Lawrence Courtenay for £199 7s. 6d.[1] He proceeded to make it his residence, and built up an attractive small estate out of its lands at Ethy, looking down upon the Lerryn River. Here they lived for two more generations, until the end of the century, were buried and remembered in St. Veep church, the rectory of which went with the estate and so remained up to our time.

At St. Anthony in Roseland, lying low down upon the waterside, in the crook of the peninsula looking across Porthcuel creek to St. Mawes, there was a cell of the monks of Plympton; in medieval times they had kept St. Anthony's light burning at the entrance to the Fal. In January 1540 the property was leased, with its house, meadows and gardens and the two dependent parsonages of St. Anthony and Gerrans, to Henry Thomas, the King's servant.[2] In 1547 another lease of the property was made for a further term, to Thomas Goodwyn, a large London dealer in church lands. At some time in the early seventeenth century the place — it retained the old monastic title of Place, as at Padstow — came into the possession of the Spry family who gave it its present modelled appearance of a small estate in a perfect natural situation.

The chief example of the transformation of a monastic barton into a large estate is, however, Lanhydrock. This property was part of the large holdings of the priory round Bodmin; there was a chapel there served by the monks, and next to it apparently, a large tithe-barn which received their grain. This was the noble property at the head of the valley running down to the river Fowey and Restormel, the old castle of the Earls of Cornwall — which the Roberts family of Truro, having made a large fortune out of the tin-trade, bought in the reign of James I and where they proceeded to build the finest Jacobean house in Cornwall. When Richard Symonds was here with the Royalist army under the King in 1644, he wrote in his diary: 'A gentleman of this county told me the original of the Lord Roberts his family. His great-grandfather was servant to a gentleman of this county, his hind. Afterwards lived in Truro, and traded in wood and fferzen: got an estate of 5 or £6000; his son was so bred and lived there too, put out his money and his debtors paid it him in tin. He, engrossing the sale of tin, grew to be worth many thousands (£300,000). His son was squeezed by the court in King James his time of £20,000: so was made a baron, and built the house at Lanhydrock, now the seat of this Lord Roberts.'[3] An unfavourable witness: for Symonds was a Cavalier and Lord Robartes, as befitted so prosperous a

---

[1] E 318/320.   [2] ibid., 497.   [3] Symonds' *Diary*, 55-6.

bourgeois, a great Puritan and Parliamentarian. But the story is substantially accurate. So the world proceeds.

The picture grows up in one's mind in concrete detail, house by house, estate by estate, of how medieval Cornwall with the large holdings of the Church became transformed into the modern Cornwall whose lines are familiar to us: St. Germans and Port Eliot, Prideaux Place at Padstow and Place at St. Anthony, Lanhydrock, Ethy, the Mount. Historical research enables us, it might be said, to photograph a social process. In other counties, where the monastic holdings were much larger, that process is even more evident and easy to trace upon the map.

Of Cornish gentry who went in for church property on a large scale, Sir Richard Grenville was the most prominent.[1] The Prideaux family, not content with their acquisitions at Padstow, made further purchases, and not only in Cornwall. In 1545 Roger Prideaux bought the manor of Trewosell, which had belonged to Launceston, and that of Lannow Sant or St. Kew, late of Plympton Priory.[2] In 1549 Nicholas and Roger Prideaux bought the lands belonging to the chantry of Week St. Mary, two more chantries at Barnstaple and a large number of rents and farms belonging to chantries in Devon and Somerset.[3] In 1553 with Richard Chamond he purchased the manor of Launcells, late of Hartland, which seems to have gone to Chamond's share, and a large number of smaller properties in several counties from Essex to Devon.[4] Under Elizabeth he was still buying: the manor and rectory of Bradock, which had belonged to the Earl of Devon, and in Devon a manor of Suffolk's and another rectory.[5] He got a renewal for life of the lease of Buckland Brewer rectory, which the abbot of Torre had made out to Humphrey and William Prideaux; and also of the lease of Tregony Martin rectory made out to Nicholas Prideaux by Merton Priory on Holy Cross Day 1534.[6] How interesting that is: it takes our mind back to that journey which Nicholas Prideaux made, upon Prior Vyvyan's death, to Merton Priory to get Mundy elected prior of Bodmin. An eventful occasion in his life; it is very lifelike to find him using the occasion to make interest for himself with the monks there. It is impossible to trace all the dealings of the Prideaux family in land now, and most of them would take us outside of Cornwall: Roger Prideaux was head of the senior line of the family at Soldon in Devon. But it is clear that of all west-country families who owed much to the dispersal of church lands, they were among the first.

The leading figure in this respect, who surpassed most others in his

[1] cf. my *Sir Richard Grenville*, 36-7. [2] E 318/1382. [3] ibid., 1890, 1891.
[4] ibid., 1485. [5] ibid., 2557. [6] Pat. Rolls Eliz. 2 March 1566.

acquisitions in the west country, was another Cornishman, altogether more highly placed than Tregonwell, namely Sir Thomas Arundell. The second son of Sir John Arundell, the most important personage in Cornwall throughout Henry's reign, on his mother's side grandson of the Marquis of Dorset (brother-in-law of Henry VII), he was himself brother-in-law by marriage to Henry VIII through his wife Margaret Howard, sister of the unfortunate Queen Catherine. In consequence he was connected with half the peerage and stood in an advantageous position close in the Court-circle. His great-grandfather had married an heiress of the Chideocks, and she brought the Arundells Chideock castle and estates in Dorset. Sir Thomas's father seems to have left the running of the Dorset interests of the family to him; and there is no doubt of the somewhat restless ability, eager and acquisitive, of the younger son. He had his first experience of the great world in the household of Wolsey, to whom he was gentleman of the privy chamber and where he became acquainted with Cromwell. In 1533 at Anne Boleyn's coronation, he was made Knight of the Bath, and in the same year he succeeded his father who had held the office since 1507, as receiver of the Duchy of Cornwall. [1]

From 1526 he had held a lease of the toll-tin on three of the large Duchy manors in Cornwall, a paying proposition. [2] His father seems to have made over Wardour castle to him in Wiltshire, which became the residence of the junior, but in time more resplendent, branch of the family. It was the Dissolution which provided him, no less than smaller fry like Tregonwell, with their major opportunity. He was not slow to take it. Officially a friend of Cromwell's — it is doubtful what his private sentiments were towards him: the great Vicar-General had few friends but a multitude of flatterers — Arundell was early concerned in the business of the monasteries. In 1534 we find the abbot of Malmesbury making out a patent for him at Cromwell's request. [3] Arundell wrote, thanking Cromwell: 'I send your bottle with a dish of partridges and rails, whereof this country was never so ill stored.' [4] Next year, there came a coolness between Cromwell and him, something which he had said grazed the sensitive skin of the man who had risen to such heights. Arundell apologised profusely: he was not so regardless of Cromwell's authority, or so ungrateful to his best master, he said, but for whose goodness he was in danger of losing the greater part of his living. There was nothing more painful than that Cromwell should misunderstand him. [5] Nothing, we may add, save the loss of the whole of his living. Cromwell

---

[1] *L.P.*, VI. 300 (14).   [2] ibid., IV. 2673.   [3] ibid., V. 990.
[4] ibid., VI. 628-9.   [5] ibid., VIII. 558.

was a dangerous person to quarrel with, as Sir Richard Grenville was to find. But Grenville and Arundell too were at daggers drawn: the shifty, insecure background of that age, a Renaissance court.

Arundell continued to be employed in monastic business in the west country, though we know little of it because not much of his correspondence has survived. We find him visiting Tavistock Abbey, and he took a hand in the tug-of-war going on over Hartland, in which he was worsted by Sir William Courtenay who had Cromwell's ear.[1] At Shaftesbury, however, he got the abbess to give Cromwell the next presentation to Tarrant Hinton: 'I advised them to do so because your letters expressed a wish she should do so', he wrote, nakedly.[2] He was one of the surveyors of the Court of Augmentations, and was given the job of suppressing the smaller houses in Somerset. He wrote to Cromwell in 1537 to know if Cleeve Abbey might be spared. Riding down to Cornwall he had heard such lamentation for the Dissolution thereof and a bruit in the country that the King had pardoned it: 'I beg in behalf of the honest gentlemen of that quarter that the house may stand.' He gave a very good report of the monks there, adding that they would give the King 1000 marks for exemption, and that he would have spoken to the King himself for them, but that 'he doubted his Grace should have noted him to have been corrupted'. He protested that he 'looked for no reward as the house was not rich'.[3] Perhaps.

With the Dissolution of the greater monasteries, Arundell's moment came and he was very fully employed. He became Receiver for the Court of Augmentations in the south-western counties at £20 a year and profits. He received a life annuity of £30, was put on all the commissions of the peace for Cornwall, Somerset and Dorset.[4] Annuities from various religious houses, like Malmesbury, accumulated; stewardships and offices like that of high bailiff of Salisbury fell to him. His purchases of lands begin now on the grand scale, to say nothing of numerous leases and farms of properties. In 1540, for £400, he bought the manor of Chesilbourne; then that of Encombe, and then, for £1761 14s. 10d., the manor and advowson of Tisbury, of Donington, and the manor of Remescombe.[5] In 1541 he bought the manor of Sedgehill from Sir Thomas Poynings, and in 1544 he put through a very large purchase, larger than any we have yet had to deal with: a number of manors and rectories in Wiltshire, Dorset and Somerset for £2609 1s. 1d., a sum twice that of Sir Richard Grenville's purchase.[6] Next year he bought

---

[1] *L.P.*, x. 1221; viii. 359, 569.   [2] ibid., xi. 1340.   [3] ibid., xii. i, 4.
[4] ibid., xiii. ii, 1520.   [5] ibid., xv. 282, 733, 831.
[6] ibid., xvi. 379; xix. ii, 340.

the lordship and manor of Fontmell and the hundred of Sexpen in Dorset for £1147 3s. 7d. [1]

By this time he is Chancellor to the Queen, very active at Court during the King's absence in France, and much concerned in ordnance matters. [2] He resigns the office of receiver of the Augmentations in the south-west, but goes on buying: in 1545, the manors of Barton and Birdsour in Dorset and Wilts with an advowson, £1097 17s. paid. [3] That same year he leased the tithes in the Scilly Isles which had belonged to Tavistock Abbey. [4] Next year he bought the college of Slapton in Devon, with various manors and rectories, including the rectory of Poundstock in Cornwall: this was for his services and for £530 6s. 0½d., evidently not the full value of the premises. [5] This was his last purchase in Henry's reign. He seems to have been in fair, though not in intimate, favour with Henry in the last years of his reign. His name was proposed for the Garter, though he did not get it; he was one of the gentlemen who attended the King at the great state-reception of the French Embassy in 1546. [6] When, on Edward VI's accession, Paget made his flattering depositions as to Henry's intentions of advancing the ranks of his councillors, Hertford to be a duke, others to be earls and so on, Sir Thomas Arundell was among those, it turned out, whom the late King would have made a baron. [7] He certainly had estates large enough to support the honour. It did not come however.

That can hardly have improved his temper, and in fact he did not approve of the Protestant direction of the new regime under Somerset. That did not prevent him from taking a lease of the college of Crantock, over which he had some difficulties in entering into possession, upon the dissolution of the chantries. [8] When the Prayer Book Rebellion broke out in the west, the Catholic sympathies of Arundell and his elder brother, Sir John, who had now succeeded at Lanherne, became evident. Sir John had mass said in his household and did not answer Lord Russell's command to serve against the rebels. [9] That summer they were bound in an enormous sum not to depart from London without licence of the Protector. [10] In the autumn, the Protector's position having been undermined by the rebellions and the failure of his policy, Sir Thomas Arundell was a prime mover in bringing about the coalition between the Catholics in the Council and the supporters of Warwick, which overthrew the Protector. [11] There was a rumour that Arundell

---

[1] ibid., xx. i, 1335. [2] ibid., App. 2. 2. 111. [3] ibid., i. 1081 (32).
[4] ibid., i. 878. [5] ibid., xxi. 149. 19.
[6] ibid., xx, i, 566; xxi. i, 1384. [7] Acts of the Privy Council, ii. 16.
[8] cf. cases in Court of Augmentations, E 321/24/27; 26/32 and 31/51.
[9] See below, p. 268. [10] A.P.C., ii. 304. [11] Cal. S.P. Spanish, 1547-49, 470.

was to succeed Paget as Comptroller, and he certainly offered his services to the Princess Mary. It was not clear at first which way Warwick intended to move. It did not take him long to double-cross his Catholic supporters. In January 1550 Arundell was a prisoner in his house; in February he was sent to the Tower, along with his brother.[1] Here he remained until October next year, during which time Arundell swung over to Somerset's side and became a leading member of the party which wanted to restore him to power.[2] Released in October, after being brought before the Council, he was re-arrested within a fortnight and sent back to the Tower with Somerset and his leading adherents.[3] This time there was no escape. He was arraigned in Westminster Hall on January 28th, 1552, but 'the quest could not find him [i.e. guilty] till the morrow. And so he went to the Tower again, then the quest were shut up till the morrow without meat or drink, or candle or fire; and on the morrow he came again, and the quest quit him of treason and cast him of felony to be hanged'.[4] He was, however, given the more polite privilege of execution on Tower Hill on February 26th.

His estates and possessions were all forfeit to the Crown; for some years on we find numerous grants of properties which had formerly been his; there is a long list of his plate that survives — it was taken to the Jewel-House.[5] He died a very rich man. The Crown valuation of his estates was £641 13s. 4¼d. a year;[6] that is at 21 years' purchase, a capital value of nearly £15,000: a fortune equal to that of some earls and most barons of the time, and which surpassed by now that of the senior branch of the family at Lanherne and Chideock. A benevolent, or approachable, government restored to his widow, Lady Margaret Arundell, a third part of the value of the lands: a more than sufficient jointure. When Mary came to the throne, a woman by temperament generous and notably loyal to old friends, she restored the whole property to his widow and son. And so the Arundells of Wardour, after these vicissitudes, came back into their own: an old Catholic family which yet, as in so many cases, reposes upon the substantial basis of monastic lands.

It is indeed worthy of comment that of the leading figures concerned in the Dissolution in Cornwall, not one was a Protestant: Sir Thomas Arundell no more than Sir John Tregonwell, neither Prideaux nor Prior Mundy. The sympathies of each were unmistakably catholic.

---

[1] *Cal. S.P. Spanish*, 1550–52, 21; *A.P.C.*, III. 27, 54, 258.
[2] ibid., 378; *Cal. S.P. Spanish*, 1550–52, 386.   [3] *A.P.C.* III, 391, 397, 484, etc.
[4] *Machyn's Diary* (Camden Soc.)   The account of Arundell's career in *D.N.B.* is not only inadequate, but inaccurate.
[5] Add. MS. 5751, 209–11.   [6] E 318/1391.

CHAPTER X

CORNWALL AND PUBLIC AFFAIRS
UNDER HENRY VIII

HENRY VIII's reign began, as so frequently in human affairs, with a war: a more than usually purposeless one, waged against France, along with other members of the 'Holy League' under the sanctified protection of the Papacy and instigated by that warlike old man whom Erasmus (rightly) hated, Julius II. It is not our business to go into this foolery as a whole. Cornwall took its part in it, as in increasing measure in the wars of the century. At its outbreak, in July 1511, commissions of array were issued to Sir John Arundell, Sir Piers Edgcumbe and all the leading gentry to muster its men.[1] As the war progressed and became more serious, a French invasion was expected early in 1513, and writs were sent down to Arundell, Edgcumbe and Willoughby to proclaim that all males between sixteen and sixty were to be levied to resist the French landing.[2] No invasion materialized, as often subsequently when there was rumour of it. Instead, the English invaded France, largely to obtain the glory of arms so coveted by a youthful and orthodox king.

When Henry made his large and opulent expedition into France, attended by the priests and singers of his chapel, his secretaries, clerks and pages, his bellicose ecclesiastics (the young Wolsey prominent among them), and his lutanist Peter Carmelianus, Arundell and Edgcumbe were among the captains of his troops.[3] The former was in command of two companies (204), the latter of one (101): the Cornish contingent in the army which captured Thérouenne and won the battle of the Spurs. Before going overseas, in December 1512, Arundell, in accordance with the pathetic belief of the time, founded a chantry in the church of St. Mawgan next door to his house of Lanherne, with a priest to pray for his soul.[4] It was not necessary. He returned home safe again, having been created a knight banneret after the fall of Thérouenne, to live out almost the span of Henry's reign and see the dissolution of the chantry he had founded.

It was in the war at sea that Cornwall figured more; and here the leading figure was Sir William Trevanion. Carhayes, the home of the Trevanions,

---

[1] *L.P.*, I. 833 (58).   [2] ibid., 1602 (38).
[3] ibid., 2053 (7).   [4] ibid., 1524 (35).

stands in a lovely situation close to the sea, convenient for both Falmouth and Fowey; and Sir William began a family connection with the sea which lasted all through and beyond our period. He was a favourite with Henry; we find him jousting in the tournaments at Court, and three times pricked for sheriff, in 1503, 1508, 1516. Controller of the coinage of tin in Cornwall and Devon, and keeper of Montorgeuil castle in Jersey, he received various grants of custody and marriage of heirs.[1] In Sir Edward Howard's fleet which kept the seas in 1512 and convoyed Dorset's army to Guienne, Trevanion was captain of the *George* of Falmouth, of 140 tons and carrying 144 men.[2] Two other Cornish ships were in the fleet, the *Peter* of Fowey, 120 tons, and the *Janet* of Penryn, of 70 tons.[3] Howard's raid upon Brest in August was made notable by the combat between two leading ships, the *Regent* and the *Cordelière*, in which both were blown up and nearly all on board perished. At the end of that year, Dorset returned from his campaign, having accomplished nothing and been thoroughly let down by Henry's father-in-law, Ferdinand; he landed at Falmouth in November.[4]

Next year the naval campaign waxed hot around the coasts of Brittany. Prégent, who had seen much Mediterranean fighting, arrived at Brest with a squadron of galleys. In Howard's fleet, which left Plymouth in April, there were the same three Cornish ships; but Trevanion was appointed to command one of the largest of the King's ships, the *Gabriel Royal*, of 800 tons, with some 600 men aboard her.[5] He had also in the fleet his little bark the *Vincent* of Fowey, of 60 tons with 32 men, commissioned by the King.[6] Howard made the mistake of ordering an attack upon Prégent's galleys in shallow water in the harbour at Brest, a mistake which cost him his life. Trevanion's bark was one of those assigned to attack the galleys and drive them aground.[7] Of the men that were to land he was to captain 300.[8] After Howard's death, the fleet returned disheartened to Plymouth.

In 1514, Trevanion offered to serve on land; but on his offer being rejected, he was content to return to the sea in command of 200 men.[9] He rigged out a balinger at his own charges, hoping that the King would employ her, and he petitioned the Lord Admiral that the poor men at Fowey, John Power and others, might be taken with their ships into the King's service again. It would be a good deed for Surrey to help the town of Fowey as he had Dartmouth; there were few better ships of her burden in England than the *George*, while Surrey himself knew the *Peter*. He requests instructions about the

---

[1] *L.P.*, 158 (16), 190 (41), 924 (32), 1221 (58). [2] ibid., 1453 (2).
[3] Spont, *Letters and Papers of the War with France*, 1512-13, 8, 10.
[4] ibid., xxix. [5] ibid., 77, 79-80; and *L.P.*, I. 1661 (3, 4, 7).
[6] ibid., 2304 (iii). [7] ibid., 1786. [8] ibid., 1869. [9] ibid., 2669.

Spanish ship and the Breton at Fowey, and asks for two or three petty captains to aid him, since for the last two or three years he had been over-burdened with the wages of his company. But peace put a stop to these employments; in December he was rewarded with the pension of 50 marks reserved to the Crown upon the Bodrugan estates.[1]

At the height of the war, invasion was expected; it was thought that Prégent had some design upon Plymouth or Falmouth.[2] Parliament passed a statute 'for the erecting of bulwarks westward': forasmuch as the French and Bretons 'by reason of their fishing upon the sea coasts know as well every haven and creek within the said county as every landing-place in as large manner as any subject of our sovereign lord the King doth', the Sheriff and Justices were to 'ride and view all the said south coast from Plymouth westward to the Land's End'.[3] At such places as they appointed the towns and parishes were to make bulwarks, the mayors and constables commanding the inhabitants to be at the sea-side with such instruments as they had. It was the first step in the long Tudor struggle to provide adequate defences along the coast.

Whether due to the disturbed conditions of war, or to the increased taxation necessary, there were riots in both Cornwall and Devon in 1514. Commissioners were appointed to inquire into them, but, alas, we know nothing more about them.[4]

In 1517 Falmouth harbour was the scene of the overthrow of a most interesting voyage, that of John Rastell for Newfoundland. This is not the place to tell its story in full, but it was intended as a follow-up of the Cabot Voyages and provides a link between those earlier and the later voyages of discovery.[5] Lawyer, dramatist, printer, promoter of voyages, brother-in-law of Sir Thomas More, Rastell was one of the most interesting and many-sided spirits of the age; he has his place in the development of the Tudor drama. In 1517 he got together a number of ships for the enterprise, and it appears that the Lord Admiral Surrey had an interest in it. This led to its undoing, for there was a division of purpose in the fleet from the start such as wrecked so many subsequent voyages. Rastell undoubtedly intended discovery, for in addition to the cargo of goods he carried, he had on board thirty or forty soldiers and brought 'tools for masons and carpenters and other engines that he had prepared for the new lands'.[6] It would seem that Surrey pre-

---

[1] *L.P.*, I. 3582.   [2] Spont, xxxii.
[3] *Statutes of the Realm*, III. 48.   [4] *L.P.*, I. 3408 (4), 3324 (42).
[5] For the full story v. Williamson, *The Voyages of the Cabots and the Discovery of North America*, 85-93, 244-8; and for Rastell, Boas, *Introduction to Tudor Drama*, 5-10.
[6] Court of Requests, bundle 3, no. 192.

ferred an ordinary trading voyage to Bordeaux. He had his representative in the fleet, one John Ravyn, who managed to wreck Rastell's plans.

The ships were delayed at Sandwich, and again at Plymouth by a leak, and Ravyn worked upon the minds of the ships' masters, who were in any case disinclined to the voyage, for the season grew late. At Falmouth things came to a head. The fleet was out of Rastell's control, though he tried all he could to get the masters to press on with the voyage. Ravyn left his ship and went on land for a week or more to get a bargain of tin for Bordeaux for his profit; he sold several pipes of flour, including one to the prior of Blackfriars at Truro. On his return, he put Rastell's factor out of his ship the *Barbara* and sold some of his goods, fine white flour, bay salt, frieses, canvas, mercery ware, and household stuff such as feather-beds, napery, pots and pans, to the value of £100. It was proposed to Rastell that he should go to Bordeaux, or even take to robbing on the seas; but he would hear none of it and insisted on his voyage. The ships got as far as Waterford, where it was finally overthrown and the project abandoned. A great pity: it might have been an important step in the history of English exploration, which Henry VIII's reign did so little to advance. We have Rastell's comment on the attempt in his *New Interlude and the Nature of the Four Elements*, evidence of his curious, inquiring mind and his interest in geographical exploration.

Henry's second French War, which began in 1522, was even more senseless than the first; it followed not long after the pompous and hypocritical exhibition of the Field of the Cloth of Gold. Not much evidence remains of Cornwall's part in it. The usual writs were sent to the J.P.s to muster the population to resist any French landing and to prepare beacons.[1] Cornish miners were sent to France, where apparently they gave no satisfaction. 'The Cornish miners are of no use', Sandys wrote to Wolsey. 'They say their faculty is to work underground, not above.'[2] Most of the evidence that remains relates to taxation, for the burden of the war was extremely heavy. For the subsidy granted by the Parliament of 1515 Cornwall seems to have been rated at £604 1s. 8d., compared with Dorset at £1138 12s.[3] The French War necessitated the levying of much larger sums. Wolsey began with a forced loan in 1522; it was in fact a tax on property which fell heaviest on the clergy. The Bishop of Exeter was rated to pay £1000, the cathedral chapter £333 6s. 8d., the priors of Bodmin and St. Germans £100 and £66 13s. 4d.[4] In fact some concession was made, and the sums paid were rather lower. The account returned by Veysey for the clergy of his diocese

[1] L.P., III. 2438.   [2] ibid., 2560.   [3] ibid., II. 1371.   [4] ibid., III. 2483.

remains, and it is pretty thorough: the tax amounted to one-tenth of the total value of the possessions and goods of all clergy worth more than £10.[1]

Next year the government was forced to apply to Parliament for money, and Wolsey proposed a staggering tax of four shillings in the pound upon every man's lands and goods. There was much resistance and discussion; the Cardinal was defeated. In May the Commons agreed to grant two shilings in the pound upon incomes of £20 and more, one shilling upon those between £2 and £20, and a poll-tax of 4d. upon those below. Payment was to be spread over two years. In Cornwall, as in other counties, a large body of commissioners for the subsidy was appointed, including practically all the J.P.s and the mayors and aldermen of the towns.[2] In November, money being slow in coming in, smaller commissions of the leading gentry were appointed to 'practise' with all persons worth £40 or more to pay their full sum beforehand.[3] Actually Cornwall was among the minority of counties which returned its account of the loan: perhaps a tribute to the business capacity of John Grenville, who brought in the money.[4] In 1524 we find a first payment for Cornwall of £1298 10s. 8d., as against £5549 11s. for Devon; and a second payment of £1651 6s. 2d.[5] A third payment of £1108 12s. 10d. appears, and then in 1525 from the Feast of the Purification (February 2nd) to May 12th a sum of £603 6s. 8d., compared with £1720 for Devon.[6] As late as 1528 there is an estimate of a fourth payment: £73 16s. 8d. for Cornwall, £423 6s. 8d. for Devon.[7] It is difficult to give these figures an exact interpretation. All one can say is that they show the resources of Devon to be about four times those of Cornwall. The war, ending in the Emperor's smashing victory at Pavia and Francis I's imprisonment in Spain, seriously altered the balance of power in Europe. So Henry and Wolsey made peace, went over to the other side and went on with the old game as before.

With Wolsey's fall the hour for the long-postponed attack on the Church struck, and the Parliament which carried through the Reformation in alliance with the King was summoned. The Cornish contingent was very representative of the two powerful, dynamic classes to whose interests that legal revolution appealed, the landed gentry and the town middle-class. It was not that Parliament was packed — that was not necessary; those out of sympathy with the new course would hardly seek return. The two knights for

---

[1] There is a transcript of the Return in Henderson, x, 366 foll.
[2] *L.P.* III. 3282.   [3] ibid.
[4] ibid., 3683. The return for the hundred of Pydar is printed by W. J. Stephens in *J.R.I.C.*, no. 61, 456-461; and cf. the *Subsidy Rolls for the Parish of Constantine* (Devon and Cornwall Record Society).
[5] *L.P.* IV. 214.   [6] ibid., 969, 1327.   [7] ibid., 3866.

the shire were Sir Piers Edgcumbe and Sir Richard Grenville,[1] both, but particularly the latter, in sympathy with the Reformation. No Arundells sat for a Cornish seat. Bodmin was represented by Gilbert Flamank, of a well-known local family, and by Thomas Treffry of Fowey, who was strong in support of the new trends and on friendly terms with Cromwell. John Rastell, also Protestant in his sympathies, sat for Dunheved, along with Edward Ringley, no doubt by arrangement with Sir Richard Grenville, who had a family interest in the borough and later succeeded Ringley as High Marshal at Calais. Truro was represented by Roger Corbet and John Thomas, a dependable serjeant-at-arms holding office in the county; Liskeard by James Trewynnard, of an old west Cornwall family interested in tin, and Henry Pyne, a local man; Lostwithiel by John Tredennick and Richard Bryan; Helston by Edward Smith and John Holditch; Newport by Simon Mounford and William Harris, the latter a Cornishman. Though it is not possible to identify every one of these, we know enough to form a reliable picture of the Cornish representation: it is typical of that which, generalized over the whole country, makes intelligible the attack on the Church, the breach with Rome, the expropriation of the monasteries, the setting up of a national church under royal authority.

Though it is anachronistic to think of Parliament then as 'packed', the government did exercise some influence in indicating candidates here and there whom it preferred or wanted to see returned. This was still more the case with the Parliament of 1539 where Cromwell needed all the support he could muster against the catholic party. And it so happens that we have a valuable bit of evidence of the influence he exercised in returning one of the knights of the shire for Cornwall. Sir William Godolphin wrote to say that he had received Cromwell's letter declaring his pleasure 'for the preferment of my son, your servant, to be a knight of the shire for Cornwall. Before it came there was great suit made by Sir Piers Edgcumbe, Sir John Chamond and John Arundell, son and heir of John Arundell, knight. The writ has not yet come.'[2] The returns for the later Parliaments of Henry's reign are lost, so that we do not know for sure if Godolphin was returned; but it is probable that Cromwell had his way. We may infer from this too how after the long duration of the Reformation Parliament and the importance of its work, a seat became more highly valued, and further perhaps, how feeling was running strongly in the country over the issues at stake.

Of the Cornish members of Henry's last Parliaments we only know William Trewynnard, member for Helston in 1542, for he gave his name to

[1] *L.P.*, iv. 6043.   [2] ibid., xiv. 598.

a leading case concerning the privilege of a member from arrest for debt.[1] He was imprisoned for a debt of £75 to John Skewes and released by the sheriff, Richard Chamond, upon receipt of a writ of privilege from the King.[2] The arguments concerning the case are long and complicated and there was some delay between the writ and Trewynnard's release. It was followed by further litigation, on the part of Skewes' executors against the sheriff, and of the sheriff against Trewynnard.[3] It gives one further insight into the duties of the sheriff and the unpleasant liabilities of the office which made people reluctant to accept it. But the upshot was, coming closely upon the similar case of Ferrers, to strengthen the privilege of M.P.s, and as such the case was cited in the Commons' debates of 1625.[4]

We have already had some indication of the attitude of the county towards the Dissolution of the monasteries: the hostility of the towns towards them, the hesitation of some of the gentry at first to see them totally destroyed, the willingness of all to profit by it when it was inevitable. There is no evidence of any opposition in Cornwall to this great property-revolution, nor, as we have seen, was there any reason for the Cornish houses to be popular. And in the crisis of the Pilgrimage of Grace, when the northern counties were in insurrection, Cornwall, like the rest of the south, was loyal and sent its contingent to the King's forces.[5] There were two companies of 100 men each under Sir William Godolphin and Sir Hugh Trevanion, and two of forty under John Arundell of Trerice and John Reskymer. Sir Piers Edgcumbe was in command of 200 and John Arundell, the heir of Lanherne, of 100 among the Devon troops, and Sir Thomas Arundell of 200 among the Dorset contingent. Altogether Cornwall provided 364 men to Devon's 968, and the Marquis of Exeter was to command an army of over 2000 men from the four south-western counties. While the situation remained critical in the north, special consideration was to be paid to the south and west lest they should be affected;[6] and in fact, at the end of the year, we find an examination at the Tower by the archdeacon of Cornwall and Dr. Layton, of a seditious writing which was shown to Cornish soldiers on pilgrimage at Walsingham on their way back from the north.[7]

It was not until the routine of their lives was affected, the saints' days and feasts and wakes, the customs of their churches, that the silly, simple people began to be disturbed. We have noticed the anxiety of Dr. Tregonwell that

[1] This must be distinguished from the later Trewynnard case concerning the jurisdiction of the Court of Stannaries, see above p. 66.
[2] Hatsell, *Precedents in the House of Commons*, I. 59-65.
[3] Early Chanc. Proc. file 1111, no. 34.
[4] Gardiner, *Commons' Debates of 1625* (Camden Soc.), 14, 60-1.
[5] L.P., XI, 580 (2, 3).   [6] ibid., 1410.   [7] ibid., 1260.

the desire of the Cornishmen to retain their patron saint's day in the parish should be met. More was involved in the matter than that: there was the deliberate policy of the Reformers to cut down holidays all round, very conveniently for the classes which profited by the Reformation and whose work it was. The importance of the question may be gathered from a curious episode which took place in Cornwall and might have come to mischief if it had not been taken in time. Early in 1537 a friend of Godolphin's who was a painter (did he, one wonders, paint the frescoes in the church at Breage?) was asked by one Carpyssack, a St. Keverne man, to make a banner for the parish with 'a picture of Christ with his wounds abroad and a banner in his hand, Our Lady in one side holding her breast in hand, St. John à Baptist in the other, the King's grace and Queen kneeling, and all the commonalty kneeling, with scripture above their heads, making their petition to the picture of Christ that it would please the King's grace they might have their holidays'.[1] Godolphin, reporting this to Cromwell, pointed out ominously that St. Keverne was a large parish where the Cornishmen first rose when they came to Blackheath: the Smith dwelled there. Carpyssack also said that when he and John Treglosack had been at Hamell by Southampton selling their fish and two men asked them why they had not risen when the northern men did, they swore upon the book that they would help them and had bought 200 jerkins, and that they would carry the banner on Pardon Monday and show it to the people. At the moment, Godolphin added, the country was in a marvellous good quiet, but all the same he begged Cromwell to move the King that they might keep the day of the head saint of their church, and the country would pray for him.

It was important that Carpyssack should not get back to rebellious and spirited St. Keverne. Nor apparently did he. Cromwell wrote at once to Godolphin to take him, and to send the names and dwelling places of those about Southampton, with the colours of the jerkins of Carpyssack and his fellow. Godolphin replied, insisting 'if you would move the King that they might have their holiday it would be a great stay'.[2] Carpyssack was taken but owing to the plague there were no assizes at Launceston. Godolphin was afraid that unless there were a special commission he would have to wait until the next assizes. He told Cromwell that he had been to every gaol delivery and assizes to give evidence against the traitor; but that Sir John Chamond had answered that he had no authority to inquire for high treason and the judge of assize had said the same. Godolphin asked Cromwell to speak to the judge 'that the traitor might be hanged in chains at Helston

[1] L.P., XII. i, 1001.   [2] ibid., 1126.

town end'.[1] No doubt it was done: such was the spirit of the time, in which Godolphin and Cromwell shared alike. When the ruling class was frightened it stuck at nothing. Someone wrote to the new dean of Exeter, who had succeeded that more exalted traitor, Reginald Pole, that Exeter was 'half afraid of a privy insurrection of Cornishmen'.[2] The dean was impressed: 'This is a perilous country, for God's love let the King's grace look to it in time'.[3] Godolphin received his reward for his good services: he and his son were granted in survivorship the office of steward of the Somerset lands in Cornwall and of the King's lands in Alverton, Penzance and Tywarnhayle.[4]

An amusing episode that same spring throws light on the customs, and perhaps the sympathies, of the people. The *Magdalen* of Truro was carrying a company of pilgrims under the conduct of two or three priests to a pardon at Lantrégar in Brittany: a 'pope-holy pilgrimage' it was called by the indignant deputy-searcher, Alexander Carvanell, who tried to search the ship and was carried off in it.[5] On entering it he 'was stricken upon the arm with a staff whereby he lost his hold and was like to perish into the salt sea'. Persevering, and with the help of his assistants, Cock and Bartholomew, he boarded her again at St. Mawes. (How well one can see the scene against that beautiful background: Percuil Creek, the end of May, the little Tudor ship with her coloured sails, the priests, the chattering Cornish company, the mouth of Falmouth haven open towards Brittany.) The ship's company answered that they would not 'for king nor queen tarry to be searched, and further "if ye search here ye shall overboard or into Brittany" and so hoisted all their sails'. Five miles out from Falmouth, Cock and Bartholomew were put into the cock-boat to make their way home; but Carvanell they carried off with them to 'learn to search in Brittany', giving him a thorough fright, 'some saying "Cast him overboard and with a rope tow him at the stern", others saying "We shall bring him whereas his father and mother shall not see him for one seven years" '. Landing at Lantrégar they caused the Bretons there 'to pick him quarrels, daily shouldering and buffeting him as though he had been a Turk or a Saracen'; and there he was for twenty-two days until rescued and brought home by Nicholas Pentecost in the *Anne* of Helford. A suitable fate one may think for an officious deputy-searcher: a not very serious episode, but it gives one the atmosphere of the time. Carvanell adds a schedule of the persons responsible: the parish priests of St. Newlyn and St. Agnes, John Mitchell of Truro, the captain, Richard Barrett of Truro, merchant, three Bretons — altogether some fifty persons.

---

[1] ibid., XII. i, 1127.   [2] ibid., pt. II, 182.   [3] ibid., 557
[4] ibid., 191 (6).   [5] ibid., 301, 1325.

Priests were apt to be troublesome when religious changes were to the fore; hence the care the Government took to see the new legislation and injunctions put in force. In the spring of 1538 Veysey made his visitation of the diocese and published his injunctions upon the clergy: all having cure of souls were every Sunday to declare in English, or in Cornish where English was not used, all or part of the epistle or gospel of the day, or else the Paternoster, Ave Maria, Creed and Ten Commandments, 'declaring especially the second and fourth commandments, for want of true knowledge thereof it is thought many of the unlearned people of the diocese have been blinded, following their own superstitious fancies and omitting to do works of mercy and other acts commanded in Holy Scripture'.[1] All curates were to set forth the King's supremacy and preach against the usurped power of Rome. Chantry priests to avoid idleness were to teach children the Paternoster, Creed, Ten Commandments with the seven works of mercy in English or Cornish. The parish clergy, especially in Cornwall, were to exhort their parishioners that at the death of their friends they have no solemn night watches or drinkings, and generally to abstain from such foolish customs not grounded in holy scripture; and also to exhort them not to make privy contracts of matrimony. The clergy were to avoid taverns, alehouses or suspicious places, and playing at dice, cards, tables or 'any other damned or unlawful game'. This was perhaps optimistic. It was the Reformation in progress.

That many of the clergy did not like the changes we shall see in the sequel. The parson of Week St. Mary was reported to Godolphin at sessions, at Bodmin for saying in church on Sunday after All Hallows day that the King and Cromwell had ordered that no parson henceforth should have more than 10 marks a year, that no more corn would be tithed, but that men should sell it at market and the tenth be paid to the King.[2] Godolphin committed him to Launceston gaol to cool his heels. But any sort of change alarmed the idiot people no less. Edgcumbe reported to Cromwell that the people in Devon and Cornwall mistrusted the King's command to the clergy to keep registers of births, marriages and deaths: they feared it meant increased taxation.[3] Old customs are hard to die, and the customary holidays were still kept in spite of royal injunctions and Convocation. In October 1539 Veysey issued a further admonition to his diocese, notifying that 'artificers and labourers, for lack of spiritual instruction, leave their work every Saturday, after the rite, custom and usage of the Jews, from noon till evensong; fishermen will not go to fish on certain Saints' days which are now abrogated;

---

[1] *L.P.*, XIII. i, 1106.   [2] ibid., XIV. i, 87.   [3] ibid., 815.

shoesmiths will not shoe horse on St. Lewis' day, nor will carriers carry hay and other things necessary to the use of man'.[1] The archdeacon was to warn all curates to instruct their parishioners against these abuses, and those who neglected to do so would be punished. It is clear that it would need more than these ecclesiastical fulminations to uproot old habits. It needed an up-heaval, and that was not long in coming.

The Parliament of this year passed an Act for the creation of new bishoprics and their endowment from monastic lands. A large scheme was sketched on paper — some dozen new dioceses, which would have been a great measure of administrative reform. Among those projected we find Bodmin noted; and in another memorandum of 'cathedral churches to be changed according to the King's new device' we find Bodmin, Launceston and St. Germans.[2] Evidently Henry had not made up his mind which to choose; and soon, with the exigencies of national defence and the cost of the third French war, there was not the money for a large scheme. Six bishoprics were founded, but Cornwall was not among them. It was a pity, for it might have made a great difference, particularly if some beloved priest and scholar like Dr. Moreman of Menheniot, who already taught his people so well in accordance with the Injunctions, had been placed at the head of it. It might have appealed to the never-forgotten days of Celtic independence and the bishopric at St. Germans, that existed before Exeter; it might have won the loyalty of the Cornish people to the new order, which, as things were, was not forthcoming until a dangerous and sanguinary barrier had been passed.

The defeat of the Pilgrimage of Grace and the quelling of all effective opposition to the new order left those members of the old nobility who were out of sympathy with it in a dangerously exposed condition; and of them particularly the Courtenays and the Poles, because of their possession of Yorkist royal blood and their relation to the Cardinal abroad. Their proximity to the throne had already got the Courtenays in trouble. Henry VII had restored the earldom of Devon for Edward Courtenay of Boconnoc; his son Lord William of Devonshire, that gallant, large-limbed man, hero of so many tournaments at Court, married the princess Catherine, daughter of Edward IV and sister of Elizabeth, Henry's queen. So long as the queen lived he was safe and in high favour; but on her death he was arrested and sent to the Tower, where he remained for the rest of Henry's life. On Henry VIII's accession he was released and restored to favour; on his father's death in 1511 he was allowed to succeed to the earldom, but died next year before his attainder could be reversed.[3]

[1] ibid., pt. II, 342.   [2] ibid., 429, 430 (11).   [3] ibid., *Addenda*, I. pp. 54-6.

His widow, the Countess, retired to live out her widowhood upon her Devonshire manors. A household book of her last years reveals her living in considerable state at Colcombe and Tiverton, receiving presents from the King and Queen, gifts of boar and swans from the abbot of Ford, oxen and red deer from the bishop, salmon from the abbot of Newenham.[1] There are payments to players for playing before my lady on New Year's eve, and to the waits of Exeter upon Twelfth Night; for a dozen points for Dick the fool, mending Dick and Mug and Kit's clothes, and to buy two coats when Mug the fool went to London. Then her ladyship fell ill and Mr. Morris, the physician, was fetched out of Cornwall; or word came that her son, the young Marquis, was coming from London, and there would be good cheer — red deer to eat and ministrels to play. And all the year through, in the church of Blackfriars in London, masses were sung for the soul of Lord William. Then too her time came: she died on Friday, November 15th, 1527, at Tiverton and lay in state in the castle, the daily offices said before her corpse.[2] On December 2nd her body was borne in great state into the church, where it was received by three abbots; the chief mourner was Lady Carew, assisted by Sir Piers Edgcumbe. Next day requiem mass was sung, and Dr. Sarsley preached from the text 'Manus Domini tetigit me'. She was buried in the Courtenay vault on the north side; all her officers broke their staves, and the company adjourned to a splendid entertainment in the castle. It must have been one of the last the place saw under the Courtenays, for her son was very little there, and then ruin came upon them all. He raised a monument to his mother in the Courtenay chapel, but after the Reformation all the tombs were destroyed; now only a fragment of the castle remains within its red walls, looking down from its terrace upon the swift-flowing Exe below.

Her son, the young earl, grew up in high favour with his cousin the King: living a great deal at Court, made early a privy councillor and gentleman of the privy chamber, he was one of the innermost circle of Henry's intimates: a dangerous proximity as many were to find. He was given the leading offices in the west country, steward of the Duchy of Cornwall, warden of the Stannaries, keeper of Restormel castle and of other chases and parks.[3] In 1522 Henry granted him the manor of Kellyland, which had belonged to the Duke of Buckingham, and the latter's town house in St. Laurence Pountney.[4] In 1525 he became constable of Windsor Castle and was created Marquis of Exeter, with a gift of the manor of Dartington.[5] A young man dandled by fortune, something of his way of life may be gathered from his books of

---

[1] L.P., IV. 771.   [2] Dunsford, *Historical Memorials of Tiverton*, 172.
[3] L.P., III. 3062; IV, 1377 (28).   [4] ibid., 2482; IV, 1610.   [5] ibid., 1431 (8), 1431.

household expenses: his journeys up from the west country, his pious offerings at churches on the way, his retinue of twenty-six men in their crane-coloured liveries, his singing-men and priests, payments for boat-hire from Greenwich to London when he went to the Savoy for confession, thence to my lord Chamberlain's to dine, from thence to the Bishop of Winchester's at St. Mary Overy's, thence to my lord Cardinal's at Westminster, and the same day back from Lyonknave to Greenwich.[1] He was young and active, given up to a round of pleasure and business, over-indulgence and mingled piety. It was rumoured that he was of 'evil rule', and that, in the atmosphere of Henry's Court, was likely enough.[2] And all the time, there was the taint of royal blood in the background, rousing hopes, suggesting suspicions.

When in 1519 there was a question of his marrying the niece of Chièvres, who governed in Flanders, Wolsey inquired secretly whether Chièvres was looking to any chance of the Earl's succession to the crown.[3] Henry's divorce proceedings were intensely unpopular in the country, and the Marquis's servants undoubtedly entertained great hopes of the future for their master. They were stirred up by that restless scheming man, William Kendall, one of the Marquis's gentlemen, whose conduct in Cornwall two emissaries from the Court, Roger Becket and John Worth, were sent down to investigate secretly in 1531.[4] They were both Cornishmen, and were ordered to repair thither as if 'to visit their friends and pass their time with the same in that country' while spying out Kendall's activities. They were to find out how many servants he kept, whether he had retained any men for his master's service, whether there was any rumour in the country that the Marquis should be heir apparent or no. Then they were to take him and his men, Quintrell and Harris, and bring them up.

They returned with a budget of rumours. Peter Coryton said that Quintrell had desired Harris to be retained for the Marquis 'who was heir apparent, and in case the King should die or marry, the Marquis should be King'.[5] Various people had heard a servant of Kendall's say that 'our master shall wear the garland at the last'; others that Kendall had said the Marquis had sent for men to the country, 'and if the King's grace marry my lady Anne, there will be need of such good fellows'. A Chard man told Becket and Worth that the Marquis was taken heir apparent in all that country; a Honiton man said likewise, and another added that he was 'the best manner of master that ever was'. The servants of the Marquis led themselves on with the thought that when the good day came, they would be 'made'.

[1] ibid., 152; IV, 1792.   [2] ibid., 312.   [3] ibid., 386.
[4] *Archaeologia*, XXII. 20 foll.   [5] *L.P.*, XII. ii, 961.

The result of these investigations was that Kendall and Quintrell were committed to the Tower, and the Marquis forbidden the Court. The Imperial ambassador wrote to Charles V that this was because he had been charged with assembling the people of Cornwall: 'the Queen (i.e. Catherine) thinks this an invention of the Lady (Anne Boleyn) because the Marquis is her humble servant'.[1] Exeter felt himself hardly treated, for in fact he was innocent, the victim of his servants' frowardness; and Kendall could explain that the retaining of men was on account of the Marquis's quarrel with Sir Anthony Willoughby. The cloud passed over; Exeter resumed his place at Court, though it was necessary to be exceedingly circumspect. And in fact he was; he fell in with the King's course, took part in the divorce proceedings, though no doubt sick at heart, presided over the trial of Anne Boleyn three years later (that must have provided some pleasure), took his part against the Pilgrimage of Grace, presided at the trial of Lords Darcy and Hussey.

Kendall had been released to return to Cornwall, where his activities were not much appreciated. He was a restless person, whose name appears frequently in Star Chamber proceedings for forcible entry or assault. Wherever he was, there was trouble. On one St. George's feast at Looe he came to blows with John Amadas, who was there as commissioner to inquire into a robbery at sea committed by some of the inhabitants upon a Breton boat.[2] Amadas accused him of breaking the peace, accompanied by a crowd of riotous persons. Kendall explained plausibly that there was 'great resort of all the country thereabout for their pilgrimage to an image in the chapel of St. George', and that he himself had come there to hear mass with his wife, attended only by a serving-lad, not knowing that the commissioners were meeting there. At their encounter high words passed between him and Amadas, and the latter laid it against Kendall that he had assembled the people. In these Tudor depositions one never knows which to believe. Kendall was a plausible person; he came to a bad end. Before that, however, his influence was sufficient to get himself and his brother named for the commission of the peace, though Edgcumbe protested to Cromwell that they had scarcely sufficient substance according to the statute, and were 'the greatest "bayhers" of lewd causes in Cornwall'.[3]

By this time the Marquis himself was in deadly danger. He had trodden as warily as might be in the intervening years, had been extremely careful of his words and kept his thoughts and hopes, whatever they were, to himself. Not so his wife. The Marchioness was a pathetic, ailing, devout, rather silly woman, with the credulous faith of the women of her kind; and she was one

[1] *L.P.*, v. 340.   [2] cf. W. J. Blake in *J.R.I.C.*, XIX. 392-4.   [3] *L.P.*, XIII. i, 1245.

of the catholic, aristocratic circle who had sought consolation in the com-promising visions and prophecies of the ridiculous Nun of Kent. So also had Queen Catherine and the Princess Mary, the Countess of Salisbury, Bishop Fisher and Sir Thomas More, and among others, Sir Thomas and John Arundell.[1] On the Nun's exposure and execution, the Marchioness had been forced to make an abject confession and apology.[2] Nevertheless she continued to keep in touch with the Princess Mary, and evidently acted as a channel of communication between her husband, the Princess and the Imperial ambassador. Henry once warned Exeter and his friends: they 'must not trip or vary for fear of losing their heads'.[3] Actually the Pilgrimage of Grace was the one and only chance for this small, aristocratic circle of seizing fortune by the forelock. They did nothing; or rather, their class-feeling made them rally to the King against the northern men, and after that they were isolated and lost.

Exeter and his friends, Lord Montague and the Poles, planned nothing. They had a good understanding among themselves and they had some com-munication with Henry's arch-enemy, the Cardinal, abroad; it exasperated Henry that he could not get at him, but at least he could get at his relations at home. Occasionally the friends met in the Marquis's garden at West Horsley, and sang of a better time to come. The Marquis said: 'Knaves rule about the King: I trust to give them a buffet one day'.[4] It fell to him to preside at the installation of Cromwell, whom he loathed, as Knight of the Garter.[5] Then in February the Marquis heard of the execution of his bear-ward at Gloucester for high treason.[6] A Breton priest who had been with Pole abroad was arrested and examined in the west country. He deposed that the Marquis had come incognito to his lodging near the Tower with six servants; hearing him speak French and Latin, he asked who he was: 'he had a long beard and a great cut upon his cheek, as with a sword, and another upon his nose'.[7] Then the unstable Sir Geoffrey Pole turned King's evidence against his family and relations, and all was lost.

There was actually very little evidence to convict Exeter; but every scrap was raked up against him, including the old charges of 1531. He was tried and condemned at Westminster on December 3rd, the day after Lord Montague, and executed on Tower Hill. Henry was determined, as he had once told the French ambassador he would, to make a clean sweep of the house of the White Rose.[8] On this occasion he practically effected it. Of

[1] ibid., VI, 1468 (i).   [2] ibid., 1464.   [3] ibid., VII. 83.
[4] q. Dodds, *The Pilgrimage of Grace and the Exeter Conspiracy*, II. 313.
[5] *L.P.*, XII. ii, 581.   [6] ibid., XIII. i, 358.   [7] ibid., pt. II, 217.
[8] ibid., 753.

the Poles there remained only a young lad who died in prison, and the celibate Cardinal; of the Courtenays, the Marchioness was in the Tower, and there only remained to her her little son Edward Courtenay, prisoner there all his boyhood and youth till the accession of Mary. The ruin of a noble house such as this was like the foundering of a great ship, so many people were involved in it. There was the Marquis's household, with its numerous west-countrymen: Thomas Godolphin, aged thirty, unmarried, 'meet and diligent in serving about a noble man with honest and decent qualities', keeper of Restormel; there was William Booth 'who can sing properly in three-man songs', Thomas Harris who 'luteth and singeth well and playeth cunningly upon the viols and divers other instruments'; there were several good wrestlers among them, and William Tremayle the fool.[1]

For William Kendall and Quintrell a worse fate waited than merely to lose their employment. Early next year they were tried at assizes in Cornwall, condemned and executed. From the judge's report to Cromwell it is clear that the old charges played a considerable part in the indictment.[2] There were others confederate with them, who were committed to ward to appear at the next assizes. A great number of the gentry appeared to see old scores paid off against Kendall and win approbation in executing the King's desires. Sir William Godolphin wrote: 'Such a cry for debt and polling and bribing I never heard of at no man's death.'[3] Cromwell thought the inventory of the Kendalls' goods very bare. Godolphin was able to add two geldings, some more cattle and one silver cup: 'yet all this is to no purpose to the port that they bare'.[4] Apparently at the arraignment of the Marquis, Kendall had been openly called a traitor; and on hearing of this, sharp birds that they were, they made conveyance of their property.

In the Parliament of 1539, the Marquis was attainted, and so all his lands and estates fell into the hands of the Crown. The Cornish manors, some thirteen in number, mostly situated in East Cornwall, were conveniently annexed to the Duchy. For the rest of the century, save during the short period of the earldom's restoration under Mary (1554-56), there are innumerable entries among official documents of property transactions, leases and sales, fines and renewals, in so great an inheritance. Early this same year, another west-countryman high in office and favour, Sir Nicholas Carew, master of the horse, was executed, for no other reason, it would seem, than that he was a friend of the Exeters and had corresponded with the lady Marquis.[5] Henry had been a particular friend of Carew's and his wife's; but

---

[1] *L.P.*, XIII. pt. II, 755. [2] ibid., XIV. i, 532. [3] ibid., 598.
[4] ibid., 599. [5] Dodds, II. 319 foll.

in their case he added meanness to his cruelty and took back the jewels, 'most beautiful diamonds and pearls', which he had given Lady Carew in the days of their favour.

It has been usual, especially since Froude wrote, to speak of 'the Exeter conspiracy'.[1] There was no such conspiracy. It is indeed anachronistic to think, in feudal terms, that the Marquis could have raised the west, even if he had tried to do so. All that was past, at any rate in the west country; it could have been done in the fifteenth century, but not under the Tudors. Henry had the gentry, the townsmen and the people generally with the monarchy, even if they did not always see eye to eye with his doings. That was the strength of his position; it was really unassailable. When the news came down to the west that Exeter was in the Tower and likely to suffer death, Sir Thomas Arundell reported, 'Some then remarked it was well, if he were a traitor'.[2] To which a tailor of Sherborne opined (he was imprisoned for his opinion) that 'Devonshire men and Cornishmen would not suffer that'. But in fact they did, and apart from the execution of the Marquis's servants, not a ripple stirred. Feudalism was over in the west; Henry had the greatest noble in the west country no less securely isolated at his Court than Louis XIV had the French nobility at Versailles.

The Marquis of Exeter struck down, it was necessary to find some one to fill the gap made in the administration of the west. Happily Henry had someone ready at hand more than capable of filling Exeter's places, and far more suitable for the King's purposes: Sir John Russell. Of a good Dorset family of middling status — they were small landowners in the fifteenth century engaged in trade at Bridport and Weymouth[3] — here was no noble of historic family with claims to independent position in the west, of royal blood that challenged the King's. It must be added that, an exact contemporary of the Marquis, Russell was altogether more experienced and more intelligent. He had seen many years of service abroad, was a good soldier, an accomplished linguist, with all the seductive manners of the born diplomat. The clue to Russell's success was that he was the perfect royal servant; he had his advantage over those men of genius, Wolsey and Cromwell, that where they were liable to insist upon their ideas and policy against the King's and so to expose themselves, Russell never put himself forward in the front line of political action, but held himself prudently in reserve. And so he survived, with all his acquisitions, where they fell; founded a great family,

[1] Froude's wholly inaccurate account of the affair in his *History* (III, c.15) was first criticized, and his inaccuracies cleared up, by W. J. Blake in *J.R.I.C.* no. 61. The account of Exeter's fall in the *D.N.B.* is equally to be corrected.
[2] *L.P.*, XIII. ii, 1134.   [3] Scott Thomson, *Two Centuries of Family History*, ii.

the only one really to compare with that other Tudor dynasty, the Cecils: the new nobility created by the monarchy, a most characteristic and lasting legacy of that age.

At the same time the government thought it necessary to make special provision for the good order and rule of the south-western counties, in view of the disturbing symptoms there, by setting up a special Council of the West on the lines of the Councils of the North and of Wales and the Marches. There was no real necessity for it in the south-west, and so it did not survive long; but it provides the most interesting development in the constitutional field in our tract of history. Actually the Dissolution had been carried through there with very little trouble. There were disturbances in Somerset in 1535, some disaffection in Dorset, and an amusing riot among the women (some said they were men dressed in women's clothing) when Dr. Tregonwell, Sir Thomas Arundell and other commissioners came to suppress St. Nicholas's Priory, Exeter.[1]

That the government was anxious about the state of feeling in the west is evident from a curious, and not wholly explicable, reproof sent by the King to Sir Thomas as one of the J.P.s for Cornwall.[2] He marvelled not a little to hear, he said, that in spite of the charge committed to them and his recent reminders of their duties, 'many things be nevertheless rather directed at will and pleasure, than either upon any just contemplation of justice' or with any regard to his previous warnings. He insisted that they were to have a principal regard that the privy maintainers of the papistical faction be brought to justice: 'there wanteth not a number that in that matter . . . retain their old fond fantasies and superstitious muttering in corners as they dare'. They were to have vigilant eyes that all spreaders of rumours, and sturdy vagabonds and beggars, be punished. They were not to hold back from inconsiderate pity for one evil person against the great multitude of the honest and law abiding. They were to advance common justice between party and party. The letter concluded with a lecture warning them to eschew from henceforth 'all disguised corruptions', and 'we shall be content the more easily to put in oblivion all your former remissness and negligence'; if they did not 'the next advice shall be of so sharp a sort as shall bring with it just punishment of those that shall be found offenders in this behalf'.

It is an extraordinary letter and it is difficult to see why it should have been directed to poor Sir Thomas Arundell. Perhaps it is only a draft, and he did not receive it in this form. But it certainly breathes the whole spirit of

[1] Oliver, *Monasticon*, 116.
[2] Printed by Blake from Stowe MS. 142, in *J.R.I.C.*, XIX. 371-4.

Cromwell's administration. No doubt there was remissness and laxity on the part of many J.P.s, a great deal of partiality in the administration of justice, and much actual injustice suffered by poor people. Cromwell's remedy was in the manner of sixteenth-century authoritarianism, a direct extension of conciliar government over the heads of local gentry, justices and common law alike.

On April 12th, 1539, the Council of the West was set up with Russell as Lord President;[1] he had been created a peer a fortnight before. There were associated with him as members, the Bishops of Exeter and Bath, the Dean of Exeter, Sir Piers Edgcumbe, Sir Thomas Denys, Sir John Arundell, Sir Giles Strangways, Sir Thomas Arundell, Sir Hugh Pollard, Sir John Horsey, Sir William Godolphin, Sir Hugh Paulet, with John Rowe, serjeant-at-law, Richard Pollard, Lewis Fortescue, William Portman and Thomas Derby evidently as officials. The Lord President had power to assemble and direct the Council, he had a veto in its proceedings and was to be treated in all respects (kneeling excepted) like the King himself. He was to receive £1000 a year for his and the Council's diets; there were directions as to the number of servants each might retain according to his status. A quorum was appointed.

The purpose of the Council was stated to be the speedy and indifferent administration of justice between party and party. Power was given to them to deal with speakers of seditious words, spreaders of rumours, and offences not amounting to treason. They were to deal with riots and unlawful retaining; to enforce conformity with the religious legislation against Rome, and to suppress the observance of vain holy days. They were to inquire into enclosures. Special regulations were made to help poor suitors and avoid the complicated appeals of the ordinary law: procedure was to be by bill of complaint and answer without replication; no attorney was to take more than 12d. for a sitting, no councillor more than 20d. Poor suitors might have counsel without payment. The Council was to meet at four places in the year, Exeter, Dorchester, Wells, and probably Tavistock.

In July Russell was appointed to Exeter's chief offices: steward of the Duchy of Cornwall, warden of the Stannaries, rider of Dartmoor forest, steward of the Duchy of Exeter lands, with a lease of Exmoor at a yearly rent.[2] At the same time he was given an enormous grant of church land to support his new dignity, sufficient to enable him to hold his own with any peer in the realm.[3] At one stroke the new Russells became richer than the

[1] *L.P.*, XIV. i, 743; and cf. Skeel, 'The Council of the West', *Trans. Roy. Hist. Soc.* (1921).
[2] *L.P.*, XIV. I. 1354 (12).   [3] ibid., (13).

old Courtenays had been: an object lesson for all to see that it was the Crown which was the sole dispenser of all good things. He was given the rich abbey of Tavistock with over twenty of its manors in Devon, Cornwall and Somerset, several of its rectories and vicarages and a large number of advowsons; the abbey of Dunkiswell, with a number of its bartons and lands, and the buildings of Blackfriars in Exeter for a town house.

. So encouraged, Russell lost no time in getting down to his task; already in April, on his way down he wrote to say that he had viewed the havens and landing places of Dorset: 'today I go to Dartmouth and so westwards'.[1] He asked that since the bishop was sore diseased with the gout, he might 'tarry here this Parliament time. It would be a pleasure to me; for when Sir Thomas Denys and other gentlemen of the country are come up, I shall have no company'. But the bishop was not spared: in May he appeared in London with a retinue of eighty horse, the extravagant old man, alighted at the Lord Privy Seal's gate at St. James's to speak with him, and rewarded his officers with twenty nobles at his departure.[2]

Russell made himself very welcome. Serjeant Rowe reported that 'Devon and the west country is singularly well content with Lord Russell's coming thither, as they find him a man of substantial wit, great experience, wisdom and gentle nature. His being here will be to the great quiet and comfort of our parts.'[3] Sir Richard and Lady Grenville, who had returned from Calais to spend the summer at Stowe, were enchanted by his hospitality. 'I have never been so gently entertained in my life as by him', Lady Grenville wrote to her aunt, Lady Lisle.[4] Sir Richard informed Lord Lisle what a great friend to him he had found Russell to be. 'He showed me all the manner of Calais and how he might have been deputy, and the advice he gave you when you wished to have it. I told him you had since found it to be true. He said if you had remained in England since your coming to Calais, it had been more to your profit.'[5] How right, how tragically right, Lisle was to find that to be! Russell had wisely chosen the better part. 'The Marquis nor none of his ancestors', Sir Richard ended, 'was never more esteemed nor better loved in these parts than his lordship is.'

It was, perhaps, not difficult to win esteem in a position of such authority, and with so much property behind it. But it was to Russell's credit that he behaved universally with such courtesy and sought to render services on every hand. In September we find him pleading the case of the Exeter leather-merchants, asking that they might have licence to export skins till

¹ *L.P.*, XIV. i, 685.   ² ibid., 967.   ³ ibid., 686.
⁴ ibid., XIV. ii, 106.   ⁵ ibid., 105

Christmas.[1] All the Council of Devon and Cornwall were then assembled at Tavistock, and there was 'great appearance of suitors', he wrote. On the same day he was granted the remainder of Exeter's offices: constable of Restormel castle, steward of the honour of Winkleigh, master of the deer-hunts of Dartmoor and Exmoor, keeper of a large number of parks, like Boconnoc with its mansion and manor, which had belonged to the Marquis and were now in the hands of the Crown.[2]

Of the business of the Council there is not much evidence, since its papers have been lost. Towards the end of October Russell wrote that they still as yet had 'much business in hearing of causes', but that when these were abated after All Hallowtide he hoped to come to Court.[3] He made himself a suitor for young Richard Edgcumbe who desired livery of his lands, for his father's sake, who 'though his body be dead, still lives in the hearts and minds of the people'. He asked Cromwell to advance the young man in the King's service; and, sure enough, we find Edgcumbe noted among Cromwell's Remembrances, and he got the livery of his lands.[4] In November Russell made his way back to Court via Wells, where he presided over the trial of the abbot of Glastonbury. In February 1540, we have an indication of the judicial activity of the Council from his letter to Thomas Trevethan: 'one John Polwhele sued a writ under the privy seal for the said West Parts against you, upon which you have not only not appeared, but have since maliciously brought an action at common-law for the same matter against the said Polwhele. I counsel you to commence your action within the King's court there, and you will be sure of justice.'[5] One or two later cases in Chancery and the Court of Requests refer to decrees of the Council;[6] in one of them a defendant says 'after the making of which decree and order the said . . . Council was dissolved by reason whereof the said decree was void and of no effect in the law'.[7]

It is not known precisely how and when the Council came to an end. As late as 1543 Russell received £927 10s. as Lord President for fees and diets of the Council, but we know nothing more of its activity.[8] Russell was now busier than ever at the centre of affairs as Lord Admiral from 1540 to 1542, and then as Lord Privy Seal. It would seem that the gentry of the west country preferred the accustomed jurisdiction of the common law

[1] ibid., XIV. ii, 190.　　[2] ibid., 264.　　[3] ibid., 371.
[4] ibid., 494 (95); xv. i, 942 (32). Lady Edgcumbe, Richard's step-mother, was made a lady of the Privy Chamber to Anne of Cleeves.
[5] ibid., 180.
[6] cf. Early Chanc. Proc. file 977, nos. 48, 44; and v. Skeel, op. cit, 75-6.
[7] Early Chanc. Proc. file 951, no. 37.　　[8] L.P., XVIII. ii, 231.

in which they were strongly entrenched and which served their interests; and about this time Henry found it necessary to conciliate the common lawyers. In any case the south-western counties, unlike Wales and the North, were so much a part of the ordinary administration of the land, and presented so little of a special problem, that the Council ceased to have any *raison d'être*, though the poorer people may well have preferred it. Russell's position was now so clear as the leading person of authority in the west, that it needed no Presidency of a Council to uphold it.

Meanwhile another family of the old dispensation, and with many west-country connections, had fallen from their high place into extreme danger: the Lisles at Calais. This is not the place to write the full story of their fall, though it was not without effect upon the wide circle of their Cornish relations. Lady Lisle, as a Grenville and the widow of Sir John Basset, had a great many west-country interests. There were the estates of her young son, the heir, for example, Tehidy in Cornwall and Umberleigh in North Devon. During her absence abroad her brother-in-law, Thomas St. Aubyn of Clowance, looked after Tehidy: a merry, facetious, delightful character. 'As for the hedges that Harry Nance made', he reported to her, 'it is now abroad like the feathers of a goose new polled with a hungry fox.'[1] He sends her a dozen puffins, 'which Bosworthogga or John Keigwin of Mount's bay' (evidently two fishermen) will deliver. He subscribes himself, on St. Blaise's day, 'your old knave, Thomas St. Aubyn'.[2] Another time, he would be glad to come to Calais he says, and 'with the good help of my good Lord, I would then trust to make you to say that I am not your pricklouse nor knave, but mercy ever cry to have': a stave no doubt from some Tudor song or other.[3] His wife writes that he often talks of Lady Lisle's great goodness, and 'though youth has ruled him before, now he is well-amended'. She concludes, 'Your loving and lowly sister, Clowance: Midsummer day.'[4]

The letters went to and fro between remote Cornwall and Calais, accompanied by presents of puffins, gulls, a kilderkin of congers from the vicar of St. Keverne[5] — there was nothing, it seems, that Tudor persons would not eat — and such delicacies as the country provided. Back would come presents from her ladyship: beads for St. Aubyn's wife, 'there is none such in Cornwall, as far as he knows',[6] an 'embracelet' for him which he wears,[7] preserves and ginger, at one time a whole 'ship of wheat and other goodness': their cousin Sir William Godolphin and many others had taken as

---

[1] *L.P.*, VI. 589 (15).   [2] ibid., (14).   [3] ibid., XV. 1030 (58).   [4] ibid., (56).
[5] ibid., VIII. 98.   [6] ibid., VI. 598 (14).   [7] ibid., XV. 1030 (57).

much as they could carry away, but the ship stands as full laded as ever.[1] Old Lady Grenville writes to her: 'I would I were one day with you. If I were as strong as when I covered you with so many clothes I would surely see you.'[2] And then, to console her in her grief — Lady Lisle's hopes of bearing a son and heir to her husband were disappointed and she had been very ill: 'Take no thought for no thing worldly of this transitory world. Ye have the love of the people as much as any woman that ever I heard of. I am sorry that you should have any grief, for I know you of old, for you would no trouble to any living creature.'[3] Lady Lisle needed all this consolation, and more, for the troubles that were in store for her.

We have seen what the canny Russell thought of the situation at Calais. It was indeed a difficult one, and Lisle was by no means capable of coping with it. In these last years of English rule hundreds of French denizens flocked into the town, undermining what English character it had and rendering it insecure in the event of war. In addition Calais was in a very exposed position in the eddies of the Reformation: Protestants and Catholics were very much to the fore with their idiot quarrels over obscure doctrinal points, which meant nothing anyway; the preaching of a very suitably named friar turned Protestant, Adam Damplip, thoroughly unsettled everybody. The Council itself was divided from top to bottom, the Lisles being devout catholics, Lady Lisle fanatically so, while her nephew Sir Richard Grenville was a man of the new dispensation. So they quarrelled, long and bitterly. What rendered the situation more dangerous was Lisle's royal blood, his kinship, if illegitimate, to the King: he was a Plantagenet, a natural son of Edward IV, and so related to the Poles and Courtenays. Then *pour comble de tout*, more by mishap than premeditation, he got into correspondence with Cardinal Pole, through the fault of his silly, busy priests rather than any will of his own.

In March he was recalled; on St. George's day he was present at a chapel of the Order of the Garter; in May he was suddenly arrested and taken to the Tower. The French ambassador reported that he 'is in a very narrow place, from which no one escapes unless by a miracle'.[4] For some time his life was in danger; it is possible that the fall of Cromwell saved him. Marillac reported that though not led to judgment, he would remain a prisoner for life in the Tower; 'some lords of this court have heard their master say the Deputy offended more through simplicity and ignorance than malice'.[5] Nearly two years passed, in which fell the tragic, the incredible episode of

---

[1] ibid., xv. 1030 (58).   [2] ibid., vi. 1154.   [3] ibid., xv. 1030 (36).
[4] ibid., 697.   [5] ibid., xvi. 1011.

Katherine Howard. After her death, it was said that Henry took a fancy to Anne Basset, Lady Lisle's eldest daughter.[1] Certainly the Garter was restored to Lord Lisle and preparations made for his release; but he died before they took effect.[2]

Such was the pathetic end of this charming group, which we know more intimately almost than any other Tudor persons because their correspondence was preserved: we owe that to their fall. Lady Lisle, after a period of confinement at Calais, returned to the west country to live out her long widowhood: she survived into the reign of Elizabeth. Though Grenville was not inculpated in the misdemeanours of his uncle, Henry determined to make a clean sweep in the administration at Calais; and Grenville returned to Cornwall to go on with his acquisitions of church lands, and take his part in the affairs of the west country. In the last years of Henry's reign, he was the leading person in the county.

Those last years were filled by Henry's third French War, a much tougher struggle, and more costly, than the first two had been, and one which affected the west country more closely. But even before it began, conditions in the Channel were disturbed by the long-continuing war between France and Spain. An episode which took place in January 1537 drew attention to the inadequate defences of our western ports, particularly of Falmouth haven which was of growing importance. A fleet of Spaniards came into the river there, and next day four French men-of-war. There was a hot encounter between them in which the French were worsted and went higher up the river, almost to Truro. The Spaniards were commanded by John Arundell of Trerice not to follow them, but their admiral said 'he would have them or die for it', and putting their ordnance into boats they attacked the French flagship which was aground. Arundell threatened to raise the country upon the Spaniards if they did not desist. He ended: 'We desire the King's help to have blockhouses made upon our haven, else we shall have more of this business.'[3] Later the sheriff reported that they had both parties up before the J.P.s at Truro, that they had allowed the Spaniards liberty to depart and detained the yards and sails of the French until the former had gone.[4]

In August there was an encounter between the King's ships keeping the seas and four Frenchmen. Godolphin wrote: 'Sir John Dudley and Sir George Carew have had a fight with four Frenchmen at Mount's bay,

---

[1] *L.P.*, XVII. 92.   [2] ibid., 34, 145, 880.
[3] ibid., XII. i, 277.   [4] ibid., 497.

from 5 p.m. till dark, and I heard their shooting. A great tempest rose at night, and Sir John Dudley's sprit-mast broke or they had taken all four. At daybreak they brought one into the quay of the Mount all to-broken with their ordnance, and departed to the sea in good health and angry with God to send them such weather.'[1]

Episodes like this, and still more the fear of invasion in 1539 when Charles and Francis made up their quarrel — it was feared at Henry's expense — brought home to the government the necessity of increasing the defences in the west, and it was not slow to act. After Russell's inspection of the coast it was decided to fortify the entrance to Falmouth with a fort on either side, at St. Mawes and upon Pendennis headland. In March 1540 Thomas Treffry was engaged in 'setting forth the fortlet on the east side of the entry to the haven', i.e. St. Mawes; he pressed his suit to have the keepership of it.[2] He would then surrender his office as customer of Cornwall, he said, by which he had lost 100 marks and had suffered much from his journeys, in consequence of a hurt from a horse. His services were duly rewarded; he was a reliable man, and he became first captain of St. Mawes. The castle was finished about 1543. Pendennis was set on foot about the same time, on top of the headland guarding the western entrance to the roads. The land belonged to the Killigrews of Arwennack and John Killigrew was made its first governor.[3] It was the beginning of the long connection of their family with the castle, with its fascinating history of imprisonments, escapes, dubious dealings at sea, its heroic holding out for the King in the Civil War. The work was finished about 1546, at the end of the French war.

These two castles were designed by a German military architect, Stephen, and were among the most important of the artillery-forts of Henry's reign.[4] They remain two of the most beautiful examples of military architecture of that time, particularly St. Mawes, which is very little changed, with its lovely trefoil pattern, the three-lobed battery for heavy guns, the circular keep with its Latin inscriptions in praise of the King, composed by Leland the King's antiquary at the request of his friend Master Treffry:

> *Semper honos Henrice tuus laudesque manebunt;*
> *Imperio Henrici naves submittite vela;*
and   *Gaudeat Eduardo duce nunc Cornubia felix.*[5]

---

[1] ibid., ii, 597.   [2] ibid., xv. 426.
[3] In 1546 a royal letter was sent to the bishop, the dean and chapter of Exeter, telling them to lease the manor of Penryn foreign to Killigrew. L.P., xxi. i, 963 (61).
[4] cf. Drake, *St. Mawes Castle and Pendennis Castle* (H.M. Stationery Office), 5; Oman, *Castles*, 113 foll.
[5] *Leland's Itinerary*, I. 248.

Two small notes among the King's payments for 1542 indicate for us the momentous change in the King's policy: an alliance with the Emperor heralding an attack upon France and Scotland. In September two messengers were sent down to Falmouth to take shipping for Spain to the court of the Emperor;[1] and in October there arrived there an envoy from Spain, the Señor de Corrierez, for whom Henry had ordered an escort, but who was brought into harbour by Killigrew and his son-in-law then bringing in a French corsair they had captured.[2]

The outbreak of war created an awkward problem in the considerable number of Frenchmen, particularly Bretons, in Cornwall, who had long inhabited there, and 'would rather die than go hence, and offer to contribute their utmost to be made denizens'.[3] The world was getting more nationalistic, and it is probable that many of these people became naturalized; for it is noticeable that the quite considerable proportion of Bretons in coastal parishes in the west of Cornwall decreases later in the century, while the surname 'Briton' becomes not uncommon.[4]

The war in France began seriously with Henry's invasion in 1544. Russell was in command of part of the army which lay before Montreuil. There were Cornishmen with him, under Sir William Godolphin the younger, for we find Russell sending 'fifty Cornish miners with their captain, as required, of the best that Mr. Godolphin can choose' to help to form the siege of Boulogne.[5] Here Godolphin distinguished himself. A mine was sprung under the castle and the town capitulated. Two years later he was appointed bailiff of the lordship and county of Boulogne.[6] It was a difficult post; there was naturally much disorder in the town, robbers were rife and prisoners escaping. But Godolphin was a man of action, and before he knew what his authority was or possessed his patent, he took measures to get the situation under control or it would have been worse.[7] In the same year we find his petty-captain paid for the conduct of sixty miners to serve at Boulogne.[8] Carew says of him that he 'demeaned himself very valiantly in a charge which he bare beyond the seas, as appeared by the scars he brought home, no less to the beautifying of his fame, than the disfiguring of his face'.[9]

Meanwhile the Emperor had contracted out of the war, leaving Henry

---

[1] *L.P.*, XVII. 880.   [2] ibid., 1017.   [3] ibid., XIX. ii. 185.
[4] cf. Matthews, *St. Ives*, 133-142; Henderson, *Constantine*, 212.
[5] *L.P.*, XIX. ii, 37. In March 1541 Russell had been commissioned to levy 400 pioneers in the west parts and transport them to Calais. *Proceedings and Ordinances of the Privy Council*, VII. 165.
[6] ibid., XXI. ii, 200 (43).   [7] ibid., XXI. i, 1444, 1476.
[8] ibid., 774.   [9] Carew, 62.

to bear the whole brunt of it. France was able to take the offensive. An enormous French fleet was being collected in the Channel, the largest they had ever had there, and in 1545 an invasion was expected. In January, as an emergency measure, the Council sent Sir Philip Hoby down to Falmouth to press into service some 600 Flemings out of a fleet of nine ships on their way to Biscay, which had been driven in there by stress of weather and were without victuals. The men were in a starving condition and ready enough to take service with the King, for food and money. The Council protested to the Emperor that this was in accordance with their treaty with him.[1] In June Russell was sent down to the west. He found the coast of Dorset unprovided for defence and Weymouth very weak.[2] In July he viewed the south coast as far as St. Michael's Mount, and reported from Bodmin that the 'gentlemen and commoners are all diligent here for the defence of the country. It is marvellous what a number of bulwarks, ditches and trenches they have made and furnished with ordnance. The weakest places are Weymouth and Plymouth, but Mr. Edgcumbe does his utmost to strengthen Plymouth'.[3] He found great lack of powder at St. Mawes and Pendennis, and begged that it might be sent on;[4] while 'Treffry's house has great miss of the ordnance which was taken away'.[5] The King's fleet was collecting at Portsmouth, and Russell wrote urgently to all the ports to send their ships and mariners thither.[6] Saltash replied that all their mariners were already in the King's service or had gone to Portsmouth, some twenty-seven of them; hence they were unable to set forth any ships, though they had one of 140 tons building which would be ready in six weeks, and a balinger of 50 tons.[7]

Some of the ships which were set forth for Portsmouth, Russell complained, had taken to robbery and spoil rather than serve. Mariners running in town were to be sent there by land at an hour's warning, he commanded; 'if any show himself unwilling I will punish him although he were mine own near kinsman'.[8] Though he had had 'great ado', he said, to set them forth, chiefly for lack of mariners, he trusted the King would soon have thirty ships out of these parts; he was glad that some had already arrived.[9] Great difficulty had been caused by scarcity of victuals and grain; 'as most of the fishermen here are taken from hence as mariners to serve the King, no fish is to be had; and women are going out fishing, and sometimes are chased home by Frenchmen'.[10] In spite of all his difficulties, with the minimum of fuss —

[1] L.P., xx. i, 106, 303, 326, 345. [2] ibid., 1104. [3] ibid., 1254.
[4] ibid., xx. ii, 53. [5] ibid., xx. i, 1254. [6] ibid., 1287.
[7] ibid., 1283. [8] ibid., 1331. [9] ibid., xx. ii, 63.
[10] ibid., 190.

Russell was both diplomatic and efficient — he collected a serviceable little fleet for the King at Portsmouth. [1]

Although Henry had under his eye there a fleet of eighty sail, 'forty of the ships large and beautiful', the French forces approaching the Solent were stronger. There was a good deal of indecisive manœuvring and some sharp engagements in which neither side gained much advantage. But these days were rendered tragically memorable by the loss of the *Mary Rose*, the vice-admiral and second largest of Henry's fleet. Suddenly on Sunday evening, July 19th, her lowest row of gunports having been left open, she heeled over in a breeze arising, with five hundred men on board. They were nearly all drowned; there must have been a great many west-countrymen who went down with her, like Sir George Carew, her commander, and the young Roger Grenville, her captain, Sir Richard's son and heir.

Sir Richard was sheriff for the last time this year and active in collecting the moneys levied for the war. We note a payment towards the benevolence of £643 2s. from Cornwall, compared with £4527 2s. 4d. from Devon. [2] No doubt the county was hit very hard by the absence of its mariners and fishermen on service. Then there were the musters, some 1117 men against Devon's 4000. [3] Next year, the war still continuing with Henry determined to hold on to Boulogne, a large west-country contingent was called on for service in France, that ever-recurring theme in our history. Devon was to send 500 men, Cornwall 300. [4] Old Sir Richard Grenville donned his armour once more to conduct his companies of men, 200 in all, from Calstock to Dover, with drum, surgeon, standard-bearer, fife and priest. [5] It was his last renewal of acquaintance with French soil, after which he might well, as he wrote himself,

> leave the seas with their annoy,
> At home at ease to live in joy.

John Reskymer and Richard Chamond conducted other companies out of Cornwall; the former brought his 'a good part of the way and was then countermanded to ship them at some port there to be at the command of the Lord Admiral'. [6]

The war naturally led to great disorder in the Channel, robbery and spoil were so difficult to distinguish from legitimate privateering, though the government did its best to repress one and encourage the other. Something

---

[1] cf. Russell's list of ships: From Truro 3, Penzance 1, Fowey 1, Looe 4, Saltash 2 (including one of his own), Milbrook 2, Mount's bay 1, Plymouth 8, Dartmouth 5, Topsham 2. (ibid., 17.)
[2] ibid., App. 4, 3.   [3] *L.P.*, xx. i, 1078.   [4] ibid., xxi. i, 91.
[5] ibid., 643.   [6] ibid., 414.

of its difficulties may be gathered from the case of the hulk *St. Olaf* of Enk-huisen, which coming from Seville with a cargo of sweet oil and white soap was first robbed by one of Sir Thomas Seymour's ships and her goods landed at Ilfracombe, and afterwards returning was spoiled, so it was alleged by her Spanish factors, by an adventurer owned by Richard Goodall of Mount's bay.[1] The Council had the latter with one Nicholas Goethyns sent up, but could not get to the bottom of the matter: the one utterly denied the fact, the other affirmed his first tale 'offering by good witness to prove it, inasmuch as the Council could not upon their bare words without other matters of proof tell certainly how to proceed'.[2] So they sent the pair back again to be further examined on the spot and to cause Ralph Couch and the Carvanells to give evidence before the Court of Admiralty. Goethyns had declared that Sir —— had offered him £50 on Goodall's behalf to surcease his suit, which if he had not been guilty he would not have offered. Goodall utterly denied the same. It is to be hoped that all this was sorted out in the end.

Michael de la Sarte complained that the captain of an unknown ship, saving 'the same goeth, he dwelt and kept an inn or hostelry in Falmouth [i.e. Penryn], and was blemished or wanteth one of his eyes', had boarded two Spanish ships laden for Antwerp with velvet and taken out certain parcels.[3] Letters were dispatched to the mayor of Penryn to apprehend him and seize the goods. A Lübeck hulk laden with grain was pirated outside of Falmouth, 'and that more cruel was, even in the main sea put the master and company of the same hulk into the boat thereof at their adventure'.[4] How little the themes change with the centuries! Off Fowey the galleon the *Trinity*, laden with cloth and pewter from Southampton, was robbed by pirates, including a ship of Rye.[5] Cases of this sort were numerous in addition to captures of licensed privateers. The privateers of Plymouth had a fine time. At the out-set of the war William Hawkins, James Horsewell and John Eliot had got licence to set out privateers to prey on French shipping.[6] We hear of as many as ten or twelve French ships being brought into Falmouth.[7] But Hawkins and his associates did not confine themselves to enemy ships; and before the year was out we find the mayor of Plymouth (Horsewell) and Hawkins in prison for a spell over one of their ships' exploits.[8] Treffry had his troubles. He lent money to Gregory Cary to rig out a ship the *Falcon Lisle*, belonging to the Lord Admiral, against the French, but he was

---

[1] *A.P.C.*, I. 459.   [2] ibid., 438, 507.   [3] ibid., 382.
[4] ibid., 468.   [5] ibid., 503.   [6] *L.P.*, XIX. ii, 340.
[7] ibid., xx. ii, 5.   [8] *A.P.C.*, I. 220.

claiming that he was still not paid in the next reign.[1] Also a son of his had been taken prisoner. He was allowed a licence to bring in French wares for the ransom of about sixty French prisoners, 'the better to compass the ransom of his son'.[2]

Nor did the trouble cease with the war. Peace was made in 1546; yet such conditions left a legacy of disturbance, so many scores to be paid off on both sides, that disorder continued on a much larger scale in the unstable conditions of Edward and Mary's reigns. In 1548 indeed a general commission was issued by the Council to the western counties permitting them to set forth ships to prey upon the French: a kind of private warfare in the Channel. In Mary's reign this even took on, with the Carews, Tremaynes, and Killigrews, a political character: the school of Elizabethan seamanship in more senses than one!

The war had been prodigiously expensive. Henry's last Parliament passed an act empowering him to take into his hands all chantries, hospitals, colleges, free chapels, fraternities, gilds and their possessions.[3] Commissioners were to be appointed to inquire into their revenue. It was left to the King to determine which should stand, which be dissolved or refounded. Inventories were to be made of all their goods, and certificates returned to the Court of Augmentations. It was but a logical step from the dissolution of the monasteries: the chantries were even less useful. For some reason, perhaps because of a scruple of conscience, or because time did not allow of it, the King did not take the final step. (In his own will, Henry made provision, pathetically, for daily masses to be said at his tomb 'while the world shall endure'.) But the exigencies of history are stronger than the will of kings. The machinery was in operation for the dissolution of the chantries and gilds; the commissions were appointed;[4] all that was necessary was the final impulse. This was provided by the financial stringency bequeathed by Henry to his son's government, the members of which, so far from nourishing any scruple on the subject of the chantries, were actively in favour of suppressing them as a further advance in the Reformation. Thus we find the two motives, economic and religious (or ideological), acting powerfully together to a common end.

---

[1] Early Chanc. Proc. file 1185, 31-2.   [2] L.P., XXI. i, 487.   [3] ibid., XXI. i, 302 (30).
[4] That for Devon and Cornwall consisted of: the Bishop, Sir Richard Edgcumbe, Sir Hugh Trevanion, Sir Gawen Carew, John Grenville, John Arscott, Nicholas Adams, Philip Lenthall, John Aylworth.

CHAPTER XI

THE PRAYER BOOK REBELLION

I<small>F</small> Henry had lived, he would, it is clear, have gone further along the course for which all was set; as it was, he bequeathed the task of continuing his work in church and state, in more difficult circumstances, to the Protestant councillors whom he set round his son, Edward. The boy's uncle, Somerset, who now held the reins of government, had, with his kindly, liberal, optimistic temperament, no idea of the difficulties of the task. Events were to give him a rude awakening and bring about his fall; and in all this the west played a leading, a sanguinary part.

The government began with a new Chantries Act, mainly re-enacting Henry's provisions, but making them more extensive and more complicated; lands given for the endowment of anniversaries, obits, lights before images, were annexed to the Crown, while various bodies — colleges, schools, chapels-at-ease, were exempted. It was all very complicated, and the Act necessitated the appointment of new commissions in every county to make surveys not only of chantry lands and goods, as Henry's commissioners had already done, but of all their plate, jewels, ornaments, bells, vestments. This was already sufficiently disturbing to remote, backward counties like Cornwall which saw in the keeping of parish registers an instrument of increased taxation. The new commissioners for Cornwall who were at work in the winter of 1547-48 were Godolphin, John Grenville and Henry Chiverton.

Godolphin had already had occasion to send up that summer a 'lewd priest', who evidently resisted the new measures, to be examined by the Council.[1] At this point, that bird of ill omen, William Body, appeared on the scene to exercise the rights of the archdeaconry he had bought, and take part in the proceedings. He had no better a reception from the people than he had had ten years before from the clergy at Launceston; there must have been something unpopular and tactless in his bearing, and a regular tumult was raised at his visitation of the hundred of Penwith. The Council in London, with its new-found lenity, rather defended the people than not.[2] They allowed that Body, to spare himself trouble, had called together a multitude of parishes in one day, whereas each one should have been taken

[1] *A.P.C.*, II. 100.   [2] ibid., 535.

separately, and further had given the impression that the church goods were to be confiscated to the Crown's use, when the purpose of the commission was to see them preserved without embezzling or private sales. The Council concluded with a conciliatory gesture: Body was to be committed to ward for a week, and bound over to appear before them; their letter was to be read to the substantial persons in each parish, declaring the real purpose of the commission, while two or three of the ringleaders were to be committed to ward. This was very mild: so different from the spirit of great Henry's government: not at all dissuasive of popular unrest.

The commission went on with its work, and in February 1548 Godolphin was able to make his return to the government.[1] The net revenues of the collegiate churches, chantries and gilds of the county, in lands and tithes, amounted to £732 19s. 3½d., compared with £1454 2s. 8¾d. for the monasteries. They possessed 235½ oz. of plate; their bells were estimated at 7600 cwt., and they had 40 fodder of lead, of which 8 had been taken away for fortifying the Scilly Isles. Much the largest of these foundations was the college of St. Mary and St. Thomas at Glasney by Penryn, founded by Bishop Walter Bronescombe in 1265. With its provost and twelve prebendaries, seven priest vicars, a bellringer, four choristers and three chantry priests, it was the largest clerical body in the county, as large as any of the monastic houses had been and with an equivalent income, though practically wholly in tithes. It possessed a number of rectories in the country round about; its net revenue was £221 18s. 4d., little less than that of St. Germans.

The picture that we have of Glasney in its last days differs little from that of the Cornish priories; it had lost something of its religious purpose, it was becoming decayed, it was an old *rentier* corporation. William Carvanyon, lessee of part of the bishop's home-farm at Penryn, brought a Star-Chamber action against the penultimate provost, James Gentle, who, he said, was 'a man of great covetousy', and 'hath not only let the college to be in decay so that the service is not ministered as it hath been, but also hath taken the chantries of the same college into his own hand and doth daily occupy them to his own use. And Sir James Gentle and his servants be men of great pleasures, more like temporal men than spiritual, do daily use hawking and hunting and do not only tread and break down hedges, corn and grass of them that be his poor neighbours there nigh him but also doth kill and slay with his spaniels, some days two sheep, some days three and divers times five in a day, and also do kill, drink and joust . . . Sir James

---

[1] E 301/9; and cf. abstract by H. M. Whitley in *J.R.I.C.* no. 25, 102-7.

is a man of great substance and being well friended, your poor orator can have no redress.'[1]

We do not need to believe the whole of this indictment, but it was a fact that the buildings were in a state of decay. We hear of several of the prebendaries' houses being ruinous; Bishop Veysey's visitation of 1542 found the church, built as it was upon a swamp at the head of the creek, much in need of repair.[2] The last provost to be appointed, John Libby, encouraged no doubt by what was happening to the church in these years, did his best to improve matters. Godolphin found that in the past year, 1547-48, the provost had spent £40 upon repairing the church and now stood bound himself for its payment. The commissioners noted that Libby was a man well-learned, and that this was 'a meet place to establish a learned man to teach a grammar school or to preach god's word, for the people thereabouts be very ignorant'. The bellringer was paid 'as well for teaching poor men's children their ABC as for ringing the bells'. We detect an unmistakable desire on the part of the commissioners to save something of Glasney for their county. Not so much, perhaps, because of any possible educational value, but rather because of its proximity to Falmouth haven and as a defended place. Leland describes the college as 'strongly walled and encastled, having three strong towers and guns at the butt of the creek':[3] these are shown in the contemporary map made of the coast.[4] The commissioners wrote that 'sometimes in the year there repaireth to the said haven for harbour 100 great ships, which being there have always used to resort to the said college to see the ministrations there. And the walls . . . on the south side well fortified with towers and ordnance . . . for the defence of the said town and the river coming to the same, which ordnance pertains to the men of the said town'.

Further suit must have been made; for the commissioners for the sale of chantry lands next year wrote that 'proceedings are now being taken by certain gentlemen of that county, to have the sale cancelled and the church (which has already been in great part dismantled) converted into a parish church'.[5] They pray that the purchasers might have the quiet enjoyment of their purchase. They had. And so the buildings were sold, the church, tower, lead, bells, the vestments, the copes of green velvet and cloth of gold with their inscription 'Pray for the soul of John Bishop', the chasubles of crimson and gold with the words '*Vero filius dei erat iste*', the altar cloths

---

[1] Star Chamber Proc. Henry VIII, vol. IX, no. 63.
[2] Oliver, *Monasticon*, 49.   [3] Leland, I. 197.
[4] Cotton MS. Aug. I, i, 38.   [5] *Salisbury MSS.*, I. 310.

of velvet and satin, the tabernacles and books — all that was requisite for the service of a large church with many priests.[1] And in time the buildings crumbled and were quarried away until now nothing remains but a piece of wall in a back garden.[2]

At St. Crantock there was a college with a dean and nine prebendaries, and an endowment of £92 11s. 9d.; here they had concealed 28 oz. of plate, afterwards found by the surveyor upon further examination. The commissioners had nothing to say in their favour. The college of St. Buryan, though its tithes had been leased by the dean to David Baugh for eighty years, did find priests to serve its dependent churches; besides it was a royal foundation: it was spared. At Week St. Mary there was a chantry with a school attached to it, founded by Dame Percival, widow of a London alderman: 'the said school in decay by reason it standeth in a desolate place and far from the market for the provision of the said scholars'. The commission recommended very sensibly that the school be transferred to Launceston. The priest was approved of as 'well-learned and a great setter-forth of God's word'. So also at Launceston where Stephen George, who had been sub-prior, was now stipendiary priest of St. Mary Magdalen, a man 'well-learned and meet for the education of children in the Latin tongue'. Stratton church had goods which 'the churchwardens refused to deliver'. Davidstow had a fraternity which possessed a store of a few sheep and kine. There had previously been some trouble about this. Some of the parishioners charged the parish constable at the time of Henry VIII's commission with selling a chalice and four oxen belonging to the store and appropriating the money to his own use, saying that the commissioners would shortly come down into the country and take away the ornaments of their churches, 'where there were three chalices they would take one with such other jewels as they listed'. He therefore advised them 'to make sale of one of their chalices and take the money for themselves'. He replied in defence that he had sold a chalice and five oxen of the store of our Lady with their consent to equip the men set forth from the parish for the French War.[3]

At Looe the inhabitants had used the money left for an obit and sold some of their plate to repair their bridge, which had been damaged by the surge of the sea. Liskeard and Bodmin the commissioners thought suitable places to maintain a preacher who would also teach school, particularly the latter which was a sessions town and populous, 'for the Lord knoweth the

[1] Whitley, loc. cit., 133-5. [2] cf. Peter, *History of Glasney Collegiate Church*.
[3] Star Chamber Proc. Edward VI, bundle 2, no. 20.

said two thousand people are very ignorant'. It was a plea that they might keep their chantry endowment, as at Saltash where there was a quay defending the town 'sore in decay, and for the maintenance thereof they have but only the premises'. At St. Austell the chantry priest acted as deacon to the vicar at the principal feasts. Again at Boscastle which depended on its quay, lately broken 'by tempest of weather and surges of the sea' (one sees the heave of the sea in that narrow inlet, that dangerous coast), the people were not able to rebuild it and prayed that they might have a part of their stipendiary priest's wages (who was a Breton), towards its maintenance. It would certainly be more useful. At St. Michael's Mount, where there were supposed to be an archpriest and two more, one of them had been put out of service by the Council's order and a gunner appointed in his place, who received the same wages. John Milliton, captain of the Mount, was still bound by his lease to find three priests, which he had done till 'the last wars'. 'Item,' the Commission minuted, 'this place of the Mount is a stronghold and a whole defence for the Mount's bay which is a great harbour and loading for ships. And this hold of the Mount is requisite to be furnished with gunners, for it is the only safeguard and defence of the whole country in these parts.' Gunners in place of priests, the protection of the angel hosts not being what it was in the Middle Ages: it is a theme very near to the heart of the Reformation.

While the commission went on with its work, in itself sufficiently disturbing, proclamations were issued in London more directly affecting the habits of mind, the usages, the penumbra of superstition and custom which was the religion of the people. Candles were no more to be borne on Candlemas day, nor ashes on Ash Wednesday, nor palms on Palm Sunday; creeping to the Cross was abolished, and the making of holy bread and holy water. This was followed in February by an order for the complete removal of all images from the churches. It would appear to have been in connection with the execution of this order that we find Body to the fore again. His presence added fuel to the flames of popular resentment. The tumultuous parish of St. Keverne took the lead in the matter, as they had in 1497 and had been prepared to do in 1537. They were headed by Martin Geoffrey, a mass-priest of St. Keverne, and William and John Kilter, yeomen, of Constantine. Other leaders came from the surrounding parishes, Grade, Mullion, Ruan minor, Gwennap, Redruth, Perranzabuloe, but most were St. Keverne men. On April 5th a large mob attacked the house in Helston where Body was, and murdered him; it seems that the blows were struck by William Kilter and Pascoe Trevian. Afterwards John Reseigh made proclamation in the market-place that 'they would have all such laws as was made by the late King Henry VIII and none other until the King's majesty accomplished the age of twenty-four years. And that whoso would defend Body, or follow such new fashions as he did, they would punish him likewise'.[1]

The argument was that of the catholic party: no change until the King was out of his minority and free to choose for himself: it was the slogan by which the Princess Mary held to her mass, and in the name of which Bishop Gardiner defied the Council. Two days later, April 7th, a larger crowd than ever assembled — it was said, three thousand people — and proclamation was made that 'on Tuesday next at the general sessions to be holden at Helston we will be there with a greater number to see if any man will be revenged herein'. In consequence, Sir William Godolphin and his fellow justices were unable to hold sessions; for the moment they were powerless before the forces of mob-law.

Letters were dispatched to the Council; but soon reinforcements for law and order began to reach the gentry from the east of the county. At Plymouth we read of payments to 'Henry Blase for him and his company 8 April when they rode with Sir Richard Edgcumbe into Cornwall against the rebels there', and for a dozen bowstrings for them.[2] Traces of the activity of the eastward parishes may be read in their certificates of church goods next year: how St. Winnow is 'indebted unto William Lower their captain when they went westward in the King's majesty's affairs against the rebellers of the west in £5 10s., whereof the said William Lower deburséd — and remaineth yet unpaid'; at Morval they sold one of their chalices to pay the charges of their men to ride west; at St. Nighton's they sold a small chalice and a bell 'by the assent of the whole parish for meat, drink and horses for the carrying of men' to the west; Lanteglos sent twenty-six men, Boconnoc eighteen.[3] There were similar payments at Launceston and Stratton in the north.[4]

If there was any resistance, it was quickly overcome; the Black Book of Plymouth says that 'the Commons were pacified by the gentlemen of the country with small trouble'.[5] The leaders in the affair were taken; six of them, including the priest, were sent up to London, and the rest reserved for trial at Launceston.[6] A special commission of oyer and terminer was sent down to Grenville, Godolphin, Trevanion and four others, a grand jury formed, which included Humphry Arundell of whom we shall hear

[1] q. from Blake, 'The Rebellion of 1549', *J.R.I.C.* no. 56, 165; and cf. Rose-Troup, op. cit., 80.

[2] Worth, *Plymouth Municipal Records*, 115. [3] Whitley, loc. cit., 108-113.

[4] cf. Rose-Troup, 83. [5] Worth, 16. [6] *A.P.C.*, II. 198.

more. Before these the pathetic band of husbandmen and fishermen appeared, their leader, William Kilter of Constantine, a strong-bodied man such as the leaders of primitive communities are made. Carew tells a characteristic anecdote of him: 'For activity, one Kilter, committed to Launceston gaol for the Cornish commotion, lying there in the Castle green upon his back, threw a stone of some pounds' weight over the tower's top which leadeth to the park.'[1] He and Trevian, who had stabbed Body to death, were condemned to be hanged, drawn and quartered; a number of others to be hanged. In June word came from the Council 'to proceed with as convenient speed as might be to the execution of the traitors there'; albeit some of the Council thought the number appointed to be executed was over-great.[2] In London they were more lenient; only the priest, Martin Geoffrey, was executed, drawn from the Tower to Smithfield to be quartered, his head being set on London bridge.[3] His five associates received pardons, and so did others of the twenty-eight originally exempted from the general pardon.[4] But there were several who died at Launceston, and that Plymouth had its share in the macabre ballet of a hanging upon the Hoe we know from the gruesome detail into which the town accounts go: faggots and timber for the gallows, 'poles to put the head and the quarter of the said traitor upon', for wine at receiving the 'traitor of Cornwall' and a dinner to the under-sheriff who was present at the execution of this nameless one.[5] No doubt the good townsfolk turned out in their hundreds to see the hanging; they had their fun. And afterwards a quarter was spared for the edification of the town of Tavistock.

How some escaped in those dangerous April days may be seen from the case of Hugh Mason, of Grade, who was arrested at Exeter on suspicion of being 'one of the stirrers of the villains of St. Keverne's'.[6] It would seem that he had been with them until April 5th and then drew back. Threatened by them with hanging and the burning of his house, he fled to Pendennis for the safeguard of his life. Advised to 'get hence eastwards until such time as the villain creatures were subdued', he was transferred to St. Mawes and thence conveyed to Exeter under suspicion. The writer of his safe-conduct (was it Killigrew or Treffry?) desired that he might be released 'unless ye have heard any further credible report of his demeanour than I have declared, for surely I found him like a true man to his prince in all points in this broil'. It may have been in consequence of this that Mason's name was erased from the bill of indictment. However the broil was over; perhaps

---

[1] Carew (ed. 1811), 177.   [2] *A.P.C.*, II. 554.   [3] *Wriothesley's Chronicle*, II. 4.
[4] Printed Rose-Troup, 422-5.   [5] Worth, 115.   [6] cf. Rose-Troup, 425.

its chief importance lay in that it led the Council to underestimate the strength of the opposition among the people. That summer the doctrinaire Somerset sent the eloquent and Protestant Dr. Tongue down to preach to the poor Cornishmen.[1]

The work of the Reformation went on. Sir Walter Mildmay and Robert Kellaway were sent down as commissioners to take order for the maintenance of schools and preachers, of curates where necessary for the service of large parishes, of money to be paid to the poor.[2] Similar commissions were appointed for other counties. It has been held that the effect of the Edwardian Chantries Act was disastrous for education.[3] It may have been disadvantageous, but that it was disastrous is not borne out by the evidence. The government sent out these commissions in order to provide for the maintenance of such schools as were in being. In Cornwall, they allowed wages for a schoolmaster at Saltash — Andrew Furlong was to continue there as schoolmaster at £7 a year — Bodmin and Penryn. The one scholastic foundation the county possessed, the school at Week St. Mary, the story of whose founding by Thomasine Bonaventure Carew tells so delightfully, was continued; the commissioners allowed £17 13s. 4½d. endowment of its previous £20. Actually the school there came to an end, greatly to Carew's regret: 'for divers the best gentlemen's sons of Devon and Cornwall were there virtuously trained up, under one Cholwell, an honest and religious teacher, which caused the neighbours so much the rather and the more to rue, that a petty smack only of Popery, opened a gap to the oppression of the whole, by the statute made in Edward VI's reign, touching the suppression of chantries'.[4] For once, Carew's information seems to have been wanting; a later chantry certificate has a note stating that the school was to be removed to Launceston, 'if it shall appear more necessary there than at St. Mary Week and upon letters directed to certain of the worshipful of the shire it is certified that the same is more meet. Whereupon it is ordained *quousque*'.[5] And this is what seems to have come about: the school was transferred under its schoolmaster Cholwell, with its manciple and laundress.[6] Nor was this the only provision: Launceston also had Stephen George, ex-monk, who acted as schoolmaster at St. Mary Magdalen, and an old usher who taught poor men's children their ABC.

Whether the stipendiary priest, who was at the same time schoolmaster,

[1] *A.P.C.*, II. 220.
[2] Their return is to be found in the Edwardian Schools Roll, E 319/1, no. 12.
[3] cf. Pollard, *Pol. History of England*, 1547-1603, 20.
[4] Carew, 119 b.   [5] E 301/10.
[6] cf. Peter, *Launceston and Dunheved*, 343 foll.

at St. Mary's, Truro, was continued, we do not know:[1] he does not appear on the roll and may have been sacrificed. The government may have considered it more properly the business of the towns to provide their own schoolmasters. Curates were allowed by the commissioners for St. Columb, St. Buryan, Sennen, St. Levan, Liskeard, Penzance, the Mount. All the rest were pensioned off, though it was open to them to become ordinary parish clergy. The total sum allowed for these purposes, schoolmasters and curates — nothing was allowed for the poor: the government was too poor itself — was £101 11s. 4½d., merely a seventh of the total value of the chantries and colleges. That was really a great saving; it represented the extinction of a non-productive interest and the direction of so much wealth into a more remunerative channel.

In January Parliament passed an Act of Uniformity: a decisive new step in the progress of the Reformation; for it reduced the previous diversity of religious usage to one measure throughout the kingdom and brought forward the first Book of Common Prayer, with its services in English to which all were to conform. The simplicity of the new services rendered unnecessary a superfluity of church ornaments and plate. Further commissions were appointed in every county, hundred by hundred, to make a survey of the goods of the parish churches, and to see that they were not alienated, except to some good use with the common assent of the parish.[2] For Cornwall the returns for six of the hundreds survive.[3] From them we can see what a large quantity of plate and vestments important parish churches like Bodmin and Liskeard had accumulated. At Liskeard there had been ten chalices weighing 80 oz. altogether, besides censers of silver, a pax and a shrine: a good deal of this was sold, partly by the parish for the common use, partly by the royal commissioners for the King's. At Bodmin there was all the paraphernalia of a big town church with dependent chapels: several chalices belonging to the parish church as well as those of the chapels, ships of silver and censers and crosses, many suits of vestments of velvet and damask and satin of Bruges, mass-books, grails, processionals, prick-song books; and with the rest, two Jesus coats and 'four tormentors' coats in keeping with John Vivian, another with Thomas Bligh, the third with Nicholas Opy, and the fourth with Richard Corant, made of a suit of vestments for Good Fridays': evidently the garments in which they enacted the scenes of the Passion in Holy Week.

[1] cf. Tregellas, 'Truro Grammar School' in *J.R.I.C.*, x, pt. II.
[2] S.P. 10/6, 25.   [3] Whitley, loc. cit., 108 foll.

The inventories show that very little plate had been stolen: at remote Warleggan on Bodmin moor, two chalices and a pyx were stolen on March 28th, 1548; and at Duloe a pyx of silver on October 20th. At Looe most of their plate had been sold to rebuild their bridge; and at Penryn they had £20 in hand from the sale of jewels to build a market-house. [1] The process by which some of the lands which had been bequeathed for obits, lights and so on slipped into private possession without being paid for — they became known as 'concealed lands' and were numerous enough to become quite a feature of Elizabethan financial administration — will be illustrated in its place. [2]

The religious changes were very disturbing to the minds of the people, and something of the state of party-feeling in the county may be gathered from Carew's anecdote of the free school at Bodmin, which he tells as a 'fore-halsening' of the rebellion next year: he had it, he says, from the mouths of some of the scholars there. They formed themselves into two factions, the old religion and the new, each with its captain; in all their games and exercises they fought each other with spirit, until one of the boys, having got hold of some gunpowder, killed a calf: 'whereupon the owner complained, the master whipped and the division ended'. [3] The divisions of their elders it was not so easy for authority to repress.

It was the Act of Uniformity in January which brought all this feeling to a head. Simple people hated change anyway, and it was a very marked breach with the past when there was substituted a new prayer book in English, in place of the mass which they had known for centuries and in which their childhood was cradled. This was the efficient cause of the rising in the west; elsewhere the risings and disturbances were mainly agrarian. The year 1549 was a very disturbed one, what with wheat quadrupled in price since 1547 — that in itself provides a leading clue — in addition to the religious changes, the agitation against enclosures and the unsettlement caused by Somerset's liberal policy directed against enclosing landlords in favour of the peasantry. His proclamation let loose riots and disturbances all over the south of England and into the Midlands and eastern counties. No wonder the gentry regarded the Protector as a traitor to his class, while he tried to propitiate the unintelligent and irresponsive people with fair words. In the Western Rebellion the ordinary class feeling is discernible, the mistrust of the peasants for the gentlemen; and there was a certain element of repining at the sheep-tax Parliament had imposed.

[1] Cal. S.P. Dom. Add. 1547-1565, 398.
[2] See below. [3] Carew, 124 b.

But, as Hooker says, the cause of the rebellion was 'only concerning religion'.[1]

The Prayer Book service was ordered to be used throughout the country on Whit-Sunday, June 9th. The first outbreak came at Sampford Courtenay, a little village in mid-Devon on the edge of the moor, on Whit-Monday, when the villagers, headed by one Underhill, a tailor, forced their priest to don his vestments and say mass instead of the new service. Immediately the news spread abroad, the people in the neighbouring parishes followed their lead and combined to have mass said too. The J.P.s who rode thither to inquire into the matter, led by Sir Hugh Pollard and Anthony Harvey, conferred a long while with the rioters, but did nothing to stop them — it may be that they, too, were disgruntled with the new service, for Harvey was an intimate of the Courtenays. Their weakness gave head to the disturbance; from that moment it spread and became something more. The Devonshire rebels joined forces with the Cornish who had already risen, though we do not know the circumstances.

In Cornwall the rising was the more formidable because it enjoyed the leadership of two gentlemen of property, Humphry Arundell of Helland and John Winslade. Arundell was named after his grandfather Humphry Calwodely, who was attainted for his part in the Rebellion of 1497: so he had rebel blood in his veins. He was now thirty-six years of age. We do not derive a very favourable impression of him either from the law-suits in which he was involved or his examination after his surrender. He was evidently an unquiet person. We find him several times charged with forcible entry upon other people's lands, with withholding moneys under his mother's will to his younger brothers, and, by a tenant and servant of his, Thomas a Leigh, with sending him four times to London and not paying his expenses.[2] John Winslade of Tregarrick was a very different sort of man: generous, impulsive, well-liked. Only a few years before, we have a picture of him at his house at Tregarrick, enfeoffing his wife with his Cornish lands by way of jointure, with the accustomed ceremony. Can he, one wonders, have been thinking of what course he might embark upon some day? Many years later an old Devonshire gentleman remembered that day, the sealing of the deeds, 'the delivery of possession to the said Agnes only by a turf and a bough at the entering in of the hall-door of the house of Tregarrick, the said John Winslade and William his son walking that while without in the court adjoining'; and after John entered the hall alone and his wife, who greatly

[1] *Hooker's History of Exeter*, ed. Harte, 56.
[2] Early Chanc. Proc. 1098/14: 1097/30; 1176/45; 1181/44.

loved him and cherished his memory, 'gave hearty thanks for that he had made her lady of the said land during her life'.[1]

After the defeat of the rebellion Arundell and Winslade deposed that they had been forced by the people to become their leaders; but that was only the usual form in such cases. Arundell told a tall story about fleeing from the rebels into a wood where he stayed in hiding for two days, and only came home at the desire of his wife who was great with child; that the rebels came to fetch him away by force to Bodmin, and that he had written to Sir Hugh Trevanion for his advice, who advised him to 'tarry with the rebels and be in their favour to the intent to admitigate their outrageous doings'; the rebels made a supplication to the King, to which he was privy, and then he feigned himself to be sick and went to his house, whence he was fetched back.[2] From all which we can discern, what we should expect, that Bodmin was the centre of the rising as it had been in 1497: Henry Bray, the mayor, and his successor, Nicholas Boyer, were among the rebel leaders; that Arundell had taken part in drafting the famous Articles the commons put forward; we can descry that — and the fear of a traitor's death before his eyes. Others among the Cornish leaders were Thomas Holmes of Blisland, yeoman, a servant of Sir John Arundell, Robert Smith of a good yeoman family of St. Germans, William Harris, James and Henry Rosogan, and a number of priests, prominent among them being Roger Barrett, John Thompson, Richard Bennett, Simon Morton.

To Bodmin men marched from all over the county, as their grandfathers had in 1497, but this time encouraged, and often accompanied, by their priests. Here they encamped in those June days, while their leaders drew up their articles of supplication to the King. These exist in different forms, the number of them being expanded from eight and nine to fifteen and sixteen; they did not reach their final form until junction was made with the Devonshire men and siege laid to Exeter. Meanwhile in Devon, too, the grievances of the people were given expression in articles which were forwarded to the government and to which Somerset replied.[3] We can only infer the character of the earlier Cornish demands from his reply; but they were almost wholly concerned with religion and no doubt the priests had a large hand in drawing them up. They were entirely conservative and demanded the retention of the old usages with regard to baptism, confirmation, communion and services in Latin. It would seem that priests were holding back and 'will do no divine service in church for frowardness and voluntary

---

[1] Excheq. K.R. Spec. Com. Eliz. 531.   [2] S.P. 10/9, 48.
[3] S.P. 10/8, 6; printed in Rose-Troup, App. G.

lacking of books'. The Cornish demanded a return to the Latin mass, because they understood no English. The Protector replied very pertinently, why should those who had no English object when they certainly understood no Latin?; and that he was informed there were very few towns in Cornwall 'but ye shall find more in them that understand English than that understand Latin'. The rebels objected to the religious changes taking place while the King was not yet of age; this was the usual Catholic platform common to the Princess Mary, Bishop Gardiner, Cardinal Pole abroad and rebels at home. Lastly they demanded remission of the relief upon sheep and cloth imposed in the last Parliament, and some remedy for the dearth and dearness of victuals, which was a serious problem in these years of want.

The rebels made their rear secure before they advanced. Some of the western gentry with their wives and families—it is likely that Godolphin was among them — took refuge in the Mount, where they were besieged. Carew tells us that the attackers first won the foot at low tide, and then carried up 'great trusses of hay before them to blench the defendants' sight and dead their shot'.[1] After which there was slender resistance and the Mount was surrendered; nobody was killed, the 'rather by God's gracious providence than any want of will', he adds unkindly. Sir Richard Grenville with his lady and followers put themselves into Trematon castle, where they were besieged, but should have been safe enough, for the rebels had no ordnance.[2] Some of those within slipped over the walls by night, 'with their bodies after their hearts', and Grenville was persuaded to go outside a postern gate to parley. A group of the besiegers got between him and the castle, and 'laid hold on his aged unwieldy body'. So Trematon was taken, and the gentry stripped of their apparel and jewels. Again no one was killed, but Grenville was carried off to Launceston where they lodged him in gaol. At Plymouth a number of the neighbouring gentry took refuge upon St. Nicholas' Island, while the castle held out.[3] The town itself surrendered. 'Then was our steeple burnt with all the town's evidence in the same by rebels', the Black Book of Plymouth says laconically.[4] In London it was thought at first that the mayor had yielded the town by treachery, but later they learned that it was rather by *force majeure*.

Earlier that month the Protector with his incorrigible optimism had been writing to Cardinal Pole, sending him a copy of the Prayer Book, and unhappily speaking of its issue 'to as great a quiet as ever was in England and as gladly received of all parts'.[5] He spoke of his rule 'so roborrated and

---

[1] Carew, 155 b.   [2] ibid., 111 b.   [3] ibid., 99 b.   [4] Worth, 17.
[5] Pococke, *Troubles connected with the Prayer Book of* 1549 (Camden Society), vi-xiv.

strengthened with faithful, true, loving and well-agreeing counsellors and subjects'. Key-words with the Protector were 'lenity' and 'liberal', even more out of keeping with his age than with ours. There were cruel surprises in store for such an obstinate idealist. Already the Protector had his hands full with the trial and execution of his brother the Lord Admiral, the complicated negotiations with Scotland, the imminent renewal of war with France. He could hardly be expected to pay much attention to remote rumblings in the west. He sent the brothers, Sir Peter and Sir Gawen Carew, down into Devonshire to see what they could do with fair words. [1] He addressed a gentle admonition to the sheriffs promising the people that all would be overlooked 'upon condition that hereafter they do behave themselves towards us as the duty is of loving and obedient subjects'. [2] More important, as the news got worse, Russell was sent down to the west at the end of the month, with such small force as could be got together. With him went Miles Coverdale, former Augustinian friar, now a militant Protestant, to preach to the people. Apart from this, the Protector's instructions were still mild: Russell was to 'bring the people with gentleness to such conformity as appertaineth by travail and gentle persuasions'. [3]

Unfortunately the Carews were hardly the people to recommend themselves to the inflamed commons: they were much too closely identified with the new order and were advanced Protestants in their views. When they arrived at Exeter and summoned the sheriff and justices, they learned that the rebels were assembled in force at Crediton. It was decided that they were to go and confer with them and attempt to pacify them. When they and their company drew near the town they found the highways entrenched, a strong rampart thrown up at the town's end and the barns on either side of it fortified. Nor would the people allow the gentlemen to pass or hold any conference with them at all; for, says the unfriendly Hooker, who was a confidant of Sir Peter and wrote his life, 'the sun being in Cancer and the midsummer moon at full their minds were embrewed in such follies and their heads carried with such vanities that as the man of Athens they would hear no man speak but themselves, and thought nothing well-said but what came out of their own mouths'. [4] The gentry, much offended by this treatment, attacked the rampart but were driven back with some loss. In the fray a servant of Sir Hugh Pollard set one of the barns on fire, which raised a panic among the defenders, who fled and the rebels evacuated the town. The gentry were able to enter; but much good it did them, for the town was deserted, and there was nobody to confer with. Discomfited they returned

[1] Hooker, 59.   [2] Pococke, 5.   [3] ibid., 9.   [4] Hooker, 61.

to Exeter, having accomplished nothing. The only result of the affair was that the rumour that the gentry had deliberately burnt the barns spread over the countryside and still more inflamed the people.

The tumult spread; people began entrenching highways, throwing down trees, barricading villages. The gentry, especially those who markedly sympathized with the new order, got everywhere into trouble. There was the case of Walter Ralegh, father of the great man, who riding from his house to Exeter on a holy day, had the misfortune, with the characteristic arrogance of that family, to upbraid an old woman on her way to church at Clyst St. Mary, who was telling her beads as she went. He had an altercation with her and threatened her with the punishment of the law if she did not conform. This put the old lady into a passion, which she succeeded in communicating to the parish when she got to church: it was not difficult with feeling running high as it was. The people all flung out of church, saying that the gentry would burn them out of their houses and spoil them: they set about erecting barricades. They first fortified the bridge across the river Clyst on the highway to Exeter: the stream flowing through the water meadows at the foot of the hill up which the village runs, the flags growing golden there by the bridge now in summer. They threw down trees across it and planted some ordnance which they got up from Topsham. A band of them pursued Ralegh and overtook him before he got into Exeter, and 'if he had not shifted himself into the chapel there and been rescued by certain mariners of Exmouth which came with him he had been in great danger of his life and like to have been murdered'.[1] He escaped this time, but later fell into the hands of the rebels again and was imprisoned in the tower of St. Sidwell's church throughout the whole rebellion. It was indeed a time when the gentry had to make themselves scarce, particularly if they were Protestants. The Drakes of Tavistock were of yeoman standing, but they were protégés of the Russells. The tradition is that Edmund Drake had to fly with his family from the west country and took refuge in Kent, where his son Francis was brought up on the banks of the Medway. The catholic peasantry, with the sympathies of the Arundells, against the Grenvilles, Raleghs, Drakes: it was the past fighting the future.

When the news of these doings so near at hand reached Exeter — Clyst was only two or three miles away, the village next the favourite manor of the bishops with its park of great oaks, now in the hands of one of Henry's grantees, Sir Thomas D'Arcy — the Carews consulted with the sheriff and the justices, and it was decided that they should ride to Clyst to confer with

[1] ibid., 63.

the people. When Sir Peter was approaching the bridge on foot, he would have been shot by a gunner if a servant of Serjeant Prideaux had not stayed his hand. Nor would the commons here either speak with the Carews, though they agreed to receive Sir Thomas Denys and Sir Hugh Pollard for a conference. The two knights were in the village all that day, while their colleagues remained outside in the water meadows on the other side of the river, getting increasingly restive as the day wore on. When they at length came away they gave no indication of what had transpired. It was not until that night after they had all supped together that the Carews and the sheriff learned that Denys and Pollard had reached an understanding that the people were to return to their obedience on condition that religion was to remain as Henry had left it and until the King came of full age. This led to a violent disagreement among the gentry—it is not difficult to see that Denys and Pollard were rather of the same mind as the people; and when this was noised abroad it encouraged the latter still further.

Several gentlemen going about on their business were trapped and kept in durance; others fled into hiding. Only some six or seven remained in Exeter. Early next morning Sir Peter Carew made his escape before the highways were stopped, and reached Hinton St. George in Somerset where Russell had by this time arrived. Russell sent him on to report to the Council. There he was very ill received. The Protector charged him with being responsible for the commotion by burning the barns at Crediton; and the Lord Chancellor said he had exceeded his warrant and by law could be hanged for his doings. Sir Peter defended himself hotly and so insisted on the dangerous state of affairs that in the end he was promised reinforcements of men and money to return to the west country.

These were some time in forthcoming, and meanwhile Russell felt himself in some danger. He considered that Sherborne was not a strong enough position strategically to stay the advance of the rebels eastward: they could pass him either to the north or the south; only an army able to withstand them in the face was any use now.[1] He reflected whether he might not even have to retire. The Council sent down secret orders to the justices and gentry to arm their servants and tenants to serve under him.[2] But Russell found the people unwilling to rally to his standard, and Sir John Arundell, who was in Dorset, ominously refused to come to him.[3] At Staines order was given to destroy the bridge if the rebels should come east.[4] Lord Arundel wrote from Surrey that the parts round him remained 'as well as may be in a quavering quiet'.[5] Other parts broke out in open disturbances, particularly Oxfordshire

[1] Pococke, 11.   [2] ibid., 13.   [3] ibid., 23.   [4] ibid., 19.   [5] ibid., 14.

and Buckinghamshire, where they reached the dimensions of a local rising and had to be repressed with a severe hand by Lord Grey. The government was half-paralysed; the infection spread into the eastern counties; the French seized the opportunity to declare war.

In the west Devonshire and Cornish men had joined forces under a common leadership. We find the Articles sent up from before Exeter signed by Humphry Arundell, [John] Bury, Thomas Underhill, John Sloeman, William Segar, as chief captains; and by John Thompson, priest, Henry Bray, mayor of Bodmin, Henry Lee, mayor of Torrington, and Roger Barrett, priest, as the four governors of the camps.[1] Several more Devonshire gentlemen had thrown in their lot with the rebels. John Bury had been one of the Marquis of Exeter's men, was now one of Sir Thomas Denys's, and had lands in various parts of Devon. One of the Coffins of Porthledge, an old family which became recusant later, was a recruit; so also was Sir Thomas Pomeroy, of Berry Pomeroy. The curious thing about him is that at the very time of his participation in the Rebellion, a large purchase for him and his brother of practically all the smaller chantry properties in Cornwall was passing through the Court of Augmentations.[2] There is no end to human complexity: how Pomeroy contrived to combine these two courses of action, buying chantry property and rebelling to retain the mass, is hard to see. Perhaps the simplest explanation is the truest: only another case of human foolery. And indeed Sir Thomas seems to have been rather a light-weight; he had sold his family estates at Berry Pomeroy to the Protector, whose family kept hold of them when everything else foundered; he was considered 'a simple gent', his chief exploit in the Rebellion more like a school-boy joke than serious warfare. Perhaps in such grim times, it was his feather-brains which saved his head.

Under this leadership the commons moved against the city of Exeter: the second time in half a century it was to undergo the ordeal of siege at the hands of the Cornishmen. Their leaders sent messages to the mayor, John Blackaller, calling upon him to join with them: the arms and money within the city would be a great acquisition to their strength, to say nothing of recruits. For the fact was that the majority in the town was Catholic; the mayor himself and his chief brethren were, for example. But the instinct of self-preservation and class-interest was stronger than religion; and in the name of God, King and country (as usual) they rejected these overtures and put the city in a state of defence. On July 2nd it was surrounded and the suburbs taken. The rebels were perhaps two thousand at first, but every day

[1] Printed in Rose-Troup, 220-222.   [2] Cal. Pat. Rolls Edward VI, III. 103.

they increased; 'many of them brought their wives, horses and panniers, persuading themselves and promising them by such a day and upon such a day tò enter into the city, and then to measure velvets and silk by the bow and to lade their horses home with plate, money and other great riches'.[1] The mayor was evidently well advised to resist. All requisite measures were taken, the armour brought out, men mustered, soldiers retained; in every ward warders by day and watchers by night were assigned; ordnance laid in every gate and upon the walls. The city upon the hill, with the river running deep at its foot, the walls intact, was a strong position to assail. Outside the rebels broke down bridges, entrenched and barred highways, brought up what ordnance they could. Markets were stopped and victuals cut off from the town, the conduits broken up to make shot and pellets. They burned the city gates; so the citizens constructed ramparts within, with fires kept up at night. A mine was laid under the wall by the west gate; but its effectiveness was ruined by a tinner within the city who flooded the workings. People appearing in garret-windows were liable to be shot by the rebels; in retaliation the citizens set some of the suburbs on fire.

Within, a great many sympathized with the rebels' cause; and the vicar of St. Thomas's, Exe Island, just outside the west gate, a Penryn man, became one of their principal leaders. Hooker gives an attractive picture of him: 'This man had many good things in him: he was of no great stature but well-set and mightily compact; he was a very good wrestler, shot well both in the long bow as also in the cross bow, he handled his handgun and piece very well, he was a very good woodsman and a hardy, and such a one as would not give his head for the polling nor his beard for the washing, he was a companion in any exercises of activity and of a courteous and gentle be-haviour'.[2] This parson was very active with the rebels and shared all their counsels. It was charged against him that he had caused a Tavistock man to be hanged, a Protestant spy, who was engaged in carrying letters between his master and Lord Russell at Honiton. Nevertheless the vicar saved the city from burning. There was among the rebels a foreigner who was so skilful a gunner that he killed a man standing in North street with a great shot from St. David's hill. He was willing and promised to set the city on fire. The vicar of St. Thomas's exerted all the force of his influence to prevent such a thing happening, and succeeded. Yet, when the siege was raised, he did not fail to be hanged upon the tower of his church for his pains.

There was a certain amount of communication between the rebels and their friends in the city, secret conferences over the walls, letters smuggled in

[1] Hooker, 68.   [2] ibid., 91.

and out, open parleys in time of truce. One day a leading merchant whose turn it was to be captain for the day and ward the gates went out to confer with the rebels, carrying the keys of the gates with him. This was thought ill of in the city; his conference came to no effect and he himself hardly escaped. At another time there was a riot set on foot at the Guildhall by a popish tailor. But the principal citizens, the mayor, John Buller, William Peryam and others, 'howsoever they were affected otherwise in religion yet they were wholly bent and determined to keep and defend the city'.[1] A special company of about a hundred citizens made a covenant together, besides their ordinary duty, to be always about the city day and night to see that no treachery could be practised: this Hooker regarded as one of the chief means to its preservation. An attempt to gain the castle by corrupting the soldiers was detected just in time.

The demands of the rebels reached their final form in the Articles to which Cranmer replied.[2] They were a complete, a pathetic manifesto of Catholic reaction. They demanded a return to the position as it had been in the last years of Henry VIII, and more, though it is interesting that they did not demand the restoration of Papal authority. It is obvious what a hand the priests had in drawing them up: they asked for a restoration of the Six Articles (the 'whip with six strings', poor fools!), the mass in Latin without anyone communicating but the priest, the sacrament to be hung over the altar and worshipped as it was wont to be, communion in one kind and then only at Easter, holy bread and holy water made every Sunday, palms and ashes at the proper times: in fact all the accustomed ceremonies of their primitive superstition. Further they said, 'we will not receive the new service because it is but like a Christmas game': very rude to the Archbishop who had expended such pains in compiling it; he felt very sore on the subject and replied hotly and to the point. 'And so we Cornish men (whereof certain of us understand no English) utterly refuse this new English.' Were there any more of them who understood Latin? he inquired. They demanded further that Dr. Moreman and Dr. Crispin 'which hold our opinions be safely sent unto us, and to them we require the King's majesty to give some certain livings to preach among us our Catholic faith'. We have already seen how greatly respected a person Moreman was in Cornwall, and from what was written of him afterwards by Carew and Hooker. He was now in the Tower, with Dr. Crispin, a fellow canon of Exeter, having been committed for their preaching in the west country.[3] Pole also they wished to be pardoned, sent for to Rome and promoted to the Council.

[1] ibid., 76.   [2] Cranmer, *Remains and Letters* (Parker Society), 163 foll.   [3] S.P. 10/9, 48.

Most interesting were the last two demands. 'We will that no gentleman shall have any more servants than one to wait upon him except he may dispend one hundred marks land, and for every hundred marks we think it reasonable he should have a man.' Cranmer had no difficulty in making hay of this, pointing out that it would lead to still more unemployment if gentlemen were not to keep house, and how rich it would make them, laying up in their coffers what they would have spent on their servants. But it is the element of class-feeling in the Rising that is interesting at this time of increasing disparity between classes, when the gentry were drawing further away from their dependents. The Archbishop was well aware of this: 'But it was not for good mind that you bare to the gentlemen that you devised this article; but it appeareth plainly that you devised it to diminish their strength and to take away their friends, that you might command gentlemen at your pleasures . . . Was it ever seen in any country since the world began, that the commons did appoint the nobles and gentlemen the number of their servants? Standeth it with any reason to turn upside down the good order of the whole world, that is everywhere and ever hath been, that is to say the commoners to be governed by the nobles, and the servants by their masters? Will you now have the subjects to govern their King, the villains to rule the gentlemen, and the servants their masters? If men would suffer this, God will not . . .' etc. For all the Archbishop's very proper acquaintance with the purposes of God, God remained (as usual) inscrutable: Cranmer can hardly have seen that but seven years and, for all his eloquent defence of the social order, he too would pass to his account in the flames that were the lot of a heretic, no less than these poor creatures for whom the hangman's rope was waiting.

Lastly they asked that half the abbey and chantry lands in every man's possession should be given back to establish two places in every county, where the two chief abbeys were, 'there to be established a place for devout persons which shall pray for the King and the commonwealth'. An interesting proposal, for though their prayers were not necessary, would in fact be rather a waste, it would have the effect of saving at least so many fabrics from destruction, so many 'bare, ruined choirs': in Cornwall, Bodmin and Launceston, in Devon, Plympton and Tavistock, in Somerset, Glastonbury. Cranmer did not reply to this article directly, but simply accused the commoners of attempting to pluck the crown from the King's head and 'to take from all other men such lands as they came to by most just title, by gift, by sale, by exchange or otherwise'. It was most fortunate for the possessors that the greatest land-revolution in English history was a legal one: all revolutions from above are legal. The commons asked that the particular griefs of their country might be so ordered as Arundell and Henry Bray 'shall inform the King's majesty', and prayed for a safe conduct for them. But they never got so far; the treachery with which Robert Aske had been treated by Henry VIII was spared them: not that the governing class would have hesitated had it been necessary.

At the beginning of July Russell had advanced from Hinton St. George to Honiton, where he remained waiting for the promised reinforcements. Having such a small escort with him — it could not have been more than a few hundred at most — he could do nothing to relieve Exeter and was in some danger himself. The Protector was prodigal of his advice, which so experienced a person as Russell hardly needed, but supplies and men were not so soon forthcoming. Hooker says: 'having long looked for the same in vain he was daily more and more forsaken of such of the common people as who at the first served and offered their service unto him; and having but a very small guard about him he lived in more fear than he was feared; for the rebels daily increased and his company decreased and shrank away and he not altogether assured of them which remained'.[1] On the rumour of a new stir about Salisbury, the Dorset gentlemen with him advised him to retreat, and next day he set out to do so. It would have been a fatal move: 'there had grown thereby a greater fire than all the waters of five shires about would have been able to quench'. Sir Peter Carew had by this time got back to his house at Mohun's Ottery, and hearing of this took horse and met Russell on Blackdown, where there was a long conference between them. Carew succeeded in convincing him of the fatal consequences of retreat, and he returned to Honiton, 'where he continued thenceforth saving one night spent at Ottery St. Mary where as it fell out he was in more fear than peril'.

In London the Council was reduced to drawing upon the foreign mercenaries which had been hired for the campaign against Scotland. Employing them against Englishmen was exceedingly unpopular, and the Imperial envoy wrote to the Emperor Charles V of the feeling in London and the popular threat not to leave a foreigner alive in England. London was closely guarded, he said, with artillery at all the gates and outlets, and they had sent for more mercenaries from Guisnes and the Boulonnais.[2] On July 10th the Council wrote to Russell promising 150 Italian arquebusiers with all speed, to be followed by three or four hundred horsemen under Lord Grey, 400 foreign horse and 1000 Almain foot; they had also ordered Sir William Herbert to march to him with the forces of Wiltshire and Gloucestershire.[3] Two days later they had to confess that the arquebusiers and Grey's horse would be

[1] Hooker, 82.   [2] Cal. S.P. Spanish 1547-1549, 406.   [3] Pococke, 22-3.

delayed by the disturbances which had broken out in Bucks and Oxfordshire 'for these matters of religion . . . (keep it to yourself)'.[1] They were very willing for Russell to levy 1600 footmen, 'yea, if it be 1700, we stick not at it'; and they gave order to the mint at Bristol for Russell to draw what money was necessary. He had asked for the appointment of the Carews as his councillors; they left it to him to choose whom he thought meet to advise him. They thought it better not to send for Sir John Arundell suddenly, which might drive him into the arms of the rebels, but that he might be quietly handed over into Herbert's charge and conveyed up to London.

The delay in sending reinforcements caused Russell great anxiety; he had practically consumed his supplies and had difficulty in levying men from Somersetshire owing to 'the evil inclination of the people'. The Council wrote him to hang two or three by way of example; and they sent him a proclamation, threatening all rebels who did not submit with forfeiture of their lands and copyholds: 'the matter of copyholds being so general a living to the number of those shires shall be as much a terror as any other thing that can be possibly devised'.[2] They thought that this threat would have good effect, particularly in Cornwall where people might step into copyholds and leases in the hands of those away taking part in the rebellion; 'a better personage to execute it cannot be devised than Sir William Godolphin who hath been a frontier man'. This proclamation was to create trouble later when Russell acted upon it. Meanwhile he did not think much of proclamations. The Council thought to counter 'Humphry Arundell's poison sent abroad by his letters' by extending the threat of forfeiture to all who received or disseminated his propaganda or aided the rebels with victual.[3] They were now engaged in examining Sir John Arundell, and because the case against him was not clear they asked Russell to 'give us notice of the full wherewith to charge him'.[4]

That Russell felt aggrieved by the delay in sending reinforcements, and no less by the superfluous advice, the tone of the Protector, is evident: the latter was made to pay for it only a few months later when he was in need of Russell's aid. But the Council could hardly help itself: by this time the eastern counties were in flame and Warwick had to be sent in command of an army to suppress an insurrection no less dangerous than that in the west. At length Russell was in a position to fend for himself. Three wealthy merchants of Exeter, Thomas Prestwood, John Bodley and John Peryam, pledged their credit to raise large sums of money from the merchants of Bristol, Taunton and elsewhere; this enabled him not only to provision himself but

[1] Pococke, 25.   [2] ibid., 32.   [3] ibid., 37.   [4] ibid., 28.

274

to raise a greater number of men.[1] At the same time supplies from the Council were beginning to come through.

Before Lord Grey's forces could reach Russell the rebels determined to attack. In the last week of July they marched out along the road to Honiton, as far as Fenny Bridges, two miles off. The Carews, as ever to the fore, advised Russell to attack them. The bridge over the Otter was in the hands of the rebels, their main force lay in the meadow beneath. Next day, which was a holiday, Russell tried various 'policies' to gain the bridge, but only succeeded at the cost of a sharp engagement in which several of his company were hurt, among them Sir Gawen Carew. They then fell upon the main force of the rebels drawn up in the meadow below the bridge and got the upper hand. The soldiers and serving men thinking the victory won took to spoil, in the midst of which a new contingent of Cornishmen, about 200 or so, arrived under the command of Robert Smith of St. Germans and set on them fiercely. Russell was forced to draw up his men in new lines of array, as the Cornishmen did, 'between whom the fight for the time was very sharp and cruel; for the Cornishmen were very lusty and fresh and fully bent to fight out the matter. Nevertheless in the end they were overthrown, and their captain whose comb was cut sheweth a fair pair of heels and fled away'.[2] Russell gave chase for some three miles and was fully minded to press on to Exeter. But Joll, his fool, coming from Honiton, reported that the bells of the churches were ringing the alarum and the country was up behind him; so he returned to Honiton, sending a secret messenger to Exeter promising to be with them shortly.

The city was by this time reduced to sad straits for want of food. It had not been provisioned for a siege; and though there was good store of dried fish, rice, prunes, raisins and wines, there was soon no bread to be had. 'In this extremity the bakers and house-holders were driven to seek up their old store of puffings and bran wherewith they in times past were wont to make horse-bread and feed their swine and poultry; and this they moulded up in cloths for otherwise it would not hold together, and so did bake it up and the people well contented therewith.'[3] But when even this gave out the common people were dangerously inclined to yield, all the more so because their sympathies were with the besiegers. The probability is that the city would have yielded before this if it had not been for the able rule of the mayor and his brethren. In this emergency they came up to the trust reposed in them and adopted wise measures for dealing with the poor people, where the danger was greatest: first a general rate was imposed for their relief,

---

[1] Hooker, 83.   [2] ibid., 84.   [3] ibid., 79.

which was doled out to them every week; such victuals as there were were issued to them free or at a low price; if any cattle came near the walls or anything was captured by a skirmish, it was divided amongst the poor; even the prisoners in gaol had their portions, though they were reduced to horse-flesh.

The siege — it had now lasted a month — got on people's nerves, and there were many quarrels. An awkward dispute broke out between John Courtenay, younger son of Sir William, and Bernard Duffield, Lord Russell's steward in Exeter. It was on the subject of skirmishing, which had brought some losses to the besieged. The mayor decided in favour of Courtenay's contention that in their extremity it was dangerous to permit individual skirmishing from the city; Duffield refused to obey and was committed to ward. His daughter insulted the mayor in public, striking him upon the face, who bore with it for the sake of the peace, and all was well. But the people were becoming weary 'and for want of victual would not endure to be pinned in any longer'.[1] Taking advantage of this feeling, some of the Catholic faction planned to raise a mutiny, on the last Sunday before the siege was raised. About eight in the morning an armed company of them turned out hoping to raise a tumult against the opposite party, crying 'Come out, these heretics and two-penny book men! Where be they? By God's wounds and blood we will not be pinned in to serve their turn: we will go out and have in our neighbours: they be honest, good and godly men', etc. As luck would have it, most of the Protestants were at home in their houses or at church, so that the news reached the mayor and the J.P.s before any harm was done. There was a little stir at the south gate; but the magistrates confined the ringleaders to their houses: and for the rest, succour was close at hand.

Shortly after the battle of Fenny Bridges Lord Grey with his horsemen and Spinola with his 300 mercenaries caught up with Russell. Feeling confident now of good success he sent a letter to the mayor to hold out but a little longer, and on Saturday, August 3rd, he set forth from Honiton. He had in all over a thousand good fighting men. Leaving the highway the army marched across the downs to Woodbury, where they pitched that night at a windmill belonging to Gregory Cary. The rebels of Clyst St. Mary came out in force to offer fight; they fought stoutly but were driven off. After the victory the militant and godly Coverdale preached a sermon at the windmill and led the general thanksgiving. (He got his reward later: Veysey was displaced to make him Bishop.)

The news of this reaching Clyst, numbers of rebels poured into the village

[1] Hooker, 75.

for its defence. On Sunday Russell pushed forward, dividing his army into three parts, each to assail one of the ramparts defending the entry. Sir William Francis, of Somerset, led the advance; the barricades were taken and the army entering the village, when Sir Thomas Pomeroy, who had hidden himself in a furze close with a trumpeter and drummer, caused them to sound the trumpet and beat the drum. Russell and his company, thinking themselves caught in an ambush, retired hurriedly; the panic spread — Tudor armies appear always to have been very temperamental; the wagons were left in the highway; the rebels brought them into the village with all their munitions and treasure. When the army learned what had happened they returned to the attack, but since every house was now full of armed men, the order was given to fire the houses. Sir William Francis was leading the way up a narrow lane on one side of the village, when he was caught in a hail of stones and killed. In the main street every house was fired by the mercenaries; the rebels were pressed back, fighting fiercely: 'very fierce and cruel and bloody was that day: for some were slain with the sword, some burned in the houses, some shifted for themselves were taken prisoners and many thinking to escape over the water were drowned'.[1] It is curious, as one goes up the quiet street of that poor little Devonshire village, with the shabby cottages and mingled thatch and slate roofs, to think of that tragic day, the burning and the slaughter.

Nor was it yet at an end. Russell crossed the river by a ford to get on to the open heath, Clyst Heath. Lord Grey's troops passed over the bridge, silencing the solitary gunner there. Arrived on the heath, Grey saw in the direction of Woodbury Hill a large company marching forward, and suspecting a renewed attack he and Russell decided to massacre all the prisoners they had taken at the windmill and in Clyst. This was the way to treat a rebellious peasantry: warfare with mercenaries on the continental model. No wonder they were so hated: even Hooker says that the foreign troops 'were abhorred of the one party and nothing favoured of the other'.[2] That night the army encamped on the top of Clyst Heath. The news of these events caused a strong body of rebels from before the city to draw off and approaching Russell's forces, entrench themselves lower down the heath. Next day Russell again drew up his army in three divisions, and having no way open for himself caused his pioners to make way over the hedges and enclosed grounds, and so came upon the rebels in the rear. Entrapped on

[1] ibid., 87. He estimates that 1000 men were killed; but all his estimates are fantastically high.
[2] ibid., 96.

every side they fought with the courage of despair. Hooker says: 'great was the slaughter and cruel was the fight, and such was the valour and stoutness of these men that the Lord Grey reported himself that he never in all the wars that he had been did know the like'.[1] After the fight Russell's army, carrying Sir William Francis's body with them, marched down the river to Topsham where they encamped.

In the night the rebels left around Exeter, discouraged by these defeats, broke their camp and marched away. The gentlemen who had been kept prisoner in the churches about the city came to the walls and informed the watch. Many of the famished inhabitants did not wait for daylight to go out and hunt for food. Next day, Tuesday, August 6th, Russell appeared before the city, but on account of the food shortage within he did not enter, nor was anyone allowed into the city, but pitched his tents in the fields by Southernhay and set up the red dragon of the royal standard upon the walls by the postern of his house. The mayor and his brethren went out in procession to greet their deliverer, who commended their faithful service and promised that it should be rewarded. Shortly after, Sir William Herbert arrived with reinforcements of 1000 men, mainly Welsh: 'who though they came late to the fray, yet soon enough to the play, and too soon as some thought, for in spoiling they were not so cruel as most insatiable'.[2] However, what they took they sold cheap enough, and largely by these means the city was revictualled in three days. One can imagine them scouring the countryside, pillaging and taking what came first to hand.

Russell remained in Exeter for ten days setting things in order, punishing rebels, taking measures for extinguishing the rebellion. He took advantage of the proclamation for forfeitures to give Sir Peter Carew Winslade's estates, Humphry Arundell's to Sir Gawen, John Bury's to William Gibbs, and to many others who had served with him both prisoners to ransom and their lands and goods. All this led to some trouble with the Council. He proceeded with severity, especially as far as the ringleaders were concerned: gallows were set up in various places in the city as well as in the country. For the vicar of St. Thomas, a gallows was erected on the top of his church tower and there he was hanged in chains in his mass-vestments, 'having a holy-water bucket, a sprinkle, a sacring bell, a pair of beads and such other like popish trash hanged about him'.[3] A grim gesture of triumphant Protestantism against the old faith. The priest took his death very patiently and with quiet courage, nor did he confess that he had been wrong in fighting for what he believed. Hooker adds that though severe to the ringleaders,

[1] Hooker, 89.   [2] ibid., 91.   [3] ibid., 94.

Russell was merciful to the common people of whom he 'did daily pardon infinite numbers'. It was like Henry VII all over again in Exeter after the 1497 Rebellion.

On August 8th, the Protector wrote to Russell that the French had declared war, and that he was to give order throughout the counties under his jurisdiction to guard the ports and landing places; licence was given to all the King's subjects to set ships to sea and prey upon French shipping.[1] The peasants' rebellion in East Anglia was still at its height, nor was it crushed till the end of the month, with great ruthlessness by Warwick. The news of the raising of the siege of Exeter brought some relief. On Saturday, August 10th, Cranmer was present at a thanksgiving service in the choir of St. Paul's, at which he made a collation:[2] perhaps that very sermon on the favourite Tudor theme of the sin of rebellion which remains. The Archbishop drew the moral: 'But herein, O good Lord, be merciful unto us; for we have been too remiss in punishing offenders, and many things we have winked at'.[3] That was not a mistake which the ruling oligarchy was going to repeat.

At the moment their chief concern was to reduce Russell's forces, which were a great charge. They pressed him specially to disband the levies from Somerset and Dorset, since they were not likely to relish fighting their Devonshire neighbours.[4] Exeter was to provide him with money for the time. Apparently Sir Thomas Pomeroy had surrendered and Russell wished to pardon him. The Council left the matter to his discretion, but wished it to be done secretly, and on condition of his betraying Arundell, Underhill and other leaders. He was also to abjure his former popish errors. The J.P.s were to make inquiry concerning papists, to burn all mass-books and cause the new service to be used everywhere. Later that month prayer-books were to be provided for Devon and Cornwall. The Council gave its grateful thanks to the mayor and gentlemen of Exeter for their faithful keeping of the city, and promised to consider any reasonable suit of theirs to their comforts.[5] They were as good as their word; and the manor of Exe Island which lay at the west gate and had for long been a source of dispute between the city and the Courtenays, was granted outright to the citizens.[6] They for their part celebrated August 6th, the day of their deliverance, with all due ceremony, the mayor and his brethren each year going to church in procession to render thanks for their preservation on that day through the centuries.

[1] Pococke, 46.
[2] *Wriothesley's Chronicle* (Camden Society), II. 20.
[3] Cranmer, op. cit., 191.   [4] Pococke, 47.
[5] ibid., 51.   [6] Hooker, 90.

The Council in London appointed a small council by whose advice Russell was to proceed in the west: Grey, Herbert, the Paulets, Sir Andrew Dudley and Sir Thomas Speke.[1] It is noticeable that the Carews were omitted. Nor did Somerset like Russell's proceedings in regard to Paget, who was a brother of Sir William Paget, a leading councillor and supporter of Somerset's. It was like the Protector to alienate a supporter in the interest of abstract justice. He wrote that Paget was manifestly known to have been a captain in the rebellion, and since he, the Protector, had not spared his own brother when charged with treason, 'it should much import us if we should spare any other man's brother'.[2] He went on pressing for Paget's punishment, but Russell, who was wiser in such matters than the Protector, does not seem to have brought him to justice. The Council insisted that Russell dismiss as many of his levies as possible, though they realized that he would need to keep his foreigners, of whom the arquebusiers had won his commendation.[3] He should take advantage of his victory to press on with all speed: 'for if you shall suffer those rebels to breathe, to catch a pride by your somewhat forbearing to follow them, and winning time so to gather strong upon you, you shall not do that with a great number that taken in time you might have done with a much fewer. At the first they were in some dismay, and then one of your men being in array was worth three of the rebels, since by some liberty to gather they may take new stomachs, wax desperate and strengthen themselves against you.'

Which was in effect what happened. Russell's delay of ten days gave opportunity to the rebels who had retreated from before the city, the bulk of them Cornish, to collect again and entrench themselves in a camp at Sampford Courtenay. The news seems to have surprised Russell, who thought all was quietening down.[4] Laying aside all business, he mustered his army, now several thousand with Herbert's Welshmen and all the gentry and people who flocked to the winning side, and on Friday, August 16th, began his march to that tiny village which has its place in history as having given the signal for the Rebellion and now was to see its last stand. Hooker says that the rebels, who were under Arundell's command, were not dismayed by the King's army, though they were 'nothing nor in order nor in company nor in experience to be compared to the others, yet they were at a point they would not yield to no persuasions, nor did, but most manfully did abide the fight'. Friday night Russell passed at Crediton.[5] On Saturday

---

[1] Pococke, 52.   [2] ibid., 54.   [3] ibid., 57.   [4] Hooker, 94.
[5] Harleian MS. 523: a copy of Russell's own report to the Council, from which the above account is taken.

there was an encounter between the scouts of both sides, in which Maunder, one of the chief rebel captains, was taken. Grey and Herbert were sent forward with the van to storm the camp, which they found in a strong position and entrenched. They played their ordnance upon it until the pioners made way for an assault on both sides, on one by the mercenary foot and on the other by the Italian arquebusiers. This was pressed home until the rebels withdrew into the village, which they had strengthened.

While Russell was behind with the main body of the army, Arundell suddenly cut in with his detachment upon the rear of the troops attacking the camp: 'the sudden shew of whom wrought such fear in the hearts of our men as we wished our power a great deal more, not without good cause'. Lord Grey was forced to leave the attack on the camp to Herbert, while he faced about to front Arundell, against whom 'was nothing for an hour but shooting of ordnance to and fro'. Herbert pressed home his attack till he had put the rebels to flight; five or six of them were slain in the chase, among them Underhill who had the charge of the camp.[1] On Russell's arrival, the hour waxing late, he ordered an attack on the village on three sides, Herbert and Kingston on one, Grey in the middle, himself on the other: evidently in order of battle. Seeing themselves about to be overwhelmed, the rebels broke and fled without further fighting. In the chase that followed seven were killed, a much larger number taken prisoner, 'great execution had followed had not the night come on so fast'.[2] Many got away, among them Arundell. All that night, fearing a renewed attack, Russell's company sat on horseback. In the morning they had word that Arundell had fled to Launceston and practised with the townsmen and the keepers of Grenville and other gentlemen for their murder. Instead the keepers set the latter at large and 'gave him their aid with the help of the town for the apprehension of Arundell, whom with four or five ringleaders they have imprisoned'. This was Russell's account of the matter. In his deposition Arundell says that after the battle he fled from the rebels to Launceston, outriding them all, and 'declared all the matter to Sir Richard Grenville'.[3] Russell reported that he had immediately sent on both Carews with a good band 'to keep the town in a stay', and was hastening there himself. They had taken sixteen pieces of ordnance. 'Of our part there were many hurt, but not passing ten or twelve slain. The Lord Grey and Mr. Herbert have served notably. Every gentleman and captain did their part so well as I wot not whom first to commend.

[1] Froude says 'five or six hundred' (*The Reign of Edward VI*, Everyman edn. 119) and is followed by Rose-Troup, and Blake, *J.R.I.C.* no. 57. But the document says 'v or vi of the rebels'.
[2] Here Froude, followed by Rose-Troup and Blake, says 700; the document says 7.
[3] S.P. 10/9, 48.

I have given order to all the ports that none of the rebels shall pass that way.'

A last detachment of Devonshiremen sought to escape up the valley of the Exe into Somerset, the way their forbears had gone in 1497. They were under the command of John Bury and Coffin. Sir Peter Carew and Sir Hugh Paulet were sent after them and caught up with them at King's Weston, where they were overthrown.[1] Coffin was captured along with some 104 other prisoners, for the gruesome accounts of the executions among the latter remain.[2] One or two of them were hanged at each Somerset town, at Bath, Frome, Mells, Beckington, Shepton Mallet, Wells, Glastonbury, Dunster, Ilminster and elsewhere. The rest were pardoned in batches.

Russell crossed the border into Cornwall to extinguish the last sparks of the rebellion and punish the offenders. Before leaving Exeter he had asked the Council to send him 1000 men to land in the rear of the rebels in Cornwall; and he had forwarded Godolphin's request for the relief of the tax on sheep.[3] The Council directed him to say that though he had no authority in the matter, he had good hope of its amendment if the people would return to their allegiance. Now these steps were not necessary. The series of defeats which Russell's forces had inflicted, their overwhelming strength, the capture of their leaders, disheartened the Cornish peasantry: there was no fight left in them, only mute resentment. The hangings and the spoils of rebels' goods by the troops began. Russell proceeded upon his former principle, singling out those who had taken any leading part for execution. The Council ordered him to send up the chief captains: not only Arundell, but Pomeroy, who was at large again, Maunder, the mayor of Bodmin, Wise and young Harris, 'whom we intend to examine here to pick out of them further matter'.[4] Russell was to defer issuing any general pardon, for fear that some of the chief offenders might escape; he might pardon rebels individually so that people might not be driven again to desperation. The Council hesitated about revoking the sheep-tax, particularly as it would benefit the clothiers whom they regarded as principally responsible for the rising by discharging their workmen, 'yea and privy incensing and encouragement' of them.

There was no danger of Russell being too lenient, and when he went back to Exeter, taking his principal prisoners with him — John Winslade had been taken at Bodmin — he left Sir Anthony Kingston, provost-marshal, to carry on the good work of hanging, a task which the latter relished: he

[1] Hooker, 95. [2] cf. Rose-Troup, 318-319.
[3] Pocock, 61. [4] ibid., 63, 66.

left an unsavoury name behind him in Cornwall. We have no account of what happened in those grim, tragic days; darkness draws down, lit only by lurid lights here and there from law-suits often many years later. We can only sense the confusion of all that time, the 'Commotion time' as they called it, the tragedy that came home to them and broke their lives. We know for instance that servants of Lord Grey, taking advantage of the licence to spoil, came to Tregarrick, where Winslade's wife was, and rifled the house. Among other things they broke up a chest in which writings were kept, though they did return the title-deed assuring her jointure of her husband's Cornish estates.[1] After his death she carried them with her to her second marriage, with John Trevanion, who saw to it that the lands never came to Winslade's son, though they were his inheritance and he tried to come by his rights. It meant the extinction of that family in Cornwall: a pretty story of reckless devotion to lost causes, of charm and fecklessness on one side, and on the other, mean, grasping avarice, not without fraud and forgery, of Trevanions, Trelawnys and Bullers alike, the determination to be in at the death and to hold on to what they had no right to.[2]

Priests who had taken a forward part in the Rebellion were specially singled out for punishment. We know that the curate of Pillaton was hanged in his parish by Russell's orders.[3] His friend the parson of Bytton, also accounted a papist, had the good sense to escape and go into hiding until trouble was over; but his goods were seized as spoil by virtue of a warrant from Russell to a man serving with him, and sold as traitor's goods at the church house. We cannot say for certain how many of those whose livings were vacated this year were hanged; but there can be no doubt about Simon Morton, vicar of Poundstock, whose activities were such as to win him a place in a popular Protestant ballad that circulated in London:

> The vicar of Poundstock with his congregation
> Commanded them to stick to their idolatry;
> They had much provision and great preparation,
> Yet God hath given our king the victory.[4]

A new vicar had to be appointed that year by Sir Thomas Arundell, the patron, on the death of Morton: he was undoubtedly hanged.[5] Robert

---

[1] Excheq. K.R. Spec. Com. Eliz. 531.
[2] The story is briefly told in my *Sir Richard Grenville*, 186-8.
[3] Early Chanc. Proc. 1369/18.
[4] *Old English Ballads*, 1553-1625 (ed. Rollins), ix.
[5] Henderson, x. 29.

Voyse, vicar of St. Cleer, was attainted.[1] Richard Bennett, the concubinous vicar of St. Veep and St. Neot, whom John Winslade had pursued so relentlessly,[2] also took part in the Rising. With his views about women's place in the vicarage, he was one of the old school. A common cause drew him and his old enemy together, and together they perished for it. The vicarage of St. Neot was filled on his death this year, that of St. Veep later.[3] The vicarage of Gulval was similarly vacated:[4] William Alsa, who was vicar in 1536, was one of the priests whose names are given by Hooker as having been executed. He gives eight names altogether; in addition to Alsa, Morton, Bennett, Roger Barrett and John Thompson, whose names we know, there are Robert Bochym, John Woolcock and John Barrow.[5] These are given as 'principal stirrers', but there must have been a number of others who took part. In the Bishop's Register, we find that the vicar of St. Keverne was attainted;[6] and a few of the other livings filled in that and the following year may have been those forfeited by rebel priests. What might happen too to those suspected may be seen from the case of Gabriel Morton, vicar of Lelant, who was given as a capture by Russell to Kingston.[7] He was not hanged; Kingston thought of a more profitable way: he made over the tithes and profits of the living to John Trewennick of Boscastle, who received them during all Morton's time.

A later law-suit gives us another glimpse of a rebel held to ransom. One Thomas Boffin was given to Roger Kemp by Russell; Boffin then compounded with John Godolphin to pay Kemp £20 for his liberty.[8] We are given several other instances of spoil, and on both sides: William Webber, a captain of the Devonshire rebels, broke into the house of Richard Pomeroy, took away his goods and certain title-deeds.[9] On the other side we find the gentry taking advantage of the forfeitures proclamation to seize the goods of the parson of Langton in Devon, who was slain in the Rising.[10] William Lower, gent., of St. Winnow, tells how he served under Russell and was one of those sent on ahead after the battle at Sampford to take the leading rebels in Cornwall.[11] He took advantage of the proclamation to apprehend a notable rebel, John Bealbury, and seize plate worth £8 along with other goods. This led to difficulties with another soldier who had a warrant for Bealbury's goods. There was a good deal of

---

[1] Henderson, x. 29.   [2] See above, pp. 156-7.
[3] Henderson, x. 29.   [4] ibid., 72.
[5] Holinshed's *Chronicles* (edn. to 1586), 1002, to which Hooker contributed the account of the Western Rebellion.
[6] Henderson, x. 72.   [7] Rose-Troup, 499.
[8] Early Chanc. Proc. 1383/2.
[9] ibid., 1253/33-43.   [10] ibid., 1387/14.   [11] ibid., 1367/82.

this sort of thing, and there must have been many private scores paid off. The tenants of one of the Duchy manors, Tywarnhayle-tyas, took advantage of the Rising to insist that their copyholds had been held in fee simple: John Grenville, the surveyor, was having none of this. [1]

Of Sir Anthony Kingston's proceedings in Cornwall after Russell left, two eloquent stories are told by Grafton. [2] Nicholas Boyer, who stepped into Henry Bray's place either as deputy or mayor of Bodmin, 'had been busy among the rebels, but some that loved him said that he was forced thereunto'. Kingston wrote to him from the field that he was coming to Bodmin and would dine with him; 'the mayor seemed to be very joyous thereof and made for him very good preparation'. On the day Kingston and his company were heartily welcomed; but before dinner he asked the mayor to have a pair of gallows set up since there must be execution done in that town. After a hearty dinner, he asked if they were ready and taking the mayor by the hand prayed to be taken to the place. Here he inquired of the mayor: 'Think you they be strong enough?' 'Yes, sir', said he, 'that they are.' 'Well then', said Sir Anthony, 'get you even up to them, for they are provided for you.' The mayor cried: 'I trust you mean no such thing to me.' 'Sir', saith he, 'there is no remedy. You have been a busy rebel, and therefore this is appointed for your reward.' 'So that without longer respite or tarrying, there was the mayor hanged.' Such was Tudor martial law: Macchiavelli could not have ordered it better.

A miller near Bodmin, who had also been in the Rebellion, did better than the mayor. Having warning that Kingston was looking for him, he called 'a good tall fellow' who was his servant, and told him that he had to go away: 'If there come any to ask for me, say that thou art the owner of the mill, and that thou hast kept the same this four years, and in no wise name not me.' When Kingston came, the servant told him that he was the miller, and when asked how long since, he answered 'three years'. Kingston then ordered him to be brought along to the next tree to be hanged as a rebel. Then he pleaded that he was not the miller, but only his servant. 'Well then,' said the provost-marshal, 'you are a false knave to be in two tales. Therefore hang him up,' and so he was hanged. Afterwards somebody by said, 'Surely this was but the miller's man?' 'What then,' said Kingston, 'could he ever have done his master better service than to hang for him?' Kingston's cynicism was not without its jovial side; and Carew, hating rebellion as a gentleman should, defends him on both scores, though he says that he left 'a name more memorable than commendable amongst the townsmen' of Bodmin.[1] Among other local persons hanged by Kingston were John Payne, port-reeve of St. Ives, and William Mayow of Clevyan, who, tradition says, was hanged at the tavern sign-post in St. Columb.[2]

The government did not approve of the confiscations and spoil going on in the west and wrote to reprove Russell for allowing it. He pleaded the authority of the forfeitures proclamation. They replied that he well understood the meaning of this and its timing: that it was intended as a device to prevent multitudes of people coming out against him at a time when he was very weak.[3] It would remain a grievance in all men's minds, not only the sufferers', if their goods were 'to be thus taken away without order of any law. We consider besides all this that your men, being in the King's wages and under your government, might have been well stayed from going to the spoil', and that the common people had been made more desperate thereby. At the same time they sent him directions for the re-establishment of order, for the better defence of the sea-coasts against the French; and, relying upon the confidence of the people, he was to restore them their arms. The bells of the churches, however, having been used to call the people to rebellion in both counties were to be taken down and sold to help defray the cost of suppressing it; only one was to remain in each tower, the least of the ring, to call the parishioners to sermons and divine service according to the Prayer Book.[4] The intentions of the Protector were merciful, except as regards Paget, for whom he kept demanding punishment; he was willing to extend the relief of the sheep-tax on all flocks less than a hundred in number to the rebellious counties as well as the good ones.[5]

In London the Articles of the rebels had called forth two replies, in addition to Somerset's, which now remain as literary memorials of the Rising: Archbishop Cranmer's and Nicholas Udall's. The leading theme of both was as much the ignorance and blindness of the westcountrymen, as it was the sin of rebellion. 'O ignorant men of Devonshire and Cornwall', said the Archbishop, 'you ask you wot not what.' How many of them knew which were the general councils and what the decrees which they wanted maintained? He deplored their deliberate walking in darkness and refusing the light when offered them; and he drew a comic picture of the old days of services in Latin, with the priest speaking what nobody understood, and some people listening, others walking up and down in church, and yet others saying their prayers in Latin 'and none understandeth other. Neither the

---

[1] Carew, 124. His defence is that the mayor was given sufficient warning, and that the miller's servant had been as much a rebel as his master. Froude inclines to doubt these stories (op. cit., 120); but they are clearly regarded by Carew as authentic.

[2] cf. Rose-Troup, 309-10.   [3] Pococke, 68 foll.   [4] ibid., 73.   [5] ibid., 74, 75.

priest nor his parish wot what they say. And many times the thing that the priest saith in Latin is so fond of itself, that it is more like a play than a godly prayer.' He instanced some of the more fantastic of the old services, for St. Valentine's day, St. Blaise, etc. After all he ought to know: he was an archbishop. His pamphlet was an effective piece of work.

So also was Udall's, who wrote as a westcountryman: 'my simple and plain-meaning countrymen (for I speak to the ignorant that have been deceived, and not to the malicious) . . .'[1] His theme was that they had been led away by the priests, and he made an excellent suggestion that the new form of service should be turned into Cornish and so enjoyed by them as well as the rest of the realm. The suggestion was never carried into effect, and the Prayer Book became a chief instrument in the spread of the English language in Cornwall. It is interesting to have this pamphlet of Udall's, even though it has, no less than Cranmer's, the character of an official reply; for, schoolmaster, dramatist, producer of Court masques, pamphleteer, Udall was one of the most remarkable minds of the time: the author of *Ralph Roister Doister*, the first of classical plays in English.[2] Besides these prose-works, several Protestant ballads appeared of which fragments remain, vigorous, vindictive, singable, with their refrains

> Whippet you priests and turn you

and

> Yet God hath given our King the victory.[3]

But before the Rebellion in the west was completely liquidated, there was a rebellion in the Council against the Lord Protector. The majority of the lords held him, the lenity of his government and his encouragement of popular causes, responsible for the disasters of that year. They resented his elevation above them all, and a liberal dictatorship was a contradiction in terms. As we have seen, in the coalition between Warwick's following and the catholics which overthrew him, Sir Thomas Arundell played a leading part behind the scenes. Early in October the Council in London moved against the Protector at Hampton Court with the King. Russell was still in the west with his army, and so in a position to determine the issue. Somerset sent him a series of urgent, then despairing appeals, 'to show the part of a true gentleman and of a very friend, the which thing we trust god

---

[1] Printed in Pococke, 141 foll.
[2] For his career, see Boas, *Tudor Drama*, 22-8.
[3] Printed in Rose-Troup, 335-9.

shall reward and the King's majesty in time to come'.[1] The wary Russell, coming up with Herbert slowly from the west, waited until he learned the posture of affairs in London, and then sent a letter of reproof: 'Your grace's proclamations and billets abroad for the raising of the Commons we mislike very much'.[2] They had reason to. With the weight of Russell's army thrown into the scale against him, it was the end of Somerset as Protector.

This crisis over, and the Council with Warwick as its guiding spirit now in control, they were free to clear up what remained over of the Rising. Pomeroy, the young Winslade, Fortescue, Wise and Harris were discharged from the Fleet on November 1st.[3] Arundell, the elder Winslade, Bury and Holmes remained in the Tower, where they were examined by members of the Council. Russell had sent up with the prisoners one Kestell, who had been Arundell's secretary, as his accuser, praying favour for him, since 'he came in of himself and in the midst of the hottest stirs he sent his secret advertisement to Mr. Godolphin and other gentlemen of so much as he knew of Arundell's proceedings and the rest'.[4] The four leaders were tried in Westminster Hall on Tuesday, November 26th; according to the indictment Arundell and Winslade had made some resistance to the very end in the streets of Launceston on August 19th. They were condemned to be hanged, drawn and quartered, at Tyburn on January 27th, 1550. In the crowd that watched them pass by on that melancholy journey were two servants of John Winslade's, faithful to the end, one a lad of nineteen, the other who had been with him for ten years.[5]

The rebellion had fatally compromised the Arundells. When at its height Sir John had been sent for to the Council, he had been kept in custody and then examined.[6] He excused himself for not responding to Russell's messages by pleading that at the time of the first he was very sick, nor had he been commanded upon his allegiance. He was minded to come as soon as he was able, but could bring no body of men as he was 'a stranger in the country where he lay'. At the first rising in Devonshire he 'caused two masses to be said, which ... he did only to appease the people, and ever since he hath heard and caused to be said the service according to the King's majesty's order. Procession he caused to be had upon Corpus Christi day, and after procession the communion according to the laws and no mass.' He was released, but bound over with his brother Sir Thomas in a large sum to remain within the city; in November the restriction was removed.[7] On December 14th, however, we find him and Sir William Godolphin bound

---

[1] Pococke, 83.   [2] ibid., 92.   [3] *A.P.C.*, II. 354.   [4] S.P. 10/9, 48.
[5] Rose-Troup, 347-9; Blake, loc. cit., 324.   [6] Pococke, 38-9.   [7] *A.P.C.*, II, 304.

in £1000 each to keep the peace, 'and neither by themselves, friends, nor servants or others, procure displeasure the one to the other', and to appear daily before the Council until the causes at variance between them were settled.[1] This can refer to nothing other than grave charges being brought by Godolphin against Sir John, probably derived from Kestell's information, relating to the Rebellion: the latter was in a favourable position for knowing what passed between Humphry Arundell and his cousin. Shortly after Sir John was in the Tower, to be followed by his brother on January 30th.[2]

In April, probably through the intervention of Somerset who had been restored to the Council, their confinement was a little relaxed, and Sir John was permitted to see his wife and talk with her in the presence of the Lieutenant.[3] In May and June the brothers, with their two attendants, were given the liberty of the Tower.[4] But still no release came. They remained there for yet another year, until in April 1551 as a protest against their 'causeless' detention, they refused to pay their diets, and in consequence were confined to strait prison as before.[5] In October Sir Thomas was brought before the Council, made a sort of submission and was released on heavy recognisances.[6] He had already formed that alliance with Somerset which both hoped would bring them back to power, but in fact brought them both to the block. The cards were in the hands of Warwick's party. If only Sir Thomas could have waited another year, till Mary's accession — he would have been a leading spirit in the government. Instead, he perished by the axe on Tower Hill on February 26th, 1552. Still his brother remained in prison, until in June he was released but not to depart from the vicinity of London.[7] The accession of Mary made all well for him, but he died before her reign was out.

A number of smaller men were affected by these events. Richard Roscarrock, of an old family near Padstow, was bound over at Exeter in November 1549 to appear before the Council.[8] What is interesting is that at least two of his children were Catholic recusants later and passed many years in prison for the old faith. The same is true of the Hore family, dependents of the Arundells, two members of which were in prison in Cornwall in 1551.[9] In the reign of Elizabeth they became whole-hearted recusants, and suffered fines and imprisonment. We see that 1549 was the parting of the ways. It left a recalcitrant fraction, mainly around the Arundells, who from this time forward never accepted the new order and would not conform. The progress of the Reformation gradually squeezed them out of public life, and in the

[1] ibid., 366.   [2] ibid., 376.   [3] ibid., 432.
[4] ibid., III. 27, 54.   [5] ibid., 258.   [6] ibid., 378.
[7] S.P. 10/14, 45.   [8] A.P.C., II. 356.   [9] ibid., III. 368.

case of the lesser people destroyed their families as such: Beckets, Tregians, Hores all vanished from their homes, others occupied their lands.

Life was good for those on the winning side. The grants to the Carews were confirmed. Sir Gawen got all Humphry Arundell's lands, the manors of Calwodely, Cadbury castle and Mere in Devon (worth £53 9s. 10d. clear per annum), in Cornwall the manors of Cassacawen, Helcett, Helland and others (worth £55 8s. 10d.).[1] Three years later he sold the Cornish estates.[2] Sir Peter Carew got all the Devon lands of Winslade, with his mansion house at Buckland Brewer: an estate of £73 14s. 10d.[3] The jointure to Winslade's widow effectually prevented him from getting the Cornish estates too. The greatest gainer of all was, of course, Lord Russell. For his services, not only, it is to be supposed, in suppressing the western Rebellion but still more for opting for the right side in the crisis which overwhelmed the Protector, he was rewarded with the earldom of Bedford and another vast grant of lands in seven counties to the value of £300 a year.[4] Among these were Thorney Abbey, the manor of Woburn; in Devon the manor of Chulmleigh, in Cornwall the great manor of Boconnoc, both of which had belonged to the Courtenays. Nor was this all: three years later we find him making another large request for properties by gift in several counties, including the manor of Boyton and barton of Bradridge which had belonged to Launceston.[5] He had already got the favourite manor of the bishops near Exeter, Bishop's Clyst, and Bishop's Tawton.[6] The promising young westcountry-man of no particular parentage had become the equivalent of a millionaire, the founder of a noble, if decidedly Protestant, house. His career, and the lot of the simple, catholic peasants over whom he won his victories suggest the moral: *Unto every one that hath shall be given, but from him that hath not shall be taken away even that which he hath.*

---

[1] *Cal. Pat. Rolls Edward VI*, III. 340; Particulars for Grants, Edward VI, 1467.
[2] Maclean, *Trigg Minor*, II. 9.
[3] Particulars for Grants, Edward VI, 1468.
[4] ibid., 1415.   [5] ibid., 1416.
[6] Scott Thomson, *Two Centuries of Family History*, 188, and see below, 294.

CHAPTER XII

THE PROGRESS OF THE REFORMATION, 1549-58

THE year 1549 was a decisive turning-point not only for the west, but for the whole country. The suppression of the Rebellion meant that there could be no further effective resistance to the measures decided upon at the centre to advance the Reformation. The issue of the struggle within the Council at the end of that year made it clear that those measures would now be rapidly proceeded with. There was in fact a strong majority in the Council, backed by the pressure of London and the forward-looking gentry and middle-class, for pushing on with the Reformation. Somerset and Northumberland, with their factions, were both on that side — their rivalry was not one of principle, but simply for power. Within the governing oligarchy the Catholics were an ineffective minority. For them the game was, for the present, lost.

During the remainder of Edward VI's reign, from 1550 to 1553, the momentum of the Reformation was free to assert itself in accordance with its own logic; those who wanted to retain the leadership of the movement had necessarily to increase the pace, whether their measures agreed with their inner convictions or no. Hence Northumberland's policy and actions. In these years were taken the measures which definitely severed the English Church from medieval Catholicism, in a way which not even the Prayer Book of 1549 had done, for that was on the whole Catholic in tendency.[1] In 1550 the new (and Protestant) Ordinal was produced, and a campaign set on foot against the bishops who refused to accept it. During this and next year the leading Catholic bishops, most prominent of them being Gardiner, were imprisoned, and at length deprived to make way for Protestants. In November 1550 order was given for the removal of altars throughout the country, and the setting-up of communion-tables. Lords-Lieutenant were appointed to overlook the counties: it was the beginning of their use as a permanent institution, and the military functions of the sheriffs were gradually absorbed by them. But no one dared to resist the government, except that privileged and Catholic person, the Lady Mary. And all the while the scrabble for the bishops' lands and church property went on: the sales and gifts and

[1] cf. Pollard, *The Political History of England, 1547-1603*, 49.

291

exchanges, the trafficking in real estate. The oligarchy pursued a regular campaign of plucking bishops of their feathers, their fattest manors: reasonably enough, since everything brought home to them that they were no longer princes of the church, but servants of the state. The strongest supporters of the new dispensation were not spared: Ridley had to surrender the best manors of the see of London; Ponet to yield up all the possessions of the see of Winchester in return for a fixed stipend.

Some years later Cecil told de Quadra that if the Church had retained its wealth, it would have gained the victory. We need not take this *au pied de la lettre*: Cecil was engaged in excusing the spoliation of the Church to a Spanish ambassador. But the remark enables us to put our finger upon the essential part in the Reformation process: the secularization of property going on concurrently with changes of doctrine and forms of worship. The latter have been studied *ad nauseam* and allotted far more than their historical importance; it is the property changes which have not been sufficiently investigated nor their fundamental importance realized. We have to keep in mind all the time, beneath the squabbles of rival ideologies — the Real Presence, the Word of God and what not — the consistent pressure bringing the property of the Church into the hands of nobility, gentry, commoners. That was the ground upon which the whole fabric rested.

The doctrinal process reached its logical conclusion with the Second Act of Uniformity and the Second Prayer Book in 1552. This Prayer Book was as definitely Protestant, with its view of the Eucharist as a commemorative supper, as the first was Catholic in doctrine. The Act which enforced it was as severe as the first Act of Uniformity had been lenient: non-attendance at church was punished by graduated terms of imprisonment. The new and simplified Protestant form of worship rendered unnecessary for the service of the church a vast quantity of valuables, jewels, crosses of gold and silver, chalices, candlesticks, censers, copes and vestments, which were confiscated to the Crown. Commissions were appointed in every town to take them in possession and return them to the Jewel House, leaving only what was necessary for the poorer rites of Protestantism. It is a double process which is under observation, a process both doctrinal and economic, but in which the latter is more important and more lasting in its consequences.

We have then to trace this process as it may be reconstructed in some detail for Cornwall, from the flickering and mostly indirect evidence that remains. And first for the bishop.

In the last years of Henry VIII Veysey had been under some pressure from the Crown to lease away the possessions of his see upon unfavourable terms.

He is credited with the responsibility for turning his see from one of the richest into one of the poorest in the country. No doubt he was compliant. But resistance would not have been of any use. His responsibility consists rather in that he used his compliance to make good terms for himself at the expense of his successors. At the time of the building of Pendennis Castle, Killigrew made suit to the King to have the lease of two of the bishop's neighbouring manors, Penryn foreign and Minster, upon favourable terms. Henry thereupon wrote a polite but unmistakable letter to Veysey and the dean and chapter to pass these leases, the manors 'being far off from you and nigh unto our said castle'.[1] Veysey was to be the recipient of many such letters in the years that followed. The lease was made out to Killigrew for 99 years, which meant a considerable loss of fines on renewal to the see. When it was entered in the bishop's register, his conscience was salved, if that is the word, with the novel formula: 'in obedience to a request made by the King'.[2]

The year 1547 saw a number of such demands upon the see of Exeter for long leases of lands to members of the inner circle at Court. On January 1st Cargoll manor was granted at a reduced rent for a period of 80 years to Clement Throckmorton, cup-bearer to Queen Catherine Parr;[3] on the twenty-fourth, while Henry lay dying, a favourite gentleman of his privy chamber, Sir Anthony Denny, obtained a lease of the great manor and lordship of Pawton for 80 years.[4] With Henry dead and the oligarchy in the saddle, the pace was quickened. On April 30th, Sir Andrew Flamock got a grant of Cuddenbeak, the episcopal half of St. Germans, for 80 years.[5] Among the enormous grants made in July to Somerset to support his dukedom, the bishop dropped the advowson of St. Clement Danes.[6] His townhouse nearby, Exeter Place, was granted next year 'in compliance with the King's letters' to Sir William Paget: very convenient for a powerful member of the Council; it was lost for ever to the see.[7] In June 1548 Sir Thomas Darcy obtained outright for himself and his heirs the splendid possession of the hundred, borough and manor of Crediton and the manor of Morchard Bishop, with all fairs and markets, and the advowsons, for a rent of only £40.[8] This was a large loss to the see, for the lands were worth more than four times as much.[9] In August several manors and advowsons in Surrey, Sussex

---

[1] cf. Pollard, *The Political History of England*, 1547-1603, 246 a; q. from *Ancient Letters*, I. 99, no. 3498.
[2] ibid., 264.
[3] ibid. The rent charged was £60 p.a. The manor was valued at £63 18s. 5½d. in *Valor Ecclesiasticus*, II. 289-291.
[4] Henderson, x. 263.   [5] ibid.   [6] *Cal. Pat. Rolls Edward VI*, I. 131.
[7] ibid., 295.   [8] ibid., II. 16.
[9] In 1553 Darcy exchanged them with the Crown for lands in Essex; ibid., v. 97.

and Middlesex were granted away to Thomas Fisher.[1] In November Veysey
made a lease of Burneyre and Tregear manors for 80 years at lower rents than
they were worth to Sir Anthony Cope, Chamberlain to Queen Catherine
Parr.[2] In April 1549 the hundred, borough and manor of Ashburton went
to Francis Pole.[3]

The Prayer Book Rebellion held up this grateful shower for a few months;
but when it was over the process was resumed, with those who had taken
leading parts in suppressing it in a strong position as claimants. In December,
Sir Thomas Speke, who was with Russell's army and of his council, got Paign-
ton manor and borough.[4] In January 1550, Bishop's Clyst and Chudleigh
went. Russell himself got a grant of Clyst and Bishop's Tawton.[5] Nor did
he fail to improve the occasion to get a grant of 30 years more beyond those
specified in the first lease; while he asked the dean and chapter to join his son
Francis with him in the patent as steward of their lands.[6] We find his son, the
second earl, occasionally using Clyst as a country house later in Elizabeth's
reign: the secular Lord-Lieutenant entrenched where the bishops had borne
rule.[7] A few days after the grant to Russell, Pawton and various manors in
Devon were alienated to Sir Andrew Dudley, Warwick's brother, who had
served with Russell.[8] To make the title clear, after the previous lease to
Denny, a recovery was made in the King's Court in 1551 whereby the whole
triple manor of Pawton, Ide and Trevose was settled upon Dudley and his
heirs for ever.[9]

Veysey was now eighty-seven, though not infirm; for many years he had
been an absentee from his diocese and was now living in opulent retirement
at his native town of Sutton Coldfield. At the end of this year we find him
buying chantry lands to support his charitable foundations there.[10] He had
evidently ceased to feel any responsibility for Exeter. In August 1551 he was,
not unnaturally, required to resign. Northumberland's government was
engaged in depriving Catholic bishops to make way for Protestants, and
they wanted to find a place for Miles Coverdale, the translator of the Bible
and a leading light of their party, both as preacher and writer. Veysey had
made good terms for himself. It is possible to discern fairly clearly what he
had done: upon the earlier leases he had reserved the usual rents to the see;
upon the latter, he granted the lands outright in return for annuities for him-

[1] Henderson, II. 403.   [2] ibid., x. 264.   [3] *Cal. Pat. Rolls Edward VI*, II. 402.
[4] ibid., III. 50.   [5] ibid., 164.
[6] Oliver, *Lives of the Bishops of Exeter*, 129.
[7] cf. Scott Thomson, *Two Centuries of Family History*, 188.
[8] *Cal. Pat. Rolls Edward VI*, III. 7.   [9] Henderson, x. 264.
[10] *Cal. Pat. Rolls Edward VI*, III. 176, 352.

self — 'which cannot be but short since he is over 87 years old'. The old man had been sharp. It cannot be denied that he had his part in impoverishing the see; and tradition is justified. The business of his resignation was conducted by Bedford, and the surrender of his see took effect on August 14th, 1551.[1] He declared the revenues that remained to him from temporalties and spiritualties, a net income of £485 9s. 3½d. He was left in possession of this magnificent income, in consideration of his long service to the Crown, and his successor was bound by oath not to disturb his enjoyment of it. In addition he had whatever he was making from his annuities. Altogether one cannot be surprised at the state with which he was enabled to surround his retirement.

On the same day Coverdale was appointed to the see by letters patent.[2] The effect of the activities of Veysey and the Crown was to reduce the revenues from £1566 14s. 6½d. to £500 a year — an income which was sufficient for the reduced figure of an Edwardian bishop. In consideration of this Coverdale was exonerated from payment of first-fruits and tenths. He was enthroned at Exeter on September 11th. A very different type from Veysey, a scholar modest in his habits, attentive to his duties, an eloquent preacher, he set to work straightaway, ordaining, preaching. He made a favourable impression in Exeter, according to the Protestant Hooker: 'He did most worthily perform the office committed unto him, he preached continually upon every holy day, and did read most commonly twice in the week in some church or other within this city'.[3] It was a very different idea of the functions of a bishop. We learn that his wife was 'a most sober, chaste and godly matron'. In that very different too: the appearance of a wife in the Palace at Exeter must have been something of a shock to old susceptibilities.

We have to imagine the changes going on in Cornwall in these last years of Edward VI, when Northumberland was the moving spirit in the government, for the evidence is mostly indirect. Veysey was still bishop when the general order went forth for the taking down of altars in the churches. In November 1550 the Council wrote that though the order had been complied with in the majority of churches, there were still cases where it had not, and requiring him to give order for its execution throughout his diocese, in places exempted as well as not exempted.[4] Tables were to be set up 'in some convenient part of the chancel'. It was done; there is hardly a stone

[1] ibid., IV. 36-7. [2] ibid., 37.
[3] q. in D.N.B. sub Coverdale. But notice that the above account corrects D.N.B. in some particulars. Coverdale did not act as coadjutor to Veysey, who did not die in his 103rd year; nor did the Prayer Book Rebellion take place in 1551.
[4] Oliver, Lives, 125-6.

altar that survives in Cornwall to-day. Lights before the rood were extinguished. We have some references to this in later years à propos of the disappearance of their endowments, the appropriation or sale of the small
properties given for their upkeep. At Liskeard in 1566 John Connock gave
evidence about a house and garden, the rent of which maintained a lamp
before the rood loft 'until such time as it was taken away in King Edward
VI's days, and it was again renewed in Queen Mary's days by order of the
mayor'.[1] At Bodmin and elsewhere there were rents to maintain a light
before the rood loft.

We may draw a picture of the kind of thing that was happening from
what we learn of the destruction of St. George's chapel and gild in Lostwithiel
church, from a case before the Court of Augmentations.[2] It would appear
that the mayor and burgesses of Lostwithiel had concealed from the Crown
the lands with which the gild was endowed. We learn that the chapel was
'defaced immediately upon the last [Commotion]' by order of the mayor.
Sir William Coles, former gild priest, deposed that the gild was 'only maintained by the devotions of them that were and would be brethren and sisters
of the same', who paid on entry 20d. for man and wife, and all foreigners, i.e.
strangers, 3s. 4d., man and wife, while each member paid 4d. yearly. It
was evidently a sort of Oddfellows Club of the time. Coles denied that there
were any lands belonging to the gild, and said that he had 'never heard it
called St. George's chantry till now of late by the adversaries of the said mayor
and brethren'. From this we may infer two things — that he had been got
at by the mayor, and that there were two factions in the town. For other
witnesses deposed that there were lands belonging to the gild: St. George's
mills, for example, and St. George's closes. There were also lands of St.
Bartholomew, patron saint of the parish church. John Halwell, the last priest
of the gild, gives us an idea of the ceremonies every year upon St. George's
riding-day: a dirige celebrated and on the morrow a mass of requiem for the
brethren. There were payments to the priest, and to the steward for scouring St. George's harness, to Nicholas the Breton for nails to fasten the harness,
for two crooks to hang a coverlet before St. George on that day, for the
dinner which took place. One sees the characteristic ceremony; was it, one
wonders, the origin of the St. George's mumming so popular in the county
up to the last century?

The chantries had been dissolved at the beginning of the reign; some of the
gilds had evidently been given, or had taken, grace till later. But these were
the years when the lands given for such parish purposes came into the hands

[1] Excheq. Depos. 9 Eliz. Hilary 4.   [2] Augmentations, Misc. Books 122, ff. 15-28.

of the local gentry. In some cases it was difficult to say when or how they were left sticking to their fingers. It was often only a matter of a small rent, a close or quillet of land, which was easily annexed: nobody noticed, or if he did, it would hardly be worth his while to bring it to the attention of the local J.P.s, who as a class were the chief offenders and not lacking in class-solidarity. Crown officials were the persons to nose out these 'concealed lands'. In May 1552, Nicholas Adams who had been one of Henry's chantry commissioners for Devon and Cornwall reported to Cecil that there was £220 a year difference to the Crown between the last survey made and the first.[1] What was lost to the Crown was a gain for somebody: not a wholly bad thing! But little bits of land here and there, little parcels of church goods, undoubtedly leaked away; and in spite of its efforts the Crown could never catch up with the leakage.

The buying of church lands continued in spate, only it tended to consist now of large numbers of smaller properties.[2] This was certainly the case in Cornwall, where the main properties of the monasteries were by this disposed of, either by sale or annexation to the Duchy. This meant that the chantry lands and tithes came to the fore as a field of investment. We find London speculators, merchants, haberdashers, joining in with the gentry to undertake large grants of petty properties dispersed over many counties. In one such grant, Edward Cowper gent. and Valentine Fairweather, haberdasher of London, bought the chantry lands of St. Stephen's by Saltash, and a parcel of those of St. Stephen's by Launceston.[3] A morsel of the latter appears in an enormous grant to Lord Clinton;[4] he was one of the greatest purchasers in the country in these years: the foundation of that great inheritance. Two Warwickshire gentlemen bought the site of the Truro Black-friars which had been rated for Henry Killigrew, servant to the Duke of Northumberland.[5] A still closer member of the Northumberland entourage, his crony Sir Henry Gate, whom the Duke set in charge of the young King to be always with him and at his ear, got the little vicarage of St. Clether.[6] In Devon he got, as a gift, the magnificent manor of Tiverton, the jewel of all the Courtenay possessions. But this was only a month before the end — Edward died in July; and Mary restored the earldom to her young cousin, Edward Courtenay, shortly after. On the execution of Sir Thomas Arundell in 1552, Gate had been appointed receiver of the Duchy.[7] His good-fortune was very short-lived: he perished with his patron the Duke. Giles Keylwey

[1] S.P. 10/18, 19.   [2] cf. Cal. Pat. Rolls Edward VI, passim.
[3] Particulars for Grants, Edward VI, no. 1550.   [4] ibid., 1515.
[5] ibid., 1595.   [6] ibid., 1627.   [7] Cal. Pat. Rolls Edward VI, IV. 386.

of Stroud, a large land-speculator, bought the farm of St. Thomas' rectory by Launceston, which was leased to Sir Gawen Carew, picking up with it various small parcels of tithes on the market.[1] Silvester Lee and Leonard Bates, speculators *pur sang*, bought the possessions of St. Crantock within the parish.[2] Among west country buyers in the market there were, as we have seen, Sir Richard Grenville and Roger Prideaux. Sir Peter Carew leased the fat rectory of St. Germans, which, wonderful to say, had been granted to the dean and chapter of Windsor in performance of Henry's will.[3] It was then worth £61 13s. 4d. p.a.; now some £1600! William Morice, of a Devon family which came to live at Werrington in the next century — he was M.P. for Looe in Edward's last Parliament, for Liskeard in Mary's first — was associated with Edward Isaac, an Exeter merchant, in buying the rectory of St. Wenn.[4] Sir John Peryam, the Exeter merchant who came to Russell's aid financially in suppressing the Rebellion in 1549, that same year bought the remaining bells, lead, stone and timber of Glasney college:[5] the end of that: its destruction was complete. Most of the lead that covered the church had already been sent over to the Scilly Isles for the fortifications being constructed there. The transition from prayer to power: the moral at the heart of the Reformation in England speaks to us from this simple story in the business of the Court of Augmentations. But after all, one is more likely to find it there than in the interminable moralizings of the Reformers.

The government was at its wit's end for money, what with the currency crisis prevailing in Europe, the expenses of the wars and civil strife, and the dispersal of so much Crown property among the supporters of the oligarchy. In December 1552 a powerful commission was appointed to inquire into these remaining sources of revenue, the lead and the bell metal of the abbeys, church goods and forfeitures: it lends an element of humour to a grim situation to think that its leading figures were Northumberland, Bedford, Clinton, Darcy.[6] But in history, as in life, human beings are rarely self-aware. The commission was to proceed by way of imprisonment and fine: a measure of its urgency. Subordinate commissions were issued for each county, that for Cornwall in January 1553.[7] It consisted of Bedford, Sir Richard Edgcumbe, Sir Hugh Trevanion, Sir William Godolphin, Thomas Treffry and John Killigrew. They were to make their survey of all church ornaments, take possession of the money, plate and jewels, and forward them

---

[1] Particulars for Grants, Edward VI, 1731.   [2] ibid., 1747.
[3] *Cal. Pat. Rolls Edward VI*, I. 149.   [4] Particulars for Grants, Edward VI, 1801.
[5] ibid., 1867.   [6] S.P. 10/15, 76.   [7] Whitley, *J.R.I.C.* no. 25, 98-9.

to the Jewel-house, leaving in each ordinary parish church one chalice, and in larger churches and cathedrals one or two. After furnishing the communion table, they might distribute the linen among the poor, and sell the vestments and bell-metal, all except one large, and one sanctus, bell. After all, it was enough for the new services: the rest was waste. The receipts were to be paid into the exchequer for the national use.

The commissioners got to work and completed their survey.[1] The Cornish churches more usually possessed two chalices than one; often they had three, and in some few cases as many as five. All had patens, but only a minority possessed crosses, censers or pyxes. The fertile hundred of Powder was much the richest in plate; and for some reason the churches in the Roseland were best provided: St. Just had a silver and gilt cross of 165 oz., besides two chalices, a paten and a pyx, St. Cuby at Tregony had a silver gilt cross of 84 oz., five chalices and a paten, 80 oz., a silver censer of 22 oz. and a pax of 3 oz.; the little church of Gerrans had a silver and gilt cross of 108 oz., besides two chalices, a paten and pyx. At Fowey and at Paul near Penzance, there were ships of silver; the latter had five chalices, a little cross, a censer and a pyx besides. At Grade, the tiny church near the Lizard, there was 'the holy cross of 18 oz.': memento of the medieval legend of Sir Roger Whalesborough.[2] Altogether the commissioners returned a total of 6241 oz. for the county. It was lodged in St. Mawes castle in the custody of Thomas Treffry; some of it had already been defaced, when the great reversal took place in London. Edward died; Mary succeeded and the Edwardian religious policy was reversed. The plate would be needed in the churches again, with the restoration of the old services.

As soon as they were well in the saddle, Mary's councillors wrote to the commissioners to restore the plate to the churches. The latter replied that they had already sent most of the plate as far as Exeter when they were countermanded by the order in Council. Matters were not straightened out until the end of 1554. The government decided to take the plate which had been defaced into the exchequer. Treffry was sent up to the Jewel-house with some 314 oz. in all. It was an inconsiderable portion of the total. All the rest was ordered by Mary's very clerical government to be restored to the churches. Some losses had taken place before; but it must be supposed that the chief losses are rather to be placed in Elizabeth's reign. An Exchequer Commission of 1578 to inquire into concealed lands and goods suggests how

---

[1] cf. Excheq., K.R. Church Goods 12/42, transcribed in Henderson, XI. 323-332.
[2] On pilgrimage to the holy sepulchre he stole a piece of the true cross, and on his return was wrecked. He vowed that he would give a piece of the true cross to the church of the parish wherever he came safely to land; and it was Grade. cf. *J.R.I.C.* for 1921.

some of these things disappeared.[1] Henry Chiverton deposed that there remained a pax of silver defaced in his mother's hands: it had been parcel of the store of St. James at St. Clere. It may have been paid for. The plate of this store was sold about 1563 for 4s. 4d. an ounce. There was a silver cross of 60¾ oz., of which John Trelawny had 44 oz. and Chiverton the rest. But Trelawny at any rate never paid; he died instead. When John Trelawny the younger was approached, he said that 'if the parish would come and reckon with him he would pay them every penny at any time for the same'. But he never did: he died too, 'and the parish never had anything for the silver'.

Edward's last Parliament was summoned early in 1553. Northumberland, feeling the need of support, exerted what influence he and his friends could to secure the return of members favourably disposed; and it was to this end no doubt that six additional Cornish boroughs were given representation. Certainly the Cornish contingent contained notable supporters of his course. Sir William Godolphin was one of the knights of the shire; Henry Chiverton the other.[2] Henry Killigrew, servant to the Duke, was a member for Launceston. It is probable that some of the non-Cornish members for the new boroughs were supporters of his, like Nicholas St. John for Camelford. Humphry Cavell who sat for Bossiney was an interesting person. A member of the group of young lawyers with whom originated the famous *Mirror for Magistrates*, a contributor himself, he was a friend of the Bedford family and in close contact with the Edwardian governing circle.[3]

But Northumberland's efforts to hold on to power were in vain: they depended on the life of the young King now obviously dying. His orders to proclaim Lady Jane Grey Queen came down to the west country. For we know that that forward man Sir Peter Carew had her proclaimed at Dartmouth;[4] and we learn indirectly years later how she was proclaimed in Cornwall, from a petition of Treffry admitting that he had been 'present at a general assize in the foresaid county when the Lady Jane was justly proclaimed Queen, as in like wise were all the gentlemen of the said county, who nevertheless came not for that purpose or knew of any such thing towards at their coming thither, nor in heart favoured the same'.[5]

For the present the Protestant game had been lost at the centre. If Northumberland had not gambled so desperately and attempted to divert the succession to the Crown itself, he might have used his power to make terms with Mary;

[1] Excheq. Comm. and Depos., 20 Eliz., 525.
[2] *Official Return*, I. 378.
[3] cf. my letter, *Times Lit. Supplt.*, April 15th, 1939.
[4] Hooker's *Life of Sir Peter Carew*, ed. Maclean, 54.
[5] Court of Requests Proceedings, bdle. 25, no. 190.

there might have been some sort of compromise: his religious convictions were flexible enough, if hers were not. As it was, the reaction from this attempt gave the opportunity to the Catholics and strengthened the Queen's position — though it was by no means a strong one and she had to go slowly. Nevertheless she came to the throne with a general access of loyalty, except for the advanced Protestant left wing. Control of the government carried nearly everybody with it in the sixteenth century, even more than to-day.

The reversal of fortunes brought back into power and place all the notabilities who had been excluded by Henry and Edward's government. On the day that Mary entered London in state, she was met at the Tower gate by Bishop Gardiner, the old Duke of Norfolk, the Duchess of Somerset and — most important from our point of view — Edward Courtenay, the Marquis of Exeter's young son who had been in prison ever since his father's fall, fifteen years ago. 'These are my prisoners', Mary said, kissing each one of them in turn as they knelt before her. Gardiner became Lord Chancellor and the leading spirit in her government. With him there came up a young westcountryman, Lady Lisle's second son, James Basset, for whom Mary's reign provided a brief moment of influence and success, and then he was dead like the Queen herself and Pole and Gardiner and young Courtenay and his mother — all the most intimate members of that prematurely old and sickly Catholic circle.

With her characteristic loyalty, Mary lost no time in restoring her friends who had sacrificed so much for her. Lady Exeter, who now became her bosom companion and shared her bed, was given a large grant of lands to support her dignity,[1] and her husband's household goods, tapestries, turkey carpets, bedsteads, hangings, which had remained impounded in the royal Wardrobe all those years, were restored to her and her son.[2] For him the earldom of Devonshire was recreated; he was invested in great state at Richmond on Sunday the third of September, the Queen herself placing the coronet upon his head and the sword round his shoulders 'hanging down before him baldric wise'.[3] The great estates of the earldom in the west country were restored,[4] and once more the goodly receipts from all those Devonshire and Cornish manors went up to an extravagant young Courtenay in London.[5] The young earl carried the sword of state at Mary's corona-

[1] Cal. Pat. Rolls Mary, I. 82.
[2] Courtenay MSS. from Trelawne.
[3] Add. MS. 6113.
[4] Particulars for Grants, Mary, 2147.
[5] Courtenay MSS.

tion, and was restored in blood by her first Parliament in October. A great future seemed to be opening before him.

A great-grandson of Edward IV and a cousin of the Queen's, he was the obvious English candidate for her hand. Moreover his long imprisonment, his tragic youth, his good looks, gave him the popular vote. Both sections in Mary's council supported his candidature, the great secular peers, Pembroke, Arundel, Bedford, and Gardiner and the churchmen still more strongly. Only Mary herself held aloof, encouraged privately by the Emperor through his ambassador; and Paget, for his own reasons,[1] was on their side. Mary had no reason to love the English, and she regarded the idea of marrying a subject with disfavour;[2] her Spanish sympathies impelled her to marriage with Philip, and there were good political reasons for it. It only turned out, in the event, to be a disaster.

But marriage with Courtenay might have proved a disaster too, and an ignominious one, like Mary Stuart's with Darnley. For all was not well with the young man. Fifteen years' imprisonment in the Tower in boyhood and youth had not been good for him. Once, early in Edward VI's reign, he had tried to escape, but failed and was put in straiter durance than before. Perhaps that had broken something in him; for what was wrong with him was that he was unreliable. To the unintelligence of his family, he added what was unusual in them, the bravado of a coward: he lacked courage and he lacked judgment. Poor lad! it was very understandable after the life, the trials he had been through. And the trouble was that the Queen understood it too well. She treated him with affection, but with the patronizing condescension of an elder sister: the worst of all combinations with such a young man, as Elizabeth was to find with Essex. Then, what genuinely shocked her, he began to run an indubitably dissolute course in London, like his father before him. Again, very understandable: who wouldn't, after a young lifetime in the Tower? The Queen's doubts of him were confirmed. Yet Gardiner went on supporting his candidature, and he was probably right. For the young man was well-educated: he spoke several languages and had employed some of his leisure in the Tower in translating from the Italian.[3] He was certainly attractive: tall, with a long auburn beard, a melancholy,

[1] Soranzo says that Courtenay had been unwise enough to say that if ever he became the Queen's husband, he would remember that Paget had proposed to have him put to death in Henry's reign. *Cal. S.P. Venetian* 1534-1554, 560.
[2] ibid.; and cf. Noailles, *Ambassades*, III. 95.
[3] He translated the *Trattato utilissimo del Beneficio di Gesu Christo Crocifisso* of Antonio della Paglia, as *The Benefit of Christ's Death*, with a dedication to the Duchess of Somerset, in 1548: evidently an appeal to the heart of the Protector.

refined expression. The French ambassador thought him 'le plus beau et agréable gentilhomme d'Angleterre',[1] and Castelnau described him as 'l'un des plus beaux entre les jeunes seigneurs de son age'. For the rest, given time and having had his fling, he might reform. Such was the situation, and the personal choice before Mary, in the first months of her reign and while she was meeting her first Parliament.

Parliament played an important part in Mary's reign, because of the necessity her government was under of getting legislative sanction for the restoration of Catholicism, while it in turn set the limits within which that restoration took place. It represented the sense of the nation, and there was comparatively little difference in composition between the last Parliament of Edward VI, which gave its support to Northumberland, and the first of Mary which reversed his policy. The large number of members from Cornwall makes the analysis of its representation interesting as a microcosm of the whole. There is nothing to show government pressure to 'pack' this Parliament, even if it had not been against Charles V's advice to Mary to do so. It is true Sir William Godolphin, who was knight for the shire in 1552-53, falls out and does not appear in any of Mary's Parliaments; on the other hand Sir Peter Carew was returned for the county of Devon.[2] Among the Cornish members were two eminent Protestants, Sir Thomas Smith, who had piloted the first Act of Uniformity through Parliament, and Dr. Alexander Nowell, compiler of the catechism and later dean of St. Paul's. As a cleric, however, he was declared unable to sit. Thomas Martin and Richard Weston, who were the earl of Devonshire's men, sat for Saltash. The bulk of the Cornish members were local men.

And so it continued through all five Parliaments of her reign. In her second, Sir John Arundell of Lanherne appeared;[3] he did not sit again: perhaps his imprisonment in the Tower had enfeebled him, for he sickened and died in 1557. His son and heir did not appear until her last Parliament. Before Mary's third Parliament, at the end of 1554, preparatory to the full reconciliation with Rome, the government sent out letters to the shires recommending the electors to choose representatives 'of the wise, grave, and catholic sort'. They do not seem to have had the slightest effect so far as Cornwall was concerned. In fact the shire returned Thomas Treffry, who was not particularly wise or grave, and was certainly not catholic.[4] On the other hand, James Basset was returned, an official member, as knight of the shire for Devon in that and the succeeding Parliaments. Humphry Cavell

---

[1] Noailles, *Ambassades*, II. 247.   [2] *Official Return*, I. 381.
[3] ibid., 385.   [4] ibid., 389.

who belonged to a by no means Catholic circle, was returned again in 1554 and in 1555, as he had been to Edward's last Parliament. What one notices of these two, the third and fourth Parliaments of the reign, is that the west country representation was overwhelmingly local in character. Even James Basset, who was a government member, was a westcountryman. The true type of west country representative at this time was Henry Chiverton, or John Kempthorne, who sat in Edward's last Parliament, and every one of Mary's except her last. Nicholas Randall and Thomas Royden, merchants, who represented Truro in 1552-53, continued to be returned, the former in 1553, in 1555 and in 1557-58, the latter in 1554 and 1557-58. Francis Roscarrock was returned in 1552-53, 1553 and to both Parliaments of 1554. Naturally two or three members of Northumberland's Parliament who were of his immediate entourage disappear from Mary's; and in her last Parliament, one or two members appear for Cornwall, a Roper and a Yaxley, who did not belong there.[1] That is the limit of government influence which is discernible. After all, it was not very necessary to exert it, since the country was prepared, within well-defined limits, to follow the government, especially if it were successful. To think too much in terms of 'influence' at this time is anachronistic: it belongs to the eighteenth century.

Mary's first parliament repealed the Edwardian religious legislation and restored the state of affairs that had existed in the last year of Henry's reign: mass and processions and holydays instead of the Prayer Book and the Protestant idea of work; marriage of the clergy was forbidden, and those who had committed this serious indiscretion were to be deprived. Beyond that, Parliament would not go. Mary remained, to her horror, Supreme Head of the Church; no means were provided for enforcing attendance at mass; she was given to understand, what really mattered, that there was no question of restoring the lands of the church. Finally, they besought her to marry an Englishman. This was greatly to her distaste; she had now made up her mind on Philip.

What was being thought by simple people in remote Cornwall about these high matters may be learned from a fascinating report sent up by Sir John Arundell of Trerice to the Lord Steward.[2] On the feast of the Epiphany, 1554, John Combe of Linkinhorne came to Efford, where Sir John lived, and gave evidence before a number of justices as to the conversation that took place at his house on Christmas eve between Sampson Jackman and John Cowlyn. Jackman asked Combe when he had come from church; to which he had replied 'One hour agone; and that he had heard and seen that thing

1 *Official Return*, 396.   2 S.P. 11/2, 2.

304

he saw not in four year before, for I have, thanked be God, heard mass and received holy bread and holy water'. Jackman said: 'I would all priests were hanged'. To which Combe replied, or said that he had — 'God forbid! for the Queen's grace hath granted it'. Cowlyn said: 'The Queen, a vengeance take her'. 'Amen', said Jackman. Cowlyn went on: 'I may say it well, for before New Year's day outlandish men will come upon our heads, for there be some at Plymouth already'. Jackman: 'Before twelve months you shall see all houses of religion up again with the Pope's laws'. Cowlyn said: 'We ought not to have a woman to bear the sword'; and Jackman added: 'If a woman bear the sword, my lady Elizabeth ought to bear it first'. Master Combe informed against his guests, a pretty turn of hospitality, at Bodmin sessions, where the offenders were given bail notwithstanding.

So much for Catholic Cornwall. It is a most revealing conversation. It has been frequently asked why it was that Cornwall, which was so devoted to Catholicism as to rebel against the Prayer Book in 1549, should have become so Protestant later. This book as a whole is the answer to that question. But here in this conversation between ordinary simple folk — it is rarely that we are given such an insight into their minds — we see Cornwall thus early ceasing to be Catholic and in course of transition to Protestantism and the age of Elizabeth. Catholicism survives by unity, and once that unity had been broken not all the Queen's horses and all the Queen's men could put Humpty-Dumpty together again. It is interesting too to observe that along with the Protestantism went the primitive xenophobia, the hatred of the foreigner, which boded ill for the Spanish marriage and to which Courtenay and the Carews hoped to appeal.

For they were now in alliance, the candidate of the English Catholics and these forward-looking Protestants. The Queen's betrothal to Philip had brought about their conjunction. The marriage was intensely unpopular, and a party drew together, Wyatt in Kent, Suffolk and his brothers in the Midlands, the Carews in the west country, to depose Mary and replace her by Elizabeth and Courtenay. Parliament over, the Carews went down to the west to spend Christmas and complete their preparations.[1] 'They drew a small party of their followers around them, including John Courtenay and the faithful William Gibbs; Sir Arthur Champernowne was sympathetic but would not join in armed revolt. In January six horses laden with harness and handguns from Dartmouth Castle, which was in Sir Peter's charge, passed through the city of Exeter; some seventy armed men were collected at his

---

[1] The documents, upon which the above is based with its quotations, are printed in Maclean, *Life and Times of Sir Peter Carew*, App. E.

fortified house of Mohun's Ottery; posts were laid all the way to Andover to meet the earl. There was a rumour that he had arrived – perhaps for the first time since childhood – in the county of his ancestors, that he was already at Mohun's Ottery. But he never came. Instead, he had allowed Gardiner to worm the secret of the enterprise out of him, though the Chancellor, who was his friend, went as far as he could to protect him from its consequences afterwards, even failing to decipher his name in a vital document.

The whole enterprise was thrown out of gear by Courtenay's revelations; Carew's move was anticipated before his preparations were complete. The Council ordered the sheriff of Devon to apprehend the Carews, who wrote from Mohun's Ottery that they were ready to submit as 'true and faithful subjects' who 'intend to observe and follow her religion as faithfully as they that most are affected unto it'. Sir Gawen Carew came late one night to Exeter, where apparently he expected to take shipping for abroad. Two nights later he escaped over the city walls 'in his boots' and made for Tiverton and Bickleigh, that pleasant house of which the great gatehouse remains in the valley of the upper Exe, where he was caught and surrendered. Gibbs likewise was rounded up. Sir Peter, assuring the sheriff that he was making his journey towards London, made for Weymouth, where Walter Ralegh put a bark at his disposal to convey him across Channel. One of the Killigrews was in command, and there went on board with him Andrew Tremayne, John Courtenay and James Kirkham. A ship's master told John Grenville, who was sent in pursuit, that three gentlemen had passed on board: 'one being a little man, the other of a mean stature, the third a more longer young man'. One of them had a chain of gold about his neck; he heard one at departing say that 'the King of Spain would come shortly: he shall be as well barked at as ever man was'.

In Kent Wyatt made his attempt unsupported, though the nearness with which he missed success showed how dangerous a coordinated effort would have been. Courtenay paid the penalty for his failure by returning to the Tower which he had so recently left, though that was exchanged shortly for Fotheringhay. His servant Edmund Tremayne was sent to the Tower with him. It is said that while there he was racked, though he would not say anything to implicate Courtenay and Elizabeth, and that this was the foundation of his favour with her when she became Queen. Sir Peter Carew arrived safely in France, where he was warmly welcomed and entertained at Court by Henry II, who harboured a nest of west country malcontents, Tremaynes and Killigrews, as useful instruments against the Spanish alliance.[1] The Killigrews,

---

[1] *Cal. S.P. Foreign*, 1553-1558, 79, 80.

in particular Peter, roamed the Channel looking out for Spanish ships to plunder, perhaps with the hope that one of them might contain Philip himself.[1]

The conspiracy out of the way, Wyatt's rebellion suppressed, the marriage was free to go forward. Bedford, who had taken a leading part against Wyatt, was now to take the foremost in the marriage negotiations. The day after Wyatt's execution he and Lord Fitzwalter, with a splendid company, set sail from Plymouth for Spain; back to Plymouth came Philip's representative, the Marquis de las Navas, who was received by Lord William Howard.[2] In July Philip himself arrived at Southampton. The Killigrews were still hovering about the Channel, and continued to give the government some anxiety. Tremaynes, Killigrews, Carews, Lord William Howard: we see the reign of Elizabeth opening out on the horizon.

The restoration of Catholic order in the Church was meanwhile proceeding. The deprived bishops returned to their sees, among them Veysey, who was now incredibly old: he had not exactly been deprived, though the patent restoring him said that he had surrendered 'pro corporis metu'.[3] Restored on September 28th, he spent Christmas at Exeter; so did Dr. Moreman, after the prominent part he had taken in the disputation on the blessed sacrament with the Protestant divines at Westminster. Coverdale was summoned before the Council, but was apparently not imprisoned; he lived quietly in retirement in or about London, and in the spring of 1555 was allowed to leave the country for Denmark.[4]

The authorities were determined to enforce clerical celibacy. In Edward's reign a considerable portion of the clergy had taken advantage of the permission to marry. Now all these were to be deprived, though on putting away their women they might be restored to their functions 'so it be not in the same place'.[5] Faced with such a choice, the great bulk of the prematurely married clergy chose their living and put away their women. It was all very disturbing. Not less than one-sixth of the beneficed clergy in the whole country were affected and had to be deprived.[6] Since such a vast number could not be replaced they were for the most part, on submission, instituted to other livings; in effect, it meant a sort of general post of the affected clergy. It meant also a vast deal of work for the diocesan authorities, much litigation and some hardship: in short, a great nuisance. The year 1554 was largely given up in the dioceses to putting the Church's house in order in this matter.

[1] ibid., 1553-1558, 66.   [2] Worth, *Plymouth Municipal Records*, 17.
[3] Pat. Rolls Mary, 28 Sept. 1553.   [4] Garrett, *Marian Exiles*, 132.
[5] Mary's Injunctions q. Frere, *The Marian Reaction*, 60-61.   [6] cf. ibid., 52-3.

In the eastern counties, as high a proportion as one fourth of the clergy were married; in London, where the disease was at its height, as many as one third. [1] Naturally in the west, which was more backward, or perhaps one should say less forward in these matters, the proportion was much lower. Dr. Frere counted some fifty deprivations in all in the diocese of Exeter, a ratio of one in a dozen. That may be slightly too low an estimate, though his general conclusion that the numbers and ratios diminish as you move further away from London remains valid. In Cornwall during this year, out of 29 institutions to livings in seven cases the outgoing incumbent had been deprived, no doubt for marriage, and in eight cases the living is described as *certo modo vacante*, which meant the same thing. In the remaining years of the reign we have three or four vacancies which may also be due to marriage. Perhaps in all some eighteen cases: a proportion of one in nine or ten. It is a sufficient indication of the conservative sympathies of the west as against the advanced tendencies of London and East Anglia.

What happened in concrete, the difficulties that arose, may be illustrated from one or two cases. Master Nicholas Nicolls, vicar of St. Kew since 1536, was deprived for marriage in 1554. [2] Some five years before, probably at the time of his marriage, he had taken the precaution of leasing his vicarage, house, gardens, glebe and tithes for five years. [3] On his deprivation John Langman was instituted, before the lease had expired, and there was trouble about it: the lessee claimed that the new vicar had renewed it by word of mouth for another five years at £20 p.a. 'in consideration of the great benevolence and friendship to him showed by this defendant'. In 1557 the living is described as *litime vacante*, perhaps because Langman had other livings in plurality, and Robert Goldsmith was instituted, who held it till his death in 1576. [4] Meanwhile in this same year 1554, the living of Marhamchurch, not many miles away from St. Kew, was vacated, probably for the same reason. [5] To it was instituted Sir Robert Hamlyn, the ex-abbot of Athelney, who, we remember, had been so anxious — years before — to become prior of Tywardreath. [6] Next year he vacated it — knowing him, we should say for a consideration; already he was well provided for. Master Nicholas Nicolls succeeded him in the rectory and so, at the cost of putting away his woman and perhaps a little more, he got another living which he kept. [7]

It was to be expected that Mary would favour ex-monks for these pro-

---

[1] cf. Miss Grieve, 'The Deprived Married Clergy in Essex, 1553-1561', *Trans. Roy. Hist. Soc.*, series 4, vol. XXII. 141.

[2] Henderson, X. 27, 31.   [3] Early Chanc. Proc. file 1366, 5-6.

[4] Henderson, X. 32, 38.   [5] ibid., 31.

[6] v. supra, p. 167.   [7] Henderson, X. 32.

motions: they were more likely to be catholic and celibate. When William Todd was deprived of Northill in 1554 he was succeeded by the old ex-prior of St. Germans, Robert Swymmer, who died in 1558.[1] The next institution recorded is in 1574, 'on the death of the last incumbent'.[2] That means that with Elizabeth's accession Todd got back his living; in this case the way was clear by Swymmer's death. But that was what usually happened, even where the way was not clear; some arrangement with the Marian intruder may have been made; the deprived incumbent usually returned, with Elizabeth, to his living: the authorities regarded him as the lawful incumbent and so no re-institution was made by which the process may be traced in the bishop's register. Take the case of Calstock, for example. Here Anthony Hunt was deprived in 1554, and the Queen, 'clementissima domina', presented Richard Eden, ex-monk of Hayles.[3] He resigned the living in 1556 to renew his profession as monk of the newly refounded abbey of Westminster, and was succeeded by John Bishop.[4] In 1573, when the next institution is entered, it is upon the death of Anthony Hunt, who must therefore have returned under Elizabeth's dispensation and Bishop given way to him.[5] In 1563 he was presented by the Queen to Linkinhorne in addition, which he only resigned in the year of his death.[6] He had done quite well: his four years in the wilderness, for marriage, were more than made up to him.

Something of the circumstances which were liable to accompany these changes may be gathered from a case brought by Nicholas Daniel of Kirton in Devon against John Chapel of St. Teath.[7] Daniel had been deprived of the rectory of St. Michael Penkivel in 1554,[8] and also, it appears, of St. Teath. He sued Chapel for breaking into his house at the latter place and taking away various goods: an iron window, a handgun, five pots of butter 'every one of them containing one gallon', 'eleven books of divers tracts': a miscellaneous cargo. Chapel retorted that 'the said complainant was married and had a woman conversant with him, being the vicar of the said parish, by the space of one year and a half, and never resident in the said parish, but was a common preacher and an unquiet person, and passed from place to place, never resident upon the said benefice nor never kept hospitality there'. He averred that the parson before his deprivation had borrowed £4 from him which he had not paid; and he claimed that with Master William Carnsew and Henry Tredenek, farmer of the tithes for the vicar, he had been appointed to receive certain fruits to pay the wages of a priest to serve the cure there, and that he had paid over 23s. 8d. to 'Sir Richard, parson of Temple', for his wages

[1] ibid., 31. [2] ibid., 37. [3] ibid., 30. [4] ibid., 32.
[5] ibid., 37. [6] ibid., 34, 37. [7] C 1/1347/16-18. [8] Henderson, x. 73.

for serving the cure for one month from Palm Sunday forward. The parson's defence does not matter: what opens before us is the background of how Cornwall became Protestant: the itinerant preacher, married, the tracts, Protestantism.

More revealing, more intimate, details of the kind of thing liable to happen to a married priest are to be found in the proceedings before the consistory court of Exeter against Elizabeth White, wife of William Lamb, former vicar of Pelynt.[1] He had been deprived of his living on account of her in 1554; but he was not badly treated, for on putting her away, he was presented to the neighbouring rectory of St. Keyne.[2] Two years later she got him into trouble again, and he forfeited St. Keyne for a time as he had previously Pelynt. To the court his wife deposed that she was married to him 'the Monday after St. Katherine's day three years ago. And on Monday before Twelfth day last hearing that Sir William was sick, she went to see how he did. And that night about ten or eleven of the clock, John Bevil, a Justice of the Peace in Cornwall, with other men took this respondent in bed with a certain Welsh woman, which dwelled in the said parsonage of Keyne in a chamber over the buttery, and took the said parson in bed within his chamber and after a little communication set the parson and this respondent in the stocks at Duloe where they both sat a night and half a day. And there nor since had not carnal copulation with him'. Mistress White was made of sterner stuff than Lamb, who had admitted to the chancellor to having 'the Friday before Twelfth day in Christmas last past within the night and within the parsonage of St. Keyne had carnal copulation with the said Elizabeth'. This she denied with double negatives, improbable as that seems: after all, why not? She stood to it that she 'never did penance for her unlawful marriage and unthrifty living'.

What a lot of fuss about nothing very much: so like human society to make it! But it gives us a picture of the time, the difficulties of the clergy torn between the call of the flesh and their calling. This little *contretemps* interfered for a time with parson Lamb's career in the church; but all was made meetly well by the accession of Elizabeth, and more was added unto him. He got both his livings back, and received another preferment, St. Martin by Looe, in 1566; it was not until 1576 that he had to resign St. Keyne, no doubt on that account.[3] He had done well.

The troubles the clergy underwent on this question must have been a con-

---

[1] Henderson, XI. 265.   [2] ibid., x. 72 b, 31, 30.
[3] ibid., 38, 34; and Transcript of Return to Archbishop Parker, c. 1561 (Corpus Christi Coll. Camb. MS. 97) at Exeter City Library.

siderable factor in inclining them to accept the changes made under Elizabeth. Clerical marriage was none too popular with the laity, as indeed it was anathema to Elizabeth herself. The natural conservatism of a simple society continued to attach vague, sacrosanct ideas to the person of a priest, to whom contact with a woman somehow brought contamination. One can think of numerous anthropological parallels: it was just a taboo. Cases before the consistory court reveal such phrases as 'old priest's whore' to be thought the vilest opprobrium addressed to a woman. As late as 1587 at Probus, when Katherine Stephens came to a house with some aqua vitae, John Dennis 'seeing her look into the door said to her, "What worketh this old priest's whore here? Get thee out of the house, or else I will hurl all that is here to thy head! Get thee out, old priest's whore".'[1] While in 1572 at Lelant, in the course of scolding together and 'multiplying of words', John Way called Agnes Davy a whore; she asked 'Whose whore?' and he said 'Sir John Vose's whore'[2] (Sir John Vose was vicar of St. Erth nearby). Marriage was indeed a more agreeable remedy for the clergy, and the Elizabethan settlement left that way open to them, though it was still not legalized. With the acceptance of the situation and their families by society, the clergy came to have a family interest in the established church. It was a great factor in its success.

Meanwhile under Mary for a bit the old order was revived. Veysey after remaining in his diocese for two months went home once more to Sutton Coldfield at the end of January 1554, where he remained till his death at the end of the year.[3] At Exeter, the bishop of Hippo performed the episcopal functions. Dr. Frere tells us that at the end of Henry's reign there had been an immense reduction in the number of ordinands, that at Exeter there were no ordinations from 1544 till Coverdale's under the new English Ordinal in 1551.[4] We may regard this as due to several causes: uncertainty as to the future and status of the clergy in those changeable years, the fact that a large number of monks were now available on the market, and the great simplification that the new English Ordinal brought about with its abolition of minor orders, in itself a reduction of the number of those who were technically 'clergy'. That there were those who doubted the sufficiency of their Edwardian orders may be seen from the case of John Grose, who, ordained deacon and priest by Coverdale in 1552, and becoming rector of Creed in 1553, had himself admitted to minor orders, was tonsured and made acolyte by the bishop of Hippo in 1554 and then went to London to receive his orders as deacon and priest from Bonner.[5] But then he was a convinced and

---

[1] ibid., x. 142.   [2] ibid., 124.   [3] Oliver, *Lives*, 124-5.
[4] op. cit., 102-4.   [5] ibid., 118, 120, 216.

doctrinaire catholic who was deprived of his living in 1559, no doubt for refusing the oath of supremacy.[1] He was very exceptional among the lower clergy in making his choice between his livelihood and his convictions.

In March 1555 James Turberville, of an old Dorset family from Bere Regis, was nominated to the see of Exeter; and later, to make all well, he was papally provided to it. Mary, whose generosity to the church exceeded the limits of discretion, restored to him the great manor and borough of Crediton,[2] the jewel of his see, and he must have recovered possession of Bishop's Clyst, for once more we find a catholic bishop dating his acts there, holding his ordinations in that chapel.[3] Other catholic rites were revived, though the routine had got a bit rusty in the interval. For example, the dean of the seven parishes round Egloshayle, which were bishop's peculiars, 'having business in Exeter chanced to meet with the substitutes of the deans rural of major and minor Trigg, who desired him to bring the holy oil from Exeter and they would please him for his pains. And so he desired Nicholas Gerves to help him to holy oil because he never fetched any holy oil before that time'.[4] Gerves delivered it to him, and he handed it over to the substitutes for two rural deans at Launceston and to a third on Good Friday at Camelford; but he could not tell 'whether it was consecrated or no, but it was the same oil he had of Gerves'. Somebody must have doubted its efficacy, for he was summoned before the consistory court.

And so the old catholic system was set once more in motion. Its worst struggle was, however, with heresy; Protestant fanatics were so very determined. They were to be found chiefly in London and the eastern counties; but the diocese of Exeter produced one martyr who insisted upon dying for her convictions, or rather her uninstructed self-will.[5] She was of the stuff of which such fanatics are usually made, a religious busybody, a poor woman of no education who could not keep her inner promptings to herself but must bore all her neighbours with her spiritual favours; there are still such in the west country: the recruits of the more fantastic and repulsive sects. She was called Agnes Prest and came from Northcote in the parish of Boyton near Launceston.[6] The teachings of Protestantism had found good soil in her; in Edward's reign she had been a devout attender of sermons, and though she could not read, she had, as such people have, a tenacious memory for texts and a fervent belief in the literal inspiration of the bible. Her husband and

[1] Henderson, XI. 132.   [2] Pat. Rolls, Philip and Mary, 18 July 1556.
[3] Oliver, Lives, 136.   [4] Henderson, XI. 267.
[5] The above account is based upon that of Hooker in Foxe's Martyrs (ed. 1583), 2050-2, from which the quotations are taken. For Hooker's authorship, cf. Harleian MS. 5827/48.
[6] Peter, Launceston and Dunheved, 200.

children, on the contrary, were strong catholics — one can see the background of family discord, the bore she had made herself to them — and they used to make her attend mass and procession with them when these were restored. This she could not abide, and one night she had a spiritual experience, 'a certain motion and feeling of singular comfort', which inspired her to 'grow in contempt of her husband and children' and to leave them, seeking her living by her own labour, mostly in spinning. 'In which time notwithstanding she never ceased to utter her mind as well as she durst.' Her chief abominations, against which she spoke her mind, were the mass and images. She was brought back to her husband, and then at length, accused by her neighbours, was sent up to Exeter to be examined by bishop Turberville and his chancellor Blackstone.

The one thing the poor bishop seems to have wanted was to avoid trouble. A propos of the sacrament of the altar, he asked her, reasonably enough, why she, an unlearned person, meddled 'with such high matters which all the doctors of the world can not define?' He referred to her husband; she answered provokingly that 'she had a husband and children, and had them not'. She was under the usual delusion with such people that Christ was her heavenly spouse, whom she greatly preferred. The chancellor and others persuaded the bishop that she was but a 'mazed creature', and very humanely set her at liberty. The keeper of the bishop's prison took her home with him, and she worked in his house as a servant, spinning and carding, and had full liberty to go about the city. 'And ever she continued talking of the sacrament of the altar, which of all things they could least abide.' A great many people had talk with her, including a number of priests with whom she disputed publicly: she must have been a public nuisance. One day entering the cathedral where a German sculptor was engaged in repairing the noses of images disfigured in Edward's time, she started on him. He called her a whore. This started a theological argument.

She was sent back to the bishop's prison, where she was visited by a number of people, some sent by the bishop for her benefit. Among them was our friend Daniel, the deprived parson of St. Teath, 'a great doer and preacher sometime of the gospel, in the days of King Edward', who, since his deprivation, had seen a light, but on the other side: him in return she earnestly 'exhorted to repent with Peter, and to be more constant in his profession'. Gregory Basset, a son of Lady Lisle and brother of James Basset, who held the catholic views of the family with the family living of Atherington, railed against her rather simple knowledge of the scriptures: he said she was mad — as, in a way, she was. The wife of Walter Ralegh on the other hand came, in an inquiring turn of mind – their sympathies were already that way – and she was much impressed by the godly chatter of the woman. The authorities did their best with kindness, trying to get her to go back to her husband and children, but 'nothing could prevail, her heart was fixed'. Foxe says that chancellor Blackstone kept a concubine – it was at any rate better than marriage – and when this lady came to his house with other gossips, he had a habit of sending for the poor fanatic to amuse them with her conversation.

Nothing could prevail with her or shake her determination, neither imprisonment, nor promises, nor reasonableness. When they saw that, they began to call her an Anabaptist, which had the same effect upon sixteenth century idiots as the word 'Bolshevik' has upon those of the twentieth century. At last she was arraigned at the Guildhall and handed over to the temporal power for execution, the gentlemen of the country to the last exhorting her to give up her fond opinions and return to her husband. She refused; she wanted martyrdom. And this she suffered with the courage of her fanaticism in the flames at Southernhay, outside the city walls, in November 1558. (The Queen's martyrdom by that time was already upon her: all her efforts in vain, her work undone.) Agnes Prest was 'as simple a woman to see to as any man might behold: of a very little and short stature, somewhat thick, about fifty-four years of age. She had a cheerful countenance, so lively, as though she had been prepared for that day of her marriage to meet the Lamb: most patient of her words and answers, sober in apparel, meat and drink, and would never be idle: a great comfort to as many as would talk with her: good to the poor; and in her trouble, money, she said, she would take none; for, she said, "I am going to a city where money beareth no mastery; whiles I am here, God hath promised to feed me".'

Deluded as she was, mistaken in her certitude, she was of the stuff of which political victories are made. It was such spirit as hers that gave Protestantism the confidence of success.

The Spanish marriage consummated, Mary's expectation – nay more, her confidence in God – of an heir to secure the catholic succession, make sure her work, meant that she could afford to be more lenient with those who had opposed it. The Earl of Devon was released from Fotheringhay in April 1555 and given leave to go to the court of the Emperor at Brussels. He was very anxious to embark upon that Italian tour which must have been such a delicious mirage during so many years of imprisonment. 'I pray you consider my going into Italy as a matter that (as this messenger shall tell you) standeth me wonderfully upon', he wrote to the faithful James Basset, asking him to press his suit for licence to travel thither upon the King.[1] The fact was that when he got to Brussels and was received kindly enough by the Emperor, he found that he was there to be supervised, detained still in a safe place in a sort of honourable exile. And there he was kept all through that summer and autumn, at great expense to himself, waiting for permission to go. There followed him the shoals of letters from great personages at court, from friends and advisers and agents, stewards of his west country estates, the press of business that accompanied a great Tudor magnate of such dangerously exalted position, upon whom such hopes rested.

His mother the Marchioness wrote him: 'I thought long till you were safe past the seas, the which I was glad to hear; assuring you I shall never be quiet till I see you well in England again; praying to our Lord to preserve you from all perils both in soul and body'.[2] He did not reply to her. She wrote again pathetically to say she was sorry to 'perceive you have so much business you have no leisure to write in your own hand to your own mother, and yet seldom to hear from you'.[3] He replied coldly to her; there was something that came between him and his mother, we do not know what; he preferred to write to Lady Berkeley as 'your son at commandment'. Nevertheless he did not forget to press upon his mother to take the chance of waiting on the Queen again, which she promised she would do: 'if my waiting can do you good, if I may get a chamber I will wait, and although my years require ease'.

The state in which he lived, and his projected journey, necessitated large advances of money: it is to this that we owe the full survey of his estates in the west from which we have drawn information earlier.[4] Nor was he at ease in Brussels on other accounts: he went in some fear of his life; his servants were attacked by Spaniards, as a reprisal for the attacks made on them in London.[5] He was desperately anxious to get away; one of his agents moved his friend, the Chancellor Gardiner, for leave from Philip to go to Italy, 'whereby your lordship should have less occasion to look homeward, and better means to advance yourself in further knowledge, and therewithal to do you more notable service at your return'.[6] But he could not escape the toils of his precarious position; all sorts of projects were discussed concerning him. At one moment there was a rumour that the Emperor and Philip would marry him to Elizabeth, on Mary's failure to produce a child:

[1] S.P. 11/5, 26.   [2] S.P. 11/5, 16.   [3] ibid., no. 35.   [4] v. above, 34 foll.
[5] Cal. S.P. Venetian, 1557-8, 123, 173, 187, 222, 245.   [6] S.P. 11/5, 27.

315

a sort of re-insurance to keep him loyal and Elizabeth catholic.[1] It would have been well for them if they had brought it to pass: as it was, Elizabeth escaped them to go on her own way. Then the word went round that he was to be sent to Spain, and Elizabeth to Brussels where she would be safe under the eye of the Emperor.[2] But the English would never have permitted that: the kingdom might be ruled by these Spaniards, but it was not yet entirely at their disposal.

At length he got permission to set out. Just before leaving in November, he had a meeting with Sir Peter Carew who had arrived from Strasburg, his peace having been made with Philip by the devoted efforts of his wife and friends.[3] There seems to have been almost a conspiracy to rehabilitate Sir Peter. Mason, the ambassador at Brussels, wrote home on his behalf saying that he was very repentant and had meant no harm, had merely been led away by his erroneous religious views and would make a good recruit to the regime since he had much influence in the west country.[4] Wotton had pleaded too on behalf of Sir Gawen Carew, who was a relation by marriage, and shortly he was liberated from the Tower.[5] Sir Peter had rejected the offers of the French court and betaken himself to Venice, where he narrowly escaped being assassinated by the contrivance of Peter Vannes.[6] He was glad to make his submission, and Philip glad to recruit a person of influence to his service in English affairs. The Earl of Devon met him at Antwerp, and wrote home to Secretary Petre a strong testimonial in his favour;[7] what was more important, Philip himself wrote to Mary asking her to pardon him. Sir Peter did not dare to venture over till her written pardon came.[8]

Before that a new conspiracy had been brought to light in England, one which was parallel in many particulars to that of the Carews two years before. The plot hatched by Sir Henry Dudley, a relative of Northumberland, was to seize the Exchequer, depose Philip and Mary, and marry Elizabeth to Courtenay.[9] The conspiracy rested upon its western wing, though there were wider ramifications and a number of important people were involved. Sir Anthony Kingston, who had spoken out against the government in the last session of Parliament and been sent to the Tower for a bit and then liberated, was in it. Sent for to court, he died on the way, it is thought by his own hand: a suitable end for a man of his type, the proper reward for his cruelty in Cornwall in 1549. Among the young men at the

[1] *Cal. S.P. Venetian*, 1557-8, 165.   [2] ibid., 178.   [3] ibid., 257, 288.
[4] *Cal. S.P. Foreign*, 1553-8, 393.   [5] ibid., 316; *A.P.C.* 1554-6, 142.
[6] Hooker's *Life of Carew*, 60-1.   [7] S.P. 11/6, 66.
[8] *Cal. S.P. Venetian*, 1557-8, 315.   [9] S.P. 11/8, 52.

centre of the conspiracy were two Horseys of Dorset, and Edmund and Nicholas Tremayne.[1] These were two of the numerous children of Thomas Tremayne of Collacombe on the Devon and Cornish border. Edmund, the ablest of them politically, had already been in the Tower for his part in the 1554 affair; Andrew and Nicholas in the Marshalsea and the Gatehouse on suspicion of piracy.[2] Yet another brother, Richard, who had been at Louvain acting as tutor to Sir Nicholas Arnold's son, was suspected in the business.[3] Anyhow they made good their escape abroad; Edmund was certainly later with Courtenay at Venice.

The affair raised all the old suspicions. Walker, an agent of Courtenay's, was arrested in London and examined.[4] Sir William Courtenay, Sir John Perrot and Sir John Pollard were taken in their beds, as the result of a letter which had come through Sir Peter Carew.[5] The last, still in Brussels, revealed all he knew of the conspiracy to Philip; notwithstanding which, he was arrested with Sir John Cheke and sent across Channel to be lodged in the Tower.[6] The rebels in Paris dispatched Henry Killigrew to Courtenay at Ferrara about Whitsuntide; he came back, so they said, with an encouraging message to the effect that the earl would join them shortly at the French court.[7] About the same time Edmund Tremayne left his service in Italy for Paris; the earl regretted his departure, which might be misinterpreted.[8] He does not seem to have committed himself this time, though his name was bandied about in all the courts of Europe. To the Imperial suggestion that Elizabeth should be married to the Archduke Ferdinand, the French King replied that he would marry Courtenay to Mary Queen of Scots.[9] But all these suggestions and possibilities foundered on a chance fever caught in the lagoons of Venice. The earl failed his friends again, this time for good: he died at Padua on September 18th, 1556, and was buried there in the nave of the famous church of Sant' Antonio.[10]

The hopes of the future rested on lesser, tougher men. The English rebels, the Tremaynes among them, were concentrating at Rouen; Peter Killigrew and his brother were at La Rochelle and careering about in the Channel preying on Spanish shipping.[11] In June, his father and brother, John the elder and John the younger, were summoned before the Council and put in close confinement in the Fleet for the depredations committed;

[1] K.B. 27/1204, m.12.   [2] A.P.C. v. 99.   [3] S.P. 11/6, 54.
[4] Cal. S.P. Venetian, 1557-8, 434, 440, 448.
[5] Noailles, Ambassades, v. 351; C.S.P. Ven., 1557-8, 482.
[6] ibid., 486.   [7] Cal. S.P. Foreign, 1553-8, 229.
[8] Garrett, Marian Exiles, 310.   [9] Cal. S.P. Venetian, 1557-8, 552.
[10] ibid., 655, 706.   [11] Cal. S.P. Foreign, 1553-8, 520.

along with some other west country merchants and gentlemen, James Killigrew, William Godolphin, John Eliot, they had to enter a bond in £2000 to answer the claims of the Spaniard.[1] In July the west country privateers, sailing under French letters of marque and in the company of Peter Killigrew, were chased by ships of the Queen: six of them were brought into Plymouth, but at the last moment Peter sheered off.[2] Next month he was captured and brought into Portsmouth, and sent up to the Tower to be examined.[3] From the political point of view his depositions were disappointing; though he had been in touch with the Tremaynes, he does not seem to have been involved in the Dudley conspiracy.[4] He was, on the other hand, communicative enough about his doings at sea: the Spanish and Flemish ships laden with wool and iron, which he had taken in the *Sacret* and the *Falcon*, in company with other French privateers. He tells us that his brother Thomas and he intended to put in hand a voyage to Guinea to make their fortune, and coming back 'to have sold their ships and then gone forth to Italy and there to have lived and rid themselves out of this misery wherein they have long lived'.[5]

This is in the highest degree interesting. The very first efforts were then being made by English merchants and seamen to break into the Portuguese monopoly of the Guinea trade; and the Killigrews were intending such a voyage ten years before Hawkins made his. But Philip supported the Portuguese and put an embargo on the English sharing in the trade: another link which drew the hostility of the west country seamen to Spain and linked them with Protestantism and France against the Spanish Empire. It was a mere straw in the wind; but in the end it brought about a profound change in the character of English policy, from the limited Channel warfare with France to the oceanic struggle for access to the New World, the twenty years' warfare with Spain.

It may seem surprising after the popular devotion to Catholicism revealed in the Rebellion of 1549, yet it is surely very significant that the most energetic and constant opposition to Mary should have come from that circle of west country gentry connected with the sea. It was to some extent a difference of class. Elizabeth's reign was to give them the opportunities which Mary's conservative, catholic and Spanish rule denied them. It was this class, not the stupid and backward-looking peasantry, which was the dynamic force in Tudor society; and Elizabeth's triumphant reign was due to her putting herself at the head of it, not trying to dam it. All these men,

[1] *A.P.C.* 1554-6, 282, 294, 307.   [2] *Cal. S.P. Venetian*, 1557-8, 554.
[3] *P.C.* 1554-6, 321, 322, 361.   [4] S.P. 11/9, 25.   [5] ibid., 26

Carews, Tremaynes, Killigrews, were in high favour with her; they had been of her party in Mary's reign and they were rewarded when she came to power.

Paradoxical as it is, it is possible then to say that the Reformation made progress under Mary. The issues became more clearly defined. The choice was henceforth a clear one between Catholicism and Spain, and Protestant nationalism. The total failure of Mary's reign — the failure of the burnings to convert the heretics, of the government to repress an irrepressible opposition, of the policy of relying upon the Spanish alliance which lost us Calais, of the Queen herself to produce an heir — left the way clear for the victory of the new, dynamic forces. In this chapter we have seen them drawing together: Protestantism, the western gentry, the sea.

CHAPTER XIII

THE ELIZABETHAN CHURCH

THE struggle between Protestants and Catholics was in the main a struggle between two parties, over the body of a mentally passive people, for the possession of power. Whichever side won, they, with variations, would follow. Mary's was a defeated party: circumstances had been too much for them: the tide was against them. One is impressed by the strength, the almost irresistible power, of the under-current which carried Elizabeth on to success. It was the House of Commons which pressed forward the legislation breaking away from Rome again, reviving the Royal Supremacy and the Prayer Book, restoring essentially the Edwardian system. The Marian party, still in control of the church, the bishops, the cathedral dignitaries, Convocation — that is the official class — waged a rearguard action throughout the first months of the reign. Isolated and defeated in detail, they at least retained their dignity: the catholic bishops could not accept the Elizabethan settlement without going back on all that they had made themselves responsible for under Mary, making nonsense of the sacrifice of lives they had exacted.

There was a new official class waiting to replace them. To it two streams contributed: the lesser Henricians and Edwardians who had contrived to survive in quiet, or had conformed, under Mary; and the more advanced body of Protestants who had gone into exile and come under the influence of continental schools of thought, predominantly that of Calvin. The dualism, the conflict between these two, becomes a main theme in the history of the Elizabethan Church: the Anglicans and the Puritans. The new state-church had a difficult path to pursue, with opposition from catholics on one side and puritans on the other. But time, as always, was on the side of power; by the end of the reign the governing circle had brought into existence the Anglican church, something neither wholly catholic, nor wholly Protestant, yet English enough.

The catholic episcopate refused the oath of supremacy and were one by one deprived of their sees. Among them Turberville: he was deprived on August 10th and sent to join his brethren in the Tower. Later he was released and handed over to the custody of the new bishop of London; in January 1564 he was liberated, on giving sureties to remain in some certain place in London, at the call of the bishop; and there he died in obscurity.[1] At Exeter the leading cathedral dignitaries similarly chose deprivation: the dean, sub-dean, Blackstone and five prebendaries; of the latter, however, two, Harpsfield and Morgan Philips, held office elsewhere, the last being bishop-elect of St. David's.[2]

Among the lower ranks of the clergy there was very little disturbance: a great contrast with the Marian deprivations of 1554: in Elizabeth's whole reign there were not so many. In Cornwall, in her first five years, there were six clear deprivations, including the bishop of St. David's from his rectory of St. Columb major.[3] Indeed it seems that only four, if that, were local Cornish clergy, the parsons of Creed, Menheniot, Lanteglos-by-Fowey, Altarnun. The sub-dean of Exeter resigned his living of Lansallos in 1561, two years after he ceased to be sub-dean. The government very wisely did not press matters in this respect: a great inducement to conform. In addition there were six livings described as *litime vacante*; but in each case the vacancy was on account of plurality. What later deprivations there were in the reign were practically all due to similar disciplinary reasons, for holding two benefices without dispensation, for refusal to pay first-fruits, or for felony. We are left then with a handful of merely three or four Cornish incumbents who did not submit to the Elizabethan change.

Of the reluctance, nevertheless, with which some of the clergy submitted we have evidence in the case of the vicar of Bodmin. This was John Dagle, ex-monk of the priory, who had got the living in 1550.[4] In Mary's time, with a Queen so partial to monks, the goodly rectory of St. Breoke was added unto him.[5] Was he to sacrifice both now? After a struggle with his conscience, common sense won. Two of the commissioners of 1559 reported:[6] 'according to our order taken concerning the recantation of the vicar of Bodmin we have here inclosed sent the same, committing the due execution by him to be done by your wisdoms', and praying them 'to inform Sir John Chichester, the mayor of Bodmin, and other the commissioners of that town how he hath behaved himself in that behalf, requiring them to see the like done by him both in the parish church of Bodmin and other places'.[7] The poor man was not to be let off public reparation, but he kept his livings.

In the summer of 1559 a royal visitation of both provinces was made to

---

[1] *A.P.C.* 1558-1570, 190.   [2] Gee, *Elizabethan Clergy*, 277.
[3] Henderson, x. 33; XI. 132.   [4] ibid., x. 29.   [5] ibid., 74.
[6] i.e. John Jewel and Henry Parry, commissioners for the visitation of the western counties, to their local colleagues.
[7] Hist. MSS. Com., *Records of City of Exeter*, 39.

set the new order in being, to see that the clergy subscribed to it, to regulate the services, take order for the removal of altars and images and the setting up of tables and prayer-books – in short, to lay down the lines that the Elizabethan church was to follow. Among the visitors of the Exeter diocese were Sir Peter Carew, Sir Richard Edgcumbe, Sir John Chichester, Sir John Pollard, Sir Arthur Champernowne, and John Jewel, that Hartland man, who became bishop of Salisbury.[1] It was obvious that the laity, the gentry, were now in control of the church, and the character of its ministrations was largely determined by them. What that character would be might be inferred from such names: they all belonged to the west country group which had been in opposition to Mary all along.

Jewel had been in exile; he now wrote to his mentor, Peter Martyr, at Zürich: 'We found everywhere the people sufficiently well disposed towards religion, and even in those quarters where we expected most difficulty. It is however hardly credible what a harvest, or rather what a wilderness of superstition had sprung up in the darkness of the Marian times. We found in all places votive relics of saints, nails with which the infatuated people dreamed that Christ had been pierced, and I know not what small fragments of the sacred cross. The number of witches and sorceresses had everywhere become enormous. If inveterate obstinacy was found anywhere, it was altogether among the priests.'[2] That was natural enough. Sir John Chichester reported from Devon to Bedford that 'the service in the church is well received and done for the most part of the shire. There wanteth nothing but preachers and some priests to serve choirs'.[3]

These, now that the affairs of the church were being put upon a sure foot, were forthcoming. Coverdale was not restored to his bishopric, though he had returned from exile. He found the government's moderate course not to his liking; at the consecration of Matthew Parker he appeared in a plain black gown, and in the vestiarian controversy that vexed Parker's first years Coverdale threw in his lot with the advanced Protestants. He remained in London preaching, with the approbation of the elect, and was presented to the living of St. Magnus the Martyr. He was followed to his grave by his patrons, the Puritan Earl of Bedford, the Duchess of Suffolk, and others who had profited by his ministrations. The government found a more amenable bishop for Exeter in William Alley, prebendary of St. Paul's, a respectable, learned man of the middle-class, from which the Elizabethan episcopate was so largely drawn. The bishops now were turned into servants of the state on a lower level, ecclesiastical J.P.s. Gone were the days when they

---

[1] Gee, 98-9.   [2] *Zürich Letters* (Parker Society), 44-5.   [3] S.P. 12/6, 17

shared in directing the policy of the nation from the council-board at White-hall. Alley was a good servant of the state, rather overmuch given to the pleasures of nepotism. In 1561 he had his son, Roger, presented to the living of St. Ervan, which was in the gift of the bishop; next year the lad — he was still only a scholar at the university — was made archdeacon of Cornwall.[1] That was in the best medieval tradition. In 1569 he was given the living of Goran, his brother Matthew that of Talland.[2] That was what they got in Cornwall; I do not know what they got in Devon, doubtless a good deal more: there was more to get. But somebody objected, for on his father's death Roger lost the archdeaconry: the new bishop pronounced against his 'pretended right' and confirmed somebody else in it.[3] Bishop Alley, like his successors, had the excuse of the impoverishment of the see: he was allowed to hold the rectory of Honiton in commendam, and it became the usual thing for bishops of Exeter to hold one or more livings to support their condition. Even so, Alley's successor Bradbridge went bankrupt, though it was really his agricultural speculations that ruined him: he died in debt to the Crown for a large sum, which he had drawn upon the first-fruits of his clergy, and 'had not the wherewith to bury him'.[4]

Under Alley, the cathedral chapter was reduced in number, in accordance with its straitened circumstances. The places vacated by the deprived Marians were filled up: Gregory Dodds became dean, and later George Carew, already dean of the Chapel Royal, a great pluralist: but he was uncle to Sir Peter Carew.[5] Blackstone's place as treasurer was taken by Richard Tremayne, who had returned from exile in the Low Countries and Germany, where he had picked up advanced protestant ideas. This did not prevent him from profiting by his association with the new governing circle to become a pluralist. In 1559 he was presented to the good living of Men-heniot;[6] he was archdeacon of Chichester for a while, and in addition to being treasurer of Exeter he was the archbishop's commissary for all the peculiars of the diocese; he held two benefices in Devon besides.[7] Not-withstanding, he was not content, but several times tried by his influence to get a commission made out to himself and his friends, for their benefit and his relations'.[8] There was a good deal of conflict between him and Bradbridge which worried the already distracted bishop into wishing, if he could, to retire. Tremayne was a strong puritan.

By 1561, when Alley made his return of the state of the clergy to Arch-

---

[1] Henderson, x. 75.   [2] ibid., 35, 77.   [3] ibid., 22.
[4] Oliver, *Lives*, 140.   [5] ibid., 276; Gee, 277.   [6] Henderson, x. 265.
[7] Boase, *Bibliotheca Cornubiensis*, II. 778; and *Reg. Coll. Exon.*, 67.
[8] Strype, *Annals*, II. pt. II, 34-5.

bishop Parker, the diocese was in fair and regular working order.[1] From this we may draw a picture of their condition. In Devon, out of some 288 beneficed clergy who are dealt with, allowing for vacancies, pluralities and peculiars not included, only 38 were as yet married, 226 were unmarried, the rest not given. There were 24 who were given as preaching, for the most part only within their own benefices; 223 did not preach. Only 58 of them had degrees. For Cornwall too the return is not quite complete: the bishop's peculiars are not returned. But we derive useful comparative figures: there were 17 married, to 104 unmarried clergy: 1 in 6, the same proportion as in Devonshire. Elizabeth did not encourage her clergy to marry: it was not even legalized; the Royal Injunctions merely laid down strenuous conditions which were to be fulfilled, the bishop's licence, leave of two neighbouring J.P.s, good will of the woman's parents: enough to put anybody off.

There were very few preachers, not more than half a dozen, but a great many pluralists. It is impossible to give exact figures, for the deaneries and counties run into each other; but one has the impression that something like a third of the benefices were held in plurality. That in turn means that at least a fifth of the livings were held by non-resident persons. And indeed non-residence continued to be, as it always had been, a scandal of the church. The dissolution of the monasteries had mitigated it a little; but in 1561 the church had not yet solved the problem of how to provide for the chapelries which had been served by the monks. For some, curates had been found; for others, as we find with the chapelries round Launceston, they had not. It was, however, exceptional to find such a state of affairs as at Davidstow, where they did not know where their vicar resided, and 'omnia sunt ruinosa'; and we know from another source that Lawhitton had not known a resident rector for sixty years.[2] Two of the beneficed clergy, the rector of Jacobstow and the vicar of Feock, resided in the household of the Earl of Pembroke. One was a royal chaplain, another chaplain to Sir William Petre, a third lived in the house of Sir Richard Edgcumbe, a fourth, the rector of Ruan minor, lived with Nicholas Vyvyan because the fruits of his benefice were not sufficient to sustain him. Yet another was treasurer of Sarum, a sixth a London incumbent, a seventh archdeacon of Oxon — but he, Dr. Kenall, did reside partly upon his benefice of St. Columb major. Two were students at Oxford, and one at Cambridge. All this besides the livings held by

---

[1] Corpus Christi Camb. MSS., transcript at Exeter City Library.
[2] *Odd Ways in Olden Days down West.* By Vic (Birmingham 1892). This curious and valuable book is based upon the archives, particularly consistory court proceedings, at Exeter.

members of the chapter at Exeter, in addition to the non-residence due to the large amount of pluralism. Of the vicar of St. Austell, for instance, Hamond Hansart, a widespread pluralist, 'it is not known where he resides'.

From the bishop's register we trace his activities, many of them carrying on the old forms under the new dispensation. We find Alley ordaining while upon visits to Cornwall in 1565 and 1569: in the first year six deacons and two priests at Budock, a few others at Truro and Egloshayle.[1] It is most interesting to find him ordaining two deacons in the Killigrews' house at Arwennack upon that visit; while upon his next, five deacons and two priests were ordained there, and a deacon at Mount Edgcumbe. What a change from the old catholic days, and the bishop performing the sacrament in the chapel of St. Gabriel at Clyst! There is a curious account of Alley ordaining in the parlour at Godolphin, where Richard Pears of Sithney saw him 'reading one book unto his kinsman, Sir Bernard John, now vicar of St. Issey, then and there being present at the time Sir William Godolphin, Mr. Retyn, esquire, Hugh Beard, servant unto the said Sir William, and one Mr. Sellack, then vicar or curate of Constantine. And after reverences and duty done by this examinate, he stayed in the parlour during the whole time that the said lord bishop was reading unto the same Sir Bernard . . . and he saw the said Sir Bernard kneel down on his knees, and the bishop to lay his hands on his head, repeating certain words, but what they be he likewise remembereth not; at the sight whereof then this deponent was certainly persuaded that the said bishop did make his said kinsman deacon.'[2]

This odd ceremony does not seem to have done the bishop's kinsman much good, for we afterwards find him with his fellow-criminal, the vicar of St. Merryn, deprived for felony. The latter was apparently a receiver of pirates' goods.[3] Together the two of them were convicted at Launceston assizes for 'certain money and writings carried away'.[4] Anthony Brown of Launceston saw Bernard John 'burned in the hand with a hot iron', in fact had bound his hand to the post; he said that the vicar had been condemned to death, but pleaded benefit of clergy. The constable of the parish said that the common report was that the vicar had paid a sum of money for his benefice, and was guilty of simony. He was a 'gamester at tables and dice for money', and had 'received into the vicarage one George Davies who doth there as they do in common taverns, sell wine whereby ill rule is kept in the same house as drunkenness and sometimes quarrelling'. Another parishioner said that 'he had lived incontinently with divers women and he confessed to this

---

[1] Henderson, x. 36.   [2] *Odd Ways in Olden Days*, xvi-xvii.
[3] cf. my *Sir Richard Grenville*, 163.   [4] Henderson, x. 143-4.

deponent that he had carnally known the body of one Thomasine Wolcock of St. Issey'. All which was much disliked by the honest men of the parish. Poor bishop Alley, it seems, was unfortunate in his kinsman. The vicar of St. Merryn was deprived in 1584, and his brother of St. Issey in 1585; yet in 1586 we find them both nominated in the mandate for the induction of the vicar of Padstow.[1] It may be that they did reparation and resumed their livings: the vicar of St. Merryn went on until 1599.[2] Nor must we forget that he owed his appointment to bishop Alley, who granted the presentation for this turn to Nicholas Nicolls, probably a relation of Matthew's, and to Dr. Kenall.[3] Perhaps some money passed. Nor had the bishop much luck with his Cornish ordinands: no less than five or six of them, a large proportion, had to be deprived later.[4] Whether it was that the bishop was careless as to their qualifications, or was pressed with other business, we do not know. More probably, it is only so much more evidence of the shortage of decent parochial clergy, and the lowness of their standard.

The old monks and chantry priests were dying out, and with them their pensions, which was a gain for the government. From time to time Exchequer commissions were sent out to see how the process was getting on. Alley sent in a return to one in 1570, from which we learn that Richard Oliver, former sub-prior of Bodmin, had died at Padstow six years since: that saved the government £8 p.a.[5] John Dagle had died as rector of St. Breoke; five of the former canons of Launceston and two ex-canons of Glasney had died since the last return.

We have to go back to 1555 for a complete picture of the remaining monastic claims upon the government, the monks that survived, their pensions and the fees to laymen still payable out of the Exchequer.[6] For Cornwall the total sum paid out for these purposes in that year was £732 4s. 4d., compared with £1751 11s. 8d. for Devon: a much larger proportion of the revenues from the church lands. However, with every year it was a diminishing charge.

Much the heaviest single items were the pensions with which, it is not too much to say, the former priors had been bribed. By 1555 the prior of Bodmin was dead: a saving of £66 13s. 4d. p.a. But the prior of St. Germans was living, on an equivalent pension plus the benefice of Northill; he died in 1558. The prior of Launceston was still going, on his grand pension of £100 p.a. The charges that came next in importance were the

[1] Henderson, x. 82.   [2] ibid., 84.   [3] ibid., 78.   [4] ibid., 78-80.
[5] v. *Devon and Cornwall Notes and Queries*, XVIII. pt. I, 45-8.
[6] Cardinal Pole's Pension Book: E 164/31, f. 35 foll.

fees to which the religious houses were committed, not only for their officials, but for their patrons and friends — all those who had taken advantage of the situation to recommend themselves. We have seen for example what a goodly revenue Dr. John Tregonwell made out of his annuities, £6 from Bodmin, £2 from Glasney, and so from all over the west country. A number of these families, Paulets, Horseys, Southcotes, Edgcumbes made something this way. From Bodmin, for example, Sir Richard Chamond got annuities of £12; from Launceston £2 13s. 4d. Bodmin, as we should expect from Prior Mundy's conduct of its affairs, had much the longest list of annuities: to Sir Richard Edgcumbe, Sir John Pollard, Sir Hugh Trevanion, the Tredennicks and many others. In short, in 1555 such sums still being paid amounted to £60 p.a., compared with £28 to the ex-monks. At Launceston they were £17 13s. 4d., compared with £32 13s. 4d. for the surviving monks and £100 for the ex-prior. At St. Germans the laymen took £14, compared with £13 13s. 4d. for the ex-monks and £66 13s. 4d. for the ex-prior. The annuities from Glasney were £12 13s. 4d., from Tywardreath £13 13s. 4d. Then come the canons and prebendaries of Glasney, St. Endellion and Crantock and the chantry priests who were still alive: they took the remainder. By the end of Elizabeth's reign they had practically all vanished and their claims were extinguished. But by that time the financial needs of the government had forced the Crown to part with the great bulk of the lands it had got by the dissolution.

Already upon her accession Elizabeth had taken back the concessions to the church made by Mary in her absurd piety: the financial stress in which her policy had left the government, Philip's war with France, rendered the resumption necessary. The first-fruits and tenths upon all benefices, which Mary had re-granted to the church, were taken back, the large number of impropriate rectories she had restored at her last gasp resumed; and in addition the new Queen 'elected to take' a number of episcopal manors into her hands. Exeter was already squeezed sufficiently dry, though when its temporalities were handed over to Alley the Queen withheld the first fruits, etc.[1] The Crown's policy of squeezing their lands out of the bishops, and replacing them, if at all, with rectories was justifiable. After all it made them bishops. This had the effect of confining the church more strictly within its own sphere; but it did not add to the popularity of the bishops to be supported by what might have gone in the better upkeep of the parochial clergy. That was a factor in the growth of Puritan feeling against them.

[1] Pat. Rolls 26 Aug. 1560

On the other hand, the increase in the return from land made the clergy better off and brought with it an improvement in their social status over the next century: after that, the eighteenth and nineteenth century heyday of the English clergy, the age of the pleasant country vicarages they built, the life portrayed in Trollope's novels.

The laity, by which we mean essentially the country gentry, did still better out of the church. In the sixteenth century, before the National Debt and the Bank of England were invented, tithes offered a ready and convenient field of investment to those who had funds to invest. Tithe was coterminous with the land itself — another, though a very different, form of investment in land.[1] The dissolution had thrown a vast amount of impropriate tithe upon the market, into which the gentry everywhere were very ready and willing to march. It was a world of wonderful opportunity for them: the age of their creative expansion, along with the merchant class: the makers of modern English history. In the basis of the social fabric they reared, the economy of their estates, their money affairs, providing for their children, securing the future, tithe remained an important factor all through the modern period till only yesterday.

From the Patent Rolls, and other sources, we can trace this process under the microscope. We see John Killigrew the younger in 1564 taking over a large lease of tithes formerly belonging to Glasney, which the college had leased to John Caplyn and Ralph Couch: the rectories of Sithney, Gluvias, and St. Allen, tithes of hay and corn in Zennor, of corn and fruits in Mylor and Mabe parishes, of the same in St. Just-in-Penwith, of corn in Feock, Kenwyn and Kea, with certain lands and sheaves (i.e. tithe-corn) in St. Enoder.[2] The lease was for twenty-one years at a rent of £132 12s. 8d. It was in effect a reversion, for the young Killigrew surrendered his interest in it during the lives of Caplyn and Couch, who were collectors of the revenues of the late college for the Crown; he agreed to pay them their annual fee and to undertake repairs up to 10 marks a year. Later, he came into possession of the lease and got it changed into one for three lives, his brothers Thomas and Simon being joined with him; an inquisition taken at 'le duchy court house' in St. Clement's, Middlesex, found that the rent had not been paid on Lady-day 1583 nor in forty days after, according to the terms of the lease.[3]

By this time Killigrew's financial affairs were going from bad to worse;

---

[1] I do not know why tithe should be regarded as so esoteric a subject. It is certainly insufficiently studied, considering its historical importance. I make my contribution in this section, and above, in c. IX.

[2] Pat. Rolls 19 June 1564.   [3] Excheq. K.R. Spec. Com. 538.

they had been greatly mismanaged, and after many years' grace due to his high connections and family influence at court, he landed in the Gatehouse. The Killigrews at Arwennack had been living beyond their resources. They were not a family with large estates: they were an old family newly engaged in trade at Penryn; one of them married the heiress of Arwennack upon Falmouth harbour, and that inheritance constituted most of their lands. They proceeded to build a fine great house there, with a superb banqueting hall: altogether more than they could manage. They were driven to all kinds of shifts to raise money, in the end to open piracy in Falmouth harbour, but their chief stand-by was the tithes formerly belonging to Glasney in the parishes roundabout. Nor was this lease their only venture in this direction: we find them leasing the tithes of Goran and Colan at this time too, while in 1602 William Killigrew purchased those of Budock.[1]

Similarly among other Cornish gentry Isobel St. Aubyn, widow, of Clowance, leased the large rectory of Breage nearby, for twenty-eight years at £47 p.a., paying a fine of £47 for it.[2] She was a catholic.[3] The rectory of Crowan next door was leased to Justinian Talkarne, governor of St. Mawes, who passed it on after a time to John Pendarves.[4] The latter took out a lease for three lives, putting his sons into it, on payment of a fine to the Crown — and whatever consideration he agreed to make Talkarne. The Pendarves family made money out of the abundant tin-streams of that district, and here we see them advancing their interests to include tithes. Later they built up an estate in the neighbourhood. The rectory of Crowan did not ultimately come into their possession, however, but into that of the St. Aubyns, who were squires of the parish. Leonard Loveys of Ogbeare, who built that Elizabethan house, and had bought the manor of Trevisquite that had belonged to the earl of Devon,[5] leased the deanery of Crantock with its tithes at £60 p.a.;[6] he paid a fine of £120 and agreed to maintain curates at Crantock and St. Columb minor at £6 and £7 p.a. respectively: an interesting scale of values, but it was usual enough. Peter Coryton leased the rectories of St. Cleer and Madron;[7] the Harrises those of Tywardreath, St. Sampson, St. Blazey, Lanlivery, Treneglos and Warbstow, which had all belonged to Tywardreath priory.[8] A groom of the Chamber leased the little rectory of St. Juliot (Hardy's St. Juliot).[9] But these are only examples, and could be easily multiplied. In general, tithes were leased, and not sold, in the reign of Elizabeth. It was not until the financial stringency of James I

[1] Grove, *Alienated Tithes*, pt. III, xiv, clxiii. [2] Pat. Rolls 28 July 1559.
[3] v. below, p. 343. [4] Pat. Rolls 22 Feb. 1580. [5] ibid., 13 May 1564.
[6] ibid., 9 July 1569. [7] ibid., 8 Jan. 1574. [8] ibid., 6 Mar. 1582.
[9] ibid., 22 Aug. 1572.

that they began to be turned into hard cash and alienated from the Crown as they had been from the Church. So it is that they came into the possession of the landed gentry, Boscawens, Eliots, Rashleighs, Bullers, Molesworths, Tremaynes being chief among their lay-owners by the nineteenth century.[1]

Not many manors remained of the original monastic estates in Cornwall which the Crown desired to sell: they had mostly been annexed to the Duchy, and the sale of these was questionable without an act of Parliament. The second Earl of Bedford bought the manor of St. Keverne in 1560, to sell three days later to Justinian Talkarne.[2] We have many instances of small church properties, tenements in Launceston or such, percolating down to small people. Towards the end of the reign the Crown got more and more hard up: that appears to be the explanation of the restitution of properties which had been taken from the dean and chapter of Exeter. They were granted a number of rectories, including Elerky, Uny Lelant, St. Breward and St. Merryn, with other lands, all of which had belonged to chantry foundations in the cathedral; but they were to pay a yearly rent of £145 and all charges for the upkeep of curates.[3] However, it was a profitable bargain for the chapter in the end, though the Crown got its cash. The college of vicars choral got a similar grant, including the rectory of Mullion, apparently ex gratia. In the last year of her reign, the Queen was driven to sell outright all the Cornish manors which had been annexed to the Duchy both from the monasteries and the earldom of Devon.[4] They were sold for large sums to London speculators. Under James, who reorganized the Duchy for his son Henry, the sale was declared illegal and the lands resumed.

How the smaller properties, the tin-doles, tenements, parcels and quillets of land given for superstitious uses, masses and obits, came into the hands of the laity, often somewhat mysteriously, we have only too much evidence from the numerous exchequer commissions to inquire into 'concealed' lands: impossible to go into them all. A comprehensive return of 1578 gives us some sidelights.[5] Some tin-works in the rich area of Polgooth had been given for annual obits and masses in the church of St. Allen. These were entered upon by John Arundell of Gwarneck, who promised to pay an annual sum for them, naming two sureties; 'but no assurance was made accordingly nor payment since to his (the witness's) knowledge'. The joke is that Arundell's sympathies were catholic; ça n'empêche pas, where property is concerned.

[1] cf. Grove, op. cit., 96–104.   [2] Pat. Rolls 15 & 18 Mar. 1560.
[3] ibid., 5 July 1585.   [4] cf. ibid., nos. 1572, 1574, 1578–9, 1581.
[5] Excheq. Coms. and Depos., 20 Eliz. no. 525.

At St. Agnes eight perches of land given to make a house for the vicar had come into the hands of Sir John Killigrew. Chantry lands at both St. Columb major and St. Columb minor had been sold to Mr. Coswarth, receiver of the Duchy, 'but by what title they know not'. We learn that at Michell there was a chapel which had been turned into a school: the bell had been taken away by Kestell, Sir William Godolphin's man, and their silver cross by one Beauchamp 'about the time of the Commotion'. Another chapel had been pulled down by Henry Rowse of St. Columb, who claimed that it 'stood on his land with some plot of ground appertaining thereunto'. The bells of St. Saviour's chapel at Polruan were taken down by order of William Mohun, when sheriff in 1572. One witness said that he 'was sent for to be at the doing thereof and at the delivery of them, but he refused the same. And for one of the bells which was broken, the same he saw in the possession of Mr. Mohun's cellar'. Another witness said that there were three bells which Mohun 'took into his own possession to his own use as he thinketh and them hath. He knoweth not of what weight they were of, but they were good big bells'. The inhabitants of Polruan evidently missed them. The gentry were doing very well. Mr. Mohun had moved up from Hall to the magnificence of Boconnoc, which had belonged to the Courtenays. William Noy of the parish of Buryan purchased all the land belonging to the deanery there: it was the beginning of his family's fortune. The next generation was able to take up residence upon the royal manor of Carnanton, and William's grandson made a large fortune at the bar and as attorney-general to Charles I. In turning over the leaves of this return, one comes on every page upon the names of Cornish gentry, Chivertons, Penroses, Sawles, Arscotts, Roscarrocks, Killigrews, who did not disdain to pick up here a morsel and there a morsel, however small it was. But the government could hardly trust commissions manned by these gentry to ferret out all the lands concealed from the Crown. Later in the reign, Tipper and Dawe, that ubiquitous couple, purchased from the Crown licence to search. and in return they were free to keep or sell what they brought to light, In this way innumerable tiny parcels were retrieved all over the country.[1]

During the first decade of Elizabeth's reign the Papacy, at Philip's instance, held its hand; the pope even made several approaches to his 'dearest daughter'. But from the moment of her accession the Protestant impulse gathered force among the classes that mattered, pressing the government, especially the Queen, further forward than she really wanted to go. Papal

[1] cf. for Cornwall, Pat. Rolls Eliz. 1340, 1370, 1386.

forbearance, however, gave the new régime and the prayer-book the benefit of the doubt for the time: an interval which was invaluable to the government in its aim of bringing about the maximum of conformity to the new order. Catholics for the most part continued to go to church, and accepted the new services. From the beginning however there was a small core of resistance. Recalcitrant priests were not imprisoned, but restricted as to residence: prebendary Halse, for instance, was not to leave Devon and Cornwall: Blackstone and Mugge went to their friends at Hereford, where they were to remain.[1] As the new bishops got their dioceses into working order, the Council used them as levers to bring about a greater measure of conformity. In 1564 they were asked to certify those J.P.s who were not well-affected to the new order, and to give the names of those who might be called to office instead.[2]

Bishop Alley consulted Sir Peter Carew and Sir John Chichester, upon whom he relied in such matters; they had been in Cornwall viewing the ports that autumn. Four J.P.s were returned as enemies to the new order: John Polwhele, John Reskymer, Richard Roscarrock and John Bevil. The last, described as a 'very great enemy', was the justice, it will be remembered, who was so hard upon parson Lamb's wife for visiting her husband. In their place, the younger Killigrew, Richard Trevanion, Peter Edgcumbe, Richard Chamond, John Trelawny, and others are suggested. Those who were not justices, 'yet being of some authority are judged no favourers of the foresaid state', are given as 'Imprimis, the great Arundell of Cornwall', i.e. John Arundell of Lanherne, John Tremayne, John Treguddick, John Hill, William Cavell.

Little as they favoured the prayer-book, it is probable that they went to church: after all the Papacy had not yet declared against it. And Arundell, who had succeeded his father in 1557, continued to occupy his family's place in county affairs. In 1566 he was knighted at Court, at the Tower.[3] In the crisis of the northern rebellion of 1569, which was rendered dangerous by the conjunction of catholicism with a candidate in the person of Mary Queen of Scots, encouraged by Spain, Sir John Arundell took his place along with Sir William Godolphin at the head of the commissioners to muster the county.[4] When the government determined to impose the oath of supremacy upon all J.P.s as a test of loyalty, Sir John forbore to subscribe. It was evidently a surprise to his fellow-justices: 'but (as we thought) not with

[1] Gee, op. cit., 181.
[2] *Camden Miscellany*, IX: Letters from the Bishops to the Privy Council, ed. Bateson, 67-70.
[3] Shaw: *The Knights of England*, II. 72.   [4] S.P. 12/51, 3.

other purpose than the accomplishment of his duty at this day of our new assembly, and he is now absent for what cause we are ignorant'.[1] Next year Sir John again put off subscribing the oath until he had 'further spoken' with the Council.[2] He must have satisfied them, or been allowed exceptional treatment like the peers — for in 1574 the Council gave order for him to view Pendennis and St. Mawes and he accompanied Bedford upon his inspection of the coastal defences.[3] The latter assembled the justices and 'declared to them her Majesty's pleasure in all things: whom, as well for Sir John Arundell as the rest I find ready and serviceable in all things'. It was not until the mission of the new seminary priests from abroad to bring catholics back to a stricter sense of their duty, and to reconcile others to Rome, that the Arundells definitely broke away. The breach became overt in 1577 with the apprehension and execution of Cuthbert Mayne, and Richard Grenville's campaign against the Cornish catholics. By then they were a small, if influential, minority outside the state church: they had become recusants.

Within the church the authorities had increasing difficulties to contend with from the puritans in these middle years of the reign: at their height from 1571 to 1584. The strength of puritanism was that it was the ideology, or if you prefer, the religion, of the forward-looking gentry and middle class, who were instinctively reaching out for power. The faction was highly favoured; it was protected by Leicester and Knollys, it had the sympathy of Walsingham and Burghley, of such people as the Carews, Killigrews, Tremaynes and all their circle. The Queen sensed the implicit threat to monarchy in their doctrines, and — it is not too much to say — despised and hated them for their narrow self-righteousness, their hypocrisy, their lack of culture, their vindictiveness, their spite against any authority that was not their own, their uncivilized intolerance: the ancestors of modern Nonconformity. The infection spread within the church among the clergy; there had always been this strain in the Reformation and it was greatly reinforced by the years of exile. Never really popular in character, it was a movement which appealed to those who had a nose for power and were denied it. It was strongly represented in the House of Commons, which was sympathetic to its demands for 'reform' of the church, its views of church order; among its leaders, Peter and Paul Wentworth sat for Cornish seats. The Queen had in the main only the bishops to rely on in the struggle, and their efforts in administration and maintaining discipline have received perhaps insufficient recognition.

[1] ibid., 12/51, 60, 27.   [2] ibid., 67, 57.   [3] Lansdowne MS. 18/93.

One of the chief instruments in the Puritan campaign was the appointment of extra-parochial preachers and lecturers. Poor bishop Bradbridge was in trouble with one such at Liskeard in 1577. There was a young man, a grammar-school master and a preacher, who had lately come there, licensed by Dr. Tremayne, a great favourer of Puritans, to catechize and expound the scriptures. This froward young man had been teaching the people that 'an oath taken upon a book on the holy evangelists is of no more value than an oath taken upon a rush or a fly, because it is nothing but ink and paper'. This degree of nominalism had greatly 'offended the ears of the simple Cornishmen'. Another preacher had arisen to contradict the doctrine, and — characteristic of the idiot people, the town was 'in great contention and heat one against another'. The bishop was perturbed lest such teaching should undermine people's belief in oaths, the sanctity of contracts: 'Truly the Cornishmen are subtle, many of them, in taking an oath; now if they shall conceive that in swearing upon a book no danger is, more than upon a rush, the obedience that we owe unto her Majesty, the trial that we have in assizes and sessions wherein the controversies are no otherwise tried but by force of a book oath, it may open a great gap and let in a flood-gate (as it were) to great disorder and many mischiefs in a commonwealth'.

The stiff-necked young man stood stoutly to what he had taught, and the bishop seeing that 'no truth could be well tried in that tumult', put over the hearing of the case to the assizes and summoned Dr. Tremayne and others of the chapter that 'I might be better able to pacify the stir that buzzeth in men's heads'. Tremayne had been busy again trying to get a special commission granted to him 'and certain his cousins and special friends'; which the bishop had always withstood as unnecessary, since he had so many officers already. The latter concluded his tale to Burghley: 'I speak somewhat of experience; my diocese is great; the puritans and sectaries daily do increase. I persuade myself I shall be able easilier to rule them, whom I partly know already, than those which by this means may get them new friends, which is the only thing that I suspect in this new commission'.

The bishop died, old and bankrupt, next year; and it was his successor John Woolton, a protégé of the Bedfords like Coverdale before him, and as such the holder of much preferment in the diocese and outside, who came in for the full brunt of the Puritan campaign. At the same time he had to deal with another, and quite different, form of religious foolery: the fascinating case of Henry Caesar, vicar of Lostwithiel. Their previous vicar had had to resign, probably because he also held the neighbouring living of Lanlivery, and in spite of the certificate which he got the burgesses and inhabitants to make to the bishop, to the effect that all the time of his curacy he has 'continued in a virtuous disposition, zealous in religion and diligent in keeping services'.[1] In his place there was appointed a young university man, the nephew of Dr. Julius Caesar, the distinguished judge of the admiralty court. They were Italian by extraction.

At Cambridge the young man — he was not much more than twenty when he got the living — was 'suspected to be popishly affected' and went over-seas.[2] On his return he recanted his popish opinions, though he continued to keep company with suspect persons. Coming to Lostwithiel, he 'used to say divine service in the chancel turning his face from the people, and at the reading of the epistle and gospel, did wear a cope to the offence of the well-affected in religion'. He was charged with seeking out the company of the vicar of St. Neot, 'being an old popish priest and a man yet suspected for his affection that way', and with maintaining that the dominion of the Pope had not decreased, 'for when Germany forsook him, then England was with him; and though England be fallen from him, he hath gotten two or three times as much in Turkey and India, so that these words are truly verified in him, *super aspidem et basiliscum ambulabis et conculcabis leonem ac draconem*'. Obviously an intelligent young man who had picked up the leading ideas of the Counter-Reformation abroad. When Alexander Fitzgeoffrey preached against the popish manner of fasting, Caesar said roundly that he preached false doctrine.

More serious than this: at dinner at Mr. Kendall's house with the vicar of St. Winnow and others, he had 'maintained the apparition of souls after their departure out of this life, and for proof affirmed that Sir Walter Mildmay was desirous to see Cardinal Pole after his death, and one by conjuration caused the said Cardinal to appear unto Sir Walter. Then the conjurer asked of Sir Walter Mildmay what he did see, and Sir Walter answered him "a man much like the cardinal" '. Caesar was charged further with giving a cope and five books to John Deviser to keep in safety for him, and when he feared that the house might be searched, he got Deviser to hide the books 'in the root of a hollow tree in his garden'. After he had been charged at sessions with what he had said about Mildmay, he sent for Deviser's wife to burn the books. There followed the usual charge that he was suspected 'to have over-much familiar acquaintance with the said Deviser's wife, who resorteth con-tinually unto him at unseasonable times albeit her husband hath often expressly commanded her to the contrary'.

The reflections upon Sir Walter Mildmay were a serious matter: he was chancellor of the exchequer and a leading patron of the puritans in govern-

---

[1] Henderson, XI. 136.   [2] Cotton MS. Titus B, III. f. 84.

ment circles. The Council wrote to the justices in Cornwall that Sir Walter was 'loth to proceed against such a lewd fellow', but that satisfaction was to be made for 'so great a wrong offered to such a person of honour'.[1] Caesar was to appear at their next sessions or assizes and confess his fault, and since he had proved a very unmeet man for the ministry in those parts, the bishop was to proceed against him and 'remove him clean out of his diocese'. Once already at sessions Caesar had stood to his report of Sir Walter Mildmay; and indeed there was nothing improbable about what he said, when one considers the superstition of the times, the belief in witchcraft, necromancy, religion. We do not know what happened further, except that at some point Caesar expressed regret at having said that Sir Walter and Secretary Wilson had desired to see the spirit of the dead cardinal, and denied that on going overseas he had become a Jesuit or seminary priest.[2] The young man ceased to be vicar of Lostwithiel, and for long remained under a cloud. Then at the end of the reign he suddenly began picking up preferments fast, and he ended his days in the odour of sanctity and approbation as dean of Ely.[3] His was an interesting case: he might be described as one of the first Anglo-Catholics.

The climax of the struggle with the Puritans came with the appointment of Whitgift as archbishop in 1583 to enforce order in the church. Under the silly and sympathetic Grindal they had made considerable headway. One of their more prominent and loquacious ministers came to Cornwall in 1580 in the person of Eusebius Paget, who was presented to the living of Kilkhampton by Sir Richard Grenville to succeed that sensible old gentleman, his great-uncle, who had gone silently, perhaps somnolently, along through all the changes since the days of Henry VIII. Paget was made of very different stuff. An educated chorister, with a crippled arm — he was in the disagreeable habit of signing himself 'lame Eusebius Paget' — an eloquent preacher, all too conscientious, this man had already once been deprived for nonconformity and had subscribed Cartwright's Book of Discipline. He was probably presented by Grenville at the request of Bedford, who was a great Puritan-fancier. Paget informed the patron and the bishop that he could not conform to all the rites ordered by the prayer-book, and for the time his ministry went forward.

He was an indefatigable preacher and writer. From the vicarage of Kilkhampton there issued his 'Godly and Fruitful Sermon . . . upon what provision ought to be made for the ministry, very necessary to be learned

---

[1] Cotton MS. Tituss B, III. f. 83.   [2] S.P. 12/176, 46.
[3] *D.N.B.* sub Henry Caesar.

of all Christians'. It dealt with tithes: very fruitful and necessary indeed for ministers. There followed his harmony upon the evangelists, with Calvin's commentary, translated from the Latin; and then his troubles, fortunately, prevented any more. The new hand at Lambeth was making itself felt in the dioceses. In 1584 Paget was called before his bishop and enjoined to an exact conformity. At the end of the year articles of accusation, based upon his preaching, were brought against him before the court of high commission and he was charged with refusing to use the prayer-book and omitting the prescribed ceremonies. He pleaded that there was not a copy of the book provided for his church, and that his conscience would not allow him to follow it in every particular. He evidently shared the Puritan objection to the use of the surplice, the cross in baptism, the ring in marriage, kneeling at communion. He was suspended, and, on his continuing to preach, deprived.

But Paget was not yet finished with. He proceeded to bring a series of counter-charges against the diocesan: charging him with never visiting his diocese in person, with not attending sermons, with nepotism, and having 'two harlots begotten with child in his own house, which accused two of his men, and none of them brought to penance, yea, the men do yet wait upon him'. This was getting pretty near the bone, and Woolton was under the necessity of satisfying the disciplinarian Archbishop as to the charges. He had, he said, been twice or thrice in most of the market towns of Devon and Cornwall. His two visitations had been interrupted by illness, his own and his wife's, yet he had taken some part in both, and his deputies were well qualified persons. He was himself a preacher, since the days of his exile in Germany, and last summer preached every Sunday upon his commendam in the country. He had never borrowed money by loan of the whole clergy, merely £5 apiece from fourteen or fifteen of them 'to prepare me necessaries for my house', eight of whom had been paid.

On the subject of nepotism the bishop had heavier going. He had presented to the vicarage of Newlyn a Mr. Blewett, who gave the bishop another living, 'and I chose that for my son in respect of the propinquity unto me'. His son was then twenty-three, a student at Cambridge and ready for it. He had chosen Mr. Barrett, a well-learned man, to be archdeacon of Exeter, and it was not until a year after that he had married the bishop's daughter. For another archdeaconry he had chosen Mr. Sweet, 'of whom I have not, nor am to have any profit'. Yet Mr. Sweet 'hath these two years last past given a son of mine in the university only, 40s. yearly: but without any desire of mine or promise binding him to continue it'. The archdeaconry of Barnstaple he had given to his cousin, Mr. Law, also a well-qualified man, though he had been forced to come upon the bishop for an advance 'for his necessaries'. As for his father-in-law, he was not responsible for him: he had entered the ministry 'ten years before I was a bishop'. He admitted to a fault in making his son a minister, for though he was of an honest disposition at that time, he 'became intractable afterwards, seduced by Nicolls the Jesuit and others', and he had 'removed him immediately from that calling, which he had never exercised, and from his little living', and laid him in irons in the common gaol.

What is evident is that the bishop had made the mistake of having too large, or too indigent, a family: a fault in bishops which the celibate Archbishop could have warned him against. But his efforts on their behalf were rewarded with success, for before he died he was enabled to purchase the eligible little estate of Pilland from the Brett family, to which his son succeeded.[1] One sees that there were both advantages and disadvantages in the dynastic clericalism that the Elizabethan church encouraged, and that became so characteristic of the church of England. But it was not essentially against this that Puritanism was a protest.

It was at this time that the Puritan campaign reached its height with the Supplication prepared to present to the Parliament of 1586. For this purpose they had made a survey of the state of the clergy in various parts of the country. The Puritan movement was highly organized rather than extensive, and they appear to have got their information by sending their own visitors into a county to consult with their sympathizers there. We have fortunately a detailed survey of Cornwall, from which we may gather what the temper of Puritanism was.[2] There were so few of the clergy of whom they could find it in their hearts to approve. As the egregious Browne said, *they* constituted the true church, 'the worthiest, were they never so few'. They were very few in Cornwall: in its way an important indication of how much of a minority movement theirs was. At the same time their survey has value: they were well-informed: they knew about the goings-on of the felonious vicar of St. Issey and the papistical vicar of Lostwithiel: only their information was somewhat highly-geared, in accordance with their temper: almost everybody is regarded as bad, except the elect.

Out of 160 livings, there were still only twenty-nine preachers. It is significant that almost all these belonged to the eastern half of the county, which was more English-speaking. The linguistic difficulty was still an

---

[1] Oliver, *Lives*, 142.
[2] Peel, *The Second Part of a Register*, II. 88-9, 98-110.

obstacle to preaching in Cornwall; at the same time, the prayer-book, the bible, sermons, were having their influence in spreading the knowledge and use of English. The survey tells us that the livings were worth £9,200 a year, and that the population was 93,690 souls: an interesting, if too generous, estimate. We are told that there are twenty-two 'notorious double-beneficed men', and 'non-residents that never come there: 3'. This was an improvement on what had been. You would not think so to judge from the comments on the clergy individually. Most of them are described as 'a very lewd fellow', 'a very worldling', 'a simple bad fellow', 'a common gamester', 'a lewd drunkard, an ignorant and very shameless fellow', 'very licentious', or, more simply, 'of bad conversation'. Only ten clergymen are given unqualified good marks: they were usually those who taught school, like the vicar of St. Winnow, who had heard Henry Caesar's indiscretions: 'his conversation honest and teacheth daily'.

The reprobates are more interesting. We learn that the vicar of Lanteglos-by-Fowey was 'the best wrestler in Cornwall', the rector of St. Mewan a good archer, of Lamorran 'a common market man and delighteth more in buying and selling than in his flock'. The rector of St. Dennis was 'a bad hireling, lately a button maker', his neighbour of St. Stephen's-in-Brannel 'lately a serving man and simple fellow'. The rector of Week St. Mary 'keepeth his house for debt, he paid so much for it to Sir Richard Grenville', while John Penkivel, vicar of St. Teath, 'by misdemeanour spoiled his patrimony, became a minstrel, and for refuge a minister'. The rector of Philleigh was 'a good dicer and carder, both night and day', and there were many like him including his brethren of St. Issey and St. Merryn, who had both been burned in the hand. The vicar of Cubert, Nicholas Arscott, who also had a family living in Devon, 'keepeth a whore, and hath had five or six bastards; he is a mass man and a known papist'. There were many like him, according to the brethren in Christ: the rector of Uny-by-Redruth was 'much suspected of popery, cometh very seldom to church, and is a whore-master'; the vicar of Gulval was merely 'a drunkard, and hath lately married a common harlot'. More *recherché* pleasures were imputed to the rector of Lanteglos and Advent, though he did not neglect the women either. He was the only person accused of his particular shortcoming: in that perhaps a contrast with pre-Reformation days. Henry Caesar is described as 'a notable papist and hath drawn the people to great idolatry': from which one would gather that his ministrations were popular. His predecessor, Batten, 'liveth as a pot companion'.

But we do not need to take the survey too literally; as Dr. Frere says 'truthfulness was never the Puritans' strong point'.[1] We may judge their ill-nature from their comments on those against whom nothing can even be alleged. The vicar of St. Austell was a clerical proctor: he is described as being 'as honest of life as such pettifoggers be'; of the much-beneficed Dr. Kenall, 'his conversation is most in hounds'. It is an additional recommendation to one in whom 'the principal love and knowledge' of the Cornish language 'lived, and with him lieth buried'.[2] Yet, on the other hand, if he had not been so attentive to his hounds, perhaps he might have left us some memorial of his knowledge of the language. The laconic comment on the rector of St. Ewe is — 'professeth physic', and that 'he hath Calverley in Devon and cometh not to the other'.

Now we happen to know from Carew's eloquent testimony that the parson of St. Ewe was one of the most bountiful and well-loved doers of good in the whole west country. He was not only well-seen in the theory of medicine but was a practitioner on a large scale with a great and deserved reputation. His success apparently lay in his modern views on diet: 'Marry, his practice is somewhat strange and varying from all others: for though now and then he use bloodletting, and do ordinarily minister *manus christi* and such like cordials of his own compounding, yet mostly for all diseases he prescribeth milk, and very often milk and apples, a course deeply subject to the exception of the best esteemed practitioners; and such notwithstanding, as whereby either the virtue of the medicine, or the fortune of the physician, or the credulity of the patient, hath recovered sundry out of desperate and forlorn extremities'.[3] His liberality was equal to his reputation: he bestowed his pains on the poor gratis, the rich he charged moderately; 'the rest together with the profits of his benefice (rather charitably accepted than strictly exacted from his parishioners) he poureth out with both hands *in pios usus*, and will hardly suffer a penny to sleep but never to dwell with him'. Carew adds that there were few towns in Cornwall, 'or any other shire between that and London, which have not in some large measure tasted of his bounty', and he pays tribute to his sound affection in religion, honesty of life, pleasantness of conversation, his voluntary poverty, by which he had won the love and honour of his neighbours.

We have other evidences of his charity, building and endowing almshouses, giving money to various parishes to set the poor to work. His fame spread far and wide: a ballad in his honour was entered at the Stationers' Company, 'The poor sailor's praise of the parson of Tue in Cornwall,

[1] Frere, *The English Church in the Reigns of Elizabeth and James I*, 175.
[2] Carew, 56.   [3] ibid., 60.

who feedeth the hungry, helpeth the sick, cureth the hurt',[1] etc. He was himself his own best recommendation for his medical skill: he lived to be over ninety, a prodigious age for that time. Presented to the living in 1559, his tenure of it extended right through the reign of Elizabeth well on into that of James I. He did not resign until 1615 and died two years later. Yet of this man, whose long life was so full of charity and healing and good works, the Puritans had no more to say than that he held two benefices. Of this a later and more sceptical generation may be sure, that such a man as this did more good in his single life than a whole lot of those disagreeable fanatics did in theirs.

It is such a life as Parson Atwell's which is itself evidence of the measure of success which the Elizabethan church had achieved. In the last two decades of the reign the Puritan challenge was definitely held, for the time defeated. Elizabeth and her archbishops, Parker and Whitgift, had held the fort until their church had come, as is the way with human institutions, to have an ethos of its own. Starting from the externals of church order and discipline, men came to find a satisfactory spiritual life within its walls and habitations. By the end of the reign several generations had been brought up in its formularies, had found consolation in its rites and services as their fathers had done in those of the old religion before them: to them it was the catholic church; the language, the very rhythms of the prayer-book services had become a habit, had entered deeply into the subconscious life of the people. Of the other side, the disciplinary and the institutional, the bishops' registers give us ample evidence: the continuance of many of the medieval forms, the ordinations and institutions, the licences to teach and preach, to keep grammar school or practice chirurgery, the customs — the parson tolling the bell at his induction, tithes rendered or unpaid, the honeycombs upon the altar, tithe fish withheld — the penances for unchastity, penalties for breach of promise, slander: all which still came within the purview of the church as in the old catholic days.[2]

By the end of the reign, acceptance and habit had made for a certain loyalty to the English church, in Cornwall as elsewhere. To the question that has been asked how it was that Cornwall which had been catholic so late became Anglican in loyalty by the Civil War, that is in part the answer. There were people who were not satisfied: a class which is reaching out towards power is never satisfied until it gets it. The Puritans spoke for it, and they were only temporarily checked. Their triumph is another story, another age.

[1] cf. G. H. Doble, *St. Ewe*, 29-31.   [2] cf. Henderson, x. and xi. *passim*.

CHAPTER XIV

THE CORNISH CATHOLICS

THE seventies saw the battle fiercely joined between militant, resurgent Catholicism and Protestantism whose aggressive impulse was not yet stemmed. The Council of Trent had rejuvenated the Catholic church and prepared it to take the offensive. We are entering the age of the Counter-Reformation. It was the decade of the religious wars in France, of the massacre of St. Bartholomew, of the Spanish Fury at Antwerp.

In England it was the end of the truce which had prevailed during the first ten years of the reign, of the lenity of which Elizabeth was so justifiably proud. The papal bull of excommunication and deposition, commanding all catholics to withhold obedience from their sovereign, was a declaration of war. The government replied with a statute making it high treason to publish or act upon any such bull, to reconcile persons to Rome, or to bring in any bull whatsoever; while those who brought in hallowed tokens, such as *agnus deis*, incurred the penalties of premunire, i.e. loss of lands, goods and liberty for life. As the conflict became sharper, so legislation became heavier and persecution fiercer against those who adhered to Rome and refused to subscribe to the state church. They became recusants – a minority which was gradually isolated and worn down by the sharp pains of the law and financial pressure. We have to see the struggle with the Catholics, their pathetic resistance, their courage, their martyrs, against this European background. They were caught between the upper and nether millstones. Their adherence to Rome, however purely religious it was in their own minds – and it was not pure with all of them – involved them in the political issue. The papal action made them choose between being heretics and being traitors. Martyrs from their own point of view, they died as traitors from the state's. And indeed one observes a close correlation between the death penalties exacted from seminary priests, the number of prisoners in the gaols, and the periods of danger to the state now opening out with the heightened tension in Europe.

The chief mainstay of Catholicism in Cornwall was the Arundell family; their influence kept a number of their friends, relations and dependents on the catholic side. There were others, too, independent of them, gentry, yeomen and even a few townsmen. A comparative table of recusants in various counties shows that there were more of them than in any other of the south-western counties: as many as in Devon, Dorset and Somerset together.[1] This refers, though, to known recusants; no doubt there were many others undiscovered. For Cornwall we are given one knight and his lady, two esquires, thirteen gentlemen, six gentlewomen, seven men and women: a total of thirty as against thirty-nine only for Lancashire. In Cornwall they had, however, been mostly brought to light; in Lancashire, where there were very many more, not. Still, this means that over and above these known recusants there was a considerable body of undiscovered papists and persons whose sympathies were catholic: in all an important minority that could not be neglected.

We have seen how the attachment of the Arundells to the old faith compromised them in the reign of Edward VI. They recovered their position under Mary and lost nothing by the accession of Elizabeth. It is possible that they went to church, so long as the papacy had not definitely pronounced; but their convictions were indubitably catholic. When Lady Elizabeth, widow of the twelfth Sir John, died in 1564 she recommended her soul to 'Almighty God and to his blessed mother the glorious Virgin our Lady Saint Mary, and to all the holy and blessed saints of Heaven'.[2] A wealthy old lady, she left, among many bequests of money and plate, sheets and bedclothes of fine Rennes cloth to Lady Stourton, who had married her son the thirteenth Sir John, a tablet of gold to her daughter Katherine Tregian, beads of jasper to her god-daughter Elizabeth Tregian, a gold ring to John Tremayne, a psalter in French and Latin to her son Edward, a nightgown of fine black cloth to her daughter-in-law Isobel St. Aubyn; twenty marks to a servant, Ursula Bray. These are all names which we shall come upon again in the sequel: they were all recusants.

Her dust has long since mouldered away in the family church of St. Mawgan next the house at Lanherne, and only a fragment of her brass remains: *Post tenebras spero lucem*. She was evidently a pious old lady, whose devotion made its impression upon the family and whose memory may have played its part in keeping them faithful. For her son Edward, a rich bachelor who died in Fleet-street in 1586, left his niece Dorothy Arundell 'my rope of pearl that was sometime her granddame's my mother, and a little diamond ring that was also hers and forty shillings to make her a signet, and I beseech God to make her a right follower of that good granddame's life'.[3] He made similar bequests, with the same prayer, to his other nieces, Elizabeth, Cicely, Margaret and Gertrude. Cicely became a Bridgettine nun; Dorothy

[1] S.P. 12/119, 20.   [2] P.C.C., 30 Stevenson.   [3] ibid., 57 Windsor.

and Gertrude, after witnessing for over twenty years the troubles brought upon their house for religion's sake, and in consequence unmarried, at length went abroad to the convent of the English Benedictine nuns at Brussels. Edward Arundell desired pathetically to be buried 'as near my lady my mother as may be'; he was, like all the Arundells, very generous, leaving sums for the poor of various parishes, and for building the new pier which gave its name to Newquay. He made bequests to his sister Katherine Tregian, a great gilt Latin chronicle to his nephew Francis Tregian, and 'my gilt curtilax which was King Henry VIII's I give unto my brother Sir John Arundell' as an heirloom. He remembers his niece Turberville, his nephew Bosgrave, his brother's servant, Humphry Powell: all recusants. And notably Richard Tremayne of Tregonan, whom 'for the especial affiance and trust' he had in him, he made assistant executor to his brother. When Richard Tremayne, who shared their troubles and imprisonment, came to die, he seems to have had a memorial along with them among the many brasses with which the church of St. Mawgan was once, alas, so rich.

Their aunt Jane, who died unmarried in 1577, and whose brass remains, formal, erect, very spinsterly with her stiff brocaded dress, left her brooch with the murrion's head to her nephew Sir Matthew Arundell, the head of the Wardour branch, son of the ambitious Sir Thomas.[1] Among many bequests of jewellery, in which she too was rich, to Arundells, Tregians, Stourtons, she left her coral beads to Mary Isham: another recusant name. There is evident among these wills not only the accustomed Arundell generosity, to servants and the poor especially, but a strong sense of family affection which bound them together and no doubt strengthened and supported them through the trials that came to them.

Aristocratic, aloof, increasingly isolated in the life of the county, they were in an exposed position: the object of much jealousy on the part of those less wealthy and well-connected, of disapproval by those who had gone in with the new régime. In the last two generations they had been making marriages which took them loftily above the ordinary flight of the Cornish gentry: a sister of Thomas Grey, Marquis of Dorset, half-brother to Henry VII's Queen; Margaret Howard, sister of Henry VIII's Queen; the present Sir John had married Lady Stourton, eldest daughter of the Earl of Derby. A further marriage was of a different, but no less successful, character.

Thomas Tregian of Truro was a very prosperous tin-merchant and shipper — he owned the *Jesus* of Truro — who by 1512 had gone into land and bought several manors from Northill to St. Ives. His son, John, was a

---

[1] P.C.C., 40 Daughtry.

man of energy and affairs: he was an esquire of the body to Henry VIII, married the heiress of the Wolvedons who brought with her the manor of Golden, and by 1525 had built up a very large estate in mid-Cornwall. He set to work to turn the old house of the Wolvedons into an appropriate residence: 'a manor place richly begun and amply, but not ended, called Wolvedon, alias Golden', Leland says of it. His daughter married Sir Richard Edgcumbe: a piece of tapestry at Cotehele used to commemorate this fortunate alliance and the bride's goodly jointure. Sir Richard Grenville of Calais would have married his daughter to Tregian's heir, but the Arundells carried off the prize: their daughter Katherine married him, and became the mother of Francis Tregian, the recusant. He in turn married the daughter of Lord Stourton, while his uncle, Sir John, married the mother, Lord Stourton's widow. The circle was complete, exclusive, *dévot*. No wonder others among the Cornish gentry were rendered envious, Grenvilles, Edgcumbes in especial; we have evidence of their rancour. They awaited their opportunity.

Devoted as the Arundells were to their religion, they gave as little offence as possible. They were cautious and they kept quiet. Nevertheless they could not approve the new course of policy. In the Anglo-Spanish crisis of 1569, when Philip backed Mary Stuart's marriage with Norfolk, their sympathies incurred unfavourable notice. A letter from a servant of Sir John's to his master, taken upon the former at the Vine, fell into Cecil's hands: it said that he had delivered Sir John's letter to Matthew Arundell, who wished him to go to the Duke of Norfolk, but he 'thinks he will find him at no great leisure, for the Queen doth stomach him because he intends to marry with the Queen of Scots'.[1] Cecil notes Matthew Arundell among those to be examined concerning the marriage. When the Spanish treasure was stayed that year on its way up Channel, of the three people at Saltash who objected, one was a servant of Sir John's.[2] Early in 1575, the report went that he was 'a great friend of the King of Spain, and also one who married Lady Stourton'.[3]

This may refer to the young Francis Tregian, who took a more open and compromising line. Some time before this he went abroad, for we find his name in a list of catholic fugitives who desire the Queen's favour to return to England;[4] and it must be in this connection that shortly after his marriage he was 'enforced by the space almost of ten months suppliantly to follow

[1] Hist. MSS. Com., *Salisbury MSS.*, I. 421, 456.
[2] S.P. 12/48, 60.
[3] *Salisbury MSS.*, II. 126.
[4] ibid., XIII. 117.

the lords of the Council'.[1] At Court, secure in his aristocratic connections, he took the opportunity to proselytise; and finally, succeeding to his estates in 1575, at Easter next year he took into his house one of the first of the seminary priests to land in this country, Cuthbert Mayne. He went about openly as Tregian's steward, travelling about the county as the latter's far-flung manors gave opportunity, performing his priestly functions in secret, sometimes remaining at Lanherne (where now his skull is) as much as a 'se'ennight or fortnight together'.[2] It could not but have been known about the county: it was courting disaster. But for the moment nothing happened.

Nevertheless for some time the Council had been pressing for greater strictness in dealing with those who refused to come to church; and in February 1576 three gentlemen of substance in Cornwall were bound in £100 each to appear before it.[3] They were Richard Tremayne of Tregonan in St. Ewe, a cousin of the Protestant Tremaynes of Collacombe: he had succeeded his uncle both in his property and in his friendship with the Arundells; Robert Becket of Cartuther, of an old armigerous family and a fair inheritance, near Liskeard; and Francis Ermyn of St. Newlyn. They pleaded for a respite of their sentence of imprisonment on the ground of lawsuits and affairs needing their attention, and for time to 'be persuaded in the causes of religion'.[4] The Council, which was always anxious to procure examples of acquiescence rather than victims, allowed them to depart home upon certain conditions, for which they were to give a bond of £400 each. They were to return after Michaelmas, and every month while away were to confer with the bishop upon those points that 'they stand in doubt of'; they were not, however, to call in question the present state of religion, or to consort with the disaffected.

Poor bishop Bradbridge was able to do no good with them. At the end of the year he wrote that 'they crave ever respite of time, and in time grow rather indurate than reformable . . . whether the cause be the boldness that they have conceived by reason of the lenity used in these our days, or rather the hope of alteration in time to come'.[5] Anyhow he could not prevail 'to work any good conformity' with them and he asked that they might be turned over to the Archbishop or the bishop of London 'who want no assistance of learned men and books'. It looks as if the bishop found them more than he could deal with intellectually: Tremayne was a lawyer and

[1] Morris, *Troubles of Our Catholic Forefathers*, I. This contemporary account I have chiefly followed in my story of Tregian's troubles.
[2] S.P. 12/118, 46.   [3] *A.P.C.*, IX. 87.
[4] ibid., 145.   [5] Lansdowne MS. 23. 8.

a bookish man. He ended: 'the whole country here longeth and desireth to hear your godly determination'.

Matters were moving to a climax. No very effective step had been taken as long as Kekewich was sheriff; but in November 1576 Richard Grenville succeeded him, a very different man. He was a member of the group actively interested in the sea and privateering, associated with William Hawkins at Plymouth, with the Edgcumbes, Killigrews, Champernownes, Raleghs: the new forward-looking school, anti-Spanish and restless at sea. Grenville had that very year been in trouble over the exploits of his ship the *Castle of Comfort*. These years when Grenville had been preparing a voyage into the Pacific and Drake made it, years of increasing hostility with Spain, saw disturbed conditions and doubtful doings in and about the Channel. It seems that Arundell and Tregian had roused the ire of this group by their attitude on a commission of piracy upon which they had served: men of inland interests against those of the sea. Their religion delivered them into the hands of their enemies.

Grenville was precisely the man to force the issue: hot-tempered, determined, energetic, harsh. He made his preparations; he would know what was going on in the household at Golden. In June 1577 the bishop was conveniently on visitation at Truro. Grenville took the excuse of a writ to search for a fugitive, one Bourne, to descend upon Golden with some nine or ten J.P.s of his party and nearly a hundred persons. There they found Mayne, and certain evidences with which to convict him: writings, an *agnus dei*, articles in use for mass, and — what was fatal — a papal bull of 1575. He was conveyed across the county to Launceston gaol, while Tregian was examined before the bishop and bound in £2000 to appear before the Council or at the next assizes. Him too Grenville conveyed to Launceston gaol where he was lodged in the filthy dungeon of which so many have recorded their experience. As the result of these proceedings and the bishop's investigations, a regular haul of recusants was made, nine or ten of the friends and servants of Tregian, together with Tremayne, Becket and others whose offences were independent. The Council wrote to the judges of assize to inquire what others there were lurking in the county and to proceed accordingly.[1] The result was that over a score of persons were charged with various indictments at the assizes in September. The affair, both because of the size and character of the haul, and of the issues involved, became a test-case important for the whole country. Sir John Arundell and Tregian were not allowed to appear: their presence might

[1] *A.P.C.*, x. 6.

347

have had an unfortunate effect upon the jury. Tregian was summoned before the Council instead. Here he attempted to justify himself, though he admitted his recusancy, and to lay the blame for what had happened to the malice of his enemies in Cornwall. Walsingham stopped him with the remark that they were expecting further advertisement from the assizes. When Tregian was departing, the earl of Sussex invited him to dinner and further discourse, the object of which was to persuade him away from his stand for catholicism. Tregian remained obdurate, as he did for the rest of his life: a confessor of the faith.

At Launceston Mayne was arraigned, and with him Richard Tremayne, John Kemp, Thomas Harris, John Williams, a schoolmaster and master of arts, and John Philips, John Hodge, James Humphreys, yeomen, for aiding and abetting Mayne. He was prosecuted by Popham, later Attorney-General, who produced notes on religious issues written by Mayne for Tregian, a letter from Gregory Martin (the translator of the Douai Bible) exhorting Mayne to acquit himself well in his function, the *agnus dei* which he wore about his neck and the papal bull found among his belongings. Mayne's defence on the last score was that the bull was merely a copy of the bull of indulgence for the Jubilee of 1575, which had already expired, and which, having bought it in a printer's shop at Douai, he had forgotten and packed up with his things. This made an impression upon one of the judges, Jefferys; but the other, Manwood, replied that the question of its expiry was not relevant, since it never had any validity in this kingdom, but it was an offence punishable as high treason to have brought it in. So it undoubtedly was; but it may be doubted whether it was an action such as this which the statute of 1571 had in mind to make high treason. It was a literal reading of the law which condemned Mayne; and there was a disagreement between the judges, Manwood, the senior, in the end giving sentence alone.

There were other indictments too upon which he was condemned, for saying Mass, for bringing in an *agnus dei*, for extolling the Romish authority; upon all these the other prisoners were charged as aiders and abetters. Against them the case had to be constructed. Tremayne was charged on the evidence of a letter which said that he had taken pains to inquire in Paul's churchyard for certain books Mayne had sent for. Both of them swore that they had never seen each other until that hour, and that no letters passed between them. Another letter declared that Kemp had conveyed to Mayne all his stuff hallowed by the late bishop of Lincoln. Against John Williams it was alleged that a child of his was christened papistically at Tregian's house, and not at church.* And so on.

Poor Hodge came off worst: he was a tailor, a servant of Tregian's, who was sent to Launceston with apparel for Mayne. The priest was lodged in a noisome place, and Hodge pledged the value of the apparel with the keeper to get him out of it and lodge him more comfortably. But at the trial, he 'would not, to save his life, say to the sheriff this money was his master's, which the sheriff had rather than all the hairs of his beard he might have extorted'. At the instant of the sentence given against Mayne, Grenville came from his seat and urged the poor man to confess the money to be Tregian's, promising not only to save his life but to give him better preferment. No doubt the money was Tregian's, but Grenville seems to have surpassed himself in his efforts to make condemnation sure. It would have been a useful bit of evidence against Tregian. The jury were long over their verdict, and when they came in still seeming doubtful, according to a catholic report, Grenville went down from his seat and in the sight of both judges and people 'talked to them and that very vehemently a long time to what effect God knoweth'. All these prisoners, save Tremayne — they stood stripped to the waist at the bar — were condemned to the penalties of premunire. Tremayne's sentence was respited, 'either at the earnest suit of some friends, or because they had no colour or cunning to cloak so manifest and palpable injustice'. It is more likely that his kinship to the clerk of the privy council was what counted.

But he was condemned along with sixteen others, including many new names, upon the seventh indictment, for not attending church. At the head of the list appears the name of John Arundell, *eques auratus*, for the first time: winged at last.[1] Along with Tremayne appear his wife, his mother (Mary Isham) and his brother and sister, Philip and Jane: the Cornish branch of the family were catholics, and long they remained so. Of the Kemps there were three: David, Margaret and Winifred. Robert Becket appears along with his brother Thomas; Robert Smith of St. Germans and his wife: his father had been a leader in the '49 Rebellion; but the son could not stay the pace: we find him reconciled shortly after. Besides Tregian and Ermyn, there are Thomas Pickford, Mary Hame and Nicholas Roscarrock, of a family which produced other recusants, for all that they were cousins of Grenville's. Nearly all these belonged to the lesser Cornish gentry, and there were more in the background, gradually brought to light as the years went on. This was but a first bunch, a warning to the others.

Because of the legal uncertainty about Mayne's condemnation, sentence was referred to the Council. Meanwhile the proceedings at Launceston having been reported to them, they summoned Tregian before them. He

---

[1] He was placed under arrest at Court. *Cal. S.P. Dom. Add. 1566-1579*, 523.

could have had immunity for himself and saved the life of his poor priest if he had been prepared to yield and go to church; but he refused, affirming that he 'would not hazard his own soul unto Hell to withhold his man's from Heaven': obviously a self-complacent, fanatic fool of the first water. He was committed to close confinement in the Marshalsea. Matters proceeded with regard to Mayne. Grenville came up to court in October to see that they did not go wrong: he was knighted for his pains. The sentence was referred to the judges for their opinion: some of the older, having catholic sympathies, agreed with Jefferys, the rest with Manwood. The Council decided to make an example of Mayne and sent down their warrant for his execution, the first of the seminary priests.

He was to die on St. Andrew's day. All the day before, from morning to night, laden with irons and fettered he held his own in discourse with the justices and ministers who came to visit him. He was a well-educated, an Oxford man: he belonged to that generation of the early seventies which increasingly found the Anglican position unsatisfactory and sent many of its best sons, particularly from Exeter, the west-country college, abroad to Douai, Rheims, Rome, Valladolid, to the English colleges there. Mayne had the whole intellectual position worked out: the complete Counter-Reformation type. He would allow of no compromise with the Anglican church, he believed that the English people might be won back to Rome by the methods of the seminary priests; he explained with candour, now that he was past hope, the ultramontane position that if any catholic prince were to invade a country to reclaim it to Rome, all catholics should be ready to aid and assist the invader.[1] It was precisely this fifth-column doctrine over-riding national sovereignty in the interest of Rome which justified the government in its repressive measures, and which by setting itself against the instinct of patriotism ultimately ensured Rome's defeat.

Next day he was dragged through the streets of Launceston on a hurdle to the gibbet erected in the market-place. A last attempt was made to get him to incriminate Sir John Arundell and Tregian, but he took all things home to himself. When he was speaking his last words to the crowd, Treffry interrupted and 'commanded the hangman to put the rope about his neck, and then, quoth he, let him preach afterward'; while Mohun ordered the ladder to be thrown off so that he had not time to finish the verse *In manus tuas, domine.*[2] While still alive he was cut down, and falling from that height against the scaffold, one of his eyes was driven out. Stripped of his clothes, his members were severed, his body ripped open and the quivering heart

[1] S.P. 12/118, 46.   [2] Morris, op. cit., I. 99.

held up to the people. His head was placed upon the castle gate, his quarters dispatched to Barnstaple, near which he was born, Bodmin, Wadebridge and Tregony, near by Tregian's house.

Tregian remained to be dealt with, a more ticklish matter since he was so well allied and it was desirable to get him to submit *pour encourager les autres*. He lay in the Marshalsea; Arundell apparently had been committed to the Gatehouse. Tregian petitioned Leicester, who was a connection of his wife's, to have his case removed into the court of Queen's Bench. The proceedings against him, he said, were due to 'envy and malice towards me (whose behaviour towards them (god knoweth) hath not deserved such recompense), first, to avoid just punishment for their own foul faults, and after in hope (by the spoil of me, if it might be) to supply the want of their own needy estates ... (not altogether impoliticly, although very wickedly)'.[1] He protested too much: he had placed himself in his enemies' hands. However Tregian was not without influence, and a most complicated series of legal manœuvres after the Elizabethan pattern thereupon ensued, of importance in beating out the track by which recusancy was pursued in the country in general.

Tregian and his friends procured a writ of *capias* directed to the sheriff of Cornwall to bring up Tregian, Mayne and the other prisoners at Launceston. This very much disturbed the Cornish J.P.s, who did not want to let them out of their clutches. The new sheriff, Mohun, returned that Mayne was dead, Tregian not to be found in his bailiwick, and the rest imprisoned and not in his custody. (Launceston castle belonged to the Duchy, which appointed the keeper.) In addition, they tried to get Judge Jefferys to stay the proceedings for removing the prisoners and harassed Tregian in what ways they could. He owed a debt of some £70 to a London goldsmith, which, in his close confinement and being short of money there, he failed to take steps to pay on the date. The sheriff thereupon seized corn and cattle to the value of £500 into his hands. Mrs. Tregian managed to raise money from her friends and got the corn and cattle back, but not until she had paid something like £200 for the debt of £70. Meanwhile Tregian's adversaries procured a writ of outlawry against him.

To the tale of his enemies was added Sir George Carey, the knight-marshal, a cousin of the Queen, in whose custody Tregian was and to whom the tenure of his lands, though not their ownership, was awarded. He exerted himself naturally to turn his enjoyment of them into full possession. By a continuation of such blows mixed with blandishments it was hoped to get

[1] Cotton MS. Titus B 7, f. 46.

351

Tregian to submit. In June 1578 he was allowed to consult two eminent lawyers, including the great Plowden who was a catholic himself, regarding his case and to see a physician in the presence of the knight-marshal. The prisoners at Launceston were brought up under a strong guard to the Queen's Bench to be arraigned upon the same indictment as at the assizes. Tregian's counsel, considering he had a strong case, petitioned the court for judgment, but the knight-marshal managed to have it put off from day to day until the term ended: very Elizabethan. The Council decided to send them all back to Cornwall to stand their trial at assizes again. A few days before their departure, Tregian was sent for to see what alteration his imprisonment had made in him. As he was leaving the council chamber, Edmund Tremayne stopped him and talked to him in a friendly way regretting his course and the treatment it called forth, and suggesting that he might win favour by asking to have some learned minister to confer with for his doubts in religion. Tregian answered that he had no doubts, and that he was willing to furnish a defence of any article of his faith to any one whatsoever. So back he went to prison, and a few days later was sent down to Cornwall under the care of a particular adversary of his.

At the assizes further evidence was procured against him. One Twigges who had come to play in an interlude at Golden at Christmas 1575 was suborned to give false evidence: he deposed to having been lodged with Mayne. Tregian pointed out that the priest did not come to him till the Easter following. Again there was disagreement between the judges, and sentence was delayed. Shortly after, a servant of Tregian's who was being sent to London with money to pay a friend who had disbursed it in his affairs was arrested by Bedford in Devon, discharged of his money and lodged in irons. Bedford had given his strong support to the proceedings the year before, from his house at Tavistock which was very convenient to Launceston. The knight-marshal was getting very restive for his prey, and at the next assizes sentence was given against Tregian by Manwood, Jefferys still dissenting, and he was condemned to the penalties of premunire. At once the sheriff and some of Sir George Carey's men made for Golden, and arriving at night broke down the gates and doors. Mrs. Tregian, who was then with child, was in her chamber with her children and her womenfolk. They turned her out of doors, and helped by friends she made her way to London, where she hoped to get some redress at the Queen's hands.

Tregian was committed to the dungeon at Launceston, some three fathom underground, infested with every sort of filth and occupied by twenty condemned persons all through that hot summer month: some of whom abused him and threatened to murder him. At the end of that time he was removed to a private room, though still kept in fetters. A commission of the exchequer came down by which all his lands and goods were seized to the use of Carey, including the lands which had been settled upon his mother as her jointure. This was questionable legally, and it led to much petitioning and litigation; in the end a composition was arrived at between Carey and Tregian's mother. Tregian consoled himself by writing verses to his wife with a pin and the snuff of a candle, 'persuaded thereunto through a very vehement and unwonted motion of the mind' — as one would suppose from the quality of the verse:

> O ever living Lord of Lords,
>   O mighty King of Kings,
> O solace of the sorrowful,
>   O glass, who gladness brings . . .
> And grant I never feed on food
>   Of thine affièd spouse,
> And that I never eat profaned
>   The Lamb without thy house.

Nor did he: through all the troubles and misfortunes it brought him and his family, a lifetime of imprisonment, he had that futile satisfaction.

Tregian now laid plans to escape overseas. It was discovered through the indiscreet forwardness of a kinsman; and Hender, a J.P. who got on the track of it, was rewarded with a licence to export 800 quarters of grain: a stage in the progress of that new family.[1] Tregian went back to his dungeon with the lice and toads, the ordure of twenty criminals. By the petition of his wife shortly after, and on giving sureties for future behaviour, he was released from irons and allowed to receive food and clothing from his kinsfolk. The Tregians insisted that his life was in danger and on this account petitioned for his removal to the Queen's Bench. He was brought up from Cornwall and confined close prisoner there for six months. The Council ordered an investigation into the threats to murder him, and found that they were untrue; Tregian's resistance was still unbroken and he had told the keeper of Launceston that 'the prison had been offered to have been broken twice for his escape in case he had wanted'. In view of this, it was ordered that Tregian should pay the charges of his removal, since it had been at his wish. Tregian had not a penny left, but his faithful wife raised the money from her friends and by selling some of her clothes. The Council, very

[1] *A.P.C.*, XI. 189.

humanely, allowed Mrs. Tregian access to her husband, 'there to remain with him at her liking, but nobody else to come unto him'.[1]

After six months of this, in January 1580, he was removed to the common gaol of the Fleet, 'among a sort of bankrupts, cozeners, and forgerers'. At the end of two years even Tregian's health gave way: he was a strong man of twenty-eight when he was first imprisoned, of a very active habit of body: his wife bore him some eighteen children all told. His illness won him better treatment, and he was moved from the common gaol to a more comfortable lodging and given the liberty of the garden for exercise. His wife lived the most part of the time with him in prison, and here he remained till within two years of the end of the reign. For six or seven years his health was affected; then he recovered. The account of his troubles, which must surely have been written from his evidence by Nicholas Roscarrock, his fellow-recusant, makes the point that he came of 'a most generous progeny planted in those western parts . . . beyond all memory to the contrary, and is, in very truth, of the natural race and remain of the ancient Britons'. Divested of his estates, he was supported by the charity of his friends and relations, and by a pension from the King of Spain.

Meanwhile in Cornwall the claims of old Mrs. Tregian disturbed Sir George Carey's enjoyment of the lands and produced much litigation. Her steward Humphrey Powell faithfully defended her interests. Carey had him committed to the Fleet, while Mohun and others of the anti-Tregian party complained of him to the Council.[2] Powell offered to stand his trial, and in the end the old lady got an amount of £60 p.a. out of the lands in Carey's occupation. What happened ultimately to the lands and the Tregians we shall see: the case is important as setting a precedent for the treatment of recusants and illustrating in detail how it was carried out. It is time to turn to the other catholics, other names and activities.

Along with the haul of Cornish Catholics taken in 1577, opportunity had been taken to include a number of others: Lewis Morley of Devon, William Wigges of London, Robert Jessop of Dorset, Simon Low of Kent, John Neale of Essex, Vincent Ingham and Thomas Scott. Ingham was mistakenly condemned for another person, and next year he was pardoned.[3] In June 1580 Richard Tremayne was pardoned; in 1581 Hodge the tailor, and James Humphreys of Launceston.[4] That summer Philip Tremayne was released from the Fleet.

[1] A.P.C., XI. 206, 274.   [2] ibid., 21, 74.
[3] Pat. Rolls, Eliz. 1172.   [4] ibid., 1186, 1208.

Sir John Arundell got more deeply into trouble. In 1579 a search was made at Lanherne and Sir George Carey brought up various things to inculpate him.[1] Arundell replied that at the time he left the house two years ago, there was nothing offensive to the law there, save certain pictures of Christ and the Virgin Mary. He could not answer for what had been brought in since, but offered to disperse the great company which sought refuge under his roof. He too, like Tregian, stated that the proceedings against him were due to the 'particular envy and malice borne him by some of that shire'. The Council thought the charges against him were 'of good moment and importance', and directed Bedford to collect further evidence in the west country.[2]

The country was on the *qui vive* now, and a sharp lookout was kept at the ports for seminary priests and suspect persons. At the end of 1578 two men landing at Plymouth from a Spanish ship were apprehended: various papist books, relics and letters were found on them. One of them was Nicholas Bawden, of a St. Mabyn family which was devoted to Catholicism, and produced the distinguished Jesuit, Fr. William Bawden. Nicholas was a young student of Exeter college who had matriculated in 1575 and gone abroad. After a number of years spent in and about London, living the underground life to which catholics were driven in these dangerous years, he went abroad once more. A tall fine man nearly forty, still unmarried, he became a gentleman of the chamber with the young Francis Tregian to Cardinal Allen at Rome.[3] He died at Valladolid, an exile, for religion's sake, like so many of his countrymen at this time.

Abroad Allen's college, founded first at Louvain, transferred to Douai and then for a while to Rheims, prospered and grew from strength to strength. Supported by the gifts of the English Catholics, and by pensions from the Pope and Philip II, it fulfilled with great success two functions: it educated the sons of the catholic gentry, withdrawing them from the English universities, and it produced a steady stream of priests, many of them to become martyrs, for the English mission. In 1576 Allen dispatched his first students to Rome, the effective beginning of the English College there, the refurbishing of the old English hospice in the hot and narrow Via Julia, the twisting cobbled streets of that little English quarter. In 1589 he was able to send students to found an English college at Valladolid. In all these activities of the exiles, the Cornish catholics had their place.

[1] *A.P.C.*, XI. 265.   [2] ibid., 345.
[3] Knox, *Letters and Memorials of Cardinal Allen*, 376.

In the first years the Cornish contingent in the college at Douai was notably large. Its gradual diminishing by persecution and financial exhaustion at home is my theme.

Allen began work with the help of several fellows of Exeter college, where catholic sympathies were strong; in 1578 the rector himself joined them. This undoubtedly influenced the west-country students at Oxford who began to follow them abroad: the Exeter diocese is much to the fore in the early Douai diaries. Thomas Ford was the first of them to be admitted: he was martyred at Tyburn in 1582. Ford and Mayne were friends at Oxford; it was Ford who gave Mayne warning in 1570 that he was suspected and the bishop of London's pursuivants out for him. Mayne slipped away into the west country, and after waiting, took shipping from the Cornish coast in 1573 and went over. He took his degree as bachelor of divinity in 1576, was ordained priest and shortly after left for England with John Payne. The news of his martyrdom reached the college and was inscribed in the margin of the Diary for November 29th, 1577.[1] That year John Curry and John Tippett, both Cornishmen, were ordained and sent to England. Curry was a poor Bodmin lad, like Kestle and Cornelius, all three of whom became Jesuits.[2] Of Kestle we know nothing, save that he was a student of the Inner Temple, went into exile at Louvain, became a Jesuit in Portugal and died at Coimbra: a brief shadow that flits across this sombre background like so many others. Of Curry we know a little more: he was a chaplain in the house of the Arundells at Chideock, for a time with John Cornelius, and was entrusted by Father Heywood with a mission to Allen at Rheims in 1583. He was then serving his novitiate in the Jesuit order. He was successful in evading capture.

John Tippett, of St. Wenn, arrived at Douai from Marchiennes college in 1576. Ordained with Curry by the bishop of Cambrai in his palace on the day before Passion Sunday 1577, he returned to England shortly after.[3] Next year he was discovered in London and brought before the bishop and recorder. He stood stoutly to his faith and was condemned to be whipped at a cart's tail and bored through the ear like any rogue, 'notwithstanding his brother with others pleaded that his father's house was his abode and that he had twenty marks by the year'.[4] He was evidently of good yeoman stock. There exists a version, translated out of Italian, of the letter which the angry, humiliated father wrote to his son from St. Wenn (Santovenno), and the edifying reply from the son in Newgate.[5] Expelled from the country,

---

[1] Knox, *First and Second Douai Diaries*, 131.
[2] Foley, *Records of the Society of Jesus*, I. 396; C.R.S., XXII. 106.
[3] Knox, *Douai Diaries*, 25, 117.   [4] ibid., 149.   [5] C.R.S., II. 80.

he went back to Rheims in March 1579 and died in exile.[1] Another John Tippett, who must have been a relation of the foregoing, was admitted a student at the English college at Rome and took the oath with John Cornelius in 1580.[2] He made his spiritual exercises in 1582, was ordained deacon and priest in 1584; he afterwards entered the Carthusian order and died in religion.

The next two Cornish recruits to the college, which was at Rheims from 1578 to 1593, are of interest as cases of Anglican clergymen leaving their livings and going into exile for the faith. Thomas Bluett became rector of St. Michael Penkivel in 1576 on the deprivation of Edward Waters; one year was enough to unsettle him.[3] He left his living and arrived at Douai a month before Mayne left: the Diary notes his accession after having had many disputes with the heretical ministers in England, and after many dangers and losses.[4] We trace his progress in the Diary, until, having been made priest at Cambrai and said his first Mass, he came back to England in 1578.[5] A year after he was taken and brought before one of the bishops to be examined: 'in which profession he took up the ministers so roundly that they were marvellously astonished at him; in so much that one of the chiefest of them, understanding that before-time he had been one of their ministers, brake into these words and said, "I have heard many times objected against us that our ministers be unlearned; but by St. Mary we have now happened on a minister with whom for his learning, I beshrew him, we be all of us much encumbered".'[6] Next year we find him among the prisoners at Wisbech, where he vanishes from view.

John Vivian was rector of St. Just-in-Roseland from 1572 to 1576, when his conscience made him quit.[7] He arrived at Rheims in 1579, where it was noted that he had been beneficed and was a good preacher. He passed through the college quickly, was made priest at Laon and left for England in September. After a time he was run to earth and imprisoned, and in 1585, the war with Spain now imminent, he was one of a large number of priests sent out of the country and back at Rheims. Return would have meant certain death. He chose rather to become a monk, and joined the order of St. Bridget (of which Cicely Arundell was a sister, now living in poverty at Rouen) and later he moved to Lisbon: in the religious life he disappears from view.[8]

[1] Knox, *Douai Diaries*, 289.
[2] *C.R.S.*, XXXVII. 19, 20.
[3] Henderson, x. 79, 80.   [4] Knox, *Diaries*, 117.
[5] ibid., 8, 26, 129, 131, 135-6.   [6] ibid., 149, 171.
[7] Henderson, x. 78, 80.   [8] Knox, *Diaries*, 9, 13, 150, 151, 154, 291, 362.

In the next few years three more Cornishmen entered the college, two of whom became martyrs. David Kemp, one of the faithful Kemps of St. Minver, arrived in 1581, became a priest at the end of that year and left for England in September 1582.[1] He was captured and held in prison at York, whence he was ordered in 1585 to leave the country; he returned to Rheims, remained a few months and left again, whither one knows not: he is lost to view. Another of the Kemps, Francis, was admitted to commons in 1589; next year he was sent, a beginner at philosophy, to the college in Spain.[2] John Cornelius did not stay long: he arrived in September 1579, was to study theology, and in February was sent on to Rome.[3] He came back to England in 1583 as a chaplain to Sir John Arundell, who was his patron and had paid for his education. Cornelius was of Irish parentage: hence perhaps the peculiarly intense quality of his religious conviction.[4] The story goes that when a boy he was reading a book under a hedge while his fellow-schoolboys played in the next field, when Sir John Arundell came by and gave him a gold piece; that he took him into his house and later sent him to Oxford. A student of Exeter, he left like so many others for Rheims, where Arundell supported him. Cornelius won golden opinions for his devotion and eloquence: on St. Stephen's day 1581 he preached before the Pope in the Sistine chapel, and to such good effect that the Pope commanded that a sermon should be preached every year on that feast by a student of the college. Curious it is to think of this poor Bodmin lad in those magnificent surroundings: the Michelangelo Last Judgment, the papal Court, Rome of the Counter-Reformation. He was well worthy of the opinions held of him. He was a most persuasive preacher and in England reconciled many to the church. The young William Bawden, who had arrived at Rheims from Oxford to go on to Rome, was a pupil of Cornelius's. There was an incessant going to and fro between England, Rheims and Rome.

Of the last of this group, John Hamley, we know much, owing to the melancholy circumstance that his capture and imprisonment broke his nerve and he made a full confession in the hope of saving his life. It is to that that we owe the most revealing document: it lifts the veil for us, throwing light into these dark places where the persecuted catholics encouraged each other to challenge and endure, the sombre and hunted lives of those faithful priests. Hamley came of a yeoman family, from the parish of St. Mabyn, and was brought up from infancy 'at divers schools in Cornwall learning

[1] Knox. *Diaries*, 10, 28, 174, 182, 184, 190, 208.   [2] ibid., 222, 234.
[3] ibid., 156, 160, 297.   [4] cf. Life of Cornelius in *R.S.J.*, III.

358

the Latin tongue'.[1] About 1582, Nicholas Bawden who had been a scholar of Exeter lent him a book called *The Reasons of Refusal* and others which he studied. One sees the picture: the scholar of Oxford, the bookish youth already 'bearing a mind to the Romish religion'. And so he began to forbear coming to church at Christmas and had never been to a service in England since. To avoid imprisonment he went to London, where he lived at the sign of the Sun and Stars in Smithfield. Here he met David Kemp and another priest, Foskew, whom he had seen before at Bawden's house in Cornwall: Foskew heard his confession, absolved and reconciled him. He heard several masses, one in the Marshalsea with Bawden present, another there said by Tippett, a third at a house near Bishopsgate at which Bawden's sister Emlyn was present. Determining to go over to Rheims, he took ship at Rye and landed at Dieppe. For the journey Bawden delivered him £10 from his brother, which was part of his father's legacy to him.

His confession describes in detail the organization of the college at Rheims, the way the work was arranged: there were altogether two hundred Englishmen, men and boys. He was there almost two years (1583 to 1585), studying among other things 'cases of conscience' and 'cases of controversies'. He received minor orders at the hands of the great Cardinal de Guise himself, in the chapel of the Holy Cross in Rheims cathedral. He was made priest at Laon, promised Dr. Allen to do his utmost to convert souls in England and received £4 and 'the apparel of a serving man, as the manner is', in which to come over. He landed on the sands beyond Ipswich and made at once for Holborn where catholics resorted. Here he was sent by Cornelius to say mass in a room in Gray's Inn, at which were nine or ten gentlemen who had everything ready for him. They were all young men and had gathered ten or twelve shillings to sustain him. Twelve months before he had been directed by Nicholas Bluett, a Cornishman, to Andrew Mundy — who must have belonged to the family of the last prior of Bodmin — who dwelt at Beaminster in Dorset, 'where he hath made his most common abode ever since'. Here he had said several masses and reconciled various people about the countryside. Some time after Easter he had ridden to Chard to meet Sir John Fulford's son — the Fulfords were Devonshire catholics — and a lady, whom he was to marry at Mundy's house. They were all apprehended in the way to Mundy's house, himself lodged in the common gaol at Ilchester while the Fulfords were allowed to return to Devon.

Hamley was arraigned and condemned at Taunton assizes but submitted

[1] S.P. 12/192, 47.

and was reprieved. He was troubled in conscience, however, and escaped to the house of a catholic at Knoyle where he was apprehended. Examined before the bishop of Salisbury he sought to win favour by a full confession: he remembered everything, recalling the names of his companions at Rheims, Vivian and Curry the Jesuit, Trewethan a student, all Cornishmen, among many others. Confronted with the fear of death, agonized in mind, young — who can blame him, though his revelations meant danger for others? In prison for nearly a year, his mind tormented with fears and doubts, he found comfort and courage in the presence and counsel of another priest, Pilcher, who helped him to die: at Salisbury about 1587. He had need of it: his case was much like that of a young fellow-catholic, of an age with Hamley, who died about the same time:

> My tale was heard and yet it was not told,
>   My fruit is fallen and yet my leaves are green,
> My youth is spent and yet I am not old,
>   I saw the world and yet I was not seen;
>   My thread is cut and yet it is not spun,
>   And now I live, and now my life is done.

> I sought my death and found it in my womb,
>   I looked for life and saw it was a shade,
> I trod the earth and knew it was my tomb,
>   And now I die, and now I was but made;
>   My glass is full and now my glass is run,
>   And now I live, and now my life is done.

Such were the circumstances of these poor hunted priests who gave their lives in order that the souls of their gentry might be saved. With the development of the European crisis, the increased tension in England, the plots against the Queen's life, the support given to Mary Stuart by Spain, severer legislation and counter-measures against catholics, priests and laity alike, were resorted to. An Act of Parliament of 1581 made it treason to reconcile any person to Rome or to be reconciled; any person saying or hearing Mass was liable to a year's imprisonment in addition to heavy fines; the fine for non-attendance at church was raised to £20 a month, which imposed a crippling burden upon any catholic family but the very richest. From now on the Arundells paid a considerable proportion of their revenues, £260 a year, for the luxury of not going to church. It was a heavy burden even for them; for lesser families it was impossible, and we watch them being slowly and inexorably reduced and in many cases ruined. All this, however, had no effect upon the religious devotion of the Arundells: they continued to be the centre, the resort of Cornish catholics, they supported priests abroad and at home, they always had catholic chaplains, sometimes two or even three serving in their household, they opened their house to the faithful remnant so that twenty or thirty persons shared the hospitality of their roof. Tregian in the Fleet continued to be the centre of a circle of recalcitrant catholics of high position, with connections at court, with priests in disguise for ever coming and going. The Arundells, owing to their high connections, got a certain measure of immunity and a great deal of forbearance, but government spies watched their activities, and those of Tregian, and at length Sir John himself was laid by the heels.

In 1584 information was laid against him of keeping an Oxford graduate at his house in Clerkenwell for a week before he went to Rheims; on the latter's return as priest Sir John would give him entertainment.[1] He had also given his consent that his nephew Charles Stourton should go to Rheims — presumably to study. Next year, after Parry's conspiracy, a little group connected with the Arundells was brought to light at Mrs. Warnford's house in Winchester where catholics harboured. Walter Trevethan of Mawgan deposed that he came there 'to bring certain congers and other dry fish to Elizabeth St. Aubyn, his mistress': she must have been George Arundell's widow.[2] He had to admit that the old gentlewoman living in the house with her was his mother, Ursula Trevethan, and the young woman his sister. On being asked whether he would go to church, he said, 'No, for his conscience will not serve him thereunto'. After this, we find him in prison.[3]

In May Sir John was in the Tower, for 'besides the old matters concerning Mayne the traitor, he hath received divers priests since the proclamation, had masses in his house in the Easter week, confessed by the priest'.[4] He was to be proceeded against in Star Chamber for his contempt of the proclamation. We hear of another west-country priest, John Brushford, visiting Arundell's house at Clerkenwell at this time, 'but for that he was then in trouble in the Star Chamber, about one Mr. Higgins a priest, I could not be received; but I was with him afterwards in the Gatehouse'.[5] As for Lady Arundell, 'she was ever fearful, and after Sir John's trouble, never bore young priests any good will. What she did to old priests I

[1] S.P. 12/168, 34.   [2] ibid., 177, 3.   [3] ibid., 189, 48.
[4] ibid., 178, 74.   [5] R.S.J., VI. 149.

cannot tell . . . I was once, I remember, entreated to ride into Cornwall, but I durst not for that I was well known by the way'.

The attempt of the Earl of Arundel to escape from the country at this dangerous time involved the Arundells in further trouble, though they were but distant connections. The French ambassador reported that this was the cause of Sir John's committal, 'un chevalier . . . de grand crédit dans ce royaume', and that their whole house was very suspect 'avec beaucoup d'amis et d'ennemis'.[1] A cadet, John Arundell of Gwarneck, that little house in the secluded valley of the river Allen dropping down among the woods to Truro, was arrested at Exeter with a large amount of money on him.[2] It was thought that he intended to fly the kingdom, but he seems to have been able to assure the government of his good faith and his money was restored. Sir John was in the Gatehouse that October, and charged with the payment of £100 to equip four light horse.[3] Richard Tremayne paid £25 for the furnishing of one.[4] He was already hard pressed to meet his fines for recusancy: he was condemned for £320, of which he had already paid £140, and offered £10 yearly to be discharged of the rest.[5] A spy reported at this time that Tremayne or his brother was engaged in bringing in and disposing of Douai New Testaments from Rouen.[6]

Two years later, in 1587, as the danger of invasion drew near, leading catholics were rounded up and put in custody as a precautionary measure. Arundell was committed to the care of the Dean of St. Paul's.[7] When the Armada crisis was over precautions were relaxed, but Sir John was not to go beyond a circuit of six miles from his house at Muswell.[8] In 1590 he was one of the prisoners at Ely Palace for whom better conditions were ordered by the Council: they were to have 'sweet and wholesome water both for the dressing of their meat and other necessary uses, and to enjoy liberty of the gardens and orchards and the leads to walk in'.[9] They were even suffered to take the air for a mile or two in the custody of some trusty persons. Sir John was one of a number of leading catholics who signed a declaration of loyalty to the Queen, protesting their readiness to imperil lives and estates in defence of her person and of the realm against the Pope and every potentate. Such declarations showed the futility of the Fifth Column activities of Parsons and the Jesuits.

At the end of the year Sir John died, at Isleworth whither he had removed,

---

[1] C.R.S., XXI. 112.
[2] Hist. MSS. Com., *Records of City of Exeter*, 311; and cf. his examination, S.P. 12/180, 2.
[3] S.P. 12/183, 23.   [4] ibid., 200, 61.   [5] ibid., 188, 42 (1).   [6] C.R.S., XXI. 75.
[7] Hist. MSS. Com., *Rutland MSS.*, I. 232.   [8] S.P. 12/226, 72 (15).
[9] Hist. MSS. Com., *Fifth Report*, Appendix, 406.

and was buried with his ancestors at St. Columb. It was not until Charles I's reign that the family fortunes recovered sufficiently to permit of a large, if debased, brass to his memory and his successor's. His will follows the old formula, calling upon the bleeding wounds of Christ, 'the intercession and mediation of our blessed Lady, the holy Virgin Mary, and of the holy angels, saints and the blessed company of heaven'.[1] He was very devout: his devotion cost the family a pretty penny, mortgaging the future. His will was a very cautious affair: he had to draw in his horns, though there were signs of the old Arundell generosity. He left small annuities to his nephew Bosgrave, his servants Edward and Richard Victor and William Hanne; the will was attested by John Williams and Henry Stephens. We find all these as recusants, under the Arundell influence. Bosgrave died along with Cornelius. Sir John charged his son to make his will at once so that he 'die not intestate whereby my goods and chattels may come into strangers' hands'. He asked that his body might rest near his grandfather in the church of St. Columb.

From the other side of the world comes a fragment of evidence about his burial. An English missionary priest in Brazil, Father John Yates who had been at work in the district of the bay of All Saints for twenty years, until his head was white and he was beginning to go rusty in writing his own language, was writing Sir Francis Englefield in Madrid news of the English expeditions along that coast: first Drake, then Waddington, then Cavendish.[2] Of the last some prisoners were taken, among them Robert Arundell who 'calls himself of kin to Sir John Arundell, and states that Sir John died a catholic in London and that his body was carried to Cornwall with great pomp to be buried'.[3] He asked Englefield if it was so, since he could not believe that a catholic would be suffered to be so buried. The young man seemed to have little knowledge of the faith; the good father had written him instructions as to what he must do to attain grace. The letter fell into the hands of the English government and lodges now in the Public Record Office.

Lady Arundell now retired to Chideock whither she was followed a few days later by her priests. In that great square moated house with its four turrets, now vanished, there collected a faithful remnant of the family, their relations and dependents. Here four years later a tragic blow fell upon them. One of the servants in the house turned informer, and in consequence

[1] P.C.C. 83 Drury.
[2] This superb subject, that of the Catholic Emigration, still awaits its historian.
[3] S.P. 12/245, 33.

Father John Cornelius was captured, the house fatally implicated.[1] Cornelius was their favourite chaplain, an intimate of the family, with whom he had mostly lived in London and at Chideock for the past eleven years. Spies had long been on his trail and information reached the government of his activities, especially among the nobility. He was intimate with Lord Vaux, and he often stayed with Lord Montagu at St. Mary Overy's. A spy told Burghley: 'Francis Browne and his brother were altogether governed by Edmunds and Cornelius. They have been by their means conveyed to sundry noblemen . . . Cornelius was thought the fittest man for to preach before ladies and gentlemen, both for his sweet and plausible tongue and for that he could best counterfeit simplicity. It was laboured that one lady should inform another and get him made famous to some of her Majesty's privy chamber.'

There were many instances of his devotion to the poor no less: visiting a poor man dying in a filthy hovel, reconciling him and giving him extreme unction; indefatigable in begging money for lights and for maintaining poor seminary priests, rigorous in his own personal discipline, in frequent fasting. Naturally such a type was given to visions: his old master, Mr. Harris, appeared to him in his sleep and entreated mass to be said for him. So also Lord Stourton, Lady Arundell's son, who had conformed but kept two priests so that he might not die unreconciled. Lady Arundell begged a mass for him, at which a vision appeared between the consecration and the memento for the dead: Lord Stourton appeared in grief and torment for his dissimulation at Court and for being one of the forty-seven who condemned Mary Queen of Scots. John Carey, the server of the mass, saw the vision too: he later died with Cornelius.

He was specially famed for his power in casting out devils, one of whom offered him 2d. to buy a halter with. The Protestants regarded him as an enchanter and a conjurer.[2] He was so bent upon the inner life of contemplation that though he lived for three years in a room which looked upon the parish church, he never noticed the fact, nor knew whether the house had a thatched or tiled roof. Living with Sir John Arundell for ten years in London and at Chideock, he knew nothing of their neighbours nor the entrance even to the house. He was so strict that he would never say grace at table when Protestants were present, nor allowed of any participation with them in worship. His innermost desire was for martyrdom; he wrote in a book of his, 'Would that I might be despoiled of this my flesh, whether by the rope, the

[1] The above account is based upon that given, and the documents cited, in *R.S.J.*, III.
[2] ibid., I. 331.

cross or the torture'. He had his way. In short his was the complete type of baroque, Counter-Reformation religion. He had always desired to become a Jesuit: at Rome he had been a member of the Jesuits' sodality in the college, but was not admitted into the society until his imprisonment. His closest affinity was to his friend, the Jesuit Southwell:

> Before my face the picture hangs,
>   That daily should put me in mind
> Of those cold qualms and bitter pangs,
>   That shortly I am like to find.

On Easter Sunday 1594 the house at Chideock was surrounded, but Cornelius, whose habit was to say mass every morning at five, had said his mass early at one o'clock and lay concealed in the woods. But his mother was in the house and he returned. He had brought her back to the church on first coming home from abroad, and since she was Irish, had devoted two hours a day to translating a book on confession into that language for her. A fortnight later the house was searched again — William Holmes the informer, a servant of fourteen years standing, who had been reproved by the priest, was sure that he was there; and after a long search he was discovered. The family refused to say anything when he was brought forth; but Dorothy Arundell spoke out her mind and Thomas Bosgrave would have defended Cornelius — a piece of bravery for which he paid with his life.

Holmes informed that Cornelius came to Sir John when he lay at Clerkenwell, that he had procured Sherwood to serve him and the two said mass daily at Clerkenwell, Muswell and Isleworth where Sir John died. Sherwood died and was buried in the chapel at Chideock, and Patenson who left for London was succeeded by Curry. When the last left, Green took his place, but when the alarm was given at Easter he went into Cornwall. We learn the names of those who daily heard mass: Lord Stourton, Charles Stourton, John Easton and his wife, Dorothy and Gertrude Arundell, Thomas Bosgrave, Anne, Margaret and Jane Tremayne, Dorothy Prideaux, Cornelius' mother and several others; the boys and hinds were not admitted. John Easton was a ward of Arundell's and brought up in his house; a spy wrote in 1587 that 'being a very tall gentleman and of great courage' he refused to come to church and drank to King Philip. Easton and Bosgrave often served at mass. We learn of the goings to and fro between the Turbervilles and Arundells with news of the executions in London, of a servant's being sent into Cornwall to fetch a priest to marry Sir John Sydenham's son to Turberville's daughter. Richard Tremayne often came to Chideock on business and heard mass.

Cornelius took leave of his mother and blessed the crowd gathered at the gates of the castle. For a fortnight he was detained at Trenchard's house, Wolfeton, where he was well treated, though he would never say grace at their table. There was a disputation between a Protestant divine and Cornelius, which Ralegh attended. It is well known that Ralegh was deeply interested in the intellectual issues concerning faith — he was by no means orthodox himself — and all one night he sat up alone with Cornelius attempting to clear up questions and doubts. The catholics thought that he was much impressed and that he offered to do what he could for Cornelius; but Ralegh, whose own position was none too secure, was unlikely to take any risk that way.[1] The Council offered inducements to Cornelius to renounce; he merely wrote to Lady Arundell: 'Et nunc ecce alligatus ego Spiritu vado in Jerusalem, quae in ea mihi ventura sunt ignorans.'

Committed to the Marshalsea and refusing to answer, he was put to the torture. Brought before the Council he refused to give any evidence that might inculpate others. He was remanded to prison, and there he was received into the Society of Jesus which he had so long desired. Sent back to Dorchester to stand his trial, he spent some days in the house of the sheriff, seeing all and sundry, but inflicting upon himself such austerities that the sheriff feared of his death. A catholic merchant offered to ransom him. The state was not to be balked of its prey: he was condemned of high treason at Dorchester assizes, and with him Arundell's nephew, Bosgrave, and two servants. Cornelius spent his last days urging Dorothy Arundell, his spiritual charge, to enter the Bridgettine convent at Lisbon: he promised to present her vow to St. Bridget in Paradise. He was, poor man, very certain of the next world.

At the execution, where all four men were to suffer, Ralegh was present and would not allow Cornelius to speak to the crowd for fear of the impression he might make on them; but he succeeded in telling them that he had been received into the Society of Jesus. He died with the words *O bona crux diu desiderata* on his lips. After the ghastly rites of dismembering, his head was placed on a pinnacle of St. Peter's church in the High Street, and the four quarters on the gates of the town. The bodies of the four were afterwards recovered by Lady Arundell, and given burial. She herself was afterwards in prison for a while. Brave Dorothy Arundell, visiting the gallows, saw it surrounded with rays of light — doubtless, poor woman, through her tears. And later, Cornelius appeared to her again in the convent at Brussels

[1] cf. *Salisbury MSS.*, IV. 510.

where she dedicated her life according to his directions.[1] Her name is inscribed in the annals of our literature through the dedication to her of Robert Southwell's prose-work *Mary Magdalen's Tears*: that curious, euphuistic work of perfervid, Tridentine piety.

Of the activities of other catholics, lesser families independent of the Arundell and Tregian circles, we have so much information, from spy reports, prison registers and examinations, that it is impossible to do justice to it here: it would require a whole book to itself. Let us take for example the Penkivells of St. Minver, an old family of the smaller gentry, who married with the Roscarrocks, Hores and Kemps, many of whom were catholics. In 1584 we find Thomas Penkivell in Newgate for hearing mass; in 1586 Peter Penkivell was in the Counter, where he was joined by Walter Penkivell and a Borlase.[2] Neither Thomas not Peter would take the oath, nor the Queen's part against a papal army.[3] One of them in the Counter was engaged in persuading a fellow-catholic to go over to Rheims: he 'greatly preferred the orders beyond sea' to those of 'our university'; he offered to put him in touch with persons who would help him over, gave him money, argued with him in favour of the real presence and prayers for the dead, and gave him the *Defence of the Censure* (of the Queen) to read.[4] Another brother was an image-maker in London.[5]

A younger brother, Mark, went to Douai in 1589, from which he proceeded to the English college at Rome.[6] Like so many of these English lads his health suffered from the climate of Rome and he was sent back to Flanders. He was ordained priest in 1599, and, a Jesuit novice, he served his probation in Germany, whence he came back to Paris.[7] Meanwhile his brother John was in an equivocal and dangerous position as a go-between in England and Spain. A catholic himself, he was sent by the government to Spain to inform as to their preparations. His intentions were honest: he meant only to inform what was already known by other channels; but it was a position which exposed him to danger from both sides. Arrived in Madrid, he was suspected by the Jesuits and thrown into prison, where he spent eleven months, six of them in a dungeon at Valladolid among thieves.[8] He was visited by Fr. Walpole who threatened him with extreme torture, to whom he told the truth: that he had been twice imprisoned in England as a spy for the King of Spain, that his eldest brother was still a prisoner, and he besought

---

[1] Here she wrote down Cornelius' Acts, from which our information chiefly come.
[2] *C.R.S.*, I. 238, 248, 252.   [3] ibid., 283.   [4] S.P. 12/195, 121.
[5] ibid., 12/241, 35.   [6] Knox, op. cit., 227, 249.
[7] *R.S.J.*, VI. 192; *C.R.S.*, X. 28.   [8] S.P. 12/284, 32.

pardon as a catholic, having a mother and brethren prisoners in England, one a Capuchin friar and all having lost their livings for religion. The Capuchin friar must have been Mark, who was now serving in the monastery at the Escorial, and he obtained the King's pardon as against the Jesuits who were his mortal enemies. All this and more emerged from the confession he made one day in June 1602 to Sir Nicholas Parker at Pendennis Castle, having arrived in a ship from Spain: one can imagine the June sun upon that blue sea, the coloured sails, the fresh wind on the headland, the scent of thyme and the little oaks in the cliffs below. John Penkivell was banished; his brother Peter followed him voluntarily into exile.[1] The family was ruined by their fidelity.

Two of the Roscarrocks were active recusants, Nicholas and Trevennor. They were both students at Exeter college, where no doubt they imbibed their catholic sympathies.[2] Nicholas was by nature a scholar and writer, and made for himself a name as an antiquarian. As a young man at the Inner Temple he contributed verses to a heraldic book of Tottel's and the prefatory verses to Gascoigne's *Steel Glass* are supposed to be his. Quit of his imprisonment for recusancy after the Mayne affair, he passed through Rheims in 1580 on his way to Rome; the college also entertained a servant of his next year, one Green.[3] He is said to have been a companion of Campion's, and at the end of the year we find him in the Tower. There he was lodged in the Martin Tower, underneath the Scottish Jesuit Crichton, with whom he found means of communication and whose letters he managed to convey out of the Tower from his chamber-window near the ground.[4] He was still there in 1585, with another, Thomas Pound: 'two dangerous men and apt for any practice: fit they should be banished'.[5] His brother Trevennor was in Newgate from 1583.[6] He continued to be a recusant and two-thirds of his small property in Cornwall were in the Queen's hands.

Released in 1586, Nicholas was in the Fleet in 1593 where he enjoyed the company of Tregian. Benjamin Tichborne, a Catholic spy,[7] watched them both: 'I cannot easily be brought out of credit with the chiefest of the papists here, for there is question of marriage between myself and one of Tregian's daughters. . . . I was with Roscarrock continually private in his study, and might have effected something ere this.'[8] Roscarrock occupied himself with his antiquarian studies; his special subject of interest was hagiography and

[1] S.P. 12/284, 43.
[2] cf. Boase, *Register of Exeter College*, 298, and *D.N.B.* sub Nicholas Roscarrock.
[3] Knox, op. cit., 169.   [4] *C.R.S.*, XXI. 71, 133.   [5] ibid., II. 238.   [6] ibid., 237.
[7] He was brother of Chideock Tichborne, who wrote the lines q. on p. 360.
[8] *Salisbury MSS.*, IV. 432.

he knew Cornish. He compiled a large folio Register of the British Saints, which now reposes in the Cambridge University Library: its particular value lies in the fact that for it he translated the lives of certain Cornish saints out of that language, thereby correcting errors current about them. In 1607 he wrote to his friend Camden 'in a small show of our ancient love' to correct a few mistakes in the last edition of his *Britannia*: for example, St. Columb in Cornwall was named after St. Columba, virgin and martyr, and not St. Columbanus.[1] He desired his service to be sent to Sir Robert Cotton; he was well spoken of by Carew. Their common devotion to antiquarian studies overrode religious divisions. By this time Roscarrock was out of prison and living in retirement with Lord William Howard at Naworth. It is probable that if his *magnum opus* had seen the light of day, he would have left an altogether more widely-known name as a scholar.

This is by no means the full tale of Cornish gentlefolk who were catholics, let alone those of simpler condition. Surprising as it may seem there were recusant Carews, Peter and William and even Lady Carew were in prison for a time: they were Carews of Haccombe.[2] Robert Becket of Cartuther continued to languish in prison for years; he would not yield and so two-thirds of his property, which was a fair inheritance of £55 p.a., fell to the Crown.[3] We find his son too, Thomas Becket, as a recusant. Their relations, the Pickfords of St. Germans, were Catholics. Edward Pickford went into exile in Spain after the Mayne trial; he was credited with the intention of returning with a party of soldiers to take Sir William Bevil out of his house.[4] In James's reign two young Pickfords were sent to study at Douai, with Peter Nanconan, who became a priest on the English mission, and Victors of Little Petherick who remained faithful to their Arundell allegiance.[5] Richard Humphrey was admitted as a student at the English college at Seville in 1595.[6] The Bawdens too had a connection with Spain. In 1590 commissions were issued from the exchequer to inquire concerning the possessions of Nicholas and William, as fugitives from the realm.[7] Nicholas was heir to his uncle, the vicar of St. Wenn. There was a good deal of litigation, Richard Victor who had married Bawden's sister following the suit on his behalf. On the other side evidence was given that the old vicar did not approve of his nephew's proceedings, that they were 'unthrifts, and he was sorry he had done so much for them'. Apparently he revoked his will in favour of Giles Hambley, and it was held that he had the right to dispose of his property.

[1] Cotton MS. Jul. C. v.   [2] *C.R.S.*, II. 140, 221.   [3] S.P. 12/229, 65.
[4] *Salisbury MSS.*, IV. 259.   [5] *C.R.S.*, X. 66, 132, 146, 288.   [6] ibid., XIV. 18.
[7] Excheq. K.R. Sp. Com. 2864; E 134, 40 Eliz. Easter 36

Among other catholics in Cornwall were John and William Bray of Camborne.[1] An agent of Burghley's travelling in the county in 1591 reported that he had found out some twenty-four recusants, among them Mr. Kemp, who 'hath his farms in the country and is there most part of the year: he is suspected to be a writer unto the enemy. There is a gentlewoman called Mrs. Bray that hath the same liberty: I call these no prisoners.'[2] There was a Scawen of St. Germans removed from the Middle Temple, and afterwards reconciled; a William Phillips of St. Key (sic) in prison in 1592; a Richard Phillips entered Douai in 1610.[3] The Cornish Tremaynes remained faithful, as opposed to the more fortunate and prosperous conformists of Collacombe. A young Thomas Tremayne entered the English college at Rome in February 1599; he died in the heat of August.[4] A cousin of his, John Tremayne of Dorset, son of Sampson Tremayne who had spent many years in prison for the faith, entered the English college in 1614; he took the oath next year, became a Jesuit and died like his cousin in August.[5] As the seventeenth century progresses, so one can watch the effect of the persecution, the penal laws and the financial pressure in the thinning out of the catholic families of Cornwall and the number of students they were able to send abroad to become priests. The tenuous line comes practically to an end by the beginning of the eighteenth century, the continuity of Catholicism in Cornwall broken, save for the Arundells and a few of their tenants and dependants.

From the Pilgrim Book of the English college we derive some further names. Several members of the Trevelyan family paid visits. They lived at Lower Basil in St. Clether, that interesting Elizabethan house with its courtyard and hall still remaining. John Trevelyan was at the college as a guest for a week in 1582, again with his son George in 1583, and for a third time in 1585.[6] It is hardly surprising that in the next generation, in Charles I's reign, a John Trevelyan was the boldest spirit among the Cornish catholics. And so the Trevelyans lost their delightful Lower Basil in that pretty valley, and the Sprys came into possession. As time went on and the first fury of the fight against the Counter-Reformation spent itself, we find Protestants increasingly accepting the hospitality of the English college. In 1632, Peter Edgcumbe was honourably received in the refectory, and in the following years two or three of the Killigrews dined with the fathers there; we find

[1] *Salisbury MSS.*, IV. 274.
[2] S.P. 12/239, 92.
[3] *C.R.S.*, XXII. 107; *Salisbury MSS.*, IV. 274; *C.R.S.*, X. 103.
[4] *R.S.J.*, VI. 206.
[5] ibid., 272.
[6] ibid., 553, 555, 556.

their names along with that of the most distinguished of all their guests, Milton, who requited their hospitality so ungratefully.[1]

In the last years of the reign a profound conflict raged within the ranks of the English catholics at home and abroad, between the secular priests and laity who wished to come to an agreement with the government on the subject of political allegiance, and the Jesuits who were uncompromising, ultramontane and pro-Spanish in their views. The latter were even opposed to religious toleration, for they were afraid that it would lead to a falling away of catholics and alienate Spanish support.[2] The seculars, however, were ready to agree to a form of oath which accepted the Queen's full sovereignty in spite of the papal excommunication.[3] This, with the dying down of the war, led to a decrease of persecution; whenever the war flared up the number of executions increased. But the campaign against the Jesuits went on.

There were two distinguished Cornish Jesuits at the end of the reign, both of whom were captured abroad and brought home to long terms of imprisonment: William Bawden and Edward Coffin.[4] Both were students at Exeter college, who followed the usual course of crossing over to Rheims and then going on to the English college at Rome. After his ordination, Bawden was penitentiary of St. Peter's for a year, but his health was affected by the climate and he was sent to Flanders. Here he became a Jesuit and was for a time professor of moral theology at Louvain. In 1594 he was summoned to Spain. English spies got wind of his journey and he was dogged all the way to St. Omer and Dunkirk; in the Channel he was intercepted, disguised as an Italian merchant, with half a dozen students and brought to England. Nothing could be proved against him, and he was released in exchange for a Hawkins imprisoned in Spain. Recalled to Rome, he was next sent to Brussels as vice-prefect of the English mission. This was a position of great authority and importance, which he occupied for the next ten years: 'the superintendent of all Englishmen', wrote a government agent of him, 'plying himself rather to be a macchiavellian than a good divine, and nothing may be done or permitted without his authority'. He was so zealous and successful that the government proclaimed him a traitor, tried to implicate him in Gunpowder Plot and to have him extradited. In 1610 while travelling past the Palatinate on his way to Rome he was seized by the Elector and handed over to the English. He was sent to the Tower and was in prison altogether for eight years.

[1] *R.S.J.*, VI. 607, 613, 615, 621.]   [2] S.P. 12/262, 28.   [3] ibid., 287, 14.
[4] *D.N.B.* sub William Bawden and Edward Coffin; *R.S.J.*, III.

Then in 1618, as part of James's reparation for Ralegh's last voyage, Bawden was released at Gondomar's request and stayed with him, where he was visited by a great number of persons. At Canterbury on his way abroad he was even received by the King. Rome made him superior of the English college at St. Omer, which he governed with great success for ten years. He was a courtly Jesuit, who had the ear of the Infanta Isabella; under his influence she conferred various privileges upon the English convent at Brussels, who regarded him as their founder. He laid down instructions for them and watched over them; they preserved the tradition of his having been racked in the Tower, which was probable enough. In addition to his executive and administrative abilities, he was a voluminous writer and left a number of manuscript treatises in both Latin and English on devotional subjects.

Edward Coffin was a less important person, except that the circumstance of his capture and examination gives us interesting glimpses of his career.[1] He was born in Cornwall of an old Devon family; his father died when he was a child and he was brought up at school at Liskeard. One of his father's kin, Christopher Turner, a catholic, took him abroad to Rheims. The college being then in straitened circumstances, he was sent to the new Jesuit college at Ingolstadt. Thence he went on to Rome, where he could not stand the summer heat and so went back to Bavaria to be ordained. In 1594 he returned to England, and here was admitted into the Jesuit order. A few years later he was in the Netherlands again and, seized by the Dutch at Lillo, was sent back and lodged in the Tower. Here he spent most of his novitiate, and in all some five years, and was not released until the accession of James I. Returning to Rome, he was for twenty years confessor to the English college; but in the end, desiring to come home to England, he set out for Flanders and died at St. Omer on the way. He too was a writer, though on a smaller scale than Bawden; but he did not publish his works — a defence of celibacy of the priesthood, an account of Bellarmine's death, and various translations.

Truly, the lives of these priests were not without adventure.

Of the laity Tregian remained all this time in the Fleet: we owe some intimate glimpses of his life there to the kindness of the catholic informer, Benjamin Tichborne, whom he nourished unsuspecting. We learn something of the anxieties of that life, of the background of priests coming and going, of their circle of friends; how one day in 1594 Tregian's two men — he lived now in some style there — went out with some of his visitors, but

[1] Hist. MSS. Com., *De L'Isle and Dudley MSS.*, II. 352-3.

they 'had no mass being so scared, but most of them went to confession'.[1] Another day at supper bad news came: 'Tregian looked wonderfully pale, went from the table and called Phillips (his man) into his study'.[2] Tichborne learned from Mrs. Tregian that it was about the taking of the Green Man, who was a seminary priest lately come over; neither Tregian nor Roscarrock would say a word about him. With Tregian's confiding lady Tichborne had the advantage of many conversations, sometimes over a bottle of good Rhenish wine at supper in the Fleet: from which we gather her view that there were as many masses said at court as about London, and that it was a very easy matter for a nobleman to conceal a priest: many did not know how many such there were about them.[3] On Easter Monday she returned from mass with a bottle of holy water; on Whit-Monday she went out to hear mass at a house near Sir Francis Tresham's.[4] The lady was as *dévote* as her husband.

Tichborne gathered other information from one Penwarne, a Cornishman, and from Farther Curry whom he met. He learned that two seminaries had landed in Cornwall last winter and that Tregian's eldest son, Francis, was shortly expected home from abroad.[5] Then comes the most interesting sentence: 'meeting with one Byrd, brother to Byrd of the Chapel, I understand that Mrs. Tregian, Mrs. Charnock and Mrs. Sybil Tregian will be here at the court [at Greenwich] at this day'.[6] This reference gives us a direct link between the Tregian circle and the greatest of English composers. Tichborne's information was accurate: the young Francis Tregian was coming home from Rome, where for the past two years he had been, with Nicholas Baldwin, a gentleman of the household to Cardinal Allen.[7] He was now twenty years old, had been educated at Douai (1586-92) and was skilled in rhetoric and music.[8] It was he who made the funeral oration on Cardinal Allen. Later, when he had succeeded his father in the Fleet for recusancy, he occupied his time compiling the great manuscript, the Fitzwilliam Virginal Book, which contains a large number of Byrd's compositions and is a chief source of our knowledge of Elizabethan key-board music.[9] For that, posterity owes him — and the good fortune of his imprisonment — a great debt. It is evident that the Tregians and Roscarrocks, with their verse-writing and music-making and scholarly tastes, were a cultivated circle. One of the best known of Byrd's compositions, Tregian's Ground, celebrates their name.[10]

[1] S.P. 12/248, 43.   [2] ibid., 83.   [3] ibid., 94, 96, 99.
[4] ibid., 116.   [5] ibid., 105.   [6] ibid., 118.
[7] Knox, *Letters and Memorials of Cardinal Allen*, 376.
[8] Knox, *Douai Diaries*, 213, 240, 246.
[9] Fellowes, *William Byrd*, 204.   [10] Howes, *William Byrd*, 132.

Tregian remained in prison several more years, until in 1601 we find him petitioning on the ground of his sciatica for liberty within five miles of London, returning to the Fleet at night.[1] He had interest at court, and apparently the Queen answered him with 'very gracious speeches and promised to talk with the Council therein'. Lord Hunsdon protested vigorously: Tregian was well known to be 'a most discontented, malicious and practising papist against Queen and state'; he had a son at Rome to negotiate all causes there, his brave buildings in the Fleet and his great housekeeping there showed whence his maintenance came; he had a wife and fair daughters to mediate for him at court.[2] They were successful; he was freed and permitted to live at Chelsea. On the day of his release he was 'enriched with a litter of greyhound whelps, and designed a brace of them' for Cecil, which he presented to him a year later.[3] Tregian was negotiating with the earl of Lincoln for his house at Chelsea, and had many conversations with him, in the course of which he upheld the Infanta's claim to the succession to the English throne.[4] Three years after James's accession he was permitted to go abroad. He passed through Douai on his way to Spain where he was well received by Philip III, who granted him a pension of 60 gold pieces a month and allowed him to live at Lisbon since it was more agreeable to his health. Here he died in 1608, and was buried in the church of St. Roch. Twenty years later his grave was opened and his body found incorrupt: such things are apt to happen in Portugal. So they buried him again, this time upright beneath the pulpit, as a confessor of the faith.

For his estates, — in 1607 Lady Hunsdon sold the younger Francis Tregian her life interest in them for £6500.[5] To raise the money he had resort to his neighbour and tenant, George Spry, in return for which he sold Spry various manors, including Trewithen, which Spry in turn was forced to sell to Ezekiel Grose, a wealthy lawyer and money-lender of Camborne, of exact Protestant opinions.[6] And so Trewithen came apart from the Tregian inheritance, became the chief estate in those parts, has now its Georgian house, a story of its own. The full sum of £6500 was handed over to her ladyship by the young Tregian in Spry's presence at her house in Blackfriars in 1613. Even so he could not maintain his hold upon what remained of the property: his own recusancy finished the family. He died in prison and was succeeded

---

[1] *Salisbury MSS.*, XI. 281.   [2] ibid., 231.   [3] ibid., XII. 248.
[4] S.P. 14/3, f. 77.   [5] Excheq. Spec. Com. 5194, 5 Chas. I.
[6] He would be; cf. the evidence of William Erick of St. Hilary: 'Grose answered that it would never be a good world until all the papists in England were hanged ... I tell you plain that the King and the Prince are both rank papists ... If it were not so why should the King send the Prince over into Spain with the arch-papist of England, the duke of Buckingham?' And more to the same effect, very proper in a Jacobean lawyer and money-lender (Henderson, I. 153).

by his brother Charles, who saw the dispersal of the estate, Spry buying Golden, himself heavily pledged to Grose and the greatest of Cornish money-lenders, Sir Richard Roberts, while various fragments flew off to Boscawens, Hawkins and others. Finally Spry had to make Golden over to Grose, who came into possession and then was buried, where formerly the Tregians had been, in Probus church. It was as it should be: nothing was wanting to make the story complete.

John Arundell had succeeded to his father's responsibilities and the family tradition of recusancy. He was among those confined at Banbury in time of crisis. In 1599 he was ordered to provide two lances and three light-horse furnished with money for their charges. He wrote to Cecil that willing as he was to do what service he could, he was about to appear before the Arch-bishop and was likely to be committed; nor could he furnish the money or raise it on credit, his estate was so low by reason of his mother's living, his 'continual charge in paying the statute and other impositions, and lending £100 on privy seal'.[1] All his armour, enough to arm 100 men, had been taken from him. He begged either liberty to accomplish what was demanded of him, or that he might be committed in or about London, since he had so many suits at law to attend to. At Michaelmas he wrote thanking Cecil for his kindness on his behalf, and willingly agreeing to the Queen's pre-emption of all tin in Devon and Cornwall.[2] On James's accession, he hoped to take advantage of the King's proclamation to 'gentlemen of spirit' to repair into their country, to return to the West.[3] He wrote to Cecil: 'the manifold favours my father and myself have received of your father and yourself encourage me to become a suitor to you by letter, being barred by the fear of breaking my confinement to attend you at the court'. He explained that it was his intention to live at Chideock, now that it was his by the death of his mother, and that he had no purpose to dwell in Cornwall — then, as now, a danger-zone — but only to repair thither sometimes to look into his estate, wherein he had sustained great loss by not being able to do so. It seems that at the death of the Queen, Arundell ceased to pay for a time the large sums due by statute for his recusancy, until a debt of some £480 to the Exchequer had accumulated.[4] It may have been that he hoped, like other catholics, for a change of policy, or at any rate greater leniency in exacting the fines. And in fact he was excused the payment of this sum, and pardoned all penalties to which he was liable for his default: in itself a signal mark of grace. But it was only a temporary relief: after Gunpowder

---

[1] *Salisbury MSS.*, IX. 275.   [2] *Cal. S.P. Dom.*, 1598-1601, 331.
[3] *Salisbury MSS.*, XV. 124.   [4] E 368/521, m. 54.

Plot the system was maintained in all its severity and the Arundells went on paying.

It remains to study the economic consequences of all this, the financial pressure upon catholic families, the process of impoverishment and extinction. Materials exist for a detailed analysis of every county.[1] Here it is only possible to illustrate from Cornwall how the system worked out.

Only the Arundells could afford to pay their regular fine of £260 a year out of their revenues, and it kept them poor. Other, lesser people went to prison for default, and from 1586 two-thirds of their lands and goods were taken into the hands of the Crown during their recusancy, leaving one-third to sustain them in prison or elsewhere. This so much increased the business of the Exchequer, so swelled the sheriff's accounts for the county, that from 1592 a separate Recusants' Roll was started, apart from the great Pipe Roll. It is from these that we can largely trace what happened to Catholic properties. In that year two-thirds of Robert Becket's barton of Cartuther were in the hands of the Crown and leased to John Wingfield for £41 6s. 8d. per annum.[2] So it continued for a number of years. Hannibal Vyvyan rented two-thirds of Tremayne's barton of Tregonan in St. Ewe; Hugh Cuffe another portion of the property. Small properties of Thomas Arundell alias Courtenay and of Trevennor and Nicholas Roscarrock, in both Cornwall and Devon, were in the hands of the Crown. Similar measures had been taken against Elizabeth Hendy of Michaelstow: the Hendys were catholics.[3] Alexander Bradley, gent. of St. Erme, and Christopher Maunsell of Launcells were liable for large sums and their lands and goods were to be seized. Since the latter does not appear again, he must have given in and conformed. Then follows a list of regular recusants: Henry Stephens and his wife, of Linkinhorne; Richard and Mary Hore, of St. Ervan; John Williams, Michael Penvose, John Bennett, all of St. Mawgan; Jane Smith of Blisland, Julian Martin of St. Gennys; William Pickford, late of St. Germans, George Arundell of Breage, Peter John of St. Columb major. Some of these, being men of substance, had paid all or part of their fines; but they could not stay the pace, though they remained obstinately catholic. Upon

[1] These mostly consist of the Recusants' Rolls in the P.R.O. They have been very little studied, though the first of them, that for 1592-3, has been printed in C.R.S., XVIII, and there is a useful treatment of procedure in Ryan and Redstone, *Timperley of Hintlesham*.
[2] C.R.S., XVIII.
[3] cf. Star Chamber 2/26/440, interrogatories 'if Hugh Powell and John Ricard have carried and conveyed the said Hendy's mother and sisters being recusants and indicted thereof from place to place and thereby now remain in unknown places'. John Hendy had been keeper of Tintagel castle; cf. my *Sir Richard Grenville*, 182.

the Dorset roll appear the names of the Arundell family, with a number of their Cornish dependants — Margaret Tremayne, Faith Victor, Dorothy Prideaux — who had taken refuge at Chideock.

Next year, 1593-4, we have a number of new names and properties: lands of Peter Coffin, William Hanne, Elizabeth Arundell, Nicholas Borlase, Digory Trevelyan.[1] In 1596-7, two-thirds of Jane Smith's lands in and around Blisland are in the hands of the Crown.[2] Next year, another small property of Nicholas Borlase's is attached.[3] In 1601 John More of Launceston is convicted: apparently he conformed.[4] It is interesting to find Robert Becket's nephew and heir, John, trying to save the family estate by leasing the forfeited part of it, with another man to help him, at an increased rent. But next year there was a renewed drive against them and further lands of Becket's were seized.[5] They could not stay the pace: in 1603, the year of his obstinate uncle's death, John Becket was outlawed for debt in both Exeter and London.[6] They had to let go, and Beckets ceased to rule at Cartuther. They were cousins of the Pickfords and Hannes, those other recusants.

The government was very hard pressed for money at this time, and in 1602 a renewed drive brings more names and properties into the net: all the Kemps of St. Minver, six in number, three Hodges of the same, Henry Bishop of Little Petherick; further lands of Trevennor Roscarrock and Thomas Arundell. In 1603, with the Puritan Sir Anthony Rowse as sheriff, pressure is increased.[7] A full muster of recusants convicted in large sums appears: Thomas Arundell and his wife, George Trevelyan of St. Cleer and his wife, Mary Tom of Little Petherick, Jane Slade of Menheniot, perhaps a dozen new names in addition to the old ones and their wives now brought in. That was the last year of the reign, and for the moment with James's accession matters rested where they were. Then in 1604-5 there was a further round-up, a number of new names being added: Denis Westcott, John Howell, Thomas Hore of St. Columb major, Drugo Warne of St. Issey, George Mawpower of Withiel, and others.[8] Lastly, in the year 1606, after Gunpowder Plot, the list reaches its greatest extent: besides the old names are Warnes and Arthurs of St. Issey, Pearses of St. Columb minor, Harrys and Trewekes of Perran-ar-worthal, Minnows of Feock, Winters of Gwennap, Duncalses of Gunwallo, Retallacks and Michells of St. Columb major, Manfields and Blakes of Padstow, a Spry of Quethiock and even the wife of a former sheriff, Sir William Wray.[9]

It is evident that there was a good deal of Catholicism, and even recusancy,

---

[1] E 377/2.   [2] ibid., 5.   [3] ibid., 6.   [4] ibid., 9.   [5] ibid., 10.
[6] Excheq. Spec. Com. 5485.   [7] E 377/11.   [8] ibid., 13.   [9] ibid., 14.

lurking about in Cornish parishes. But what is no less evident is that the parishes chiefly affected were those where the Arundell estates were concentrated. Far the greater number of recusants were to be found in parishes like St. Columb major, St. Columb minor, St. Mawgan, St. Ervan, St. Issey, where they held a great deal of land. Even the Duncalse family of Gunwallo were almost certainly tenants of their great manor of Winnianton. The ordinary fool — so characteristic of life — simply followed in these matters the ways of his master. It may not have been even that the Arundells favoured catholics for tenants, though they were certainly considerate of them when they were. For instance, Peter John of St. Columb, who had to pay heavily for his recusancy, was given some property by John Arundell — not to much avail, since two-thirds of it were soon in the hands of the Crown.[1] Then, too, the Arundells employed catholics for their stewards. We find John Arundell writing to Cecil in 1602 on behalf of Richard Tremayne and Henry Stephens, who stood bound to appear at the next assize.[2] He begged the Council's letters to the judges not to convict them, since they were no meddlers, but men of good carriage; the Queen had already enjoyed for fourteen years Tremayne's living, while the other had nothing to lose but Arundell's service. These two had the whole charge of his estate.

From this we may gather that the authorities were not above making exceptions in some cases; there were gaps in the execution of the law, sometimes a measure of leniency made a hole in its severity,[3] or there were dodges to evade its full force. Nicholas Borlase, for instance, two-thirds of whose property were in the hands of the Crown, passed to his brother-in-law the remainder and went to live with him, with his family of ten or eleven, for their maintenance.[4] They all resided together at Treluddro, and it was very difficult to say that any of the goods and chattels were his or to bring home to him any further fines for recusancy. When another conviction was brought against him, the jury found that he had no goods or chattels. When they knew that Exchequer commissions were on the way, it seems that recusants disposed of what goods they could beforehand.

Nevertheless, the burden was too heavy to be borne. We have an illuminating example of how catholics gave way and conformed from a long entry in the Memoranda Roll for 1639.[5] Thomas Arundell alias Courtenay, of Clerkenwell and St. Breoke, remained a recusant all his life; there were numerous convictions against him. He died in 1632 and was buried with his

<hr>

[1] E 377/15.
[2] *Salisbury MSS.*, XII. 210.
[3] cf. the government's clemency to Thomas Smith of St. Germans in 1587, S.P. 12/202, 57.
[4] E 134, 12 James I, Easter 8.
[5] E 368/649, m. 238.

ancestors at St. Columb. Shortly after, his son conformed and received the Sacrament according to the statute. The bishop of Exeter gave his certificate of having seen him at service at St. Breoke, and after at St. Goran, and 'this very day I can testify for him that he was at the sermon in the church of St. Peter in Exeter, and yesterday at the said cathedral at divine service, so as he hath given full assurance of his perfect conformity to the religion established'. In consequence, his father's properties were restored to him, and he was exonerated from all debts for recusancy upon them. That was how it was done. All the same we notice, not without a certain pathos, that the son goes away from the old home to start anew at Goran.

So these families conformed or came to an end. The Beckets of Cartuther, the Trevelyans of St. Clether, the Borlases of Newlyn are no more — any more than Hardy's Turbervilles. Only the Tremaynes have survived, at Heligan; and though they carried on their Catholicism a good way into the seventeenth century, in the end they conformed, and came even to own the tithes of St. Austell. The Tregians are farmers where once they owned the land; the only Bawden I have known in Cornwall was a steeple-jack, the only Becket a library-assistant. Even the Arundells have long left the county, and Lanherne is no longer theirs.

CHAPTER XV

DEFENCE AND WAR, 1569–1603

Two exciting events marked the end of the Anglo-Spanish alliance which, in spite of the Queen's deviation from the faith, subsisted for the first ten years of the reign: these were the action at San Juan de Ulloa and the seizure of the Spanish treasure in the western ports. In the first, Philip's viceroy had fired upon the Queen's officer, John Hawkins, in a Spanish port when sailing under her flag upon an expedition in which she had invested. When, in December 1568, William Hawkins at Plymouth heard a rumour that his brother had been killed, he at once wrote to Cecil desiring that the treasure on board the Spanish ships, which had taken refuge from French rovers in Saltash and Fowey, should be seized.[1] This treasure amounted to some £400,000 and was in fact a loan from Genoese bankers intended to pay Alva's troops in the Netherlands.

Since Cecil was at that moment engaged in a life and death struggle with all the conservative and catholic forces gathered round Mary Stuart and Norfolk, backed by Philip, he hardly needed the suggestion. And in fact his letters went down to the west country ordering his trusty instruments, Champernowne and Killigrew, 'under colour of friendship' to 'use all policy' to acquire the treasure for the Queen.[2] Champernowne reported his activity in the matter with a smack of self-satisfaction. Fowey being outside his liberties he had sent down for order to be taken, while he himself took in hand the two barks at Saltash laden with 65 chests containing 600,000 ducats. He persuaded the Spaniards not to depart till the French who were lying in wait for them had gone, 'that it might well appear unto them how careful her grace is in giving of order for their safeguard'. The Spaniards were duly grateful. Meanwhile Champernowne was of the opinion, 'great pity it were that such a booty should escape her grace'; and since the treasure at Fowey was easier to take than that at Saltash, he wished to have Mr. Treffry joined with him in commission, 'who will be both ready and willing'. Otherwise he would himself enterprise that at Saltash, leaving the French admiral to attempt the other at Fowey.

The government had no intention of allowing any part of the treasure to escape them, and there were landed at Saltash 'three score and four cases of reals of plate and out of two pinnaces that lay at Fowey thirty-two cases of

[1] S.P. 12/48, 50.   [2] ibid., 60.

reals of plate, every of which cases doth contain as the Spaniards inform about the number of 20,000 of the said reals'.[1] The Saltash treasure was taken to the town hall at Plymouth where it was sealed and guarded. At Fowey the unlading was 'done by the Spaniards and by themselves carried to the house of Mr. John Treffry and there locked and sealed with their seals and ours, and four or six of the Spaniards with some of our men with watch guarding the same did so remain until her grace's commandment of the general stay'.[2] The proceedings there are described in detail: how every case was opened in the presence of the Spaniards, the officers and the honest merchants of the town, each bag taken out and weighed by merchant beam, then numbered and the contents entered in a book before it was taken up and safely stowed in the house at Place. What a spectacle it must have been for the good townsmen of Fowey! Some £50 were assigned for keeping the sailors and paying their debts for meat and drink in the town.

By this the Netherlands government had answered with an embargo upon English shipping, to which the reply was a general stay of all Spanish ships in English ports. Those in Devon and Cornwall were estimated to be worth £40,000. At Falmouth there was a Flemish hulk of 140 tons, laden with sugar, molasses, canary wine, and 5000 odd reals of plate; a Spaniard of 80 tons laden with figs, and a Portuguese of 50 tons laden with sugar and some silver plate. The Cornish commissioners proceeded to argue the case against Alva, whose embargo enabled the English government to annex the treasure and at the same time keep themselves right with international morality. Killigrew and Treffry professed to believe that the money belonged to 'the bishop of Rome's clergy' and 'should not appertain unto the King'.

In the midst of these enchantments arrived the remnants of Hawkins' expedition, Francis Drake with the *Judith* at Plymouth[3] and Hawkins with the *Minion* in Mountsbay, many of his men dead, the rest starving, the ship in a hopeless condition unable to move farther. It was from here, January 25th, 1569, that he wrote his letter to the Queen, with its moving ending: 'All is lost, save only honour'.[4] William Hawkins heard of his arrival and of his terrible straits not from him or any of his company, but from one of the Mount.[5] He at once sent down a bark with men, fresh victuals, cables and tackle to enable him to get to Plymouth.

Next day Champernowne set out from Plymouth with the treasure on the way to the Tower, attended with fifty horse and fifty foot and artillery for its protection. And so trundling along the highroad to London it passes out of our picture. The English government had greatly got the better in the ex-

[1] ibid., 12/49, 1. [2] ibid., 30. [3] ibid., 36. [4] ibid., 40. [5] ibid., 42.

change of embargoes and by the seizure of the treasure. The Hawkinses were amply avenged. But that was the starting-point of a new age of Anglo-Spanish enmity in place of the old amity. It is symptomatic that at once we observe a greater activity than hitherto in all matters of defence – taking of musters, provisioning forts, preparing beacons – the machinery of which had rather lapsed during the long peace. There was some danger of war, still more of Spanish reprisals. William Hawkins reported the poor state of Plymouth, unable to provide 2 cwt. of powder of itself 'without a collection among ourselves'.[1] The government sent down artillery and stores for Pendennis – it could well afford to now with what should have gone to supply Alva's troops. The captain, John Killigrew, received a gun 'complete with slivers of brass', two culverins, two demi-culverins, two sacres, with powder and shot, a quantity of bows and arrows, bills and pikes.[2]

Musters were ordered to be taken throughout the country, Godolphin and Arundell being at the head of the commission for Cornwall.[3] As the result of their efforts a complete volume was compiled, containing the muster-books for the county parish by parish.[4] The number of men returned, they wrote, was greater than in any previous certificate, due to their having abled their own servants and those of all other gentlemen fit to be abled: 'the residue being the common sort are (in effect) all husbandmen, tinners and fishers upon whose daily labours the relief of this poor country dependeth and also the defence of the same when need shall require'. They found great want of good armour and weapons; the people were very willing to be better furnished, but were for 'the most part in such extreme poverty, grown by a late general loss of cattle, horses and sheep (the like whereof by a great part hath not been seen nor heard of in this shire within the memory of man)' that they were unable to provide themselves with armour. They thought good to provide for sending down 500 corselets, 200 calivers, 500 bows and sheaves of arrows, which the county would pay for within a month of arrival. There follow the detailed returns: Walter Carlyon of St. Blazey has a bow, 12 arrows and a jack, William Sawle of Luxulyan a corselet, an almain rivet, a pike and a bill; the best armed man was John Treffry, who had a light horse, 2 pair of corselets, 10 pair of almain rivets, 20 pikes, 4 long bows, 4 sheaves of arrows, 3 harquebuses and 3 halberds: evidently a well-armed household for the defence of Fowey.

All this activity required money and the government was forced next year to resort to privy seals for loans from private citizens. For the sheriff, Peter Edgcumbe, returning the names of suitable recipients was an ungrateful task:

---

[1] S.P. 12/49, 37.   [2] ibid., 74.   [3] ibid., 51, 1, 3.   [4] ibid., 52, 2.

'Your honour knoweth how unthankful an office it is to persuade the greater number to depart with moneys much more to prefer them' — except in so far as it gave opportunity for getting himself and his friends off, and placing the burden upon those of whom he disapproved. [1] Of these there were two classes: 'divers of meaner calling who are of great wealth and may spare very well, by reason of their great usury and not charged any way to serve the prince'. (Edgcumbe as a gentleman, engaged up to the hilt in mining speculations, could hardly regard such townspeople with any charity.) Secondly, 'there be divers papists of great wealth whose moneys will better serve the Queen's majesty than their hollow hearts; for it were better their moneys were in her Highness' custody than their heads to be troubled with the superfluity thereof'. The bearer was to give Cecil their names.

There can be no doubt what names he gave, for shortly afterwards we find a tart letter from Edward Arundell to Edgcumbe on behalf of Lady Arundell saying that 'her ladyship doth very well know that my brother, Sir John Arundell, hath taken order for the payment of £100 to the Queen's majesty's use upon receipt of her grace's privy seal. And that she is assured my said brother is furnished either with ready payment, or with sufficient discharge to be showed or paid, being required at his hand by such as have authority. And thus I leave you in haste.' [2] Such cold formality between cousins, underneath which resentment burns, shows how far the breach between the Arundells and the rest over religion had gone: on one side jealousy, on the other a lofty contempt. At the same time Edgcumbe begged release from his privy seal for himself and for his friends, Mr. Milliton, Mr. Bevil and Mr. Killigrew, on account of the 'vehement burdens' lying upon them. [3] In their place he sent the names of six persons 'such as may very well spare that which may be lacking in this behalf'.

It is only possible here to sketch the development of the system of defensive fortifications in the west which marked the period. In the Middle Ages, upon the coast there was only the Mount and the defences of Fowey. Henry VIII added St. Mawes and Pendennis castles to guard Falmouth haven. The French war of Edward VI gave the impulse to fortify the Scilly Isles, at the same time as the government made an agreement with the town of Plymouth to fortify St. Nicholas' Island. [4] The town was very remiss in starting the work, but at length with the aid of the government's admonitions and financial help it was done, and the custody of the little fort was committed to the mayor and the town. In this duty the long years of peace, and perhaps restricted

[1] ibid., 12/52, 67, 62.   [2] ibid., 73, 9.   [3] ibid., 27.   [4] ibid., 10/6, 24.

resources, made them negligent. When war came, the government had to take away its charge from the citizens; defence was increasingly professionalized everywhere, and a military man, Ferdinando Gorges, was appointed first governor of the fort built on the mainland, with charge of the island.[1] This led to a bitter, if now rather comic, quarrel with the town authorities: a typical Elizabethan conflict of jurisdictions which Gorges's successor, Sir John Gilbert, inherited. In Cornwall there was no such trouble: no town was sufficiently large to stake out an independent claim. The chief difficulties were the shortcomings or the misdemeanours of the Crown's representatives.

In 1547 Lord Admiral Seymour went from the Mount to Scilly to view the ground:[2] charges in connection with Scilly, piracy and what not, formed part of the accusations which led to his execution. In the succeeding years the work went forward and a great deal of money was spent, under John Killigrew's supervision. He was to 'make the fort in our lady's isle at Scilly upon the little hill betwixt fresh water and St. Mary's Road . . . and to set the new house without the fort near unto the fresh water and in the end thereof a horse mill for victualling'.[3] There seem to have been two works in Scilly at this time, the fort upon St. Mary's of which Thomas Godolphin was captain, and another upon Tresco in charge of one Guy. Under Mary the latter got into trouble and was removed.[4] Having the protection of the Spanish alliance she was anxious to cut down charges: Scilly had a garrison of 150 men; so John Grenville was sent to survey the works and report on them. To that we owe the beautifully written survey of his now in the British Museum.[5] He was to allot 30 men to garrison Tresco, while Guy was removed to Agnes. When Mary died, the wages of the men were several months in arrear — it may be wondered how they supported themselves upon those small islands; Elizabeth was glad to accept Sir William Godolphin's offer to farm them.[6] And so began the long association of the Godolphin family with Scilly which came to an end only in the last century.

At first there were some difficulties with the Berkeleys who claimed the title. Francis Godolphin wrote that the isles were nothing but a 'bushment of briars and a refuge for pirates' before King Edward bestowed his charges upon fortifications and maintaining a guard, whereby 'by erecting houses and manuring the place had been made more beneficial'.[7] Still it yielded little profit, the tenants being all free tenants, and shipwrecks in all the time of his captaincy yielding no more than £20. Godolphin held on, and, a reliable and public-spirited man, had the confidence of the government; by the end

---

[1] S.P. 12/256, 114.   [2] ibid., 10/1, 37.   [3] A.P.C., III. 282.   [4] ibid., IV. 12, 18, 24.
[5] Add. MS. 25, 300.   [6] A.P.C., VII. 33.   [7] S.P. 12/122, 23.

of the reign, after the departure of Sir Richard Grenville for wider horizons, he was the leading spirit, and the most trusted, in county affairs. The defence of the islands was left to his responsibility; ordnance and ammunition were provided him from the Tower — for which he was charged and held responsible.[1] He was given the right to impress his own tenants and servants to defend the islands in time of war, and licence to provision them from Cornwall at the Queen's prices. The system arrived at worked satisfactorily: under Godolphin there were no, or few, complaints. During the war it became an important strategical outpost, whence watch was kept upon movements at sea and the first news came of ships approaching the Channel. In the last years of the war when the Spaniards were intrenched in Brittany and the fortifications in the west were extended, a new and bigger fort was built upon the hill at St. Mary's commanding the roadstead, and its custody committed to Godolphin's son.[2]

The personal history of St. Mawes and Pendennis was chequered. Of the former, the first captain, Thomas Treffry, was removed on Mary's accession: he was a notorious Protestant; his place was taken by Thomas Arundell.[3] He was succeeded by Justinian Talkarne, who ultimately came to grief, like his colleagues across the water at Pendennis, through his questionable dealings with pirates.[4] Hannibal Vyvyan took his place and he proved trustworthy. The first John Killigrew, captain of Pendennis, got into trouble under Mary, but kept his office upon giving a bond of £1000 to keep the castle with 'all his power, cunning and industry'.[5] Later we find him and his son in the Fleet prison for an action against a Spanish ship.[6] But still he kept his charge in spite of the privateering activities of his Protestant family in the Channel. His son, Sir John, maintained his keepership for life, though he got more and more deeply involved financially and was hand in glove with the pirates who frequented Helford. At the end there was a grave scandal, an open attack upon a Spanish ship in harbour by his servants, from the consequences of which not all his high connections at Court could save him.[7] His son inherited an already embarrassed position, which went from bad to worse; his debts dragged him down, he squeezed and oppressed his tenants and small men lawlessly, he continued the association with the Helford pirates. He ended up in the Gatehouse and his place was taken by Sir Nicholas Parker, a professional soldier, who proceeded to root himself in the county by marrying an Erisey.

The earlier, medieval castles were of not much importance from the point

---

[1] ibid., 74, 48.   [2] ibid., 262, 92.   [3] A.P.C., IV. 372.   [4] ibid., XIV. 318.
[5] ibid., v. 12.   [6] ibid., 294, 307.   [7] v. my Sir Richard Grenville, 164-8.

of view of the sea-war with Spain, though we find Grenville agitating about the keepership of Tintagel, in the hands of John Hendy, a catholic, and pressing his cousin George Grenville for the position. [1]

The equipment of Menendez's fleet at Santander in 1574, with its uncertain objective, sent a preliminary tremor through the west country, as if it might have been an anticipation of 1588. The alarm passed, and in fact the outstanding disputes between England and Spain were regulated by the Convention of Bristol. But the government were taking no risks, and Bedford was sent down as Lieutenant to the west — a position in which he succeeded his father — to survey the defences. He was met by Sir John Arundell and the leading J.P.s, who accompanied him to Fowey and then to Falmouth. [2] At Pendennis the gun-platform was 'much decayed and almost unserviceable'. He went as far as the Mount, and returning, assembled the J.P.s to give them the government's instructions, as to which he found them 'very ready and serviceable in all things'. He sent two barks to sea 'to discover this navy; but have heard nothing of them'. On his return the Council sent a letter of thanks to the leading gentlemen for 'their forwardness, diligence and good conformity to the Queen's service'. [3]

At the same time Bedford had been charged with the levy of 1000 men from the western counties for service in Ireland. [4] This is a first indication of a theme which becomes monotonously regular in later years, with the enormous task undertaken by Elizabeth's government, with inadequate resources, to subjugate Ireland. War, and of a very fearful character, accompanied by disease and famine and mutual cruelties, became endemic there; Ireland was for twenty years one of the chief battlefields in which the struggle with Spain was fought out. It cost the government sums of money which were all but ruinous to the stability of its finances; it swallowed up successive harvests of men; the war seemed never-ending; it sickened the Queen. A totally disproportionate burden fell upon the western counties, especially considering that they were in the front liｎe in the sea-war, and also had to supply some levies for the war in Normandy and Brittany. Still, the western counties, with Wales, Lancashire and Cheshire, were the most conveniently situated to supply Ireland with men and provisions, and the great bulk went from western ports from Chester to Plymouth. Padstow and Barnstaple became increasingly used for this purpose, and at the end of the reign a system of fast posts was organized from Ireland via Padstow to Exeter and London.

In this year, 1574, Cornwall was to provide 100 men, of whom 64 were

---

[1] v. my *Sir Richard Grenville*, 181-2.   [2] Lansdowne MS. 18/93.
[3] *A.P.C.*, VIII. 304.   [4] Add. MS. 5754/133.

armed with pikes, 18 with bows and 18 with bills; Devon 300, Somerset 150, Dorset 100. [1] In 1578, Cornwall had to provide 200, Devon 400, Somerset 300, Dorset 100, Wales north and south 1000. [2] Next year, upon the landing of James Fitzmaurice of Desmond to stir up a quasi-national revolt, another 1000 men were called for from the four western counties: 200 from Cornwall, 400 from Devon to be embarked at Barnstaple for Cork or Waterford. [3] A boat was to be laid at one of these western ports, and posts laid thence to Exeter for speedy communication between the Council and the authorities in Ireland. Next year again, 1580, 100 men were called for from Cornwall, to be embarked at Padstow or Ilfracombe. The J.P.s, with Grenville at their head, felt bound to register a protest: 'it hath pleased her Majesty to take knowledge of the late charge our county was at in sending 200 men into Ireland, whereby this little shire has been greatly charged and unfurnished of weapon and armour; so taking 100 more will leave us bare for defence of the sea-coasts', and not knowing where to turn for money to refurnish the same. [4] The government could not help itself: the great Desmond rebellion had broken out, all Munster was in a flame. The new Lord Deputy was promised 200 men from Cornwall, 200 from Devon, and licence was given for transporting 200 quarters of wheat from the two counties. [5] Next year 100 men went from each. [6] After that, with the extinguishing of the Desmond rebellion, there came a respite from that service — though Devon and Cornwall were now occupied with more urgent attentions upon their own doorstep. Then in the last years of the reign, with renewed rebellion in Ireland, the unpleasant necessity was clamped down again, and large numbers were dispatched from the west. Back too from the indescribable condition of chaos that prevailed in that unhappy country came crowds of deserters and vagrants. No wonder Carew waxed so indignant on the subject: a good, responsible J.P.'s point of view. The Irish war was a great drain.

In the seventies the government made a determined effort to improve, like everything else through the machinery of the J.P.s, the system of home defence. Year by year progress was made in organization; bit by bit more professional standards introduced, experienced military men sent down as muster-masters to train the men, and more up to date weapons provided. The expenses, of course, were met by the county. From 1572 we have a return from the Cornish hundreds which shows that practically all the men were armed with bills and bows. [7] The hundred of Powder, which was the

---

[1] S.P. 12/95, 68.   [2] *A.P.C.*, x. 240.   [3] ibid., xi. 219, 224, 230.
[4] S.P. 12/140, 21.   [5] *A.P.C.*, xii. 106, 227.   [6] ibid., xiii. 45.
[7] S.P. 12/89, 34, 41, 43-5.

largest and wealthiest, had 1008 able men, of whom only 46 were armed with corselets and pikes; in Pydar, of 575 able men, only 8. Each hundred had two or three chief captains, and from six to ten captains: all naturally drawn from the gentry. The idea was to select a certain number for training: for 1573-74, out of a total of 6800 for Cornwall, some 400; out of 10,000 for Devon, some 2000, 'to be trained as the county may bear the charges'.[1] These for comparative figures. As for armour, in 1577 there were 3988 longbows, 2973 sheaves of arrows, 571 morions, 260 pikes, 27 black bills and halberds.[2] There were only 6 demi-lances, 29 light horsemen with corselets and 43 furnished otherwise. Those would be the gentry; but indeed there was a great lack of horses, it was the constant refrain of replies from the J.P.s to the Council: the county simply did not grow them. ·There were 2585 able men unfurnished.

That year 200 soldiers were to be levied and trained; exercises were ordered to begin on the eve of St. George's day and to end on St. Mark's day.[3] The county was divided into four parts, with a trainer to train 50 men in each; though 'in truth we find the country very much destitute of men of good service and much unprovided of furniture for this service'. That was the state of affairs to be remedied as time went on. The county was poor, but every commissioner of musters would contribute £1, and the rest raised from the gentlemen of wealth, the whole charge being estimated at £400. Later that summer came orders for general musters to be held. The J.P.s kept the order till after harvest, which was followed by the plague, 'very great in divers places in this shire'.[4] So musters were put off, and instead the constables ordered to view their men parish by parish. Next year, the plague 'doth still continue, but (god be thanked) not so vehement, so as thereby the numbers of our able men are greatly reduced'.[5] The total of able men for the county was now 7043, of whom 1971 were furnished, 2585 unfurnished; 2160 were pioners and labourers, 2175 selected men.

Great efforts were made to improve the position, in training, weapons and dispositions. By 1580 there were 4000 selected men; 2000 appointed for supply into Devon in case of need, and three companies of 100 for Pendennis, St. Mawes and the Mount.[6] There were four generals, Grenville at the head. A new system of training was then being instituted. Instead of two days twice in the year, by which the men profited little, they were to be trained ten times in the year by captains travelling from one group of three parishes to another.[7] More efficient, less chargeable. The muster-master

---

[1] S.P. 12/99, 56. [2] ibid., 104. [3] ibid., 112, 22. [4] ibid., 115, 26.
[5] ibid., 123, 22. [6] ibid., 138, 5, 6. [7] ibid., 140, 22.

appointed for the county was Captain Dowdall. In 1584, on the eve of war, when Captain Horde was sent down to view the trained bands he still found 'the country much unfurnished of serviceable armour, but the people very willing to have it supplied, not respecting any reasonable charge, so it might be had for money'.[1] There were all sorts of minor difficulties, like the right exercised by John Killigrew to muster the five parishes around Pendennis and command them for the castle's defence.[2] The practice had been discontinued, and on its revival with the approach of war, its exercise led to loud complaints from the surrounding country: the townsmen of Penryn feared that it would leave their precious town uncovered, and others complained of Killigrew making excessive demands upon them. Not unlikely. Then there was the major complication of the Stannaries, which had the right to muster separately. This led to great rows in Devon, where many people took the opportunity to evade their obligation by claiming the privilege of the stannary. In Cornwall the difficulty was solved, from 1585 with the war beginning, by appointing Ralegh, already Warden of the Stannaries, as Lord Lieutenant, and so combining both jurisdictions.

The growing international instability led to increasingly disturbed conditions at sea. The revolt of the Netherlands against Philip was the beginning of Dutch sea-power, and many privateers, English as well as Dutch, sailed the seas preying upon shipping under the licence of the Prince of Orange. Others sailed under letters of marque from Huguenot Rochelle or the Prince of Condé. There was a silent league of amity between Protestant Plymouth and Huguenot Rochelle, and much coming and going between the two.[3] In 1569 Philip Budockshide played a beautiful trick upon a number of Barbary hulks, Flemings subject to the King of Spain, in Plymouth Sound.[4] They were a strong force, but he went out to them flying the Queen's flag and persuaded them to submit on the ground of the stay of shipping, saying that they could not escape the Queen's ships waiting outside for them anyway. Which they did. He then placed four men aboard each of them and brought them into Saltash water, where that night they were rifled. They had a goodly cargo of sugar, molasses and chests of ostrich feathers. Three of the hulks Budockshide carried over to Rochelle: the last we hear of him is from someone who 'saw him ride in Charles du bois with a hulk or two in his company'.[5] Around this mass of privateering — actually Budockshide sailed under

[1] ibid., 171, 8.   [2] ibid., 185, 54.
[3] The Hawkinses gave substantial help to Rochelle when besieged in 1573. Williamson, *Sir John Hawkins*, 275–9.
[4] H.C.A. 13/16.   [5] H.C.A. Exams. 17.

licence from the Prince of Condé — there was a wide margin of plain piracy. Privateering was more the concern of the gentry and shipping families like the Hawkinses; piracy was the occupation of poorer men, shadier figures. Often enough one merged into the other, and it was difficult to tell under which heading some exploits came. Hence the cases in the court of admiralty, that came before the Council, that troubled the wits, if not the consciences, of the local J.P.s. In the grimy file of admiralty indictments remaining for 1575-77, almost half the cases are of piracies committed round the Cornish coast or by Cornish pirates.[1] Impossible to go into much detail over what remains: think how numerous they would be if the records survived in full!

The government did what it could in the matter; it was always out to check, and if possible suppress, piracy. The trouble was that so many of the local gentry upon whom they had to rely as instruments were hand in glove with the pirates and friendly receivers of their goods. In 1564 Sir Peter Carew and Sir John Chichester were sent down to view the coasts of Devon and Cornwall and to inquire concerning certain piracies and their perpetrators.[2] Next year two commissions of piracy were appointed for these counties in a determined attempt to enforce order. Reynold Mohun brought a formidable list of charges against Sir William Godolphin and the Killigrews, which were to be investigated by Carew: it does not follow that they were true or that they were not capable of explanation.[3] A relative of Chichester's went to the seas from Penryn on Shrove Tuesday 1569 in a bark of fifty tons with fifty men aboard.[4] He had with him Richard Reskymer and Richard Bevill of Budock, gentlemen. They lay about Scilly for a while, then came into Mounts Bay. Off Beachy Head they met a French ship laden with coals, 'which in some part they lightened of her lading'. William Hawkins, head of the family shipping business at Plymouth, was several times in trouble over the doings of his ships — once along with Grenville over the *Castle of Comfort* which they jointly owned.[5] Martin Frobisher made his début in Cornwall, along with his brother and Richard Erisey, which caused the first two to be landed in Launceston gaol: all three were summoned before the Council.[6]

The state of affairs became deplorable in the later seventies with the activities round our coasts of Captain Hicks of Saltash, Diggory Piper gent. of Launceston, William Batts of Cardiff and Saltash, John Callice of Tintern. In 1577, sailing in a Danish ship, the *Red Lion*, Hicks had a succession of good catches off Cape Finisterre, the coast of Portugal, and in the Bay of Biscay.[7]

[1] H.C.A. 1/2.   [2] *A.P.C.*, VII. 202.   [3] ibid., 225, 292.   [4] H.C.A. 1/39.
[5] H.C.A. Exams. 22.   [6] *A.P.C.*, VII. 153.   [7] H.C.A. 1/2.

Next year, sailing with a Dutchman in the *Flying Hart*, he continued his depredations off the coasts of Brittany and Portugal, coming into Cawsand Bay where John Callice then lay with twenty men aboard.[1] William Batts of Saltash sailed from his home port in his own ship, the *William Bonaventure* (indeed!), under licence from the King of Navarre. Off Ushant he took a French ship with a cargo of Newfoundland fish, a Norman laden with Guinea grains and elephants' teeth, and straightway 'fell into the lap of her Majesty's ships under the charge of George Winter esquire'. The situation had got so bad that the government had had to equip a squadron to clear the seas. Batts was charged with having taken a Biscayan, the *Maria Concepcion* of Allaredo, laden with Spanish wools for Dunkirk in St. Mary's Roads at Scilly. But this seems to have been Callice's doing, who got a large haul of 200 sacks worth £2000 thereby; Batts merely received some 16 or 20 of them 'upon his bill to pay for the same', so he said.

Disturbing as such proceedings were to good order, they are not without their attractive side in the depositions of the mariners, the adventures they recall. Here is a Cornish merchant, Edward Rowe of Tregony, travelling back from San Lucar with Andrew Fownes of Plymouth, in a ship laden with the latter's goods.[2] Thwart of Start they were attacked by three Flushingers, and both Rowe and Fownes wounded by caliver shot – in the right shoulder, it is pleasant to record. The Flushingers 'searched also with candlelight every corner of the same ship and left not the same night nor day until they came thwart of Flushing. And as they passed from one ship to another the reals of plate shed and dropped out of their sleeves . . . The mariners of the said ships which were left on board the *Minion* . . . did play at dice and cards for Spanish reals, of iv and ii the piece, being of the money gotten in the said ship.' The poor Englishmen they spoiled of their clothes and gunpowder and two popinjays.

Upon the coast there was not only the receiving of pirates' goods, a temptation which no one could resist, but also the profits from wrecks. In 1575 some Spanish ships were driven in by tempest upon the rocks of Stonehouse: the spoil came mainly into the tenacious hands of Mistress Edgcumbe, her husband being away.[3] The vice-admiral of Devon was ordered to sequester the goods to the benefit of the owners. Mrs. Edgcumbe utterly refused to give them up, 'and hath otherwise misused herself by disobeying the commission, and since the coming home of her husband hath been by him maintained in her ill-doings'.[4] He was commanded to restore the goods and to appear before the Council. At the end of 1577 the Council made a

[1] ibid., 1/40.   [2] ibid., 13/22.   [3] *A.P.C.*, IX. 27.   [4] ibid., 42.

drive to rout out offenders in these ways; instructions were sent to the commissioners of piracy to inquire and make a return of them.[1] Only it happened that Sir John Killigrew was at the head of the commission. No reply was forthcoming. The Council sent down a stern rebuke. But the rest of the commissioners had never heard from Sir John and 'by reason of the long keeping of the said commission from us by the said Sir John Killigrew, who first received the same, we could not do our duties'.[2] They had to proceed without him.

Nor was that surprising; for when at length the return was made, Peter Killigrew appears as one of the chief offenders.[3] When Captain Fenner came from Rochelle to grave his ship at Helford — the chief resort of such persons—he had desired Killigrew 'for the lighting of his ship to lend him the key of his cellar; and before his departure . . . he had of the gift of the said Fenner 500 of newland fish'. A nice way of putting it: in fact he was engaged in aiding and provisioning his friends, the sea-rovers: it was a business. When Captain Hicks was at Helford, Killigrew had supplied him with beeves, in return for which he had two tons of iron horseshoes, some hogsheads of wine, and thirty or forty sacks of rye.[4] He declared that for the iron he had since satisfied the Spanish, and for the wine the French, owner. The horseshoes he sold to Thomas Davy of Truro, merchant, who was a receiver of such goods on his own account: he had had a fardel of white narrow cloth from Thomas Lower, brother to the vice-admiral, 'from whence Lower had the cloth he knoweth not'. Captain Fenner had also sent Justinian Talkarne 200 of his newland fish, while Talkarne's cellar at St. Mawes housed the iron horseshoes for Davy. One sees the sort of mutual services performed between those at sea and the coast-dwellers. Quite a number of names among the latter were brought to light: John Tregose of Trewotheck had had hogsheads of wine from Robert Hicks, while Hicks's wife and two other women came to his house from Saltash and he sent them back in his boat. Other receivers of Hicks's wine were Walter and John Rashleigh of Manaccan; William Bawden, tailor there, had had fifty Caen stones and 5 cwt. of plaster of Paris 'for to make millstones' from Captain Callice, and some Scottish cloth of Captain Court. Altogether a score of persons were brought to light and fined in this haul.[5] There must have been many, many more: a regular, if also irregular, part of the economy of the county.

[1] S.P. 12/122, 6. [2] ibid., 49. [3] ibid., 130, 44.
[4] The evidence of Killigrew's man, Penrose (S.P. 12/122, 30), gives larger quantities than Killigrew confesses to have received. I naturally follow Penrose.
[5] S.P. 12/120, 79.

It is not my purpose, nor would it be possible here, to recount the story of the war with Spain, but to sketch briefly some of its consequences for Cornwall and its part in it. That part was necessarily an important one, since the county was an advance-post in the sea-struggle, exposed to the greatest danger. The outbreak of war is usually dated to the Spanish embargo upon English shipping in 1585. This was replied to by the seizure of their Newfoundland fishing fleet; Bernard Drake was ordered to bring the ships into west country ports.[1] But for years relations had been worsening, especially at sea where rivalry had redoubled since Philip's acquisition of the Portuguese Empire in 1580: for his was a world-empire now. The west-country seamen, led by the great captain, Drake, had for years been conducting their own campaign against that ponderous, monopolistic imperialism, interloping, trespassing, getting blows in where they could. They suffered their casualties: Edward Rowe of Fowey, owner of a small bark which was employed in spying upon Spanish preparations, was caught, his goods confiscated, himself landed in the prisons of the Inquisition where he languished and died.[2] He was only one of many. At Plymouth in 1583-84 considerable sums were spent by the town upon fortifying and entrenching St. Nicholas' Island.[3] In 1584 ordnance was sent down to the Mount.[4]

On the outbreak of war new commissions of lieutenancy were issued — for the western counties to Bedford.[5] Five deputy-lieutenants were appointed for Devon, and two for Cornwall: Sir Francis Godolphin and Sir William Mohun. This was a new departure. Actually Bedford was dying, and in draft instructions made out for him for Cornwall Ralegh's name was inserted. He was made Lord Warden of the Stannaries, and later Lord Lieutenant of Cornwall. Ralegh naturally relied a great deal on his cousin Grenville, and we find the latter given special charge by the government in relation to the defences of Cornwall. In 1586 preparations had been considerably advanced under the care of the deputy-lieutenants, who found themselves more and more occupied with government work. They were able to reply that they had 'already erected the bulwarks and defences on the sea-coast, also the beacons are sufficiently erected and watched'.[6] A new training of the trained bands was set on foot, and the exercise of the light horsemen begun. To the clergy and the richer recusants, who in this respect were placed in the same category, it fell to provide the money to equip

[1] ibid., 179, 21.   [2] *A.P.C.*, XII. 36.
[3] Worth, *Plymouth Municipal Records*, 125.
[4] Add. MS. 5752.   [5] S.P. 12/186, 50-2.   [6] ibid., 188, 42.

light horse. The bishop was rated at three lances, so also Sir John Arundell — in this respect alike if in no other; the Archdeacon of Cornwall — and Richard Tremayne, at one; Dr. Kenall, parson of St. Columb and holding many other preferments, rated at three, was 'sorry that he is not able to contribute any more' than £35.[1] From the Cornish clergy there was collected a sum of £63 6s. 8d.

In 1587 additional orders were sent down 'because of the increasing danger of the times'.[2] Likely landing places were to be covered with stakes and ramparts thrown up — just as to-day, after so many years, the long Victorian peace, this return to Elizabethan dangers. Ammunition would be supplied by the Queen — this was a great concession, tribute to the gravity of the crisis and suitably recognized by Carew as coming from her 'provident and gracious care'; but they were 'not to use it for pleasure or it will be charged to them'. Horses for transport as other costs the counties were to discharge 'as it is for their own defence'; one observes the curious localism of the times. The watch on the beacons and training the men to shoot at boards were to go forward according to the orders sent out in 1585; nor are things so very different around our coasts to-day (July 1940). The J.P.s were ordered to take steps to supply the markets with grain:[3] there had been a bad harvest the year before, and, the sheriff wrote, 'there is found a great scarcity within the county, but the people very willing to do their best for the relief of their poor neighbours'.[4] Schedules were drawn up of what might be spared for elsewhere, from which we can see how much greater the production of corn was in the eastern half of the county.

Drake was at Plymouth preparing for his descent upon the coast of Spain. The year before he had been in the Indies, where — so John Spark forwarded the news from Plymouth — he 'runneth through the country like a conqueror'.[5] Now, 'if your honour did now see the fleet under sail and knew with what resolution men's minds do enter into this action as your honour would rejoice to see them, so you would judge a small force would not divide them . . . There was never more likely in any fleet of a more loving agreement than we hope the one of the other, I thank God . . . Each wind commands me away, our ship is under sail. God grant we may so live in his fear as the enemy may have cause to say that God doth fight for her majesty as well abroad as at home'.[6] He did. In his raid upon Cadiz, Drake burnt a Biscayan of 1200 tons, a ship of the Marquis of Santa Cruz of 1500 and thirty-one smaller vessels.[7] He brought back a great East Indies carrack, the

---

[1] S.P. 12/186, 36.   [2] ibid., 198, 63.   [3] ibid., 197, 42.   [4] ibid., 199, 37.
[5] ibid., 188, 1.   [6] ibid., 200, 2.   [7] ibid., 46.

San Felipe, laden with calicoes and silks and spices, with which he covered the cost of singeing Philip's beard. She lay in Saltash water, while her jewels and stuff were brought into the little town to be inventoried by Sir John Gilbert and Godolphin. Beneath their eyes were heaped the chains of gold, the forks and hafts, the pendants, rings, bowls, hoops of gold, the stones 'which we esteem to be garnets', the 'agates small and great, and other stones of a green colour with spots of red'.[1] What was more important was Drake's news: 'the like preparation was never heard of nor known as the King of Spain hath and daily maketh to invade England'.

That summer there was a false alarm given from the west country of the approach of the Armada to these shores. The J.P.s forwarded to the Council the report of a gentleman who thought he descried a fleet of 120 ships not far from Scilly. The Council gave order to put all in readiness 'with as little bruit and trouble to the people that shall be occupied in harvest as may be'.[2] The ordnance and ammunition appointed for each maritime county, two sacres, two minions, two falcons, with their equipment, were set under way.[3] As the danger increased Burghley, who thought of everything, turned over in his mind what officers were best to meet the emergency: we may read his thoughts from his memoranda, like Cromwell's.[4] Instead of Carmynow he would prefer Hugh Trevanion for sheriff. (In fact that safe Protestant, Anthony Rowse, Drake's friend, was made sheriff for 1588.) He would remove Harris, farmer of the Mount, and place someone in his stead; the ordnance out of the great carrack was to be bestowed where needful in Devon and Cornwall; so with that of the *New Bark* which perished near Padstow; the deputy-lieutenants were to 'confer with Sir Richard Grenville for the trenching of places upon the sea-coast where most danger is of landing'. Grenville was duly sent down to view the trained bands and inspect the defences: he brought back a full report to the Council.

In November there was a second alarm: the Lord Lieutenant of Devon was ordered to look specially to Plymouth, the deputies in Cornwall to look to Falmouth, as places 'aptest for landing'.[5] To advise the government a council of war was set up in London, upon which Ralegh and Grenville served. The plan for the west was to draw together an army of 2000 foot and 200 horse from the trained bands of Devon and Cornwall to serve where most needed. Ralegh was sent down to his lieutenancy in December, and in Devon found great discord and unwillingness to bear the burden forced upon them.[6] Exeter totally refused to do its share, and Ralegh greatly

---

[1] ibid., 200, 53. [2] ibid., 203, 7. [3] ibid., 17.
[4] ibid., 205, 28. [5] *A.P.C.*, xv. 288. [6] S.P. 12/206, 40.

suspected the religion and spirit among other Devonshire J.P.s. (He was a hot-tempered, impatient, tactless person.) On the other hand, 'it is most assured that the careful usage of the action by the deputies in their several divisions will easily induce the inferior sort to whatsoever shall be thought necessary for her Majesty's safety and their own defence'. And, of course, it was so. A sensitive government, faced with these difficulties, forbore to put into operation the plan devised by the military men. The Council protested they were 'loth to lay any burden other than necessary for defence'.[1] The bands were to be viewed separately. Various difficulties, especially that of mustering the Stannaries, were left to be dealt with by Ralegh, who held a Stannary Parliament at Lostwithiel in January, which registered several resolutions and affirmed their customs.[2]

As the result of all this activity fuller certificates of musters were returned: for Cornwall, 5560 men furnished, 1395 shot, 633 corselets, 1956 bills and halberds, 1528 bows, 4 lances and 96 light horse: a great increase in equipment on the earlier years.[3] There were still gaps: 'no pioners appointed, no carriage nor petronels, neither what provision they have made in the county of match and powder for their men, neither yet in the corporate towns'.[4] The Council of War regarded Plymouth as the most likely place for a landing, 'for that it is unlikely the King of Spain will engage his fleet too far within the Sleeve before he have mastered some one good harbour, of which Plymouth is the nearest to Spain'.[5] To meet this it was thought good to arrange for 6000 of the trained bands, 2000 from Cornwall, to converge upon Plymouth if attacked; if Falmouth, 4000 from Cornwall and a similar proportion from Devon.[6] It was fortunate that these elaborate provisions were not put to the test; but so far as they could be made so, the land-defences were ready.

Drake was at Plymouth chafing for permission to make another descent upon the Spanish coast. The government was too fearful of invasion to permit him, and he was kept on the defensive, gathering the west country ships that volunteered for service from the little ports. The five ships that Grenville was fitting out at Bideford for another Virginian expedition were ordered around Cape Cornwall to serve under Drake. He was in command of a subsidiary fleet to that of the Queen now on its way down Channel under Howard 'with a pleasant gale all the way long'.[7] Captain Polwhele had been off Cape Finisterre, where he had taken some French prizes and a fly-boat with news of the Spaniards.[8] They were expected to come out

[1] A.P.C., xv. 302, 307. [2] Add. MS. 6713. [3] S.P. 12/209, 43. [4] ibid., 42.
[5] ibid., 49. [6] ibid., 51. [7] ibid., 210, 28. [8] ibid., 17.

at any time. The summer turned to storms. Only the Queen's great ships, well and truly built by John Hawkins, could ride out in the Sound — there was no breakwater then; the small merchant ships took refuge in Cattewater; Drake lay between St. Nicholas' Island (now it is called by his name) and the shore. The unseasonable south-westerly gales locked the English ships in the Sound while their victuals were exhausted. The Spaniards took advantage of a lull to come out. On Thursday, June 20th, a bark of Mousehole encountered 'nine sail of great ships between Scilly and Ushant bearing north-east . . . their sails were all crossed over with a red cross'.[1] Godolphin sent up the news to the Lord Admiral. Another boat of West Cornwall had been chased and shot at; so too an Exeter vessel. These last had met groups of six and fifteen ships: contingents of the great Armada forced back by the storms. Howard now disposed his ships in three squadrons to keep watch at the entrance to the Channel: himself in the middle, Drake in the vanguard off Ushant, Hawkins near Scilly.[2] But the south-westerly gale drove them back, and the same wind 'that brought us back from the coast of Spain brought them out'.

On Friday, July 19th, fifty ships of the Armada were spied off Scilly 'hovering in the wind as it seemed to attend the rest of the fleet'.[3] That night Howard got the news at Plymouth of their having been seen off the Lizard: the whole Armada, 130 ships strong, coming slowly up-Channel in unbroken formation, a great coloured crescent moon. One can imagine the excitement in the Cornish parishes, the stir of which traces remain here and there (like the pikes of Napoleonic days in Hardy's Dorset churches), in the entries in parish account-books, the letters sent from Launceston to Stowe to fetch Sir Richard Grenville to Plymouth.[4] Next day the fleet warped with difficulty against the wind out of the harbour, under the lee of Mount Edgcumbe, and about three in the afternoon Howard first got sight of the Spaniards.[5] That day and night the English ships hugged the coast of Whitsand Bay, until they caught up with the Armada off Looe, having recovered the wind of the Spaniards.[6] At nine o'clock on Sunday morning they first gave fight, when the two fleets were thwart of Plymouth: a spectacle which the Mayor and citizens beheld for themselves, sending out reinforcements and victuals as they could.[7] Howard snatched a moment aboard the *Ark* off Plymouth to write to Walsingham, 'there shall nothing be either neglected or unhazarded that may work their overthrow'. Nor

[1] ibid., 211, 47.   [2] ibid., 212, 18.   [3] ibid., 214, 42.
[4] cf. my *Sir Richard Grenville*, 263.
[5] S.P. 12/212, 80.   [6] ibid., 213, 67.   [7] ibid., 212, 81.

was there, as we well know. So the two fleets passed on, out of western waters.

Of the Cornish ships and captains that served under Drake that memorable summer there were three of Grenville's: the *Galleon Dudley*, a Spanish prize, 250 tons, 96 men, commanded by James Erisey; the *Virgin Save Her*, 200 tons and 70 men, under Grenville's son John; and the *Tiger*.[1] The *Bark Hawkins* was commanded by a Prideaux, the *Bark Mannington* by Ambrose Mannington.[2] Saltash and Tavistock provided the *John Trelawney*, of 150 tons and 30 men, under Thomas Meek: she served for six weeks beginning July 19th and ending August 29th, and was paid £169 10s. for victuals, tonnage, etc.[3] John Rashleigh sailed his ship, the *Francis* of Fowey, to Plymouth to serve under Drake after the fighting had begun: she was 140 tons with 60 men on board and was chartered from July 22nd to September 1st. Rashleigh had great difficulty in raising from the neighbouring towns and hundreds the money, some £600, which he had disbursed to equip the ship and her pinnace. The Council had to give order for the sum to be raised by an equal tax upon Fowey and Looe, and the hundreds adjoining those ports and Plymouth; nor were the tinners to be exempt for all their privileges.[4] Similar letters were addressed to the towns of Truro, Tregony, Penryn, Penzance for payments to a Dartmouth captain who had served with his ship.[5] A little vessel, the *Minion* of Fowey, laden with provisions, biscuit, beer, beef, was sunk that summer by tempest within the pier at Dover.[6]

How the parishes contributed to the upkeep of the trained bands that summer, their victuals and carriage, their expenses at Bodmin and Liskeard, may be seen from the Green Book of St. Columb: not only money but butter and cheese. What remained of the former went into the parish stock, of the latter it 'remaineth in the hands of divers of the parishioners to be yielded again upon demand'.[7] While the Armada was rounding the north of Scotland and danger remained of a descent upon Ireland, a levy of 100 soldiers was made from Cornwall, 200 from Devon for service there:[8] they were countermanded when the danger passed.[9] Like the last little waves when some great ship has passed by.

The reply to the Armada was the large Norris-Drake expedition to the coast of Portugal next year. Though the Queen contributed six of her

[1] S.P. 12/213, 91.
[2] Laughton, *Defeat of the Spanish Armada*, II. 324.
[3] S.P. 12/217, 37.   [4] *A.P.C.*, XVI. 159, 279.   [5] ibid., 404.   [6] S.P. 12/219, 69.
[7] *J.R.I.C.* (supplt. to vol. XIX), 'St. Columb Green Book', 37–8.
[8] *A.P.C.*, XVI. 317.   [9] S.P. 12/218, 3.

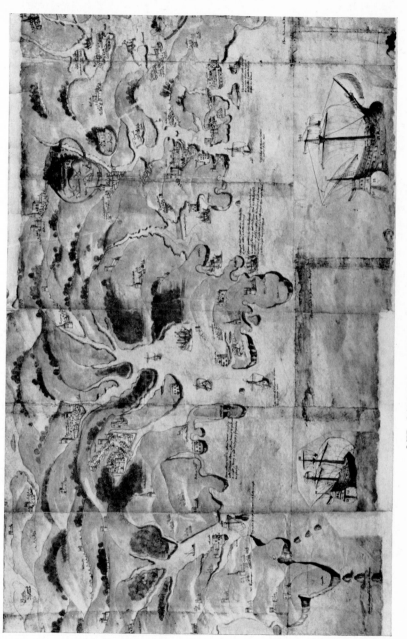

MID-CORNWALL IN THE TIME OF HENRY VIII

ST. MAWES CASTLE

ships, the voyage had something of the character of a private venture. The reputations of our most famous sailor and soldier of the time brought scores of ships and thousands of men to volunteer under their flag. Among the Cornish ships which served again under Drake were the *John Trelawny*, and the *Minion* of Fowey, which was recovered from Dover harbour, and probably too John Rashleigh's *Francis*.[1] At Plymouth there was a concourse of 20,000 soldiers and sailors waiting, and the difficulty of provisioning them was doubled by the bad weather which held them up while they consumed their victuals. Some strain was placed upon the resources of the west country: William Hawkins wrote, 'we cannot find in all these parts above 12 tons of oil, and by reason it is now seed time we cannot both in peas and beans furnish above 400 quarters'.[2] They could get no more than 2000 dry newland fish. Beef, however, could be got, and butter and cheese 'which the country yieldeth readily'. The Council was forced to come to their aid, and ordered Godolphin to pay over direct as much of the loan then being collected as he could get, 'which we hope will be £1000'.[3]

The effect of this growing business of provisioning fleets must have been to expand trade and credit in the west country, particularly at Plymouth. It may be regarded as the chief factor in the town's growing prosperity; the bulk of the business was done by the Hawkins family, though other merchants, like Fownes, Spark, Trelawny, shared in it. To them too fell the business of selling the cargoes of captured prizes. Norris complained on his return that 'the mayor and Mr. Hawkins who carry the greatest sway in the town, under colour of their authority do hinder both town and country from buying of anything to the end to bring all things to base prices and then to take them into their own hands'.[4] So familiar a complaint, so well-known a situation; but somebody profited. The great expedition achieved nothing like what was expected of it, in fact was rather a fiasco. Thousands of men died of disease. Its chief result was that Drake henceforth was left on the shelf, employed not at sea, but in overlooking affairs at Plymouth. The failure of the expedition led to renewed fear of invasion in retaliation. The ships that returned were to be taken into the Hamoaze to be cleansed, 'safe from danger of any enemy'; west country fishermen were warned that if at any time when abroad they sighted more than ten ships in company they were to return and report at once.[5]

As the war progressed its conduct became professionalized. The government put in being a blockade, so far as it could, upon all contraband going

---

[1] ibid., 222, 89; 223, 76. [2] ibid., 224, 7. [3] ibid., 223, 91, 92.
[4] ibid., 225, 30. [5] *A.P.C.*, XVII. 397.

to Spain, particularly the products of the Scandinavian countries — pitch, tar, cordage, sails, wood — and, of course, upon corn. The trade policy pursued may be seen fully in the interesting instructions sent down to Godolphin.[1] It was designed to cut off all imports into Spain, and all trade on the part of Spanish subjects. Neutral ships coming from Spain were to be allowed to pass. The rights of English subjects to make reprisal for losses were expressly affirmed. The economic war entailed a great burden of business upon the west country J.P.s, and a vast correspondence of which much remains in state papers and Privy Council records. Innumerable ships were brought into our ports, especially into Falmouth, to be examined, their goods sold if contraband, war-material reserved to the government. If a neutral suffered against the rules, he was generally compensated — like Martin Heithusen whose ship the *Flower de Luce* was taken on the coast of Portugal that year: he was given licence to freight a ship with 'some good quantities of pilchards in the west country to pass to Leghorn, being in good terms of amity with her Majesty'.[2] It would seem that this business was the chief factor in causing Falmouth to grow at the end of the century.

The failure to finish the war by any decisive blow on either side, either by the Armada of 1588 or the Lisbon expedition of 1589, meant the extension of the conflict on land and a settling down to a prolonged war of attrition. Already Philip had had a long war on his hands in the Netherlands and Elizabeth was deeply engaged in aiding Dutch resistance. Now he took a step towards extending the area of conflict by openly intervening in the civil war in France. In the autumn of 1590 Parma invaded France from the east, while in October 3000 Spanish troops were landed in Brittany. These moves forced the English government to counter them with active intervention in France, and for the next few years there were constantly some 10,000 English troops serving abroad, strung out along the continental coast of Brittany and Normandy to Holland.[3] Philip's acquisition of a foothold in Brittany was a matter of the utmost concern for the west country, and an important factor in governing the future conduct of the war: it necessitated the fortification of the town of Plymouth (besides the fort and the island), and similarly of the Scilly Islands; it kept Cornwall each summer on the alert for raids and invasion; it imposed an additional burden for levies to go across the Channel; it influenced Philip's plan of campaign in the last Armadas which he sent against this country in 1596 and 1597.

[1] *A.P.C.*, XVI. 421.   [2] ibid., XVIII. 69.
[3] Cheyney, *History of England from the Defeat of the Armada to the Death of Elizabeth*, I. 260.

The Spaniards held Blavet, the modern Port Louis, and fortified it as a base. Here they kept a small squadron of fast galleys to maintain communications across the bay of Biscay, and to prowl round the entrance to the Channel. Rumour greatly exaggerated the number of both their ships and men; but in 1591, 2000 more troops disembarked. Sir John Norris was placed in command of an army of 3000 men which was sent across to Brittany. Half of them were raw levies, of whom Cornwall supplied 100; Norris complained bitterly of the ill-equipment of the Somerset contingent.[1] Probably the rest were not much better. Lord Thomas Howard was just departing upon that expedition to the Azores in which Grenville won such glory; a pinnace was sent after him to instruct him that there was an enemy fleet between Ushant and Scilly and to take all that passed in or out of the Channel.[2] It was thought that Scilly was in danger, and the Council, in a panic, displayed great activity: Ralegh was to be sent down with a commission to take up shipping and men 'to save Scilly if it be not taken and to defend the coasts of Devon and Cornwall'.[3] Godolphin was to repair at once to Scilly with sufficient forces, the Council 'marvelling very much of his not advertising the late attempts of the enemy in those parts'. London was full of rumours: 'the speech is here all of the coming of certain (twenty sail of) Spaniards upon the Scillies and coast of Cornwall, for resistance whereof all that country is in arms . . . The Queen hath been very much moved with these news and was very melancholy at my Lord Treasurer's.'[4]

The Queen and Council recovered their usual good spirits; but the result of the jar they had had was that the fortification of Plymouth and the Scillies was undertaken in good earnest. The engineer, Robert Adams, was sent west to survey the ground, and submit plans in consultation with Ralegh and Drake at Plymouth, and with Godolphin at Scilly.[5] The town accounts at Plymouth note payments to him coming and going between London and Cornwall, and to his men for levelling the ground.[6] At Plymouth the plan was to finish the castle at one end of the Hoe, then to surround the town with a ditch and a wall, entrenching the sea side, and to knit the castle to the town with a bulwark so that it might be more easily approached from the town.[7] The cost was estimated at £5000; and to raise this sum the government after much cogitation decided to levy 18d. upon every hogshead of pilchards exported by foreigners, 12d. for Englishmen;[8] to grant £100 a year out of the Plymouth and Fowey customs, and to collect benevolences from

[1] ibid., 246.   [2] S.P. 12/238, 152.   [3] A.P.C., XXI. 131.   [4] S.P. 12/238, 159.
[5] A.P.C., XXII. 345.   [6] Worth, Calendar, 134.   [7] S.P. 12/241, 75-81.
[8] The pilchard fishery was at this time greatly expanding; v. my 'Dispute concerning the Plymouth Pilchard Fishery, 1584-1591', in Economic History, II. 461-72.

persons of credit in the west country.[1] So financed, the work went forward. In overseeing the work, and other town business, leasing the corn-mills and bringing in a sufficient water-supply from the Meavy, Drake consumed the years of inactivity in a tamer sphere than that to which he was accustomed. Eighteen months later, the government had to complain of the slackness of the west country gentry in contributing to the fortification: which 'yourselves ought rather to be suitors for in regard of your own good and safety than anyways to be moved hereunto by her Majesty or us'.[2] Drake wrote that the inhabitants of Plymouth would contribute more willingly if the continual government of the fortification were committed to the mayor: a spirit that looks forward to 1640. The government made the concession, except for times of doubt and danger, when expert men were to have charge.

The fortification of Scilly was slower in getting under way. In 1592 the little English army was cut to pieces by Mercoeur, and in November 2000 more Spaniards were landed. Next year there was a truce between Henry IV and Philip, but the latter, determined to keep his foothold in Brittany, landed 2000 more troops, who proceeded to advance on Brest. In these years driblets of English levies were sent abroad, among them now a company from Cornwall, now fifty miners for the siege of Rouen — thereby keeping up an old tradition of using Cornish tinners for such works.[3] The threat to Brest necessitated sending larger reinforcements before it was finally overcome in 1594. But it was not until 1593 that Godolphin's annual petitions for proceeding with the works on Scilly were attended to, the advance of Spain's power in Brittany bringing danger ever closer to the islands. It was decided to fortify St. Mary's, as the largest and most important island: a fort and two sconces upon Hugh hill to command the shipping in the roads.[4] Adams was to perform the work, under Godolphin's supervision, and £400 was granted out of the customs of Plymouth and Cornwall to meet the cost. A garrison of a lieutenant, three gunners, and twenty-six soldiers was allowed in summer-time; ten were thought sufficient for the winter. Ordnance was sent down, four demi-culverins and two brass minions. The inhabitants were to assist the garrison in building and defence; while Ralegh was to arrange for a force of 100 men to be in readiness upon the mainland to go to the defence of the islands upon warning from the beacons.[5]

---

[1] S.P. 12/242, 31.   [2] A.P.C., XXIV. 477.
[3] cf. S.P. 12/242, 113; A.P.C., XXI. 192; ibid., XXIII. 68, 225, 250.
[4] ibid., XXI. 200; XXII. 344; XXIV. 223.   [5] ibid., XXIV. 375.

By August the work was well advanced, though Adams found it necessary to keep a continual eye upon the masons 'who do not conceive such walling, and also to attend the laying of every stone, whose hardness and difficulty to dig out, from their bigness, he dares not express'.[1] Godolphin reported that the work had been done speedily, and that it was well since in the last week there had been very many ships near the isles, 'sometimes as many as twenty sail, one an exceeding great one, but could not discover whether friends or enemies'.[2] This increased his desire to be furnished with artillery. He enumerated the works remaining to be done when the fort was finished: three blockhouses, four platforms, 'a trench and a bank to compass the hill near the sea to shadow the men from discovery by the shipping', a windmill, houses for brewing and baking, dwellings for the soldiers, and a pier for the safety of ships, 'for which there is a very apt place under command of the fort'.[3] Later in the year he sent in his accounts for that summer: they were to finish off in the spring.[4] And so there took shape the little fort on St. Mary's of which something still remains, notably the gateway with Elizabeth's and Godolphin's initials upon it, overlooking the little harbour (with all the brown and tawny sails of the fishing luggers) which his pier made.

In January 1595 the English troops in Brittany, having prevented the Spaniards from capturing Brest, were withdrawn. That set the galleys at Blavet free to prowl round the Cornish coast, and what happened in consequence drove home with force Godolphin's representations. The fortification of Scilly was only just in time. At Plymouth Drake and Hawkins were fitting out their last voyage to the West Indies, upon which both were to die. The Spaniards were very anxious to learn its destination. In May a shallop from Blavet, manned by sixteen sailors and twenty-four soldiers, appeared in Falmouth Bay and captured a fisher-boat of St. Keverne, carrying the men over to Brittany.[5] There they were examined, but fortunately could tell the Spanish general nothing of the objectives of the expedition, but that it consisted of 100 sail and was under Drake's command. An English gunner, a Bristol man, whom the Spaniards would not release, told the fishermen to report to the first J.P. they could upon their return that there were four galleys and ten ships of war at Blavet, and that they

---

[1] S.P. 12/245, 70.   [2] ibid., 71.   [3] ibid., 72.
[4] ibid., 133. The interesting accounts in detail to the end of the year are to be found in S.P. 12/251, 56 and 56 (1). There are payments for 50 planks of walnut tree from Mr. Rashleigh, £3, 40 deal boards from Mr. Killigrew, £2, 300 pineapple planks to be paid to Henry Trevelleck, £20, etc.
[5] S.P. 12/252, 79. The *Calendar* wrongly says 20 soldiers.

were expecting seven more galleys and ten ships with which to surprise shipping at Scilly. The fishermen on their return told their story to Anthony Rowse.

On July 10th Godolphin wrote to Essex that more men would be needed for the defence of Scilly: 'I rest still of the same mind that it needeth a stronger garrison, for the gathering of those Spaniards seemeth as a cloud that is like to fall shortly in some part of her Majesty's dominions'.[1] A week later the galleys were off the Cornish coast. Apparently they first appeared on the north coast, and threatened to land some men at St. Eval, near Padstow; but Grenville's son assembled the bands under his charge to impeach their landing, and the Spaniards held off.[2] On July 21st, two men of St. Keverne sent on the intelligence to Godolphin that 'there is 60 sail of ships within the Manacles in our bay turning off and on all this day . . . There was also seen two pinnaces at our harbour's mouth hulling, and returning towards the said fleet. Thus in haste we bid you farewell at 9 of the clock this Monday evening'.[3]   Next day, the news took more probable proportions: 'this last night after sunset, these ships made in to the sea somewhat east of our harbour, and one tall ship coming west presently drew towards her and drew together to the number of 20 sail or upwards. And afterwards hovered up and down not regarding what course they took, being seen by divers fishermen.'[4]

Whatever they were, Godolphin had more immediate matters to attend to. Soon after sunrise on July 23rd, the four galleys appeared out of the mist off Mousehole and landed half their men, some 200 pikes and shot, who proceeded to fire the little fishing town and the hamlets round about, including the church-town of Paul, whose church was ruined by the fire.[5] The inhabitants were taken completely by surprise and fled, some towards Penzance, where Godolphin, who had ridden over that morning from his house, met them upon the green to the west of the town and tried to put them in order to resist. For all the efforts of the government in past years, they were virtually unarmed. Godolphin sent a messenger post haste to Drake and Hawkins at Plymouth 'to consider what is to be done for your own safety and our defence'.[6] He clearly thought that the raid, and the ships in Falmouth Bay, were the prelude to invasion; and 'here is assembled 200 naked men. I attend the coming of more and so to make head towards the enemy.'

1 Hist. MSS. Com., *Salisbury MSS.*, v. 274.
2 ibid., 285.   3 S.P. 12/253, 26.   4 ibid., 27.
5 My account is based mainly on Carew, p. 156 foll., who clearly had it from Godolphin himself: how often the tale was told at their meetings, for they were friends, one may imagine.
6 S.P. 12/253, 31.

But the Spaniards disconcerted his plan by returning to their galleys and landing their whole force at Newlyn, next Penzance. They were some 400 men in all. They sent two ranks of soldiers to the top of the hill to spy out the country, and when they saw the smallness of Godolphin's forces, they made for Penzance. The galleys kept up a fire upon the Cornishmen, who by this time were in a panic. Godolphin hoped to make a stand at the market place; but nothing could induce them to stay, neither his persuasions nor threats with his drawn rapier. Only a dozen or so of his own servants stood with him in the rear of the retreating mob. The Spaniards were in possession of three parts of the town; there was nothing for him to do but withdraw. The enemy then set fire to Penzance as they had fired Newlyn and Mousehole. It was reported afterwards that they had a mass said on the western hill, where they vowed to build a friary upon the conquest of England.[1] They then returned once more to their galleys.

That evening greater numbers — they had been all too few at first — flocked in under Godolphin's command, and they encamped upon the green outside Marazion, further along the bay, for the defence of that place and the Mount. Hannibal Vyvyan sent word to Drake of the state of affairs, asking him to send down some of his leaders who had commanded in war and to put some ships in readiness.[2] The success of the Spaniards might encourage them to land elsewhere further to the east, as well as on the north coast. Next day they made show to land again on the west side of Mounts Bay; but the Cornish made a better show of resistance, and the galleys moved farther off out of range. The day after, Sir Nicholas Clifford and other captains arrived from Plymouth, while Drake sent down some of his ships to the Lizard. The plan was to cut off the retreat of the Spaniards if they should land again, as they would shortly have to, for they were hard pressed for water. The wind was strong at south-east, which prevented them getting away. But within an hour of the captains' arrival from Plymouth, it suddenly shifted north-west, and the galleys seized a heaven-sent opportunity to get clear away.

The episode was over, except for the examination of English prisoners who had been landed by the Spaniards in Mounts Bay.[3] They told Godolphin that the galleys would have stayed longer and done more spoil along the coast, had they not stood in fear of Drake's fleet; they meant to have gone to St. Ives and Padstow, and thence into the Bristol Channel, but they were much in want of fresh water when the change of wind enabled them to get away. The Spaniards purposed to take Scilly, where they would keep their

[1] ibid., 33.   [2] ibid., 30.   [3] ibid., 33.

galleys under the protection of the fort. Godolphin drew the moral of the affair: two good pieces of ordnance to beat them from the Roads, a better store of ammunition, and some skilful leaders in places where they might land. Sir Nicholas Clifford reported well of Godolphin's conduct: 'For the town of Penzance, had the people stood with Sir Francis Godolphin, who engaged himself very worthily, it had been saved; but the common sort utterly forsook him, saving four or five gentlemen'.[1] Those same common people took refuge in 'an ancient prophecy, in their own language . . . that hath long run amongst them, how there should land upon the rock of Merlin, those that would burn Paul church, Penzance and Newlyn. And indeed so is the rock called where the enemy first stepped on shore . . .

> Ewra teyre a war meane Merlyn
> Ara Lesky Pawle Pensans ha Newlyn.'[2]

From a letter of Thomas Treffry we learn what happened further to the galleys.[3] On their way back they encountered a fleet of seventy hulks and gave chase to fourteen of them which were severed from the rest. They sank one of the hulks, but in the fight lost 140 men and 'had one of their galleys so torn as they could not carry her to Blavet'. The other three were still there. Two Spanish fly-boats had recently chased a Bristol ship into Fowey, while there were Spanish men-of-war at Conquet.

For the government the affair, unimportant as it was, administered a shock: it was the only time in the whole course of the war that the Spaniards effected a landing in any force in any part of the country. Its effect was salutary. The whole defence position of the country was carefully surveyed by Burghley,[4] and a spate of new instructions sent down to the west country in particular.[5] Ralegh was to go down and view all the levies in Cornwall and see them trained. Meanwhile the deputy-lieutenants were to see to the barricading of the port towns, and receive Captain Peyton who was to train the levies. They were unwilling to bear the charge of this, but the Council insisted: without his advice, 'haply such as dwell amongst you either for favour or some other private cause would not be so fit'. Later new measures were ordered: the deputy-lieutenants were to select certain numbers to go under their captains to the threatened places on the coast, these were to be supported by the adjoining land forces as opportunity served. The same principle was extended to the counties as such: Devon was to aid Cornwall with 4000 men upon invasion, and vice versa. Somerset and Dorset also

---

[1] *Salisbury MSS.*, v. 290.   [2] Carew, 159.   [3] *Salisbury MSS.*, v. 322.
[4] S.P. 12/254, 65.   [5] *A.P.C.*, xxv. 57, 64, 302, 342.

were to lend (and receive) aid. Those who owned houses and castles on the coast were to inhabit them for defence, 'as by the law of nature and of the land they are bound to do in time of danger, upon pain of forfeiture of their livelihoods and further punishment'. Inquisition was to be made of those who had moved away in the past year and their names certified.

Ralegh, who had to make what he described to his friend Cobham as his 'miserable journey into Cornwall' — away from the pleasant pursuits of Sherborne — wrote a powerful criticism of these measures to the Council at the end of November.[1] He showed in detail that the situation of Cornwall was much more exposed and difficult than that of Devon, though their liabilities under the scheme were equal, and he argued that Devon should be reinforced from Somerset, from which access was broad and easy, and not from Cornwall. He recalled the difficult geography of the county, eighty miles in length, virtually an island so that it would be very difficult to get forces round the Tamar to aid Plymouth, and itself broken into three parts by deep river-estuaries so that communication inside it was hard enough. He concluded that 'there is no part of England so dangerously seated, so thinly manned, so little defenced and so easily invaded, having the sea on both sides, which no other county of England hath, and is withal so narrow that if an enemy possess any of the two or three straits, neither can those of the west repair eastward nor those of the east westward'. He drew attention to the Falmouth estuary, 'which is as much of Cornwall as the enemy should need, for within so much as lieth to the west . . . are the best ports, and are very sufficient to receive the greatest fleet that ever swam, and containeth 27 miles of length very guardable, which in my simple judgment is every way more to be sought for by the enemy than Plymouth, at least if the same were so well understood by them, which is not unlikely'. His prognostication proved correct: the objective of the Adelantado's Armada of 1597 was Falmouth. But indeed the whole paper is evidence of his very superior powers of intellect.

No less insistent were the governors of the western forts. The government had sent down some supplies of powder, shot and muskets; but Hannibal Vyvyan wrote from St. Mawes, 'where I will not dwell unless I have better supply', demanding a culverin, four demi-culverins and three sacres.[2] When he and Killigrew mustered the five parishes around Pendennis assigned for its defence, of 270 men there came fifty unarmed 'though often admonished these six years to supply arms'.[3] This right to muster the five parishes led, as usual, to contention: it was challenged by Penryn, which

[1] *Salisbury MSS.*, v. 466.   [2] S.P. 12/254, 41.   [3] ibid., 256, 21.

complained that it was left naked of defence.[1] John Trefusis supported it against Killigrew, and the deputy-lieutenants sympathized with its case. The Council left the controversy to Ralegh to settle, 'not meaning that the said parishes should be utterly disfurnished of their own safeguard or molested unnecessarily with service or attendance on Mr. Killigrew'. Killigrew replied that he was rather to blame for acting too mildly with them, for 'those five parishes are not prepared for war, nor have provided arms, nor keep watch as they should do; thus the castle is in continual danger'.[2] He asked that the place might be fortified, for which he had been twelve months a suitor.[3] To add point to his petition, he enclosed a curious story of a Spanish attempt to fire the castle and Arwennack. A Penryn fisherman who had been captured was employed by the Spaniards to lead the attempt: 'they landed near the castle and tried to fire it, and returning to their ship, rejoiced when they heard a great clap. They had twelve barrels of like fireworks to bang aboard ships in harbour, and fire another house near, and carry away Killigrew's wife and children'. The Spanish captain on his return boasted of his success in firing the house and was given a gold chain and a pension by the King.

Godolphin followed suit with a petition for an increase in the winter guard for Scilly, for more muskets and allowance for the money he had expended on the fortifications.[4] The government did something in these matters: it went through their establishments and paid up their accounts.[5] Most important, it took order for finishing the altogether larger works at Plymouth: £800 more was needed, and six persons were appointed to oversee the spending of it.[6] A commission was granted to Sir Ferdinando Gorges as captain and commander of the fort, carefully delimiting his sphere of authority from the town's: which did not prevent them from starting an embittered quarrel. In March a Spanish pinnace came into Cawsand Bay and landed a party to fire the village: they fixed barrels of powder with a train to several houses, but one man having a caliver put them to flight before the fire took effect.[7] And, sure enough, among the Plymouth accounts we find note of one of the barrels sent up to London.[8]

The effect of these accidents in the west country upon minds beginning to weary of the war may be seen in the defeatist talk of a goldsmith at the Mitre in Cheapside: of the landing at Penzance he said 'what a valiant exploit it was to come into our own coast under Sir Francis's nose; and that within one fortnight after they came within twenty miles of Plymouth

[1] *A.P.C.*, xxv. 15, 153, 306.   [2] S.P. 12/256, 39.   [3] ibid., 40.   [4] ibid., 56.
[5] ibid., 108.   [6] ibid., 65.   [7] ibid., 89.   [8] Worth, *Calendar*, 137.

and there burnt a house, and after came to a gentleman's house and set a barrel of gunpowder to his gate; it was a worthy exploit and worthy to be chronicled twice or thrice'.[1] Nor did he think well of the behaviour of the Cornishmen; the tale lost nothing in the telling — how the Spaniards on their flight rang the bells and said masses in our churches.

During the years 1595 to 1597 the war at sea woke up again and large-scale operations were resumed as in the years 1586 to 1589. Nine years after his successful campaign of 1586 in the West Indies, Drake was called out from his retirement and placed, with Hawkins, in command of another expedition, their last, to that familiar scene of their activities where they had made their début thirty years before. The expedition accomplished little; both Drake and Hawkins died upon it and were buried at sea; disease ravaged the fleet. In April 1596 several of their ships reached Falmouth in great want and distress.[2] A new generation had come to the fore: that summer Essex and Ralegh made their brilliant attack upon Cadiz, in which the city was captured and of which the effect was to bankrupt Philip's credit in Europe. In the absence of the fleet upon the coast of Spain, the Council took the usual measures of precaution against invasion, orders being sent down for strict musters to be kept and select forces assembled upon the coast.[3]

And in fact in these years, with infinite labour and cost, in altogether more unfavourable conditions, the indomitable, obstinate Philip was preparing another great armada to reduce the heretic country. In October it set sail: the revenge for Cadiz. At once something of the measures of 1588 was put into force: there was to be a royal army at the centre round the Queen, to which Cornwall and Devon were to contribute 2000 men.[4] It was not necessary: the Protestant winds which saved us in 1588 repeated their good work in 1596, no doubt to the perplexity of devout catholics. The armada was struck by fierce gales off Finisterre; a number of fine galleons were lost and hundreds of good fighting men. Undismayed, like something termite in the habit of his mind, Philip went on gathering what remained for another effort next year. At Plymouth Gorges raised his garrison to 100, while under his supervision many more hundreds of pounds were spent upon the fortifications.[5] The strain was being felt: notification was given that there would not be sufficient out of the revenue of Devon and Cornwall to meet his half-yearly charges, now amounting to £900.[6] At Scilly Godolphin's son was given the post of lieutenant in the absence of his father, and allowed ten more men for the fort.[7]

[1] *Salisbury MSS.*, VI. 51.   [2] S.P. 12/257, 48, 50.   [3] ibid., 259, 111.
[4] ibid., 261, 55.   [5] ibid., 262, 44, 56, 57.   [6] ibid., 62.   [7] ibid., 92.

Ralegh and Essex were fitting out another joint expedition at Plymouth, this time for the Azores, to intercept the Plate fleet. Meanwhile information was coming into the west country of the renewed preparations in Spanish harbours: an armada of 100 sail, Killigrew reported pretty accurately, but waiting for the King's greatest vessels to convoy them.[1] It was thought that, as in 1588, they were for Calais. Treffry reported four Spanish war-ships scouting in the Channel, picking up small boats to gain information of the English fleet at Plymouth.[2] It was rumoured that ten galleys were coming to attack some western town. At the same time Essex and Ralegh put to sea to run into a great storm in the mouth of the Channel. They were parted and lost sight of each other. Ralegh returned with his ships to Plymouth, afraid that Essex with his temperament 'will either wrestle with the seas to his peril, or if forced to come back, will be utterly heart-broken'.[3] He and his ships were driven to take refuge in Falmouth, whence he wrote off to Cecil: 'In haste, in passion, and yet hope of change, I send the bearer to acquaint her Majesty with my state, and what I know of the fleet'.[4] Ralegh got news of him there, reported that he had been 'in great extremity at sea, and in imminent peril of sinking which I knew would betide him before he would yield to sea or wind'.[5] At Falmouth Essex met with Sir Ferdinando Gorges in the *Dreadnought*, and with the *Foresight*, which had been driven to take shelter. He sent off Sir Thomas Gates to the Queen to report, 'for as my industry to overcome the difficulties in which I find my-self, gives me no time to write, so my sad spirit is not fit to indite anything that your fair eyes should read'.[6] On hearing news that Ralegh with most of the fleet was at Plymouth, he set off at once riding 'all night post over the rugged mountains of Cornwall'. Urgent repairs were put in hand, and soon the fleet was ready to set out again.

In the Azores they just missed the Plate fleet: the narrowest escape Philip had had. Essex and Ralegh quarrelled bitterly, and, their fleet battered by the gales of that summer and in no condition to fight, made for home. Two days before they left, the Adelantado weighed anchor from Ferrol and with all his armada kept company 'with great joy' until within twenty-five leagues from Scilly. Then it transpired what his objective was: not Calais at all, but Falmouth.[7] His instructions were a new and elaborated version of the great Menendez's plan of the seventies: to seize, fortify and garrison Pendennis, then take his station off Scilly and destroy the English ships returning from

[1] S.P. 12/263, 3.   [2] ibid., 264, 26.   [3] ibid., 32.   [4] ibid., 34.
[5] ibid., 40.   [6] Devereux, *Lives and Letters of the Devereux Earls of Essex*, I. 433-4.
[7] *Salisbury MSS.*, VII. 495; S.P. 12/264, 148; 266, 69; 268, 24, etc.

the Azores. If successful in this, he was with the other half of his forces, some 10,000 men, to march eastward and capture Plymouth. It was an ambitious plan, and some part of it might have achieved success. But again the anti-Catholic, anti-Spanish winds of the Channel prevented it being put to the test. It was October when the armada put out; it was within two days' sail of Land's End when the autumn gales struck it and forced it to turn back.

In the west country the alarm was up: Gorges drew 500 men into the fort and the island at Plymouth.[1] The Lord Chamberlain was sent down to head the levies in resisting a Spanish landing. Ralegh and Essex on landing were shocked to learn how narrow had been their and their country's escape. Ralegh at once went ashore to assist the land preparations; Essex, less usefully, wrote — so like him! — 'though we eat ropes' ends and drink nothing but rain-water, we will out . . . to make a final end of this proud nation. For life, for life, Essex.'[2]

The immediate consequence of it, when the objective of the armada was bit by bit learned, was that the fortification of Pendennis was undertaken in real earnest. Essex gave his opinion that it was not defensible as it was against an army landed, and that an engineer should be employed to make the ground better to resist fire.[3] It was reported that the Adelantado had meant to establish himself on the headland and turn it into an island by cutting the narrow neck of the peninsula.[4] At the moment of danger, Ralegh had drawn 500 levies into Pendennis; it was a great strain for a poor county.[5] When it had passed Godolphin wrote him: 'Our country poor people do and will much repine at the burden of maintaining these small forces of 400 or 500 at Penryn for guard thereof, which guard to the intended force is of ineffectual moment'.[6] He suggested a further garrison to lie in readiness about Truro. 'But what speak I of beggarly country aid against princes' royal armies, which cannot but by our prince's purse and munition be resisted?' That put the gist of the matter in a sentence. The strain of defence, the constant responding to calls on levies, maintaining them in service, was becoming too much for the county's resources; the government would have to come to the rescue. To its credit, it did. The 500 levies were allowed to go home; in their place the government sent two companies of professional soldiers from the Low Countries to Pendennis, and three to Plymouth; and hard pressed as it was financially, it maintained them.[7]

While in Cornwall, Ralegh surveyed the ground for the new fortifica-

---

[1] ibid., 443. [2] ibid., 445. [3] ibid., 480. [4] ibid., VIII. 58.
[5] A.P.C., XXVIII. 108. [6] Salisbury MSS., VII. 466. [7] A.P.C., XXVIII. 131, 183, 244, 306.

tions with Gorges and Sir Nicholas Parker, an experienced cavalry commander from the Netherlands who was called in specially for this job.[1] Gorges
reported of Pendennis: 'It is now the dangerous(est) place that ever I saw,
and the worst provided for. (If the enemy should descend there before these
defences be made, I protest I do not see (and yet I do assure myself I do
understand something) how without great difficulty they will be gotten
out again).)'[2] That was what Killigrew had been pleading for some years.
But it did not fall to him to remedy it. He was bidden to London to confer
with Parker about the measures necessary.[3] In February the latter was given
charge of the new fortifications and appointed colonel of the companies
guarding it;[4] he was made a deputy-lieutenant of the county, a motion of
which Ralegh heartily approved, since he did 'exceedingly well allow of the
gent'.[5]

Killigrew found himself in prison: his own misdemeanours and extravagance, and those of his father, had at last, in spite of the family influence at
Court which protected them so long, caught up with him. Against many
warnings and narrow escapes, he continued his associations with pirates at
Helford. Only a year before, when a Queen's ship was at Falmouth on the
look out for them, he had given a warning to the notorious Captain Elliott
who had taken service with Spain.[6] That enabled Elliott to show a clean
pair of heels and get away: Killigrew received nine bolts of holland cloth —
which must have become a sort of currency in the Killigrew circle — and a
chest for his services. These connections led to a rumour much more serious
in its implications. It was being said openly in Spain that Pendennis was to
have been rendered if the Adelantado had got there, that the governor of
the castle was bought.[7] The report was very persistent, and though it is
hardly likely to have been true, what is probable is that Killigrew's despair
at his own position and his failure to get the government to pay any heed
to his demands for Pendennis had made him unwise in his talk with such
dubious go-betweens as Captain Elliott. His own financial position was
deeply involved: he owed debts everywhere, to his uncle Sir Henry, to
Mr. Lock, to the Crown — and it was that, rather than any proof of treason,
or any suggestion on the part of the government that they believed the
charge, that laid him by the heels and kept him in and out of prison for the
next few years.[8] He was loud in complaints of his innocence: was this the
reward for thirty years' service at Court? Happy it were, if when the Spaniards

---

[1] S.P. 12/265, 5. [2] ibid., 45. [3] *A.P.C.*, xxviii. 149. [4] S.P. 12/266, 45.
[5] *Salisbury MSS.*, viii. 18. [6] S.P. 12/265, 13 (ii).
[7] *Salisbury MSS*, viii. 63. [8] ibid., 155.

were at his house, they had had the spoil of it; was it so heinous an offence, to have bought and sold with men of war in the Queen's service? Later, as imprisonment lengthened, he become more lachrymose, and regretted his past vanities.[1] A curious, unstable figure, not altogether clear to us; anyhow we have no further concern with him.[2]

With Killigrew out of the way, and a competent professional soldier in his place, very anxious to give satisfaction and root himself in the county – he lost not much time in marrying an Erisey – the fortifications went ahead. Paul Ivy was employed as engineer; the whole area was to be trenched and walled, as at Plymouth, but in particular there was to be a bulwark from which to command the shipping in harbour.[3] £1000 was Ivy's estimate, and £200 was set aside from the impost on pilchards with which to begin work; the financial side was to be dealt with by Godolphin. During the danger period before the fortifications were complete four more companies were sent down to Falmouth, and Gorges was ordered to go to its assistance if it were threatened. Very soon the inevitable happened: the estimates were exceeded, and Parker and Ivy appealing for more money.[4] Four hundred men were at work upon the site, and they pleaded the 'exceeding hardness of the work, being a main rock'; the £1000 allowed them would not pay the labourers above fourteen days. But Ivy, after the manner of experts, had changed his plan, having been mistaken in the ground. The Council wrote that her Majesty was grievously offended that the work was not finished according to the estimate.[5] A full report was to be sent, and care taken to safeguard the interests of Killigrew whose woods at Arwennack were being entrenched upon. Somebody high up – in all probability Ralegh – patched the matter up and saw that the extra £1000 was forthcoming to finish the work. It was done, and £191 10s. 1d. provided in addition for the ordnance which Parker found so sadly wanting when he entered upon his charge.[6]

We naturally find Ralegh's hand, as Lord Lieutenant, in all matters concerning the defence of Cornwall in these years. Rashleigh had erected a battery at his house by the quay at Fowey, and himself furnished it with ordnance; in recompense Ralegh granted him liberty to muster his family, servants and twelve of his tenants for its defence, and exemption from all other watching and warning, training and mustering.[7] In 1598 he drew up new and detailed instructions for training the levies, instituting a new system

[1] ibid., XI. 151.   [2] I hope to deal with him in detail elsewhere.
[3] A.P.C., XXVIII. 51, 132, 145, 244, 280.   [4] S.P. 12/266, 74, 75.
[5] ibid., 424.   [6] ibid., 270, May 17, 1599.
[7] I first published this letter, from the Henderson MSS., in the Spectator, May 5th, 1939.

which prevailed during the last years of the reign.[1] The old was lamentably inefficient, though burdensome; it broke down whenever a test was imposed upon it. The keystone of the new was the selection of some fifteen hundred men to be given proper training, officers and men alike, by two full-time muster-masters, Captains Dowdall and Hughes, who knew their job. (How like the Home Guard to-day, and how little human activities change!) These trained bands were 'to be chosen of the better sort, whereby they are also favoured from foreign employment'; the muster-masters were to dismiss from them 'such as are poor and uncertain dwellers, or known to be of bad religion; and that of the best farmers' and wealthy men's sons you make up your numbers'. Nor were they to admit deputies, by which vagrant and poor persons had been hired to pass muster on muster days. The officers of untrained companies were to attend to learn their business when the muster-masters made their circuit of the county once in two months. So that we arrive at the full-flown system described by Carew with some pride — for he was part of it: a deputy-lieutenant and treasurer of the forces.[2]

In these last years Tyrone's rebellion made Ireland a main theatre of the struggle with Spain, and that too had important consequences for Cornwall, since by its geographical position it was closely concerned. In 1597 100 men were sent there, 300 from Devon.[3] The rebellion became a national revolt, encouraged by Spain's promises of armed intervention. Next year there was an urgent demand for 300 men from Cornwall (400 from Devon), to be sent from Fowey or Padstow as Ralegh and his deputies thought best.[4] There was an apologetic note in the Council's letters: only urgent necessity forced them to levy from the counties nearest Ireland. Cornwall was very hard pressed by the long continuance of the war, and Christopher Harris, deputy-lieutenant, was driven to protest. He would do his duty, 'yet I know the country will greatly grieve at the charge and be hardly brought unto it'.[5] He humbly intreated 'that such favour may be yielded hereafter to that poor county, which of late has sundry ways been very much charged at the fort of Falmouth, furnishing the defects of arms of the six companies late sent for Ireland, which indeed was much. [Those were the companies at Pendennis.] And now these 300 will be more burdensome than any charge that I have known heretofore levied on them, for Cornwall has seldom been more than a third part unto Devon, and now almost equal.' Nor was this the end of the charges they had been at. Yet later he wrote of the 'special regard the gentlemen of the county have had in the choice of men,

[1] S.P. 12/265, 113.   [2] Carew, 83-4.   [3] S.P. 12/268, 124.
[4] A.P.C., xxix. 240, 243.   [5] Salisbury MSS., viii. 427.

who are very well furnished; and the gentlemen of Fowey have had great care for the provision of shipping, and especially Mr. Rashleigh, who gave entertainment to the captains at his own cost.'[1] Out of the profits of his prospering shipping business he could well afford to.

Parker on the other hand found the public service 'somewhat hindered by private factions, too much reigning in this country, so that they do not stick to forsake the captains under whom they have been formerly enrolled and put themselves under others. There should be speedy reformation, lest by these means they absent themselves from both.'[2] They sometimes did, like some of the Devon levies who ran away from Plymouth where they were to embark for Ireland. The fortifications at Pendennis dragged on, though by the summer of 1599 Parker was able to report that the work was now reasonably forward. He was apprehensive of surprise and kept careful watch: he was always sending word of any doubtful shipping in the bay and reports of movements in Spain. Usually the ships were trading vessels, difficult to make out in the distance and bad weather, like the sixty vessels he described in July thwart of the Manacles.[3] He at once sent to the deputy-lieutenants and captains to stand to at their appointed posts — measures which had as often to be countermanded. He had his own quarrel with Hannibal Vyvyan, captain of St. Mawes — though he was not a quarrelsome man.[4] But in the later conditions of the war it was realized that St. Mawes was not a good defensive position — it was dominated by the hill above it. Better therefore to take away its ordnance for the use of Pendennis. Such a simple operation was immensely difficult in Elizabethan times. Vyvyan appealed against the decision; some members of the Council supported him. The Council's letters were then countermanded and the ordnance stayed.[5] Parker pressed again and again, and so on; after infinite delays he finally got the guns. He was a competent, professional person who could be relied on. In the end he got the works at Pendennis completed: they must have considerably altered the appearance of that lovely, familiar headland.

As it became clear that the Spaniards were preparing to intervene in Ireland, Godolphin became increasingly anxious for the Scillies. They were a key-position strategically, he wrote to Cecil, as cutting the line from Corunna to Dublin and the Irish ports.[6] The harbour there was not inferior in capacity to Falmouth or Plymouth; Lord Admiral Nottingham had heard his captains commend it — 'here hath been harboured at once above 120 sail, and some Venetian argosies of the greatest sort'. If the Spaniards once took the Scillies,

[1] ibid., 449.   [2] S.P. 12/272, 48.   [3] *Salisbury MSS.*, IX. 223.
[4] ibid., 207.   [5] ibid., 228.   [6] ibid., 292.

they would not be driven out with a force ten times greater.[1] (This said nothing of the difficulty they would have to feed themselves there — in fact, its impossibility. It would seem that all these men were unduly, perhaps professionally, apprehensive.) He did not wish to appear importunate. But in fact he was. In April 1600 he submitted a long memorandum on the state of Scilly.[2] In Edward VI's time, when it was first fortified, it had a garrison of 150; now there were only 50 in summer and 25 in winter, though the entrances into the isles were better known, 'the Spaniards more powerful and spiteful than the French were . . . navigation being also grown into more perfection'. He proposed that a pinnace should be stationed there, to convey victuals, munitions, news, most of the barks in west Cornwall and some of the fishing boats of Scilly having been taken by the Spaniards for want of such a guard. He indicated the defects of the fort, which was too small, and he enclosed his proposals for further works, sconces to command St. Mary's and Crow Sounds, and the harbour at Tresco. He sent an admirable plan of what subsequently became Star castle, on the highest point on St. Mary's, dominating the old fort, the Sound and looking out over miles of reefs to Bishop's Rock against the setting sun. The fact was that the Godolphin lease of the islands was nearing its term with the reign of Elizabeth: it had been granted in her first year for fifty years. Sir Francis offered £500 towards the cost of the fortifications for a further term like that of his uncle, Sir William.[3] The lease was renewed, though the building of Star castle falls outside our period.

The landing of the Spaniards at Kinsale provided Godolphin with an admirable argument for drawing the attention of the government to the dangerous state of the islands, 'being the fairest inn in the direct way between Spain and Ireland'.[4] From Carew we gather that Sir Francis had not done so badly with his fort, 'who with his invention and purse, bettered his plot and allowance, and therein hath so tempered strength with delight, and both with use, as it serveth for a sure hold and a commodious dwelling'.[5] Here, looking out upon those delightful, coloured waters, Godolphin had spent 'some idle hours last summer' framing a project for the Irish wars which would have saved all her Majesty's charges. If only her Majesty and the Council, at their wits' ends for money, could have believed in it! Godolphin was rather given to projects — after all was he not a projector, a mining capitalist, by calling? He forwarded them all to Cecil — plans for raising the treasure in the Spanish galleys sunk off Dunkirk, suggestions for block-

[1] *Salisbury MSS.*, IX. 171.   [2] S.P. 12/274, 122.   [3] ibid., 283, 58.
[4] *Salisbury MSS.*, XI. 412.   [5] Carew, 85.

ading Kinsale: 'may a dutiful mind offer the service of an inferior workman to a master builder?' he wrote to the Secretary in the exaggerated, but no less revealing, language of the time.[1]

Still their pre-occupations in the Channel continued. The failure of the Armada of 1597 did not mean that further attempts might not be made. There were concentrations of ships from time to time at Corunna or Ferrol; they were as often reported with apprehension in the west country. The Spanish galleys caused particular concern. In the summer of 1599 six arrived in Brittany: at once Parker set pen to paper and the messengers sped up from Pendennis, Fowey, Plymouth to London with the news.[2] Or again a Spanish man of war made depredations in the Channel, captured a bark of Fowey or appeared off Plymouth; once we hear of four boats taken by them. The war at sea was degenerating into its last phase: the Dunkirk pirates were a great nuisance off the coast in these last years.[3] On the other side a new generation of seamen, Monson, Leweson, were following their predecessors' example and sending prizes, an Indiaman laden with hides and ginger, a Hamburger laden with copper and hardware, into Fowey or Falmouth.[4]

At the end Ireland held the centre of attention. When he learned that Essex was going over as Lord Deputy, Godolphin's son petitioned him to command his attendance by letters to his father, lest his voluntary departure might prejudice him in the lieutenancy of Scilly which he held under Sir Francis.[5] He would have delivered his petition to Essex's ear, 'but the majesty of his presence causes him to speak in too much fear'. This gives some measure of the devotion of the younger military men to that brilliant, fatal figure next the throne. William Godolphin was one of the band of them who accompanied Essex to Ireland, and one of those, a considerable number, who owed their knighthood to him. But Sir William, a competent and hardheaded soldier, did not involve himself as Sir Ferdinando Gorges did in Essex's conspiracy and fall; he remained on in Ireland doing his duty efficiently and well, and winning the favour of Mountjoy, the new Lord Deputy, an able soldier who accomplished the task of subduing the rebellion.[6] But that was after the Queen's death.

Meanwhile, with resistance at its height and involving most of the country, it was necessary to send reinforcements. The government, aware of popular feeling and the general dislike of the Irish service, sent small bodies of men from a number of counties: from Cornwall in December 1600, 20, in the

---

[1] *Salisbury MSS.*, XI. 427.
[2] S.P. 12/272, 62, 63, 64, 65.
[3] cf. *Salisbury MSS.*, X. 425.
[4] ibid., XII. 181, 185.
[5] ibid., VIII. 450.
[6] ibid., XI. 428.

spring 20 more, in summer 25, then 50, then 100.[1] It was necessary to send over wheat, since the country was laid waste, to supply the army: Cornwall, having a considerable surplus of corn now in good years, was scheduled to send 1200 quarters, Devon 1000 quarters.[2] The levies deserted wholesale and came back and in at the ports whenever they could. The Council ordered that they were not to be allowed to land without passports granted in case of sickness.[3] It may be imagined that these were somehow forthcoming, for the number of loiterers, vagrants, maimed soldiers coming over from Ireland into the county presented a serious problem which vexed Carew, Godolphin and the J.P.s and reflected itself in the accounts of the parishes. The unemployment problem became the most serious question in internal affairs; measures agreed upon by the Cornish justices at quarter sessions were forwarded by Godolphin to Cecil.[4] No doubt they reflected the general experience, for the statutory legislation which followed, the great Elizabethan poor-law code, followed very much these lines, with the careful distinction between the deserving and undeserving poor.

Nevertheless when the Spaniards landed at Kinsale in October 1601, the government could not help itself: at once 500 mariners were ordered to be impressed in the west, 300 from Devon, 200 from Cornwall.[5] A horse and man, armed and furnished, were to be provided by every gentleman in the southern counties.[6] In November 100 Cornish levies went from Barnstaple, in December another 100 from Padstow.[7] Horses were shipped from Padstow; the mayors of these ports were ordered to provide shipping and fodder, lodging for the men. For the benefit of the Irish service, in December fast running posts were laid, to carry packets and letters, between Plymouth and Falmouth.[8] After the landing at Kinsale a like service was established between Plymouth and Padstow.[9] At Padstow there was a post-bark ready: one hears of it leaving with letters from the Lord Admiral to the Fleet, or someone fears it has been lost in the vehement storms of that December, and is providing another 'to sail this night, weather permitting'.[10] One day at Falmouth Parker made a very good catch: a loquacious Irishman, whose uncle was bishop of Santiago, could not help confiding to Robert Mundy of Penryn (father of Peter Mundy, the traveller) that he was carrying letters from Spain to Tyrone.[11] Mundy rushed with the news to Pendennis, where Parker's ordnance was in time to stay the ship: so presumably he had got his guns at last.

[1] A.P.C., XXX. 789; XXXI. 315, 365, 444; XXXII. 82.   [2] ibid., XXX. 795.
[3] ibid., 55.   [4] Salisbury MSS., VII. 160.   [5] A.P.C., XXXII. 255.
[6] ibid., 278.   [7] ibid., 239, 444.   [8] ibid., XXXI. 20, 418.
[9] ibid., XXXII. 304.   [10] Salisbury MSS., XI. 519, 534.   [11] ibid., 119.

So the weary war went on and on: old Burghley, who had his ear to the ground, had known to what accompaniment of increasing war-weariness, despondency, sickness, misery, disenchantment. All that remains now are the schedules of payments to maimed soldiers from the parishes, entries of relief to them, of their deaths, in the registers.[1] Essex, the darling of the younger generation, would not realize this: it was what led him to his fall. That fall, and the tragic manner of it, increased the disenchantment. There is evidence of that in the plays of Shakespeare, as also in the speech of a Cornish captain, home from abroad, his tongue loosed by the wine that flowed when his friends flocked about him, in an inn at Padstow.[2] He swore that 'if Sir Ferdinando Gorges had not been, the Earl of Essex had yet been living and a true subject', and he added, 'the crows will eat his flesh whatsoever the dogs do with his bones'. These were dangerous sentiments, though true enough: Gorges, persuaded by Ralegh, only saved his life by turning queen's evidence against his friend and patron.

To the idiot people, Essex could do nothing wrong, Ralegh nothing right. In fact, of course, the case was almost exactly the reverse: everything that Essex did was ill-judged and ill-executed, whereas Ralegh was a man of profound intuition, great abilities and intellectual power. He was not a good politician, but a genius; and as such disliked and — because he knew and resented that — hated. A court-ballad of this time says:

> Ralegh doth time bestride,
> He sits twixt wind and tide,
> Yet uphill he cannot ride
> For all his bloody pride;
> He seeks taxes in the tin,
> He polls the poor to the skin,
> Yet he swears 'tis no sin,
> Lord for thy pity.[3]

There is no evidence that he polled the tinners: as Lord Warden he made himself a means to the Queen for the favourable treatment of the poor tinners.[4] When he was made Lord Lieutenant of Cornwall, somebody protested because he did not reside there. Nobody had objected that against two generations of Russells. Yet Ralegh was closely related in Cornwall and was very attentive to his duties — as this chapter proves. Carew dedicated his

---

[1] cf. S.P. 12/288, 36 for an account of payments to maimed soldiers in five hundreds of Cornwall.
[2] *Salisbury MSS.*, XI. 267.   [3] S.P. 12/278, 23.   [4] *Salisbury MSS.*, X. 374.

book to him in language which was deserved; Sir John Eliot, a later generation, was inspired by his life and his melancholy end. His memory in later
ages, his undying fame, have more than made up for his want of popularity
in his own.

His period of power in the state, of highest office in Cornwall, came to an
end with the Queen's life. Parker published the proclamation of James,
'which with a general joy and applause was then received and so continues'.[1]
The accession of James meant peace. To the war-weary, overburdened
county of Cornwall, it must have come as a blessed relief: the end of the
fighting Elizabethan age.

[1] *Salisbury MSS.*, xv. 29.

CHAPTER XVI

THE LIFE OF THE SOCIETY AND OF THE INDIVIDUAL

We have now exposed, in some detail, the structure and character of Tudor society as it is to be seen in microcosm in Cornwall; we have shown the fabric in which men lived their lives, studied the foundations upon which it was reared, described the external conditions of men's actions, recounted the story of the actions themselves. It remains to ask what was the inner content of the lives lived within that fabric. What sort of men were these? What were their loves, hopes, passions, fears, beliefs? In what light, in so far as it expresses itself unconsciously in their actions, did they view life? Is it possible to discern any change in the character of their society, in the quality of their common life, in the course of that age which saw such profound historic changes externally? Has there been any progress that we can witness?

These are the ultimate and most difficult questions for the historian to answer. Indeed the answers can only suggest themselves, slowly and patiently, as the picture forms in our mind from the evidences of that vanished age. Even now we still must proceed from an external approach, exploring inward, laying an occasional finger where we can upon some fragment of experience in which life once pulsed.

We are exceedingly fortunate in having as the *terminus ad quem* of our studies Carew's *Survey of Cornwall*, for it is in itself a portrait of Cornish society as it was at the end of our period. Of the distinguished antiquarian works of the time from the pens of such men as Camden, Stow, Spelman, Lambarde, Carew's is not the least worthy of renown, nor the least distinctive. Indeed it is not too much to say that it is the best written and has the most character. Carew has left to posterity an admirable portrait of himself in his book. An Elizabethan gentleman of ancient family and fair estates, devoted to the duties of his station, justice of the peace, sheriff of his county, member of Parliament, treasurer and colonel of the forces, he was, what was more, a man of scholarly tastes and attainments, well-versed in languages, with considerable literary abilities, a style of his own, a certain charming Elizabethan quaintness of conceit, a scribbling man. From his portrait there speak to us the wide-awake, intelligent eyes, the trim-cut hair of the country-gentleman of moderate Protestant inclinations, the neat beard; from his beautiful Italian signature we discern the man of taste, of the new education.

But it is from his book above all that we see the kind of man he was: his kindliness and tolerance (except where pettifogging lawyers were concerned) his insatiable curiosity, his liking for a good story, like that of Martin Trewynnard's snake, or of the building of church and barn at Sheviock, his eye for any oddity of place or person or thing, the mixture of credulity and scepticism which describes the man of the Renaissance. He tells us, for example, 'that in the west parts of Cornwall, during the winter season, swallows are found sitting in old deep tinworks and holes of the sea cliffs: but touching their lurking places, Olaus Magnus maketh a far stranger report. For he saith that in the north parts of the world, as summer weareth out, they clap mouth to mouth, wing to wing, and leg in leg, and so after a sweet singing, fall down into certain great lakes or pools amongst the canes, from whence at the next spring, they receive a new resurrection'.[1] He adds gravely that he had seen this confirmed by a Venetian ambassador to Poland and heard it 'avowed by travellers in those parts: wherethrough I am induced to give it a place of probability in my mind, and of report in this treatise'. He was evidently touched by the pathetic story of devotion of Sir William Bevil's dwarf, the deaf-mute, John Size.[2] He had the usual Elizabethan feeling for landscape, liking it trim and orderly, which made Essex complain of the 'rugged mountains of Cornwall'. A touch of personal feeling comes into his description of Tintagel: 'Under the Island runs a cave, through which you may row at full sea, but not without a kind of horror at the uncouthness of the place'.[3] He had a good eye for the picturesque scene, as we may see from his descriptions of Plymouth Sound and Fowey haven, opening out to 'the vast ocean, sparkled with ships, that continually this way trade forth and back to most quarters of the world'.[4] He preferred the valleys and cultivated lowlands, especially where there were good rivers to fish, like his own Lynher, upon the tidal waters of which his own pleasant house of Antony looked down, the spire of Merrifield church near by among the trees.

He was an enthusiastic angler, very much of a Cornish Walton in spirit, and many of the verses with which his book is sprinkled are devoted to his favourite sport.

---

[1] *Survey*, 25 b.
[2] ibid., 130.
[3] ibid., 121.
[4] ibid., 133.

I wait not at the lawyers' gates,
Ne shoulder climbers down the stairs;
I vaunt not manhood by debates,
I envy not the miser's fears:
　　But mean[1] in state, and calm in sprite,
　　My fishfull pond is my delight.

In heat the top, in cold the deep:
In spring the mouth, the midst in neap:
With changeless change by shoals they keep,
Fat, fruitful, ready, but not cheap:
　　Thus mean in state, and calm in sprite,
　　My fishfull pond is my delight.

When he comes to deal with his own fishponds at Antony he spreads himself: it is to be feared that, like most fishermen, he was a bore about fishing. His verses do not rise above this level, pleasant and ambling; they often fall below it. He was the kind of poet that well-educated country gentlemen of that day were apt to be. In these verses, the influence of his reading is apparent: the first reminds one of Sir Richard Grenville's poem 'In Praise of Seafaring Men', following a common model; the second, in rhythm and its antitheses, brings to mind Southwell's

The sea of Fortune doth not ever flow.

But then Carew was very much a reading man. He was well versed in the classics; we find him citing naturally and easily Herodotus — with whom his own temper was so much akin — Diodorus Siculus, Aesop and many such.[2] And not only these, but the chroniclers: he quotes Matthew of Westminster, Roger Hoveden and others, upon points of Cornish history, for all was grist to his mill that bore upon Cornwall. In his account of the tin-industry, he refers to Munster's Cosmography and Francis Leandro's writings on minerals; but these references he probably owes to Sir Francis Godolphin, who, like Carew, knew and read Italian. Carew refers familiarly several times to the histories of Macchiavelli and Guicciardini; his preference in contemporary literature, following the taste of the time, was for Italian, though he read French also. Nor was he above taking note of the legend of some obscure little Cornish saint, such as the parish churches preserved in

---

[1] In the Elizabethan sense, meaning 'moderate'.
[2] cf. pp. 125-6 for a whole section exhibiting his classical and other reading.

pre-Reformation days: would he had made a collection of them, as Nicholas Roscarrock set out to do! Perhaps his Protestantism prevented him from thinking of it — though his religion was of no exclusive, polemical cast. He was genuinely pious, after an Anglican pattern; a man after Archbishop Parker's own heart, to whose Society of Antiquaries he was elected nineteen years after the Archbishop's death. He loved the past: 'I reverence antiquity', he wrote. What is more, he had the gift of style by which to express his love upon every page of his book, and so his work lives.

Carew was sent at the age of eleven, early even for those days, to Oxford where he was entered at Broadgates Hall. When a scholar of three years' standing, he tells us, 'upon a wrong conceived opinion touching my sufficiency I was there called to dispute *ex tempore* (*impar congressus Achilli*) with the matchless Sir Philip Sidney, in presence of the Earls Leicester, Warwick and divers other great personages'.[1] He was clearly a clever lad. From Oxford he went to the Middle Temple, and then early inherited the family estates, so that he did not travel abroad like his much-travelled kindred. Staying at home, he married a Coswarth, got with her some property, attended to his family and county affairs, and learned modern languages for himself from books. In addition to Latin and Greek, he knew Italian, French, Spanish and apparently German.[2] About the time he became a member of the Society of Antiquaries, he took in hand the task of compiling his *Survey*. But first, in 1594, he published his translation of Tasso's *Gerusalemme Liberata*, by which he made for himself a respectable place among the Tudor translators. In the same year appeared his version of Juan de la Huarte's *Examen de Ingenios*, from the Italian translation lent him by Godolphin. The loan was repaid by a dedication: 'Good sir, your book returneth unto you clad in a Cornish gabardine'. This work appealed to the Elizabethan public, and three editions were issued in Carew's lifetime. Next came a poem, *The Herring's Tail*, published anonymously in 1598, and there were various other verses that came from his pen to celebrate local and personal occasions.[3]

Then, in 1602, appeared the *Survey*. In his dedication to Ralegh, Carew calls it 'this mine ill-husbanded Survey, long since begun, a great while discontinued, lately reviewed, and now hastily finished', and there are indications in the text that this represents the state of the case. From his epistle to the reader, we gather that a few copies of the book in manuscript had early been passed round among his friends, and that it was 'Master Camden's

---

[1] *Survey*, 102 b.
[2] cf. his epitaph in Gilbert, *History of Cornwall*, IV. 378-9.
[3] cf. article in *D.N.B.*; Boase and Courtney, *Bibliotheca Cornubiensis*, I. 56-8; III. IIII.

often-mentioning this work, and my friends' persuasions', that brought him to publish it. It was printed for John Jaggard, and was to be bought at the sign of the Hand and Star near Temple Bar. Four years later he was meditating a second edition; he had learned that the Solicitor-general, Doddridge, 'hath compiled a treatise of our Cornish Duchy, and dedicated it to the Prince; this I much long to see and heartily pray by your means to obtain a copy thereof'.[1] He prepared a second edition of the *Survey*, 'not so much for the enlarging it, as the correcting mine and the printer's oversights ... I imagine that I may cull out of Mr. Solicitor's garden many flowers to adorn this other edition; and if I wist where to find Mr. Norden, I would also fain have his map of our shire, for perfecting of which he took a journey into these parts'. The letter concludes with a postscript: 'I pray, sir, make me beholden unto you for occurrents'. In his remote country-seat, which he did not now much leave, he was interested in what passed in the world.

However, he never brought his second edition to pass. About this time he contributed to the second edition of Camden's *Remains* 'An Epistle concerning the Excellencies of the English Tongue', which has its place in Elizabethan criticism, for it is a wholehearted statement of the case for the English language for all literary purposes, of all the greater force coming with such sincerity and conviction from one well qualified to speak of languages both ancient and modern. The essay is famous for one of the earliest references to Shakespeare: 'Will you read Vergil? take the Earl of Surrey; Catullus? Shakespeare, and Marlowe's fragment; Ovid? Daniel; Lucan? Spenser; Martial? Sir John Davies and others ... Will you have all in all for prose and verse? take the miracle of our age, Sir Philip Sidney.' At some time too he wrote an essay on the best method of learning Latin, which was printed in the Commonwealth time, with a dedication to Francis, son of his old friend across the water and up the Tamar to Halton, Sir Anthony Rowse. Carew lived on, honoured and remembered by the circle of antiquaries he had frequented in London: Spelman dedicated to him an Epistle concerning Tithes; John Dunbar addressed two Latin epigrams to him, Charles Fitzgeoffrey a Latin poem, Henry Lock an English sonnet; Ben Jonson named him along with Selden and Cotton. Such were the courtesies which reached him in his quiet retreat, reading, angling, keeping his bees. He died on November 6th, 1620, 'as he was at his private prayers in his study (his daily practice) at four in the afternoon', and was buried in sweet Antony church hard by his house.

Such was the life of our chief literary light in that age: a plain country

[1] Cotton MS. Jul. C., v.

gentleman of no great worldly importance or fame, unlike his cousins Ralegh and Grenville. Yet he has left his abiding memorial, no less than they.

He was not the only writing man in Cornwall even in that day. There was the young poet, Charles Fitzgeoffrey, who was born at Fowey in the seventies; like other young Cornishmen of the time — they went naturally to Oxford, being westcountrymen — he followed Carew at Broadgates Hall.[1] While there, in 1596, he published a spirited poem on 'Sir Francis Drake, his honourable Life's Commendation and his tragical Death's Lamentation'. It was dedicated to the Queen, had commendatory verses prefixed to it by his fellow students at Broadgates Hall, Francis and Richard Rowse of Halton, and immediately won him favourable notice: Francis Meres refers to him as 'that high-towering falcon', and many passages from his poems are included in England's Parnassus of 1600. Next year appeared a volume of his Latin poems and epigrams, in which comes that addressed to Carew along with those to Drayton, Daniel, Sir John Harington and others. He took holy orders and was presented by Sir Anthony Rowse to the living of St. Dominick, the parish church of Halton. Henceforth he only published sermons on godly subjects and such occasions as the funerals of Sir Anthony and his wife. She, by her first husband, was the mother of John Pym; and there in the nineties, among the cherry-orchards of Tamarside, the young Pym was growing up. In 1599 he followed his foster-brother, Francis Rowse, who later became one of the more voluminous of Puritan writers, Speaker of Barebones' Parliament and Provost of Eton, to Broadgates Hall. In these same years, only a few miles away, a still younger lad was growing up in the great house of the monks at St. Germans: John Eliot. A new age that is opening out before us; between them these two lads were to shatter the old landmarks of the Elizabethan world.

If we would explore further, more intimately, into the life of a country gentleman of the time, there is the fascinating fragment of William Carnsew's diary for 1576-77.[2] We have already looked into his mining ventures; his private life is even more interesting. He was of an old family of Mabe parish near Penryn, where he had lands.[3] But for some time the family had been living at Bokelly in St. Kew, that house in the grove of trees from which it derives its name, in sight of Rowtor on the uplands of Bodmin moor on one side, and of Pentire Point at the entrance to Padstow haven on the other.

---

[1] cf. art. in D.N.B., and Boase and Courtney, op. cit., I. 148-150.
[2] S.P. 46/16.   [3] Henderson, History of Mabe, 31-3.

Carnsew was a person of no particular importance in the county's affairs: that is his interest to us. He was just a plain J.P., who went about his grounds, overlooked his men at their shearing or hedging or delving, went to church, visited his friends, scolded his children, read a good deal, and like most diarists was plainly an inveterate gossip. It would seem that occasionally a story was put upon him, as appears from his entry: 'The Saracens took Cadiz in Spain in January, as heard (a lie) Sessions at Exeter 10 April. At Launceston 9 April it was told me in mirth that the Great Turk was dead and the Lord John d'Austria was in Barbary laying siege to Algiers.' But his information about public affairs, for all his remoteness from the centre of them, was usually correct; for example, 'one Wentworth, committed to prison for his speech and his carriage in the Parliament house'. At the end of the year he tells us there was 'great resort of stately gentlemen' to Exeter to keep Christmas there, as Sir William Courtenay, Sir Arthur Basset, Sir John Gilbert, Sir Gawen Carew and others, besides the Bishop and canons of the Close.

But let us take his daily routine. January he spent at home, going to church on New Year's eve (he calls it Christmas eve); he notes an 'extreme storm: my houses torn with winds'; he dines at St. Mabyn at Glynn's wedding. Next day: 'about my lambs; many died'. Humphry Nicolls' sheep from Penvose 'trespassed me much'; the day after he meets Humphry whose wife has had a young daughter. At the beginning of February, on the Feast of the Purification, he goes over to Roscarrock; it is very wild weather and he stays the night: 'won at play, lost health'. When he comes home, his wife and sister, Jane Penkivell, go 'agossiping to Penvose': no doubt to see the new baby and perhaps attend its christening. On their return he goes on a journey westward to see to his affairs, stopping the first night at Trerice, where he heard that the bishop of Exeter was to be removed to Salisbury. The second night he stopped at Roscrow, then with the St. Aubyns at Clowance: meanwhile 'at home Jane Penkivell's boy ran away with her money'. John St. Aubyn and he rode to see the mine at Binnerton and arranged about working it, for they were partners in the enterprise. At John Nance's, one Richardson 'delivered unto me a Book of Discipline, I think put forth by Cartwright, *incerto authore sine nomine*'. Two months later we find him handing the book over to Ford, the preacher. It is interesting to see the works of the great Puritan passing from hand to hand in the country.

Carnsew was very interested in medical matters — this month he is reading Montanus' *De Febre Sanguinis* — and prided himself upon his skill as a physician. There was a potion which he made, called 'skilly', with which he was very fond of dosing his patients: his daughter Frances received a draught, 'wherewith she was not much molested, but wrought well so as she had three vomits, one stool and amended'. When the vicar was sick, it wrought well too at first; then he fell extremely ill, and in a few days was dead. Carnsew saw him ripped: a putrefaction of the lungs, he said. This mishap in no wise abated his confidence: while at St. Germans for the wedding of Jane Penkivell, he wrote out 'a diet and order for batheing'; next day he 'wrote to Adrian Gilbert for congratulating of my lord of Berry,[1] wherein I wrote of betain to be applied to his nose'. He observed his own symptoms with equal interest: in June he was 'much diseased with rheums, eating milk and cream', or he is diseased with eating fish, or 'troubled in my urine'. In May 'stronger beer did me no good'; in June he is making a conserve of roses, and distilling rose water. News was brought him secretly that poor Mary Roscarrock was frantic; shortly after she was buried *ex melancholico humore*.

But there is no doubt that he enjoyed life: he played bowls and quoits with his friends, he won or lost at saint, sometimes stopping up all night and feeling not much the worse for it; at visitation time he played in Bodmin and won. Then in July he made an excursion to the bishop's at Newton Ferrers, stopping at Port Eliot on the way; he was at the bishop's with Ralph Callard 'and divers greedy gulls gaping for Egloshayle benefice'. He came back through Plymouth, 'saw Mary Langford like a fool', and missing John Eliot, 'dined at a husbandman's house in St. Germans parish; met there with Robert Smith, played at bowls with him, at saint and quoiting with even hand'. Arrived home, a few days later he met Lord Stourton riding, 'after whom I came to Lanherne, dined, played at bowls there and supped; but lay at Trerice'. The week after, 'I am written to to meet Mr. Mohun at Bodmin plays. Spent there 12s., whereof I gave wrastlers 5s. Dined at Killigrew.' Next day he dined there again and played at bowls. The day after, 'walked to Lanseague; saw my meadows cut, my oats almost ripe, my wheat thin, thin. Read upon the Commentaries of Luther to Galatians in English, translated *incognito authore*.'

Carnsew too was a great reading man; he read religious works, medicine, history and current affairs. Early that year he read the history of the Turks newly set forth; in the intervals of chiding his son Richard for sloth, grafting trees, and watching his hedgers, he read to Richard and William from Vegetius and Whithorne. In April he was reading 'Ridley's end and Latimer's and his friendly Farewell', the bishop of Winchester's sermon before Edward VI and Bullinger against the Pope's bull. From a visit to St. Merryn he brought back a Foxe, in which he read a great deal. He exchanged books

---

[1] i.e. Lord Edward Seymour, lord of Berry Pomeroy.

with Lord Mountjoy upon a visit into Devonshire: he left with him Woolton's *An Armour of Proof*, while there read Sir Humphry Gilbert's book — evidently the newly published *Discourse on the North West Passage to Cathay* — and 'had Arbatell *Magiae* of Lord Mountjoy wherein I read. Lord Mountjoy told me of Doctor Julio and how he fled into France'. In the autumn he was reading Marsilio Ficino's *De Triplice Vita*, '*lectu dignissime*', Calvin's Epistles and Life, Foxe again, the Acts of the Council of Basel, a book on astrology, and the Destruction of Antwerp by the Spaniards. Nor does that exhaust the tale of his reading; it is evident that books meant more to him, and some of his friends, than to the average country gentleman of to-day.

His greatest pleasure was, perhaps, in the amenities of friendship and company. He was for ever visiting and being visited, going over to Roscarrock, or to Trerice, where in May 'Francis Godolphin and his wife *cum multis aliis* dined. Talked with Francis Go. of tin and tin works'. Sir John Killigrew calls in on him on his way to the assizes; his horse is tired and Carnsew lends him one of his own. Or Mr. Erisey comes up from the Lizard to ask his help in the matter of the presentation to St. Tudy; together they rode to see the scapegrace parson of St. Merryn, 'who said his son had answered him that he would keep it, sith God hath provided it for him; and was I bobbed and mocked'. At the end of the year he was planting pear-trees, and on January 1st, 'at home all day the worse for play'. Over Twelfth Night he had many guests with him: George Grenville and Richard Carew among them; there was much play at night and Carnsew lost heavily. One morning in December he had got up early, 'sent to the fair, reckoned with my servants, paid them wages and so to bed again, when I left but 2s. 6d. in my purse'. In the summer he had had to send Matthew westwards to look for moneys; fortunately he brought back some. Then there were weddings to be arranged and attended: the festivities lasted over several days; church affairs — the communion plate to be made more commodiously, talking over pulling down the rood loft, his interest in the vicar's son riding hurriedly to London to get his father's benefice, and returning in triumph with the broad seal for it. There were his affairs about the house: removing trees, 'setting hops and raisin trees', tilling oats, shearing sheep, watching his hay being made up into cocks, selling his wool, riding over to Port Isaac to buy fish; at the end of the year noting the shipwrecks upon that terrible north coast, 'three hulks at Widemouth, one at Treledroke, a Frenchman from Guinea, all between the 23rd and 26th this November'.

So life passes for William Carnsew: one night he dreamed of his elder brother, who must have been long dead; another time he notes a strange dream of Winchester's box. He goes to communion once a quarter, noting that he passed the day 'temperate', reading in Calvin or Luther or the Scriptures. He was anxious to do his best for his boys, writing to his friend Lord Mountjoy on behalf of Matthew. On October 20th, 'Matthew departed towards Lord Mountjoy with weeping tears. The wind south-east.' Nine days later, on a morning of rain, he came home again. He and his brother were to return to Oxford. 'John Kenall with me for to have William go to Oxford, and lent me a nag, promised to write his letters for placing of him.' On November 7th, 'Matthew and William went away towards Oxford'. In December the letters begin to come down from thence; John Nance's son dies and is buried there. The image of William Carnsew, so clear to us for just this year 1576-77, that tells us so much about that vanished life, withdraws into shadows and so into silence. It is for his sons to speak.

It happens that we possess a few leaves of the diary and accounts which Richard and Matthew kept, evidently on their father's instructions, for a part of the years 1573-74 at Oxford: a rare, perhaps a unique thing, for I do not know any other source from which we can reconstruct the life of an undergraduate of that time.[1] In May, they 'received letters out of Cornwall and with them 40d'. Next day: 'made definitions of *homo* by the five ways. Bought paper 4d.' Then: 'our Principal went to the Parliament'; 'made exercises to master vice-Principal'. At the end of the month they were reading Sallust; Richard's shoes were mended for 2d., and they bought Calvin, Melanchthon, Calton on Logic bound in one volume for 12d. In June they bought Foxe's Sermons and were engaged in translating them into Latin; Richard was polled for 1d., and the cook's wages paid (8d.). August was mostly filled with exercises in logic; both lads were polled, they bought a pound of candle for 4d., two pairs of gloves for 12d., and Richard a pair of garters (12d.). In October the brothers parted, the one leaving the other 20d. Matthew heard Mr. Curry's public lectures in natural philosophy — presumably the fellow of Exeter who later became a Jesuit. He wrote into Cornwall twice this month, when Mr. Tregose came to town by his man, and by Mr. Arscott's man. At the end of October Mr. Doctor Kenall came home, we learn. In November the brothers were together again. John Goldsmith, the parson of St. Kew's son, who was up with them, fell sick: 'we were with him all the time of his sickness, which was a cause of defect in reading as you willed us'.

Next year Matthew entered into commons at Christ Church, from Broadgates Hall where they were entered. He began to translate Cebes' Table, for

1 S.P. 46/15.

Ann° dñi. 1586

Chi verace durera

Ætatis suæ 32.

RICHARD CAREW

TRERICE

which he borrowed the book of John Goldsmith. 'What needed that, sith you had one of your own?' is the careful father's comment in the margin. Richard began to translate Cicero's *De Amicitia*. They removed into 'an higher chamber, the rent 13s. 4d.' After this extravagance they borrowed 14d. of John Cole, and began to read Peter Martyr on Aristotle's Ethics — 'borrowed the book of Sir Matthew'. In April, 'my brother very sick'; then 'we laid in 40d. to the common stock of the house because our manciple gave over his office'. On April 22nd 'we were sworn in to observe the statutes of the house which were read to us'. In December they wrote into Cornwall by Kenall's man; and on Christmas Eve were reading 'the books set forth by the Puritans to the parliament'.

So their education proceeded: any amount of logic — no wonder the Crown found the country gentlemen of England such tough nuts to crack in Parliament — Cicero and Aristotle's Ethics, the great Reformers, Parliament affairs. And all the while, there are innumerable small expenses for 'making of our gowns', fustian for the back, fur for the front, a pair of shoes, two dozen of points, a cap for 2s. 4d. We hear no more of Richard, the elder brother, at the university: during the period covered by his father's diary we find him living at home. Matthew took his B.A. in 1575, his M.A. in June 1579.[1] Dr. Kenall, who took an interest in the youngest lad William, was as good as his word: he was an influential person in the university, and William went up to Broadgates Hall like his brothers. He became a Fellow of All Souls in 1579, and, following in the Doctor's footsteps, took his B.C.L. in 1588.[2] He was M.P. for Camelford in the parliaments of 1597-98 and 1601.

The kind of fellow he was may be seen in his letters from his chambers in London home to Bokelly, particularly the affectionate, chaffing ones he wrote to his brother Richard of whom he was fond. 'Messor Richardo carissimo', he writes in October 1583, 'my father wrote to me by this bearer that you should come to London about Allhallowtide, which I think is called Christmas. I pray you forget not to bring £3 of good and lawful moneys of England with you for me, for I want it. And if you can speak to my father conveniently for it, you may do me a great pleasure; the like and greater pains must I do for you one day. If you bring more it must be welcome, if less, yet all is fish that comes to the net.'[3] He sends commendations to his friend 'Mr. Nicholls of Penvose, that is to say as well friends as foes, my cousin Mo. Hill and his wife, all at Roscarrock, Tregear and every other where: all the good hurlers in St. Kew with whom perchance I shall hurl this next year'. Did he? one wonders: one would so like to know.

[1] *Reg. Univ. Oxon.* (O.H.S.), II. 50.   [2] Foster, *Alumni Oxonienses*, I. 239.   [3] S.P. 46/71.

In fact his father came up to London in November. After he left, a Mr. Mordant showed young William great courtesy: insisting that William's father was a connection of his wife's, he hired a horse for the young man and took him down to his house to stay for three days near Oxford. 'While I was there he used me with all kind of familiarity and at my departure thence he lent me one of his own geldings to me to come home to Oxford withal.' It is obvious that young William was an attractive lad, whom people took a fancy to. 'By his means I spent nothing in London save 12s., wherewith I bought a hat, a shirt and a pair of stockings, and a little book of law places entitled *Topica Legalia*.' William reports that he has paid his battels and his debts out of the £7 his father gave him on departing: he has 28s. left in his purse, with which he must 'buy a load of wood to burn this winter and buy a doublet also if I may, for I have great need thereof'. He complains that the London carrier has forgotten to bring down to Oxford the books his father left with him there, so that he could not send them down to Cornwall by 'this carrier'. To his mother he sends thanks in December for two shirts and a powder: 'I have done wonderful cures for the green sickness and am much sought unto by divers, for they call me the best physician in England for that disease, and all is through your powder which hath so much increased my credit'. Evidently there was a strong streak of his father in him.

Two years later there is a high-spirited, chaffing letter to Richard: he has no news for him, 'yet you may not, nor shall not be unsaluted', and sending commendations to all the good friends at home: 'to old and young Roche, to Bokelly, Tregear and by west the bridge though unacquainted and never thought on, generally to all your acquaintance wheresoever, not forgetting my very good friends of Roscarrock, their courteous guests and gentle frump. Oh, Heigh-ho: why, Mathy, what occasion hadst thou to go etc. O love, love! I fear me, Richard, this whoreson love will kill us all. Sustine pro nunc. If there can be a letter to Braband, I pray let it be speedily delivered. Vale. . . .'[1] Two years later, the summer of 1587 — Drake is on the coast of Spain — William is writing: 'Mr. Justinian and I have made such a league as that the one is bound to take the other's part in any indifferent cause. He hath given his promise and I my hand never to fail our friends in any just cause. Would Juno and you were such catercousins as Pallas and I mean to be, then would I come home to sing a song to Hymen and would not doubt but to help to fill your new consort with good concord. My bow served my turn passing well and Will thanks you for him. God keep you.'[2]

And that is all. For all his merry chaff, the brothers did not marry until

---

[1] S.P. 46/17.   [2] ibid., 71.

late: William himself setting an example by marrying Ann Arundell of Trerice in 1610.[1] His brother did not follow suit until 1619, Matthew not at all: he died in 1613. The brothers were all childless, their sisters unmarried; and so old William's line died out at Bokelly, and silence descends upon them all. And yet as one passes by on the roadside, the view of Rowtor opening out on the right, and one looks left across the fields to that house among the trees, one seems to hear an echo of those long vanished voices: the dead place comes alive for a moment with the thought of all that happy crowded life, old William and his whims, Jane Penkivell and her boy running away with her purse, Richard Grenville coming over to discuss a match, the vicar sick, and young William in London longing to come home and hurl once again with all the good hurlers of St. Kew.

Carew tells us that in his time the sea-coast towns were thriving, the inland ones decaying.[2] He meant by the latter such places as Tregony and St. Germans, which had never been anything much, but the relative importance of which in the Middle Ages was greater. Of Lostwithiel he says, in spite of its 'mayoralty, markets, fairs, and nomination of burgesses for the Parliament', its coinage, keeping of the stannary gaol and county courts — 'yet all this can hardly raise it to a tolerable condition of wealth and inhabitance.'[3] There were two exceptions to this: Launceston, the county town, and Truro. Launceston had picked up since the days of Henry VIII: 'a new increase of wealth expresseth itself in the inhabitants' late repaired and enlarged buildings'.[4] Of Truro: 'I hold it to have got the start in wealth of any other Cornish town, and to come behind none in buildings, Launceston only excepted, where there is more use and profit of fair lodgings, through the county assizes'.[5] He regarded Saltash as the most 'healthfully situated' of Cornish towns, and Bodmin as the most unhealthily.[6] He goes on to a whole attack on the latter, its siting, the sun excluded by the hills, its 'filth by every great shower washed down through their houses into the streets', its water supply coming through the churchyard, 'the ordinary place of burial for town and parish. It breedeth little cause of marvel that every general infection is here first admitted and last excluded. Yet the many decayed houses prove the town to have been once very populous'. True enough, there were three visitations of the plague in these years, 1576, 1581 and 1590, and there was a great mortality at Bodmin.[7]

For the life of the towns, let us look into what was going on at Launceston,

---

[1] Vivian, *Visitations*, 77.   [2] *Survey*, 65 b.   [3] ibid., 137.   [4] ibid., 116.
[5] ibid., 142.   [6] ibid., 123.   [7] *Bodmin Register*, 15.

and, at the other end of the county, at St. Ives which was growing into a thriving, self-conscious township. As we should expect, there is reflected in all such town accounts as survive the increasingly secular trend of the age. Where the earlier town-accounts of Launceston were dominated by payments for the church of St. Mary Magdalen, for quantities of wax for its services, torches for funerals, for vestments and making the Easter sepulchre and cord for mass-bells, for celebration of obits and all the paraphernalia of medieval Catholicism, now a great simplification and a saving had been wrought in all that. Not that the conduct of the town's affairs was any less paternal than it had been, or the eye and hand of the burgesses any less prying or interfering. Nothing was too small to escape them. Thomas Batten is fined 12d., 'for that he keepeth a mastiff bitch, and that William Hocken standeth in fear of his life for him'.[1] They 'remember master Mayor, to see some order for Harry Bere, because he is betrothed unto Jane Cornish and doth not marry her, which is contrary to any good order'.[2]

Nor do church affairs escape their attention, though they play a less dominating part: other interests and concerns have grown up. But the church is still coterminous with society: 'We present such as do not come to church to serve God, not in long time; their excuse is that they be in debt, so that by that means they displease God more ways than ii or iii: we pray you, Mr. Mayor, to see an order for it, or else to rid the town of such persons.' There is still music in church, though we find nothing about the organs, which were a frequent item of expense in pre-Reformation days: in 1574, 'paid for pricking a Magnificat, a Nunc Dimittis, an anthem and a psalm, v s'. That same year there was paid for 'paper to prick songs which were sent from Torrington, 4d.'; no doubt secular music: did the mayor and his brethren sing them, one wonders? The bishop still comes to his manor of Lezant: 6s. 8d. was paid for a 'banquet' to him this year; not an over-liberal allowance: perhaps it meant only a drink all round on his arrival. Nowadays he comes on the same footing as other gentlemen visiting the town, as for example the year before: 'Gave to Sir Gawen Carew, half a pound of sugar, 8d.; to Sir John Arundell, a quarter of a pound of sugar, 4d.; to Mr. Mohun, half a pound of sugar, 8d.' But the year before they had presented the bishop with a hogshead of wine, which with the carriage cost 52s.

There were innumerable little works of charity, of good fellowship and good cheer, as well as those of a disciplinary nature, which testify to that close-knit life, where everybody knew everybody else's business, where there was little privacy, for they lived on top of one another: the warm,

[1] Peter, *Launceston*, 220.   [2] ibid., 203 et seq. for the following paragraphs.

huddled life of a numerous family living in a small space, rich in the smells of humanity. Jeffery's two boys are paid 4d. for leasing stones; Pears's wife 2d. 'for boiled apples given the children that leased stones'. There are small payments to 'one that was robbed upon London way', to another that was whipped 4d. (Was a groat sufficient compensation for his smarts?) 'To two men and a woman of Stratton which had their houses overthrown with a mighty wind and flood, 27 February 1574, 18d.' Again there are payments for songs: 'For a song which I brought from Exeter, at the request of Mr. Parr, 18d.'; 'to Mr. Parr for songs he bought, 3s.' The good burgesses must have been very fond of music, since they laid out more upon it than upon most items. Carew tells us how fond the Cornish were of their three-men songs, 'cunningly contrived for the ditty and pleasantly for the note'. There was a famous one sung at Fowey which celebrated the prowess of one Nicholas, a widow's son, who fought against a Doria set forth by the French King, and in the end took and slew him.[1] Presumably these three-men songs were the ancestors of such songs as 'I will sing you one, O' and 'I saw three ships come sailing by' that went on being sung right up to the time of my grandparents.

Launceston had its share of festivities: a good dinner for the mayor and burgesses, and neighbouring gentlemen, on Coronation day; payments in 1577 to the interlude players, Lord Stafford's men, 13s. 4d. At Plymouth contemporaneously the town was often visited by the players; until the time came, after the accession of James, when half a crown was given to 'the interlude players to depart the town without playing'.[2] The growth of Puritan feeling among the burgesses made them willing to pay far more to preachers for their interminable sermons. Launceston, as the assize town, had its more gruesome festivities. We find in 1577 — the year of Mayne's martyrdom — payments for rushes for the hall and speech house, for the Queen's arms painted in cloth, for making the gibbet.[3] And then, the sorry end to these proceedings, in St. Thomas's churchyard in the valley beneath the castle: payments for horses to 'bring home' the prisoners, to the men for 'helping of them home', for 'washing of the prisoners', for 'making of the pits', for burying them.[4]

Life at St. Ives, allowing for the different conditions of a new and growing seaport town which lived chiefly by fishing, was in essentials the same. Probably even more intimate and close, however — the fishermen's cottages packed together upon the narrow neck of the Island — than with an inland town, owing to the conditions of its livelihood, as is still more noticeably the

[1] Carew, 135.   [2] Worth, op. cit., 145.   [3] Peter, 212.   [4] ibid., 373.

case to-day. (Perhaps the difference was less then.) From the Borough Accounts we see what a large place was taken in the social life of that little community by the summer games and the miracle plays; they also were a chief source of revenue from which to provide money for charitable purposes. In 1573 the head warden received £1 os. 11d. of John Clark for the interlude; 6d. of William Trenwith for 'six score and three foot of elm boards in the playing place', of Harry Hayne for boards 1s. 6d.; and from the king and queen of the summer games, £1 os. 4d.[1] Next year there is a more detailed and profitable account of the returns from the play: 12s. the first day, the second £1 12s. 2d., the third £4 10s. 11d., the fourth £1 19s. 6d., the fifth £3 2s., the sixth £3 os. 1d.; more received for drink money 1s. 2d., of William Trenwith in the churchyard — that would be for the church-ale — £1 16s. 2d., and for drink money after the play 2s. 8d.[2] It was evidently a very successful, rollicking, riotous week they made of it; it so exhausted the resources of the townsfolk that the summer games only made 14s. 6d. that year.

Carew tells us how much the Cornish loved their guary-miracles; and how they would come from several parishes together to spend several days enjoying themselves. 'The country people flock from all sides, many miles off, to hear and see it; for they have therein devils and devices to delight as well the eye as the ear.'[3] There are no details given of the scenery employed at St. Ives, except obliquely on one occasion: 'spent upon the carpenters that made Heaven, 4d.', no doubt for drink to encourage the good work.[4] Sometimes the town received a visit from other performers: in 1588, 'gave the Robin Hood of St. Columb the lower by the appointment of Mr. Tregenna, 5s.'[5] It is pleasant to find that in spite of Sir John Arundell's Catholicism and absence now from Cornwall, ten horseloads of moor-rushes went from his manor of Connerton to strew the church with fresh rushes at Christmas, as they had been given by him and his ancestors 'time out of mind'.[6] As the years go by we observe the times becoming more grim and earnest, reflected as in a mirror in the accounts: the place formerly occupied by the plays comes to be taken by the necessities of the war, there are frequent payments on account of the soldiers going to Ireland, for their equipment and feeding, bulwarks are erected upon the coast, a gun set up in the churchyard. Sir Francis Godolphin comes to and fro over these matters; he is regaled with wine; mutual courtesies pass between him and the townsmen. And then infallibly as we pass from the age of Elizabeth to that of James,

---

[1] Matthews, *History of St. Ives, Lelant, etc.*, 144-5. [2] ibid., 147.
[3] *Survey*, 71 b. [4] Matthews, 148. [5] ibid., 157. [6] ibid., 154.

from the heroic age to that of reflection, speculation, heart-searching, we find the sermons multiplying, here as at Plymouth. The vicar of Gwinnear, a preaching man, is given a dinner for himself and his friends, 'when he gave us a sermon gratis'; 'more at his next sermon, for his pains and dinner 6s. 6d.'[1] He was evidently much appreciated; the sermons of the godly were, alas, taking the place of the old miracle-plays; society in the towns was coming under the control of the Protestant bourgeois, in the country of the Puritan gentry. We are over the threshold of the seventeenth century: we see Puritanism, the Civil War looming before us, the Wesleyanism of the eighteenth century, the Nonconformity of the nineteenth, that dank cloud upon the life of modern Cornwall.

The growth of Puritan sentiment may be seen in the curious discussion which Carew includes on the subject of parish feasts and church-ales.[2] 'Of late times', he says, 'many ministers have by their earnest invectives both condemned these Saints' feasts as superstitious and suppressed the church-ales as licentious'. Yet the latter at any rate had the justification of serving a useful purpose, 'raising a store, which might be converted partly to good and godly uses, as relieving all sorts of poor people, repairing of churches, building of bridges, amending of highways'. To which Carew replies — the discussion is in dialogue-form — that 'the very title of ale was somewhat nasty, and the thing itself had been corrupted with such a multitude of abuses, to wit idleness, drunkenness, lasciviousness, vain disports of minstrelsy, dancing and disorderly night-watchings, that the best curing was to cut it clean away'. It is difficult to know whether this exactly represented Carew's own opinion, or whether he was merely stating a case.

Anyhow we may be sure that whatever he thought, there were still cakes and ale in the Cornish parishes. In the Green Book of St. Columb major, from which we can reconstruct the social life of the parish, the wardens carry over from year to year among the parish goods, '5 coats for dancers, 1 friar's coat, 24 dancing bells, a streamer of red mocado and lockram'.[3] There were plenty of occasions for feasting and jollity in the course of the year: had not the Reformers made a point of attacking the undue number of Saints' days observed in the county? But nothing persuaded the Cornish to abandon the celebration, with appropriate junketings, of their own particular parish feast at the anniversary of their patron saint or dedication: as for instance at St. Austell in Trinity week, for the church was re-dedicated by Bishop Bronescombe to the Holy Trinity. Almost everywhere it still continues,

---

[1] ibid., 174.   [2] *Survey*, 69-71.
[3] *J.R.I.C.* no. 59 (Supplement 1912).

though its original rationale, as always in the sleeping minds of the people, has long been forgotten. At Mevagissey, at St. Peter's-tide, the procession still wends its way down to the quay, as in the Middle Ages when the image of the Saint was carried down to bless the waters and their increase, though nothing is remembered of the purpose for which they go — a partly instinctive and wholly customary impulse, an empty, unmeaning gesture with a pathos of its own.

There were so many other occasions of good cheer, about which Carew and others tell us, many of which have survived down to to-day, or yesterday.[1] There were harvest dinners, the custom of 'crying the neck', when a shock from the last sheaf to be gathered in was brought into the farmhouse bound with ribbons and escorted by the harvesters singing and crying 'A-neck, A-neck': my father remembered it still observed upon the farm at Tregonissey; it had gone by my time. There was the Christmas mumming when players came to perform 'St. George and the Dragon' in the inn or inn-yard: again it had not died out at St. Austell when my father was a lad, and it is pleasant to think that it must have been the same mumming that William Carnsew saw when Elizabeth was alive. There were all sorts of local festivals like the Bodmin Riding, Hobby-horse day at Padstow, Furry Day at Helston, the last two of which still survive. There was the custom, then universal, of the young men and maidens going round the parish serenading and hanging boughs early on May morning. In short there were all the pleasures of a rural society, simple, child-like, elemental.

Carew gives us a good account of its recreations, 'hunting, hawking, shooting, wrastling, hurling and such other games'.[2] His account of hurling is especially interesting, and of both sorts, 'in the east parts of Cornwall to goals, and in the west, to the country'. He tells us that 'these hurling matches are mostly used at weddings, where commonly the guests undertake to encounter all comers'. No wonder wedding festivities were so prolonged, often over several days and sometimes for a week, so that William Carnsew could leave a wedding, cross the Tamar into Devonshire for a day or two and come back to the wedding, which was still being celebrated. We know how his son loved hurling. Carew describes hurling to the country as 'a play (verily) both rude and rough, and yet such as is not destitute of policies, in some sort resembling the feats of war'. The game has everywhere died out in Cornwall now, save only at St. Columb, and until recent years at

[1] For a full account of these customs, v. Hamilton Jenkin, *Cornish Homes and Customs*, and *Cornwall and the Cornish*.

[2] *Survey*, 71-6.

St. Ives. Still more popular and ubiquitous was wrestling, in which the Cornish acquired such skill that neither the ancient Greeks, according to Carew, nor the Turks, 'nor their once countrymen and still neighbours, the Bretons, can bereave them of this laurel'. Which was only to be expected, for 'you shall hardly find an assembly of boys in Devon or Cornwall, where the most untowardly amongst them, will not as readily give you a muster of this exercise, as you are prone to require it'.

The gentry took great delight in hawking and pride in their eyries. When James succeeded to the English throne, Sir William Godolphin happened to tell him that Mr. Reskymer's hawks at Merthen were wont to prey upon sea-fowl, such as the redshank and others. At once his Majesty, who was much interested in the sport, commanded some of these hawks to be procured for him. Sir Francis wrote down somewhat anxiously — everybody wanted to make a good impression upon the new King — asking Mr. Reskymer to send them up: 'which request I doubt not if it lie in you, you will with all dutiful readiness most willingly yield unto and rejoice that your eyrie is so honoured as to be desired by his majesty, and let this also satisfy the most earnest desire of your ancient good friend'.[1] It looks as if Sir William's credit with the sporting King was rather engaged in the matter.

From the simple entries in parish registers we learn something: the names of those who lived then, their children, whom they married, and when, with an occasional insight into how, they died. In Catholic days children were frequently called after the patron saint of the parish: Columb at St. Columb, Perran in Perranzabuloe, Denis at St. Dennis. (Would the old custom might be revived to-day!) In west Cornwall it was the usual thing, as in Wales, for children to take the Christian name of their father as their surname. At Constantine in 1522 one family of three men are charged in the subsidy roll to provide a whole suit of armour: Nicholas Vicar, Nicholas Nicholl and John Nicholl, the two latter being sons of the first.[2] Nor was that due to the father being what his surname implies. It was the regular thing. The western Cornish, as Carew tells us, were apt to combine their own with their father's name 'and conclude with the place of their dwelling: as John, the son of Thomas, dwelling at Pendarves is called John Thomas Pendarves'.[3] And he adds that through this means various families have changed their names by removing their dwellings, as Trengrove to Nance, 'two brethren of the Thomases, the one to Carnsew, the other to Roscrow'. In the earlier sixteenth century it is quite usual to find John Arundell of Trerice referred to as John Arundell Trerice: only the superior pull of the Arundell name

[1] S.P. 46/61. [2] Henderson, *History of Constantine*, 212. [3] *Survey*, 54 b.

prevented them from becoming Trerices. The fact was that it was in this period that Cornish names were becoming regularized and settling down; by the end of the century the process was practically complete.

We learn when epidemics swept the county, the rate of bastardy, the numbers of the people. There was a fearful pestilence in the year 1547, to judge from the early registers of St. Columb which survive.[1] It began at the end of June, got a terrible hold in July, was at its height in August, was still raging in September, and only subsided at the end of October. Whole families were wiped out, or so one would say from the pathetic, laconic entries: July 30th, Janet the wife of John Clerk is buried, their son John on the same day; on August 5th, their daughter Jane, next day John Clerk himself, next day another son. And so on for other families. There was, as usual in such a society, a high rate of bastardy: poor Margery Rowe seems to have had a whole family of bastard children, several of whom died. Occasionally a child is buried, who was baptised by the midwife at home a day or so before. (It is like the scene in Hardy's *Tess*, and oddly enough a year or two later in this parish we find a John Turberfield buried.) There were the usual poor boys buried, a strange man out of Lancashire, or a 'poor man that died in Bostarnan's stable'. In the coastal parishes one finds entries of the poor sailors' bodies washed up by the waves or at Gerrans of the five people drowned by the overturning of a boat when crossing Anthony passage at the mouth of the Fal at Christmas time.[2]

Life was indeed hard, but it was not altogether heartless. It had nothing of the impersonality of modern life; it was very personal. The parishes with their wardens, their collectors for the poor, their twelve men to look after the parish store did what they could to help their poorer neighbours, lending out a cow, giving a ewe to Jane Glyn widow, a shovel to a poor man to work with, money for shoes to a soldier going to Ireland. Forth from these parishes went men to the wars, to the Netherlands, Brittany, Ireland, with Norris and Drake to the coast of Portugal. The sailors went on their more astonishing adventures with Drake on the voyage round the world, or with Grenville to Virginia, to fight under Rashleigh or Erisey against the Armada, or underwent the incredible experiences, if indeed they are to be believed, of Peter Carder, mariner, of Veryan.[3] The fascinating career of Peter Mundy, who travelled several times to the east, drank tea at Canton, saw Shah Jehan go by in procession at Agra with the beautiful Mumtaz Mahal (to whose memory he raised the Taj Mahal), who saw a great deal of

---

[1] A. J. Jewers, *Registers of St. Columb Major*, 182-5.   [2] Hambly Rowe in *West Briton*.
[3] cf. Purchas, *Pilgrims* (ed. 1625), IV. 1187-90.

Europe travelling overland from Constantinople, and what was more important, kept a careful diary of all that he saw: the career of Peter Mundy, of the family of the last prior of Bodmin, is already upon the horizon: he was born about the turn of the century. [1]

At home no less exciting, pathetic, revealing, were the things that happened to men and women in their inner lives. For the most intimate of their concerns, their passions, we have to go to the records of the courts, particularly of the consistory court at Exeter, which dealt with their matrimonial affairs, breach of promise, slander, adultery: a most intimate source, hardly yet drawn upon, which brings these folk face to face before us across the centuries, for there was the scribe taking down in his rapid, illegible hand the very words they said. [2] Here is Anne Collins of Tregony who was married by her father to Edward Pascoe when she was twelve years of age. [3] That same day a friendly woman of twice her age found her walking by 'a certain tin-work, wherein was a great deep pit of water . . . She said, "I will drown myself in this pit". That night she would not lie with him to die for, until two women went to bed with her; and she desired this deponent and other company present, saying, "For the Passion of God, tarry here and dance in the chamber for I will not go to bed with him" . . . The next night following she would not go to bed with him at all; and then her father with weeping eyes took her by the hair of the head and threw her into the bed. Yet she crying out, crope out of the bed again, and never lay with him after this deponent's knowledge, neither had carnal copulation together, for she was not able thereunto for lack of age, for she was not full twelve years of age.' She went back to her father's house, but whenever her husband tried to come near her she ran away, sometimes to her good friends', and hid under the bed. Thomas Mallett who had a good influence over her and whom she loved dearly 'rebuked her and tried in vain to get her to lie with her husband. But she would not go to bed until her elder brother lay between her and her husband. Then she went into service with Sir Hugh Trevanion and after to Mr. Arundell Talvern [i.e. of Talvern] until his death. And it fortuned that Edward her husband had committed a rape, and after that she could never abide to hear of him.'

Nicholas Gill of Lasack forced his daughter to marry Thomas Penhallick who frequently came to those parts to buy wool and fish. [4] When the father

---

[1] v. *The Travels of Peter Mundy* (Hakluyt Society).
[2] For the transcripts of these I draw upon the Henderson MSS., vols. x and xi.
[3] Henderson, x. 118 b.   [4] ibid., 114-15.

discovered that Penhallick 'had a good bargain of the Queen's holt, he was very desirous that his daughter might be well pleased with a good living because he had no more daughters'. So when she was only eleven years old, he forced her to contract with Thomas and beat her until she agreed thereto. Penhallick deposed that he did not lie with her the first night because her mother came to him and said, 'Thomas, thou shalt not lie with thy wife this first night because it is said that if thou do not thou shalt have plenty of horn-beasts'. The second night poor Thomas consoled himself with 'two queans in one bed and she never lay with him afterwards'. Next day Penhallick took 13s. 4d. out of her purse and sent her home to her father's; she had lived there, an honest woman, ever since.

There would obviously have been other cases of child-marriage, which did not come before the courts and may have been successful enough. But it is clear from these two cases that it was exceptional, and not approved of among the neighbours. We hear of Elizabeth Gill's marriage, that 'the bride being not above eleven years old, it caused great stir'.

Such was the compulsion of circumstances in that huddled, close-knit, close-lived life. How close it was may be gathered from Samson Stephens' suit to Mary Tredenham of St. Ewe in 1587.[1] Samson offered to give her a new pair of gloves, but she refused saying 'I would wish you to bestow your gloves where you may get something by them for you be not like to get a pair of gloves by me'. (There is a hidden meaning in the lady's un-friendly sentiment here.) ' "I pray you," quoth the said Samson, "yet take them", and she received them.' She was not always so coy about his attentions. One evening when the parson of St. Mewan was away, she sent for the parson's wife to keep her company that night. After a while Samson turned up, came in to supper with them and 'lay there that night in the very same chamber' where she and Mary lay. 'And in the morning about an hour before day Samson came out of his own bed where he lay with a lad, a kinsman of the said Mary's, and came into the bed to the said Mary and there lay by her by the space of an hour or so.'

The question of betrothal was responsible for a great many cases, for according to custom a verbal pledge exchanged between a man and a woman before witnesses was almost equivalent to marriage. (It is the situation upon which the action turns in Webster's *Duchess of Malfi*.) A pre-contract of this kind was a sufficient obstacle to marriage with a third person: hence so many cases and the careful inquisition into the exact circumstances of the pledge, whether it had been exacted by force or no.

[1] Henderson, x. 142.

There was an interesting breach of contract case tried at Padstow in 1596 between Nicholas Treffry and Elizabeth Ash.[1] Mrs. Ash was a well-to-do widow with a portion of £40 a year of her own. She seems to have had a good liking for Nicholas and was well inclined to his suit: but she was afraid of her Padstow relations, John Prideaux and John Flamock, if she married a poor man. One day Mrs. Ash was walking with her friend Tomiris Leonard, the parson's wife of St. Minver — parsons' wives seem very much to the fore in these matters: naturally they were all in favour of matrimony; these two had got as far as St. Saviour's stile near Padstow when they met Treffry. Together they went along to Richard Prideaux's garden to invite him and his wife along to Treffry's house to eat cream and strawberries. 'A cloth was laid on the table in the hall with cream and strawberries upon it and a quart of wine and sugar.' There was also a dish of raisins, which Nicholas offered to Mrs. Ash, 'who refused them saying she loved no raisins. Unto whom Treffry answered saying, "Then I pray you give me one good reason: you know that I have borne you good will a long time and now I pray you let me know your mind either to deny me or else to yield to me." '

The widow provokingly replied that she loved him as well as ever she loved Mr. Ash, but that she was afraid her friends would never give their consents. Treffry took this for a kind of consent on her part, and holding her hand in his swore 'I give you my faith and troth to be your husband'. She answered, 'I likewise give you my consent thereunto'. Then Treffry took 'a ring from his finger and put it on her finger, and they two kissed oftentimes together, which ring she threw from her upon the board in mirth once or twice and there took it again and did wear the same again upon the finger' when Mrs. Prideaux left the house. Treffry said: 'Now you are my wife before God as well as if it were done in the church'. Mrs. Ash answered 'Yea, truly'. After this scene, the engaging widow was got at by her relations and went back on her word. Shut up in the house of Mr. Nicholas Prideaux at St. Breoke she deposed that when Treffry put his ring upon her finger she had cast it back again; that the gifts she had made him, a toothpick of silver and a couple of shirt bands, were in recompense for his gifts to her, 'a pair of gloves, a pair of knives and a silver instrument for her hair . . . because she would not be beholding to him'. It sounded suspicious; she was evidently a desirable *parti* and as such the subject of dispute among her relatives. The question was whether she was betrothed or no?

Joan Daniel's case in 1584 was a different one.[2] John Trevanion had long

---

[1] ibid., 176-181.   [2] ibid., 145-7.

entertained a suit for her hand, but she was sweet on a kinsman of hers, Richard Rawe, a young connection of the Arundells who was in service with her father. Rumour was that they had been found in bed together. John Arundell of Veryan said he would procure out citations for both Rawe and Joan, for, quoth he, 'he hath occupied her an hundred times'. A girl friend of Joan's reported that 'she, the said Joan, and the said Richard Rawe did tumble together in the sheephouse'. At Probus Midsummer fair Joan 'rode behind her father to the fair and in the fair left her father behind and went away with Richard and rode home behind him and her father knew not which way she was gone'. When Richard went back to his uncle's service he was frequently out of the way when he was wanted about 'affairs touching husbandry' — it was not the kind of husbandry that most interested him — he was off to some wedding with Joan or at her father's house. He spent all one night in the kitchen there with her and a maidservant.

Pressure was put upon Joan by her people to go into North Devon to one Mr. Garland's 'to have sight of his son, one Thomas Garland, for marriage'. She was loth to go, but promised Richard she would do nothing. Richard fell very sick at the news and went to bed; in the afternoon Joan went up to his chamber to see him 'and continued with him an hour thereabout and leaned in upon the side of the bed by him'. When he recovered, his uncle asked him the cause of his sickness; Richard told him and added, 'Truly, uncle, she can never marry with any man of right but with me'. ' "Why", said his uncle, "then I marvel that being so familiar as ye two have been together, thou didst never seek to have the pleasure of her." "Truly, uncle," quoth he, "and so I have and for this two year I have had her continually at my pleasure." Quoth this deponent, "Where had you such places of meeting?" He answered between Tregeswan and Gueniter, and laughing said "That is a bawdy place".' Richard asked his uncle to do his best for him with her father, but he was denied, and after that left her company; notwithstanding Joan would occasionally send for him to go to markets or weddings with her. She must have been a desirable baggage — or perhaps she was her father's heir — for several suitors were after her. Richard Langhorn was turned down, but John Trevanion was accepted: they were betrothed and 'the matrimony was solemnized in the face of the church'.

Joan was more fortunate than her contemporary, Christian Gayer, daughter of John Gayer, of an old St. Keverne family, who was the subject of a case that must have been the talk of Cornwall in 1577.[1] She was to have married Henry Pomeroy, a Truro merchant, who was taking her — such

[1] Henderson, X. 119-22, 155-65.

was her reputation for good housewifery — without any portion. Then rumours began to reach his ear which caused him to hold off and ask for the tokens he had given her to be redelivered. She said: 'If I be such a one, I be not fit for you'. Her cousin, Henry Gayer, promoted a cause of correction to establish her reputation. It was a very expensive and unwise proceeding: literally scores of witnesses were examined all through the month of May at various churches; the commission travelled from Helston to St. Keverne, then back to Helston, to Truro, Fowey, St. Winnow, Fowey again, then back to St. Keverne and Helston. The evidence occupies scores of pages, and the total upshot may be described in the words of a St. Keverne peasant woman, Margery Sampson alias Walter, relict of Sampson Walter: 'A foul thing, the more it is stirred the more it will stink'.

The rumour was the usual one that Christian Gayer had had a child — a rumour for spreading which Christian had already sued Jane Namble in the Archdeacon's Court. 'Why shall I not send my daughter as well as Mr. Gayer hath sent his daughter?' said Jane, but 'Jane's daughter was known to be pregnant although Christian was never so spotted'. It was impossible to catch up with a rumour like this; it was on everybody's lips. Anne Kent, quarrelling with another woman, wished her 'at St. Keverne where Mistress Christian Gayer might use her like a drab'; for herself, 'I am an honester woman than Christian Gayer, for I did never run out of the parish to Mr. Treffry's as she did to sling a child'. The rumour ran through the fields, from the lips of the women as they worked 'drying of malt' or a-spinning, and was exchanged by the men as they met at market in Helston. It was all over the Lizard district, naturally, for the Gayers were one of the best old families there. It reached Falmouth, and one man told another 'as he was passing in a boat between Falmouth and Penryn'. 'God's wounds', said one Penryn woman to another, 'Mrs. Christian Gayer is either gone east or going eastwards to empty her belly'. To whom the other lady replied: 'Out upon the whore, it is not true'. The first answered, 'God's blood, with us over the water, it is full of it'. (The incomparable foolery: as if it mattered: human idiocy changes little from one age to another.)

As the rumour spread it took a new turn. Mr. Tregose had been heard to say that 'her father, Mr. John Gayer, was the father of the child'. A mason of Landewednack near the Lizard heard 'one which paid our wages say that the father of Mistress Christian Gayer's child was the grandfather and laughed withal'. Innumerable persons heard the rumour in this form; whether it was true it is impossible to say. All that we know is that Christian Gayer did go east to stay in the houses of her relations, the Treffrys at Fowey, the Lowers at St. Winnow. When John Roskrege of St. Anthony-in-Meneage went up to Lostwithiel he inquired how she was doing and who was in childbed at Mr. Lower's, he was told Mistress Calwodely was 'in childbed of a young son' and Mistress Christian was in health: and so he reported to her father when he came back.

A pitiful story all told; for though we do not know the sentence of the court, or whether Christian's name was cleared, we do know that she never married.[1]

Marriage too had its accidents, its misfortunes, dangers. Katherine Drew was betrothed before witnesses at Pieworthy in Devon to Walter Wydes.[2] Six months after, he 'went out of the country and was absent eight or nine years and no man could tell where he was becomed'. About three years ago her banns were called and she was married at Jacobstow to William Pearce, 'and dwelt with him by the space of a quarter of a year and he begot a child by her'. Shortly after, the provoking Walter returned, and Pearce hearing of it 'took all her goods and clothes from her and beat her most piteously with a staff and had killed her with an axe if her mother had not been, which rid them and was shrewdly cut with the axe in the ridding of them'. Not content with this Pearce bought rats' bane for her, and at length carried her away saying, 'Go to thy husband; I will not keep another man's wife'.

There was, too, simple adultery, for which cause John Watt sought divorce from his Joan.[3] A St. Tudy man said she had 'on Tuesday before All Hallows day last in the dawning of the day in her father's sheephouse in the parish of Luxulyan committed adultery with a certain man whom this deponent knew not. For this deponent had lodged at her father's house, and coming out to do his easement in the fields went into the sheephouse because it was wet weather and there saw them commit adultery . . . The common speech of the country is that she is a common whore and Mr. Coryton's whore and Hendy's whore, for she was fet out of her house by the constables.' John Hony, who also 'before the sun rising was passing along by the sheephouse', put his head in at the door and said to Joan that she kept the laws of matrimony well and that she should hear of it. She did.

The passions no doubt were simpler, stronger, more immediate with such people than now, held in check by no reason, their only control the fears, the superstitions of their religion. Frequently they led them to their death; then there were the consolations of religion for these poor fools who had wrecked their lives. Here is the case of a quarrel between uncle and nephew,

---

[1] cf. Vivian, *Visitations*, 172.   [2] Henderson, XI. 266.   [3] ibid., 268.

Nicholas and William Lower, over the succession to property in 1546: it ended in the death of one of them.[1] The manor of Treloske had come into the possession of Nicholas Lower and his brother, William's father, through their marriages to two Upton sisters. William's parents were dead and he proceeded to claim his moiety of the manor for himself. He was a very young man and had already had an open quarrel with his uncle in Lewannick church. After which his uncle tried to pacify him, inviting him home to breakfast with him to partake of a goose. William refused to go, but demanded his rights of his uncle.

On September 3rd he proceeded to enforce them himself: with a band of his men he took distress of the cattle upon Treloske down, driving away over thirty beasts. His uncle hearing of this assembled a band of his tenants and servants with arms and started in pursuit. He came up with his nephew in Trewithy lane; the latter does not appear to have wished to fight, but he was driven up against a bank and in self-defence struck and gave his uncle a deep wound in the knee so that he fell from his horse to the ground. There had been a regular fray in the lane, and William was getting away when he was called back by the cries of his uncle's servants 'for the Passion of God, to save the gentleman's life, saying that it was shame to kill him and to run away and not to help him'. When William realized what he had done, he came back to his uncle 'weeping and lamenting his fortune that ever he should do such a deed, and desired him heartily to forgive him'.

They then carried the wounded man to Northill church and laid him in the chancel, where the priest heard his confession; and afterwards Nicholas exonerated his nephew who was 'there present weeping and sighing, saying unto him "Cousin William, why do ye lament thus? Ye do me no pleasure therein, and here before God and my ghostly father I do clearly forgive you and if I have offended you I pray you forgive me likewise".' He then declared to the people who had remained in the church that his death was his own seeking and that he did not wish his nephew to be troubled for it. He was removed to Northill parsonage where he lingered. He remained of the same mind towards his nephew, saying 'It was the devil's chance', and 'It came of my own seeking'; and to his wife 'Jane, lift up my head' and then bidding her not to trouble or sue his nephew for his death. At the end he said 'I marvel my cousin William Lower cometh not to me; it should do me more good to see him than any surgeons that cometh to me'. One day the boy attending him told him that 'as he was riding by the way he was taken up in the air, horse and man, and was let fall again by a sprite'.

[1] Star Chamber 2/30/40.

They jested together at this and so he died. His wife, of course, sued the coroner for bringing in a verdict that William had killed his uncle in self-defence.

Such, so far as the evidence remains to us, were their lives and deaths.

At the end of our investigation a certain change in the circumstances of life, perhaps even in its tone and quality, is discernible between the beginning of our period, when Cornwall had not yet emerged from the Middle Ages, and its term, the threshold of our modern world. We learn from Carew the evidences of material progress in the course of that century. Wealth had increased, and with it there was a greater differentiation between classes, more variety in standards. He tells us of the great improvement in building, particularly in the houses of the gentry, which was taking place in his time. More, many more, ships were entering and clearing from our ports. Notable progress in agriculture was being made. There was more to eat. Though life was hard for the people, it was not quite so hard.

One can even discern a certain progress not only in material affairs, but in the realm of the spirit. Innumerable as were the accidents to life and limb, a greater value was coming to be set upon human life. Men emerge more distinctly as individual souls from the background of the community. They are a shade more self-reliant: such is the impression one derives from town and parish accounts. Though the continuity of group life and tradition goes on, it changes, hardly perceptibly, there a shade, here a tone, in emphasis and composition rather than in character and constituents. Life has become, in a hardly definable way, more secular. Not that it was not secular, and grossly so, in the Middle Ages. But still the claims of a universal religion swaddled the whole life of man and were everywhere accepted. By the end of the period it was no longer so. The claims of religion had a reduced, though still a very important place. They had come into closer conformity with the actual facts of social life. The English church still contained the bulk of society; but there were as the result of the struggle over the Reformation, people who were outside, and on both wings, Catholics and extreme Protestants. It was that which opened the way ultimately to liberty for the individual soul. The Reformation, though some precious things were dropped by the way, and there was, as is the way in human affairs, much suffering in the process, was on the whole a reform: a most significant stage in the evolution of English society, which this book has illustrated in concrete fact, or it has done nothing.

When you consider the superstitions and imaginings of the old Cornish country-folk up to my grandmother's day, how their lives were swaddled in them from the cradle to the grave, their daily actions in large part determined by them — so many things you would not think of doing, like starting a journey on a Friday, or looking at the moon through a pane of glass, or failing to wear something new on Whitsunday — their minds haunted by ghosts and fears, you have a fair idea of what the minds of these people in the sixteenth century were like. It was a life full of shadows that frightened them and dangers that might come home to them: how much more so in those days when their fears had the sanction, and even the corroboration, of the elect and the intelligent; when a uniform religion existed to enforce its lessons and draw the moral. However, no doubt it filled up life for them, made it more interesting and exciting, more mysterious and incalculable; it added a dimension to it, where the modern uneducated, rid of their fears and ghosts, are apt to find life empty and void of meaning.

Impossible as it is to reconstruct at all fully those vanished lives, we may reflect that they as we felt the heat of noonday, lay down tired with their labour at night, watched the stars come out over the familiar hillsides and hang the night with creation; they too heard the wind in the trees, the smouldering seas lapping our coasts in summer, or thundering upon the rocks in winter. Or perhaps their lives were for the most part of sterner, simpler stuff, their lot harder, filled almost wholly with labour and endurance, the struggle to wrest a living from the soil, the begetting of their children, birth, marriage, death. In the end their lives can never be wholly without interest for us: for they were our forefathers.

ABBREVIATIONS

A.P.C.	*Acts of the Privy Council*
C.R.S.	Publications of the Catholic Record Society
Carew	Richard Carew, *Survey of Cornwall* (ed. 1769)
Henderson	Henderson MSS. at County Museum, Truro
J.R.I.C.	*Journal of the Royal Institution of Cornwall*
L.P.	*Letters and Papers of Henry VIII*
Leland's Itinerary	Edition of Toulmin Smith
R.S.J.	*Records of the Society of Jesus*

INDEX

INDEX

INDEX

Wolvedon family, 345
Woolcock, John, 284
Woolton, John, bishop, of Exeter, 334, 337-8, 429
Worth, John, 235
Wray, Sir William, 377
Wydes, Walter, 446

Yates, John, 363
Yaxley, Francis, 93
Young, John, 210; Thomas, 112

Zennor, 96, 328
Zouche, lord, 118